Yamaha YZF-R6
Service and Repair Manual

by Matthew Coombs

Models covered
YZF-R6. 600cc. 2003 to 2005

(4601-272)

© Haynes Publishing 2007

A book in the Haynes Service and Repair Manual Series

All rights reserved. No part of this book may be reproduced or transmitted in any form or by any means, electronic or mechanical, including photocopying, recording or by any information storage or retrieval system, without permission in writing from the copyright holder.

EAN/ISBN-13: 978-1-84425-601-3

British Library Cataloguing in Publication Data
A catalogue record for this book is available from the British Library.

Library of Congress Control Number 2006932595

ABCDE
FGHIJ
KLMNO
PQRST

Printed in the USA

Haynes Publishing
Sparkford, Yeovil, Somerset BA22 7JJ, England

Haynes North America, Inc
861 Lawrence Drive, Newbury Park, California 91320, USA

Editions Haynes
4, Rue de l'Abreuvoir
92415 COURBEVOIE CEDEX, France

Haynes Publishing Nordiska AB
Box 1504, 751 45 Uppsala, Sweden

Contents

LIVING WITH YOUR YAMAHA YZF-R6

Introduction
Yamaha – Musical instruments to motorcycles	Page	0•4
Acknowledgements	Page	0•8
About this manual	Page	0•8
Identification numbers	Page	0•9
Buying spare parts	Page	0•9
Model development and Bike spec	Page	0•10
Safety first!	Page	0•12

Pre-ride checks
Engine oil level	Page	0•13
Suspension, steering and drive chain	Page	0•13
Coolant level	Page	0•14
Brake fluid levels	Page	0•14
Tyres	Page	0•16
Legal and safety	Page	0•16

MAINTENANCE

Routine maintenance and servicing
Specifications	Page	1•2
Lubricants and fluids	Page	1•2
Maintenance schedule	Page	1•3
Component locations	Page	1•4
Maintenance procedures	Page	1•6

Contents

REPAIRS AND OVERHAUL

Engine, transmission and associated systems

Engine, clutch and transmission	Page	2•1
Cooling system	Page	3•1
Engine management system	Page	4•1

Chassis components

Frame and suspension	Page	5•1
Brakes, wheels and final drive	Page	6•1
Bodywork	Page	7•1

Electrical system

Page 8•1

Wiring diagrams

Page 8•22

REFERENCE

Tools and Workshop Tips	Page	REF•2
Security	Page	REF•20
Lubricants and fluids	Page	REF•23
Conversion factors	Page	REF•26
MOT Test Checks	Page	REF•27
Storage	Page	REF•32
Fault Finding	Page	REF•35
Fault Finding Equipment	Page	REF•43
Technical Terms Explained	Page	REF•47

Index

Page REF•51

Yamaha
Musical instruments to motorcycles

**The FS1E -
first bike of many sixteen year olds in the UK**

The Yamaha Motor Company

The Yamaha name can be traced back to 1889, when Torakusu Yamaha founded the Yamaha Organ Manufacturing Company. Such was the success of the company, that in 1897 it became Nippon Gakki Limited and manufactured a wide range of reed organs and pianos.

During World War II, Nippon Gakki's manufacturing base was utilised by the Japanese authorities to produce propellers and fuel tanks for their aviation industry. The end of the war brought about a huge public demand for low cost transport and many firms decided to utilise their obsolete aircraft tooling for the production of motorcycles. Nippon Gakki's first motorcycle went on sale in February 1955 and was named the 125 YA-1 Red Dragonfly. This machine was a copy of the German DKW RT125 motorcycle, featuring a single cylinder two-stroke engine with a four-speed gearbox. Due to the outstanding success of this model the motorcycle operation was separated from Nippon Gakki in July 1955 and the Yamaha Motor Company was formed.

The YA-1 also received acclaim by winning two of Japan's biggest road races, the Mount Fuji Climbing race and the Asama Volcano race. The high level of public demand for the YA-1 led to the development of a whole series of two-stroke singles and twins.

Having made a large impact on their home market, Yamahas were exported to the USA in 1958 and to the UK in 1962. In the UK the signing of an Anglo-Japanese trade

Introduction 0•5

agreement during 1962 enabled the sale of Japanese lightweight motorcycles and scooters in Britain. At that time, competition between the many motorcycle producers in Japan had reduced numbers significantly and by the end of the sixties, only the big-four which are familiar with today remained.

Yamaha Europe was founded in 1968 and based in Holland. Although originally set up to market marine products, the Dutch base is now the official European Headquarters and distribution centre. Yamaha motorcycles are built at factories in Holland, Denmark, Norway, Italy, France, Spain and Portugal. Yamahas are imported into the UK by Yamaha Motor UK Ltd, formerly Mitsui Machinery Sales (UK) Ltd. Mitsui and Co. were originally a trading house, handling the shipping, distribution and marketing of Japanese products into western countries. Ultimately Mitsui Machinery Sales was formed to handle Yamaha motorcycles and outboard motors.

Based on the technology derived from its motorcycle operation, Yamaha have produced many other products, such as automobile and lightweight aircraft engines, marine engines and boats, generators, pumps, ATVs, snowmobiles, golf cars, industrial robots, lawnmowers, swimming pools and archery equipment.

Two-strokes first

Part of Yamaha's success was a whole string of innovations in the two-stroke world. Autolube engine lubrication, torque induction, multi-ported engines, reed valves and power valves kept their two-strokes at the forefront of technology. Many advances were achieved with the use of racing as a development laboratory. They went to the USA in the late 1950s with an air-cooled 250cc twin but didn't hit the GPs until the early 1960s when Fumio Ito scored a hat-trick of sixth places in the Isle of Man TT, the Dutch TT and the Belgian GP. This experiment gave rise to the idea of the over-the-counter racer, an idea that became reality in the TD1, the first in an unmatched series of two-stroke racers that were the standard issue for privateers at national and international level for years and helped Yamaha develop their road engines. While privateers raced the twins, Yamaha built the outrageously complicated vee-four 250 for Phil Read and followed it with a vee-four 125 that Bill Ivy lapped the Isle of Man on at over 100mph! When the FIM regulations were changed to limit the smaller GP classes to two cylinders, these exotic bikes died but set the scene for an unparalleled dynasty of mass-produced racers based on the same technology as the road bikes.

In the 1960s and 70s the two-stroke engined YAS3 125, YDS1 to YDS7 250 and YR5 350 formed the core of Yamaha's range. By the mid-70s they had been superseded by the RD (Race-Developed) 125, 250, and 350 range of two-stroke twins, featuring improved 7-port engines with reed valve induction. Braking was improved by the use of an hydraulic brake on the front wheel of DX models, instead of the drum arrangement used previously, and cast alloy wheels were available as an option on later RD models. The RD350 was replaced by the RD400 in 1976.

Running parallel with the RD twins was a range of single-cylinder two-strokes. Used in a variety of chassis types, the engine was used in the popular 50 cc FS1-E moped, the V50 to 90 step-thrus, RS100 and 125, YB100 and the DT trail range.

The TD racers got water-cooling in 1973 to become the TZs, the most successful and numerous over-the-counter racers ever built. That same year, Jarno Saarinen became the first rider to win a 500cc GP on a four-cylinder two-stroke on the new in-line four which was effectively a pair of TZs side-by-side. TZs won everywhere – including the Daytona 200 and 500 races when overbored to 351cc. A 700cc TZ also appeared, one year later taken out to 750cc. Steve Baker won the first Formula 750 world title – one of the precursors of Superbike – on one in 1977. The following year Kenny Roberts won Yamaha's first world 500 title and would be succeeded by Wayne Rainey and Eddie Lawson before Mick Doohan and the NSR500 took over.

The air-cooled single and twin cylinder RD road bikes were eventually replaced by the LC series in 1980, featuring liquid-cooled engines, radical new styling, spiral pattern cast wheels and cantilever rear suspension (Yamaha's Monoshock). Of all the LC models, the RD350LC, or RD350R as it was later known, has made the most impact in the market. Later models had YPVS (Yamaha Power Valve System) engines, another first for Yamaha – this was essentially a valve located in the exhaust ports which was electronically operated to alter port timing to achieve maximum power output. The RD500LC was the largest two-stroke made by Yamaha and differed from the other LCs by the use of its vee-four cylinder engine.

With the exception of the RD350R, now manufactured in Brazil, the LC range has been discontinued. Two-stroke engined models have given way to environmental pressure, and thus with a few exceptions, such as the TZR125 and TZR250, are used only in scooters and small capacity bikes.

The Four-strokes

Yamaha concentrated solely on two-stroke models until 1970 when the XS1 was produced, their first four-stroke motorcycle. It was perhaps Yamaha's success with two-strokes that postponed an earlier

The distinctive paintwork and trim of the RD models

0•6 Introduction

move into the four-stroke motorcycle market, although their work with Toyota during the 1960s had given them a sound base in four-stroke technology.

The XS1 had a 650 cc twin-cylinder SOHC engine and was later to become known as the XS650, appearing also in the popular SE custom form. Yamaha introduced a three cylinder 750 cc engine in 1976, fitted in a sport-tourer frame and called the XS750, TX750 in the USA. The XS750 established itself well in the sport tourer class and remained in production with very few changes until uprated to 850 cc in 1980.

Other four-strokes followed in 1976, with the introduction of the XS250/360/400 series twins. The XS range was strengthened in 1978 by the four-cylinder XS1100.

The 1980s saw a new family of four-strokes, the XJ550, 650, 750 and 900 Fours. Improvements over the XS range amounted to a slimmer DOHC engine unit due to the relocation of the alternator behind the cylinders, electronic ignition and uprated braking and suspension systems. Models were available mainly in standard trim, although custom-styled Maxims were produced especially for the US market. The XJ650T was the first model from Yamaha to have a turbo-charged engine. Although these early XJ models have now been discontinued, their roots live on in the XJ600S and XJ900S Diversion (Seca II) models.

The FZR prefix encompasses the pure sports Yamaha models. With the exception of the 16-valve FZR400 and FZR600 models, the FZ/FZR750 and FZR1000 used 20-valve engines, two exhaust valves and three inlet valves per cylinder. This concept was called Genesis and gave improved gas flow to the combustion chambers. Other features of the new engine were the use of down-draught carburetors and the engine's inclined angle in the frame, plus the change to liquid-cooling.

The XS650 led the way for Yamaha's four-stroke range

Yamaha's XS750 was produced from 1976 to 1982 and then uprated to 850 cc

Lightweight Deltabox design aluminium frames and uprated suspension improved the bikes's handling. The Genesis engine lives on in the YZF750 and 1000 models.

The Genesis concept was the basis of Yamaha's foray into four-stroke racing, first with a bike known simply as 'The Genesis', an FZ750 motor in a TT Formula 1 bike with which the factory attempted to steal the Honda RVF750's thunder at important events like the Suzuka 8 Hours and the Bol d'Or although they never fielded it for a whole World Championship season. That had to wait for the advent of the World Superbike Championship, although there was no full works team until 1995, instead it was left to individual importers to support teams. It was the Australian Dealer Team Yamaha which scored the factory's first World Superbike win in the series debut year of 1988. The rider? Mick Doohan. Slightly, embarrassingly, it was the steel framed FZ750 rather than the FZR homologation special that won races. The OW01 was a race winner, mainly in the hands of Fabrizio Pirovano, the factory's most successful Superbike racer with ten victories, but national success in the UK, Japan, and in the Daytona 200 has not been translated into World Championships for any of Yamaha's 750s.

The vee-twin engine has been the mainstay of the XV Virago range. Since 1981 XVs have been produced in 535, 700, 750, 920, 1000 and 1100 engine sizes, all using the same basic air-cooled sohc vee-twin engine. Other uses of vee engines have been in the XZ550 of the early 1980s, the XVZ12 Venture and the mighty VMX-12 V-Max.

Yamaha has always been a sporting-orientated company whose motto could be 'Racing Improves the Breed', so it's no surprise that the latest generation of lightweight sportsters are at the cutting edge of performance on and off the track. The R6 won more races than any other machine in the inaugural year of the World Supersports Championship, the R7 won a race in its debut year in World Superbike in the hands of the mercurial Noriyuki Haga, and the mighty 1000cc R1 ended Honda's domination of the Isle of Man F1 TT when David Jefferies won three races in a week in 1999.

In Grand Prix racing, the factory took several years to get over the shock of Wayne Rainey's crippling accident. and first 500cc win since the American's enforced retirement didn't come until 1998 when Simon Crafar won at Donington Park. For 1999, Yamaha refocussed their ambitions and signed Italian superstar Max Biaggi plus Spanish trier Carlos Checa for the works team, while dashing young Frenchman Regis Laconi and tough little Aussie Gary McCoy rode for the WCM satellite team. Both teams got a win in the '99 season and with a new TZ250 being developed for 2000 it looks as if Yamaha's spirit of competition will go on unabated into the new Millenium.

A new family of four-strokes was released in 1980 with the introduction of the XJ range

The discrete R6

In many ways it's difficult to rationalise the Yamaha R6 that appeared in the dealerships from 2003 to '05 with the models that appeared before and afterwards. The first and latest R6s were uncompromising, hard-edged racers for the road but the models this manual is concerned with occupied the middle ground of the highly competitive 600cc supersports class for three years. In many ways it took the title of best all-rounder from the Honda CBR600F, the bike that historically has been regarded as the jack-of-all-trades of this class.

That's even more surprising when you look at the specification of the Yamaha. This was the first R6 to get fuel injection, a stacked gearbox and the third-generation Deltabox chassis. The frame and swinging arm were the first to be made by Yamaha's Controlled Filling die-casting system. This very clever piece of production engineering manages to send more liquid metal to where it is needed, normally very difficult because the material cools quickly. The result is that one casting can have varying wall thicknesses so where the old frame consisted of enough separate parts to need sixteen welds to hold them together, the new frame needed just two. That means greater precision, which means rigid rather than adjustable engine mountings. Controlled Fill was also used for the swinging arm, which in places has a wall thickness of only 2.5mm.

The factory pointed out that the lateral stiffness of the chassis was improved by 50%, making it nearly as rigid as the 750cc R7's chassis.

Along with the new fuel injection, talk of lateral stiffness provided echoes of the buzz

The XV535 Virago vee-twin

Introduction

The 2003 R6

The re-modelled 2005 R6

words in the MotoGP paddock. The 990cc four-stroke formula had arrived in 2002 and with it came the wholesale adoption of fuel-injection in the blue-riband class of motorcycle racing. Getting the resulting power to the ground saw further investigation of the usefulness of deliberately making some parts of the chassis, notably the swinging arm, much stiffer torsionally than laterally. CF technology was clearly going to be helpful in that area and feedback from the tracks drove rapid progress in that area. Most of the R6 stayed unchanged for the three-year life of this model, but the fuel-injection mapping was modified every year.

The only significant changes came for the 2005 model year when the R6 got its suspension and brakes uprated. Upside down forks and radially-mounted calipers brought a more racy look to the front end but all contemporary roadtests are agreed that the most important modification was much more subtle. The 120/60x17 front tyre was replaced with a slightly chunkier 120/70. The higher aspect ratio put a slightly bigger footprint on the tarmac and made the bike (and rider) much less nervous going into corners.

Despite the R6's usability and comfort compared to the other sports 600s, it would be a mistake to think of it as a sports tourer or anything less than a full-on sports bike. It may have the longest seat you'll find on a supersports 600 but that doesn't mean that you'd want to carry a passenger on it, and far less be that passenger. The gaps between bikes in this class are very small and fine nuances make a big difference and this R6 is sporty enough for just about everyone who is more concerned with the street than the race track.

Acknowledgements

Our thanks are due to Bransons Motorcycles of Yeovil, Somerset, who supplied the machines featured in the illustrations throughout this manual. We would also like to thank NGK Spark Plugs (UK) Ltd for supplying the colour spark plug condition photographs, the Avon Rubber Company for supplying information on tyre fitting and Draper Tools Ltd for some of the workshop tools shown.

Thanks are also due to Yamaha Motor (UK) Ltd who supplied model photographs, and to Julian Ryder who wrote the introduction 'Musical Instruments to Motorcycles'.

About this Manual

The aim of this manual is to help you get the best value from your motorcycle. It can do so in several ways. It can help you decide what work must be done, even if you choose to have it done by a dealer; it provides information and procedures for routine maintenance and servicing; and it offers diagnostic and repair procedures to follow when trouble occurs.

We hope you use the manual to tackle the work yourself. For many simpler jobs, doing it yourself may be quicker than arranging an appointment to get the motorcycle into a dealer and making the trips to leave it and pick it up. More importantly, a lot of money can be saved by avoiding the expense the shop must pass on to you to cover its labour and overhead costs. An added benefit is the sense of satisfaction and accomplishment that you feel after doing the job yourself.

References to the left or right side of the motorcycle assume you are sitting on the seat, facing forward.

We take great pride in the accuracy of information given in this manual, but motorcycle manufacturers make alterations and design changes during the production run of a particular motorcycle of which they do not inform us. No liability can be accepted by the authors or publishers for loss, damage or injury caused by any errors in, or omissions from, the information given.

Illegal copying

It is the policy of Haynes Publishing to actively protect its Copyrights and Trade Marks. Legal action will be taken against anyone who unlawfully copies the cover or contents of this Manual. This includes all forms of unauthorised copying including digital, mechanical, and electronic in any form. Authorisation from Haynes Publishing will only be provided expressly and in writing. Illegal copying will also be reported to the appropriate statutory authorities.

Identification numbers 0•9

Frame and engine numbers

The frame serial number is stamped into the right-hand side of the steering head. The engine number is stamped into the rear of the crankcase, and is repeated on a sticker attached to the ECU which is under the rider's seat. The model code label is on the rear sub-frame under the rider's seat. These numbers should be recorded and kept in a safe place so they can be given to the police in the event of a theft.

The frame serial number, engine serial number, and model code should also be kept in a handy place (such as with your driver's licence) so that they are always available when ordering parts for your machine.

The procedures in this manual identify the bikes by model and year (e.g. YZF-R6 (S) 2004). The model codes for all years and models covered are tabled below.

Buying spare parts

Once you have found all the identification numbers, record them for reference when buying parts. Since the manufacturers change specifications, parts and vendors (companies that manufacture various components on the machine), providing the ID numbers is the only way to be reasonably sure that you are buying the correct parts.

Whenever possible, take the worn part to the dealer so direct comparison with the new component can be made. Along the trail from the manufacturer to the parts shelf, there are numerous places that the part can end up with the wrong number or be listed incorrectly.

The two places to purchase new parts for your motorcycle – the accessory store and the franchised dealer – differ in the type of parts they carry. While dealers can obtain virtually every part for your motorcycle, the accessory dealer is usually limited to normal high wear items such as shock absorbers, tune-up parts, various engine gaskets, cables, chains, brake parts, etc. Rarely will an accessory outlet have major suspension components, cylinders, transmission gears, or cases.

Used parts can be obtained for roughly half the price of new ones, but you can't always be sure of what you're getting. Once again, take your worn part to the breaker's yard for direct comparison.

Whether buying new, used or rebuilt parts, the best course is to deal directly with someone who specialises in parts for your particular make.

UK/Europe models	Year	Code
YZF-R6 (R)	2003	5SL1 (5SL2 – France, 5SL6 – Austria)
YZF-R6 (S)	2004	5SLB (5SLC – France, 5SLG/LL – Austria)
YZF-R6 (T)	2005	5SLM (5SLN – France, 5SLP – Austria)
US models	**Year**	**Code**
YZF-R6 (R) 49-state	2003	5SL3
YZF-R6 (RC) California	2003	5SL4
YZF-R6 (S) 49-state	2004	5SLD
YZF-R6 (SC) California	2004	5SLE
YZF-R6 (T) 49-state	2005	5SLR
YZF-R6 (TC) California	2005	5SLS

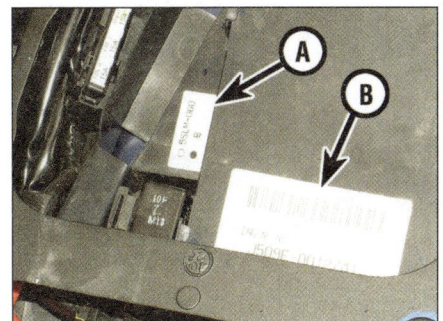

The model code label (A) is stuck to the rear sub-frame, and the engine number is repeated on a sticker (B) on the ECU

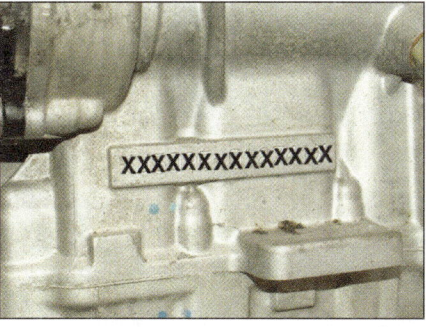

The engine number is stamped into the rear of the crankcase

The frame number is stamped into the right-hand side of the steering head

Model development and Bike spec

2003

The R6 features an extremely lightweight in-line four cylinder engine. Drive to the hollow double overhead camshafts which actuate the four valves per cylinder is by chain from the right-hand end of the crankshaft. The engine is liquid-cooled. The clutch is a conventional wet multi-plate unit and the gearbox is 6-speed. Engine length is kept to a minimum by 'stacking' the transmission shafts, thus enabling a short wheelbase. Drive to the rear wheel is by chain and sprockets.

The engine is fed by four 38 mm throttle bodies, and this is ignited by combined 'stick' type ignition coils and spark plug caps and twin-electrode spark plugs. Control of the fuelling and ignition parameters is by a digital electronic engine management system. The exhaust system is a four-into-two-into-one design and incorporates a catalyser to reduce emissions and meet regulations. Yamaha's air induction system (AIS) feeds fresh air into the exhaust ports to improve exhaust end-gas burning.

The engine sits in a twin spar aluminium Deltabox III style frame which uses the engine as a stressed member. Front suspension is by oil-damped 43 mm forks which have cartridge type dampers. Rear suspension is by a single shock absorber via a rising rate linkage to the truss-type aluminium swingarm. Braking is via Sumitomo calipers front and rear, with twin 298 mm floating discs at the front and a single 220 mm disc at the rear.

Colours: Blue/black, yellow/black, silver/black and red/black.

2004

Changes amounted to revised fuel injection mapping to improve throttle response and a larger silencer to increase flow. Colours: Blue/white/black, silver/white/black and red/white/black.

2005

Modifications were made to the camshafts and intake funnels, and this combined with larger 40 mm throttle bodies and revised fuel injection and ignition mapping led to a power increase across the range. Cooling was improved using a new radiator with twin fans.

Changes to the front end amounted to 41 mm USD forks and new yokes along with radially mounted brake calipers and a wider section front tyre. To complement this at the rear modifications were made to the frame and the suspension linkage. The front disc size was increased to 310 mm and a radial master cylinder was fitted. Minor styling changes were made to the lower fairing and headlight lens.

Colours: Blue/white, red/white/black and black.

Engine

Type	Four-stroke 16V in-line four
Capacity	600 cc
Bore	65.5 mm
Stroke	44.5 mm
Compression ratio	12.4 to 1
Cooling system	Liquid cooled
Clutch	Wet multi-plate
Transmission	Six-speed constant mesh
Final drive	Chain and sprockets
Camshafts	DOHC, chain-driven
Throttle bodies	
YZF-R6 (R and S) 2003 and 2004 models	4 x Mikuni 38EIS
YZF-R6 (T) 2005 model	4 x Mikuni 40EIS
Ignition system	Digital electronic CDI

Chassis

Frame type	Twin spar aluminium Deltabox III
Rake and trail	
YZF-R6 (R and S) 2003 and 2004 models	24°, 86 mm
YZF-R6 (T) 2005 model	24.5°, 95 mm
Fuel tank capacity (including reserve)	17 litres (3.74 Imp gal, 4.5 US gal)
Reserve capacity (with fuel light on)	3.5 litres (0.77 Imp gal, 0.92 US gal)
Front suspension	
YZF-R6 (R and S) 2003 and 2004 models	
Type	43 mm oil-damped conventional telescopic forks
Travel	120 mm (4.7 in)
Adjustment	Pre-load, compression and rebound damping
YZF-R6 (T) 2005 model	
Type	41 mm oil-damped USD telescopic forks
Travel	120 mm (4.7 in)
Adjustment	Pre-load, compression and rebound damping
Rear suspension	
Type	Single shock absorber, rising rate linkage, box-section aluminium swingarm
Travel	120 mm (4.7 in)
Adjustment	Pre-load, compression and rebound damping
Wheels	17 inch 5-spoke alloys
Tyres	
Front	
YZF-R6 (R and S) 2003 and 2004 models	120/60 x 17 Tubeless radial
YZF-R6 (T) 2005 model	120/70 x 17 Tubeless radial
Rear	180/55 x 17 Tubeless radial
Front brake	
YZF-R6 (R and S) 2003 and 2004 models	Twin 298 mm discs with Sumitomo 4-piston opposed calipers, conventionally mounted
YZF-R6 (T) 2005 model	Twin 310 mm discs with Sumitomo 4-piston opposed calipers, radially mounted
Rear brake	Single 220 mm disc with Sumitomo single piston sliding caliper

Bike spec 0•11

Dimensions and weights
Overall length
    YZF-R6 (R and S) 2003 and 2004 models .... 2025 mm (79.7 in)
    YZF-R6 (T) 2005 model .... 2045 mm (80.5 in)
Overall width. .... 690 mm (27.2 in)
Overall height
    YZF-R6 (R and S) 2003 and 2004 models .... 1090 mm (42.9 in)
    YZF-R6 (T) 2005 model .... 1105 mm (43.5 in)
Wheelbase
    YZF-R6 (R and S) 2003 and 2004 models .... 1380 mm (54.3 in)
    YZF-R6 (T) 2005 model .... 1385 mm (54.5 in)
Seat height
    YZF-R6 (R and S) 2003 and 2004 models .... 820 mm (32.3 in)
    YZF-R6 (T) 2005 model .... 830 mm (32.7 in)
Ground clearance
    YZF-R6 (R and S) 2003 and 2004 models .... 135 mm (5.3 in)
    YZF-R6 (T) 2005 model .... 145 mm (5.7 in)
Dry weight (no fluids and empty fuel tank)* .... 162 kg (357 lb)
Wet weight (with all fluids and full fuel tank)*
    YZF-R6 (R and S) 2003 and 2004 models .... 182 kg (401 lb)
    YZF-R6 (T) 2005 model .... 183 kg (404 lb)
Maximum load (rider, passenger, luggage, accessories)**
    YZF-R6 (R and S) 2003 and 2004 models .... 193 kg (426 lb)
    YZF-R6 (T) 2005 model .... 192 kg (423 lb)
California models add 1 kg
*** California models subtract 1 kg*

Safety First!

Professional mechanics are trained in safe working procedures. However enthusiastic you may be about getting on with the job at hand, take the time to ensure that your safety is not put at risk. A moment's lack of attention can result in an accident, as can failure to observe simple precautions.

There will always be new ways of having accidents, and the following is not a comprehensive list of all dangers; it is intended rather to make you aware of the risks and to encourage a safe approach to all work you carry out on your bike.

Asbestos

● Certain friction, insulating, sealing and other products - such as brake pads, clutch linings, gaskets, etc. - contain asbestos. Extreme care must be taken to avoid inhalation of dust from such products since it is hazardous to health. If in doubt, assume that they do contain asbestos.

Fire

● Remember at all times that petrol is highly flammable. Never smoke or have any kind of naked flame around, when working on the vehicle. But the risk does not end there - a spark caused by an electrical short-circuit, by two metal surfaces contacting each other, by careless use of tools, or even by static electricity built up in your body under certain conditions, can ignite petrol vapour, which in a confined space is highly explosive. Never use petrol as a cleaning solvent. Use an approved safety solvent.

● Always disconnect the battery earth terminal before working on any part of the fuel or electrical system, and never risk spilling fuel on to a hot engine or exhaust.
● It is recommended that a fire extinguisher of a type suitable for fuel and electrical fires is kept handy in the garage or workplace at all times. Never try to extinguish a fuel or electrical fire with water.

Fumes

● Certain fumes are highly toxic and can quickly cause unconsciousness and even death if inhaled to any extent. Petrol vapour comes into this category, as do the vapours from certain solvents such as trichloro-ethylene. Any draining or pouring of such volatile fluids should be done in a well ventilated area.
● When using cleaning fluids and solvents, read the instructions carefully. Never use materials from unmarked containers - they may give off poisonous vapours.
● Never run the engine of a motor vehicle in an enclosed space such as a garage. Exhaust fumes contain carbon monoxide which is extremely poisonous; if you need to run the engine, always do so in the open air or at least have the rear of the vehicle outside the workplace.

The battery

● Never cause a spark, or allow a naked light near the vehicle's battery. It will normally be giving off a certain amount of hydrogen gas, which is highly explosive.

● Always disconnect the battery ground (earth) terminal before working on the fuel or electrical systems (except where noted).
● If possible, loosen the filler plugs or cover when charging the battery from an external source. Do not charge at an excessive rate or the battery may burst.
● Take care when topping up, cleaning or carrying the battery. The acid electrolyte, evenwhen diluted, is very corrosive and should not be allowed to contact the eyes or skin. Always wear rubber gloves and goggles or a face shield. If you ever need to prepare electrolyte yourself, always add the acid slowly to the water; never add the water to the acid.

Electricity

● When using an electric power tool, inspection light etc., always ensure that the appliance is correctly connected to its plug and that, where necessary, it is properly grounded (earthed). Do not use such appliances in damp conditions and, again, beware of creating a spark or applying excessive heat in the vicinity of fuel or fuel vapour. Also ensure that the appliances meet national safety standards.
● A severe electric shock can result from touching certain parts of the electrical system, such as the spark plug wires (HT leads), when the engine is running or being cranked, particularly if components are damp or the insulation is defective. Where an electronic ignition system is used, the secondary (HT) voltage is much higher and could prove fatal.

Remember...

✗ **Don't** start the engine without first ascertaining that the transmission is in neutral.
✗ **Don't** suddenly remove the pressure cap from a hot cooling system - cover it with a cloth and release the pressure gradually first, or you may get scalded by escaping coolant.
✗ **Don't** attempt to drain oil until you are sure it has cooled sufficiently to avoid scalding you.
✗ **Don't** grasp any part of the engine or exhaust system without first ascertaining that it is cool enough not to burn you.
✗ **Don't** allow brake fluid or antifreeze to contact the machine's paintwork or plastic components.
✗ **Don't** siphon toxic liquids such as fuel, hydraulic fluid or antifreeze by mouth, or allow them to remain on your skin.
✗ **Don't** inhale dust - it may be injurious to health (see Asbestos heading).
✗ **Don't** allow any spilled oil or grease to remain on the floor - wipe it up right away, before someone slips on it.
✗ **Don't** use ill-fitting spanners or other tools which may slip and cause injury.
✗ **Don't** lift a heavy component which may be beyond your capability - get assistance.

✗ **Don't** rush to finish a job or take unverified short cuts.
✗ **Don't** allow children or animals in or around an unattended vehicle.
✗ **Don't** inflate a tyre above the recommended pressure. Apart from overstressing the carcass, in extreme cases the tyre may blow off forcibly.
✓ **Do** ensure that the machine is supported securely at all times. This is especially important when the machine is blocked up to aid wheel or fork removal.
✓ **Do** take care when attempting to loosen a stubborn nut or bolt. It is generally better to pull on a spanner, rather than push, so that if you slip, you fall away from the machine rather than onto it.
✓ **Do** wear eye protection when using power tools such as drill, sander, bench grinder etc.
✓ **Do** use a barrier cream on your hands prior to undertaking dirty jobs - it will protect your skin from infection as well as making the dirt easier to remove afterwards; but make sure your hands aren't left slippery. Note that long-term contact with used engine oil can be a health hazard.
✓ **Do** keep loose clothing (cuffs, ties etc. and long hair) well out of the way of moving mechanical parts.

✓ **Do** remove rings, wristwatch etc., before working on the vehicle - especially the electrical system.
✓ **Do** keep your work area tidy - it is only too easy to fall over articles left lying around.
✓ **Do** exercise caution when compressing springs for removal or installation. Ensure that the tension is applied and released in a controlled manner, using suitable tools which preclude the possibility of the spring escaping violently.
✓ **Do** ensure that any lifting tackle used has a safe working load rating adequate for the job.
✓ **Do** get someone to check periodically that all is well, when working alone on the vehicle.
✓ **Do** carry out work in a logical sequence and check that everything is correctly assembled and tightened afterwards.
✓ **Do** remember that your vehicle's safety affects that of yourself and others. If in doubt on any point, get professional advice.
● If in spite of following these precautions, you are unfortunate enough to injure yourself, seek medical attention as soon as possible.

Pre-ride checks

Note: *The Pre-ride checks outlined in the owner's manual covers those items which should be inspected before riding the motorcycle.*

Engine oil level

Before you start:
✔ Support the motorcycle in an upright position, using an auxiliary stand if required. Make sure it is on level ground.
✔ Start the engine and let it idle for several minutes to allow it to reach normal operating temperature.
Caution: Do not run the engine in an enclosed space such as a garage or workshop.
✔ Leave the motorcycle undisturbed for a few minutes to allow the oil level to stabilise.

Bike care:
● If you have to add oil frequently, you should check whether you have any oil leaks. If there is no sign of oil leakage from the joints and gaskets the engine could be burning oil (see *Fault Finding*).

The correct oil:
● Modern, high-revving engines place great demands on their oil. It is very important that the correct oil for your bike is used.
● Always top up with a good quality oil of the specified type and viscosity and do not overfill the engine.
Caution: Do not use chemical additives or oils with a grade of CD or higher, or use oils labelled 'ENERGY CONSERVING II'. Such additives or oils could cause clutch slip.

Oil type	API grade SE, SF or SG
Oil viscosity	SAE 10W30 or 20W40*

*Refer to the viscosity table to select the oil best suited to your conditions.

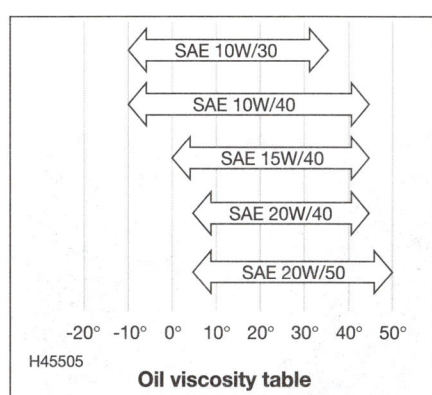

Oil viscosity table

1 Remove the dipstick from the right-hand side of the crankcase and use clean rag or paper towel to wipe off all the oil.

2 Insert the clean dipstick back into the engine, but do not screw it in.

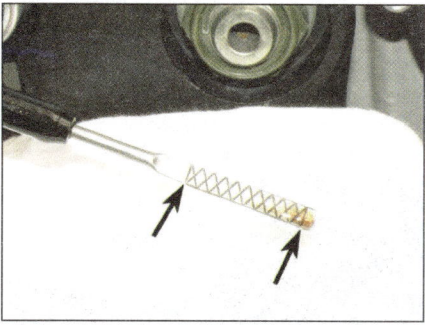

3 Remove the dipstick and check the level of the oil, which should be somewhere between the upper and lower level lines (arrowed).

4 If the level is below the lower line, remove the filler cap from the top of the clutch cover.

5 Add the recommended grade and type of oil, to bring the level almost up to the upper line on the dipstick. Do not overfill. Install the filler cap and the dipstick.

Suspension, steering and drive chain

Suspension and Steering:
● Check that the front and rear suspension operates smoothly without binding.
● Check that the suspension is adjusted as required.
● Check that the steering moves smoothly from lock-to-lock.

Final drive:
● Check that the drive chain slack isn't excessive, and adjust it if necessary (see Chapter 1).
● If the chain looks dry, lubricate it (see Chapter 1).

0•14 Pre-ride checks

Coolant level

Before you start:
✔ Make sure you have a supply of coolant available – a mixture of 50% distilled water and 50% corrosion inhibited ethylene glycol anti-freeze is needed. **Note:** *Yamaha specify that soft tap water can be used if necessary, but NOT hard water. If in doubt, boil the water first or use only distilled water.*
✔ Always check the coolant level when the engine is cold.
✔ Support the motorcycle in an upright position, using an auxiliary stand if required. Make sure it is on level ground.

⚠ **Warning: DO NOT remove the cooling system pressure cap to add coolant. Topping up is done via the coolant reservoir tank filler. DO NOT leave open containers of coolant about, as it is poisonous.**

Bike care:
● Use only the specified coolant mixture. It is important that anti-freeze is used in the system all year round, and not just in the winter. Do not top the system up using only water, as the system will become too diluted.
● Do not overfill the reservoir. If the coolant is significantly above the FULL level line at any time, the surplus should be siphoned or drained off to prevent the possibility of it being expelled out of the overflow hose.
● If the coolant level falls steadily, check the system for leaks (see Chapter 1). If no leaks are found and the level continues to fall, it is recommended that the machine be taken to a Yamaha dealer for a pressure test.

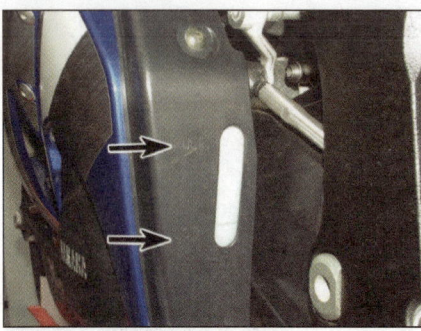

1 The reservoir is mounted on the left-hand side of the motorcycle, inside the fairing side panel. The coolant FULL and LOW level lines (arrowed) are marked on the reservoir.

2 If the coolant level does not lie between the FULL and LOW level lines, undo the screws (arrowed) and remove the reservoir cover, noting how the hoses route through the guide on its base.

3 Remove the reservoir filler cap and draw the hose out, catching any drops of coolant with a rag.

4 Top the coolant level up with the recommended coolant mixture then fit the cap securely.

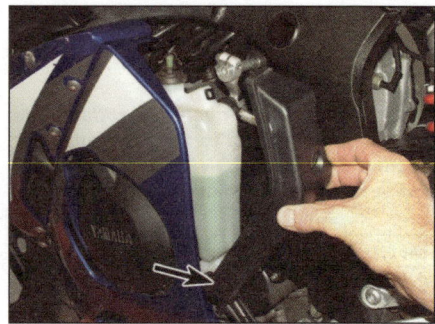

5 Refit the cover, feeding the hoses through the guide in the bottom (arrowed).

Brake fluid levels

⚠ **Warning: Brake hydraulic fluid can harm your eyes and damage painted surfaces, so use extreme caution when handling and pouring it and cover surrounding surfaces with rag. Do not use fluid that has been standing open for some time, as it absorbs moisture from the air which can cause a dangerous loss of braking effectiveness.**

Before you start:
✔ The front brake fluid reservoir is on the right-hand handlebar. The rear brake fluid reservoir is located under the rider's seat on the right-hand side.
✔ Make sure you have the correct hydraulic fluid. DOT 4 is recommended.
✔ Wrap a rag around the reservoir being worked on to ensure that any spillage does not come into contact with painted surfaces.
✔ When checking the fluid level in the front reservoir, place the motorcycle on its sidestand and turn the handlebars as required so the reservoir is level.
✔ When checking the fluid in the rear reservoir support the motorcycle upright, if available using an auxiliary stand.

Bike care:
● The fluid in the front and rear brake master cylinder reservoirs will drop as the brake pads wear down. If the fluid level is low check the brake pads for wear (see Chapter 1), and replace them with new ones if necessary (see Chapter 6). Do not top the reservoir(s) up until the new pads have been fitted, and then check to see if topping up is still necessary – as the caliper pistons are pushed back to accommodate the extra thickness of the pads some fluid will be displaced back into the reservoir.
● If either fluid reservoir requires repeated topping-up there could be a leak somewhere in the system, which must be investigated immediately.

Pre-ride checks

FRONT BRAKE

Steps 1-5

REAR BRAKE

Steps 6-11

1 The front brake fluid level is visible through the reservoir body – it must be between the UPPER and LOWER level lines (arrowed).

2 If the level is below the LOWER level line, undo the reservoir cap clamp screw and remove the clamp, then unscrew the cap and remove the diaphragm plate and the diaphragm.

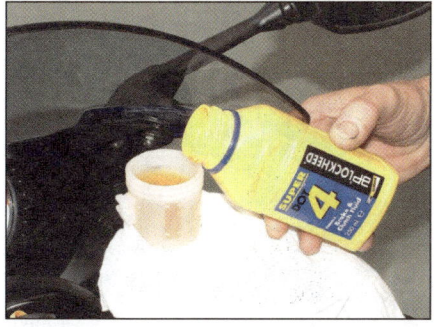

3 Top up with new, clean DOT 4 hydraulic fluid, until the level is between the level lines. Take care to avoid spills (see **Warning**) and do not overfill.

4 Wipe any moisture out of the diaphragm using a clean lint-free cloth.

5 Ensure that the diaphragm is correctly seated before installing the plate and cap. Secure the cap with its clamp.

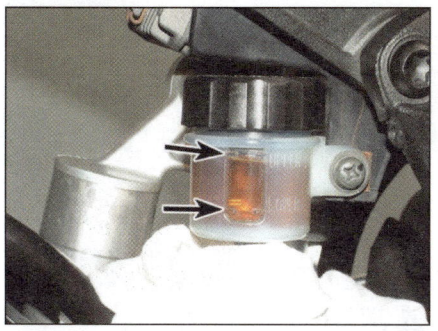

6 The rear brake fluid level is visible through the reservoir body – it must be between the UPPER and LOWER level lines (arrowed).

7 If the level is below the LOWER level line, slacken the reservoir mounting screw enough to tilt the reservoir so the cap clears the frame.

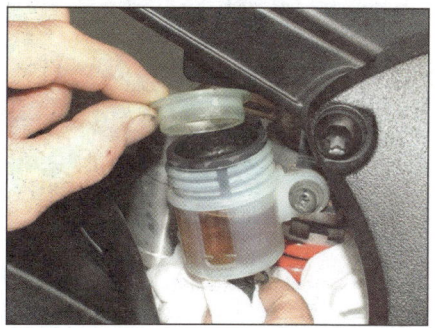

8 Hold the reservoir, then unscrew the cap and remove the plate and the diaphragm.

9 Top up with new, clean DOT 4 hydraulic fluid, until the level is between the level lines. Take care to avoid spills (see **Warning**) and do not overfill.

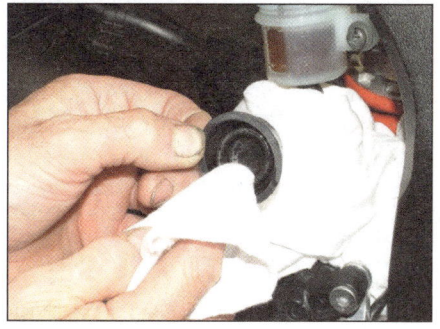

10 Wipe any moisture out of the diaphragm using a clean lint-free cloth.

11 Refit the diaphragm, plate and cap and tighten the reservoir screw.

Pre-ride checks

Tyres

Tyre tread depth:
- At the time of writing UK law requires that the tread depth must be at least 1 mm over the entire tread breadth all the way around the tyre, with no bald patches. Many riders, however, consider 2 mm tread depth minimum to be a safer limit. Yamaha recommend a minimum of 1.6 mm.
- Many tyres now incorporate wear indicators in the tread. Identify the triangular pointer or TWI mark on the tyre sidewall to locate the indicator bar and renew the tyre if the tread has worn down to the bar.

The correct pressures:
- The tyres must be checked when **cold**, not immediately after riding. Note that low tyre pressures may cause the tyre to slip on the rim or come off. High tyre pressures will cause abnormal tread wear and unsafe handling.
- Use an accurate pressure gauge. Many garage forecourt gauges are wildly inaccurate. If you buy your own, spend as much as you can justify on a quality gauge.
- Correct air pressure will increase tyre life and provide maximum stability, handling capability and ride comfort.

YZF-R6 (R and S) 2003 and 2004 models		
Loading*/speed	Front	Rear
Up to 90 kg (198 lb) load	36 psi (2.5 Bar)	36 psi (2.5 Bar)
90 kg (198 lb) up to max. load	36 psi (2.5 Bar)	42 psi (2.9 Bar)
High speed riding	36 psi (2.5 Bar)	36 psi (2.5 Bar)

YZF-R6 (T) 2005 model		
Loading*/speed	Front	Rear
Up to 90 kg (198 lb) load	36 psi (2.5 Bar)	42 psi (2.9 Bar)
90 kg (198 lb) up to max. load	36 psi (2.5 Bar)	42 psi (2.9 Bar)
High speed riding	36 psi (2.5 Bar)	42 psi (2.9 Bar)

*Load is the total weight of the rider, passenger, luggage and any accessories

Tyre care:
- Check the tyres carefully for cuts, tears, embedded nails or other sharp objects and excessive wear. Operation of the motorcycle with excessively worn tyres is extremely hazardous, as traction and handling are directly affected.
- Check the condition of the tyre valve and ensure the dust cap is in place.
- Pick out any stones or nails which may have become embedded in the tyre tread. If left, they will eventually penetrate through the casing and cause a puncture.
- If tyre damage is apparent, or unexplained loss of pressure is experienced, seek the advice of a tyre fitting specialist without delay.

1 Remove the cap from the valve – if there isn't one there buy a new one.

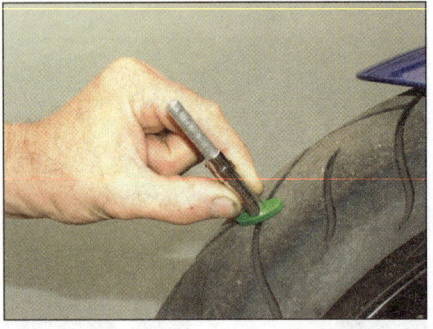

2 Check the tyre pressures when the tyres are cold and keep them properly inflated. Fit the cap on completion

3 Measure tread depth at the centre of the tyre using a tread depth gauge.

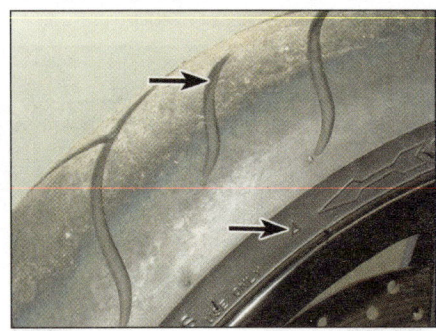

4 Tyre tread wear indicator bar and its location marking (usually either an arrow, a triangle or the letters TWI) on the sidewall.

Legal and safety

Lighting and signalling:
- Take a minute to check that the headlight, tail light, brake light, instrument lights and turn signals all work correctly.
- Check that the horn sounds when the switch is operated.
- A working speedometer graduated in mph is a statutory requirement in the UK.

Safety:
- Check that the throttle grip rotates smoothly and snaps shut when released, in all steering positions. Also check for the correct amount of freeplay (see Chapter 1).
- Check that the steering moves freely from lock-to-lock.
- Check that the brake lever and pedal, clutch lever and gearchange lever operate smoothly. Lubricate them at the specified intervals or when necessary (see Chapter 1).
- Check that the engine shuts off when the kill switch is operated.
- Check that the sidestand return spring holds the stand up securely when it is retracted.

Fuel:
- This may seem obvious, but check that you have enough fuel to complete your journey. If you notice signs of fuel leakage – rectify the cause immediately.
- Ensure you use the correct grade fuel – see Chapter 4 Specifications.

Chapter 1
Routine maintenance and Servicing

Contents

	Section number
Air filter and air intake	3
Battery	18
Brake fluid levels	see Pre-ride checks
Brake system	12
Clutch	8
Coolant level	see Pre-ride checks
Cooling system	10
Drive chain and sprockets	1
Engine oil and filter	11
Engine oil level check	see Pre-ride checks
Engine wear assessment	see Chapter 2
Fuel system and emission control	6

	Section number
Idle speed	4
Nuts and bolts	17
Sidestand and starter safety circuit	16
Spark plugs	2
Stand, lever pivots and cable lubrication	9
Steering head bearings	15
Suspension	14
Throttle body synchronisation	5
Throttle cables	7
Valve clearances	19
Wheels, wheel bearings and tyres	13

Degrees of difficulty

| **Easy,** suitable for novice with little experience | **Fairly easy,** suitable for beginner with some experience | **Fairly difficult,** suitable for competent DIY mechanic | **Difficult,** suitable for experienced DIY mechanic | **Very difficult,** suitable for expert DIY or professional |

Specifications

Engine
Spark plugs
    Type .... NGK CR9EK or CR10EK
    Electrode gap .... 0.6 to 0.7 mm
Engine idle speed .... 1250 to 1350 rpm
Cylinder identification .... numbered 1 to 4 from left to right
Throttle body synchronisation – intake vacuum at idle .... 180 mmHg
Throttle body synchronisation – max. difference between bodies .... 10 mmHg
Valve clearances (COLD engine)
    Intake valves .... 0.13 to 0.20 mm
    Exhaust valves .... 0.23 to 0.30 mm

Cycle parts
Drive chain slack .... 35 to 45 mm
Drive chain stretch limit (see text)
    R and S (2003 and 2004) models .... 150.1 mm
    T (2005) models .... 239.3 mm
Drive chain type .... see Chapter 6
Brake pad friction material wear limit
    Front calipers .... 0.5 mm
    Rear caliper .... 1.0 mm
Rear brake pedal height .... 7 to 11 mm
Throttle cable freeplay .... 6 to 8 mm
Clutch cable freeplay .... 10 to 15 mm
Tyre pressures (cold) .... see Pre-ride checks

Lubricants and fluids
Fuel .... see Chapter 4
Engine oil type .... see Pre-ride checks
Engine oil capacity
    Oil change .... 2.4 litres
    Oil and filter change .... 2.6 litres
    Following engine overhaul – dry engine, new filter .... 3.4 litres
Coolant type .... 50% distilled water, 50% ethylene glycol anti-freeze with corrosion inhibitors for aluminium engines. **Note:** *Yamaha specify that soft tap water can be used, but NOT hard water. If in doubt, boil the water first or use only distilled water.*
Coolant capacity
    Radiator .... 2.15 litres
    Reservoir .... 0.44 litre
Brake fluid .... DOT 4
Drive chain .... Engine oil or chain lubricant suitable for O-ring chains
Steering head bearings .... Lithium-based multi-purpose grease
Swingarm pivot and bearings .... Lithium-based multi-purpose grease
Suspension linkage bearings .... Lithium-based multi-purpose grease
Bearing seals .... Lithium-based multi-purpose grease
Gearchange lever, clutch lever, front brake lever,
    rear brake pedal, sidestand pivots .... Lithium-based multi-purpose grease
Cables .... Aerosol cable lubricant
Throttle twistgrip .... Lithium-based multi-purpose grease

Torque wrench settings
Cooling system drain plug .... 10 Nm
Fork clamp bolts (top yoke) .... 26 Nm
Handlebar positioning bolts .... 13 Nm
Handlebar clamp bolts .... 33 Nm
Oil drain plug .... 43 Nm
Oil filter .... 17 Nm
Rear axle nut .... 110 Nm
Spark plugs .... 13 Nm
Steering head bearing adjuster nut
    Initial setting .... 52 Nm
    Final setting .... 14 Nm
Steering stem nut .... 113 Nm
Ignition rotor/pick-up coil cover bolts .... 12 Nm

Maintenance schedule

Pre-ride
- [ ] See Pre-ride checks at the beginning of this manual.

After the initial 600 miles (1000 km)
Note: *This check is usually performed by a Yamaha dealer after the first 600 miles (1000 km) from new. Thereafter, maintenance is carried out according to the following intervals of the schedule.*

Every 500 miles (800 km)
- [ ] Check, adjust, clean and lubricate the drive chain (Section 1)

Every 6000 miles (10,000 km)
- [ ] Check and adjust the spark plugs (Section 2)
- [ ] Clean and check the air filter element and drain the intake surge tanks (Section 3)
- [ ] Check and adjust the idle speed (Section 4)
- [ ] Check/adjust throttle body synchronisation (Section 5)
- [ ] Check the fuel system and the air induction system (AIS) (Section 6)
- [ ] Check and adjust the throttle cables (Section 7)
- [ ] Check and adjust the clutch and clutch cable (Section 8)
- [ ] Lubricate the clutch/gearchange/brake lever/brake pedal/sidestand pivots and the throttle/choke cables (Section 9)
- [ ] Check the cooling system (Section 10)
- [ ] Change the engine oil (Section 11)
- [ ] Check the brake pads (Section 12)
- [ ] Check the brake system and brake light switch operation (Section 12)
- [ ] Check the condition of the wheels and tyres (Section 13)
- [ ] Check the wheel bearings (Section 13)
- [ ] Check the suspension (Section 14)
- [ ] Check and adjust the steering head bearings (Section 15)
- [ ] Check the sidestand and starter safety circuit (Section 16)
- [ ] Check the tightness of all nuts, bolts and fasteners (Section 17)
- [ ] Check the battery (Section 18)

Every 12,000 miles (20,000 km)
Carry out all the items under the previous interval, plus the following:
- [ ] Fit new spark plugs (see Section 2)
- [ ] Fit a new air filter element (see Section 3)
- [ ] Check the EVAP system (Section 6) – California models only
- [ ] Fit a new engine oil filter (Section 11)
- [ ] Re-grease the steering head bearings (Section 15)
- [ ] Re-grease the suspension linkage bearings (Section 14)

Every 25,000 miles (40,000 km)
- [ ] Check and adjust the valve clearances (Section 19)

Every 30,000 miles (50,000 km)
- [ ] Re-grease the swingarm bearings (Section 14)

Every two years
- [ ] Change the brake fluid (Section 12)
- [ ] Renew the seals in the brake master cylinders and calipers (Section 12)

Every three years
- [ ] Change the coolant (Section 10)

Every four years
- [ ] Fit new brake hoses (Section 12)

Non-scheduled maintenance
- [ ] Fit new fuel hoses (Section 6)
- [ ] Change the front fork oil (Section 14)

1•4 Component locations

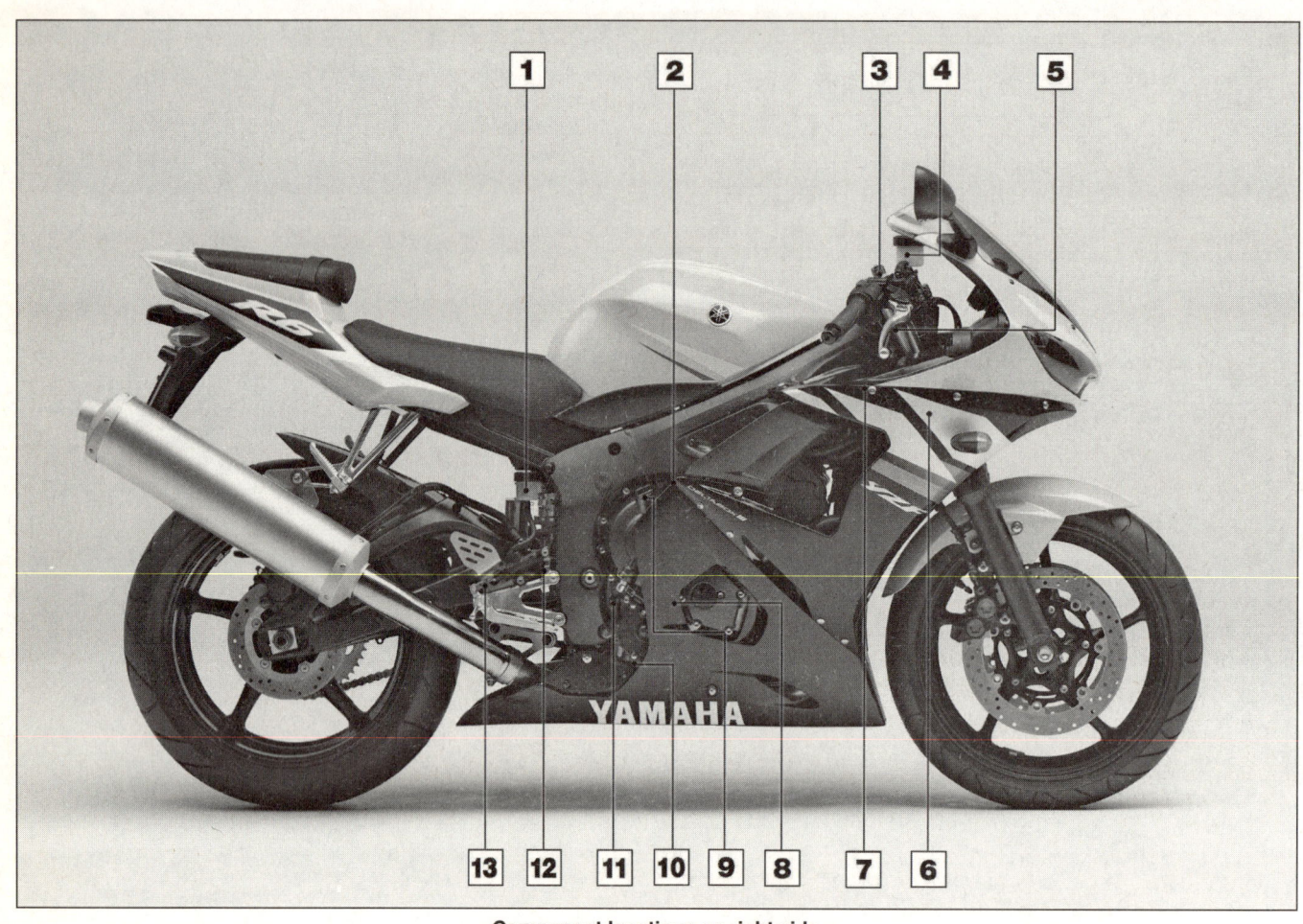

Component locations on right side

1 Rear brake fluid reservoir
2 Idle speed adjuster
3 Steering head bearing adjuster
4 Front brake fluid reservoir
5 Throttle cable upper adjuster
6 Air intake surge tanks
7 Radiator pressure cap
8 Clutch cable lower adjuster
9 Engine oil filler cap
10 Coolant drain bolt
11 Engine oil level dipstick
12 Rear brake light switch
13 Rear brake pedal height adjuster

Component locations 1•5

Component locations on left side

1 Clutch cable upper adjuster
2 Front fork rebound damping and pre-load adjuster
3 Air filter
4 Battery
5 Drive chain adjuster
6 Rear shock compression damping adjuster
7 Rear shock rebound damping adjuster
8 Rear shock spring pre-load adjuster
9 Engine oil drain bolt
10 Engine oil filter
11 Coolant reservoir cap
12 Throttle cable lower adjuster
13 Front fork compression damping adjuster

1•6 Routine Maintenance and Servicing

1 This Chapter is designed to help the home mechanic maintain his/her motorcycle for safety, economy, long life and peak performance.

2 Deciding where to start or plug into the routine maintenance schedule depends on several factors. If the warranty period on your motorcycle has just expired, and if it has been maintained according to the warranty standards, you may want to pick up routine maintenance as it coincides with the next mileage or calendar interval. If you have owned the machine for some time but have never performed any maintenance on it, then you may want to start at the beginning and include all frequent procedures to ensure that nothing important is overlooked. If you have just had a major engine overhaul, then you should start the engine maintenance routines from the beginning. If you have a used machine and have no knowledge of its history or maintenance record, you should combine all the checks into one large initial service and then settle into the maintenance schedule prescribed.

3 Before beginning any maintenance or repair, the machine should be cleaned thoroughly, especially around the oil filter, drain plugs, spark plugs and valve cover. Cleaning will help ensure that dirt does not contaminate the engine and will allow you to detect wear and damage that could otherwise easily go unnoticed.

4 Certain maintenance information is sometimes printed on decals attached to the motorcycle. If any information on the decals differs from that included here, use the information on the decal.

⚠️ *Warning: Read the Safety first! section of this manual carefully before starting work.*

Maintenance procedures

1 Drive chain and sprockets

Chain slack check

1 A neglected drive chain won't last long and can quickly damage the sprockets. Routine chain adjustment and lubrication isn't difficult and will ensure maximum chain and sprocket life.

2 To check the chain, support the bike upright, but do not have someone sit on it to do this, and shift the transmission into neutral.

3 Push up on the bottom run of the chain and measure the slack midway between the two sprockets **(see illustration)**, then compare your measurement to that listed in this Chapter's Specifications. As the chain stretches with wear, adjustment will periodically be necessary (see below). Since the chain will rarely wear evenly, roll the bike forward so that another section of chain can be checked (having an assistant to do this makes the task a lot easier); do this several times to check the entire length of chain, and mark the tightest spot.

Caution: Riding the bike with excess slack in the chain could lead to damage.

4 In some cases where lubrication has been neglected, corrosion and dirt may cause the links to bind and kink, which effectively shortens the chain's length and makes it tight **(see illustration)**. Thoroughly clean and work free any such links, then highlight them with a marker pen or paint. Take the bike for a ride.

5 After the bike has been ridden, repeat the measurement for slack in the highlighted area. If the chain has kinked again and is still tight, replace it with a new one (see Chapter 6). A rusty, kinked or worn chain will damage the sprockets and can damage transmission bearings. If in any doubt as to the condition of a chain, it is far better to install a new one than risk damage to other components and possibly yourself.

6 Check the entire length of the chain for worn or damaged rollers and side plates, loose links and pins, and missing O-rings and replace it with a new one if necessary. **Note:** *Never install a new chain on old sprockets, and never use the old chain if you install new sprockets – replace the chain and sprockets as a set.*

7 Inspect the drive chain slider on the front of the swingarm for excessive wear and damage and replace it with a new one if necessary.

Adjustment

8 Rotate the rear wheel until the chain is positioned with the tightest point at the centre of its bottom run. Support the bike upright (but not by having someone sit on it).

9 Loosen the nut on the right-hand end of the rear axle.

10 Loosen the locknut on the adjuster bolt on each side of the swingarm, then turn the

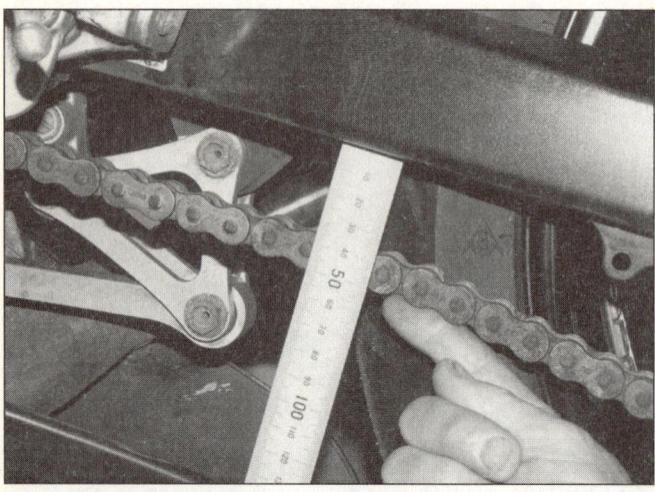
1.3 Push up on the chain and measure the slack

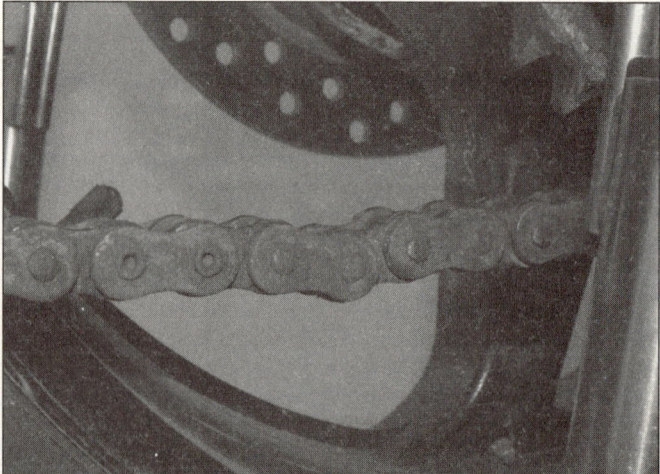
1.4 Neglect has caused the links in this chain to kink

Routine Maintenance and Servicing

1.10a Slacken the locknut (arrowed) on each side ...

1.10b ... and turn each adjuster by an equal amount ...

1.10c ... then check the alignment of the adjuster plate with the index marks on the swingarm as described

adjuster bolts evenly, a small amount at a time, until the specified chain tension is obtained **(see illustrations)**. Following chain adjustment, check that the back edge of each adjuster plate is in the same position in relation to the marks on each side of the swingarm **(see illustration)**. It is important that each plate aligns with the same mark; if not, the rear wheel will be out of alignment with the front.

> **HAYNES HiNT** *Refer to Chapter 6 for information on checking wheel alignment.*

11 If there is a discrepancy in the position of the plates, correct it with the adjusters and then check the chain tension as described above. Also check that there is no clearance between the adjuster bolt head and the front of the adjuster plate – push the wheel forwards to eliminate any clearance.

12 Tighten the axle nut to the torque setting specified at the beginning of this Chapter, then tighten the adjuster locknuts securely. Recheck the adjustment.

Cleaning and lubrication

13 If required, wash the chain using a dedicated aerosol cleaner or in paraffin (kerosene), then wipe it off and allow it to dry, using compressed air if available. If the chain is excessively dirty, remove the rear wheel (see Chapter 6) and soak the chain in paraffin. *Caution: Don't use petrol (gasoline), solvent or other cleaning fluids which might damage the internal sealing properties of the chain. Don't use high-pressure water. The entire process shouldn't take longer than five to six minutes – if it does, the O-rings in the chain rollers could be damaged.*

14 The best time to lubricate the chain is after the motorcycle has been ridden. When the chain is warm, the lubricant will penetrate the joints between the side plates better than when cold. **Note:** *Yamaha specifies engine oil or chain lube that is specifically for O-ring chains; do not use chain lube that is not specifically for O-ring chains, as it may contain solvents that*

> **HAYNES HiNT** *Apply the lubricant to the top of the lower chain run, so centrifugal force will work it into the chain when the bike is moving. After applying the lubricant, let it soak in a few minutes before wiping off any excess.*

could damage the O-rings. Apply the lubricant to the area where the side plates overlap – not the middle of the rollers and protect the tyre from overspray with a rag **(see illustration)**.

 *Warning: Take care not to get any lubricant on the tyres or brake system components. If any of the lubricant inadvertently contacts them, clean it off thoroughly using a suitable solvent or dedicated brake cleaner before riding the machine.*

Drive chain stretch and sprocket wear check

15 Check the entire length of the chain for worn or damaged rollers and side plates, loose links and pins, and missing O-rings. Fit a new chain if damage is found.

16 Remove the front sprocket cover (see Chapter 6). Check the teeth on the front sprocket and the rear sprocket for wear **(see illustration)**. If the sprocket teeth are worn excessively, renew the chain and both sprockets as a set. Check that the lockwasher is correctly installed on the front sprocket nut and that the nut is tight. Check that the rear wheel sprocket nuts are tight (refer to Chapter 6 Specifications for torque settings).

17 Inspect the drive chain slider on the

1.14 Apply the lubricant to the overlapping sections of the sideplates

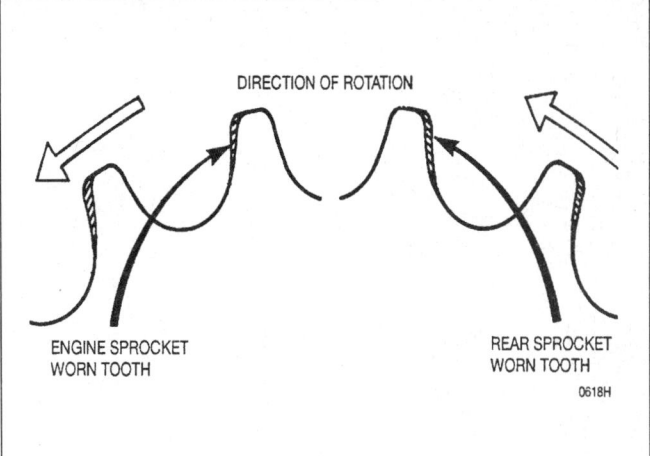

1.16 Check the sprockets in the areas indicated to see if they are worn excessively

1•8 Routine Maintenance and Servicing

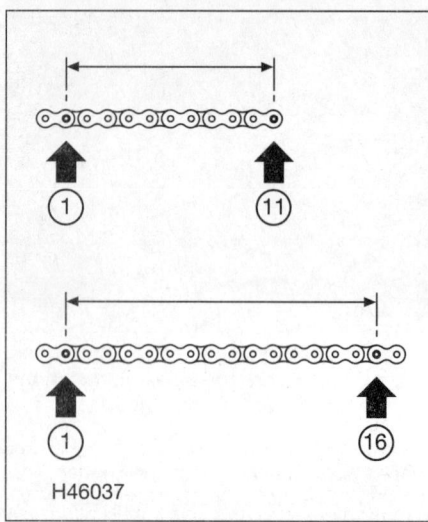

1.20 Measure chain link sections as shown to determine chain stretch

On R and S (2003 and 2004) models measure a 10-link section – between the 1st and 11th pins

On T (2005) models measure a 15-link section – between the 1st and 16th pins

front of the swingarm for excessive wear and damage and replace it with a new one if necessary.

18 Measure the amount of chain stretch as follows:

19 Loosen the nut on the right-hand end of the rear axle.

20 Slacken the adjuster bolt locknuts, then turn the adjuster bolts out evenly until all slack is taken up, but not so much that the chain is taut **(see illustrations 1.10a and b)**. Measure along the bottom run of the chain, a 10 link section on R and S (2003 and 2004) models or a 15 link section on T (2005) models **(see illustration)**. Rotate the rear wheel so that several sections of the chain can be measured, then calculate the average and compare it to the stretch limit specified at the beginning of the Chapter. If the chain stretch measurement exceeds the service limit it must be replaced with a new one (see Chapter 6).

21 If the chain is good, reset the adjusters so that there is the correct amount of freeplay (see Steps 8 to 12).

Caution: *Never install a new chain on old sprockets, and never use the old chain if you install new sprockets – replace the chain and sprockets as a set.*

2 Spark plugs

Check and adjustment

1 Make sure your spark plug socket is the correct size (16 mm) before attempting to remove the plugs – a special plug spanner is supplied in the motorcycle's tool kit which is stored under the passenger seat.

2 Remove the air filter housing, and for best access the air duct joint pieces (see Chapter 4). Note the routing of all cables, wiring and hoses over and around the radiator cover. Release the cables ties to free the wiring **(see illustration)**. Release the trim clips securing the cover and remove it, noting how it fits **(see illustration)**.

3 Clean the area around each ignition coil to prevent any dirt falling into the spark plug channels. Check that the cylinder location is marked on each wiring sleeve, then disconnect the coil wiring connectors **(see illustration)**. Pull the coil off each spark plug **(see illustration)**. If compressed air is

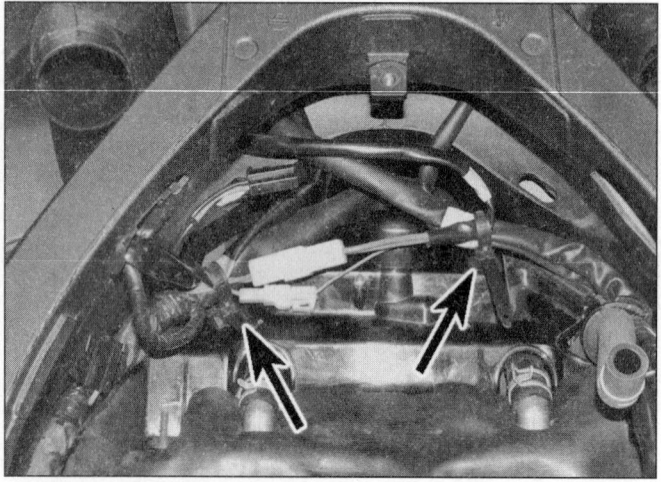

2.2a Release the cable ties (arrowed) . . .

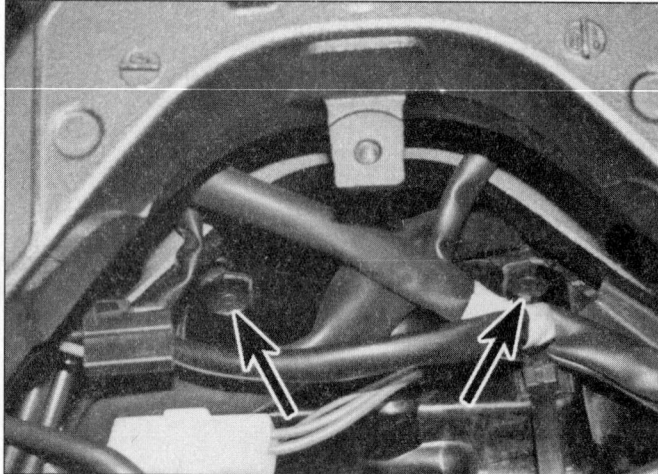

2.2b . . . then move the wiring aside and release the trim clips (B) . . .

2.2c . . . and remove the cover

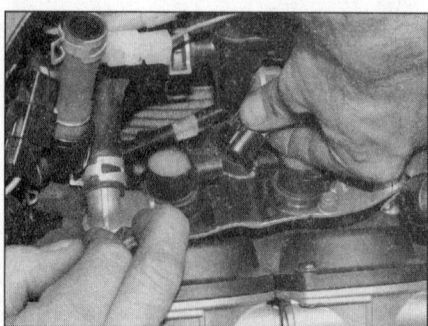

2.3a Disconnect the coil wiring connector . . .

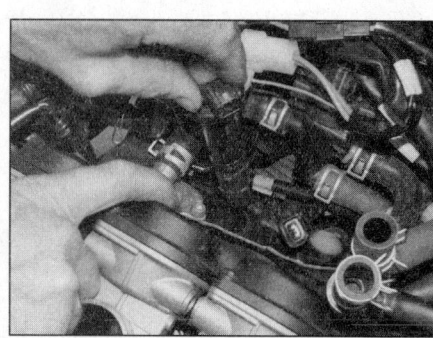

2.3b . . . then pull the coil up off the plug

Routine Maintenance and Servicing 1•9

2.4 Unscrew the plug and lift it out with the tool – the rubber insert should grip around the plug top

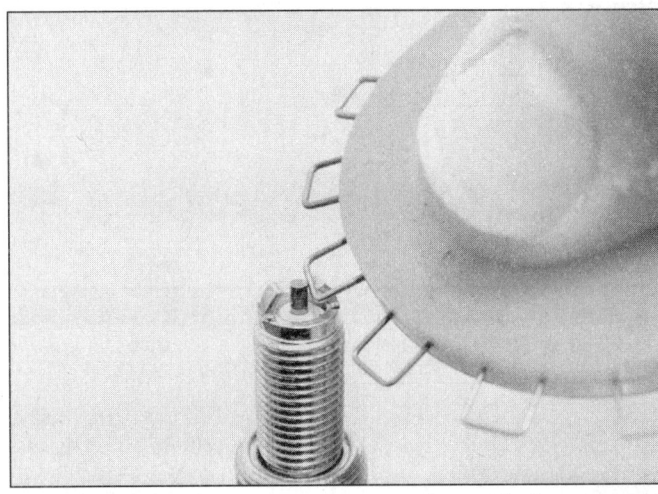

2.7a Using a wire type gauge to measure the spark plug electrode gap

available blow away any accumulated dirt lying in the bottom of each spark plug well to prevent any falling into the engine when the plug is removed.

4 Using either a plug spanner or a deep socket type wrench, unscrew the plugs from the cylinder head **(see illustration)**. Lay each plug out in relation to its cylinder so that, if any plug shows up a problem, it will be easy to identify the troublesome cylinder.

5 Inspect the electrodes for wear. Both the centre and side electrodes should have square edges and the side electrodes should be of uniform thickness. Look for excessive deposits and evidence of a cracked or chipped insulator around the centre electrode. Compare your spark plugs to the colour spark plug reading chart at the end of this manual. Check the threads, the washer and the ceramic insulator body for cracks and other damage.

6 If the electrodes are not excessively worn, and if the deposits can be easily removed with a wire brush, and there are no cracks or chips visible in the insulator, the plugs can be re-gapped and re-used. If in doubt concerning the condition of the plugs, replace them with new ones, as the expense is minimal. Note that new spark plugs should be fitted at every second service interval, i.e. every 12,000 miles (20,000 km).

7 Before installing the plugs, make sure they are the correct type and heat range and check the gap between the side (earth) electrodes and the centre electrode **(see illustration)**. Compare the gap to that specified and adjust as necessary **(see illustration)**. If the gap must be adjusted, bend the side electrodes only and be very careful not to chip or crack the insulator nose **(see illustration)**. Make sure the sealing washer is in place on the plug before installing it.

8 Since the cylinder head is made of aluminium, which is soft and easily damaged, thread the plugs into the head and turn the tool by hand **(see illustration 2.4)**. Once the

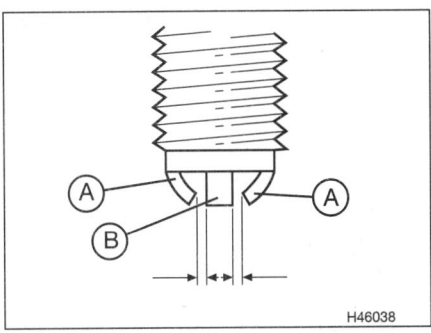

2.7b The gaps between the two earth electrodes (A) and the centre electrode (B) must be equal and as specified

plugs are finger-tight, the job can be finished with a spanner on the tool supplied or a socket drive. If a torque wrench is available, tighten the spark plugs to the torque setting specified at the beginning of this Chapter. Otherwise tighten them by 1/4 to 1/2 turn after they have been fully hand tightened and have seated. Do not over-tighten them.

 *As the plugs are quite recessed, you can slip a short length of hose over the end of the plug to use as a tool to thread it into place. The hose will grip the plug well enough to turn it, but will start to slip if the plug begins to cross-thread in the hole – this will prevent damaged threads.*

9 Install the coils, making sure they locate correctly onto the plugs **(see illustration 2.3b)**. Reconnect the coil wiring connectors, making sure they are securely connected to the correct cylinder – each wiring sleeve should be marked with its cylinder number **(see illustration 2.3a)**.

10 Install the radiator cover **(see illustrations 2.2c, b and a)**. Install the air duct joint

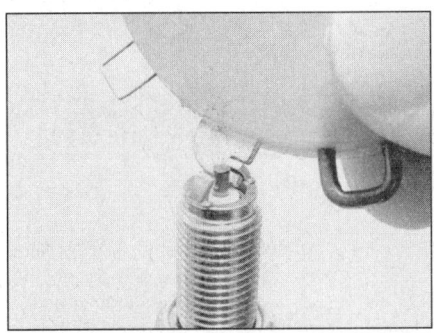

2.7c Adjust the electrode gap by bending the side electrodes only

pieces if removed and the air filter housing (see Chapter 4).

 Stripped plug threads in the cylinder head can be repaired with a thread insert – see Section 2 of 'Tools and Workshop Tips' in the Reference section.

Renewal

11 At the prescribed interval, whatever the condition of the existing spark plugs, remove the plugs as described above and install new ones.

3 Air filter and air intake

Note: *If the machine is continually ridden in dusty conditions, clean the filter more frequently than specified.*

Air filter

Cleaning

1 Raise the fuel tank, or remove it if required for better access (see Chapter 4).

1•10 Routine Maintenance and Servicing

3.2a Undo the screws . . .

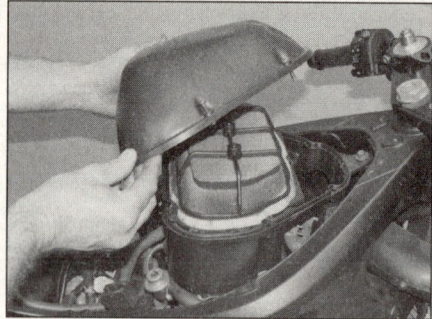
3.2b . . . and remove the cover . . .

3.2c . . . the filter element . . .

3.2d . . . and the seal

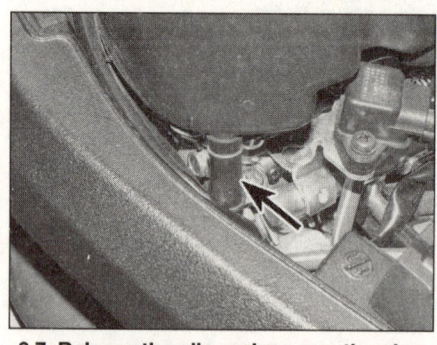
3.7 Release the clip and remove the plug (arrowed) to drain the collector

3.8 Crankcase breather hose (arrowed)

2 Remove the screws securing the air filter housing cover, then remove the cover, the filter element and the seal (see illustrations).
3 Check the element for signs of damage. If the element is torn or is obviously beyond further use, replace it with a new one.
4 If the element is undamaged but dirty, tap it on a hard surface to dislodge any dirt, then wash it in solvent. Gently squeeze out all solvent (do not wring it out!), then dry the element, using compressed air if available.
5 Soak the element in clean engine oil, then gently squeeze out any excess oil – it should be wet but not dripping.
6 Clean out any dirt from the filter housing and cover. Install the seal and the filter element and fit the cover, making sure the components locate correctly in the rim of the housing (see illustrations 3.2d, c, b and a).
7 Remove the plug from the end of the air filter housing drain hose and drain the collector

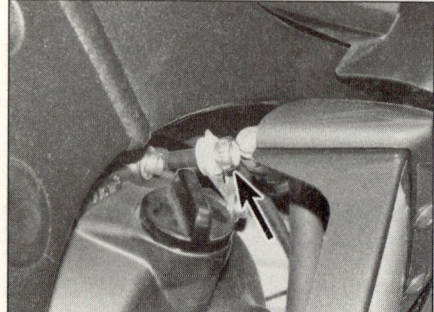
4.3 Idle speed adjuster (arrowed)

(see illustration). Check that the collector is not blocked.
8 Check the crankcase breather hose between the engine and the rear of the air filter housing for loose connections, cracks and deterioration, and replace it with a new one if necessary (see illustration).
9 Install the fuel tank (see Chapter 4).

Renewal

10 At the prescribed interval, whatever the condition of the existing filter element, remove the element as described above and install a new one.

Air intake

11 Remove the fairing, then remove the air duct intake pieces from the fairing (see Chapter 7).
12 Drain any water from the tanks, then flush out any debris with clean water. Allow the tanks to drain and dry completely before installing them.

4 Idle speed

1 Check and adjust the idle speed before and after the throttle bodies are synchronised (balanced), after checking the valve clearances, and when it is obviously too high or too low. Before adjusting the idle speed, make sure the valve clearances were checked at the previous prescribed interval, and the spark plug gaps are correct and the air filter

is clean. Also, turn the handlebars back-and-forth and see if the idle speed changes as this is done. If it does, the throttle cables may not be adjusted or routed correctly, or may be worn out. This is a dangerous condition that can cause loss of control of the bike. Be sure to correct this problem before proceeding.
2 The engine should be at normal operating temperature, which is usually reached after 10 to 15 minutes of stop-and-go riding. Make sure the transmission is in neutral, and place the motorcycle on its stand.
3 The idle speed adjuster is located on the right-hand side of the motorcycle above the clutch cover (see illustration). With the engine idling, turn the adjuster until the speed listed in this Chapter's Specifications is obtained. Turn the knob clockwise to increase idle speed, and anti-clockwise to decrease it.
4 Snap the throttle open and shut a few times, then recheck the idle speed. If necessary, repeat the adjustment procedure.
5 If a smooth, steady idle cannot be achieved, the throttle bodies may need synchronising (see Section 5). Also check the intake manifold rubbers for cracks which will cause an air leak, resulting in a weak mixture.

5 Throttle body synchronisation

⚠ **Warning:** *Petrol (gasoline) is extremely flammable, so take extra precautions when you work on any part of the fuel system.*

Routine Maintenance and Servicing 1•11

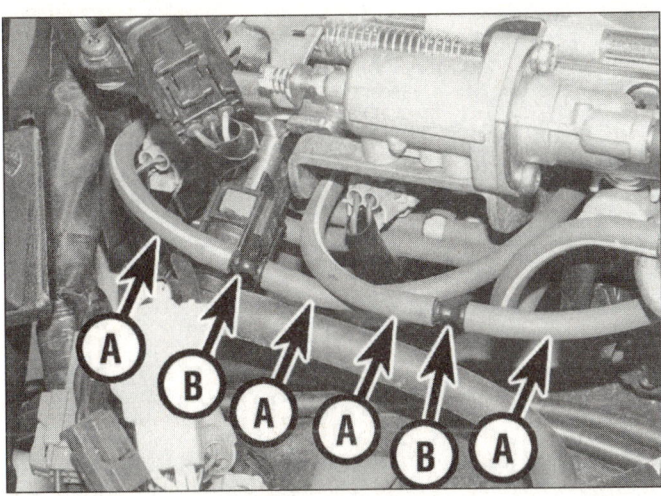

5.4 Detach the balance hoses (A) from the joining plugs (B) and connect them to the gauges

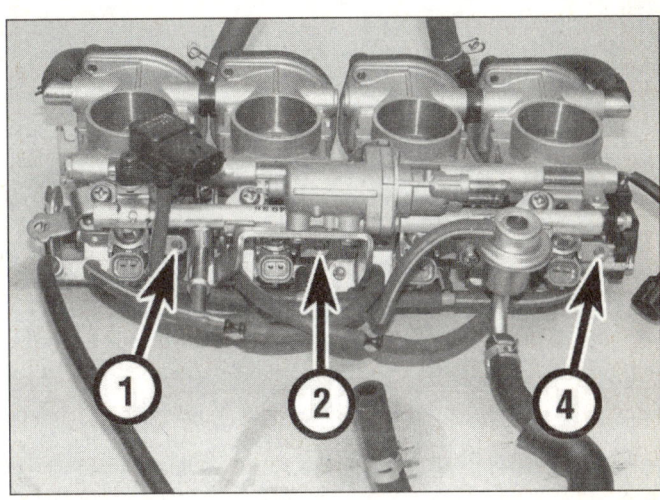

5.7a Synchronise the throttle bodies using the air screws for Nos. 1, 2 and 4 (arrowed) . . .

Don't smoke or allow open flames or bare light bulbs near the work area, and don't work in a garage where a natural gas-type appliance is present. If you spill any fuel on your skin, rinse it off immediately with soap and water. When you perform any kind of work on the fuel system, wear safety glasses and have a fire extinguisher suitable for a Class B type fire (flammable liquids) on hand.

⚠ **Warning:** *Do not allow exhaust gases to build up in the work area; either perform the check outside or use an exhaust gas extraction system.*

Special tool: *A set of vacuum gauges or a manometer is necessary for this job.*

1 Throttle body synchronisation ensures each throttle body passes the same amount of fuel/air mixture to each cylinder. This is done by measuring the vacuum produced in each cylinder. Throttle bodies that are out of synchronisation will result in increased fuel consumption, higher engine temperature, less than ideal throttle response and higher vibration levels. Before synchronising the throttle bodies, make sure that the valve clearances and idle speed are properly adjusted and that the ignition timing has been checked.

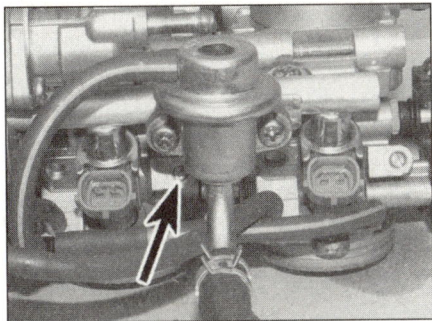

5.7b . . . do not disturb the air screw for No. 3 throttle body (arrowed)

2 To synchronise the throttle bodies you will need a set of vacuum gauges or a manometer. These instruments measure engine vacuum, and can be obtained from motorcycle dealers or mail order parts suppliers. The equipment used should be suitable for a four cylinder engine and come complete with the necessary adapters and hoses to fit the take-off points.

3 Start the engine and let it run until it reaches normal operating temperature, then shut it off. Support the machine upright on level ground using an auxiliary stand. Raise the fuel tank (see Chapter 4).

4 Locate the balance hoses between the intake manifolds for Nos. 1 and 3 cylinders **(see illustration)**. Detach the hoses from the joining plug midway between them and remove the plug. Fit suitable adapters to the hose ends if necessary and connect them to the appropriate vacuum gauge or manometer hoses. Make sure the No. 1 gauge is attached to the hose from the No. 1 (left-hand) intake manifold, and so on. Now locate the balance hoses for Nos. 2 and 4 cylinders and connect them to the vacuum gauge or manometer hoses.

5 Start the engine and let it idle, making sure the speed is still correct. If the gauges are fitted with damping adjustment, set this so that the needle flutter is just eliminated but so that they can still respond to small changes in pressure.

6 The vacuum readings for the Nos. 1, 2 and 4 cylinders should be the same as the No. 3 cylinder, or at least within the maximum difference specified at the beginning of the Chapter. The No. 3 cylinder is the base to which all the others are matched, and cannot itself be adjusted.

7 If the vacuum readings vary, locate the air screws in the throttle bodies **(see illustrations)** and adjust the Nos. 1, 2 and 4 throttle bodies as required by turning the appropriate air screw until the readings are the same as No. 3. If an air screw is inadvertently removed, screw it in until it seats, then screw it out ¾ of a turn (standard position), and make any fine adjustment to its setting according to the gauge readings. **Note:** *Do not disturb the throttle valve adjustment screws situated in the linkage between the throttle bodies.*

8 When all the throttle bodies are synchronised, open and close the throttle quickly to settle the linkage, and recheck the gauge readings, readjusting if necessary.

9 When the adjustment is complete, adjust the idle speed (see Section 4). Remove the gauges and connect the hoses together using the joining plugs **(see illustration 5.4)**. Lower the fuel tank (see Chapter 4).

6 Fuel system and emission control

⚠ **Warning:** *Petrol (gasoline) is extremely flammable, so take extra precautions when you work on any part of the fuel system. Don't smoke or allow open flames or bare light bulbs near the work area, and don't work in a garage where a natural gas-type appliance is present. If you spill any fuel on your skin, rinse it off immediately with soap and water. When you perform any kind of work on the fuel system, wear safety glasses and have a fire extinguisher suitable for a Class B type fire (flammable liquids) on hand.*

Fuel system

1 Raise the fuel tank (see Chapter 4) and check the tank, the fuel supply and return hoses, the tank overflow and breather hoses and the throttle body vacuum hoses, for signs of leaks, cracking, hardening, kinks or

Routine Maintenance and Servicing

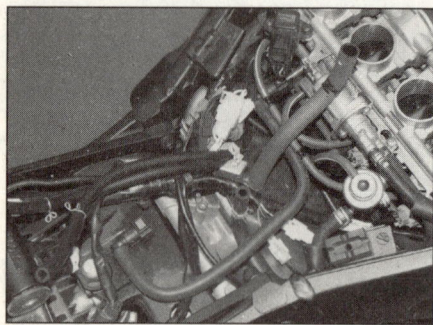

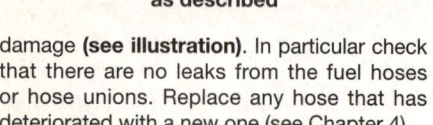
6.1 Check the various fuel system hoses as described

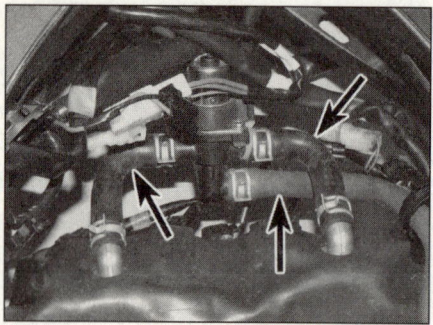
6.7 Check the AIS system hoses (arrowed)

any hoses that are damaged or deteriorated.
10 Check the EVAP canister and the valve for cracks or other damage.
11 Refer to your dealer for further information and tests on the system. Note that there is an emission control system hose routing diagram on a label under the passenger seat.

Exhaust gas (carbon monoxide) density

12 Have the exhaust gases analysed by a Yamaha dealer.

7 Throttle cables

damage **(see illustration)**. In particular check that there are no leaks from the fuel hoses or hose unions. Replace any hose that has deteriorated with a new one (see Chapter 4).
2 If the joint between the fuel pump mounting plate and the tank is leaking, ensure the mounting bolts are tightened to the specified torque setting (see Chapter 4); if the leak persists, remove the pump and fit a new gasket (see Chapter 4).
3 Inspect the joints between the fuel rail, the injectors and the throttle bodies. If there are any leaks, remove the fuel rail and fit new seals and O-rings to the injectors (see Chapter 4).
4 Make sure the joints between the air filter housing and the throttle bodies and the intake adapters between the throttle bodies and the cylinder head are in good condition and that the clamp screws securing the throttle bodies in them are tight. Also make sure the bolts securing the intake adapters to the cylinder head are tight.

Air induction system (AIS)

5 To reduce the amount of unburned hydrocarbons released in the exhaust gases, an air induction system (AIS) is fitted. The system consists of the control valve (mounted under the front of the air filter housing), the reed valves (fitted in the valve cover) and the hoses linking them. The control valve is actuated electronically by the ECU.
6 Under certain operating conditions, a signal from the ECU opens up the AIS control valve which then allows filtered air to be drawn through the reed valves and cylinder head

passages and into the exhaust ports. The air mixes with the exhaust gases, causing any unburned particles of the fuel in the mixture to be burnt in the exhaust port/pipes. This process changes a considerable amount of hydrocarbons and carbon monoxide into relatively harmless carbon dioxide and water. The reed valves in the valve cover are fitted to prevent the flow of exhaust gases back up the cylinder head passages and into the air filter housing.
7 The system is not adjustable and requires little maintenance. Remove the air filter housing (see Chapter 4). Remove the radiator cover (see Section 2, Step 2). Check that the hoses are not kinked or pinched, are in good condition and are securely connected at each end **(see illustration)**. Replace any hoses that are cracked, split or generally deteriorated with new ones.
8 If the valve clearances are all correct and the throttle bodies have been synchronised and have no other faults, but the idle speed cannot be set properly, it is possible that the AIS is faulty. Refer to Chapter 4 for further information on the system and for checks if it is believed to be faulty.

EVAP system (California models)

9 Raise the fuel tank (see Chapter 4). Visually inspect all the system hoses between the fuel tank, the roll-over valve, the purge control solenoid valve, and the canister for kinks and splits and any other damage or deterioration. Make sure that the hoses are securely connected with a clamp on each end. Replace

1 Make sure the throttle twistgrip rotates easily from fully closed to fully open with the front wheel turned at various angles. The twistgrip should return automatically from fully open to fully closed when released.
2 If the throttle sticks, this is probably due to a cable fault. Remove the cables (see Chapter 4) and lubricate them (see Section 9). If the inner cables still do not run smoothly in the outer cables, replace the cables with new ones.
3 With the cables removed, check that the twistgrip turns smoothly around the handlebar – dirt combined with a lack of lubrication can cause the action to be stiff. If necessary, unscrew the handlebar end-weight and slide the twistgrip off the handlebar **(see illustration)**. Clean any old grease from the bar and the inside of the tube. Smear some new grease of the specified type onto the bar, then refit the twistgrip. Install the lubricated or new cables, making sure they are correctly routed (see Chapter 4). If this fails to improve the operation of the throttle, the fault could lie in the throttle bodies. Remove them and check the action of the throttle linkage and butterflies (see Chapter 4).
4 With the throttle operating smoothly, check for a small amount of freeplay in the cables, measured in terms of the amount of twistgrip rotation before the throttle opens, and compare the amount to that listed in this Chapter's Specifications **(see illustration)**. If it is incorrect, adjust the cables as follows:
5 Initially adjust freeplay using the adjuster in the throttle opening cable where it leaves the throttle/switch housing on the handlebar. Loosen the lock ring and turn the adjuster until the specified amount of freeplay is obtained, then retighten the lock ring **(see illustration)**. Turn the adjuster in to increase freeplay and out to reduce it.
6 If the adjuster has reached its limit of adjustment, reset it so that the freeplay is at a maximum, then adjust the cables at the throttle body end as follows. Remove the fuel tank and air filter housing (see Chapter 4) and the fairing left-hand side panel and its inner trim section (see Chapter 7).
7 The upper cable in the bracket on the throttle bodies is the decelerator (throttle

7.3 Unscrew the end-weight (arrowed) to free the twistgrip

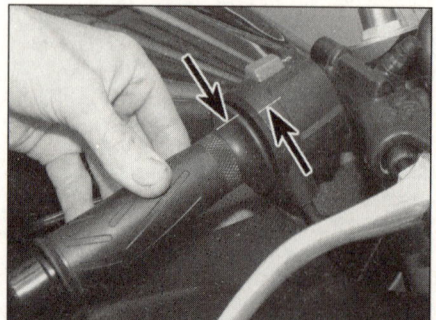
7.4 Throttle cable freeplay is measured in terms of twistgrip rotation

Routine Maintenance and Servicing 1•13

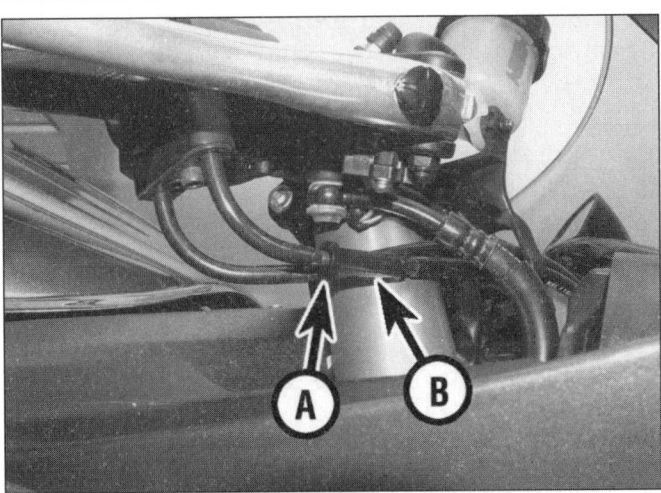

7.5 Slacken the adjuster locknut (A) and turn the adjuster (B) as required – handlebar end

7.7 Throttle cable adjusters (arrowed) – throttle body end

closing) cable, and the lower cable is the accelerator (throttle opening) cable. Loosen the locknut on the upper cable adjuster and turn the adjuster nut until any slack is removed, but not so it is tight, then tighten the locknut **(see illustration)**.

8 Loosen the locknut on the lower cable adjuster and turn the adjuster nut until the specified amount of freeplay is obtained, then tighten the locknut. Further adjustments can now be made at the twistgrip (see Step 5). If the cables cannot be adjusted as specified, replace them with new ones (see Chapter 4).

⚠ **Warning: Turn the handlebars all the way through their travel with the engine idling. Idle speed should not change. If it does, the cables may be routed incorrectly. Correct this condition before riding the motorcycle.**

9 Check that the throttle twistgrip operates smoothly and snaps shut quickly when released.

8 Clutch

1 Check that the clutch lever operates smoothly and easily.
2 If the lever action is heavy or stiff, remove the cable (see Chapter 2) and lubricate it (see Section 9). If the inner cable still does not run smoothly in the outer cable, replace the cable with a new one. Install the lubricated or new cable (see Chapter 2).
3 If the lever itself is stiff, remove the lever from its bracket (see Chapter 5) and check for damage or distortion, or any other cause, and remedy as necessary. Clean and lubricate the pivot and contact areas (see Section 9).
4 If the lever and cable are good, refer to Chapter 2 and check the release mechanism in the clutch cover and the clutch itself.
5 With the clutch operating smoothly, check that the clutch lever is correctly adjusted. Periodic adjustment is necessary to compensate for wear in the clutch plates and stretch of the cable. Check that the amount of freeplay at the clutch lever end is within the specifications listed at the beginning of this Chapter **(see illustration)**.
6 If adjustment is required, turn the adjuster in or out until the required amount of freeplay is obtained **(see illustration)**. To increase freeplay, turn the adjuster clockwise (into the lever bracket). To reduce freeplay, turn the adjuster anti-clockwise (out of the lever bracket). Tighten the locking ring securely.
7 If all the adjustment has been taken up at the lever, reset the adjuster to give the maximum amount of freeplay, then set the correct amount of freeplay using the adjuster on the lower end of the cable in the bracket on the right-hand side of the engine.
8 Remove the lower fairing (see Chapter 7). Slacken the rear adjuster nut, then turn the front nut as required to obtain the correct freeplay **(see illustration)**. To increase freeplay, thread the front nut towards the front of the motorcycle. To reduce freeplay, thread the front nut towards the back of the motorcycle. When the correct amount of freeplay has been achieved, locate the front nut against the bracket, then tighten the rear nut against the bracket.
9 Subsequent adjustments can now be made using the clutch lever adjuster only.

9 Stand, lever pivots and cable lubrication

Pivot points

1 Since the controls, cables and various other components of a motorcycle are exposed to the elements, they should be checked and lubricated periodically to ensure safe and trouble-free operation.
2 The footrest pivots, clutch and brake lever

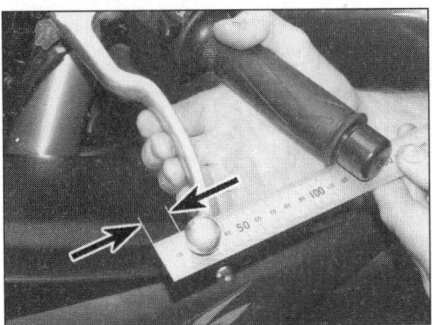

8.5 Measure the amount of freeplay at the clutch lever end as shown

8.6 Turn the adjuster in or out as required

8.8 Slacken and adjust the nuts (arrowed) as described

1•14 Routine Maintenance and Servicing

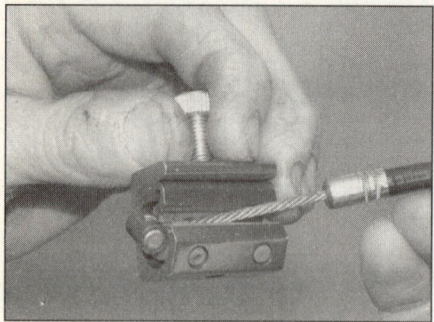

9.3a Fit the cable into the adapter . . .

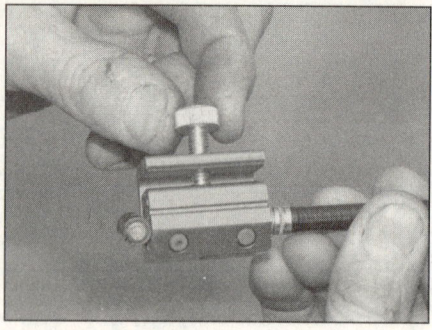

9.3b . . . and tighten the screw to seal it in . . .

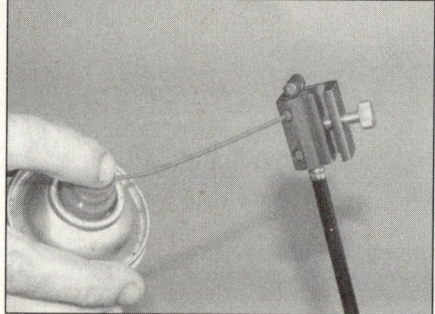

9.3c . . . then apply the lubricant using the nozzle provided inserted in the hole in the adapter

pivots, brake pedal and gearchange lever pivots and linkage and sidestand pivot should be lubricated frequently. In order for the lubricant to be applied where it will do the most good, the component should be disassembled (see Chapter 5). The lubricant recommended by Yamaha for each application is listed at the beginning of the Chapter. If chain or cable lubricant is being used, it can be applied to the pivot joint gaps and will usually work its way into the areas where friction occurs, so less disassembly of the component is needed (however it is always better to do so and clean off all corrosion, dirt and old lubricant first). If motor oil or light grease is being used, apply it sparingly as it may attract dirt (which could cause the controls to bind or wear at an accelerated rate). **Note:** *An alternative lubricant for the control lever pivots is a dry-film lubricant (available from many sources by different names).*

Cables

Special tool: *A cable lubricating adapter is necessary for this procedure (see illustration 9.3c).*

3 To lubricate the cables, disconnect the relevant cable at its upper end, then lubricate it with a pressure adapter and aerosol cable lubricant **(see illustrations)**. See Chapter 4 for throttle cable removal procedures, and Chapter 2 for the clutch cable.

10 Cooling system

Check

⚠️ **Warning:** *The engine must be cool before beginning this procedure.*

1 Check the coolant level in the reservoir (see *Pre-ride checks*).
2 Remove the fairing side panels and the lower fairing (see Chapter 7). Check the entire cooling system for evidence of leakage. Examine each rubber coolant hose along its entire length **(see illustration)**. Look for cracks, splits, abrasions and other signs of deterioration. Squeeze each hose at various points. They should feel firm, yet pliable, and return to their original shape when released. If they are cracked or hard, replace them with new ones.
3 Check for evidence of leaks at each cooling system joint. If necessary, tighten the hose clips carefully to prevent future leaks.
4 Examine the oil cooler inlet and outlet hoses for damage and signs of deterioration – the cooler is on the front of the engine. Ensure that the hose clips are secure and that there is no sign of leakage of either coolant or oil at the oil cooler-to-crankcase joint. If there is, refer to Chapter 2 – if coolant is leaking replace the cooler with a new one, and if oil is leaking first make sure the cooler bolt is tightened to the specified torque, and if it is, or if leakage persists, remove the cooler and replace the O-ring with a new one.
5 Check for leakage around the pump on the right-hand side of the engine **(see illustration)**. If it is leaking around the cover, check that the bolts are tight. If they are, remove the cover and replace the O-ring with a new one (see Chapter 3). If it is leaking around the crankcase, remove the pump and replace the body O-ring with a new one (see Chapter 3). To prevent leakage of water from the cooling system to the lubrication system and vice versa, two seals are fitted on the water pump shaft. If either seal fails, a drain hole in the underside of the pump body allows the coolant or oil to escape and prevents them mixing. Look for tell-tale signs of leakage where the water pump body enters the crankcase.
6 The water seal on the pump shaft is of the mechanical type and bears on the inner face of the pump body and the rear face of the pump impeller. The oil seal, which is mounted in the pump body, is of the normal feathered lip type. If there are signs of coolant leakage, remove the pump and replace the mechanical seal with a new one. If it is oil that is leaking, or if the leakage is white and with the texture of emulsion, replace both seals with new ones (the mechanical seal has to be removed in order to remove the oil seal, and it cannot be reused). Refer to Chapter 3 for seal renewal.
7 Check the radiator for leaks and other damage. Leaks in the radiator leave tell-tale scale deposits or coolant stains on the outside of the core below the leak. If leaks are noted, remove the radiator (see Chapter 3) and have it repaired by a specialist.

Caution: *Do not use a liquid leak stopping compound to try to repair leaks.*

8 Check the radiator fins for mud, dirt and insects, which may impede the flow of air through the radiator. If the fins are dirty, remove the radiator (see Chapter 3) and clean it, using water or low pressure compressed air directed through the fins from the back. If the fins are bent or distorted, straighten them carefully with a screwdriver. Bent or damaged fins will restrict the air flow and impair the efficiency of the radiator causing the engine to overheat. Where there is substantial damage to the radiator's surface area, renew the radiator.
9 Remove the pressure cap from the radiator filler neck by turning it anti-clockwise until it reaches a stop. If you hear a hissing sound

10.2 Check the cooling system hoses as described

10.5 Check for leakage around the pump (arrowed)

Routine Maintenance and Servicing 1•15

10.9 Remove the pressure cap as described

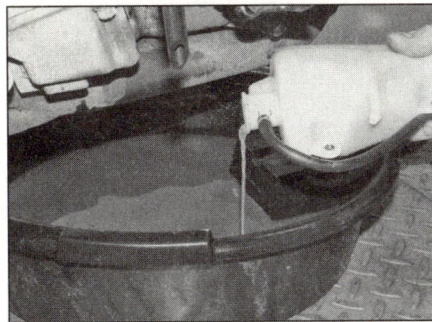

10.16 Remove the reservoir and drain it

(indicating that there is still pressure in the system), wait until it stops. Now press down on the cap and continue turning until it can be removed **(see illustration)**.

10 Check the condition of the coolant in the system. If it is rust-coloured or if accumulations of scale are visible, drain, flush and refill the system with new coolant (see below). Check the cap seal for cracks and other damage. If in doubt about the pressure cap's condition, have it tested by a Yamaha dealer or replace it with a new one.

11 Check the antifreeze content of the coolant with an antifreeze hydrometer (see Specifications). A mixture with less than 40% antifreeze (40/60 antifreeze to distilled water) will not provide proper corrosion protection. Sometimes coolant looks like it's in good condition, but might be too weak to offer adequate protection. If the hydrometer indicates a weak mixture, drain, flush and refill the system (see below). A higher than specified concentration of antifreeze decreases the performance of the cooling system and should only be used when additional protection against freezing is needed.

12 Install the cap by turning it clockwise until it reaches the first stop then push down on the cap and continue turning until it will turn no further.

13 Start the engine and let it reach normal operating temperature, then check for leaks again. As the coolant temperature increases beyond normal, the fan should come on automatically and the temperature should begin to drop. If it does not, refer to Chapter 3 and check the fan switch, fan motor and fan circuit carefully.

10.18a Unscrew the drain bolt (arrowed) . . .

14 If the coolant level is consistently low, and no evidence of leaks can be found, have the entire system pressure-checked by a Yamaha dealer.

Change the coolant

> **Warning:** Allow the engine to cool completely before performing this maintenance operation. Also, don't allow antifreeze to come into contact with your skin or the painted surfaces of the motorcycle. Rinse off spills immediately with plenty of water. Antifreeze is highly toxic if ingested. Never leave antifreeze lying around in an open container or in puddles on the floor; children and pets are attracted by its sweet smell and may drink it. Check with local authorities (councils) about disposing of antifreeze. Many communities have collection centres where antifreeze can be disposed of safely. Antifreeze is also combustible, so don't store it near open flames.

Draining

15 Secure the motorcycle upright on a level surface using an auxiliary stand. Remove the fairing side panels and the lower fairing (see Chapter 7).

16 Remove the coolant reservoir (see Chapter 3). Empty the contents of the reservoir into a suitable container, rinse the inside with clean water and refit it to the motorcycle **(see illustration)**.

17 Remove the pressure cap from the radiator filler neck by turning it anti-clockwise until it reaches a stop **(see illustration 10.9)**. If you hear a hissing sound (indicating there is

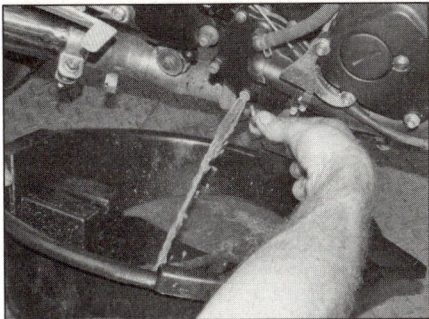

10.18b . . . and allow the coolant to drain

still pressure in the system), wait until it stops. Now press down on the cap and continue turning until it can be removed.

18 Position a suitable container beneath the drain bolt on the water pump. Remove the bolt, noting that the coolant will spurt out (so hold the container up to it) and allow the coolant to completely drain from the system **(see illustrations)**. Retain the old sealing washer for use during flushing.

Flushing

19 Flush the system with clean tap water by inserting a garden hose in the radiator filler neck. Allow the water to run through the system until it is clear when it flows out of the drain hole. If there is a lot of rust in the water, remove the radiator (see Chapter 3) and have it professionally cleaned. If the drain hole appears to be clogged with sediment, remove the water pump cover and clean the inside of the pump (see Chapter 3).

20 Install the drain bolt using the old sealing washer. Fill the system via the radiator with clean water mixed with a flushing compound. Make sure the flushing compound is compatible with aluminium components, and follow the manufacturer's instructions carefully. Install the pressure cap. Fill the coolant reservoir to the FULL mark with clean water.

21 Start the engine and allow it to reach normal operating temperature. Let it run for about ten minutes.

22 Stop the engine. Let it cool for a while, then cover the pressure cap with a heavy rag and turn it anti-clockwise to the first stop, releasing any pressure that may be present in the system. Once the hissing stops, push down on the cap and remove it completely. Drain the system once again.

23 Drain the system again.

24 Repeat Steps 20 to 23, filling the system with clean water only.

Refilling

25 Fit a new sealing washer onto the drain bolt and tighten it to the torque setting specified at the beginning of this Chapter.

26 Fill the system via the radiator with the proper coolant mixture (see this Chapter's Specifications). **Note:** *Pour the coolant in slowly to minimise the amount of air entering the system.* When the system appears full, move the bike off its stand and shake it slightly to dissipate the coolant, then place the bike back on the auxiliary stand and top the system up.

27 When the system is full (all the way up to the top of the radiator filler neck), install the pressure cap. Now fill the coolant reservoir to the FULL mark and fit the cap (see *Pre-ride checks*).

28 Start the engine and allow it to run for several minutes. Flick the throttle open 3 or 4 times, so that the engine speed rises to approximately 4000 – 5000 rpm, then stop the engine. Any air trapped in the system should bleed back to the top of the radiator, and the level will drop.

1•16 Routine Maintenance and Servicing

11.3 Unscrew the oil filler cap to act as a vent...

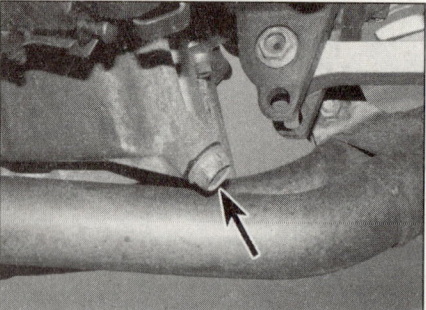

11.4a ... then unscrew the oil drain plug (arrowed) ...

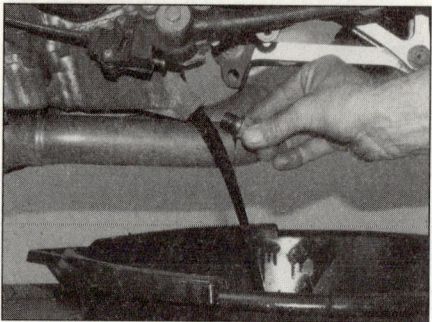

11.4b ... and allow the oil to completely drain

29 Wait a few minutes for the coolant to settle, then check the coolant level in both the radiator and the coolant reservoir. If necessary, top up the radiator to the base of the filler neck, then install the pressure cap. Also top up the coolant reservoir to the FULL mark.
30 Check the system for leaks.
31 Do not dispose of the old coolant by pouring it down the drain. Instead pour it into a heavy plastic container, cap it tightly and take it into an authorised disposal site or service station – see **Warning** at the beginning of this Section.
32 Install the fairing panels (see Chapter 7).

Hose renewal

33 The hoses will deteriorate with age and should be replaced with new ones regardless of their apparent condition (see Chapter 3).

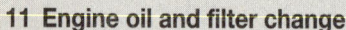

11 Engine oil and filter change

 Warning: Be careful when draining the oil, as the exhaust pipes, the engine, and the oil itself can cause severe burns.

Engine oil

1 Regular oil changes are the single most important maintenance procedure you can perform on a motorcycle. The oil not only lubricates the internal parts of the engine, transmission and clutch, but it also acts as a coolant, a cleaner, a sealant, and a protector. Because of these demands, the oil takes a terrific amount of abuse and should be replaced often with new oil of the recommended grade and type. Saving a little money on the difference in cost between a good oil and a cheap oil won't pay off if the engine is damaged. The oil filter should be changed with every second oil change (see Steps 10 to 14).
2 Before changing the oil, warm up the engine so the oil will drain easily. Remove the lower fairing (see Chapter 7).
3 Position a clean drain tray below the engine. Unscrew the oil filler cap from the clutch cover to vent the engine unit and to act as a reminder that there is no oil in the engine **(see illustration)**.
4 Unscrew the oil drain plug from the underside of the engine and allow the oil to flow into the drain tray **(see illustrations)**. Discard the sealing washer and replace it with a new one **(see illustration)**.
5 When the oil has completely drained, fit the plug with its new washer and tighten it to the torque setting specified at the beginning of this Chapter **(see illustration)**. Avoid overtightening, as you will damage the sump.
6 Refill the engine to the proper level using the recommended type and amount of oil (see *Pre-ride checks*). With the motorcycle vertical, the oil level should lie between the maximum and minimum level lines on the dipstick (see *Pre-ride checks*). Install the filler cap **(see illustration 11.3)**. Start the engine and let it run for two or three minutes. Stop the engine, wait a few minutes, then check the oil level. If necessary, add more oil to bring the level almost up to the maximum level line on the dipstick. Check that there are no leaks around the drain plug.

7 Every so often, and especially as Yamaha do not fit an oil pressure switch and warning light (the system fitted uses an oil level sensor), it is advisable to perform an oil pressure check (see Chapter 2, Section 3).
8 The old oil drained from the engine cannot be re-used and must be disposed of properly. Check with your local refuse disposal company, disposal facility or environmental agency to see whether they will accept the used oil for recycling – most will. Don't pour used oil into drains or onto the ground.
9 Install the lower fairing (see Chapter 7).

 **HAYNES HiNT** *Check the old oil carefully – if it is very metallic coloured, then the engine is experiencing wear from break-in (new engine) or from insufficient lubrication. If there are flakes or chips of metal in the oil, then something is drastically wrong internally and the engine will have to be disassembled for inspection and repair. If there are pieces of fibre-like material in the oil, the clutch is experiencing excessive wear and should be checked.*

Oil filter

Special tool: *A filter removing tool is necessary for this job (see illustration 11.11a).*
10 The oil filter is on the lower left-hand side of the engine Drain the engine oil as described in Steps 2 to 5. Displace the coolant reservoir cover and draw the fuel tank drain and breather hoses out of their guide **(see illustration)**.

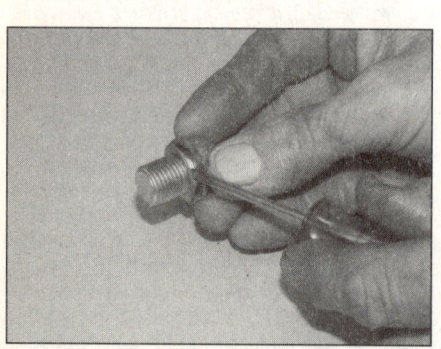

11.4c Remove and discard the sealing washer

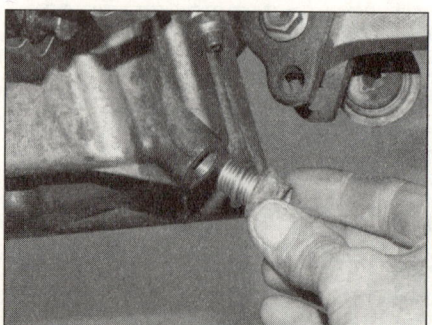

11.5 Install the drain plug using a new sealing washer

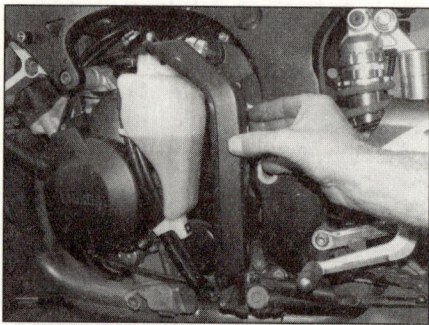

11.10 Unscrew the bolts and remove the reservoir cover

Routine Maintenance and Servicing 1•17

11.11a Fit the filter removing tool . . .

11.11b . . . then unscrew the filter . . .

11.11c . . . and allow the oil to drain

11.12a Smear clean oil onto the seal . . .

11.12b . . . then install the filter and tighten it as described

Note: it is antisocial and illegal to dump oil down the drain. To find the location of your local oil recycling bank, call this number free.

In the USA, note that any oil supplier must accept used oil for recycling

11 Place the drain tray below the oil filter. Clean the crankcase around the filter, then unscrew the filter using a filter removing tool (several types are available, but the socket-type hex-wrench is the best as it allows the new filter to be tightened to the correct torque - make sure you purchase the correct size as many are available) **(see illustrations)**. Tip any residual oil into the drain tray **(see illustration)**.
12 Clean the sealing surface on the crankcase with a suitable solvent, then smear clean engine oil onto the rubber seal on the new filter, and screw the filter onto the engine until the seal just seats **(see illustrations)**. If a socket-type hex-wrench is being used, tighten the filter to the torque setting specified at the beginning of this Chapter. Otherwise, tighten the filter as tight as possible by hand, or by the number of turns specified on the filter or its packaging. **Note:** *Do not use a strap or chain wrench to tighten the filter as you will damage it.*

13 Refill the engine to the proper level (see Step 6).
14 Remember to drain all the old oil from the filter into the drain pan. Note that the old filter should be taken to the oil disposal facility rather than disposed of with the household rubbish.
15 Fit the drain and breather hoses into their guide and install the coolant reservoir cover **(see illustration 11.10)**.

12 Brake system

Brake system check

1 A routine general check of the brake system will ensure that any problems are discovered and remedied before the rider's safety is jeopardised.

2 Check the brake lever and pedal for looseness, improper or rough action, excessive play, bends, and other damage. Replace any damaged parts with new ones (see Chapter 5). Clean and lubricate the lever and pedal pivots if their action is stiff or rough (see Section 9).
3 Make sure all brake fasteners are tight. Check the brake pads for wear (see Steps 9 to 13) and make sure the fluid level in the reservoirs is correct (see *Pre-ride checks*). Look for leaks at the hose connections and check for cracks in the hoses themselves **(see illustration)**. If the lever or pedal is spongy, bleed the brakes (see Chapter 7). The brake fluid should be changed every two years (see paragraph 12) and the hoses renewed if they deteriorate, or every four years irrespective of their condition (see paragraph 15). The master cylinder and caliper seals should be renewed every two years, or if leakage from them is evident (see paragraph 17).
4 Make sure the brake light operates when the front brake lever is pulled in. The front brake light switch, mounted on the underside of the master cylinder, is not adjustable. If it fails to operate properly, check it (see Chapter 8).
5 Make sure the brake light is activated just before the rear brake takes effect. The switch is mounted behind the rider's right-hand footrest bracket. If adjustment is necessary, hold the switch and turn the adjuster nut on the switch body until the brake light is activated when required **(see illustrations)**. If the brake light comes on too late, turn the nut clockwise. If the brake light comes on too

12.3 Check the hoses and all joints for leaks and deterioration

12.5a Hold the rear brake light switch body (arrowed) . . .

1•18 Routine Maintenance and Servicing

12.5b ... and turn the adjuster ring (arrowed) as required

12.6a Front brake lever span adjuster (arrowed) – R and S models

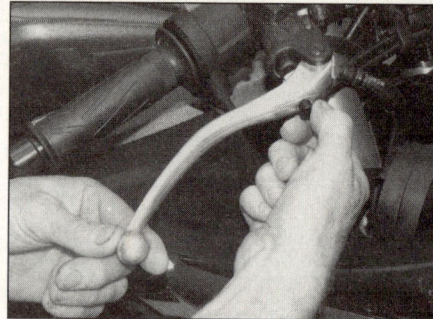

12.6b Adjusting front brake lever span – T model type

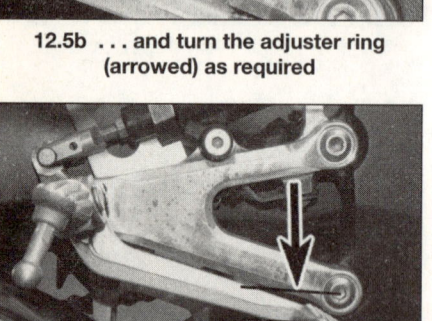

12.7 Measure the brake pedal height between the two points (arrowed)

soon or is permanently on, turn the nut anti-clockwise. If the switch doesn't operate the brake light, check it (see Chapter 8).

6 The front brake lever has a span adjuster which alters the distance of the lever from the handlebar. Each setting is identified by a number on the adjuster which aligns with the arrow on the lever bracket. Pull the lever away from the handlebar and turn the adjuster until the setting which best suits the rider is obtained **(see illustrations)**. There are five settings on R and S (2003 and 2004) models and four on T (2005) models – setting 1 gives the largest span, and setting 5 or 4 the smallest. When making adjustment make sure the marks between the lever and the adjuster align to ensure correct engagement of the adjuster setting.

7 Check the position of the brake pedal (brake pedal height). Yamaha recommend the distance between the front edge of the brake pedal and the centre line of the lower footrest bracket bolt should be as specified at the beginning of this Chapter **(see illustration)**.

8 If the pedal height is incorrect, or if the rider's preference is different, loosen the locknut on the master cylinder pushrod, then turn the pushrod using a spanner on the hex at the top of the rod until the pedal is at the correct or desired height **(see illustration)**. After adjustment check that the pushrod end is still visible in the hole in the clevis. On completion tighten the locknut securely. Adjust the rear brake light switch after adjusting the pedal height (see Step 5).

Brake pad wear check

⚠ **Warning: The dust created by the brake system may contain asbestos, which is harmful to your health. Never blow it out with compressed air and don't inhale any of it. An approved filtering mask should be worn when working on the brakes.**

9 Each brake pad has wear indicators that can be viewed without removing the pads from the caliper.

10 On the front brake pads the turned-in corners of the pad backing material indicate the wear limit – when the corners are almost contacting the disc the pads must be replaced with new ones. The indicators are visible by looking up at the bottom corners of the pads **(see illustration)**.

Caution: Do not allow the pads to wear to the extent that the indicators contact the disc itself, as the disc will be damaged.

11 On the rear brake pads a cut-out in the friction material indicates the wear limit – replace the pads with new ones when the friction material has worn to the cut-out. The cut-outs are visible by looking at the back edge of the pads **(see illustration)**. **Note:** *Some after-market pads may use different wear indicators; always check with your supplier before fitting.*

12 If the pads are worn to the limit, new ones must be installed. If the pads are dirty or if you are in doubt as to the amount of friction material remaining, remove them for inspection

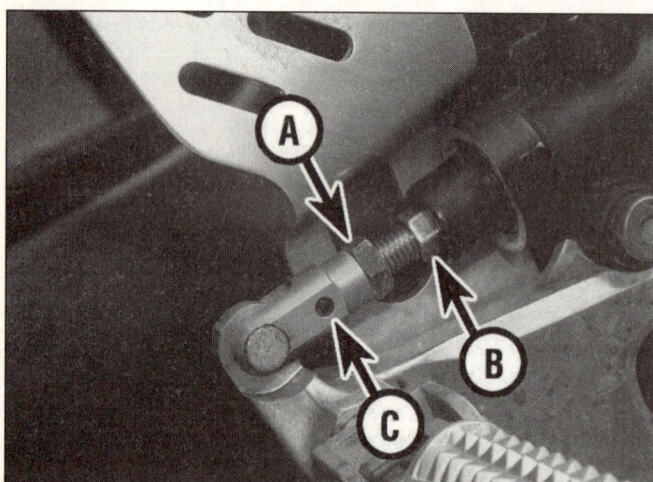

12.8 Slacken the locknut (A) and turn the pushrod using the hex (B) to adjust pedal height. Check that some of the pushrod is still visible in the hole (C)

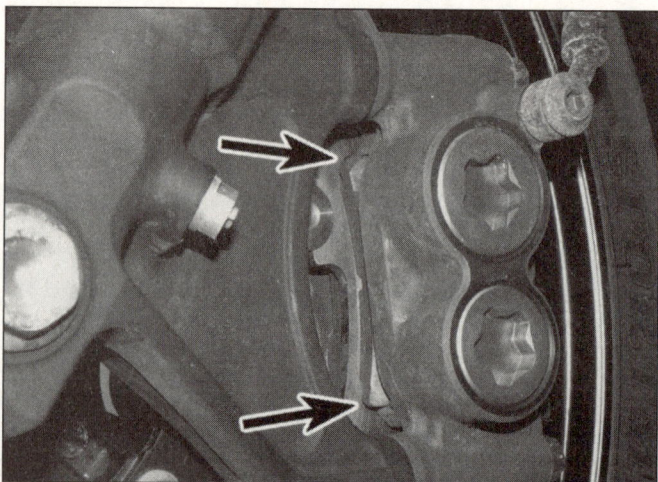

12.10 Check the proximity of the turned in corners (arrowed) of the pad backing to the disc

Routine Maintenance and Servicing 1•19

12.11 Check the amount of friction material remaining and whether it has worn to the cut-out

13.2a Make sure there is a cap on each valve

13.2b Check the security of any wheel balance weights (arrowed)

(see Chapter 6). If required, measure the amount of friction material remaining – the minimum is 0.5 mm (front) or 1.0 mm (rear). **Note:** *It is not possible to degrease the friction material; if the pads are contaminated in any way they must be renewed.*

13 Refer to Chapter 6 for details of pad removal and installation.

Brake fluid change

14 The brake fluid should be changed at the prescribed interval or whenever a master cylinder or caliper overhaul is carried out. Refer to Chapter 6 for details. Ensure that all the old fluid is be pumped from the hydraulic system and that the level in the fluid reservoir is checked and the brakes tested before riding the motorcycle.

Brake hoses

15 The hoses will deteriorate with age and should be replaced with new ones regardless of their apparent condition (see Chapter 6).

16 Always replace the banjo union sealing washers with new ones when fitting new hoses. Refill the system with new brake fluid and bleed the system as described in Chapter 6.

Brake caliper and master cylinder seals

17 Brake system seals will deteriorate over a period of time and lose their effectiveness, leading to sticky operation of the brake master cylinders or the pistons in the brake calipers, or fluid loss. The seals should be replaced at the specified mileage interval or beforehand if fluid leakage or a sticking caliper action is apparent.

18 Replace all the seals in each caliper as a set – a rebuild kit for each caliper is available; master cylinder seals are supplied as a kit along with a new piston and spring (see Chapter 6).

13 Wheels and tyres

Wheels

1 Cast wheels are virtually maintenance free, but they should be kept clean and checked periodically for cracks and other damage. Also check the wheel runout and alignment (see Chapter 6). Never attempt to repair damaged cast wheels; they must be replaced with new ones.

2 Check the tyre valve rubber for signs of damage or deterioration and have it replaced with a new one if necessary. Also, make sure the valve cap is in place and tight **(see illustration)**. Check that the wheel balance weights are fixed firmly to the wheel rim **(see illustration)**. If the weights have fallen off, have the wheel rebalanced by a motorcycle tyre specialist.

Tyres

3 Check the tyre condition and tread depth thoroughly – see *Pre-ride checks*.

Wheel bearings

4 Wheel bearings will wear over a period of time and result in handling problems.

5 Support the motorcycle upright using an auxiliary stand. Check for any play in the bearings by pushing and pulling the wheel against the hub **(see illustration)**. Also rotate the wheel and check that it rotates smoothly and quietly, but do not mistake brake pad-to-disc noise for noisy bearings.

6 If any play is detected in the hub, or if the wheel does not rotate smoothly (and this is not due to brake or chain drag), the wheel must be removed for thorough inspection of the bearings (see Chapter 6).

14 Suspension

1 The suspension components must be maintained in top operating condition to ensure rider safety. Loose, worn or damaged suspension parts decrease the motorcycle's stability and control.

Front suspension check

2 While standing alongside the motorcycle, apply the front brake and push on the handlebars to compress the forks several times. Check that they move up and down smoothly without binding. If binding is felt, the forks should be disassembled and inspected (see Chapter 5).

3 Inspect the fork tubes (R and S (2003 and 2004) models) or sliders (T (2005) models) for signs of scratches, corrosion and pitting, and oil leakage **(see illustration)**. On R and S (2003 and 2004) models displace the stoneguard from the top of the fork slider On all models carefully lever the dust seals out using a flat-bladed screwdriver and inspect the area around the fork seals (see Chapter 5). Any scratches, corrosion and pitting will cause premature seal failure. If the damage

13.5 Checking for play in the wheel bearings

14.3 Check for scratches, pitting and oil leakage on the tube or slider (arrowed)

1•20 Routine Maintenance and Servicing

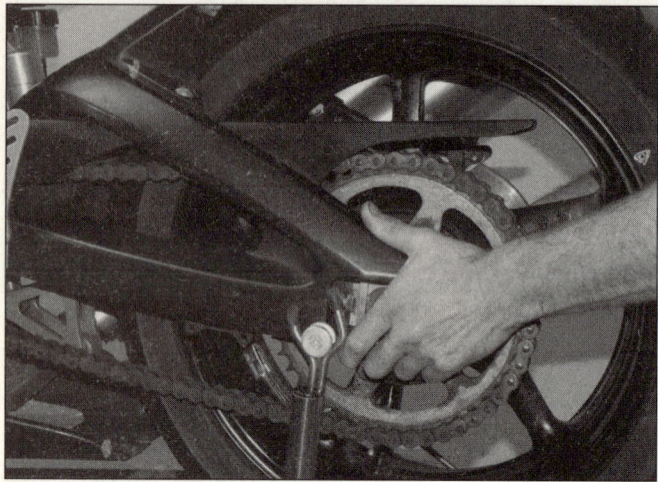

14.8 Checking for play in the swingarm bearings

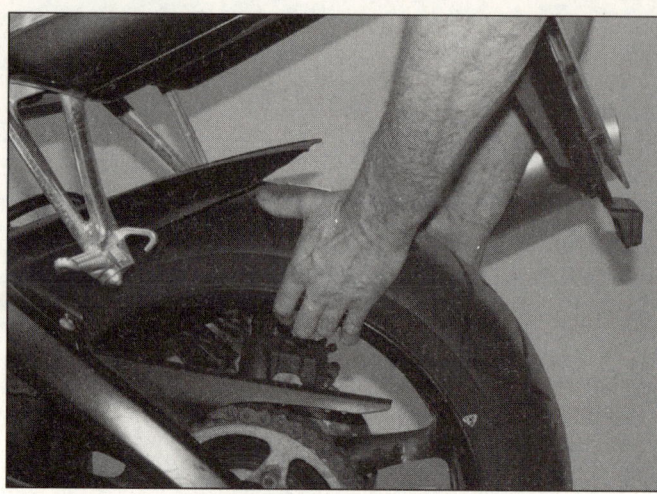

14.9 Checking for play in the rear shock mountings and suspension linkage bearings

is excessive, new tubes or sliders (according to model) should be installed (see Chapter 5). If oil leakage is evident, new seals must be fitted (see Chapter 5). If there is evidence of corrosion between the seal retaining ring and its groove in the fork slider spray the area with a penetrative lubricant, otherwise the ring will be difficult to remove if needed. Press the dust seal back into place on completion.

4 The forks are adjustable for spring pre-load, rebound damping and compression damping and it is essential that both fork legs are adjusted equally. Refer to Chapter 5 and check the settings on each fork if in doubt.

5 Check the tightness of all suspension nuts and bolts to be sure none have worked loose, referring to the torque settings specified at the beginning of Chapter 5.

Rear suspension check

6 Inspect the rear shock for fluid leakage and tightness of its mountings. If leakage is found, a new shock should be installed (see Chapter 5).

7 With the aid of an assistant to support the bike, compress the rear suspension several times. It should move up and down freely without binding. If any binding is felt, the worn or faulty component must be identified and checked. The problem could be due to either the shock absorber, the suspension linkage components or the swingarm components (see Chapter 5).

8 Support the motorcycle using an auxiliary stand so that the rear wheel is off the ground. Grab the swingarm and rock it from side to side – there should be no discernible movement at the ends of the swingarm (Yamaha specify a maximum of 1 mm sideplay) **(see illustration)**. If there is a little movement or a slight clicking can be heard, inspect the tightness of all the rear suspension mounting bolts and nuts, referring to the torque settings specified at the beginning of Chapter 5, and re-check for movement.

9 Next, grasp the top of the rear wheel and pull it upwards – there should be no discernible freeplay before the shock absorber begins to compress **(see illustration)**. Any freeplay felt in either check indicates worn bearings in the suspension linkage or swingarm, or worn shock absorber mountings. The worn components must be identified and checked (see Chapter 6).

10 To make an accurate assessment of the swingarm bearings it is necessary to remove the rear wheel (see Chapter 6) and the bolt securing the suspension linkage plates to the swingarm (see Chapter 5). Grasp the rear of the swingarm with one hand and place your other hand at the junction of the swingarm and the frame. Try to move the rear of the swingarm from side to side. Any wear (play) in the bearings should be felt as movement between the swingarm and the frame at the front. If there is any play, the swingarm will be felt to move forward and backward at the front (not from side-to-side). Next, move the swingarm up and down through its full travel. It should move freely, without any binding or rough spots. If any play in the swingarm is noted or if the swingarm does not move freely, remove the swingarm for inspection of the bearings (see Chapter 5).

11 The rear shock is adjustable for spring pre-load, rebound damping and compression damping (See Chapter 5).

Front fork oil change

12 Although there is no set interval for changing the fork oil, note that the oil will degrade over a period of time and lose its damping qualities. Refer to Chapter 5, Sections 6 and 7 for details of front fork removal, oil draining and refilling. The forks do not need to be completely disassembled to change the oil.

Rear suspension bearing lubrication

13 Over a period of time the grease in the swingarm and suspension linkage bearings will be washed out (especially if pressure washers are used) or will harden allowing the ingress of dirt and water.

14 The suspension linkage and the swingarm should be disassembled at the specified mileage interval and the bearings cleaned and re-greased as necessary (see Chapter 5, Sections 12, 14 and 15).

15 Steering head bearings

Freeplay check and adjustment

1 Steering head bearings can become dented, rough or loose during normal use of the machine. In extreme cases, worn or loose steering head bearings can cause steering wobble – a condition that is potentially dangerous.

Check

2 Support the motorcycle in an upright position using an auxiliary stand. Raise the front wheel off the ground either by having an assistant push down on the rear, or by placing a support under the engine, in which case remove the lower fairing first (see Chapter 7).

3 Point the front wheel straight-ahead, and slowly turn the handlebars from side to side. Any dents or roughness in the bearing races will be felt and if the bearings are too tight the bars will not move smoothly and freely. If the bearings are damaged or the action is rough, they should be replaced with new ones (see Chapter 5). If the bearings are too tight they should be adjusted as described below. Again point the wheel straight-ahead, and tap the front of the wheel to one side. The wheel should 'fall' under its own weight to the limit of its lock, indicating that the bearings are not too tight (take into account the restriction that cables and wiring may have). Check for similar movement to the other side.

4 If a spring balance graduated zero to 600 g

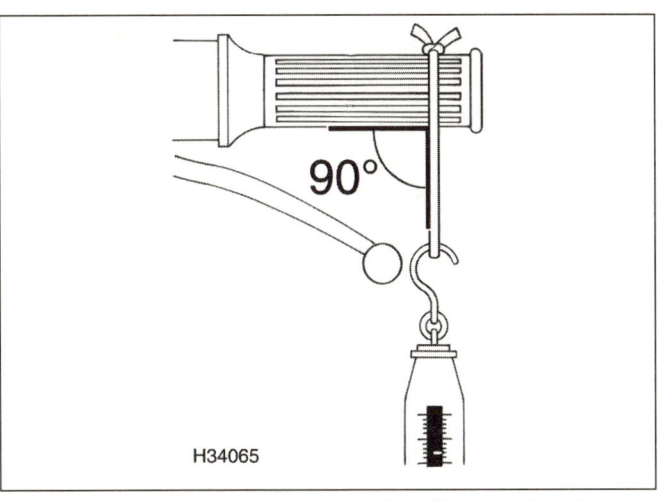

Routine Maintenance and Servicing 1•21

15.4 Hook the spring balance to the handlebar end as shown

15.5 Checking for play in the steering head bearings

is available, loosely fit a cable tie around the end of one handlebar, then hook the end of the spring balance to the tie as shown **(see illustration)**. With the steering straight-ahead and the balance at 90° to the handlebar, pull on the balance and check the reading at which the handlebars start to turn. Repeat on the other handlebar. If the reading on either side is below the minimum value specified in the pre-load range given in the Specifications at the beginning of the Chapter, the steering head is too loose, if the reading is above the maximum value specified the steering head is too tight. If the steering doesn't perform as described, and it's not due to the resistance of cables or hoses, then the bearings should be adjusted as described below.

5 Next, grasp the fork sliders and try to pull and push them forwards and backwards **(see illustration)**. Any looseness in the steering head bearings will be felt as front-to-rear movement of the forks. If play is felt in the bearings, adjust them as follows.

> **HAYNES HiNT** *Freeplay in the fork due to worn fork bushes or rocking of the bike on its stand can be misinterpreted as steering head bearing play – do not get them mixed up.*

Adjustment

Special tool: *A suitably sized C-spanner is useful for this procedure (see illustration 15.11a).*

6 Position the motorcycle in an upright position using an auxiliary stand. Remove the fuel tank (see Chapter 4) and the fairing (see Chapter 7). **Note:** *Although it is not strictly necessary to remove the fuel tank and fairing, doing so will prevent the possibility of damage, should a tool slip.*

7 Displace each handlebar from its fork (see Chapter 5). Slacken the fork clamp bolts in the top yoke **(see illustration)**.

8 Unscrew the steering stem nut and remove

it along with its washer **(see illustration)**, then ease the top yoke upwards off the fork tubes and lay it to one side on some rag.

9 Remove the tabbed lockwasher, noting how it fits, then unscrew and remove the locknut, using either a C-spanner, a peg spanner or a drift located in one of the notches if necessary, though it should only be finger-tight **(see illustrations)**. Remove the rubber washer **(see illustration)**.

10 To adjust the bearings as specified by Yamaha, a special service tool (Pt. No. 90890-01403 for Europe, or YU-33975 for USA) and a torque wrench are required. If the tool is available, first slacken the adjuster nut slightly

15.7 Unscrew the fork clamp bolt (arrowed) on each side

15.8 Unscrew the steering stem nut and remove the washer

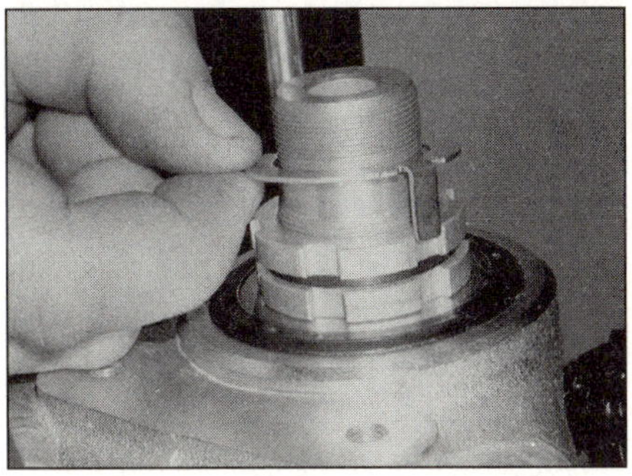

15.9a Remove the tabbed lockwasher . . .

15.9b . . . then unscrew the locknut . . .

15.9c . . . and remove the rubber washer

1•22 Routine Maintenance and Servicing

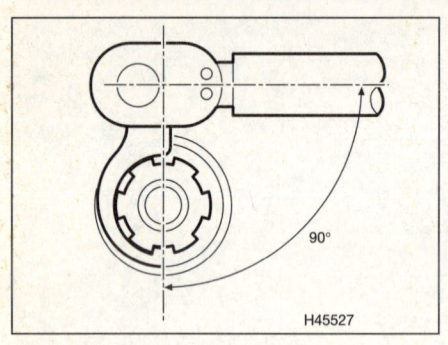

15.10 Make sure the torque wrench arm is at right angles (90°) to the service tool

15.11a Alternatively loosen . . .

15.11b . . . and then tighten the adjuster nut as described to remove bearing freeplay

to take pressure off the bearing, then tighten the nut to the initial torque setting specified at the beginning of this Chapter. Make sure the torque wrench handle is at right-angles (90°) to the centre line between the adjuster nut and the service tool wrench socket **(see illustration)**. Now slacken the nut, then tighten it to the final torque setting specified.

11 If the Yamaha tool is not available, using either a C-spanner, a peg spanner or a drift located in one of the notches, slacken the adjuster nut slightly to take pressure off the bearing then tighten the nut until all freeplay is removed **(see illustrations)**. Now tighten the nut a little more to pre-load the bearings. Now slacken the nut and retighten it, setting it so that all freeplay is just removed from the bearings, yet the steering is able to move freely from side to side. Tighten the nut only a little at a time, and after each adjustment repeat the checks outlined in Steps 3 to 5.

12 Turn the steering from lock to lock five times to settle the bearings, then recheck the adjustment or the torque setting depending on your method used. The object is to set the adjuster nut so that the bearings are under a very light loading, just enough to remove any freeplay.

Caution: Take great care not to apply excessive pressure because this will cause premature failure of the bearings.

13 With the bearings correctly adjusted, install the rubber washer and the locknut **(see illustrations 15.9c and b)**. Tighten the locknut finger-tight, then tighten it further until its notches align with those in the adjuster nut, making sure the adjuster nut does not turn as well. Install the tabbed lockwasher so that the tabs fit into the notches in both the locknut and adjuster nut **(see illustration 15.9a)**. Recheck the bearing adjustment as described in Steps 3 to 5 to ensure the adjuster nut hasn't moved.

14 Fit the top yoke onto the steering stem and the fork legs. Install the washer and steering stem nut and tighten it to the torque setting specified at the beginning of this Chapter **(see illustration 15.8)**. Now tighten the fork clamp bolts in the top yoke to the specified torque **(see illustration)**.

15 Fit the handlebars over the forks and onto the yoke, then align them correctly and fit the positioning bolts, tightening them to the specified torque setting. Now tighten the handlebar clamp bolts to the specified torque.
16 Recheck the bearing adjustment as described in Steps 3 to 5 and re-adjust if necessary.

Lubrication

17 Over a considerable time the grease in the bearings will be dispersed or will harden allowing the ingress of dirt and water.
18 At the specified interval the steering head should be disassembled and the bearings cleaned and re-greased (see Chapter 5, Section 10).

16 Sidestand and starter safety circuit

1 The stand return spring must be capable of retracting the stand fully and holding it retracted when the motorcycle is in use. If a spring has sagged or broken, it must be replaced with a new one **(see illustration)**.
2 Lubricate the stand pivot regularly (see Section 9).
3 The sidestand switch prevents the motorcycle being started if the transmission is in gear and the stand is down, and cuts the engine if the stand is put down while the engine is running and in gear.

16.1 Check the spring (arrowed) is securely anchored and in good condition

4 Check the operation of the safety circuit (which incorporates the sidestand, clutch and neutral switches, and the starter circuit cut-off relay and diodes) by shifting the transmission into neutral, retracting the stand and starting the engine. Pull in the clutch lever and select a gear. Extend the sidestand. The engine should stop as the sidestand is extended. Also make sure that the engine cannot be started while in gear unless the stand is up and the clutch lever is pulled in. If the circuit does not operate as described, check the incorporated components (see Chapter 8).

17 Nut and bolt tightness check

1 Since vibration of the machine tends to loosen fasteners, all nuts, bolts, screws, etc. should be periodically checked for proper tightness.
2 Pay particular attention to the following:
   Spark plugs
   Engine oil drain plug
   Lever and pedal bolts
   Footrest and sidestand bolts
   Engine mounting bolts
   Shock absorber and suspension linkage bolts; swingarm pivot adjuster bolt and nut
   Handlebar positioning and clamp bolts
   Front fork clamp bolts (top and bottom yoke) and fork top bolts
   Steering stem nut
   Front axle bolt and axle clamp bolts
   Rear axle nut
   Front and rear sprocket nuts
   Chain adjuster bolt locknuts
   Brake caliper and master cylinder mounting bolts
   Brake hose banjo bolts and caliper bleed valves
   Brake disc bolts
   Exhaust system bolts/nuts
3 If a torque wrench is available, use it along with the torque specifications (where given) at the beginning of this and other Chapters.

Routine Maintenance and Servicing 1•23

18 Battery check

1 All models are fitted with a sealed, gel-type maintenance-free battery. **Note:** *Do not attempt to open the battery as resulting damage will mean it will be unfit for further use.*

2 All that should be done is to check that the terminals are clean and tight and that the casing is not damaged or leaking. See Chapter 8 for further details.

Caution: *Be extremely careful when handling or working around the battery. The electrolyte gel is very caustic and an explosive gas (hydrogen) is given off when the battery is charging.*

3 If the machine is not in regular use, disconnect the battery and give it a refresher charge every month to six weeks (see Chapter 8, Section 4).

19 Valve clearances

1 The engine must be completely cool for this maintenance procedure, so let the machine sit overnight before beginning.

2 Remove the fairing side panels and the lower fairing (see Chapter 7). Remove the radiator (see Chapter 3). Remove the spark plugs (see Section 2).

3 Remove the valve cover (see Chapter 2). Each cylinder is referred to by a number. They are numbered 1 to 4 from left to right, viewed as normally seated on the bike.

4 Make a chart or sketch of all valve positions so that a note of each clearance can be made against the relevant valve.

5 Place an oil pan under the timing rotor cover on the right-hand side of the engine to catch any oil as it is removed. Unscrew the bolts and remove the cover, noting the clamp for the coolant hose and the bracket for the clutch cable **(see illustration)**. Discard the gasket, as a new one must be used and remove the dowels from either the crankcase or the cover if they are loose. If the cam chain tensioner blade pivot pin comes away with the cover, remove it, then realign the blade and slide the pin back into place.

6 Using a spanner on the timing rotor bolt and rotating in a clockwise direction only, turn the engine until the 'T' mark on the ignition rotor faces to the rear and aligns with the crankcase mating surfaces and the camshaft lobes for the No. 1 (left-hand) cylinder face away from each other **(see illustrations)**. If the cam lobes are facing towards each other, rotate the engine clockwise 360° (one full turn) so that the 'T' mark again aligns with the crankcase mating surfaces. The camshaft lobes will now be facing away from each other and the No. 1 cylinder will be at TDC (top dead centre) on the compression stroke.

7 Check the clearances on the four No. 1 cylinder intake and exhaust valves. Insert a feeler gauge of the same thickness as the correct valve clearance (see Specifications) between the camshaft lobe and follower of each valve and check that it is a firm sliding fit – you should feel a slight drag when the you pull the gauge out **(see illustrations)**. If not,

19.5 Unscrew the bolts (arrowed) and remove the cover

19.6a Turn the engine clockwise using the bolt . . .

19.6b . . . until the line next to the T mark faces back and aligns with the crankcase mating surfaces . . .

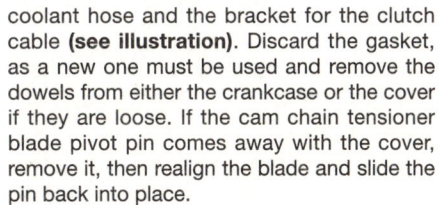

19.6c . . . and the camshaft lobes are as shown

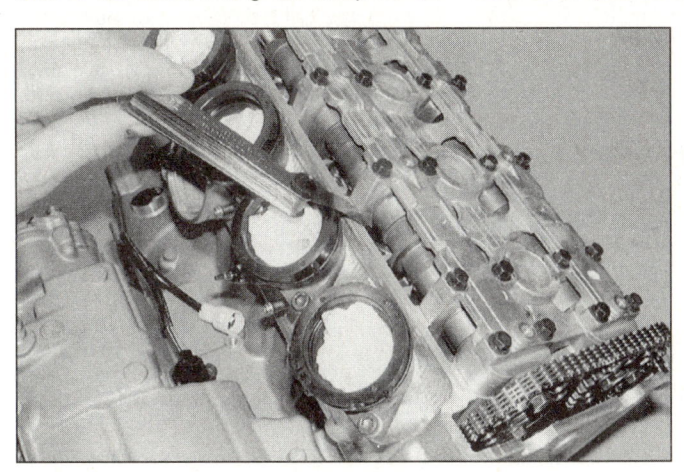

19.7a Insert the feeler gauge . . .

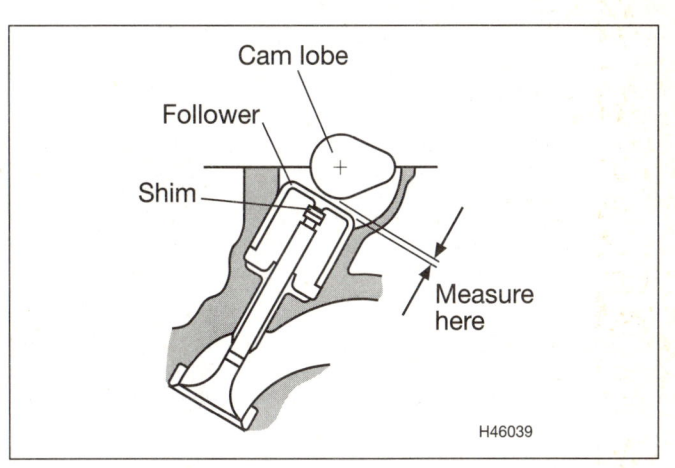

19.7b . . . between the base of the cam lobe and the top of the follower as shown

1•24 Routine Maintenance and Servicing

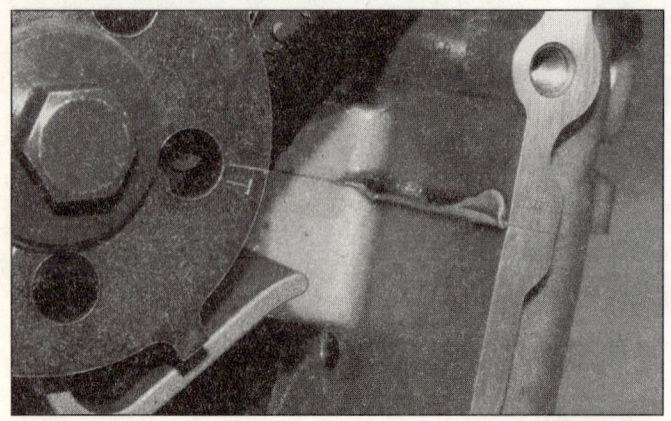

19.8a Turn the engine until the line next to the T mark faces forwards and aligns with the crankcase mating surfaces . . .

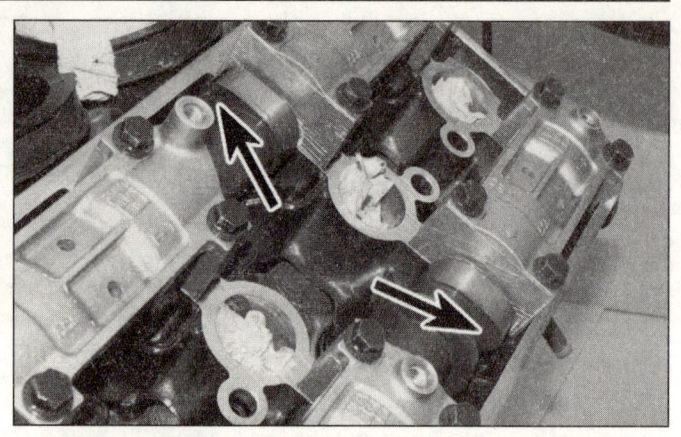

19.8b . . . and the camshaft sprocket lobes are as shown

19.13a Carefully lift out the follower using your fingers, grips, a lapping tool or a magnet . . .

19.13b . . . and retrieve the shim from inside it . . .

use the feeler gauges to measure the exact clearance. Record the measured clearance on your chart.

8 Now turn the engine clockwise 180° (half a turn) so that the 'T' mark faces forward and aligns with the crankcase mating surfaces and the camshaft lobes for the No. 2 cylinder are facing away from each other **(see illustrations)**. The No. 2 cylinder is now at TDC on the compression stroke. Measure the clearances of the No. 2 cylinder valves using the method described in Step 7.

9 Now turn the engine clockwise 180° (half a turn) so that the 'T' mark faces to the rear and aligns with the crankcase mating surfaces and the camshaft lobes for the No. 4 cylinder are facing away from each other. The No. 4 cylinder is now at TDC on the compression stroke. Measure the clearances of the No. 4 cylinder valves using the method described in Step 7.

10 Now turn the engine clockwise 180° (half a turn) so that the 'T' mark faces forward and aligns with the crankcase mating surfaces and the camshaft lobes for the No. 3 cylinder are facing away from each other. The No. 3 cylinder is now at TDC on the compression stroke. Measure the clearances of the No. 3 cylinder valves using the method described in Step 7.

11 When all clearances have been measured and recorded, identify whether the clearance on any valve falls outside that specified. If it does, the shim between the cam follower and the valve must be replaced with one of a thickness which will restore the correct clearance.

12 Shim replacement requires removal of the camshafts (see Chapter 2). There is no need to remove both camshafts if shims from only one need replacing. Place rags over the spark plug holes and the cam chain tunnel to prevent a shim from dropping into the engine on removal.

13 With the camshaft removed, remove the cam follower of the valve in question, then retrieve the shim from inside the follower **(see illustrations)**. If it is not in the follower, pick it out of the top of the valve using either a magnet, a small screwdriver with a dab of grease on it (the shim will stick to the grease), or a screwdriver and a pair of pliers. Do not allow the shim to fall into the engine.

14 A size should be marked on the upper face of the shim – a shim marked 175 is 1.75 mm thick. If the mark is not visible, the shim thickness will have to be measured. It is recommended that the shim is measured anyway, to check that it has not worn **(see illustration)**.

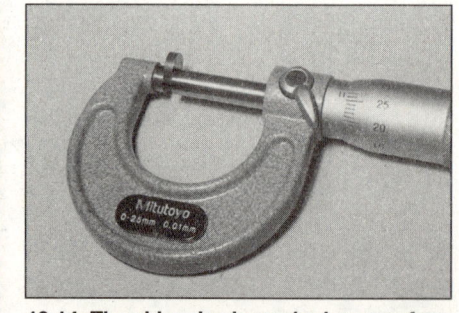

19.13c . . . or from the top of the valve

19.14 The shim size is marked on one face but check the thickness of the shim using a micrometer

Routine Maintenance and Servicing 1•25

15 Using the appropriate shim selection chart, find where the measured valve clearance and existing shim thickness values intersect and read off the shim size required **(see illustrations)**. *Note: If the existing shim is marked with a number not ending in 0 or 5, round it up or down as appropriate to the nearest number ending in 0 or 5, so that the chart can be used.* Shims are available in 0.05 mm increments from 1.20 mm to 2.40 mm. *Note: If the required replacement shim is greater than 2.40 mm (the largest available), the valve is probably not seating correctly due to a build-up of carbon deposits and should be checked and cleaned or resurfaced as required (see Chapter 2).*

16 Obtain the replacement shim, then

MEASURED INTAKE VALVE CLEARANCE	\multicolumn{25}{c}{EXISTING SHIM SIZE (mm)}
	1.20	1.25	1.30	1.35	1.40	1.45	1.50	1.55	1.60	1.65	1.70	1.75	1.80	1.85	1.90	1.95	2.00	2.05	2.10	2.15	2.20	2.25	2.30	2.35	2.40
0.00 – 0.02 mm				1.20	1.25	1.30	1.35	1.40	1.45	1.50	1.55	1.60	1.65	1.70	1.75	1.80	1.85	1.90	1.95	2.00	2.05	2.10	2.15	2.20	2.25
0.03 – 0.07 mm			1.20	1.25	1.30	1.35	1.40	1.45	1.50	1.55	1.60	1.65	1.70	1.75	1.80	1.85	1.90	1.95	2.00	2.05	2.10	2.15	2.20	2.25	2.30
0.08 – 0.12 mm		1.20	1.25	1.30	1.35	1.40	1.45	1.50	1.55	1.60	1.65	1.70	1.75	1.80	1.85	1.90	1.95	2.00	2.05	2.10	2.15	2.20	2.25	2.30	2.35
0.13 – 0.20 mm	\multicolumn{25}{c}{SPECIFIED CLEARANCE/NO ADJUSTMENT REQUIRED}
0.21 – 0.25 mm	1.25	1.30	1.35	1.40	1.45	1.50	1.55	1.60	1.65	1.70	1.75	1.80	1.85	1.90	1.95	2.00	2.05	2.10	2.15	2.20	2.25	2.30	2.35	2.40	
0.26 – 0.30 mm	1.30	1.35	1.40	1.45	1.50	1.55	1.60	1.65	1.70	1.75	1.80	1.85	1.90	1.95	2.00	2.05	2.10	2.15	2.20	2.25	2.30	2.35	2.40		
0.31 – 0.35 mm	1.35	1.40	1.45	1.50	1.55	1.60	1.65	1.70	1.75	1.80	1.85	1.90	1.95	2.00	2.05	2.10	2.15	2.20	2.25	2.30	2.35	2.40			
0.36 – 0.40 mm	1.40	1.45	1.50	1.55	1.60	1.65	1.70	1.75	1.80	1.85	1.90	1.95	2.00	2.05	2.10	2.15	2.20	2.25	2.30	2.35	2.40				
0.41 – 0.45 mm	1.45	1.50	1.55	1.60	1.65	1.70	1.75	1.80	1.85	1.90	1.95	2.00	2.05	2.10	2.15	2.20	2.25	2.30	2.35	2.40					
0.46 – 0.50 mm	1.50	1.55	1.60	1.65	1.70	1.75	1.80	1.85	1.90	1.95	2.00	2.05	2.10	2.15	2.20	2.25	2.30	2.35	2.40						
0.51 – 0.55 mm	1.55	1.60	1.65	1.70	1.75	1.80	1.85	1.90	1.95	2.00	2.05	2.10	2.15	2.20	2.25	2.30	2.35	2.40							
0.56 – 0.60 mm	1.60	1.65	1.70	1.75	1.80	1.85	1.90	1.95	2.00	2.05	2.10	2.15	2.20	2.25	2.30	2.35	2.40								
0.61 – 0.65 mm	1.65	1.70	1.75	1.80	1.85	1.90	1.95	2.00	2.05	2.10	2.15	2.20	2.25	2.30	2.35	2.40									
0.66 – 0.70 mm	1.70	1.75	1.80	1.85	1.90	1.95	2.00	2.05	2.10	2.15	2.20	2.25	2.30	2.35	2.40										
0.71 – 0.75 mm	1.75	1.80	1.85	1.90	1.95	2.00	2.05	2.10	2.15	2.20	2.25	2.30	2.35	2.40											
0.76 – 0.80 mm	1.80	1.85	1.90	1.95	2.00	2.05	2.10	2.15	2.20	2.25	2.30	2.35	2.40												
0.81 – 0.85 mm	1.85	1.90	1.95	2.00	2.05	2.10	2.15	2.20	2.25	2.30	2.35	2.40													
0.86 – 0.90 mm	1.90	1.95	2.00	2.05	2.10	2.15	2.20	2.25	2.30	2.35	2.40														
0.91 – 0.95 mm	1.95	2.00	2.05	2.10	2.15	2.20	2.25	2.30	2.35	2.40															
0.96 – 1.00 mm	2.00	2.05	2.10	2.15	2.20	2.25	2.30	2.35	2.40																
1.01 – 1.05 mm	2.05	2.10	2.15	2.20	2.25	2.30	2.35	2.40																	
1.06 – 1.10 mm	2.10	2.15	2.20	2.25	2.30	2.35	2.40																		
1.11 – 1.15 mm	2.15	2.20	2.25	2.30	2.35	2.40																			
1.16 – 1.20 mm	2.20	2.25	2.30	2.35	2.40																				
1.21 – 1.25 mm	2.25	2.30	2.35	2.40																					
1.26 – 1.30 mm	2.30	2.35	2.40																						
1.31 – 1.35 mm	2.35	2.40																							
1.36 – 1.40 mm	2.40																								

19.15a Shim selection chart – intake camshaft

MEASURED EXHAUST VALVE CLEARANCE	\multicolumn{25}{c}{EXISTING SHIM SIZE (mm)}
	1.20	1.25	1.30	1.35	1.40	1.45	1.50	1.55	1.60	1.65	1.70	1.75	1.80	1.85	1.90	1.95	2.00	2.05	2.10	2.15	2.20	2.25	2.30	2.35	2.40
0.00 – 0.02 mm						1.20	1.25	1.30	1.35	1.40	1.45	1.50	1.55	1.60	1.65	1.70	1.75	1.80	1.85	1.90	1.95	2.00	2.05	2.10	2.15
0.03 – 0.07 mm					1.20	1.25	1.30	1.35	1.40	1.45	1.50	1.55	1.60	1.65	1.70	1.75	1.80	1.85	1.90	1.95	2.00	2.05	2.10	2.15	2.20
0.08 – 0.12 mm				1.20	1.25	1.30	1.35	1.40	1.45	1.50	1.55	1.60	1.65	1.70	1.75	1.80	1.85	1.90	1.95	2.00	2.05	2.10	2.15	2.20	2.25
0.13 – 0.17 mm			1.20	1.25	1.30	1.35	1.40	1.45	1.50	1.55	1.60	1.65	1.70	1.75	1.80	1.85	1.90	1.95	2.00	2.05	2.10	2.15	2.20	2.25	2.30
0.18 – 0.22 mm		1.20	1.25	1.30	1.35	1.40	1.45	1.50	1.55	1.60	1.65	1.70	1.75	1.80	1.85	1.90	1.95	2.00	2.05	2.10	2.15	2.20	2.25	2.30	2.35
0.23 – 0.30 mm	\multicolumn{25}{c}{STANDARD CLEARANCE/NO ADJUSTMENT REQUIRED}
0.31 – 0.35 mm	1.25	1.30	1.35	1.40	1.45	1.50	1.55	1.60	1.65	1.70	1.75	1.80	1.85	1.90	1.95	2.00	2.05	2.10	2.15	2.20	2.25	2.30	2.35	2.40	
0.36 – 0.40 mm	1.30	1.35	1.40	1.45	1.50	1.55	1.60	1.65	1.70	1.75	1.80	1.85	1.90	1.95	2.00	2.05	2.10	2.15	2.20	2.25	2.30	2.35	2.40		
0.41 – 0.45 mm	1.35	1.40	1.45	1.50	1.55	1.60	1.65	1.70	1.75	1.80	1.85	1.90	1.95	2.00	2.05	2.10	2.15	2.20	2.25	2.30	2.35	2.40			
0.46 – 0.50 mm	1.40	1.45	1.50	1.55	1.60	1.65	1.70	1.75	1.80	1.85	1.90	1.95	2.00	2.05	2.10	2.15	2.20	2.25	2.30	2.35	2.40				
0.51 – 0.55 mm	1.45	1.50	1.55	1.60	1.65	1.70	1.75	1.80	1.85	1.90	1.95	2.00	2.05	2.10	2.15	2.20	2.25	2.30	2.35	2.40					
0.56 – 0.60 mm	1.50	1.55	1.60	1.65	1.70	1.75	1.80	1.85	1.90	1.95	2.00	2.05	2.10	2.15	2.20	2.25	2.30	2.35	2.40						
0.61 – 0.65 mm	1.55	1.60	1.65	1.70	1.75	1.80	1.85	1.90	1.95	2.00	2.05	2.10	2.15	2.20	2.25	2.30	2.35	2.40							
0.66 – 0.70 mm	1.60	1.65	1.70	1.75	1.80	1.85	1.90	1.95	2.00	2.05	2.10	2.15	2.20	2.25	2.30	2.35	2.40								
0.71 – 0.75 mm	1.65	1.70	1.75	1.80	1.85	1.90	1.95	2.00	2.05	2.10	2.15	2.20	2.25	2.30	2.35	2.40									
0.76 – 0.80 mm	1.70	1.75	1.80	1.85	1.90	1.95	2.00	2.05	2.10	2.15	2.20	2.25	2.30	2.35	2.40										
0.81 – 0.85 mm	1.75	1.80	1.85	1.90	1.95	2.00	2.05	2.10	2.15	2.20	2.25	2.30	2.35	2.40											
0.86 – 0.90 mm	1.80	1.85	1.90	1.95	2.00	2.05	2.10	2.15	2.20	2.25	2.30	2.35	2.40												
0.91 – 0.95 mm	1.85	1.90	1.95	2.00	2.05	2.10	2.15	2.20	2.25	2.30	2.35	2.40													
0.96 – 1.00 mm	1.90	1.95	2.00	2.05	2.10	2.15	2.20	2.25	2.30	2.35	2.40														
1.01 – 1.05 mm	1.95	2.00	2.05	2.10	2.15	2.20	2.25	2.30	2.35	2.40															
1.06 – 1.10 mm	2.00	2.05	2.10	2.15	2.20	2.25	2.30	2.35	2.40																
1.11 – 1.15 mm	2.05	2.10	2.15	2.20	2.25	2.30	2.35	2.40																	
1.16 – 1.20 mm	2.10	2.15	2.20	2.25	2.30	2.35	2.40																		
1.21 – 1.25 mm	2.15	2.20	2.25	2.30	2.35	2.40																			
1.26 – 1.30 mm	2.20	2.25	2.30	2.35	2.40																				
1.31 – 1.35 mm	2.25	2.30	2.35	2.40																					
1.36 – 1.40 mm	2.30	2.35	2.40																						
1.41 – 1.45 mm	2.35	2.40																							
1.46 – 1.50 mm	2.40																								

19.15b Shim selection chart – exhaust camshaft

1•26 Routine Maintenance and Servicing

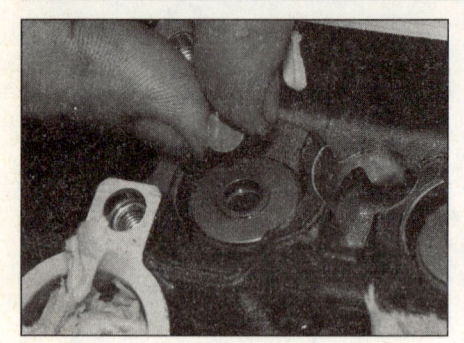

19.16 Fit the shim into its recess

19.18a Fit a new gasket onto the dowels (arrowed) . . .

19.18b . . . then install the cover, making sure it locates correctly

lubricate it with molybdenum disulphide grease and fit it into its recess in the top of the valve, with the size marking facing up **(see illustration)**. Check that the shim is correctly seated, then lubricate the follower with molybdenum disulphide oil (a 50/50 mixture of molybdenum disulphide grease and engine oil) and fit it onto the valve **(see illustration 19.13a)**. Repeat the process for any other valves until the clearances are correct, then install the camshafts (see Chapter 2).

17 Rotate the crankshaft clockwise several turns to seat the new shim(s), then check the clearances again **(see illustration 19.6a)**.

18 Install the valve cover (see Chapter 2). Ensure the dowels for the timing rotor cover are in place and that the cam chain tensioner blade pivot pin locates in the hole in the cover **(see illustrations)**. Install the cover bolts, the clamp for the coolant hose and the bracket for the clutch cable and tighten the bolts to the torque setting specified at the beginning of this Chapter – the longer bolts secure the clutch cable bracket **(see illustration 19.5)**.

19 Install all remaining components (see Step 2). On completion, check and adjust the idle speed (see Section 4).

Chapter 2
Engine, clutch and transmission

Contents

	Section number
Alternator	see Chapter 8
Cam chain tensioner	7
Cam chain, tensioner blade and guides	9
Camshafts and followers	8
Camshaft position (CMP) sensor	see Chapter 4
Clutch	13
Clutch cable	12
Clutch check	see Chapter 1
Component access	2
Connecting rods and bearings	21
Crankcases and cylinder bores	28
Crankcase separation and reassembly	19
Crankshaft and main bearings	24
Crankshaft position (CKP) sensor	see Chapter 4
Cylinder head and valve overhaul	11
Cylinder head removal and installation	10
Engine overhaul general information	5
Engine removal and installation	4
Engine wear assessment	3
Gearchange mechanism	15
General information	1

	Section number
Idle speed	see Chapter 1
Main and big-end bearing information	20
Neutral switch	see Chapter 8
Oil and filter change	see Chapter 1
Oil cooler	16
Oil level check	see *Pre-ride checks*
Oil level sensor	see Chapter 8
Oil pump	18
Oil sump, strainer and pressure relief valve	17
Pistons	22
Piston rings	23
Running-in procedure	29
Selector drum and forks	27
Spark plugs	see Chapter 1
Starter clutch and gears	14
Starter motor	see Chapter 8
Transmission shaft overhaul	26
Transmission shaft removal and installation	25
Valve clearances	see Chapter 1
Valve cover	6
Water pump	see Chapter 3

Degrees of difficulty

Easy, suitable for novice with little experience	Fairly easy, suitable for beginner with some experience	Fairly difficult, suitable for competent DIY mechanic	Difficult, suitable for experienced DIY mechanic	Very difficult, suitable for expert DIY or professional

Specifications

General
Type	Four-stroke in-line four
Capacity	600 cc
Bore	65.5 mm
Stroke	44.5 mm
Compression ratio	12.4 to 1
Cylinder numbering	1 to 4 from left to right
Cooling system	Liquid cooled
Clutch	Wet multi-plate
Transmission	Six-speed constant mesh
Final drive	Chain

Cylinder head
Warpage (max)	0.05 mm

Camshafts
Intake lobe height	
Standard	33.45 to 33.55 mm
Service limit (min)	33.4 mm
Exhaust lobe height	
Standard	32.55 to 32.65 mm
Service limit (min)	32.50 mm
Journal diameter	22.967 to 22.980 mm
Holder diameter	23.008 to 23.029 mm
Journal oil clearance	0.028 to 0.062 mm
Service limit (all models)	0.08 mm
Runout (max)	0.06 mm

Valves, guides and springs

Valve clearances.. see Chapter 1
Intake valve
  Stem diameter
    Standard.. 3.975 to 3.990 mm
    Service limit (min)... 3.950 mm
  Guide bore diameter
    Standard.. 4.000 to 4.012 mm
    Service limit (max).. 4.042 mm
  Stem-to-guide clearance
    Standard.. 0.010 to 0.037 mm
    Service limit (max).. 0.08 mm
  Stem runout... 0.04 mm
  Head diameter... 24.9 to 25.1 mm
  Face width.. 1.14 to 1.98 mm
  Seat width
    Standard.. 0.9 to 1.1 mm
    Service limit (max).. 1.6 mm
  Margin thickness
    Standard.. 0.6 to 0.8 mm
    Service limit (min)... 0.5 mm
Exhaust valve
  Stem diameter
    Standard.. 3.960 to 3.975 mm
    Service limit (min)... 3.935 mm
  Guide bore diameter
    Standard.. 4.000 to 4.012 mm
    Service limit (max).. 4.042 mm
  Stem-to-guide clearance
    Standard.. 0.025 to 0.052 mm
    Service limit (max).. 0.10 mm
  Stem runout... 0.04 mm
  Head diameter... 21.9 to 22.1 mm
  Face width.. 1.14 to 1.98 mm
  Seat width
    Standard.. 0.9 to 1.1 mm
    Service limit (max).. 1.6 mm
  Margin thickness
    Standard.. 0.6 to 0.8 mm
    Service limit (min)... 0.5 mm
Valve spring free length
  Intake (inner)
    Standard.. 35.7 mm
    Service limit (min)... 33.9 mm
  Intake (outer)
    Standard.. 40.3 mm
    Service limit (min)... 38.3 mm
  Exhaust
    Standard.. 41.7 mm
    Service limit (min)... 39.6 mm
Valve spring bend (max)
  Intake (inner).. 1.6 mm
  Intake (outer)... 1.8 mm
  Exhaust... 1.8 mm

Lubrication system

Engine oil pressure (at 96°C)............................... 34.8 psi (2.4 Bars) @ 6000 rpm
Relief valve opening pressure.............................. 65.3 to 79.8 psi (4.5 to 5.5 Bars)
Oil pump
  Inner rotor tip-to-outer rotor clearance
    Standard.. 0.03 to 0.09 mm
    Service limit (max).. 0.15 mm
  Outer rotor-to-body clearance
    Standard.. 0.03 to 0.08 mm
    Service limit (max).. 0.15 mm

Clutch

Friction plates
- Quantity
  - Outer plates (Brown colour code) ... 6
  - Inner plates (Purple colour code) ... 2
- Thickness
  - Standard ... 2.9 to 3.1 mm
  - Service limit (min) ... 2.8 mm

Plain plate
- Outer plates
  - Quantity ... 7
  - Thickness ... 1.9 to 2.1 mm
  - Warpage (max) ... 0.1 mm
- Inner plate
  - Quantity ... 1
  - Thickness ... 2.2 to 2.4 mm
  - Warpage (max) ... 0.1 mm

Clutch springs
- Free length ... 50 mm
- Service limit ... 49 mm

Cylinder bores

Bore ... 65.50 to 65.51 mm
Ovality (max) ... 0.05 mm
Taper (max) ... 0.05 mm
Cylinder compression
- Standard ... 220.5 psi (15.5 Bars)
- Maximum ... 247 psi (17.4 Bars)
- Minimum ... 192 psi (13.5 Bars)
- Max. difference between cylinders ... 14.5 psi (1.0 Bar)

Piston-to-bore clearance
- Standard ... 0.010 to 0.035 mm
- Service limit ... 0.055 mm

Pistons

Piston diameter (measured 4 mm up from skirt, at 90° to piston pin axis) ... 65.475 to 65.490 mm
Piston-to-bore clearance
- Standard ... 0.010 to 0.035 mm
- Service limit ... 0.055 mm

Piston pin diameter
- Standard ... 15.991 to 16.000 mm
- Service limit (min) ... 15.971 mm

Piston pin bore diameter in piston
- Standard ... 16.002 to 16.013 mm
- Service limit (max) ... 16.043 mm

Piston pin-to-piston pin bore clearance
- Standard ... 0.002 to 0.022 mm
- Service limit ... 0.072 mm

Piston rings

Top compression ring
- Type ... Barrel
- Ring width ... 2.45 mm
- Ring thickness ... 0.90 mm
- Ring end gap (installed)
  - Standard ... 0.25 to 0.35 mm
  - Service limit ... 0.60 mm
- Piston ring-to-groove clearance
  - Standard ... 0.030 to 0.065 mm
  - Service limit ... 0.115 mm

2nd compression ring
Type .... Taper
Ring width .... 2.5 mm
Ring thickness .... 0.8 mm
Ring end gap (installed)
   Standard .... 0.70 to 0.80 mm
   Service limit .... 1.15 mm
Piston ring-to-groove clearance
   Standard .... 0.030 to 0.065 mm
   Service limit .... 0.115 mm
Oil ring
   Ring width .... 2.0 mm
   Ring thickness .... 1.5 mm
   Side-rail end gap (installed) .... 0.10 to 0.35 mm

Crankshaft and bearings
Main bearing oil clearance
   Standard .... 0.034 to 0.058 mm
   Service limit .... 0.10 mm
Runout (max) .... 0.03 mm

Connecting rods
Big-end side clearance .... 0.160 to 0.262 mm
Big-end oil clearance
   Standard .... 0.028 to 0.052 mm
   Service limit (max) .... 0.09 mm

Transmission
Gear ratios (no. of teeth)
   Primary reduction .... 1.955 to 1 (86/44T)
   Final reduction .... 3.000 to 1 (48/16T)
   1st gear .... 2.846 to 1 (37/13T)
   2nd gear .... 1.947 to 1 (37/19T)
   3rd gear .... 1.555 to 1 (28/18T)
   4th gear .... 1.333 to 1 (32/24T)
   5th gear .... 1.190 to 1 (25/21T)
   6th gear .... 1.083 to 1 (26/24T)
Shaft runout (max) .... 0.02 mm

Gearchange mechanism
Gearchange linkage rod installed length .... 290 mm
Selector fork shaft runout (max) .... 0.05 mm

Torque wrench settings
Alternator cover bolts .... 12 Nm
Cam chain tensioner cap bolt .... 7 Nm
Cam chain tensioner mounting bolts .... 12 Nm
Camshaft holder bolts .... 10 Nm
Camshaft sprocket bolts .... 24 Nm
Clutch centre nut
   R and S (2003 and 2004) models .... 70 Nm
   T (2005) models .... 90 Nm
Clutch cover bolts .... 12 Nm
Clutch pressure plate bolts .... 8 Nm
Connecting rod cap nuts
   Initial setting .... 15 Nm
   Final setting (see Section 21) .... + 150°
Crankcase 6 mm bolts .... 12 Nm
Crankcase 8 mm bolts (see Section 19)
   Nos. 1 to 10
      1st stage .... 12 Nm
      2nd stage .... 25 Nm
      3rd stage .... 27 Nm
   Nos. 11 and 12 .... 24 Nm

Engine, clutch and transmission 2•5

Torque wrench settings (continued)

Cylinder head bolts	
10 mm (stage 1)	19 Nm
10 mm (stage 2)	50 Nm
6 mm	12 Nm
Engine mounting adjuster bolts	7 Nm
Engine mounting bolts	
Engine bracket bolts	45 Nm
Front mounting bolts	45 Nm
Rear mounting bolt nuts	45 Nm
Front sprocket cover bolts	10 Nm
Gearchange shaft centralising spring locating pin	22 Nm
Oil baffle plate bolts	12 Nm
Oil cooler bolt	63 Nm
Oil level sensor bolts	10 Nm
Oil gallery bolt	8 Nm
Oil pipe (U-shaped) bolts	12 Nm
Oil pump drive chain guide bolts	12 Nm
Oil pump housing bolts	12 Nm
Oil pump mounting bolts	12 Nm
Oil sump bolts	12 Nm
Selector drum retaining plate bolts	10 Nm
Starter clutch bolts	32 Nm
Timing rotor bolt	35 Nm
Timing rotor cover bolts	12 Nm
Transmission input shaft bearing housing Torx screws	12 Nm
Valve cover bolts	12 Nm

1 General information

The engine is a liquid-cooled in-line four, with four valves per cylinder. The valves are operated by double overhead camshafts which are chain driven off the right-hand end of the crankshaft. The engine assembly is constructed from aluminium alloy. The crankcase is divided horizontally.

The crankcase incorporates a wet sump, pressure-fed lubrication system which uses a chain-driven, dual-rotor oil pump, an oil filter, a relief valve and an oil level sensor. The pump is chain-driven from the back of the clutch housing. The oil is circulated through a cooler which is located on the front of the crankcases.

The alternator is on the left-hand end of the crankshaft, and the starter clutch is on the back of the alternator.

Power from the crankshaft is routed to the transmission via the clutch. The clutch is of the wet, multi-plate type and is gear-driven off the crankshaft. The transmission is a six-speed constant-mesh unit. Final drive to the rear wheel is by chain and sprockets.

Read the *Safety first!* section of this manual carefully before starting work.

2 Component access

Operations possible with the engine in the frame

The components and assemblies listed below can be removed without having to remove the engine assembly from the frame. If however, a number of areas require attention at the same time, removal of the engine is recommended.
Valve cover
Camshafts
Cam chain
Cylinder head
Water pump and thermostat
Clutch and starter clutch
Gearchange mechanism
Alternator
Starter motor
Crankshaft position (CKP) sensor
Oil filter and cooler
Oil sump, oil strainer and oil pressure relief valve
Oil pump

Operations requiring engine removal

It is necessary to remove the engine/transmission assembly from the frame to gain access to the following components.
Crankshaft and bearings
Connecting rods and bearings
Cylinder bores, pistons and piston rings
Transmission shafts
Selector drum and forks

3 Engine wear assessment

1 Poor engine performance may be caused by leaking valves, incorrect valve clearances (see Chapter 1), a leaking head gasket, or worn pistons, rings and/or cylinder walls. A cylinder compression check will confirm the existence of a problem and can also indicate the presence of excessive carbon deposits in the combustion chambers, and a leakdown test (for which special equipment is needed – consult a Yamaha dealer) will pinpoint the actual cause(s) of the problem.
2 If there is any doubt about the performance of the engine lubrication system an oil pressure check must be carried out. The check provides useful information about the state of wear of the engine.

Cylinder compression check

Special tool: *A compression gauge is required to perform this test.*

2•6 Engine, clutch and transmission

3.9 Oil gallery bolt (arrowed)

3 The only tools required are a compression gauge (with a threaded end to match the spark plug hole size – 10 mm) and a spark plug wrench. Depending on the outcome of the initial test, a squirt-type oil can may also be needed.

4 Make sure the valve clearances are correctly set (see Chapter 1) and that the cylinder head bolts are tightened to the correct torque setting (see Section 10).

5 Refer to *Fault Finding Equipment* in the Reference section for details of the compression test. Refer to the specifications at the beginning of this Chapter for compression figures.

Engine oil pressure check

Special tool: *An oil pressure gauge is required to perform this test.*

6 This engine is fitted with an oil level sensor and warning light. The function of the circuit is described in Chapter 8.

7 To check the oil pressure, a suitable pressure gauge (which screws into the crankcase) will be needed. Yamaha provide a gauge (part no. 90890-03153 in Europe, YU-03153 in the US) and gauge adapter (part no. 90890-03139) for this purpose.

8 Place the bike upright on level ground using an auxiliary stand. Remove the lower fairing (see Chapter 7). Warm the engine up to normal operating temperature then stop it. Check the engine oil level and top up if necessary (see *Pre-ride checks*).

9 Unscrew the oil gallery bolt in the left-hand side of the crankcase below the alternator cover **(see illustration)** and quickly screw the adapter into the crankcase threads. Connect the pressure gauge to the adapter.

⚠️ **Warning:** *Take great care not to burn your hand on the hot engine unit, exhaust pipe or with engine oil when accessing the gauge take-off point on the crankcase. Do not allow exhaust gases to build up in the work area; either perform the check outside or use an exhaust gas extraction system.*

Discard the oil gallery bolt O-ring as a new one must be fitted on reassembly.

10 Start the engine and increase the engine speed to 6600 rpm whilst watching the pressure gauge reading. The oil pressure should be similar to that given in the Specifications at the beginning of this Chapter.

11 If the pressure is significantly lower than the standard, either the pressure relief valve is stuck open, the oil pump is faulty, the oil strainer or filter is blocked, or there is considerable engine wear. Begin diagnosis by checking the oil filter, strainer and relief valve, then the oil pump (see Sections 17 and 18). If those items check out okay, the engine bearing oil clearances are likely to be excessive and the engine needs to be overhauled.

12 If the pressure is too high, either an oil passage is clogged, the relief valve is stuck closed or the wrong grade of oil is being used.

13 Stop the engine and unscrew the gauge and adapter from the crankcase.

14 Lubricate the oil gallery bolt O-ring with clean engine oil and install the bolt. Tighten the bolt to the specified torque setting, then check the oil level (see *Pre-ride checks*).

15 Refer to Chapter 2 and rectify any problems before running the engine again. Install the lower fairing (see Chapter 7).

4 Engine removal and installation

Caution: The engine is very heavy. Engine removal and installation should be carried out with the aid of at least one assistant. Personal injury or damage could occur if the engine falls or is dropped. An hydraulic or mechanical floor jack should be used to support and lower or raise the engine, if possible.

Removal

Note: *If you intend to remove the alternator, clutch or timing rotor with the engine removed from the frame, it is best to slacken the alternator rotor bolt, clutch nut and timing rotor bolt while the engine is still in the frame – the bolts are tight and the engine needs to be held securely while they are unscrewed. Refer to Chapter 8 for the alternator and to Sections 13 and 9 for the clutch nut and timing rotor.*

1 Support the motorcycle securely in an upright position using an auxiliary stand. Work can be made easier by raising the machine to a suitable working height on an hydraulic ramp or a suitable platform. Make sure the motorcycle is secure and will not topple over (see Section 1 of *Tools and Workshop Tips* in the *Reference* section). When disconnecting any wiring, cables and hoses, it is advisable to mark or tag them as a reminder of where they connect.

2 Remove the seats (see Chapter 7) and disconnect the negative (–) lead from the battery, then disconnect the positive (+) lead (see Chapter 8).

3 Remove the fairing side panels and their inner trim sections, the lower fairing, fairing, and the seat cowling (see Chapter 7). **Note:** *Removal of the fairing and seat cowling is not strictly necessary, although it is wise to remove them as they could be damaged accidentally.*

4 If the engine is dirty, particularly around its mountings, wash it thoroughly before starting any major dismantling work. This will make work much easier and rule out the possibility of dirt falling inside.

5 Drain the engine oil and the coolant and remove the coolant reservoir (see Chapters 1 and 3).

6 Remove the fuel tank and the air filter housing (see Chapter 4). Slacken the clamps securing the air ducts and draw the ducts out **(see illustration)**. Detach the crankcase breather hose and remove it **(see illustration)**.

7 Remove the throttle bodies (see Chapter 4). Plug the intake manifolds with clean rag. Remove the rubber heat shield, noting how it fits **(see illustration)**.

4.6a Slacken the clamp (arrowed) securing each duct and remove the ducts

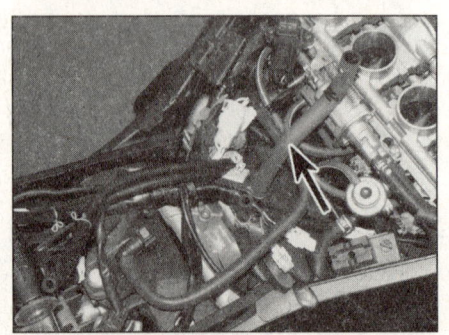

4.6b Remove the crankcase breather hose (arrowed)

4.7 Remove the rubber heat shield

Engine, clutch and transmission 2•7

4.8a Release the cable ties (arrowed) . . .

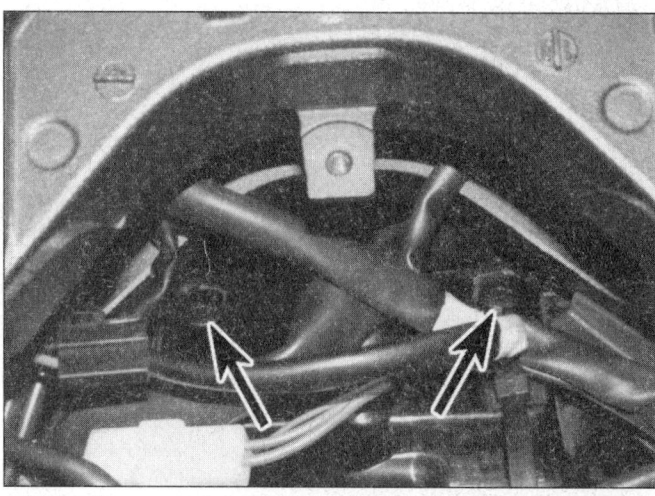

4.8b . . . then move the wiring aside and release the trim clips (B) . . .

8 Note the routing of all cables, wiring and hoses over and around the radiator cover. Release the cables ties to free the wiring **(see illustration)**. Release the trim clips securing the cover and remove it, noting how it fits **(see illustration)**.
9 Release the cable tie securing the clutch cable to the coolant hose on the right-hand side **(see illustration)**. Remove the radiator along with the coolant hoses to the engine, water pump and oil cooler, (see Chapter 3).
10 Remove the AIS control valve along with the hoses (see Chapter 4). Remove the ignition coils (see Chapter 4). Disconnect the camshaft position (CMP) sensor wiring connector **(see illustration)**. Disconnect the front sub-loom wiring black connectors and remove the loom **(see illustration)**.
11 Remove the exhaust system (see Chapter 4). Unscrew the bolt securing the radiator mounting bracket to the front of the engine and remove it, noting how it fits **(see illustration)**.
12 Detach the clutch cable from the release mechanism arm (see Section 12).
13 Trace the oil level sensor wire from underneath the engine and disconnect it at the white single pin connector **(see illustration)**. Trace the sidestand switch wiring from the switch and disconnect it at the blue two-pin connector **(see illustrations)**. Release the

4.8c . . . and remove the cover

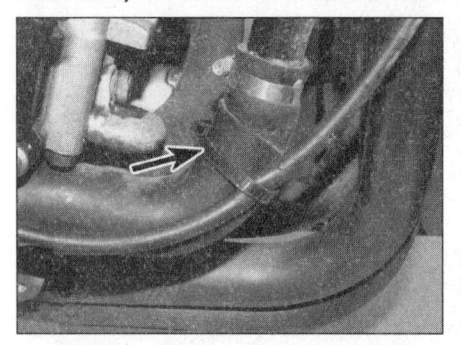

4.9 Release the cable tie (arrowed)

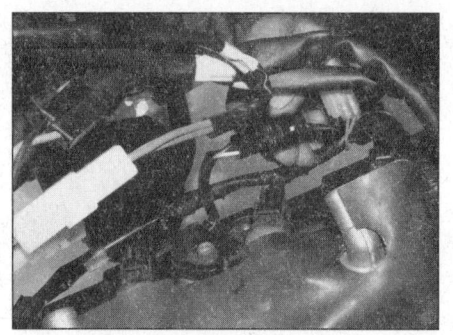

4.10a Disconnect the CMP sensor wiring connector . . .

4.10b . . . then disconnect the front loom connectors and remove the loom

4.11 Unscrew the bolt (arrowed) and remove the bracket

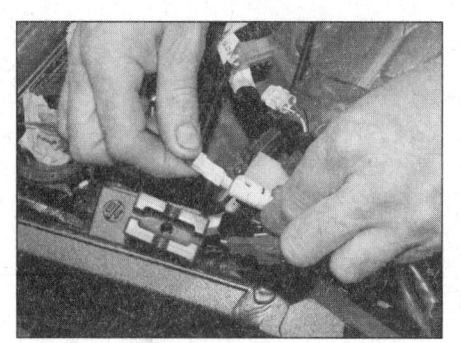

4.13a Disconnect the oil level sensor wiring connector . . .

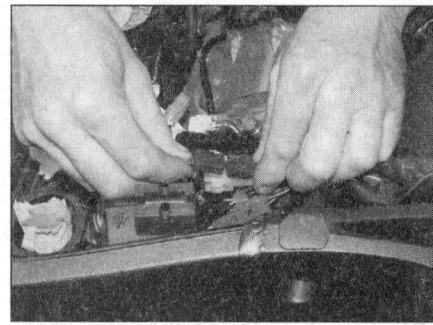

4.13b . . . the sidestand switch wiring connector . . .

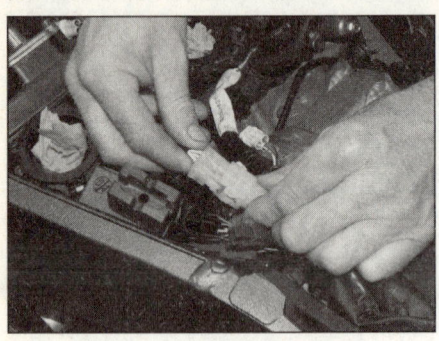

2•8 Engine, clutch and transmission

4.14 ... the alternator wiring connector ...

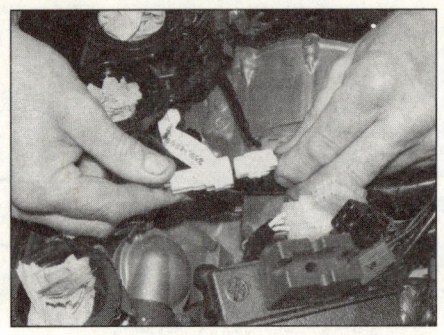

4.15 ... the speed sensor wiring connector ...

4.16a ... and the rear brake light switch wiring connector

wires from any ties and coil them so that they do not impede engine removal.

14 Trace the alternator wiring from the top of the alternator cover on the left-hand side of the engine and disconnect it at the off-white, three-pin connector **(see illustration)**. Coil the wiring so that it does not impede engine removal.

15 Trace the speed sensor wiring from the sensor on the top of the transmission case and disconnect it at the white three-pin connector **(see illustration)**.

16 Trace the wiring from the rear brake light switch mounted behind the rider's right-hand footrest bracket and disconnect it at the brown two-pin connector **(see illustration)**. Feed the wiring down to the switch, noting its routing under the frame and ahead of the engine mount.

17 Peel back the boot on the starter motor terminal, then unscrew the starter motor terminal nut and detach the lead **(see illustration)**.

18 Unscrew the bolt securing the crankcase earth (ground) lead and detach the lead **(see illustration)**. Secure the lead clear of the engine.

19 Trace the crankshaft position (CKP) sensor wiring from the timing rotor cover on the right-hand side of the engine and disconnect it at the off-white, two-pin connector. Coil the wiring so that it does not impede engine removal **(see illustration)**.

20 Disconnect the wiring from the neutral switch on the back of the engine **(see illustration)**.

21 Make sure the transmission is in neutral. Loosen the gearchange linkage rod locknuts, then unscrew the rod and separate it from the lever and the arm (see Section 15). Withdraw the rod from the frame.

22 Remove the front sprocket and disengage the chain from the gearbox output shaft (see Chapter 6). Unscrew the bolt securing the chain guide to the sidestand bracket, noting the collar, and remove the guide, noting how it locates **(see illustrations)**.

4.16b Note the routing of the wiring and feed it down to the switch

4.17 Unscrew the nut (arrowed) and detach the lead

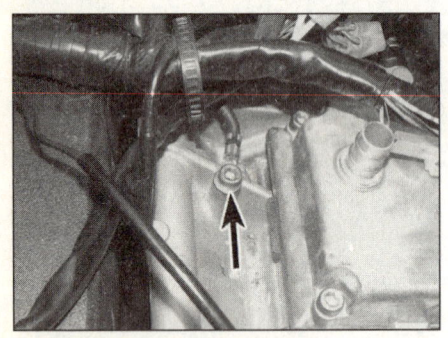

4.18 Unscrew the bolt (arrowed) and detach the lead

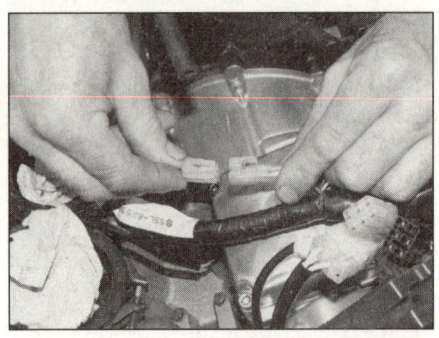

4.19 Disconnect the CKP sensor wiring connector

4.20 Pull the connector off the neutral switch

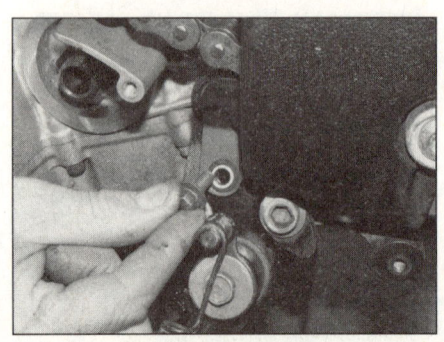

4.22a Unscrew the bolt ...

4.22b ... and remove the guide ...

Engine, clutch and transmission 2•9

4.22c ... noting how the peg locates in the hole (arrowed) on the rear of the frame section

4.23 Support the engine using a jack

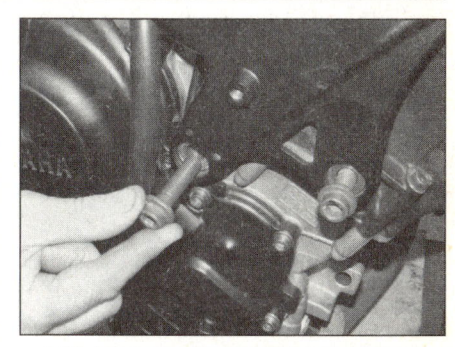

4.25 Unscrew the two right-hand front mounting bolts

23 At this point, position an hydraulic or mechanical jack under the engine with a block of wood between the jack head and crankcase **(see illustration)**. Make sure the jack is centrally positioned so the engine will not topple in any direction when the last mounting bolt is removed and the engine is supported only by the jack. Take the weight of the engine on the jack. It is also advisable to place a block of wood between the rear wheel and the ground in case the bike tilts back onto the rear wheel when the engine is removed.
24 Check around the engine and frame to make sure that all the necessary wiring, cables and hoses have been disconnected, and that any that remain connected to the engine are not retained by any clips, guides or brackets on the frame. When removing the engine mounting bolts note which fits where as there are different lengths and sizes.
25 Unscrew and remove the engine front mounting bolts on the right-hand side **(see illustration)**.
26 Unscrew and remove the engine front mounting bolts on the left-hand side, and slacken the bracket bolts but do not yet remove them **(see illustration)**.
27 Remove the frame blanking cap from each end of the upper rear mounting bolt **(see illustration)**. Unscrew the nuts from the right-hand end of the upper and lower rear mounting bolts, but do not withdraw the bolts **(see illustration)**. Make sure the engine is properly supported on the jack, and have an assistant support it as well, then withdraw the mounting bolts **(see illustration)**. Note that the upper bolt is shorter than the lower bolt.
28 Unscrew the bolts securing the engine bracket to the front left-hand side of the engine **(see illustration 4.26)**.
29 Thread the engine rear mounting adjusters away from the engine until they lightly contact the inside of the frame **(see illustrations)**. Yamaha provide a shaft wrench and socket adapter for this purpose (part Nos. 90890-01471 (YM-01471 in the US) and 01476), or alternatively a suitable tool for use with a socket can be made **(see Tool Tip** relevant to swingarm removal in Chapter 5, Section 14, noting that the bar should be 12 mm wide instead of 22 mm**)**.

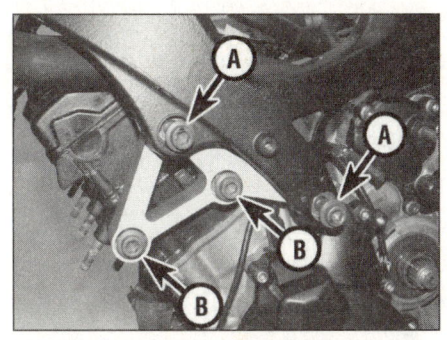

4.26 Unscrew the two left-hand front mounting bolts (A) and slacken the bracket bolts (B)

4.27a Remove the blanking cap from each side

4.27b Unscrew nut from each rear mounting bolt

4.27c With the engine properly supported withdraw the rear mounting bolts

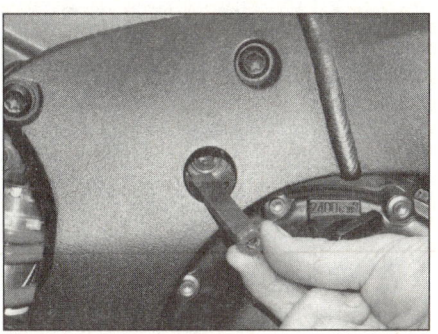

4.29a Thread the adjusters away from the engine ...

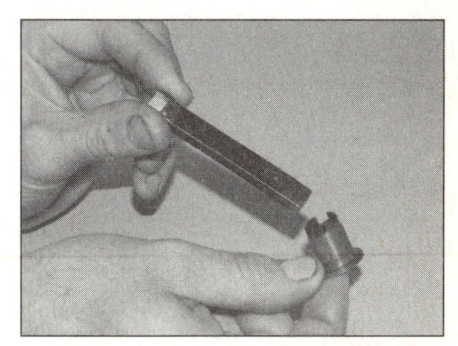

4.29b ... using a home-made tool if required to fit in the adjuster

2•10 Engine, clutch and transmission

4.30 Remove the engine bracket when it becomes free

4.31 Remove the mounting adjusters if required

30 Carefully lower the engine and bring it forward, collecting the engine bracket as you do, then manoeuvre it out of the frame from the right-hand side **(see illustration)**.

31 If required thread the engine rear mounting adjusters out of the frame from the inside **(see illustration)**.

Installation

32 Installation is the reverse of removal, noting the following points:
- Before lifting the engine into position, if removed screw the engine rear mounting adjusters finger-tight all the way into the right-hand side of the frame **(see illustration 4.31)**. Fit the engine bracket onto the left-hand side of the engine and tighten its bolts to the torque setting specified at the beginning of the Chapter.
- With the aid of an assistant, place the engine unit onto the jack and block of wood and carefully raise it into position so that the mounting bolt holes align. Make sure no wires, cables or hoses become trapped between the engine and the frame. The engine mounting bolts are of different sizes and lengths. Make sure the correct bolt is installed in its correct location.
- Lubricate the threads of the upper and lower rear mounting bolts with lithium based grease and slide them into place **(see illustration 4.27c)**.
- Install the front mounting bolts on the left-hand side and tighten them to the specified torque setting, tightening the rearmost bolt first **(see illustration 4.26)**.
- Displace first the upper and then the lower rear engine mounting bolts sufficiently to use the engine mounting adjuster tool, and tighten the adjusters, lower one first, to the torque setting specified at the beginning of this Chapter **(see illustrations 4.29b and a)**. Push the bolts back through.
- Fit the nuts onto the ends of the upper and lower rear mounting bolts and tighten them to the specified torque, tightening the lower one first **(see illustration 4.27b)**.
- Tighten the front mounting bolts on the right-hand side to the specified torque, tightening the rearmost bolt first **(see illustration 4.25)**.
- Make sure all wires, cables and hoses are correctly routed and connected, and secured by any clips or ties.
- Refill the engine with oil and coolant to the correct levels (see Chapter 1 and *Pre-ride checks*).
- Check the throttle and clutch cable freeplay (see Chapter 1).
- Adjust the drive chain tension (see Chapter 1).
- Tighten all nuts and bolts to the specified torque settings where given.
- Start the engine and check that there are no oil or coolant leaks before installing the fairing panels.
- Adjust the engine idle speed (see Chapter 1).

5 Engine overhaul general information

1 Before beginning the engine overhaul, read through the related procedures to familiarise yourself with the scope and requirements of the job. Overhauling an engine is not all that difficult, but it is time consuming. Check on the availability of parts and make sure that any necessary special tools are obtained in advance.

2 Most work can be done with a decent set of typical workshop hand tools, although a number of precision measuring tools are required for inspecting parts to determine if they are worn.

3 To ensure maximum life and minimum trouble from a rebuilt engine, everything must be assembled with care in a spotlessly clean environment, using the correct lubricant where directed.

Disassembly

4 Before disassembling the engine, thoroughly clean and degrease its external surfaces. This will prevent contamination of the engine internals, and will also make the job a lot easier and cleaner. A high flash-point solvent, such as paraffin (kerosene) can be used, or better still, a proprietary engine degreaser such as Gunk. Use old paintbrushes and toothbrushes to work the solvent into the various recesses of the casings. Take care to exclude solvent or water from the electrical components and intake and exhaust ports.

⚠ **Warning:** *The use of petrol (gasoline) as a cleaning agent should be avoided because of the risk of fire.*

5 When clean and dry, position the engine on the workbench, leaving suitable clear area for working. Gather a selection of small containers, plastic bags and some labels so that parts can be grouped together in an easily identifiable manner. Also get some paper and a pen so that notes can be taken. You will also need a supply of clean rag, which should be as absorbent as possible.

6 Before commencing work, read through the appropriate section so that some idea of the necessary procedure can be gained. When removing components note that great force is seldom required, unless specified (checking the specified torque setting of the particular bolt being removed will indicate how tight it is, and therefore how much force should be needed). In many cases, a component's reluctance to be removed is indicative of an incorrect approach or removal method – if in any doubt, re-check with the text.

7 When disassembling the engine, keep 'mated' parts together (including gears, pistons, connecting rods, valves, etc, that have been in contact with each other during engine operation). These 'mated' parts must be reused or replaced as an assembly.

8 A complete engine disassembly should be done in the following general order with reference to the appropriate Sections (or Chapters, where indicated).

Remove the valve cover
Remove the cam chain tensioner
Remove the camshafts
Remove the cylinder head
Remove the clutch
Remove the alternator and starter clutch
Remove the starter motor (see Chapter 8)
Remove the gearchange mechanism
Remove the water pump (see Chapter 3)
Remove the oil cooler
Remove the oil sump
Remove the oil pump
Separate the crankcase halves
Remove the crankshaft
Remove the connecting rods and pistons
Remove the transmission output shaft
Remove the selector drum and forks
Remove the transmission input shaft

Reassembly

9 Reassembly is accomplished by reversing the general disassembly sequence.

6 Valve cover

Note: *This procedure can be carried out with the engine in the frame. If the engine has been removed, ignore the steps that do not apply.*

Engine, clutch and transmission 2•11

6.3a Unscrew the bolts (arrowed) . . .

6.3b . . . and remove the cover

Removal

1 Remove the throttle bodies (see Chapter 4). Remove the radiator (see Chapter 3).
2 Remove the AIS control valve along with the hoses (see Chapter 4). Disconnect the camshaft position (CMP) sensor wiring connector **(see illustration 4.10a)**. Remove the ignition coils (see Chapter 4).
3 Unscrew the bolts securing the valve cover and remove them with their sealing washers **(see illustration)**. Lift the cover off the cylinder head – if it is stuck, break the gasket seal by tapping gently around the edge with a soft-faced hammer or block of wood **(see illustration)**. Do not lever the cover off as this will damage the sealing surface.
4 Remove the gasket. Note the four AIS system air passage dowels and remove them if they are loose **(see illustration)**.

Installation

5 Examine the valve cover gasket rim and circular spark plug seals for signs of damage or deterioration and fit a new one if necessary. Similarly check the sealing washers on the cover bolts for cracks, hardening and deterioration and use new ones if necessary.
6 Clean the mating surfaces of the cylinder head and the valve cover with a suitable solvent.

7 Apply a smear of a suitable sealant to the valve cover and into the cut-outs in the cylinder head. Make sure the AIS system dowels are pushed fully into place **(see illustration 6.4)**. Fit the gasket onto the valve cover, making sure it locates correctly **(see illustrations)**. If the gasket has a bridge piece between the cam chain end and the adjacent spark plug seal cut it away using a sharp knife **(see illustration)**.
8 Position the valve cover on the cylinder head, making sure the gasket stays in place **(see illustration 6.3b)**. Fit the sealing washers with the cover bolts and tighten the bolts to the torque setting specified at the beginning of this Chapter **(see illustration)**.

9 Install the remaining components in the reverse order of removal.

7 Cam chain tensioner

Note: *This procedure can be carried out with the engine in the frame. If the engine has been removed, ignore the steps that do not apply.*

Removal

1 Remove the fairing right-hand side panel and its inner trim section, and the lower fairing (see Chapter 7).

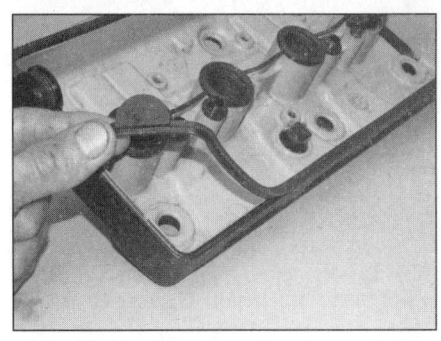

6.4 Take care not to lose the dowels (arrowed)

6.7a Fit the gasket into the groove in the rim of the cover . . .

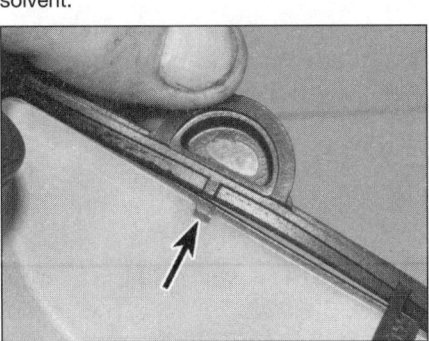

6.7b . . . making sure it locates correctly (arrowed)

6.7c Cut the bridge piece (arrowed) away

6.8 Use new sealing washers with the bolts if necessary

2•12 Engine, clutch and transmission

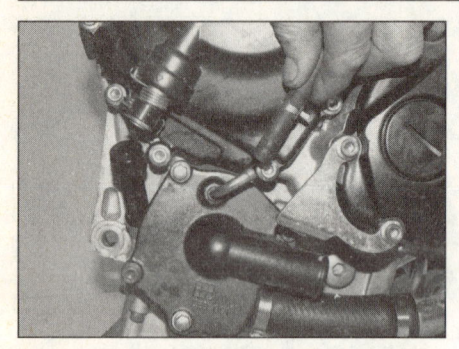

7.2a Release the clamp and detach the by-pass hose from the top of the water pump...

7.2b ... and free the hose from its guide (arrowed)

7.3 Unscrew the cap bolt (arrowed) and remove the washer

2 To access the tensioner, either drain the cooling system (see Chapter 1), then detach the by-pass hose from the water pump, free it from its guide and position it clear of the tensioner **(see illustrations)**, or remove the throttle bodies (see Chapter 4), or if required do both.

3 Unscrew the tensioner cap bolt and remove the bolt and the sealing washer **(see illustration)**. Note the 'UP' mark on the tensioner body.

4 Slacken the tensioner mounting bolts slightly **(see illustration)**. Insert a small flat-bladed screwdriver into the tensioner so that it engages the slotted plunger **(see illustration)**. Turn the screwdriver clockwise until the plunger is fully retracted and hold it in this position while unscrewing the tensioner mounting bolts and removing the tensioner.

5 Release the screwdriver – the plunger will spring back out once the screwdriver is removed, but can be easily reset on installation.

6 Discard the gasket, as a new one must be used on reassembly. Do not dismantle the tensioner.

Inspection

7 Apply hand pressure to the end of the tensioner plunger and wind it into the tensioner body by turning the screwdriver **(see illustration)**. Hold the plunger under pressure and remove the screwdriver, then slowly release the plunger. Check that the plunger moves smoothly and springs out freely when released.

8 If the tensioner is worn or damaged, or if the plunger does not run smoothly in the body, the tensioner must be replaced with a new one – individual components are not available.

Installation

9 Ensure the tensioner and cylinder block surfaces are clean and dry. Lightly smear the new gasket with grease. Insert a small flat-bladed screwdriver into the tensioner so that it engages the slotted plunger, then turn it clockwise until the plunger is fully retracted **(see illustration 7.7)**. Fit the gasket onto the tensioner **(see illustration)**. Fit the bolts into their holes in the tensioner.

10 Hold the screwdriver so the plunger remains retracted and fit the tensioner into the cylinder block with the 'UP' mark facing up, and tighten its bolts to the torque setting specified at the beginning of this Chapter **(see illustration)**.

11 Release the tension on the screwdriver and remove it – the plunger will spring out (which you should hear) and tension the chain. Install the tensioner cap bolt with a new

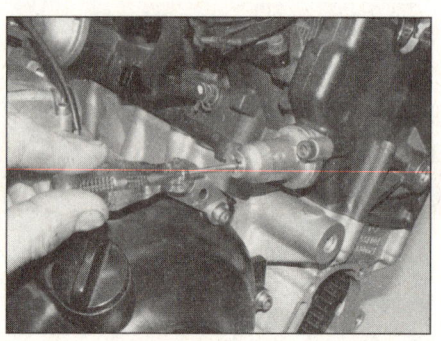

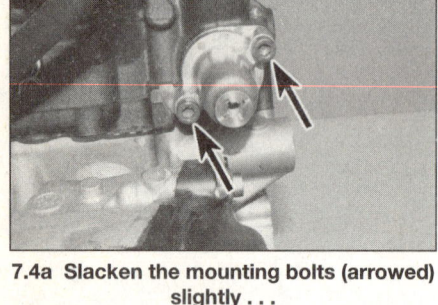

7.4a Slacken the mounting bolts (arrowed) slightly...

7.4b ... then insert the screwdriver and retract the plunger and unscrew the mounting bolts

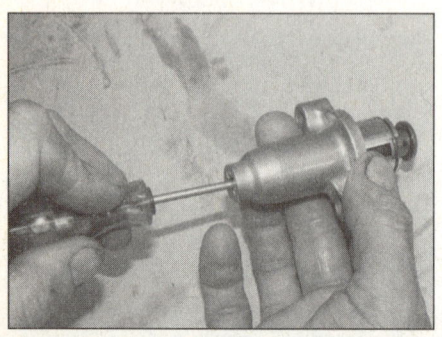

7.7 Check the action of the plunger as described

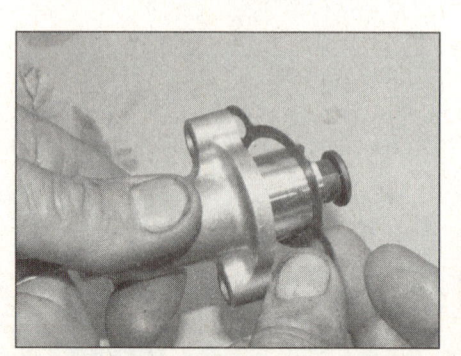

7.9 Fit a new gasket onto the tensioner...

7.10 ... then install the tensioner, all the time holding the screwdriver to keep the plunger retracted

Engine, clutch and transmission 2•13

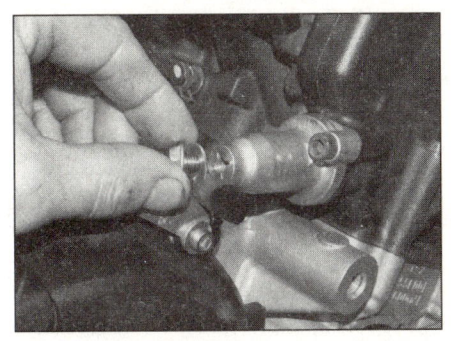

7.11 Fit the cap bolt using a new sealing washer

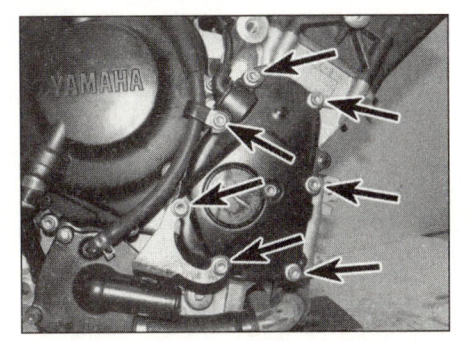

8.2 Unscrew the bolts (arrowed) and remove the cover

8.4a Turn the engine clockwise using the bolt . . .

sealing washer and tighten it to the specified torque **(see illustration)**.
12 Install the remaining components in the reverse order of removal.

8 Camshafts and followers

Note: *This procedure can be carried out with the engine in the frame. If the engine has been removed, ignore the steps that do not apply.*

Removal

1 Remove the valve cover (see Section 6). Remove the spark plugs (see Chapter 1). Place rags in the spark plug holes and the cam chain tunnel to prevent anything dropping into the engine.
2 Place an oil pan under the timing rotor cover on the right-hand side of the engine to catch any oil as it is removed. Unscrew the bolts and remove the cover, noting the clamp for the coolant hose and the bracket for the clutch cable **(see illustration)**. Discard the gasket, as a new one must be used and remove the dowels from either the crankcase or the cover if they are loose. If the cam chain tensioner blade pivot pin comes away with the cover, remove it, then realign the blade and slide the pin back into place.
3 The engine must now be turned to position the No. 1 cylinder at TDC (top dead centre) on the compression stroke. To turn the engine, use a spanner on the ignition rotor bolt and turn it in a clockwise direction only.
4 Turn the engine clockwise until the 'T' mark on the ignition rotor faces to the rear and aligns with the crankcase mating surfaces **(see illustration)**. The camshaft lobes for the No. 1 (left-hand) cylinder should face away from each other **(see illustrations)**; if the cam lobes are facing towards each other, rotate the engine clockwise 360° (one full turn) so that the 'T' mark again faces to the rear and aligns with the crankcase mating surfaces. The camshaft lobes should now be facing away from each other and the No. 1 cylinder will be at TDC (top dead centre) on the compression stroke.
5 Before disturbing the camshafts, ensure that the timing marks on the camshaft sprockets face away from each other and align with the cylinder head mating surface **(see illustration)**. If you are in any doubt as to the alignment of the markings, or if they are

8.4b . . . until the line next to the T mark faces back and aligns with the crankcase mating surfaces . . .

not visible, make your own alignment marks between all components, and also between a tooth on each sprocket (including the timing sprocket) and its corresponding link on the chain, before disturbing them. These markings ensure that the valve timing can be correctly set up on assembly. As it is easy to be a tooth out on installation, marking between a tooth on each sprocket and its link in the chain is especially useful.
6 Remove the cam chain tensioner (see Section 7).
7 There are three camshaft holders for each

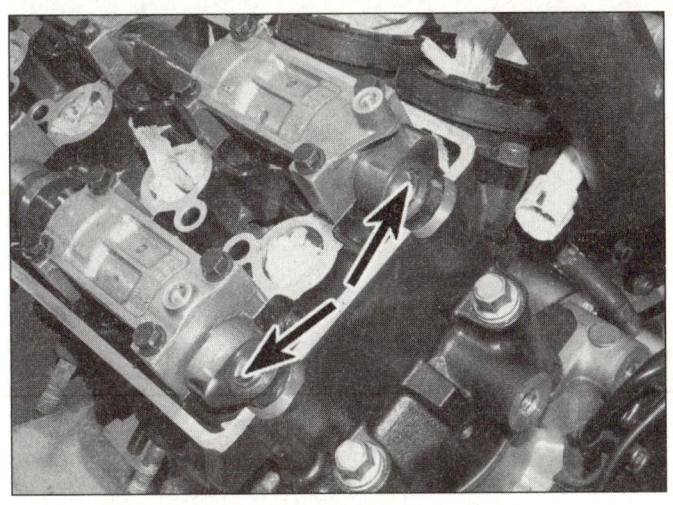

8.4c . . . the camshaft lobes are as shown . . .

8.5 . . . and the camshaft sprocket marks (arrowed) are as shown

2•14 Engine, clutch and transmission

8.7a There are three holders (arrowed) for each camshaft

8.7b Note the arrows pointing to the right-hand side of the engine, and the E1 marks for the two right-hand exhaust camshaft holders . . .

8.7c . . . and the E2 mark for the left-hand holder

8.9 Unscrew the bolts as described and remove the holders

camshaft **(see illustration)**. Each has an identity mark (I1 or I2 on the intake side and E1 or E2 on the exhaust side) and an arrow which points to the right-hand side of the engine **(see illustrations)**. Note the position of each holder for correct installation later. If the marks are unclear make your own.

8 Working on one camshaft at a time and starting with the intake shaft if removing both, unscrew the camshaft holder bolts evenly and a little at a time in a criss-cross pattern, starting from the outside and working towards the centre. Slacken the bolts above any cam lobes that are pressing onto a valve last in the sequence so that the pressure from the open valves cannot cause the camshaft to bend.

Caution: *If the bolts are loosened carelessly and the holders do not come away from the head squarely, a holder is likely to break. If this happens the complete cylinder head assembly must be replaced with a new one as the holders are matched to the head and cannot be obtained separately. Also, the camshaft could be damaged if the holder bolts are not slackened evenly and the pressure from a depressed valve causes a shaft to bend.*

9 Remove the bolts, then lift off the camshaft holders **(see illustration)**. Retrieve the dowels from either the holder or the cylinder head if they are loose.

10 Note the camshaft identification markings – the intake camshaft has two small rings between the lobes on the left-hand end, and the exhaust camshaft has one large ring at its centre **(see illustrations)**.

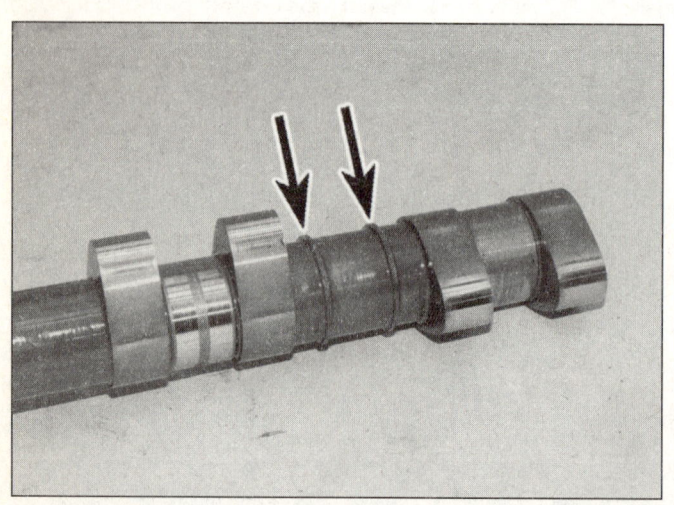

8.10a Note the small rings (arrowed) on the intake camshaft . . .

8.10b . . . and the large ring (arrowed) on the exhaust

Engine, clutch and transmission 2•15

8.13a Carefully lift out the follower using your fingers, grips, a lapping tool or a magnet . . .

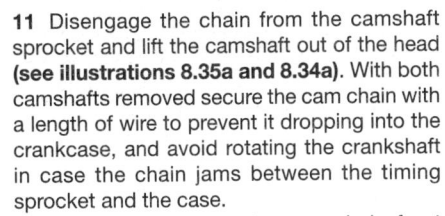

8.13b . . . and retrieve the shim from inside it . . .

8.13c . . . or from the top of the valve

11 Disengage the chain from the camshaft sprocket and lift the camshaft out of the head **(see illustrations 8.35a and 8.34a)**. With both camshafts removed secure the cam chain with a length of wire to prevent it dropping into the crankcase, and avoid rotating the crankshaft in case the chain jams between the timing sprocket and the case.
12 If required remove the cam chain front guide blade, the tensioner blade and the cam chain (see Section 9).
13 If the followers and shims are being removed from the cylinder head, obtain a container which is divided into sixteen compartments, and label each compartment with the location of its corresponding valve in the cylinder head. If a container is not available, use labelled plastic bags (egg cartons also work very well). Remove the cam follower of the valve in question, then retrieve the shim from the inside of the follower **(see illustrations)**. If it is not in the follower, pick it out of the top of the valve using either a magnet, a small screwdriver with a dab of grease on it (the shim will stick to the grease), or a screwdriver and a pair of pliers **(see illustration)**. Do not allow the shim to fall into the engine.

Inspection

14 Inspect the bearing surfaces of the cylinder head and camshaft holder and the corresponding journals on the camshaft **(see illustration)**. Look for score marks, deep scratches and evidence of spalling (a pitted appearance). If damage is noted or wear is excessive, the relevant parts must be renewed. The cylinder head and holder must be replaced as a new matched set – individual parts are not available.
15 Check the camshaft lobes for heat discoloration (blue appearance), score marks, chipped areas, flat spots and spalling **(see illustration)**. Measure the height of each lobe with a micrometer **(see illustration)** and compare the results to the minimum lobe height listed in this Chapter's Specifications. If damage is noted or wear is excessive, the camshaft must be replaced with a new one. Also check the condition of the cam followers.
16 Check the amount of camshaft runout by supporting each end of the camshaft on V-blocks, and measuring any runout at the journals using a dial gauge. If the runout exceeds the specified limit the camshaft must be replaced with a new one.

HAYNES HINT *Refer to Tools and Workshop Tips (Section 3) in the Reference section for details of how to read a micrometer and dial gauge.*

17 The camshaft journal oil clearance should now be checked. There are two possible ways of doing this, either by direct measurement (see Steps 18 to 21) or by the use of a product known as Plastigauge (see Steps 22 to 27).

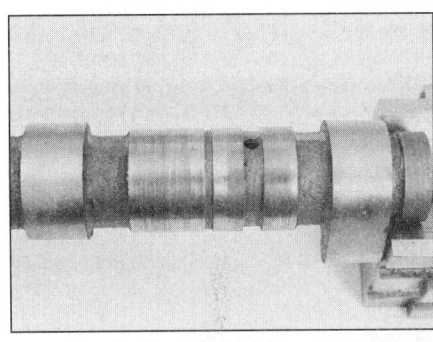

8.14 Check all related bearing surfaces as described

18 If the direct measurement method is to be used, make sure the camshaft holder dowels are fitted then install the holders in their correct location (see Step 7). Lubricate the threads of the holder bolts with clean engine oil, then tighten the bolts evenly and a little at a time in a criss-cross pattern to the torque setting specified at the beginning of this Chapter. Using telescoping gauges and a micrometer (see *Tools and Workshop Tips*), measure the inside diameter of the holder journals.
19 Now measure the diameter of the corresponding camshaft journals with a micrometer **(see illustration)**. To determine the journal oil clearance, subtract the journal diameter from the holder diameter and compare the result to the clearance specified. If any clearance is greater than specified, it is an indication of wear on the camshaft, the holder, or both.

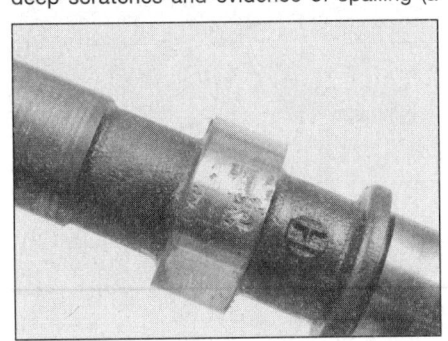

8.15a Check the camshaft lobes as described – damage as shown requires immediate attention

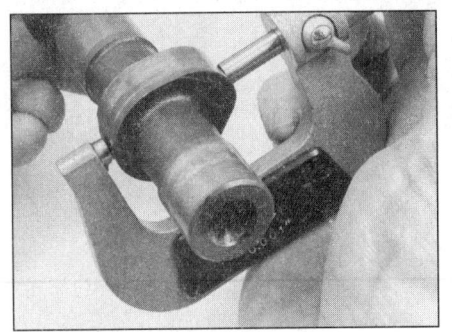

8.15b Measure the height of the camshaft lobes with a micrometer

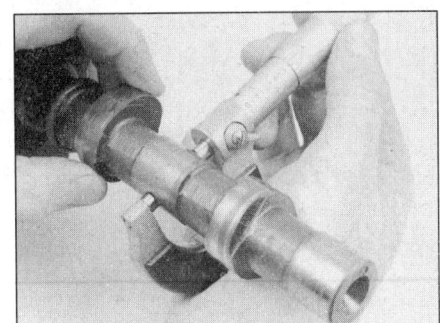

8.19 Measure the journals with a micrometer

8.23 Lay a strip of Plastigauge across each bearing journal parallel with the centreline

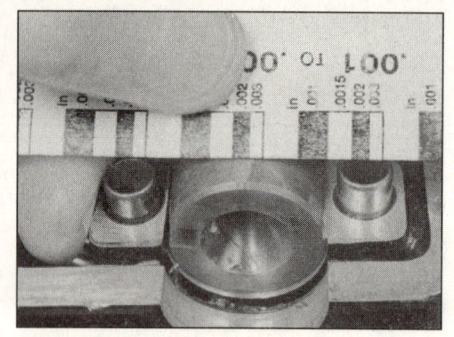

8.25 Compare the width of the crushed Plastigauge with the scale printed on the container

> **HAYNES HiNT** *Before fitting new camshafts, cylinder head or holders because of damage, check with local machine shops specialising in motorcycle engine work. In the case of the camshafts, it may be possible for cam lobes to be welded, reground and hardened, at a cost far lower than that of a new camshaft. Due to the cost of new components it is recommended that all options are explored!*

20 First check to see if the camshaft journals are worn below the service limit. If they are, a new camshaft must be fitted. However, since it is likely that the holder is also worn, ensure that the specified journal diameter for a new camshaft will restore the oil clearance to within specification before buying a new camshaft.

21 If the camshaft journals are good, or if fitting a new camshaft will not restore the oil clearance to within specification, the holders and cylinder head will have to be replaced as a new matched set.

22 If the Plastigauge method is to be used, clean the camshaft being checked (work on one at a time), the bearing surfaces in the cylinder head and camshaft holder with a suitable solvent and a clean, lint-free cloth, then lay the camshaft in place in the cylinder head, making sure the timing marks are correctly aligned (see Step 4 and 5).

23 Cut some strips of Plastigauge and lay one piece on each journal, parallel with the camshaft centreline **(see illustration)**. Make sure the camshaft holder dowels are fitted then install the holders in their correct location (see Step 7) **(see illustrations 8.7a, b and c, 8.9 and 8.37)**. Lubricate the threads of the holder bolts with clean engine oil, then tighten the bolts evenly and a little at a time in a criss-cross pattern to the torque setting specified at the beginning of this Chapter. Work from the centre of the camshafts outwards (i.e. starting with the bolts that are above valves that will be opened when the camshafts are tightened down). Whilst tightening the bolts, make sure each holder is being pulled down squarely and is not binding on the dowels. Whilst doing this, don't let the camshaft rotate.

24 Now unscrew the bolts evenly and a little at a time in a criss-cross pattern, starting from the outside and working towards the centre, and carefully lift off the camshaft holders.

25 To determine the oil clearance, compare the crushed Plastigauge (at its widest point) on each journal to the scale printed on the Plastigauge container **(see illustration)**. Compare the results to this Chapter's Specifications. Carefully clean away all traces of Plastigauge using a fingernail or other object which will not score the bearing surfaces. If any clearance is greater than specified, it is an indication of wear on the camshaft, the holder, or both.

26 First check to see if the camshaft journals are worn below the service limit by measuring them with a micrometer **(see illustration 8.19)**. If they are, a new camshaft must be fitted. However, since it is likely that the holder is also worn, ensure that the specified journal diameter for a new camshaft will restore the oil clearance to within specification before buying a new camshaft.

27 If the camshaft journals are good, or if fitting a new camshaft will not restore the oil clearance to within specification, the holders and cylinder head will have to be replaced as a matched set.

28 Inspect the cam chain guide blade, tensioner blade and cam chain (see Section 9).

29 Inspect the camshaft sprockets; if they show signs of wear, cracks or other damage, replace them and the cam chain with a new set. The camshaft sprockets are retained by two bolts **(see illustration)**; unscrew the bolts and remove the sprockets, noting how they fit. Install the new sprockets on their respective camshafts with the marks facing out, and tighten the bolts to the specified torque setting.

30 Inspect the outer surfaces of the cam followers for evidence of wear, scoring or other damage. If the side of a follower is in poor condition, it is probable that the bore in which it works is also damaged. Check for clearance between the followers and their bores. Whilst no specifications are given, if slack is excessive, replace the followers with new ones. If the bores are seriously out-of-round or tapered, then replace the cylinder head and followers with new ones.

Installation

31 If removed, lubricate each valve shim and follower with molybdenum disulphide oil (a 50/50 mixture of molybdenum disulphide grease and engine oil) and fit each shim into its recess on the top of the valve, with the size marking on the shim facing up **(see illustration)**. Make sure the shim is correctly seated, then install the follower, making sure it fits squarely in its bore **(see illustration 8.13a)**. **Note:** *It is most important that the shims and followers are returned to their original valves, otherwise the valve clearances will be inaccurate.*

8.29 Camshaft sprocket bolts (arrowed)

8.31 Fit each shim into its recess

Engine, clutch and transmission 2•17

8.34a Install the exhaust camshaft as described . . .

8.34b . . . and fit the chain round the sprocket

8.35a Install the intake camshaft as described . . .

32 Make sure the camshaft journals and the bearing surfaces in the cylinder head are clean, then apply molybdenum disulphide oil to them and to the camshaft lobes.

33 If removed, install the cam chain, the tensioner blade and the front guide blade (see Section 9).

34 Ensure that the 'T' mark on the ignition rotor still aligns with the crankcase mating surfaces (see Step 4). Fit the exhaust camshaft, making sure the timing mark on the sprocket faces forward and aligns with the cylinder head mating surface **(see illustrations)**. Fit the cam chain around the sprocket as you install the camshaft, pulling up on the chain to remove all slack in the front run between the crankshaft and the camshaft. If alignment marks were made prior to disassembly (see Step 5), check that the marks on the cam chain and sprocket align.

35 Now fit the intake camshaft, making sure the timing mark on the sprocket faces to the rear and aligns with the cylinder head mating surface **(see illustrations)**. Fit the cam chain around the sprocket, aligning the marks (if made) between sprocket and chain. When fitting the chain, pull it tight to make sure there is no slack between the two camshaft sprockets – any slack in the chain must lie in the rear run, so that it is taken up by the tensioner.

36 Fit the camshaft holder dowels into the holders or cylinder head if removed. Make sure the bearing surfaces in the holders are clean, then lubricate them with molybdenum disulphide oil.

37 Lubricate the threads of the holder bolts with clean engine oil and fit them into the holders. Install the holders in their correct location (see Step 7). Ensure that the holders locate correctly over the rims of the locating bosses on the camshafts **(see illustration)**. Tighten the bolts evenly and a little at a time in a criss-cross pattern to the torque setting specified at the beginning of this Chapter. Work from the centre of the holder outwards (i.e. starting with the bolts that are above valves that will be opened when the camshafts are tightened down). Whilst tightening the bolts, make sure each holder is being pulled down squarely and is not binding on the dowels.

Caution: The camshaft holder is likely to break if it is not tightened down evenly and squarely and the camshaft is likely to bend if it is tightened down onto the closed valves before the open ones.

38 Using a piece of wooden dowel, press on the back of the cam chain tensioner blade via the tensioner bore in the crankcase to take up any slack in the cam chain. Check that all the timing marks are still in **exact** alignment as described in Steps 4 and 5. If it is necessary to turn the engine slightly to align the marks with the engine mating surfaces, keep the wooden dowel pressed onto the tensioner blade as without the tensioner in place, the chain may slip on the sprockets. Note that it is easy to be slightly out (by one tooth on a sprocket) without the marks appearing drastically out of alignment.

39 If the camshaft marks are out, release the tension on the chain and remove the cam chain front guide, slip the chain around the relevant sprocket to correct the alignment, install the guide and recheck the timing marks.

Caution: If the marks are not aligned exactly as described, the valve timing will be incorrect and the valves may strike the pistons, causing extensive damage to the engine.

40 With everything correctly aligned, install the cam chain tensioner (see Section 7). Turn the engine clockwise through two full turns and check again that all the timing marks still align (see Steps 4 and 5).

41 Check the valve clearances and adjust them if necessary (see Chapter 1).

42 Ensure the dowels for the timing rotor cover are in place and install the cover using a new gasket, making sure the cam chain tensioner blade pivot pin locates in the hole in the cover **(see illustrations)**. Install the guide for the coolant hose and the clutch cable adjuster bracket and tighten the cover bolts to the torque setting specified at the beginning of this Chapter – the longer bolts secure the clutch cable bracket **(see illustration 8.2)**.

43 Install the valve cover (see Section 6).

8.35b . . . and fit the chain round the sprocket

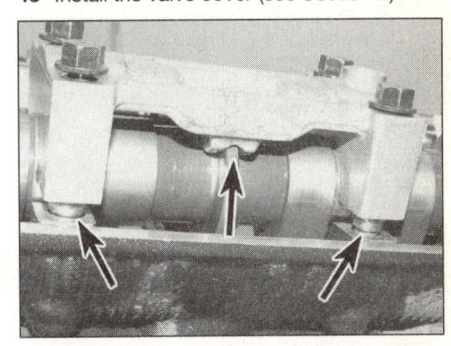

8.37 Install the holders making sure the dowels and rim locate correctly (arrowed)

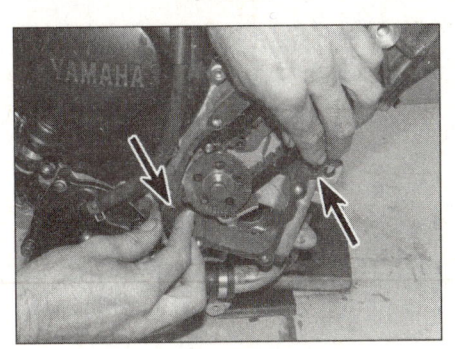

8.42a Fit a new gasket onto the dowels (arrowed) . . .

8.42b . . . then install the cover, making sure it locates correctly

2•18 Engine, clutch and transmission

9.1 The top guide (arrowed) is fixed in the valve cover

9.2 Lift the front guide blade out of the engine

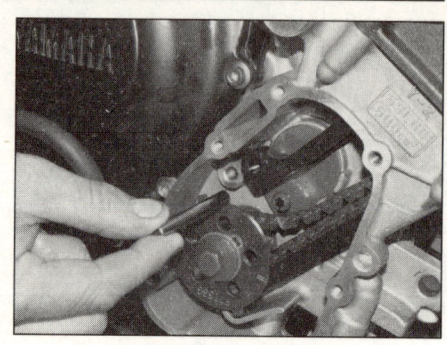

9.3a Withdraw the pivot pin . . .

9 Cam chain, tensioner blade and guides

Note: *This procedure can be carried out with the engine in the frame. If the engine has been removed, ignore the steps that do not apply.*

Tensioner blade and guides

Removal

1 Remove the valve cover (see Section 6), the timing rotor cover (see Section 8, Step 2) and the cam chain tensioner (see Section 7). The cam chain top guide is fixed in the valve cover and should not be removed **(see illustration)**.
2 To remove the cam chain front guide, lift it out of the front of the cam chain tunnel, noting which way round it fits and how it locates – it is a fairly tight fit but can be removed with the exhaust camshaft in place **(see illustration)**.
3 To remove the cam chain tensioner blade, first remove the intake camshaft (see Section 8). Withdraw the tensioner blade pivot pin, then draw the blade out of the top of the engine, noting which way round it fits **(see illustrations)**.

Inspection

4 Check the sliding surfaces of the tensioner blade and guides for excessive wear, deep grooves, cracking and other obvious damage, and replace them with new ones if necessary.

Installation

5 Apply some clean engine oil to the tensioner blade pivot pin, then install the tensioner blade and insert the pin **(see illustrations 9.3b and a)**. Install the intake camshaft (see Section 8).
6 Slide the front guide into the front of the cam chain tunnel, making sure it locates correctly onto its seat at its lower end and its lugs at the top locate in their cut-outs **(see illustrations)**.
7 Install the cam chain tensioner and the valve and timing rotor covers.

Cam chain

Removal

8 Remove the camshafts (see Section 8).
9 Unscrew the bolt securing the timing rotor **(see illustration)**. To prevent the crankshaft turning, either select a gear and apply the rear brake (if the engine is in the frame), or remove the alternator cover (see Chapter 8) and use a rotor holding strap to counter-hold the crankshaft. Remove the bolt, washer and the rotor, noting how it fits **(see illustrations)**.
10 Lift the cam chain off the crankshaft sprocket and out of the engine. The sprocket is an integral part of the crankshaft.

Inspection

11 Except in cases of oil starvation, the cam chain wears very little. If the chain is stiff or the links are binding, or if the links are loose, discard the chain. A chain in poor condition will wear the sprocket teeth and ideally a chain and sprockets should be replaced as a set. The camshaft sprockets are easily renewed, but if the crankshaft sprocket is unfit for further use the crankshaft will have to be renewed.

Installation

12 Installation of the chain is the reverse of removal. Make sure the marked side of the

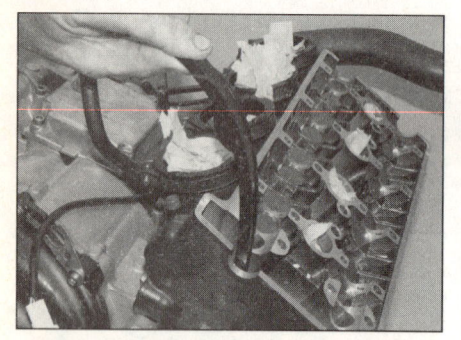

9.3b . . . and draw the blade out of the engine

9.6a Make sure the blade locates correctly in its seat . . .

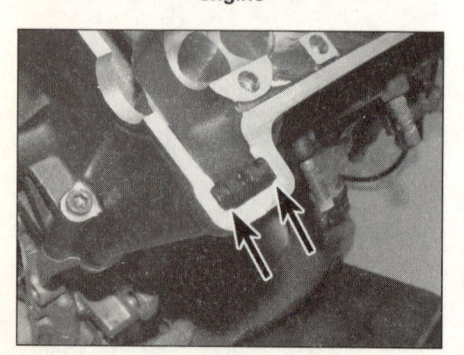

9.6b . . . and in the head

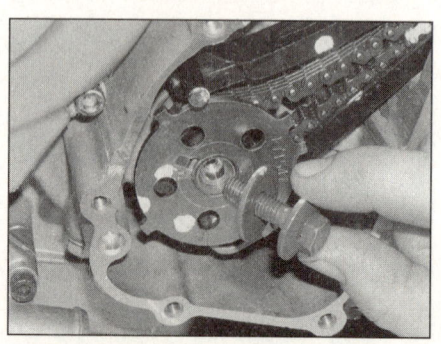

9.9a Remove the bolt and the washer . . .

9.9b . . . then remove the rotor, noting how its keyway (A) locates in the rotor slot (B)

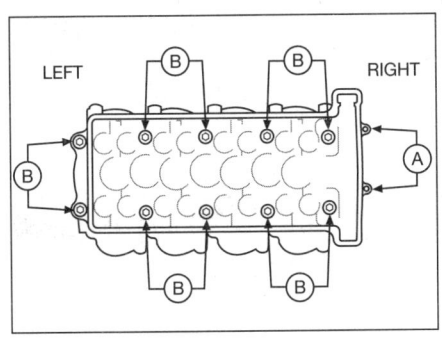

Engine, clutch and transmission 2•19

10.3a Cylinder head 6 mm bolts (A) and 10 mm bolts (B)

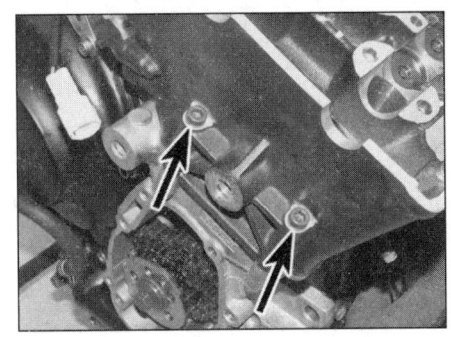

10.3b First unscrew the 6 mm bolts (arrowed)

10.3c Unscrew the 10 mm bolts (arrowed) as described . . .

ignition rotor faces out and that the key on the rotor locates in the keyway on the crankshaft. Tighten the rotor bolt to the torque setting specified at the beginning of this Chapter, counter-holding the crankshaft as on removal.

10 Cylinder head removal and installation

Note: *To remove the cylinder head with the engine in the frame you need an Allen bit that is 75 mm long to reach the rear 6 mm bolt on the right-hand end.*

Removal

1 Unscrew and remove the engine front mounting bolts on the left-hand side **(see illustration 4.26)**. Unscrew the bolts securing the engine bracket to the front left-hand side of the engine and remove the bracket **(see illustration 4.30)**.
2 Remove the valve cover (see Section 6) and the camshafts and followers (see Section 8).
3 The cylinder head is secured by twelve bolts **(see illustration)**. First unscrew and remove the 6 mm bolts on the right-hand end of the head **(see illustration)**. Now unscrew the 10 mm bolts evenly and no more than a half turn at a time in a criss-cross pattern, starting from the outside and working inwards (see *Tools and Workshop Tips* (Section 4) in the *Reference* section) **(see illustration)**. When all the bolts are loose, remove them.
4 Pull the cylinder head up off the cylinder block **(see illustration)**. If it is stuck, tap

around the joint faces of the head with a soft-faced hammer or block of wood to free it. Do not attempt to free the head by inserting a lever between it and the cylinder block – you will damage the sealing surfaces.
5 If they are loose, remove the dowels from the cylinder block **(see illustration 10.9)**. If they appear to be missing they are probably stuck in the underside of the cylinder head.
6 Check the cylinder head gasket and the mating surfaces on the cylinder head and block for signs of leakage from the cylinders, the oil or coolant passages, which could indicate that the head is warped. Refer to Section 11 and check the flatness of the cylinder head.
7 Remove the old cylinder head gasket and discard it as a new one must be fitted on reassembly. Lay a clean cloth over the cylinders and pistons while the head is off to prevent any dirt getting in.

Installation

8 Clean all traces of old gasket material from the cylinder head and block with a suitable solvent. If you need to use a scraper, take care not to scratch or gouge the soft aluminium. Be careful not to let any of the gasket material fall into the crankcase, the cylinder bores or the oil or coolant passages. Check that the oil nozzle on the right-hand underside of the head is clear **(see illustration 11.11)**.

> **HAYNES HiNT** *Refer to Tools and Workshop Tips (Section 7) for details of gasket removal methods.*

9 Lubricate the cylinder bores with clean engine oil. If removed, fit the dowels into the crankcase, then lay the new head gasket in place, making sure it locates correctly over the dowels, and all the holes are correctly aligned **(see illustration)**.
10 Carefully fit the cylinder head onto the crankcase, making sure it locates correctly onto the dowels **(see illustration 10.4)**.
11 Lubricate the threads and seating surfaces of the 10 mm cylinder head bolts with clean engine oil. Install the bolts and tighten them finger-tight **(see illustrations 10.3c)**. Now tighten the bolts evenly and in two stages, working in a criss-cross pattern starting from the centre and moving outwards (see *Tools and Workshop Tips* (Section 4) in the *Reference* section), to the torque setting specified at the beginning of this Chapter.
12 Install the 6 mm bolts and tighten them to the specified torque setting **(see illustration 10.3b)**.
13 Install the remaining components in the reverse order of removal.

11 Cylinder head and valve overhaul

1 Because of the complex nature of this job and the special tools and equipment required, most owners leave servicing of the valves, valve seats and valve guides to a professional. However, you can make an initial assessment of whether the valves are seating correctly, and therefore sealing, by pouring a small amount of solvent into each of the valve ports. If the solvent leaks past any valve into the combustion chamber area the valve is not seating correctly and sealing.
2 With the correct tools (a valve spring compressor is essential – make sure it is suitable for motorcycle work), you can also remove the valves and associated components from the cylinder head, clean them and check them for wear to assess the extent of the work needed, and, unless seat cutting or guide replacement is required, grind in the valves and reassemble them in the head.
3 A dealer service department or engine specialist can replace the guides and re-cut the valve seats.

10.4 . . . then lift the head up off the block and remove it

10.9 Fit the dowels (arrowed) then lay the new gasket on the block

2•20 Engine, clutch and transmission

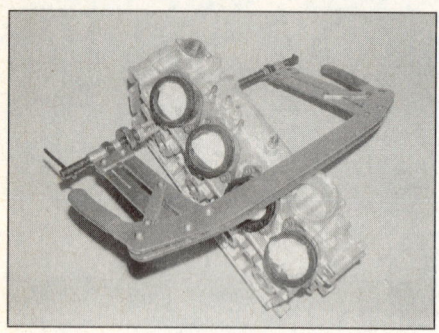

11.7a Compressing the valve springs using a valve spring compressor

11.7b Make sure the compressor is a good fit on the top . . .

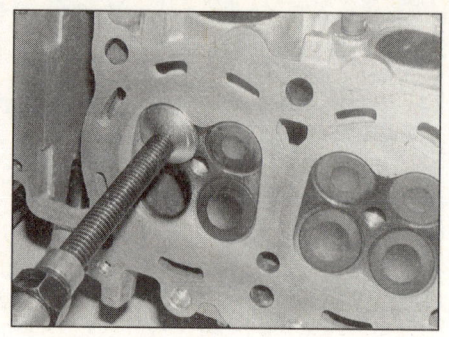

11.7c . . . and the bottom of the valve

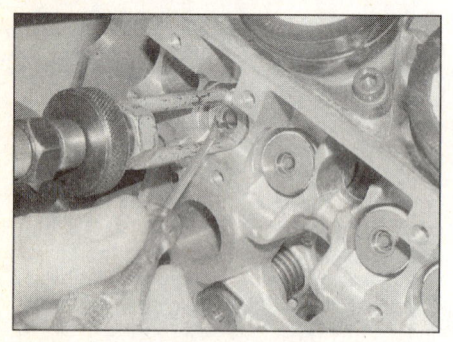

11.8a Remove the collets taking care not to drop them into the engine

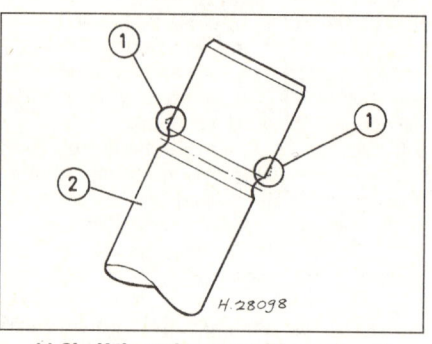

11.8b If the valve stem (2) won't pull through the guide, deburr the area above the collet groove (1)

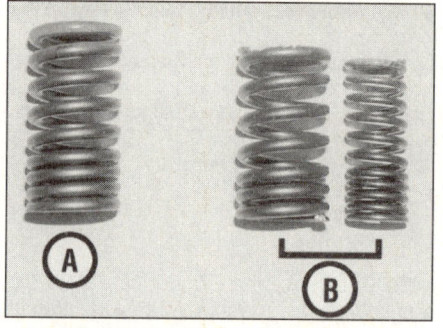

11.8c Exhaust (A) and intake (B) valve springs differ in length. Springs are fitted with the closer-wound coils into the head

4 After the valve service has been performed, be sure to clean it very thoroughly before installation on the engine to remove any metal particles or abrasive grit that may still be present from the valve service operations. Use compressed air, if available, to blow out all the holes and passages.

Disassembly

5 Before proceeding, arrange to label and store the valves along with their related components in such a way that they can be returned to their original locations without getting mixed up. Either use the same container as the valve shims and followers are stored in (see Section 8), or obtain a separate container which is divided into sixteen compartments, and label each compartment with the identity of the valve which will be stored in it. Alternatively, labelled plastic bags will do just as well.

6 Clean all traces of old gasket material from the cylinder head with a suitable solvent. If you need to use a scraper, take care not to scratch or gouge the soft aluminium.

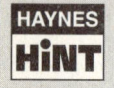

> **HAYNES HINT** *Refer to Tools and Workshop Tips (Section 7) in the Reference section for details of gasket removal methods.*

7 Compress the valve spring on the first valve with a spring compressor, making sure it is correctly located onto each end of the valve assembly **(see illustrations)**. On the underside of the head, make sure the plate on the compressor only contacts the valve and not the soft aluminium of the head – if the plate is too big for the valve, use a spacer between them **(see illustration)**. Do not compress the springs any more than is absolutely necessary.

8 Remove the collets, using either needle-nose pliers, tweezers, a magnet or a screwdriver with a dab of grease on it **(see illustration)**. Carefully release the valve spring compressor and remove the spring retainer, noting which way up it fits, the spring(s) and the valve **(see illustrations 11.30c, b and a)**. If the valve binds in the guide (won't pull through), push it back into the head and deburr the area around the collet groove with a very fine file or whetstone **(see illustration)**. **Note:** *There are two springs fitted with each intake valve and one with each exhaust valve. Note the difference in length between the exhaust and intake valve springs – do not mix them up* **(see illustration)**.

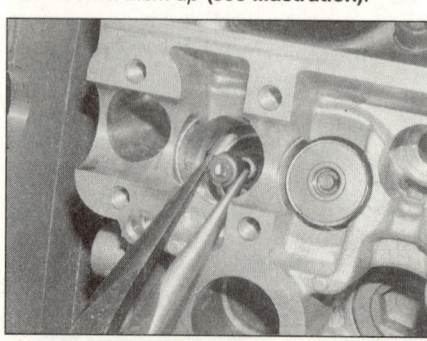

11.9 Pull the stem seal off with long nosed pliers

9 Pull the valve stem seal off the top of the valve guide with pliers and discard it (the old seals should never be reused) **(see illustration)**. Remove the spring seat, noting which way up it fits – using a magnet is the easiest way to lift the seat off the head **(see illustration 11.29a)**.

10 Repeat the procedure for the remaining valves. Remember to keep the parts for each valve together and labelled so they can be reinstalled in the correct location.

11 Next, clean the cylinder head with solvent and dry it thoroughly. Compressed air will speed the drying process and ensure that all holes and recessed areas are clean. Check that the oil nozzle on the right-hand underside of the head is clear **(see illustration)**.

12 Clean all the valve springs, collets, retainers and spring seats with solvent and dry them thoroughly. Clean the parts from one valve at a

11.11 Blow compressed air through the oil nozzle (arrowed) to ensure it is clear

Engine, clutch and transmission 2•21

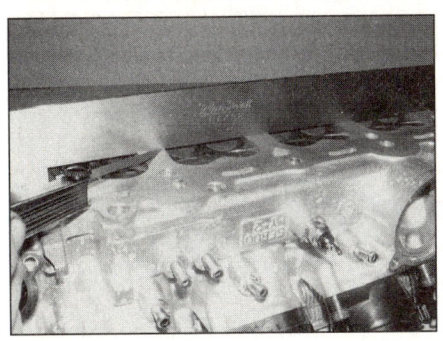

11.14 Checking the head for warpage with a straight-edge

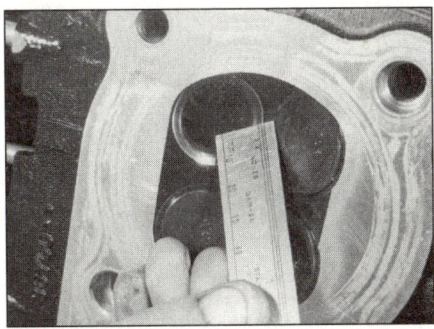

11.15 Measure the valve seat width with a ruler (or for greater accuracy use a Vernier caliper)

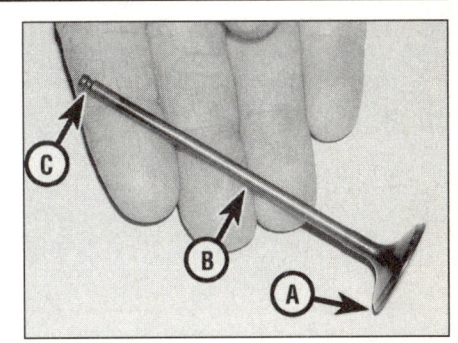

11.16 Check the valve face (A), stem (B) and collet groove (C) for wear and damage

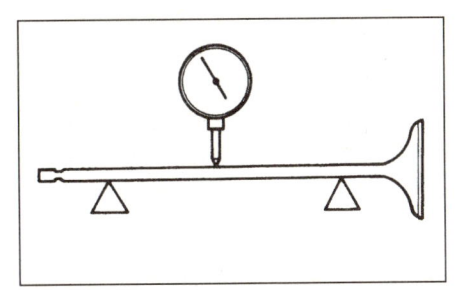

11.17 Measure valve stem runout with V-blocks and a dial gauge

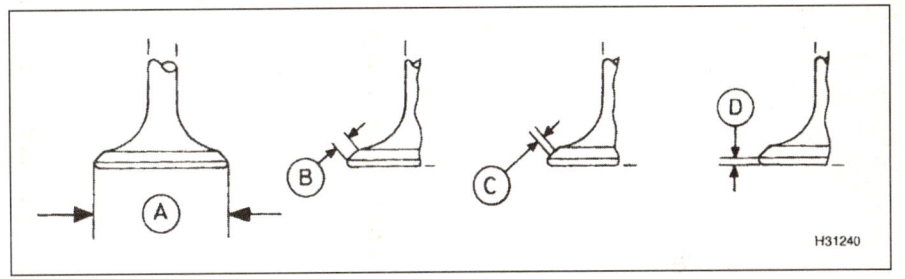

11.18 Valve head measurement points
A Head diameter   B Face width   C Seat width   D Margin thickness

time so that no mixing of parts between valves occurs. Scrape off any deposits that may have formed on the valves, then use a motorised wire brush to remove deposits from the valve heads and stems. Again, make sure the valves do not get mixed up.

Inspection

13 Inspect the head very carefully for cracks and other damage. If cracks are found, a new head will be required. Check the cam bearing surfaces for wear and evidence of seizure. Check the camshafts for wear as well (see Section 8).

14 Using a precision straight-edge and a feeler gauge, check the head gasket mating surface for warpage **(see illustration)**. Refer to *Tools and Workshop Tips* (Section 3) in the *Reference* section for details of how to use the straight-edge. If the head is warped beyond the limit specified at the beginning of this Chapter, consult your Yamaha dealer or take it to an engineer for rectification.

15 Examine the valve seats in the combustion chamber. If they are pitted, cracked or burned, the head will require work beyond the scope of the home mechanic. Measure the valve seat width and compare it to this Chapter's Specifications **(see illustration)**. If it exceeds the service limit, or if it varies around its circumference, consult your Yamaha dealer or take the head to an engineer for rectification.

16 Examine each valve face for cracks, pits and burned spots **(see illustration)**. **Note:** *Slight imperfections between the valve face and seat may be overcome by grinding the valve (see Steps 24 to 28).*

17 Rotate the valve and check for any obvious indication that it is bent. Using V-blocks and a dial gauge if available, measure the valve stem runout and compare the results to the specifications at the beginning of this Chapter **(see illustration)**. If the measurement exceeds the service limit specified, the valve must be replaced with a new one. Note that a slightly bent valve stem will prevent the valve from seating properly in the head.

18 Measure the various aspects of the valve head and compare them with the listed specifications **(see illustration)**. If the valve is worn it should be replaced with a new one.

19 Measure the valve stem diameter **(see illustration)**. Clean the valve guides to remove any carbon build-up, then measure the inside diameters of the guides (at both ends and the centre of the guide) with a small hole gauge and micrometer (see *Tools and Workshop Tips* (Section 3) in the *Reference* section). The guides are measured at the ends and at the centre to determine if they are worn in a bell-mouth pattern (more wear at the ends). Subtract the stem diameter from the valve guide diameter to obtain the valve stem-to-guide clearance. If the stem-to-guide clearance is greater than listed in this Chapter's Specifications, replace whichever components are worn beyond their specified limits with new ones. If the valve guide is within specifications, but is worn unevenly, it should be renewed.

20 Inspect the valve stem and collet groove area for scuffing and cracks **(see illustration 11.16)**. Check the end of the stem for pitting and wear. The presence of any of the above conditions indicates the need for fitting new valves.

21 Check the end of each valve spring for wear. Measure the free length of each spring, making sure you identify each one correctly as to its location, and compare it to that listed in the specifications **(see illustration)**. If any

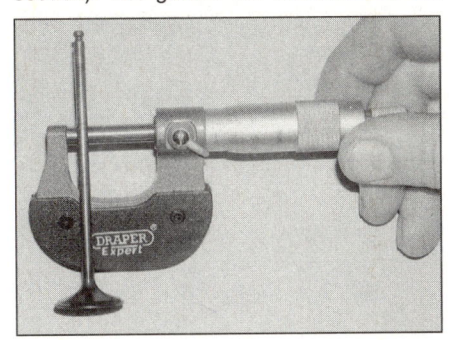

11.19 Measuring valve stem diameter with a micrometer

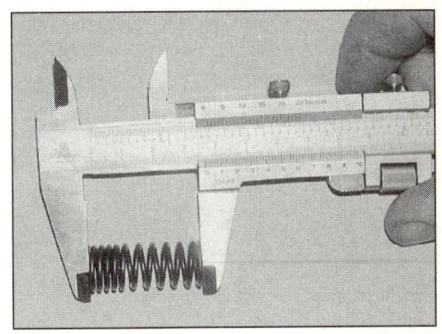

11.21 Measuring spring free length with a Vernier caliper

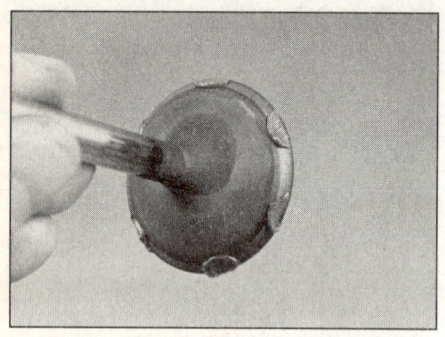

11.25 Apply small dabs of grinding compound to the valve face only

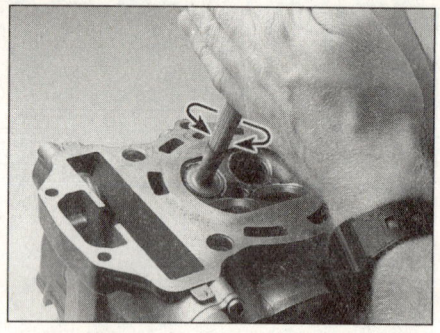

11.26a Rotate the valve grinding tool back and forth between the palms of your hands

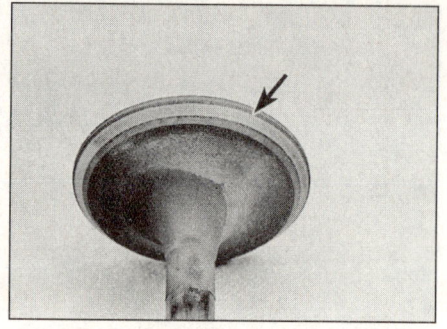

11.26b The valve face (arrowed) and seat should appear as a uniform, unbroken ring ...

spring is shorter than specified it has sagged and must be replaced with a new one. Also place the spring upright on a flat surface and check it for bend by placing a ruler or engineer's square against it. If the bend in any spring exceeds the specified limit, it must be replaced with a new one.

22 Check the spring retainers and collets for obvious wear and cracks. Any questionable parts should not be reused, as extensive damage will occur in the event of failure during engine operation.

23 If the inspection indicates that no overhaul work is required, the valve components can be reinstalled in the head.

Reassembly

24 Unless a valve service has been performed, before installing the valves in the head they should be ground in (lapped) to ensure a positive seal between the valves and seats. **Note:** *Do not grind in the valves after the seats have been re-cut. The valve seat must be soft and unpolished for final seating to occur when the engine is first run.* This procedure requires coarse and fine valve grinding compound and a valve grinding tool (either hand-held or drill driven – note that some drill-driven tools specify using only a fine grinding compound). If a grinding tool is not available, a piece of rubber or plastic hose can be slipped over the valve stem (after the valve has been installed in the guide) and used to turn the valve.

25 Apply a small amount of coarse grinding compound to the valve face **(see illustration)**. Smear some molybdenum disulphide oil (a 50/50 mixture of molybdenum disulphide grease and engine oil) to the valve stem, then slip the valve into the guide **(see illustration 11.30a)**. **Note:** *Make sure each valve is installed in its correct guide and be careful not to get any grinding compound on the valve stem.*

26 Attach the grinding tool to the valve and rotate the tool between the palms of your hands. Use a back-and-forth motion (as though rubbing your hands together) rather than a circular motion (i.e. so that the valve rotates alternately clockwise and anti-clockwise rather than in one direction only) **(see illustration)**. If a motorised tool is being used, take note of the correct drive speed for it – if your drill runs too fast and is not variable, use a hand tool instead. Lift the valve off the seat and turn it at regular intervals to distribute the grinding compound properly. Continue the grinding procedure until the valve face and seat contact area is of uniform width, and unbroken around the entire circumference **(see illustrations)**.

27 Carefully remove the valve from the guide and wipe off all traces of grinding compound. Use solvent to clean the valve and wipe the seat area thoroughly with a solvent soaked cloth.

28 Repeat the procedure with fine valve grinding compound, then repeat the entire procedure for the remaining valves.

29 Working on one valve at a time, lay the spring seat in place in the cylinder head so that its shouldered side faces upwards **(see illustration)**. Fit a new valve stem seal onto the guide and use an appropriate size deep socket to press the seal over the end of the valve guide until it is felt to clip into place **(see illustration)**. Don't twist or cock the seal, or it will not seal properly against the valve stem. Also, don't remove it again or it will be damaged.

30 Coat the valve stem with molybdenum disulphide oil, then install it into its guide, rotating it slowly to avoid damaging the seal **(see illustration)**. Check that the valve moves up and down freely in the guide. Next, install the spring(s) (two springs on the intake valves), with the closer-wound coils facing down into the cylinder head

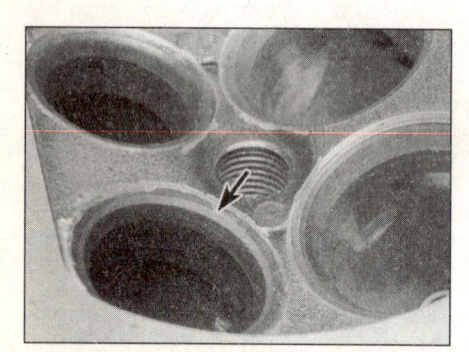

11.26c ... and the seat (arrowed) should be the specified width all the way round

11.29a Install the valve spring seat

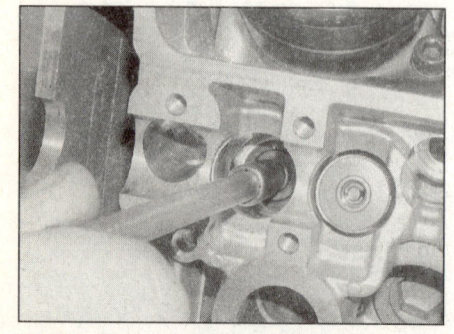

11.29b Press the new stem seal into place with a suitable deep socket

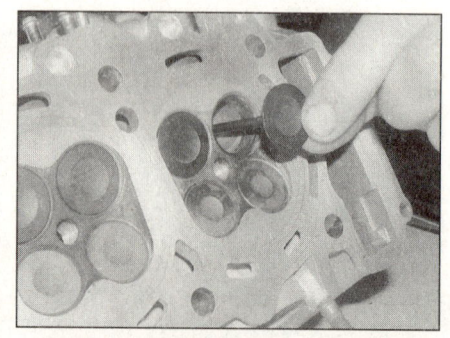

11.30a Lubricate the valve stem then install the valve

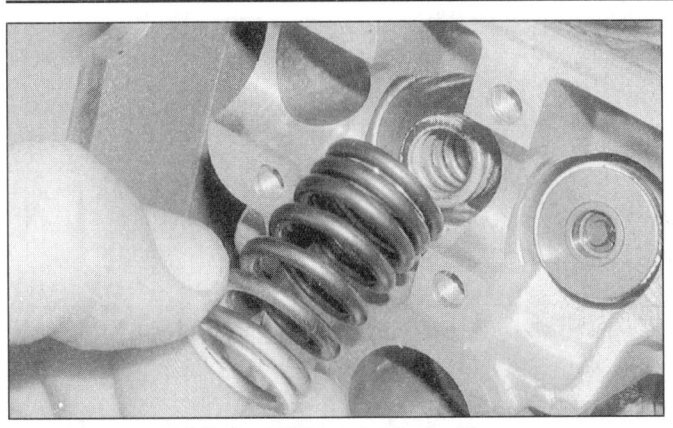

Engine, clutch and transmission 2•23

11.30b Install the valve spring(s) . . .

11.30c . . . and the spring retainer

(see illustration). Fit the spring retainer, with its shouldered side facing down so that it fits into the top of the spring (see illustration).
31 Apply a small amount of grease to the inside of the collets – this will help to help hold them in place when fitting them on the valve stem (see illustration). Compress the spring with the valve spring compressor and install the collets (see illustrations 11.7a, b and c and 11.8a). When compressing the spring, do so only as far as is necessary to slip the collets into place. Make certain that the collets are securely located in the collet groove and release the spring compressor.
32 Repeat the procedure for the remaining valves. Remember to keep the parts for each valve together and separate from the other valves so they can be reinstalled in their original locations.
33 Support the cylinder head on blocks so the valves can't contact the workbench top, then very gently tap the top of each valve stem to seat the collets in the groove (see illustration).

HAYNES HiNT *Check for proper sealing of the valves by pouring a small amount of solvent into each of the valve ports. If the solvent leaks past any valve into the combustion chamber the valve grinding operation on that valve should be repeated.*

12 Clutch cable

Removal

1 Remove the lower fairing and the fairing right-hand side panel (see Chapter 7).
2 Bend back the tab in the cable retainer on the end of the clutch release mechanism arm, then loosen the rear nut on the adjuster (see illustrations).
3 Slip the adjuster out of the bracket on the engine cover and release the cable end from the retainer, noting how it fits (see illustration).

11.31 A small dab of grease will help to keep the collets in place on the valve while the spring is released

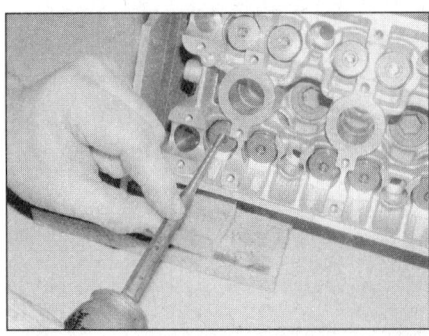

4 Screw the adjuster at the handlebar end of the cable fully into the lever bracket and align the slot in the adjuster with that in the

11.33 Tap the valve stem gently to seat the collets in the groove

lever bracket (see illustration). Pull the outer cable end from the socket in the adjuster and release the inner cable nipple from the lever.

12.2a Bend back the tab in the cable retainer . . .

12.2b . . . then loosen the adjuster nut, free the cable from the bracket . . .

12.3 . . . and release the clutch cable end from the retainer

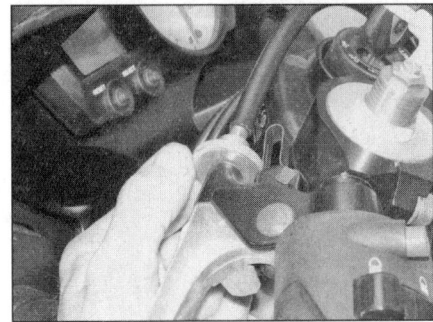

12.4 Thread the adjuster into the bracket and align the slots as described

2•24 Engine, clutch and transmission

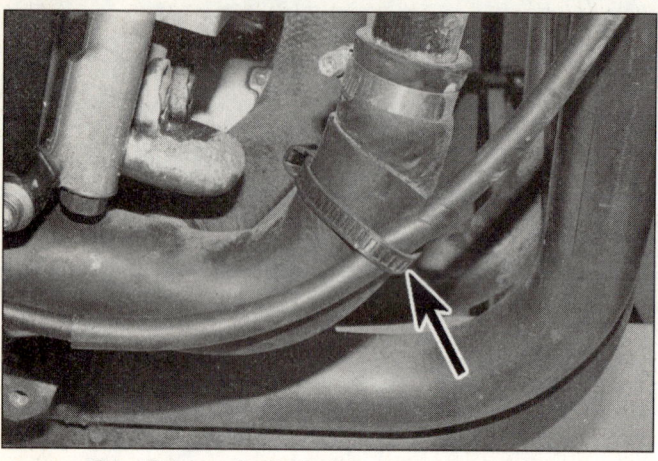

12.5a Release the cable from the tie (arrowed) . . .

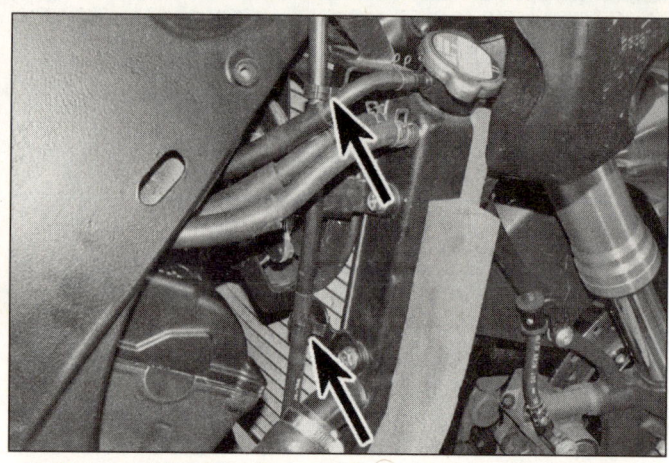

12.5b . . . and the clips (arrowed) on the back of the radiator . . .

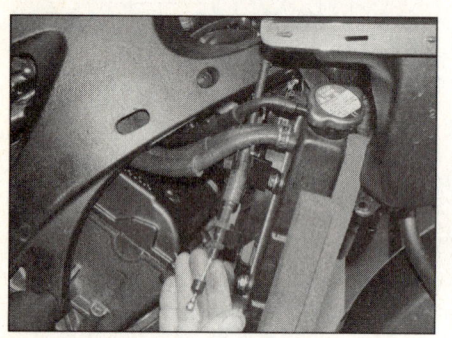

12.5c . . . then draw it out . . .

12.5d . . . noting its routing through the guide on the top yoke

5 Release the cable tie that holds the clutch cable to the radiator lower hose and release the clips on the back of the radiator **(see illustrations)**. Remove the cable from the machine, noting its routing through the guide on the top yoke **(see illustrations)**.

> **HAYNES HiNT**
> When fitting a new cable, tape the lower end of the new cable to the upper end of the old cable before removing it from the motorcycle. Slowly pull the lower end of the old cable out, guiding the new cable down into position. Using this method will ensure the cable is routed correctly.

Installation

6 Installation is the reverse of removal. Apply grease to the cable ends and make sure the cable is correctly routed and clipped into place. With the cable installed, turn the adjuster on the lever bracket so that the slots are not aligned **(see illustration 12.4)** and bend the retainer on the release mechanism arm to secure the cable end **(see illustration 12.2a)**. Check the clutch release mechanism for smooth operation and any signs of wear or damage. Remove it for cleaning and re-greasing if required (see Section 13).

7 Adjust the clutch lever freeplay (see Chapter 1). Install the fairing panels (see Chapter 7).

13 Clutch

Note: *This procedure can be carried out with the engine in the frame. If the engine has been removed, ignore the steps that do not apply.*
Special tool: *A clutch centre holding tool is useful, although not essential – see Step 8.*

Removal

1 Remove the fairing right-hand side panel and the lower fairing (see Chapter 7). Drain the engine oil and the coolant (see Chapter 1).
2 To allow clearance for removing the clutch cover, unscrew the bolt on the timing rotor cover that retains the coolant hose guide and release the guide **(see illustration)**. Release the clamp and detach the coolant by-pass hose from the water pump **(see illustration)**.
3 Detach the clutch cable from the release mechanism arm (see Section 12). Detach the engine idle speed adjuster from its bracket **(see illustration)**. Remove the oil dipstick.
4 Working evenly in a criss-cross pattern, unscrew the clutch cover bolts and remove the cover and the idle adjuster bracket, being prepared to catch

13.2a Displace the coolant hose guide (arrowed) . . .

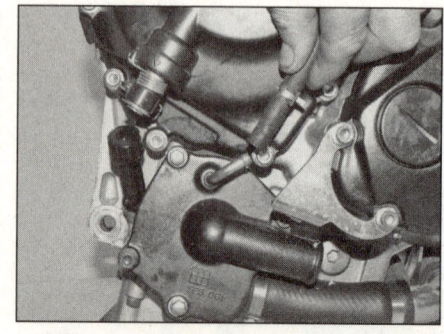

13.2b . . . and detach the hose from the pump

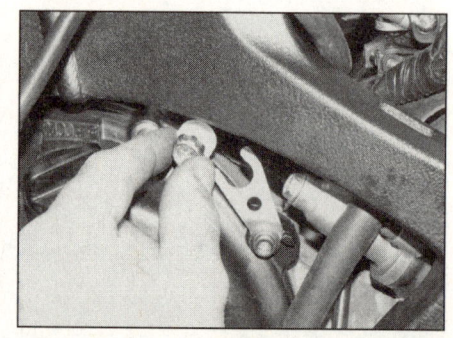

13.3 Free the engine idle speed adjuster from its bracket

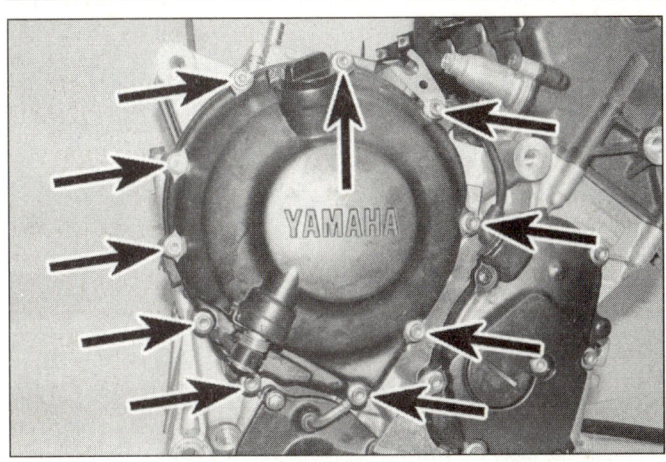

Engine, clutch and transmission 2•25

13.4 Unscrew the bolts (arrowed) and remove the cover

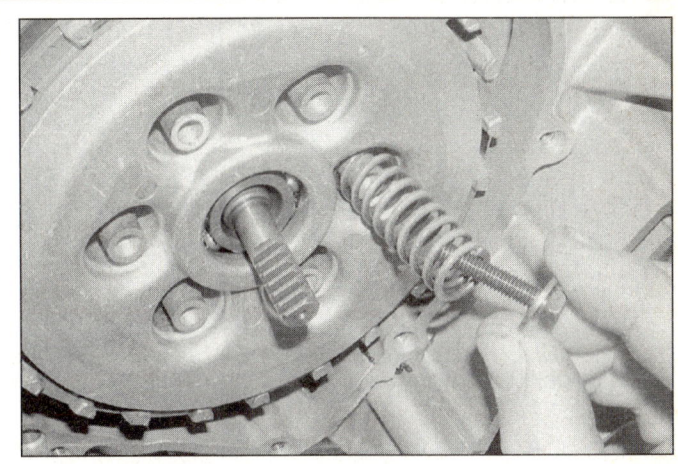

13.6a Remove the clutch bolts and springs . . .

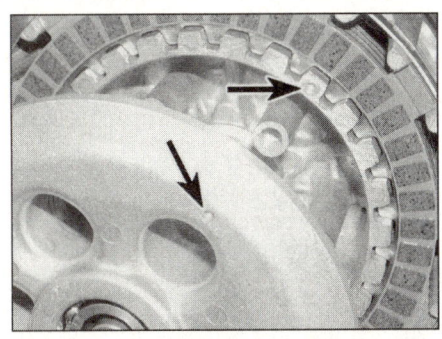

13.6b . . . and the pressure plate, noting the reference marks (arrowed)

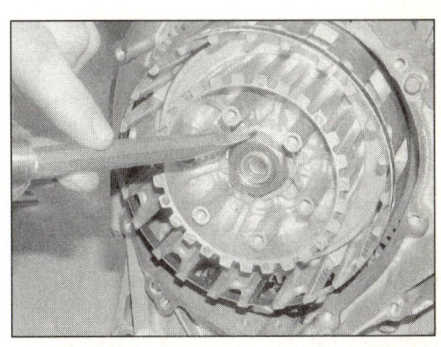

13.8a Bend back the lockwasher tabs

any residual oil **(see illustration)**. If the cover will not lift away easily, break the gasket seal by tapping gently around the edge with a soft-faced hammer or block of wood. Note how the teeth on the clutch pull-rod engage on the actuating shaft in the clutch cover.

5 Remove the cover gasket and discard it as a new one must be fitted on reassembly. Note the position of the two locating dowels and remove them for safe-keeping if they are loose – they could be in either the cover or the crankcase **(see illustration 13.37)**.

6 Working in a criss-cross pattern, gradually slacken the clutch spring bolts until the spring pressure is released, counter-holding the clutch using a rag. Remove the bolts, springs and clutch pressure plate, noting the alignment marks on the clutch pressure plate and the clutch centre **(see illustrations)**. Remove the pull-rod from the pressure plate, noting the bearing **(see illustration 13.34)**.

7 Grasp the complete set of clutch plates and remove them as a pack. Unless the plates are being replaced with new ones, keep them in their original order. Note that the innermost plain plate is thicker than the rest, and the two innermost friction plates have a purple colour-code and thinner tabs, while all the rest are brown.

8 Bend back the tabs on the clutch centre nut lockwasher **(see illustration)**. To remove the clutch centre nut, the transmission input shaft must be locked. This can be done in several ways. If the engine is in the frame, engage 1st gear and have an assistant hold the rear brake on hard with the rear tyre in firm contact with the ground. Alternatively, the Yamaha service tool – Pt. No. 90890-04086 (European models) or YM-91042 (US models) – or a similar commercially available tool, can be used to stop the clutch centre from turning while the nut is loosened. Protect the engine casing with a piece of wood if the clutch holding tool bears against it **(see illustration)**.

9 With the transmission input shaft locked, unscrew the nut and remove the lockwasher, noting how it fits **(see illustration 13.32b)**. Discard the lockwasher, as a new one must be fitted on reassembly.

10 Slide the clutch centre and the thrust washer off the input shaft **(see illustrations 13.32a and 13.31)**.

11 Note how the primary driven gear on the clutch housing engages with the primary drive gear on the crankshaft. Note also the position of the oil pump drive chain which engages on a sprocket on the back of the clutch housing **(see illustration)**.

13.8b Remove the clutch nut as described

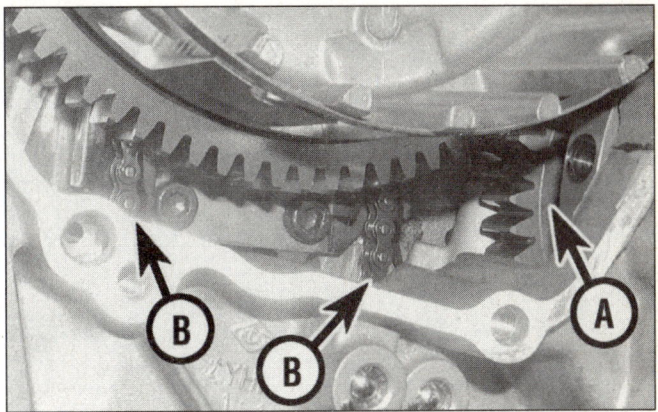

13.11 Note the primary drive gear engagement (A) and the position of the oil pump drive chain (B)

2•26 Engine, clutch and transmission

13.12a Use a tool to dislodge the bearing centre from the clutch housing . . .

13.12b . . . then remove the bearing centre . . .

13.12c . . . and the needle roller cage

12 Ease out the bearing centre and needle bearing from between the clutch housing and the input shaft – this can be done using a magnet and by sliding the housing on the shaft to help push them along **(see illustrations)**.

13 There is now enough clearance to pull the clutch housing out along the input shaft and expose the oil pump drive chain behind it **(see illustration)**. Disengage the chain from the drive sprocket and remove the clutch housing, the thrust washer and spacer. **Note:** *It may be necessary to rotate the crankshaft to obtain clearance between the primary driven gear and the connecting rod of No. 4 cylinder or the right-hand web on the crankshaft (see illustration). To rotate the crankshaft, unscrew the inspection plug in the ignition rotor cover and turn the rotor bolt on the end of the crankshaft in a clockwise direction only.*

14 If required, unscrew the bolts that retain the oil pump drive chain guide to the crankcase and remove the guide **(see illustration)**.

Inspection

15 After an extended period of service the clutch friction plates will wear and promote clutch slip. Measure the thickness of each friction plate using a Vernier caliper **(see illustration)**. If any plate has worn to or beyond the service limit given in the Specifications at the beginning of this Chapter, the friction plates must be replaced with a new set. Also, if any of the plates smell burnt or are glazed, they must be replaced as a set.

16 The plain plates should not show any signs of excess heating (bluing). Check for warpage using a flat surface and feeler gauges **(see illustration)**. If any plate exceeds the maximum permissible amount of warpage, or shows signs of bluing, all the plain plates must be renewed as a set.

17 Measure the free length of each clutch spring **(see illustration)**. If any spring is below the service limit specified, renew all the springs as a set.

18 Inspect the clutch assembly for burrs and indentations on the edges of the protruding tangs of the friction plates and/or slots in the edge of the housing with which they engage. Similarly check for wear between the inner teeth of the plain plates and the slots in the clutch centre. Wear will cause clutch drag and slow disengagement during gear changes, as the plates will snag when the pressure plate is lifted. With care, a small amount of wear can be corrected by dressing with a fine file, but if

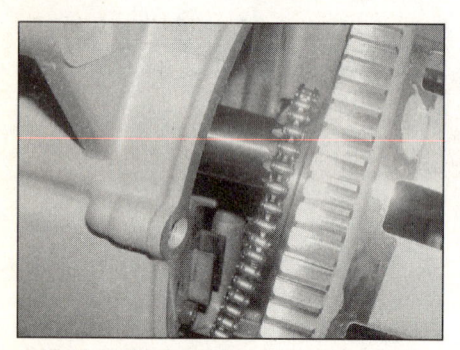

13.13a Withdraw the clutch housing to expose the oil pump drive chain

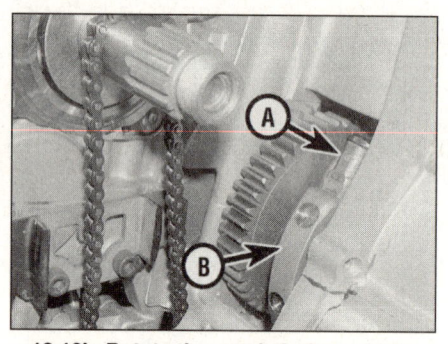

13.13b Rotate the crankshaft to obtain clearance from the connecting rod (A) and crankshaft web (B)

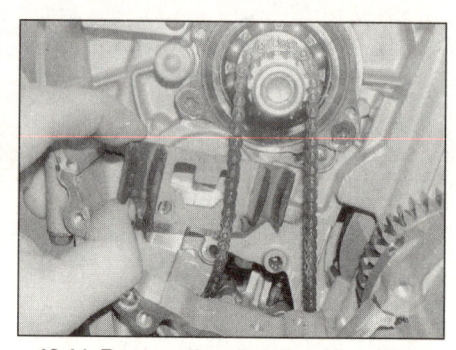

13.14 Remove the oil pump drive chain guide if required

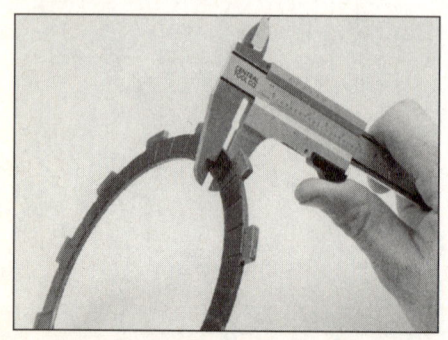

13.15 Measuring clutch friction plate thickness

13.16 Checking the plain plates for warpage

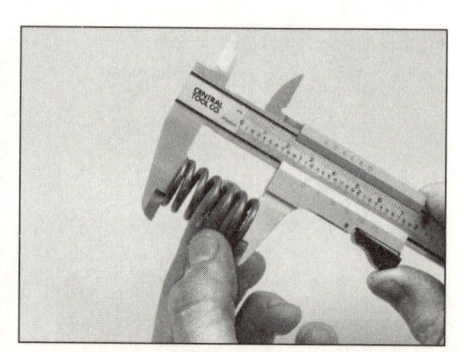

13.17 Measure the free length of the clutch springs as shown

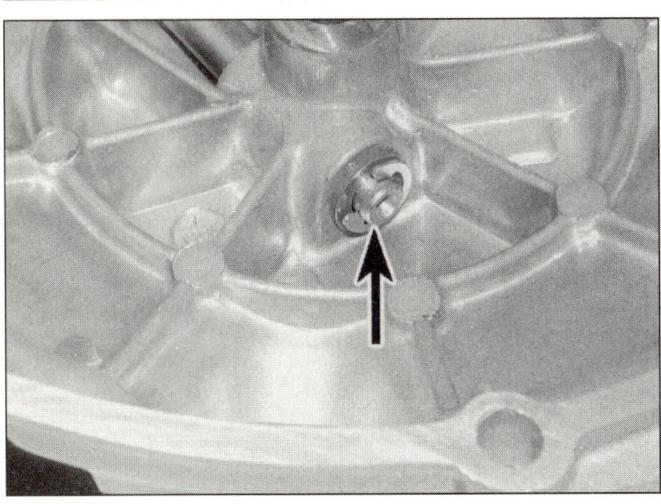

Engine, clutch and transmission 2•27

13.24a Remove the E-clip (arrowed) and washer securing the clutch actuating shaft

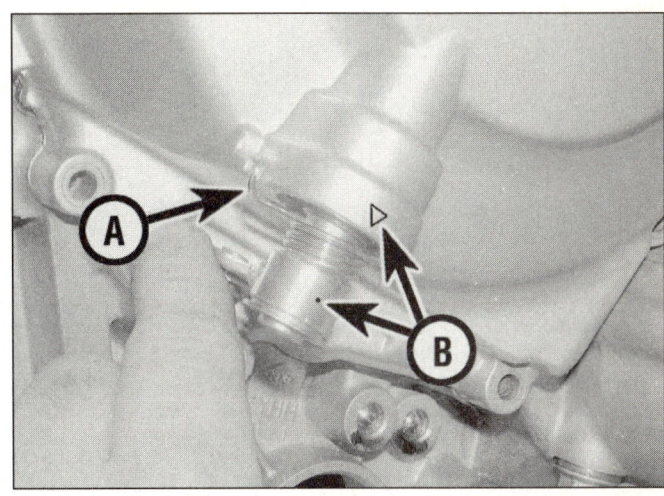

13.24b Note the position of the spring (A) and the alignment marks (B)

it is excessive the worn components should be replaced with new ones.

19 Inspect the needle roller bearing in conjunction with the internal bearing surface of the clutch housing and the external surface of the bearing centre. If there are any signs of wear, pitting or other damage the affected parts must be replaced with new ones.

20 Check the teeth of the primary driven gear on the clutch housing and the corresponding teeth of the primary drive gear on the end of the crankshaft. Replace the clutch housing with a new one if any teeth are worn or chipped. The primary drive gear is an integral part of the crankshaft (see Section 24 for removal of the crankshaft).

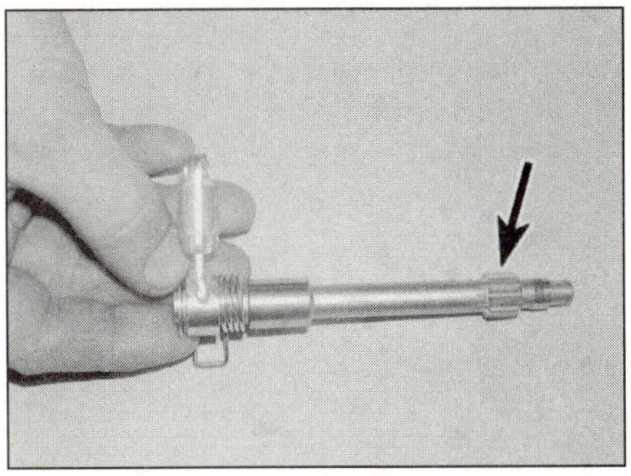

21 Check the teeth of the oil pump drive sprocket on the back of the clutch housing. If any are worn or chipped, replace the housing with a new one and remove the oil pump and chain for inspection (see Section 18).

22 The clutch housing incorporates a cush-drive mechanism – check that the springs are not loose and that there is no backlash between the centre of the housing and the primary driven gear.

23 Check the pressure plate and its bearing for signs of wear or damage and roughness. Check the pull-rod for signs of wear or damage. Replace any parts, as necessary, with new ones.

24 Check the clutch release mechanism shaft pinion and the pull-rod teeth for signs of wear and damage. Check that the shaft turns smoothly in the clutch cover. If necessary, remove the E-clip and washer securing the shaft and withdraw the shaft **(see illustration)**. Note the position of the return spring and the alignment marks on the clutch cover and release mechanism arm **(see illustration)**.

25 Check the condition of the shaft, oil seal and two bearings, and fit new parts if necessary **(see illustration)**. If the bearings need to be removed, first remove the oil seal **(see illustrations)**, then heat the cover in very hot water to ease removal and drive the bearings out (see *Tools and Workshop Tips* (Sections 5 and 6) in the *Reference* section). Discard the oil seal as a new one must be fitted on reassembly.

26 If required, remove the E-clip and washer securing the arm on the end of the shaft. Note the position of the arm and return spring, then slide the arm off the shaft and remove the spring.

27 Clean all components and lubricate the seal and bearings with grease. Installation is the reverse of removal. Before installing the arm on the shaft, fit the spring and ensure that the 'UP' mark on the arm is facing up when the shaft is installed in the cover.

Installation

28 Remove all traces of old gasket from the crankcase and clutch cover surfaces. If removed, install the oil pump chain guide, applying a suitable non-permanent thread locking compound to its bolts and tightening them to the torque setting specified at the beginning of this Chapter **(see illustration 13.14)**.

29 Slide the spacer and the thrust washer onto the transmission input shaft **(see illustration)**. Slide the clutch housing along the shaft to a position where the oil pump

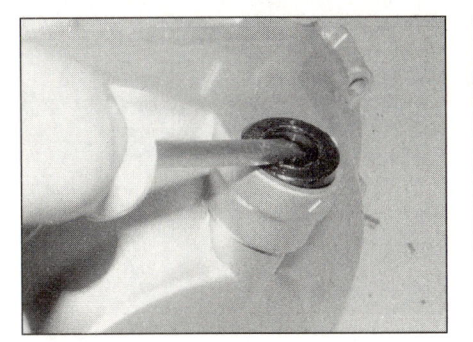

13.25a Examine the actuating shaft pinion (arrowed) and bearing surfaces

13.25b Lever the oil seal out . . .

13.25c . . . before removing the actuating shaft bearing

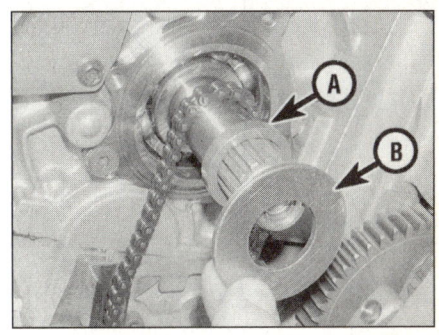

13.29a Install the spacer (A) and thrust washer (B)

2•28 Engine, clutch and transmission

13.29b Rotate the clutch housing to engage the oil pump drive chain

13.31 Install the thrust washer . . .

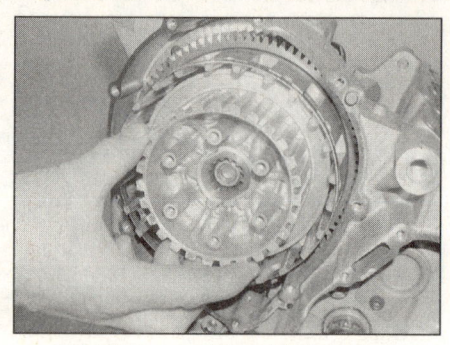

13.32a . . . and the clutch centre

drive chain can be located onto the drive sprocket on the back of the clutch housing. Slowly rotate the housing and feed the chain onto the sprocket **(see illustration)**. Ensure that the chain is correctly routed between the guides on the inside of the crankcase.

30 Lubricate the needle roller bearing with clean engine oil. Support the clutch housing and engage the primary driven and drive gears, then slide the bearing and the bearing centre into place on the input shaft **(see illustrations 13.12c and 12b)**.

31 Lubricate the thrust washer with clean engine oil and slide it onto the shaft **(see illustration)**.

32 Slide the clutch centre onto the shaft splines, then fit the new lockwasher. Note how two of the lockwasher tabs locate on flats on the clutch centre boss **(see illustrations)**. Install the clutch centre nut with the shouldered side on the inside, and tighten the nut to the torque setting specified at the beginning of this Chapter using the method employed on removal to lock the input shaft (see Step 8) **(see illustration)**. **Note:** *Check that the clutch centre rotates freely after tightening.* Bend up the tabs of the lockwasher to secure the nut **(see illustration 13.8a)**.

33 Coat each clutch plate with clean engine oil prior to installation. Build up the plates as follows: first fit the thick plain plate, then a purple-coded/thin tabbed friction plate, then a standard plain plate, then the second purple-coded/thin tabbed friction plate, then alternate plain and brown-coded friction plates until all are installed **(see illustrations)**.

34 Lubricate the bearing in the pressure plate with clean engine oil. Fit the pull-rod into the back of the pressure plate **(see illustration)**.

35 Align the reference marks on the clutch pressure plate and the clutch centre and fit the pressure plate, making sure the castellations in its rim locate into the slots in the clutch centre **(see illustration 13.6b)**.

36 Install the clutch springs and bolts **(see illustration 13.6a)**, and tighten the bolts evenly and a little at a time in a criss-cross sequence to the specified torque setting **(see**

13.32b Align the new lockwasher tabs with the flats on the clutch centre boss

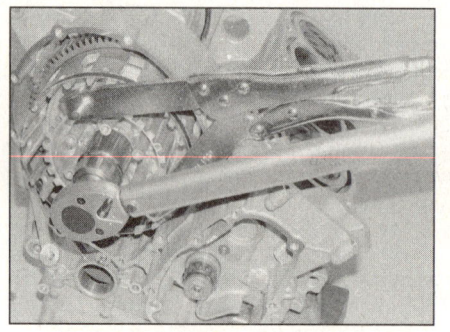

13.32c Tighten the clutch nut to the specified torque and secure it with the lockwasher tabs

13.33a First install the thick plain plate . . .

13.33b . . . then a friction plate, and so on

13.33c Make sure the different thickness plates are installed in the correct order as described

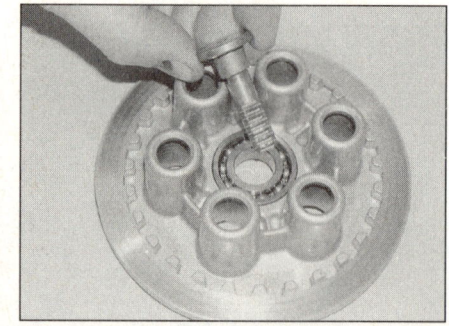

13.34 Fit the pull-rod into the back of the pressure plate

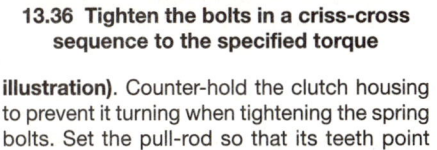

Engine, clutch and transmission 2•29

13.36 Tighten the bolts in a criss-cross sequence to the specified torque

13.37a Fit a new gasket onto the dowels (arrowed)

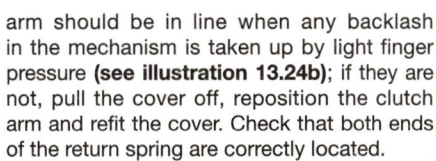

13.37b Install the cover as described

illustration). Counter-hold the clutch housing to prevent it turning when tightening the spring bolts. Set the pull-rod so that its teeth point towards the rear and are angled up slightly.

37 If removed, insert the dowels in the crankcase and fit the new gasket onto them **(see illustration)**. When installing the clutch cover, getting the actuating shaft to engage correctly with the pull-rod teeth can be tricky. Set the release arm so that it is pointing to the rear, then as the cover is installed and the teeth engage, the arm should turn in **(see illustration)**. With the cover fully installed, the alignment marks on the cover and the clutch arm should be in line when any backlash in the mechanism is taken up by light finger pressure **(see illustration 13.24b)**; if they are not, pull the cover off, reposition the clutch arm and refit the cover. Check that both ends of the return spring are correctly located.

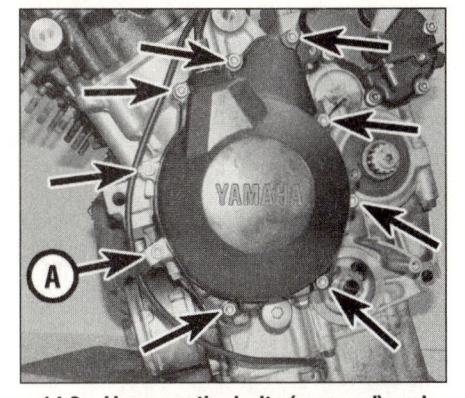

38 Install the cover bolts and the idle speed adjuster bracket and tighten the bolts evenly in a criss-cross sequence to the specified torque setting **(see illustration 13.4)**.

39 Install the idle speed adjuster and the coolant hose and guide **(see illustrations 13.3, 2b and 2a)**.

40 Fit the clutch cable onto the release arm and adjust the cable as necessary (see Section 12).

41 Refill the engine with oil to the correct level (see Chapter 1 and *Pre-ride checks*).

42 Install the fairing side panel and the lower fairing (see Chapter 7).

14 Starter clutch and gears

Note: *This procedure can be carried out with the engine in the frame. If the engine has been removed, ignore the steps which do not apply.*

1 Remove the fairing left-hand side panel and the lower fairing (see Chapter 7). Drain the engine oil (see Chapter 1). Remove the coolant reservoir (see Chapter 3). Remove the fuel tank (see Chapter 4).

2 Trace the alternator wiring from the top of the alternator cover on the left-hand side of the engine and disconnect it at the white, three-pin connector **(see illustration 4.14)**. Feed the wiring through to the left-hand engine cover, noting its routing.

3 Unscrew and remove the bolts securing the alternator cover, noting the wiring guide **(see illustration)**. Remove the cover, being prepared to catch any residual oil. If the cover will not lift away easily, break the gasket seal by tapping gently around the edge with a soft-faced hammer or block of wood, or by levering carefully with a screwdriver on the tab as shown **(see illustration)** – do not try to lever between the cover/crankcases mating surfaces as they could be damaged. Discard the gasket as a new one must be used. Remove the dowels from either the cover or the crankcase if they are loose.

Check

4 The operation of the starter clutch can be checked while it is in place. Check that the idler gear is able to rotate freely anti-clockwise as you look at it from the left-hand side of the bike, but locks when rotated clockwise **(see illustration)**. If not, the starter clutch is faulty and should be removed for inspection.

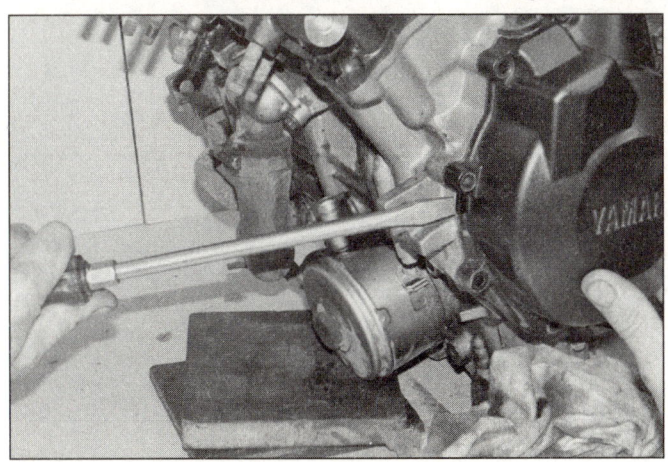

14.3a Unscrew the bolts (arrowed) and remove the wiring guide (A)

14.3b Some leverage can be applied to the purpose made tab if required

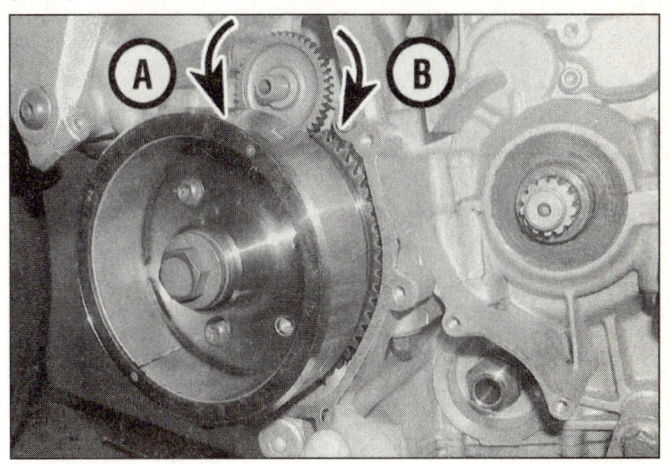

14.4 Idler gear should rotate freely anti-clockwise (A), and lock when turned clockwise (B)

2•30 Engine, clutch and transmission

14.5a Withdraw the shaft and the idler gear

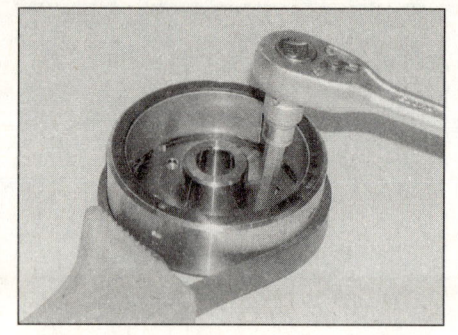

14.5b Remove the bolts to separate the starter clutch from the alternator rotor

14.7 Examine the idler gear teeth for wear and damage

Removal

5 Withdraw the idler gear shaft from the crankcase and remove the gear **(see illustration)**. Remove the alternator rotor – the starter clutch is mounted on the back of it (see Chapter 8). **Note:** *Before removing the alternator rotor, slacken the three starter clutch bolts while holding the rotor centre bolt. If the rotor has already been removed from the bike, hold the rotor with a strap wrench to slacken the bolts* **(see illustration)**.

6 Lay the alternator rotor face down on the work surface and withdraw the starter driven gear from the starter clutch. If the gear appears stuck, rotate it anti-clockwise as you withdraw it to free it from the starter clutch. If the starter driven gear does not come away with the alternator rotor, slide it off the crankshaft.

Inspection

7 Inspect the teeth on the idler gear and replace it with a new one if any are chipped or worn **(see illustration)**. Check the idler shaft bearing surfaces for signs of wear or damage, and replace with a new one if necessary.

8 Fit the starter driven gear into the starter clutch, rotating it anti-clockwise to spread the sprags and allow the gear hub to enter. With the alternator rotor face down, check that the starter driven gear rotates freely in an anti-clockwise direction and locks against the rotor in a clockwise direction **(see illustration)**. If it doesn't, the starter clutch should be dismantled.

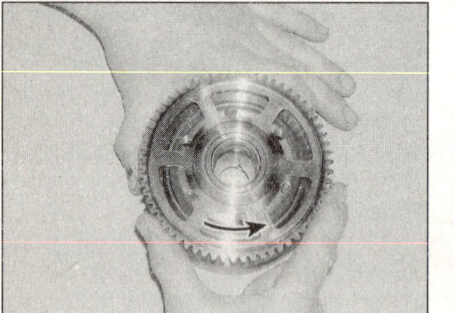

9 Unscrew the three bolts and remove the clutch housing from the back of the alternator rotor **(see illustration)**. Depress the spring lock on the outside edge of the clutch sprag assembly and withdraw it from the housing **(see illustration)**.

10 Inspect the condition of the sprags and their cage inside the clutch assembly **(see illustration)**. If they are damaged or worn at any point, the starter clutch should be replaced with a new one.

11 Inspect the driven gear bearing surfaces for signs of wear and scoring. If the bearing surfaces show signs of excessive wear, replace the gear with a new one and inspect the surface of the crankshaft for damage. Inspect the teeth of the driven gear and replace the gear with a new one if they are worn or damaged.

Installation

12 Fit the clutch sprag assembly into its housing and ensure that the spring lock engages **(see illustration 14.9b)**. Clean

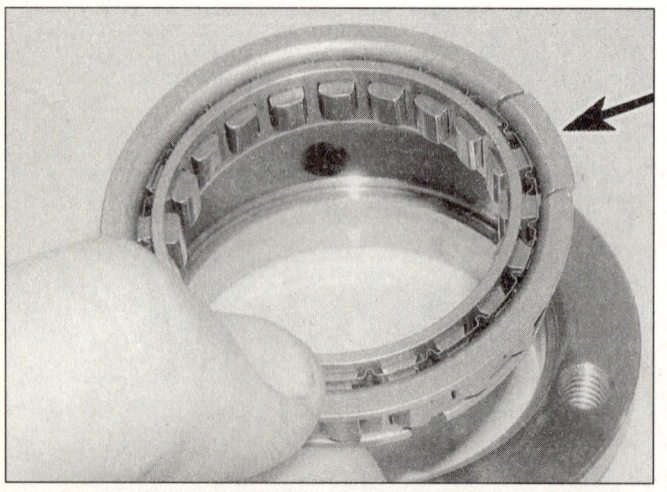

14.8 Check that the driven gear turns freely anti-clockwise

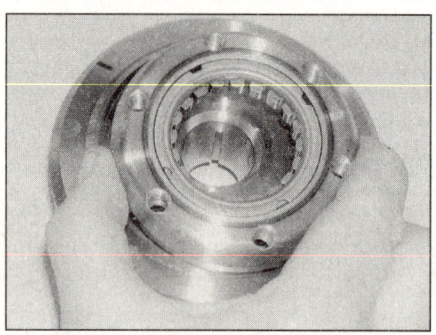

14.9a Remove the clutch housing from the back of the rotor

14.9b Depress the spring lock (arrowed) to release the clutch assembly from its housing

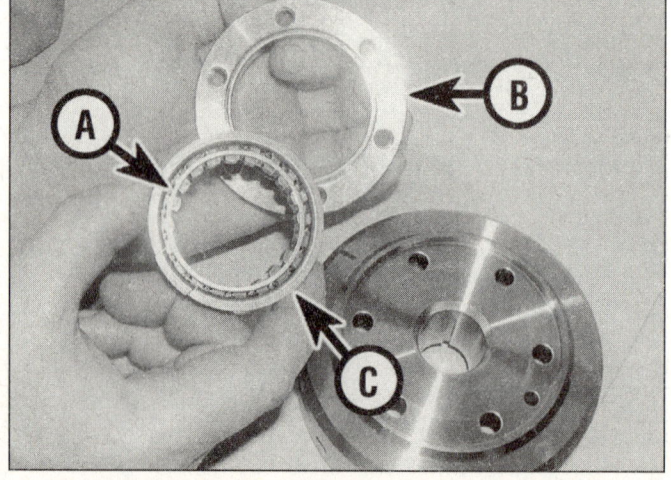

14.10 Inspect the starter clutch sprags (A), cage (C) and housing (B)

Engine, clutch and transmission 2•31

14.12 Apply locking compound to the starter clutch bolts and tighten them securely

14.16a Fit a new gasket onto the dowels (arrowed) . . .

14.16b . . . and make sure the cover locates correctly on the shaft

the starter clutch bolts and apply a drop of locking compound to their threads. Fit the housing onto the back of the alternator rotor, then install the bolts and tighten them to the specified torque setting **(see illustration)**. *Note: If a strap wrench is not available to hold the alternator rotor, final tightening of the bolts can take place once the rotor has been fitted to the crankshaft.*

13 Lubricate the starter driven gear hub with clean engine oil, then fit it into the starter clutch, rotating it anti-clockwise to spread the sprags and allow the hub to enter **(see illustration 14.8)**. Check the operation of the starter clutch as described in Step 8.

14 Install the alternator (see Chapter 8).

15 Lubricate the idler gear shaft with clean engine oil. Slide the gear onto the shaft, making sure the smaller pinion faces inwards, and the teeth of the larger pinion mesh with the teeth of the starter motor shaft **(see illustration 14.5a)**.

16 If removed, insert the dowels in the crankcase, then install the alternator cover using a new gasket, making sure the cover locates correctly onto the dowels and the idle gear shaft **(see illustrations)**. Install the cover bolts, not forgetting the wiring guide, and tighten the bolts evenly in a criss-cross sequence to the torque setting specified at the beginning of this Chapter **(see illustration 14.3a)**.

17 Install the remaining components in the reverse order of removal.

18 Refill the engine with oil to the correct level (see Chapter 1 and *Pre-ride checks*).

15 Gearchange mechanism

Note: This procedure can be carried out with the engine in the frame. If the engine has been removed, ignore the steps which do not apply.

Removal

1 Remove the lower fairing and the fairing left-hand side panel (see Chapter 7). Remove the coolant reservoir (see Chapter 3).

2 Make sure the transmission is in neutral. Note how far the gearchange linkage rod is threaded into the lever and arm, as this determines the height of the lever relative to the footrest. Loosen the rod locknuts, then unscrew the rod and separate it from the lever and the arm (the rod is reverse-threaded on the lever end, so will unscrew from both lever and arm simultaneously when turned in the one direction) **(see illustrations)**. Withdraw the rod from the frame **(see illustration)**.

3 Unscrew the pinch bolt on the gearchange linkage arm and slide the arm off the shaft, noting how the punch mark on the shaft aligns with the slot in the arm **(see illustration)**. If no mark is visible, make your own before removing the arm so that it can be correctly aligned with the shaft on installation.

4 Remove the front sprocket cover (see Chapter 6).

5 Unscrew the bolts securing the gearchange mechanism cover and remove it **(see illustration)**. Discard the gasket, as a new one must be used. Remove the dowels from either the cover or the crankcase if they are loose.

6 Note how the gearchange shaft centralising spring ends fit on each side of the locating pin

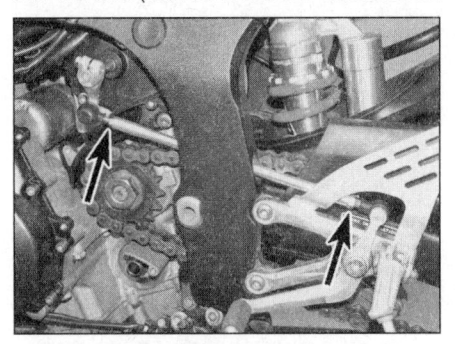

15.2a Slacken the locknuts (arrowed) . . .

15.2b . . . counter-holding the shaft as you do . . . .

15.2c . . . then unscrew the rod and withdraw it from the frame

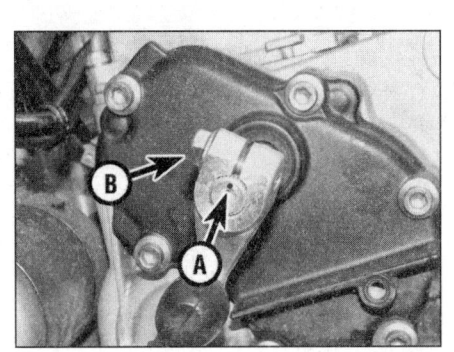

15.3 Note the alignment of the punch mark (A) with the slot then unscrew the bolt (B) and remove the arm

15.5 Unscrew the bolts (arrowed) and remove the cover

2•32 Engine, clutch and transmission

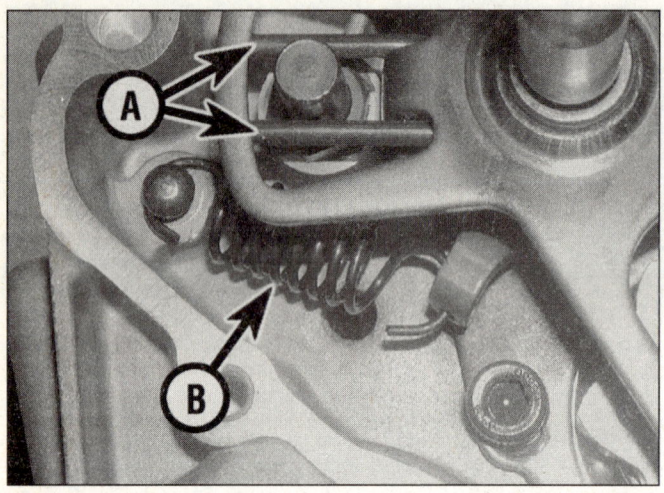

15.6a Note the location of the centralising spring ends (A) and the stopper arm spring (B)

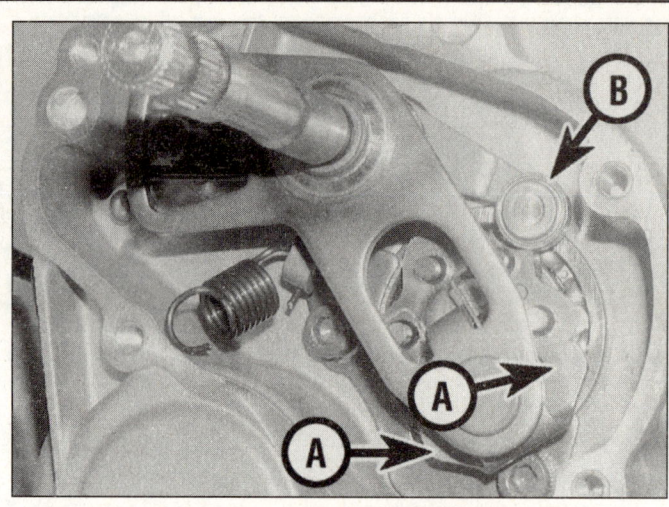

15.6b Note the position of the selector arm pawls (A) and the stopper arm roller (B)

in the crankcase, and where the stopper arm spring locates **(see illustration)**. Note how the pawls on the selector arm locate onto the pins on the end of the selector drum and how the roller on the stopper arm locates in the neutral detent on the selector drum **(see illustration)**.

7 Unhook the stopper arm spring from its anchor pin, then withdraw the gearchange shaft assembly **(see illustration)**. Ensure the washer is on the inner end of the shaft as you remove the assembly – it may stick to the crankcase wall.

8 Slide the washer off the gearchange shaft, then remove the circlip, the second washer and the stopper arm **(see illustrations)**.

Inspection

9 Inspect the splines on the gearchange shaft; if they are worn or damaged, or if the shaft is bent, replace the shaft with a new one. Check the shaft selector arm for cracks, distortion and wear of its pawls, and check for any corresponding wear on the selector pins on the selector drum **(see illustration)**.

10 Check the stopper arm roller and the detents in the selector drum for any wear or damage, and make sure the roller turns freely. Replace any components that are worn or damaged with new ones.

11 Inspect the centralising spring, the pawl spring and the stopper arm return spring for fatigue, wear or damage. If any faults are found, replace the components with new ones. Note how the ends of the centralising spring locate each side of the tab on the selector arm.

12 Check that the centralising spring locating pin in the crankcase is securely tightened. If it is loose, remove it and apply a non-permanent

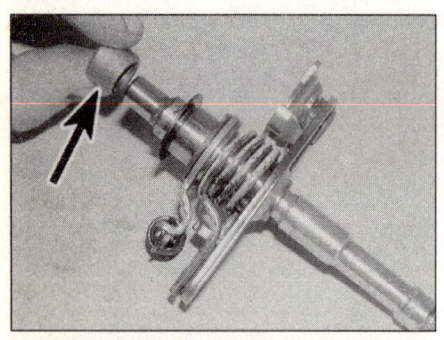

15.7 Remove the complete gearchange shaft assembly and collar (arrowed)

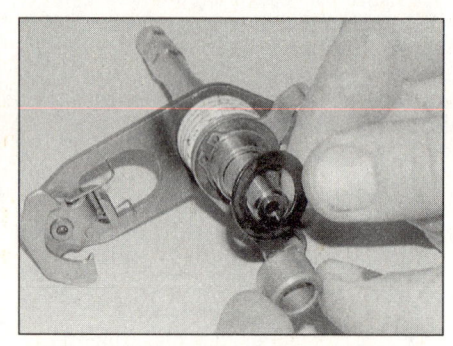

15.8a Slide the collar and the washer . . .

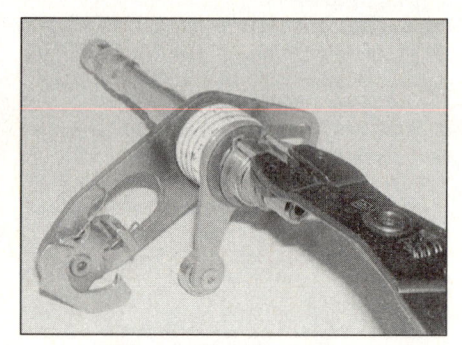

15.8b . . . then the circlip . . .

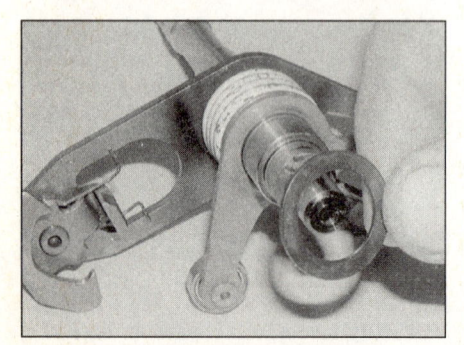

15.8c . . . and the second washer . . .

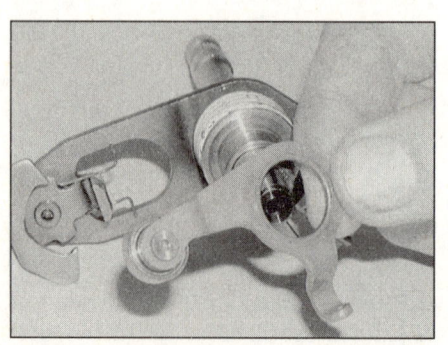

15.8d . . . and the stopper arm off the shaft

15.9 Check the selector pins for wear

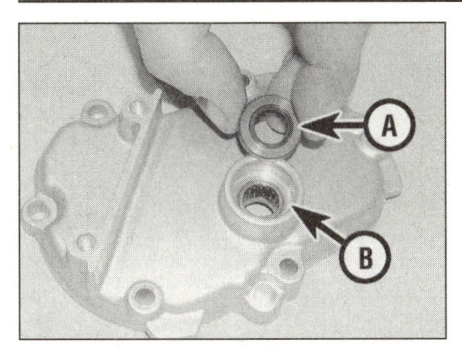

Engine, clutch and transmission 2•33

15.13 Examine the oil seal (A) and bearing (B) for wear and damage

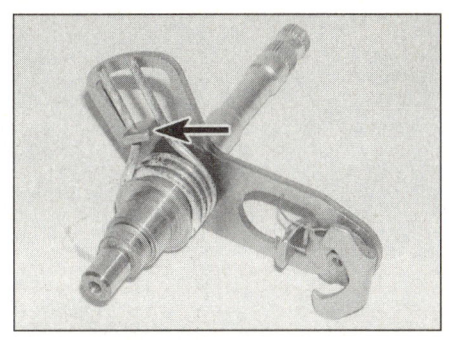

15.14 Centralising spring ends locate on each side of tab (arrowed)

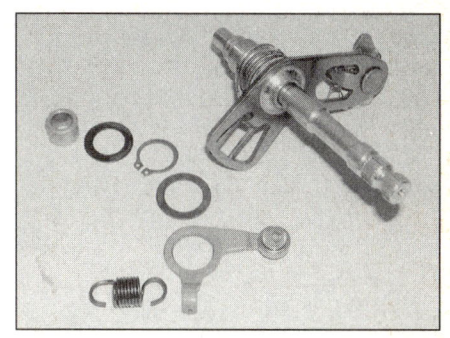

15.15 Gearchange shaft stopper arm components

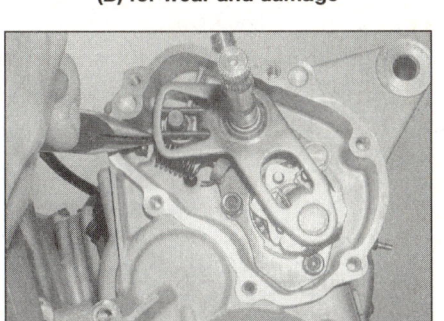

15.18 Hook the stopper arm spring over its anchor pin

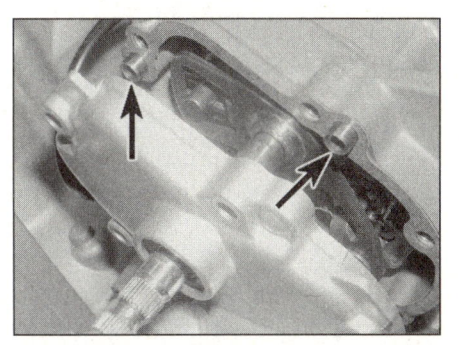

15.19 Make sure the cover locates over the dowels (arrowed)

thread locking compound to its threads, then tighten it to the torque setting specified at the beginning of this Chapter.
13 Check the condition of the gearchange shaft oil seal and bearing in the cover. If the oil seal is damaged, deteriorated or shows signs of leakage it must be replaced with a new one. Lever out the old seal with a flat-bladed screwdriver. If the bearing is damaged or does not run smoothly and freely, it must be replaced with a new one (see Section 5 of *Tools and Workshop Tips* in the *Reference* section) **(see illustration)**. Drive the new seal squarely into place, with its lip facing inward, using a seal driver or suitable socket.

Installation

14 Lubricate the gearchange shaft with clean engine oil. If removed, slide the centralising spring onto the gearchange shaft, making sure the ends are correctly positioned each side of the selector arm tab **(see illustration)**.
15 Slide the stopper arm onto the shaft, making sure it is the correct way round, then fit the washer and the circlip **(see illustration)**.
16 Fit the washer onto the shaft, and the stopper arm spring onto the stopper arm, then install the gearchange shaft assembly into the crankcase.
17 Ensure that the centralising spring ends fit on each side of the locating pin and that the selector arm pawls engage the pins on the selector drum. Locate the stopper arm roller onto the neutral detent on the selector drum **(see illustrations 15.6a and b)**.
18 Hook the stopper arm spring over its anchor pin **(see illustration)**.
19 If removed, fit the dowels into the crankcase and lubricate the gearchange shaft oil seal with grease. Install the gearchange mechanism cover using a new gasket, ensuring the gasket and cover locate correctly onto the dowels, and tighten the cover bolts securely **(see illustration)**.
20 Install the remaining components in the reverse order of removal. **Note:** *To adjust the gearchange lever position, first loosen both locknuts on the linkage rod. Rotate the rod in one direction or the other to either raise or lower the lever height. Make sure the linkage rod length is within specification, then tighten both locknuts securely.*
21 Check the engine oil level and top up if necessary (see *Pre-ride checks*).

16 Oil cooler

Note: *This procedure can be carried out with the engine in the frame. If the engine has been removed, ignore the steps that do not apply.*

⚠ **Warning: Allow the engine to cool completely before starting work.**

Removal

1 The cooler is located on the front of the engine. Drain the engine oil and the coolant (see Chapter 1). Leave a drain tray under the cooler to catch residual oil and coolant as the cooler is removed.
2 Remove the radiator (see Chapter 3) and the exhaust system (see Chapter 4).
3 Loosen the clips securing the coolant inlet and outlet hoses to the oil cooler and detach the outlet hose from the top **(see illustrations)**.

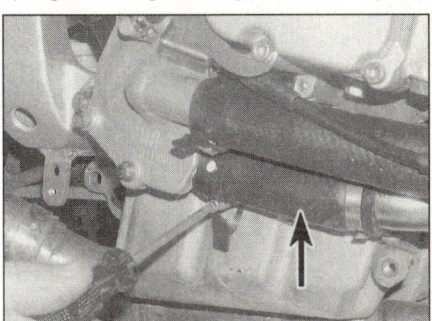

16.3a Loosen the clips on the water pump outlet hose (arrowed) . . .

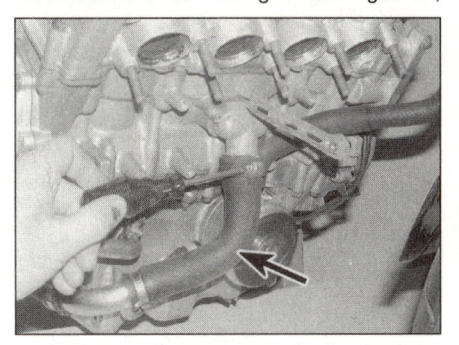

16.3b . . . the front water jacket hose (arrowed) . . .

16.3c . . . the oil cooler inlet hose . . .

2•34 Engine, clutch and transmission

16.3d ... and the oil cooler outlet hose ...

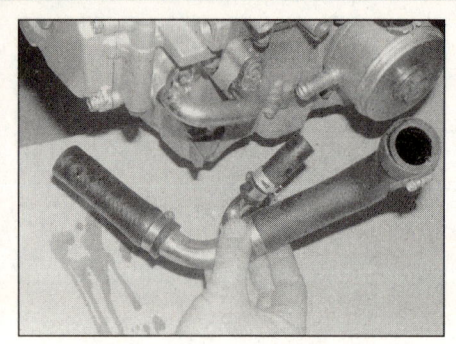

16.3e ... and detach the hoses

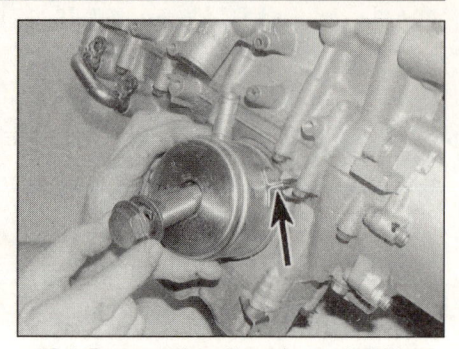

16.4 Remove the oil cooler, noting how the tab (arrowed) locates against the crankcase

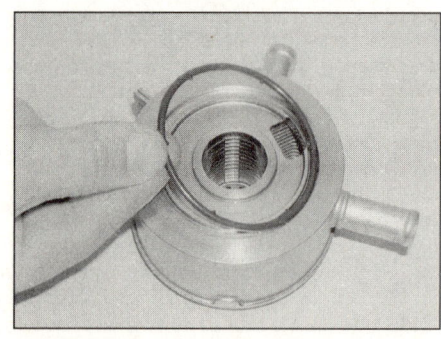

4 Unscrew the oil cooler centre bolt and remove the bolt, washer and oil cooler, detaching it from the inlet hose as you do. Note how the tab on the cooler body locates between the lugs on the crankcase **(see illustration)**.
5 Discard the washer and the O-ring from the cooler body as new ones must be fitted on reassembly.
6 Check the cooler body for cracks and dents and any evidence of coolant leakage and replace it with a new one if necessary. Also check the hoses for splits, cracks, hardening and deterioration and fit new ones if required.

Installation

7 Installation is the reverse of removal, noting the following:
- Clean the mating surfaces of the crankcase and the cooler with a rag and solvent.
- Before reassembly, lubricate the new O-ring with clean engine oil and ensure it seats correctly on the cooler body **(see illustration)**.
- Locate the tab on the cooler body between the lugs on the crankcase **(see illustration 16.4)**.
- Use a new washer on the centre bolt and lubricate its threads, and tighten it to the torque setting specified at the beginning of this Chapter.

- Make sure the coolant hoses are pressed fully onto their unions and tighten the clips securely.
- Refill the engine with oil and refill the cooling system, both to the correct levels (see Chapter 1 and *Pre-ride checks*).
- Start the engine and check that there are no leaks before taking the machine on the road.

17 Oil sump, oil strainer and pressure relief valve

Note: *This procedure can be carried out with the engine in the frame. If the engine has been removed, ignore the steps which do not apply.*

⚠️ **Warning: Allow the engine to cool completely before starting work.**

Removal

1 Raise or remove the fuel tank. Remove the radiator (see Chapter 3). Remove the exhaust system (see Chapter 4).
2 Drain the engine oil (see Chapter 1). Trace the wire from the oil level sensor underneath the sump and disconnect it at the connector **(see illustration 4.13a)**. Feed the wire through to the underside of the engine, noting its routing.

16.7 Use a new O-ring on the oil cooler body

3 Unscrew the sump bolts, noting there is one in the middle as well (13 in all), slackening them evenly in a criss-cross sequence to prevent distortion, and remove the sump **(see illustration)**. **Note:** *Do not unscrew the two bolts retaining the oil level sensor*. If necessary, break the gasket seal by tapping gently around the edge of the sump with a soft-faced hammer or block of wood; do not lever the sump off as this will damage the sealing surface. Note the position of the oil level sensor wiring clamp and the two lower fairing fixing brackets **(see illustration)**. Discard the gasket, as a new one must be

17.3a Unscrew the bolts (arrowed) and remove the sump

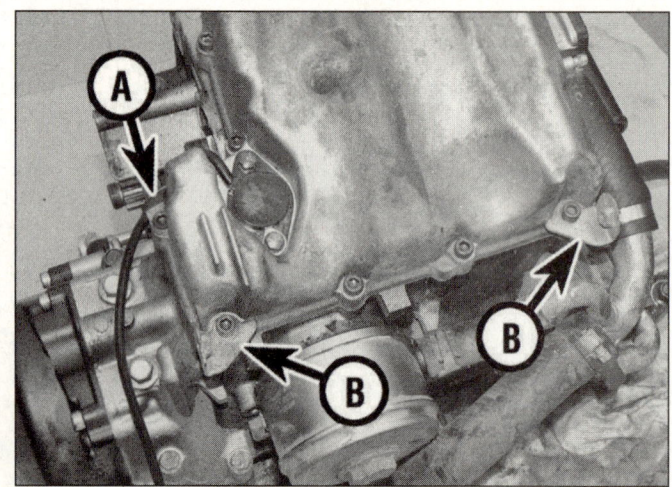

17.3b Note the position of the wiring clamp (A) and lower fairing brackets (B)

Engine, clutch and transmission 2•35

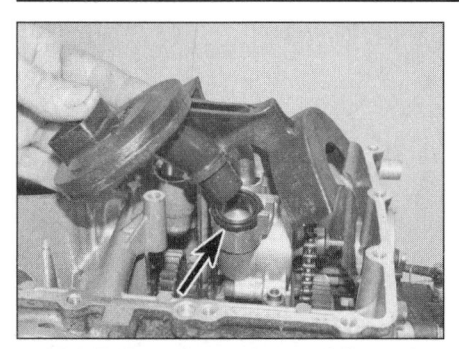

17.4 Pull out the strainer and the seal (arrowed)

17.5 Pull the pressure relief valve out of its socket

17.6 Clean the inside of the sump thoroughly

used. Note the positions of the dowels and remove them if they are loose.

4 Pull the oil strainer out of its socket in the oil pump, noting how the tab on the strainer locates between the lugs on the pump. Remove the seal and discard it as a new one must be fitted on reassembly **(see illustration)**.

5 Pull the pressure relief valve out of the crankcase **(see illustration)**. Discard the O-ring, as a new one must be fitted on reassembly.

Inspection

6 Remove all traces of gasket from the sump and crankcase mating surfaces, and clean the inside of the sump with a suitable solvent **(see illustration)**. Do not remove the oil level sensor unless it is necessary for testing the unit (see Chapter 8).

7 Clean the strainer in solvent, flushing it through from the inside, and remove any debris caught in the strainer mesh. Inspect the mesh for any signs of wear or damage and replace the strainer with a new one if necessary.

8 Push the relief valve plunger into the valve body and check that it moves smoothly and freely against spring pressure **(see illustration)**. If not, remove the circlip, noting that it is under spring pressure, and remove the spring seat, spring and plunger **(see illustrations)**. Clean all the components in solvent and check them for scoring, wear or damage. If any is found, replace the relief valve with a new one – individual components are not available. Otherwise, coat the inside of the valve body and the plunger with clean engine oil, then insert the plunger, spring and spring seat and secure them with the circlip. Check the action of the valve plunger again – if it is still suspect, replace the valve with a new one.

Installation

9 Fit a new O-ring onto the relief valve and smear it with grease **(see illustration)**. Push the valve into its socket in the crankcase **(see illustration 17.5)**.

10 Lubricate the new seal for the oil strainer with grease and fit it into the pump **(see illustrations)**. Fit the strainer into the seal and onto the pump, making sure the tab locates between the lugs and the arrow points to the front of the engine **(see illustration 17.4)**.

11 If removed, fit the sump dowels into the crankcase. Lay a new gasket onto the sump (if the engine is in the frame) or onto the crankcase (if the engine has been removed and is upside down on the work surface) **(see illustration)**. Make sure the holes in the gasket align correctly with the bolt holes.

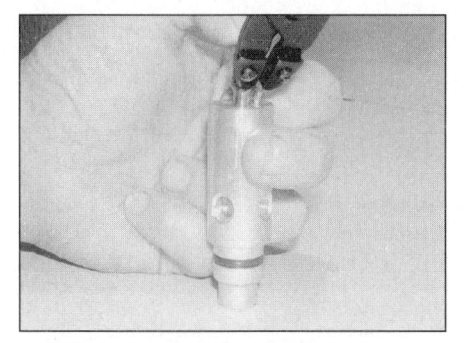

17.8a Press down on the spring seat to remove the circlip

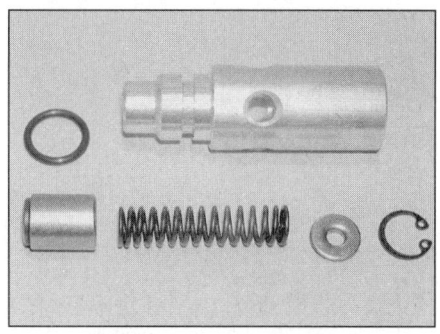

17.8b Disassemble the relief valve and examine the components

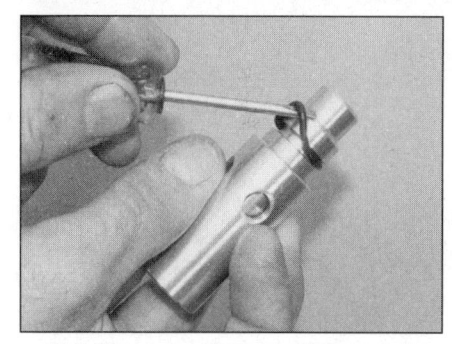

17.9 Fit an new O-ring and lubricate it

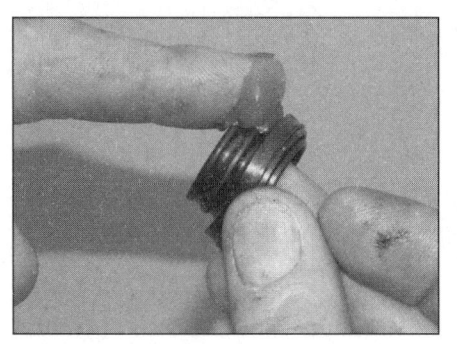

17.10a Lubricate the new seal . . .

17.10b . . . and fit it into the pump

17.11 Ensure the new gasket aligns with the dowels (arrowed) and sump bolt holes

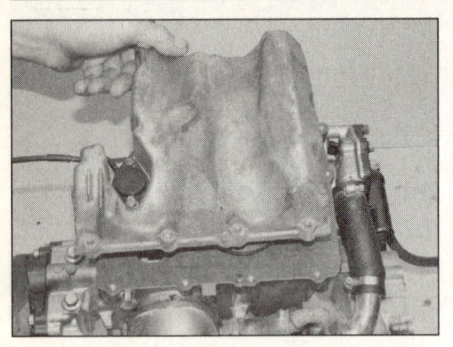

2•36 Engine, clutch and transmission

17.12a Fit the sump . . .

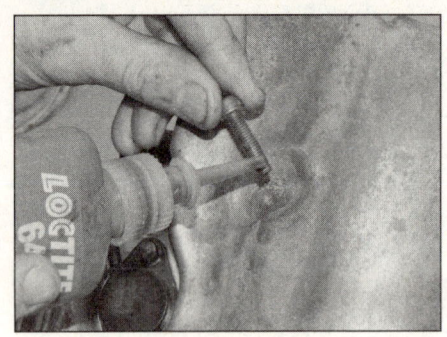

17.12b . . . and apply a thread lock to the central bolt

12 Position the sump on the crankcase, then install the bolts, the oil level sensor wiring clamp and the lower fairing fixing brackets **(see illustration and 17.3b)**. Apply a suitable non-permanent thread locking compound to the central bolt and tighten all bolts evenly and a little at a time in a criss-cross pattern to the specified torque setting **(see illustration)**.
13 Connect the oil level sensor wire at the connector **(see illustration 4.13a)**.

14 Install the exhaust system and the fuel tank (see Chapter 4), and the radiator (see Chapter 3).
15 Fill the engine with the correct type and quantity of oil and coolant (see Chapter 1 and *Pre-ride checks*).
16 Start the engine and check that there are no leaks around the sump before taking the machine on the road.

18 Oil pump

Note: *This procedure can be carried out with the engine in the frame. If the engine has been removed, ignore the steps which do not apply.*

⚠ **Warning: Allow the engine to cool completely before starting work.**

Removal

1 Remove the water pump (see Chapter 3).
2 Remove the sump and the oil strainer (see Section 17). If the engine is upside down on the bench, from here on take care not to drop any bolts as you remove them.
3 Unscrew the U-shaped oil pipe retaining bolts and pull the pipe out of its sockets in the crankcase **(see illustration)**. Discard the O-rings as new ones must be fitted on reassembly.
4 Unscrew the bolt retaining the oil return pipe and pull out the pipe **(see illustration)**.
5 Unscrew and remove the bolts securing the oil pump **(see illustration)**.
6 Tilt the pump to disengage the drive chain from the driven sprocket, then remove the pump from the engine **(see illustration)**. If the engine is upside down on the work surface, secure the chain with a length of wire to prevent it dropping into the crankcase. Note the dowels in the pump mounting lugs and remove them if they are loose.

Inspection

7 Unscrew the bolts securing the two halves of the oil pump body, then separate the body halves and remove the dowels **(see illustrations)**.
8 Remove the outer and inner pump rotors from the housing, noting how they fit **(see illustrations)**. The outer rotor is not marked

18.3 Unscrew the bolts (arrowed) and remove the U-shaped oil pipe . . .

18.4 . . . and the oil return pipe

18.5 Unscrew the bolts . . .

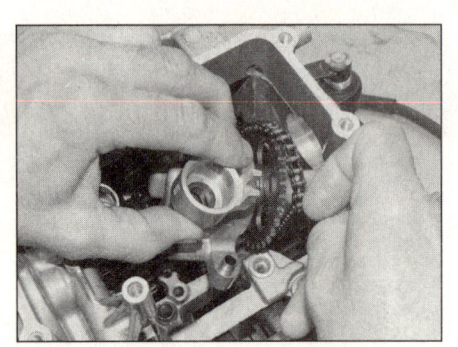

18.6 . . . then disengage the chain and remove the pump

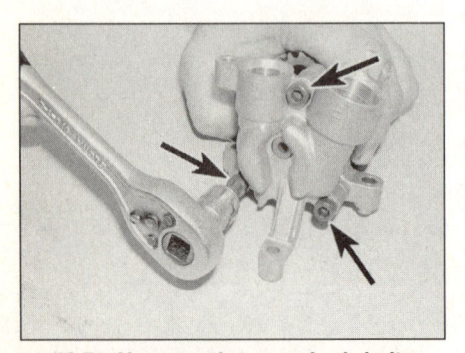

18.7a Unscrew the pump body bolts (arrowed) . . .

18.7b . . . and separate the body halves. Remove the dowels (arrowed)

18.8a First slide the outer . . .

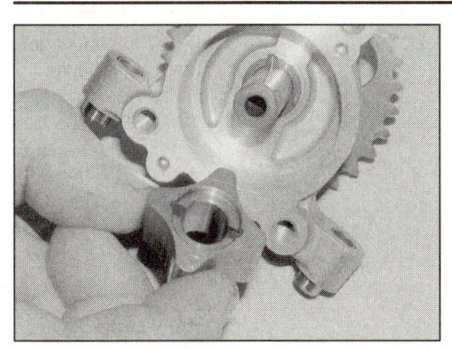

Engine, clutch and transmission 2•37

18.8b ... and then the inner rotor off the pump shaft

18.9a Withdraw the drive pin ...

18.9b ... and then remove the washer ...

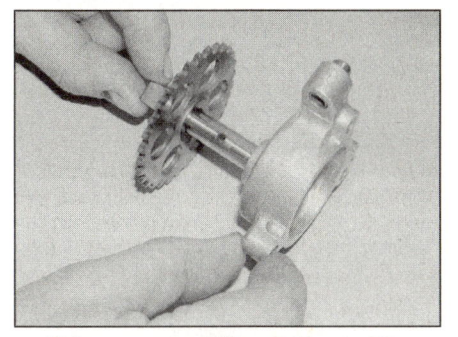

18.9c ... and pull the shaft out of the pump body

18.12 Measure the outer rotor to body clearance as shown

18.13 Measure the inner rotor tip to outer rotor clearance as shown

but it should be installed in the pump the same way round on reassembly.

9 Withdraw the drive pin from the shaft, noting how it locates in the slots in the inner rotor, then slide the washer off the shaft and pull the shaft out of the pump body **(see illustrations)**.

10 Clean all components in solvent. Check that the oilways in the body are clear by blowing them through with compressed air.

11 Inspect the components for scoring and wear. If any damage, scoring or uneven or excessive wear is evident, replace the pump with a new one – individual components are not available.

12 Reassemble the pump rotors in the housing and measure the clearance between the outer rotor and the pump body with a feeler gauge and compare it to the maximum clearance listed in the specifications at the beginning of this Chapter **(see illustration)**. If the clearance measured is greater than the maximum listed, replace the pump with a new one.

13 Measure the clearance between the inner rotor tip and the outer rotor with a feeler gauge and compare it to the maximum clearance listed in the specifications at the beginning of the Chapter **(see illustration)**. If the clearance measured is greater than the maximum listed, replace the pump with a new one.

14 Check the pump driven sprocket and the chain for wear or damage, and replace them with new ones if necessary. **Note:** *When replacing the chain and driven sprocket, also check the condition of the drive sprocket on the back of the clutch housing (see Section 13).*

15 If the pump is good, make sure all the components are clean, then lubricate them with clean engine oil. Fit the pump shaft through the pump body and install the washer and drive pin **(see illustration 18.9c, b and a)**. Slide the inner rotor onto the shaft so that the slots in the rotor locate over the drive pin then fit the outer rotor onto the inner rotor, remembering to install it the same way round as noted on removal **(see illustrations 18.8b and a)**.

16 Fit the dowels into the body, then fit the other half of the pump body over the rotors and the shaft **(see illustration 18.7b)**.

17 Install the bolts and tighten them to the torque setting specified at the beginning of this Chapter. Rotate the pump shaft by hand and check that the rotors turn freely. If not, strip and reassemble the pump.

Installation

18 Before installing the pump, prime it with clean engine oil and ensure that the dowels are in place on the mounting lugs.

19 Install the pump, tilting it to engage the driven sprocket with the drive chain **(see illustration 18.6)**. Ensure the chain is correctly routed between the guides on the inside of the crankcase **(see illustration 13.14)**.

20 Apply a suitable non-permanent thread locking compound to the pump bolts and tighten them to the torque setting specified at the beginning of this Chapter **(see illustration 18.5)**.

21 Fit the oil return pipe and tighten its bolt **(see illustration)**. Smear the new O-rings for the U-shaped oil pipe with grease and fit them onto the pipe **(see illustration)**. Fit the U-shaped pipe, then apply a suitable non-

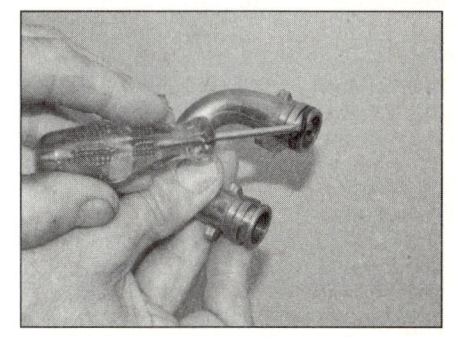

18.21a Fit the oil return pipe ...

18.21b ... then fit new O-rings onto the U-shaped pipe ...

2•38 Engine, clutch and transmission

permanent thread locking compound to its bolts and tighten them to the specified torque **(see illustration)**.

22 Install the oil strainer and the sump (see Section 17), then the water pump (see Chapter 3).

23 Fill the engine with the specified quantity and type of new engine oil and coolant (see Chapter 1 and *Pre-ride checks*).

19 Crankcase separation and reassembly

Note: *To separate the crankcase halves, the engine must be removed from the frame.*

Separation

1 To gain access to the connecting rods, pistons and rings, crankshaft, bearings, transmission shafts and selector drum and forks, the crankcase must be split into two parts.

2 Remove the engine from the frame (see Section 4). **Note:** *To reduce the weight of the engine, where possible remove as many of the components listed below before removing the engine from the frame.*

3 Before the crankcases can be separated the following components must be removed:

Camshafts and cam chain tensioner (Sections 7 and 8).
Cylinder head (Section 10).
Alternator rotor (Chapter 8).
Thermostat (Chapter 3).
Starter motor (Chapter 8).
Cam chain (Section 9).
Clutch (Section 13).
Gearchange mechanism (Section 15).
Oil cooler (Section 16).
Water pump (Chapter 3).
Oil sump, strainer and pressure relief valve (Section 17).
Oil pump and drive chain (Section 18).

4 Remove the oil filter and unscrew the filter fitting from the crankcase to gain access to crankcase bolt No. 12 **(see illustration)**.

> **HAYNES HINT** Make a cardboard template of the crankcase and punch a hole for each bolt location. Number the holes according to the cast numbers in the crankcase. As each bolt is removed, store it in its relative position, with its washer where applicable, in the template. This will ensure all bolts are installed correctly on reassembly – this is important, as many bolts differ slightly in length.

5 Turn the engine upside down. The crankcases are joined by twelve 8 mm bolts (Nos. 1 to 12) and fifteen 6 mm bolts (Nos. 13 to 27). Unscrew the bolts a quarter turn at a time in a **reverse** of the numerical sequence shown and as marked on the crankcase (the number of each bolt is cast into the crankcase), until they are finger-tight, then remove them and store them in the template to ensure correct installation (see **Haynes Hint**) **(see illustrations)**. Note the washers fitted to bolts Nos. 1 to 10.

6 Carefully lift the lower crankcase half off the upper half, using a soft-faced hammer or block of wood to tap around the joint to initially separate the halves, if necessary **(see illustration)**. **Note:** *If the halves do not separate easily, make sure all fasteners have been removed. Do not try and separate the halves by levering between the sealing surfaces as they are easily damaged and will leak oil on reassembly.*

7 Remove the three locating dowels from the

18.21c . . . and fit it into the crankcase

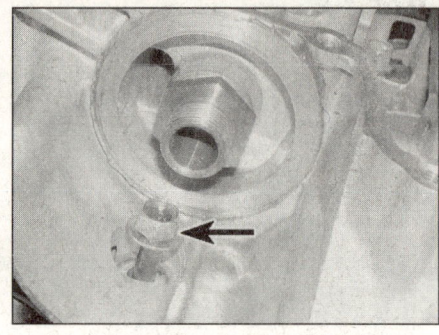

19.4 Remove the oil filter and fitting to access crankcase bolt No. 12 (arrowed)

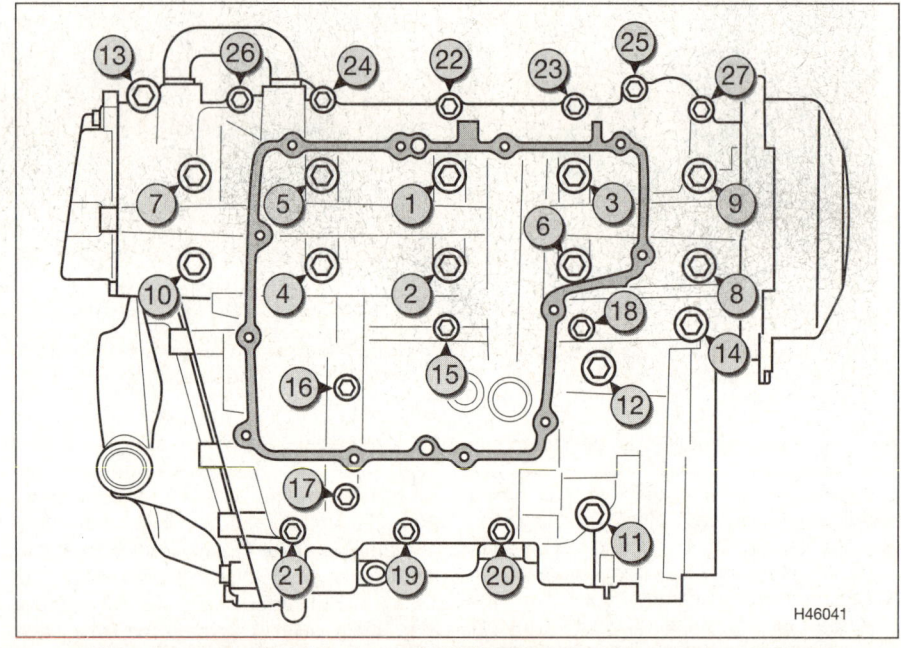

19.5a Crankcase bolt location and TIGHTENING sequence. Loosen bolts in REVERSE order

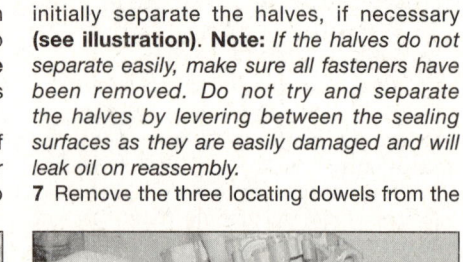

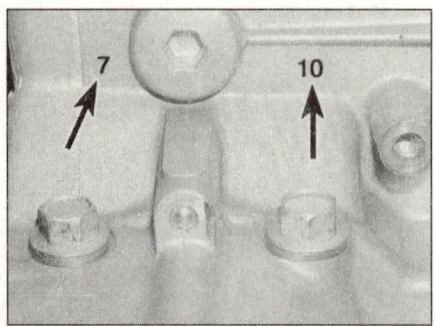

19.5b Bolt numbers (arrowed) are cast into the crankcase

19.6 Lift the lower half of the crankcase off the upper half

Engine, clutch and transmission 2•39

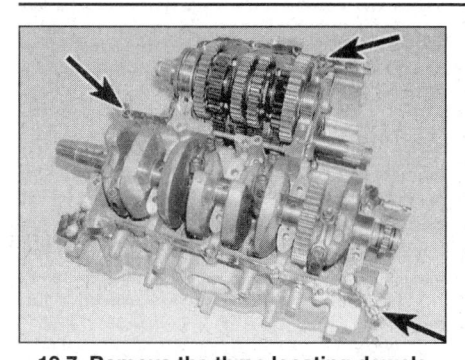

19.7 Remove the three locating dowels (arrowed) shown in the upper crankcase

19.10 It is best to fit a new output shaft oil seal before reassembly

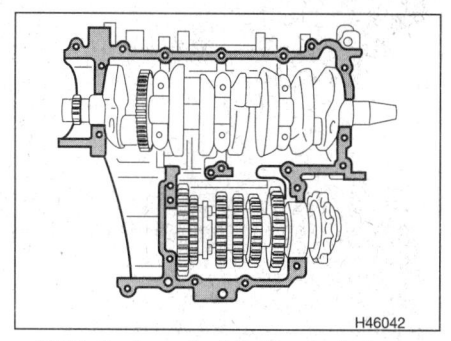

19.12 Apply sealant to the shaded area

crankcase (they could be in either half) **(see illustration)**.

8 Refer to Sections 20 to 28 for the removal and installation of the components housed within the crankcases.

Reassembly

9 Remove all traces of sealant from the crankcase mating surfaces.

10 Ensure that all components and their bearings are in place in the upper and lower crankcase halves. If the transmission shafts have not been removed, check the condition of the oil seal on the left-hand end of the output shaft and replace it with a new one if it is damaged, deformed or deteriorated – it is wise to fit a new seal whatever the perceived condition of the existing one (you wouldn't want to discover a leak after the engine has been rebuilt and put back in the frame) **(see illustration)**. Apply some grease to the inside of the new seal on installation. Check that the selector drum is in the neutral position.

11 Generously lubricate the crankshaft, transmission shafts and selector drum and forks, particularly around the bearings, with clean engine oil, then use a rag soaked in high flash-point solvent to wipe over the mating surfaces of both crankcase halves to remove all traces of oil.

12 Apply a small amount of suitable sealant (such as Yamaha Bond 1215) to the mating surface of one crankcase half as shown **(see illustration)**.
Caution: Do not apply an excessive amount

of sealant as it will ooze out when the case halves are assembled and may obstruct oil passages. Do not apply the sealant on or too close (within 2 to 3 mm) to any of the bearing shells or surfaces.

13 If removed, fit the three locating dowels into the crankcase **(see illustration 19.7)**.

14 Check again that all components are in position, particularly that the bearing shells are located in their seats in the lower crankcase half, then fit the lower crankcase half onto the upper crankcase half, making sure the dowels locate correctly.

15 Check that the lower crankcase half is seated correctly. **Note:** *The crankcase halves should fit together without being forced. If the casings are not correctly seated, remove the lower crankcase half and investigate the problem. Do not attempt to pull them together using the crankcase bolts as the casing will crack and be ruined.* Rotate the transmission selector drum to ensure that the gears select correctly and investigate any problems before bolting the crankcase halves together.

16 Clean the threads of the crankcase bolts and lubricate the threads of all except bolt No 18 **(see illustration 19.5a)** with clean engine oil. Lubricate the underside of the heads and washers of bolt Nos. 1 to 10. Apply a suitable thread locking compound to the threads of bolt No. 18.

17 Install the bolts in their correct locations and secure them finger-tight **(see illustration)**. First tighten bolt Nos. 1 to 10 in the correct numerical sequence as marked and as shown

(see illustration 19.5a) to the first stage torque setting specified at the beginning of the Chapter, then tighten them in the same sequence to the 2nd stage torque setting. Now reverse the sequence (i.e. 10 to 1) and loosen the bolts. Now tighten them in the correct sequence (1 to 10) to the 3rd stage torque setting specified. Now tighten bolts 11 to 27, evenly and a little at a time, in the correct numerical sequence as marked on the crankcase and as shown **(see illustration 19.5a)**, to the torque settings specified at the beginning of this Chapter **(see illustration)**.

18 With all crankcase bolts tightened, check that the crankshaft and transmission shafts rotate smoothly and easily. Check that all gears can be selected and that the shafts rotate freely in every gear. If there are any signs of undue stiffness, rough spots, or of any other problem, the fault must be rectified before proceeding further.

19 Install all the removed assemblies in the reverse order of removal, according to your procedure (see Steps 2 and 3).

20 Main and big-end bearing information

1 Even though main and connecting rod bearings are generally replaced with new ones during an engine overhaul, the old bearings should be carefully examined as they can reveal valuable information about the condition of the engine.

2 Bearing failure occurs mainly because of lack of lubrication, the presence of dirt or other foreign particles, overloading the engine and/or corrosion. Regardless of the cause of bearing failure, it must be corrected before the engine is reassembled to prevent it from happening again.

3 When examining the bearings, match them with their corresponding journal on the crankshaft to help identify the cause of any problem.

4 Dirt and other foreign particles get into the engine in a variety of ways. They may be left in the engine during assembly or they may pass through filters or breathers, then get into the oil and from there into the bearings. Metal

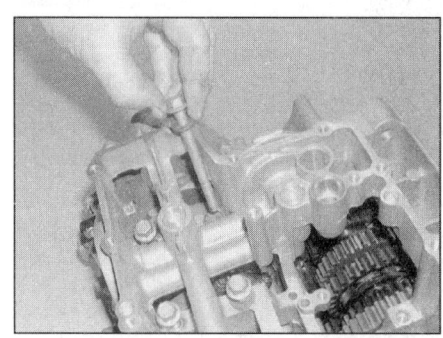

19.17a Ensure the bolts are refitted in their correct locations, with washers as required . . .

19.17b . . . and then tightened in sequence to the specified torques

chips from machining operations and normal engine wear are often present. Abrasives are sometimes left in engine components after reconditioning operations, especially when parts are not thoroughly cleaned using the proper cleaning methods. Whatever the source, foreign objects often end up imbedded in the soft bearing material and are easily recognised. Large particles will not imbed in the bearing and will score or gouge the bearing and journal. The best prevention for this type of bearing failure is to clean all parts thoroughly and keep everything spotlessly clean during engine reassembly. Regular oil and filter changes are also essential.

5 Lack of lubrication or lubrication breakdown have a number of interrelated causes. Excessive heat (which thins the oil), overloading (which squeezes the oil from the bearing face) and oil leakage or throw off (from excessive bearing clearances, a worn oil pump or high engine speeds) all contribute to a breakdown of the protective lubricating film. Blocked oil passages will starve a bearing of lubrication and destroy it. When lack of lubrication is the cause of bearing failure, the bearing material is wiped or extruded from the steel backing of the bearing. Temperatures may increase to the point where the steel backing and the journal turn blue from overheating.

HAYNES HiNT *Refer to Tools and Workshop Tips (Section 5) in the Reference section for bearing fault finding.*

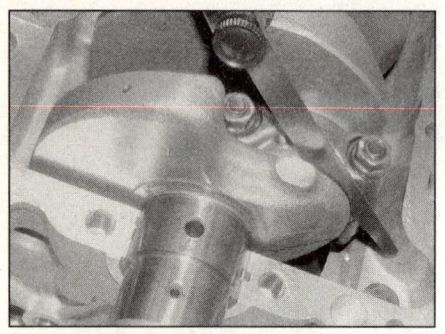

6 Riding habits can have a definite effect on bearing life. Full throttle, low speed operation, or labouring the engine, puts very high loads on bearings, which tend to squeeze out the oil film. These loads cause the bearings to flex, which produces fine cracks in the bearing face (fatigue failure). Eventually the bearing material will loosen in pieces and tear away from the steel backing. Short trip riding leads to corrosion of bearings, as insufficient engine heat is produced to drive off the condensed water and corrosive gases produced. These products collect in the engine oil, forming acid and sludge. As the oil is carried to the engine bearings, the acid attacks and corrodes the bearing material.

7 Incorrect bearing installation during engine assembly will lead to bearing failure as well. Tight fitting bearings which leave insufficient bearing oil clearances result in oil starvation. Dirt or foreign particles trapped behind a bearing insert result in high spots on the bearing which lead to failure.

8 To avoid bearing problems, clean all parts thoroughly before reassembly, double check all bearing clearance measurements and lubricate the new bearings with clean engine oil during installation.

21 Connecting rods and bearings

Note: *To remove the connecting rods the engine must be removed from the frame.*

21.2 Measuring the connecting rod side clearance with a feeler gauge

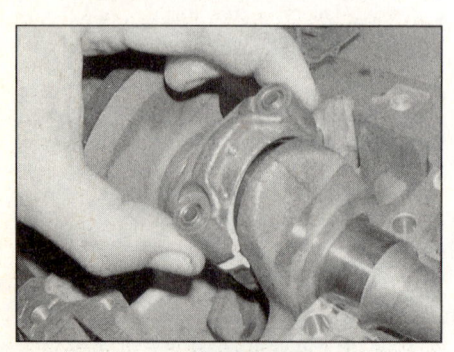

21.4a Unscrew the nuts (arrowed) . . .

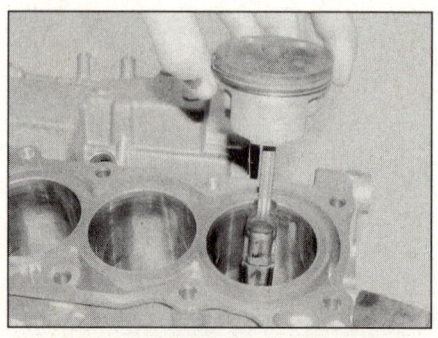

21.4b . . . and pull the cap off the connecting rod

21.6 Remove each piston and connecting rod from the top of its bore

On installation new rod bolts and nuts must be used, so it is wise to obtain them before commencing work.

Removal

1 Remove the engine from the frame (see Section 4) and separate the crankcase halves (see Section 19).

2 Before separating the rods from the crankshaft, measure the side clearance on each rod with a feeler gauge **(see illustration)**. If the clearance on any rod is greater than the service limit listed in this Chapter's Specifications, replace that rod with a new one.

3 Using paint or a marker pen, mark the cylinder identity on the top of each piston and on each connecting rod and cap. Cylinders are numbered 1 to 4 from the left-hand side of the motorcycle (as seated). Note that the number and letter already written on the rod and cap are the rod size code and weight grade respectively, not the cylinder number.

4 Unscrew the connecting rod cap nuts and separate the caps, complete with the lower bearing shells from the crankpins **(see illustrations)**. If a cap appears stuck, tap it on one end with a hammer while pulling it.

5 Detach the connecting rods, complete with the upper bearing shells, from the crankpins, then lift the crankshaft out of the upper crankcase half, taking care not to dislodge the main bearing shells **(see illustration 24.2)**. If required, remove the main bearing shells from the crankcase halves by pushing their centres to the side, then lifting them out **(see illustration 24.3)** – it is imperative that the shells are kept in order so that they can be returned to their original locations.

6 Raise the front of the crankcase and rest it on some wood, or turn it onto its side. Push each piston/connecting rod assembly to the top end of the cylinder bore and remove it, making sure the connecting rod does not mark the bore walls **(see illustration)**. Note the 'Y' mark on each connecting rod that must face to the left-hand side of the engine **(see illustration 21.27)**, and the arrow on the top of each piston which points to the front of the engine **(see illustration 22.2)**. If this is not visible, mark the piston accordingly so that it can be installed the correct way round.

HAYNES HiNT *To ease removal of the pistons, carefully remove any ridge of carbon built up on the top of each cylinder bore using a scraper. If there is a pronounced wear ridge, remove it using a ridge reamer.*

Caution: *Do not try to remove the piston/connecting rod from the bottom of the cylinder bore. The piston will not pass the crankcase main bearing webs. If the piston is pulled right to the bottom of the bore the oil control ring will expand and lock the piston in position. If this happens it is likely the ring will be broken.*

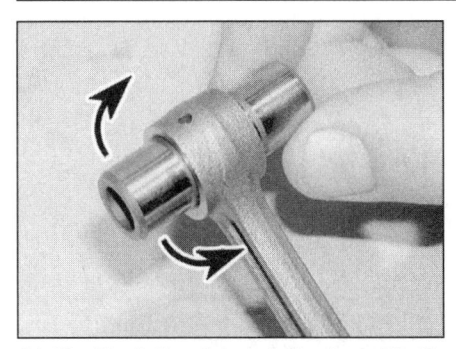

21.10a Rock the piston pin back and forth in the small-end to check for looseness

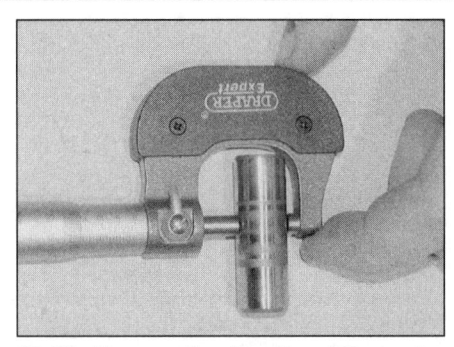

21.10b Measure the diameter at the centre of the pin

7 Fit the related bearing shells (if removed), bearing cap, and bolts on each piston/connecting rod assembly so that they are all kept together as a matched set. **Note:** *New big-end bolts must be used on final assembly. Use the old bolts and nuts for the oil clearance check, then discard them.*

8 Separate the pistons from the connecting rods (see Section 22).

Inspection

9 Check the connecting rods for cracks and other obvious damage.

10 Apply clean engine oil to the piston pin, insert it into its connecting rod small-end and check for any freeplay between the two **(see illustration)**. If freeplay is excessive, measure the external diameter at the centre of the pin **(see illustration)**. Compare the result to the specifications at the beginning of this Chapter. Replace the pin with a new one if it is worn beyond its specified limits. If the pin diameter is within specifications, replace the connecting rod with a new one. Repeat the measurements for all the pins and rods.

11 Refer to Section 20 and examine the connecting rod bearing shells. If they are scored, badly scuffed or appear to have seized, new shells must be installed. Always renew the shells in the connecting rods as a set. If they are badly damaged, check the corresponding crankpin. Evidence of extreme heat, such as bluing, indicates that lubrication failure has occurred. Be sure to thoroughly check the oil pump and pressure relief valve as well as all oil holes and passages before reassembling the engine.

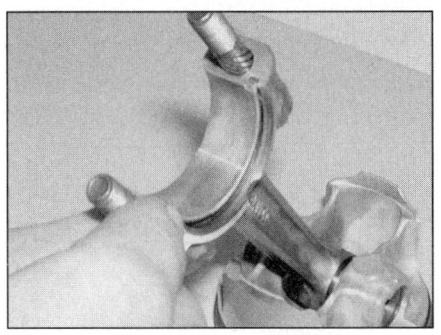

12 Have the rods checked by a Yamaha dealer if you are in doubt about their straightness.

Oil clearance check

Note: *It is essential that, throughout this procedure, the connecting rod does not rotate on the crankshaft. If the procedure is being carried out on a bench find some way of clamping the crankshaft so it cannot move, and also the connecting rod once it has been fitted onto its journal. The alternative is to fit the rod and piston back into its bore and lay the crankshaft in the crankcase to keep them held.*

13 Whether new bearing shells are being fitted or the original ones are being re-used, the connecting rod big-end bearing oil clearance should be checked prior to reassembly. Bearing oil clearance is measured with a product known as Plastigauge.

14 Remove the bearing shells from the rods and caps, keeping them in order **(see illustration)**. Clean the backs of the shells, the bearing locations in both the connecting rod and cap, and the crankpin journal with a suitable solvent.

15 Press the bearing shells into their locations, ensuring that the tab on each shell engages the notch in the connecting rod or cap **(see illustration)**. Make sure the bearings are fitted in the correct locations and take care not to touch any shell's bearing surface with your fingers.

16 Working on one rod at a time, cut an appropriate size length of Plastigauge (it should be slightly shorter than the width of the crankpin) and place it on the crankpin journal to be checked **(see illustration 24.12)**. Do not place Plastigauge over the oil holes in the journal.

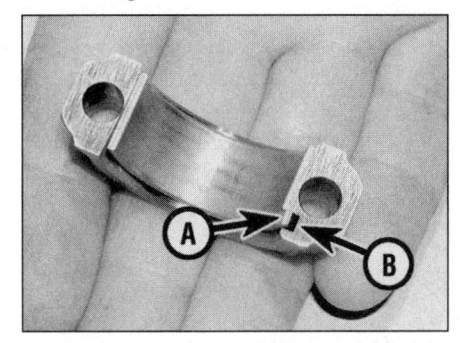

17 Apply molybdenum disulphide grease to the shanks and threads of the bolts and to the seats of the nuts. Fit the connecting rod and cap onto the crankpin **(see illustration 21.34)**. Make sure the cap is fitted the correct way around so the previously made markings align (see Step 3), and that the 'Y' mark on the rod is facing to the left-hand end of the crankshaft (see Step 6). Fit the nuts and tighten them finger-tight. **Note:** *It is essential that, throughout this procedure, the connecting rod does not rotate on the crankshaft.*

18 Tighten the nuts to the initial torque setting specified at the beginning of this Chapter with a torque wrench **(see illustration 21.36a)**. Now tighten each nut in turn and in one continuous movement through the specified angle using a torque angle gauge **(see illustration 21.36b)**. If tightening is paused between the initial and final settings, slacken the nut to below the initial setting and repeat the procedure. **Note:** *If a torque angle gauge is not available, paint a small reference mark on one point of the nut hex after tightening the nut to the initial torque setting, then go clockwise around the nut a distance of two and a half flats and paint another mark corresponding to this on the connecting rod – the angle between two flats is 60°, so going through two and a half flats is 150°. Now, using a ring spanner so that you can see the two marks, tighten the nut clockwise until the marks align.*

19 Slacken the nuts and remove the cap and rod from the crankshaft.

20 Compare the width of the crushed Plastigauge on the crankpin to the scale printed on the Plastigauge envelope to obtain the connecting rod bearing oil clearance **(see illustration 24.16)**. Compare the reading to the specifications at the beginning of this Chapter. If the clearance is within the range specified and the bearings are in perfect condition, they can be reused.

21 Carefully clean away all traces of the Plastigauge from the crankpin journal and bearing shells using a fingernail or other object which will not score the bearing surfaces.

22 If the clearance is beyond the service limit, replace the bearing shells with new ones (see Steps 25 and 26) and check the oil clearance once again. Always renew all of the shells at the same time.

23 If the clearance is still greater than the service limit listed in this Chapter's Specifications, the big-end bearing journal is worn and the crankshaft should be replaced with a new one.

24 Repeat the procedure for the remaining connecting rods, then discard the old big-end bolts and nuts.

21.14 To remove a big-end bearing shell, push it sideways and then lift it out

21.15 Ensure tab (A) locates in notch (B)

2•42 Engine, clutch and transmission

21.25a Main bearing journal numbers (A) and big-end bearing journal numbers (B)

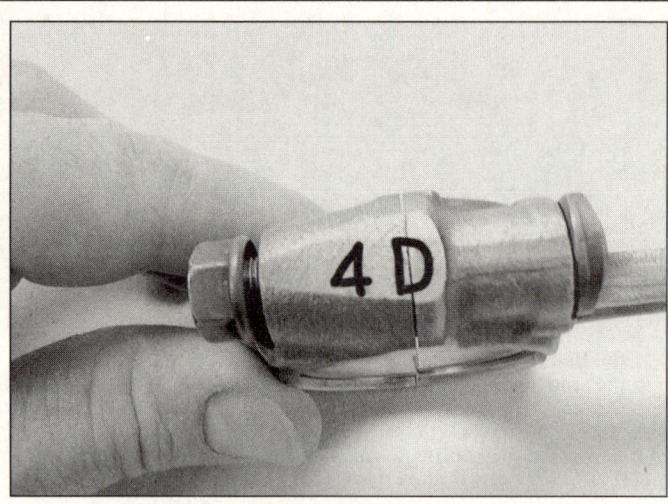

21.25b Connecting rod size code number

Bearing shell selection

25 Replacement bearing shells for the big-end bearings are supplied on a selected fit basis. Code numbers for the crankshaft journals are stamped on the outside of the crankshaft web on the left-hand end of the crankshaft **(see illustration)**. The right-hand block of four numbers are the size codes for the big-end bearing journals (the left-hand block of five numbers are the size codes for the main bearing journals). The first number of the block is for the left-hand (No. 1 cylinder) journal, and so on. Each connecting rod size code number is marked in ink on the flat face of the connecting rod and cap **(see illustration)**.

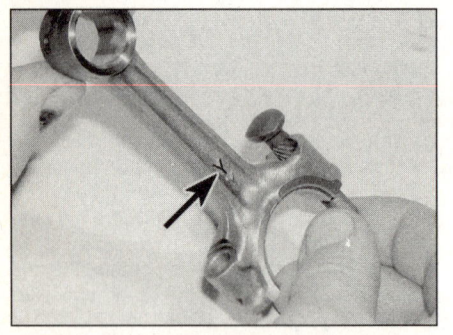

26 A range of bearing shells are available. To select the correct shells for a particular journal, subtract the big-end bearing journal number from the connecting rod number and compare the result with the table below to find the colour coding of the replacement shells, e.g. connecting rod number 4 minus journal number 2 = 2; No. 2 bearing shells are colour coded black. The colour code is marked on the side of each bearing shell.

Number	Colour
1	blue
2	black
3	brown
4	green

Installation

27 New big-end bolts and nuts must be used on reassembly. Note the alignment of the bolt head with the recess in the connecting rod, then press the old bolt out of the rod. Align the head of the new bolt with the recess in the rod and press the bolt into place **(see illustration)**.

28 Fit the pistons onto the connecting rods (see Section 22).

29 Ensure that the backs of the bearing shells, the bearing seats in the caps and rods and the crankpin journals are clean. If new shells are being fitted, ensure that all traces of protective grease are removed using paraffin (kerosene). Dry the shells, caps, rods and journals with a clean, lint-free cloth. Install the shells, making sure the tab on each shell engages the notch in the cap or rod **(see illustration 21.15)**.

30 Make sure the bearings are fitted in their correct locations and take care not to touch any bearing surfaces with your fingers. Lubricate the shells with clean engine oil.

31 Lubricate the pistons, rings and cylinder bores with clean engine oil. Insert the piston/connecting rod assembly into the top of its bore, taking care not to allow the connecting rod to mark the bore. Make sure the arrow on the top of the piston points to the front and the 'Y' mark on the rod faces the left-hand side of the engine (see Step 6).

32 Stagger the piston ring end gaps (see Section 23) and carefully compress and feed each piston ring into the bore until the piston crown is flush with the top of the bore. If available, a piston ring compressor makes installation a lot easier **(see illustrations)**.

33 Lower the crankshaft into position in the upper crankcase, making sure all the main bearing shells are in place (see Section 24).

34 Working on one connecting rod at a time, lubricate the crankpin and the shells in the connecting rod and cap with clean engine oil. Apply molybdenum disulphide grease to the

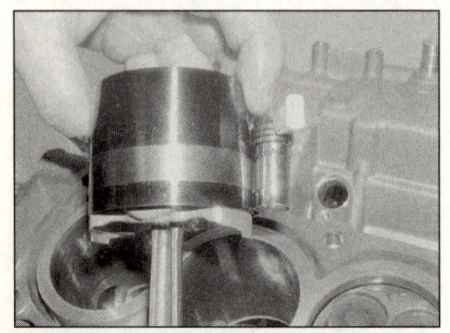

21.27 Align the bolt head with the recess in the rod. Note the 'Y' mark (arrowed)

21.32a With the ring ends staggered, fit the ring compressor over the piston...

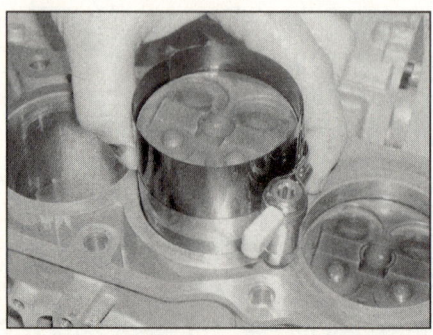

21.32b ...then insert the rod assembly into the top of the bore...

21.32c ...and carefully press the piston into the bore

Engine, clutch and transmission 2•43

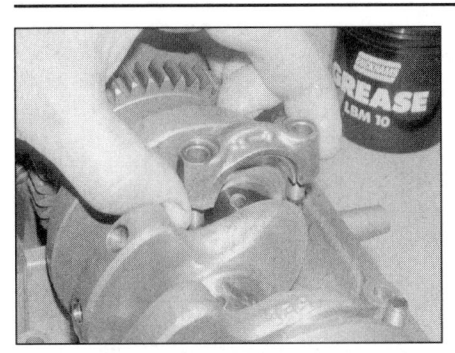

21.34 Align the markings and fit the big-end cap onto the rod . . .

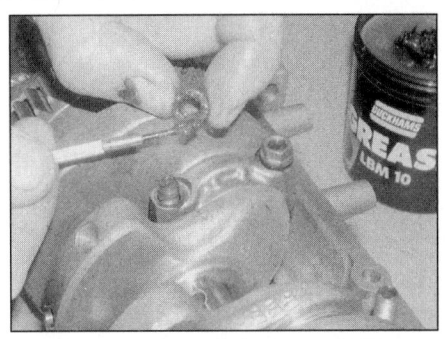

21.35 . . . then install the cap nuts finger-tight

21.36a Tighten the nuts to the initial torque setting with a torque wrench . . .

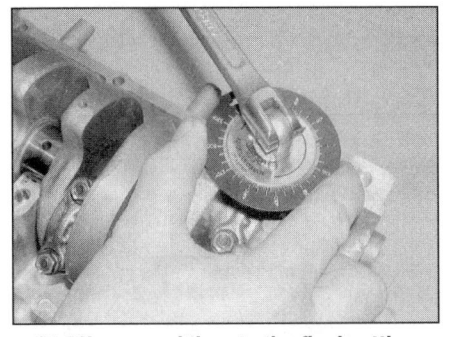

21.36b . . . and then to the final setting with a torque angle gauge

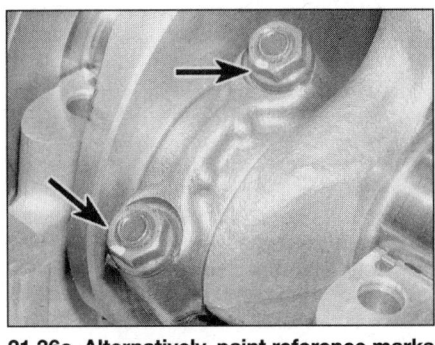

21.36c Alternatively, paint reference marks (arrowed) on the nuts . . .

21.36d . . . and tighten them finally with a ring spanner as described

shanks and threads of the new big-end bolts. Pull the rod onto the crankpin and fit the cap onto the rod **(see illustration)**. Make sure the cap is fitted the correct way around so the previously made markings align (see Step 3).

35 Apply molybdenum disulphide grease to the seats of the new nuts, then fit the nuts and tighten them finger-tight **(see illustration)**. Check that all components have been returned to their original locations using the marks made on disassembly.

36 Tighten the nuts to the initial torque setting specified at the beginning of this Chapter with a torque wrench **(see illustration)**. Now tighten each nut in turn and in one continuous movement through the specified angle using a torque angle gauge **(see illustration)**. If tightening is paused between the initial and final settings, slacken the nut to below the initial setting and repeat the procedure. Fit the remaining rods onto the crankshaft in the same way. **Note:** *If a torque angle gauge is not available, paint a small reference mark on one point of the nut hex after tightening the nut to the initial torque setting, then go clockwise around the nut a distance of two and a half flats as shown and paint another mark corresponding to this on the connecting rod – the angle between two flats is 60°, so going through two and a half flats is 150°. Now, using a ring spanner so that you can see the two marks, tighten the nut clockwise until the marks align* **(see illustrations)**.

37 Lubricate the bores liberally with clean engine oil and check that the crankshaft rotates smoothly and freely. If there are any signs of roughness or tightness, detach the rods and recheck the assembly. Sometimes tapping the bottom of the connecting rod cap will relieve tightness.

38 Reassemble the crankcase halves (see Section 19).

22 Pistons

Note: *To remove the pistons the engine must be removed from the frame.*

Removal

1 Remove the engine from the frame (see Section 4), separate the crankcase halves (see Section 19). Remove the piston/connecting rod assemblies (see Section 21).

2 Before removing the piston from the connecting rod, ensure it is marked with its cylinder identity. If the piston is going to be cleaned, scratch the identity lightly on the inside of the piston skirt. Each piston must be installed in its original cylinder on reassembly. Note the arrow on the top of each piston that points to the front of the engine **(see illustration)**. If this is not visible, mark the piston accordingly so that it can be installed the correct way round.

3 Carefully prise out the circlips on each side of the piston pin using needle-nose pliers or a small flat-bladed screwdriver inserted into the notch **(see illustration)**. Check for burring around the circlip grooves and remove any with a very fine file or knife blade, then push

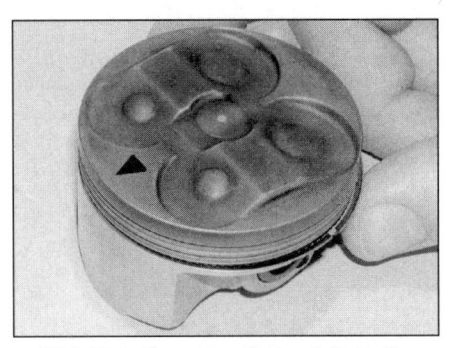

22.2 Note the arrow that points to the front of the engine

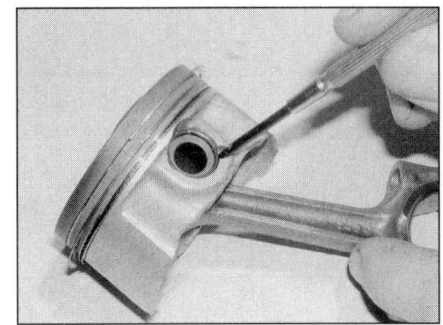

22.3a Prise out the circlip . . .

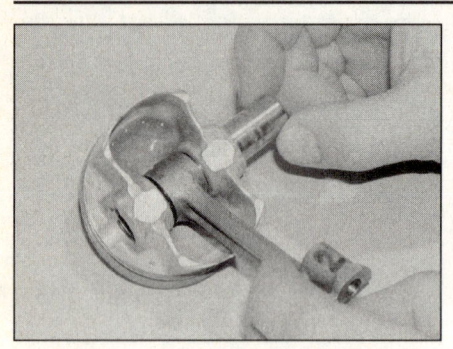

2•44 Engine, clutch and transmission

22.3b . . . then push out the pin and remove the piston

22.4a Removing the piston rings using a ring removal and installation tool

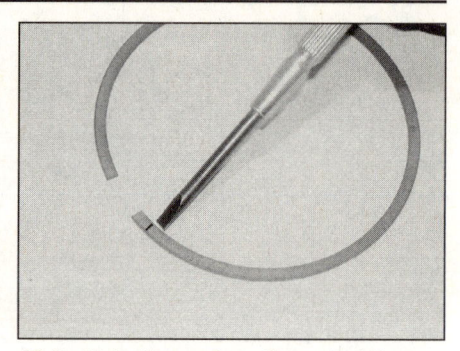

22.4b Note the mark on the end of the two top rings (compression)

the piston pin out to free the piston from the connecting rod **(see illustration)**. Discard the circlips as new ones must be used on reassembly. When the piston has been removed from the rod, keep the piston and its pin together so that related parts do not get mixed up.

HAYNES HiNT *If a piston pin is a tight fit in the piston, soak a rag in boiling water then wring it out and wrap it around the piston – this will expand the alloy piston sufficiently to release its grip on the pin. If the piston pin is particularly stubborn, extract it using a drawbolt tool, but be careful to protect the piston's working surfaces.*

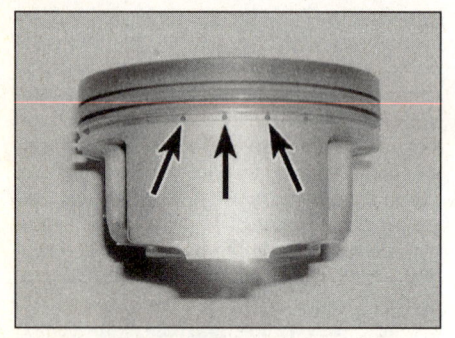

4 Using your thumbs or a piston ring removal and installation tool, carefully remove the rings from the pistons, working on one piston at a time **(see illustration)**. Do not nick or gouge the pistons in the process. Note which way up each ring fits and in which groove, as they must be installed in their original positions if being re-used. The upper surface of the two top rings (compression rings) should have a manufacturer's mark or letter at one end – if the mark on each ring is different, note which mark is for the top ring and which is for the second **(see illustration)**.

5 Scrape all traces of carbon from the tops of the pistons. A hand-held wire brush or a piece of fine emery cloth can be used once most of the deposits have been scraped away. Do not, under any circumstances, use a wire brush mounted in a drill motor; the piston material is soft and is easily damaged.

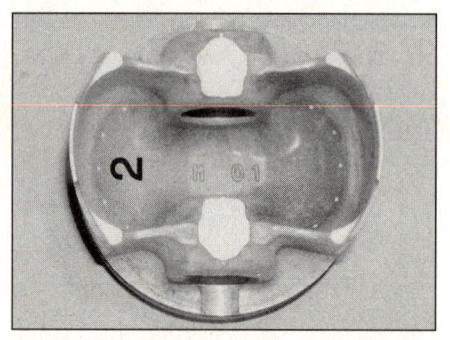

6 Use a piston ring groove cleaning tool to remove any carbon deposits from the ring grooves. If a tool is not available, a piece broken off an old ring will do the job. Be very careful to remove only the carbon deposits. Do not remove any metal and do not nick or gouge the sides of the ring grooves.

7 Once the carbon has been removed, clean the pistons with a suitable solvent and dry them thoroughly. Make sure the oil return holes at the back of the oil ring groove are clear **(see illustration)**. If the identification mark previously applied to the piston is cleaned off, be sure to re-mark it correctly **(see illustration)**.

Inspection

8 Inspect each piston for cracks around the skirt, at the pin bosses and at the ring lands. Normal piston wear appears as even, vertical wear on the thrust surfaces of the piston and slight looseness of the top ring in its groove. If the skirt is scored or scuffed, the engine may have been suffering from overheating and/or abnormal combustion, resulting in excessively high operating temperatures.

9 A hole in the top of the piston (only likely in extreme circumstances), or burned areas around the edge of the piston crown, indicate that pre-ignition or knocking under load have occurred. If you find evidence of any problems the cause must be corrected or the damage will occur again (see *Fault Finding* in the *Reference* section).

10 Check the piston-to-bore clearance by measuring the bore (see Section 28) and the piston diameter. Make sure each piston is matched to its correct cylinder. Measure the piston 4 mm up from the bottom of the skirt and at 90° to the piston pin axis **(see illustration)**. Subtract the piston diameter from the bore diameter to obtain the clearance. If it is greater than the figure specified at the beginning of this Chapter, check whether it is the bore or piston that is worn beyond its service limit. If the bores are good, install new pistons and rings. If the bores are worn, replace the crankcases, pistons and rings.

11 Measure the piston ring-to-groove clearance by laying each compression ring in its groove and slipping a feeler gauge in beside it **(see illustration)**. Make sure you have the

22.7a Ensure that the oil return holes (arrowed) are clear . . .

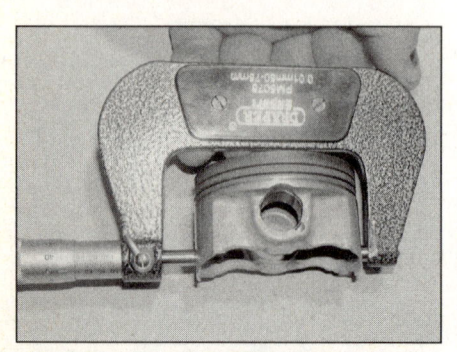

22.7b . . . and that the piston is still clearly marked

22.10 Measuring the piston diameter with a micrometer

22.11 Measuring the piston ring-to-groove clearance with a feeler gauge

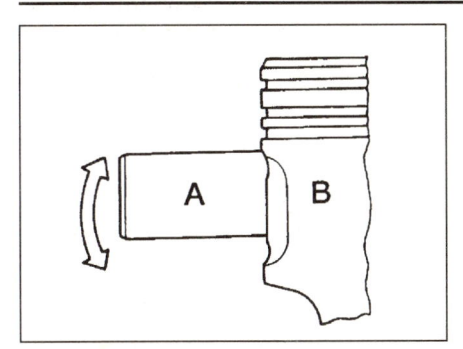

Engine, clutch and transmission 2•45

22.12a Insert the pin (A) into the piston (B) and try to rock it back and forth. If the pin is loose . . .

22.12b . . . measure the pin external diameter and the pin bore in the piston

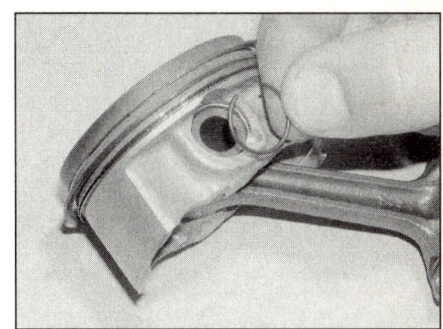

22.15 Fit the circlip with the open end away from the removal notch

correct ring for the groove (see Step 4). Check the clearance at three or four locations around the groove. If the clearance is greater than specified, renew both the piston and rings as a set. If new rings are being used, measure the clearance using the new rings. If the clearance is greater than that specified, the piston is worn and must be replaced with a new one.

12 Apply clean engine oil to the piston pin, insert it part way into the piston and check for any freeplay between the two **(see illustration)**. Measure the pin external diameter at each end, and the pin bores in the piston **(see illustration)**. Subtract the pin diameter from the bore diameter to obtain the clearance. If it is greater than the specified figure, check whether it is the bore or pin that is worn beyond its service limit and replace them with new ones as required. Check for excessive play between the pin and the connecting rod small-end (see Section 21).

Installation

13 Inspect and install the piston rings (see Section 23).
14 Install a **new** circlip into one side of the piston (never re-use old circlips), then lubricate the piston pin, the piston pin bore and the connecting rod small-end bore with clean engine oil.
15 Line up the piston on its connecting rod so that the arrow on the top of the piston will point to the front and the 'Y' mark on the rod will face the left-hand side of the engine when they are installed. Insert the piston pin from the side without the circlip **(see illustration 22.3b)**. Secure the pin with the other **new** circlip. When installing the circlips, compress them only just enough to fit them in the piston, and make sure they are properly seated in their grooves with the open end away from the removal notch **(see illustration)**.
16 Install the connecting rods (see Section 21).

23 Piston rings

1 It is good practice to fit new piston rings when an engine is being overhauled. Before installing the rings on the pistons, the ring end gaps must be checked with the rings installed in the cylinder.

Inspection

2 Lay out each piston with its new ring set so the rings will be matched with the same piston and cylinder during the measurement procedure and engine reassembly. The upper surface of the two top rings (compression rings) should have a manufacturer's mark or letter at one end – if the mark on each ring is different, note which mark is for the top ring and which is for the second **(see illustration 22.4b)**. The rings are also identifiable by their different profiles.
3 To measure the ring end gap, fit the ring into the top of the cylinder and square it up with the cylinder walls by pushing it in with the top of the piston. The ring should be about 5 mm below the top edge of the cylinder. Slip a feeler gauge between the ends of the ring and compare the measurement to the specifications at the beginning of this Chapter **(see illustration)**.
4 If the gap is larger or smaller than specified, double check to make sure that you have the correct rings before proceeding.
5 Excess end gap is not critical unless it exceeds the service limit. Check that the bore is not worn (see Section 28).
6 Repeat the procedure for each ring and each cylinder in turn. Note that the end gaps differ between the top, second and oil ring. When checking the oil ring, only the side-rails can be checked as the ends of the expander ring should contact each other. Remember to keep the rings together with their matched pistons and cylinders.

Installation

7 Once the ring end gaps have been checked and corrected as necessary, the rings can be installed on the pistons.
8 The oil control ring (lowest on the piston) is installed first. It is composed of three separate components, namely the expander and the upper and lower side rails. Slip the expander into the ring groove, then install the lower side rail **(see illustrations)**. Do not use a piston ring installation tool on the oil ring side rails as they may be damaged. Instead, place one end of the side rail into the groove between the expander and the ring land. Hold it firmly in place and slide a finger around the piston

23.3 Measuring piston ring end gap

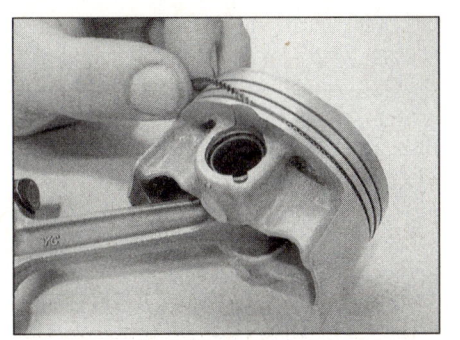

23.8a Fit the oil ring expander in its groove . . .

23.8b . . . then fit the lower side rail . . .

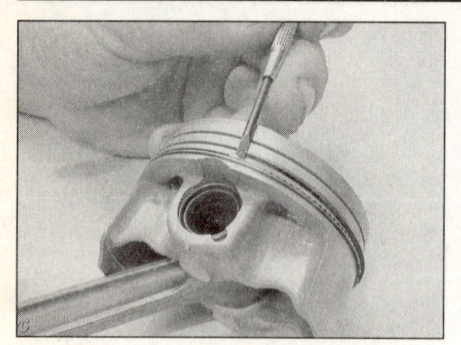

2•46 Engine, clutch and transmission

23.8c ... and the upper side rail as described

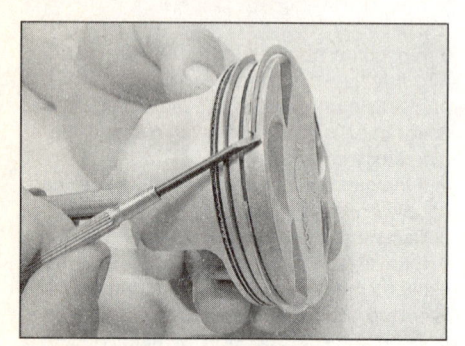

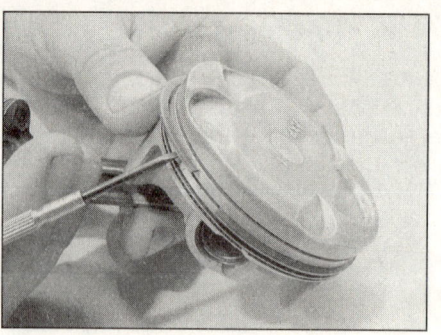

23.10a Carefully feed the second ring into its groove

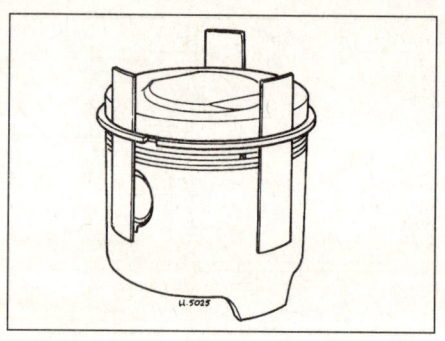

23.10b Old pieces of feeler gauge blade can be used to guide the ring over the piston

23.11 Finally, install the top ring ...

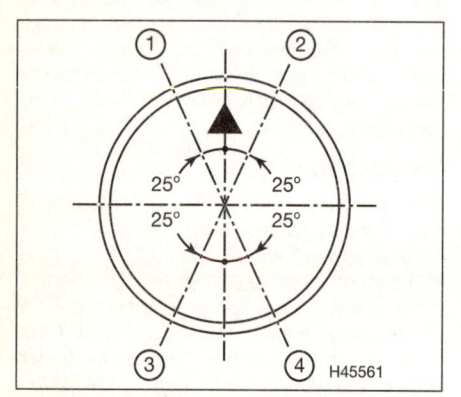

23.12 ... and then stagger the ring end gaps as shown

1 Top ring
2 Oil ring lower side rail
3 Oil ring upper side rail
4 Second ring

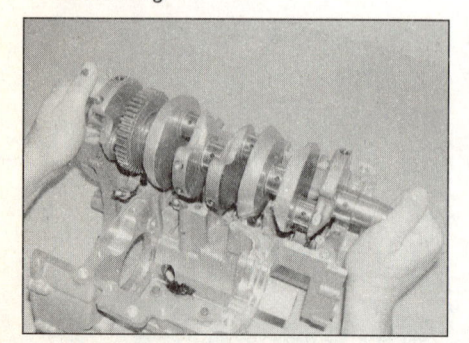

24.2 Lift the crankshaft out of the crankcase carefully

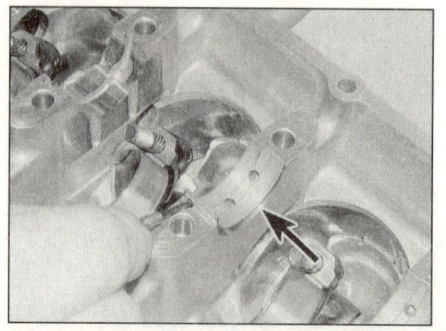

24.3 To remove a main bearing shell, push it sideways and lift it out

while pushing the rail into the groove. Next, install the upper side rail in the same manner **(see illustration)**. Make sure the ends of the expander touch but do not overlap.

9 After the three oil ring components have been installed, check to make sure that both the upper and lower side rails can be turned smoothly in the ring groove.

10 The upper surface of each compression ring should have a mark or letter at one end which must face up when the ring is installed on the piston (see Step 2). Fit the second ring into the middle groove in the piston. Do not expand the ring any more than is necessary to slide it into place **(see illustration)**. To avoid breaking the ring, use a piston ring installation tool **(see illustration 22.4a)**, or pieces of old feeler gauge blades **(see illustration)**.

11 Finally, fit the top ring in the same manner into the top groove in the piston **(see illustration)**.

12 Once the rings are correctly installed, check they move freely without snagging and stagger their end gaps as shown **(see illustration)**.

24 Crankshaft and main bearings

Note: *To remove the crankshaft the engine must be removed from the frame.*

Removal

1 Remove the engine from the frame (see Section 4), separate the crankcase halves (see Section 19) and disconnect the piston/connecting rod assemblies from the crankshaft (see Section 21). There is no need to remove the piston/connecting rod assemblies from the cylinders; push them up the bores so that the connecting rod ends are clear of the crankshaft and wrap clean rag around the rod ends to prevent damage to the bores. **Note:** *New big-end bolts and nuts must be used on reassembly.*

2 Lift the crankshaft out of the upper crankcase half, taking care not to dislodge the main bearing shells **(see illustration)**.

3 If required, remove the bearing shells from the crankcase halves by pushing their centres to the side, then lifting them out **(see illustration)**. Keep the shells in order so that they can be fitted in their original locations for the oil clearance check.

Inspection

4 Clean the crankshaft with a suitable solvent, paying particular attention to flush out the oil passages. If available, blow the crank dry with compressed air, and also blow through the oil passages. Check the primary drive gear for wear or damage. If any of the teeth are excessively worn, chipped or broken, the crankshaft must be replaced with a new one. Check the primary driven gear on the clutch housing for corresponding wear or damage. Also check the cam chain sprocket, the sprockets on the camshafts and the cam chain itself and replace them with new ones, if necessary.

5 Refer to Section 20 and examine the main bearing shells. If they are scored, badly scuffed or appear to have seized, new bearings must be installed. Always renew the main bearings as a set. If they are badly damaged, check the corresponding crankshaft journals. Evidence of extreme heat, such as bluing, indicates that lubrication failure has occurred. Be sure to thoroughly check the oil pump and pressure relief valve as well as all oil holes and passages before reassembling the engine.

6 Give the crankshaft journals a close visual examination, paying particular attention where damaged bearings have been discovered. If the journals are scored or pitted in any way, a new crankshaft will be required. Note that undersized bearing shells are not available,

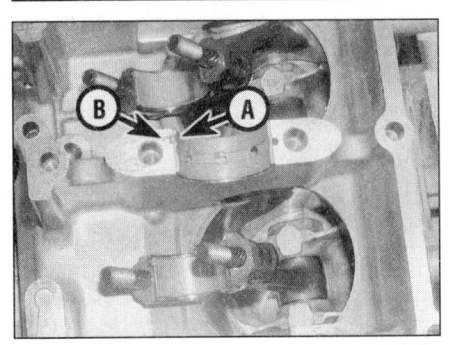

Engine, clutch and transmission 2•47

24.10 Ensure tab (A) locates in notch (B)

24.12 Place a strip of Plastigauge on each bearing journal

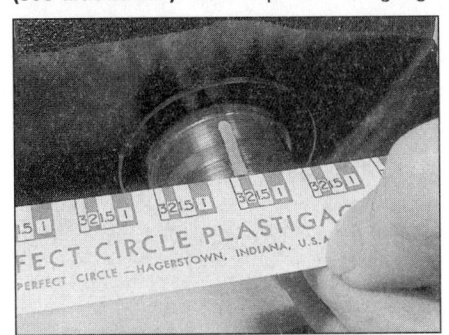

24.16 Measure the crushed Plastigauge using the scale on the pack

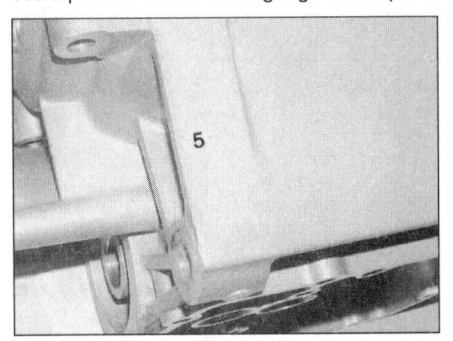

24.21 Main bearing size code(s) (arrowed)

precluding the option of re-grinding the crankshaft.

7 Place the crankshaft on V-blocks and check the runout at the main bearing journals using a dial gauge (see *Tools and Workshop Tips* in the *Reference* section). Compare the reading to the maximum specified at the beginning of this Chapter. If the runout exceeds the limit, the crankshaft must be replaced with a new one.

Oil clearance check

8 Whether new bearing shells are being fitted or the original ones are being re-used, the main bearing oil clearance should be checked before the engine is reassembled. Main bearing oil clearance is measured with a product known as Plastigauge.

9 If not already done, remove the bearing shells from the crankcase halves (see Step 3). Clean the backs of the shells and the bearing seats in both crankcase halves, and the main bearing journals on the crankshaft.

10 Press the bearing shells into their seats, ensuring that the tab on each shell engages in the notch in the crankcase **(see illustration)**. Make sure the bearings are fitted in the correct locations and take care not to touch the bearing surfaces with your fingers.

11 Ensure the shells and crankshaft are clean and dry. Lay the crankshaft in position in the upper crankcase.

12 Cut five appropriate size lengths of Plastigauge (they should be slightly shorter than the width of the crankshaft journals). Place a strand of Plastigauge on each journal **(see illustration)**. Do not place Plastigauge over the oil holes in the crankshaft. Make sure the crankshaft is not rotated.

13 If removed, fit the dowels into the crankcase **(see illustration 19.7)**. Carefully fit the lower crankcase half onto the upper half, making sure the dowels locate correctly and the Plastigauge is not disturbed. Check that the lower crankcase half is correctly seated. **Note:** *Do not tighten the crankcase bolts if the casing is not correctly seated.*

14 Clean and lubricate the threads and underside of the heads and washers of the crankcase bolts Nos. 1 to 10 **(see illustration 19.5a)** with clean engine oil. Install the bolts in their correct locations and secure them finger-tight. Now tighten bolt Nos. 1 to 10 in the correct numerical sequence as marked and as shown **(see illustration 19.5a)** to the first stage torque setting specified at the beginning of the Chapter, then tighten them in the same sequence to the 2nd stage torque setting. Now reverse the sequence (i.e. 10 to 1) and loosen the bolts. Now tighten them in the correct sequence (1 to 10) to the 3rd stage torque setting specified.

15 Unscrew the bolts a quarter turn at a time in a **reverse** of the numerical sequence shown in illustration **19.5a** and as marked on the crankcase, until they are loose, then remove them. **Note:** *As each bolt is removed, store it in its relative position in the cardboard template of the crankcase halves.* Carefully lift off the lower crankcase half, making sure the Plastigauge is not disturbed.

16 Compare the width of the crushed Plastigauge on each crankshaft journal to the scale printed on the Plastigauge envelope to obtain the main bearing oil clearance **(see illustration)**. Compare the reading to the specifications at the beginning of this Chapter. If the clearance is within the range specified and the bearings are in perfect condition, they can be reused.

17 Carefully clean away all traces of the Plastigauge from the journals and bearing shells using a fingernail or other object which will not score the bearing surfaces.

18 If the clearance is beyond the service limit, replace the bearing shells with new ones (see Steps 20 to 22) and check the oil clearance once again. Always renew all of the shells at the same time.

19 If the clearance is still greater than the service limit listed in this Chapter's Specifications, the crankshaft journal is worn and the crankshaft should be renewed.

Bearing shell selection

20 Replacement bearing shells for the main bearings are supplied on a selected fit basis. Code numbers for the crankshaft journals are stamped on the outside of the crankshaft web on the left-hand end of the crankshaft **(see illustration 21.25a)**. The left-hand block of five numbers are the size codes for the main bearing journals (the right-hand block of four numbers are the size codes for the big-end bearing journals). The first number of the block is for the left-hand (No. 1) journal, and so on.

21 The main bearing size codes are stamped into the back of the lower crankcase half **(see illustration)**. The first number of the five is for the left-hand (No. 1) bearing, and so on. **Note:** *If there is only one number stamped into the crankcase, it means that all the bearings are the same number.*

22 A range of bearing shells are available. To select the correct shells for a particular journal, subtract the crankshaft journal number from the crankcase number, and then subtract 1. Compare the result with the table below to find the colour coding of the replacement shells, e.g. crankcase number 5 minus crankshaft journal number 2 minus 1 = 2; No. 2 bearing shells are colour coded black. The colour code is marked on the side of each bearing shell.

Number	Colour
0	white
1	blue
2	black
3	brown
4	green

Installation

23 Ensure the backs of the bearing shells, the bearing seats in both crankcase halves, and the main bearing journals on the crankshaft are clean. If new shells are being fitted, ensure that all traces of the protective grease are cleaned off using paraffin (kerosene). Wipe the shells and crankcase halves dry with a lint-free cloth. Make sure all the oil passages and holes are clear, and blow them through with compressed air if it is available.

2•48 Engine, clutch and transmission

25.2a Note the locating pin (arrowed) on the output shaft bearing

25.2b Lift the output shaft out of the crankcase

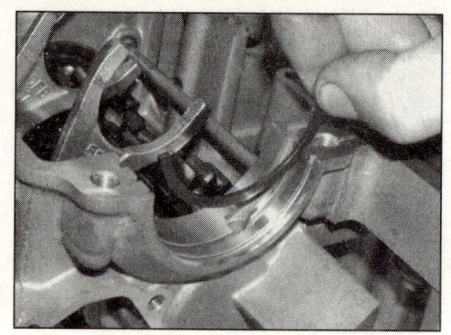

25.3a Remove the bearing retainer . . .

24 Press the bearing shells into their seats. Make sure the tab on each shell engages in the notch in the casing **(see illustration 24.10)**. Make sure the bearings are fitted in the correct locations and take care not to touch any bearing surfaces with your fingers. Lubricate the shells with clean engine oil.
25 Fit new bolts into the connecting rods – note the alignment of the bolt head with the recess in the connecting rod, then press the old bolt out of the rod. Align the head of the new bolt with the recess in the rod and press the bolt into place. Lower the crankshaft into position in the upper crankcase, making sure all bearing shells remain in place **(see illustration 24.2)**.
26 Refer to Section 21, Steps 34 to 37, and fit the connecting rods onto the crankshaft using new big-end nuts.

25.3b . . . and discard the shaft oil seal

27 Reassemble the crankcase halves (see Section 19).

25 Transmission shaft removal and installation

Note: *To remove the transmission shafts the engine must be removed from the frame.*
Special tool: *Although not strictly a tool, this procedure requires the use of two M6 x 1.0 bolts of 30 mm thread length and three M6 x 1.0 bolts of 25 mm thread length with plain washers – see Steps 5 and 7.*

Removal

1 Remove the engine from the frame (see Section 4). Temporarily install the gearchange linkage arm and shift the transmission into neutral. Remove the gearchange mechanism (see Section 15) and separate the crankcase halves (see Section 19).
2 Note how the pin on the output shaft bearing locates in the upper crankcase half, and how the output shaft selector forks locate in the grooves on the 5th and 6th gear pinions and how the guide pins on the forks locate in the grooves in the selector drum **(see illustration)**. Lift the output shaft out of the crankcase **(see illustration)**; if it is stuck, use a soft-faced hammer and gently tap on the ends of the shaft to free it.

3 Remove the bearing half-ring retainer from the crankcase or bearing, noting how it fits **(see illustration)**. Discard the oil seal from the left-hand end of the shaft as a new one must be fitted on reassembly **(see illustration)**.
4 Remove the selector drum and forks (see Section 27).
5 Undo the Torx screws securing the input shaft bearing housing. Discard the screws as new ones must be fitted on reassembly. Obtain two 6 mm bolts, 30 mm long excluding the bolt head, and with a 1 mm thread pitch, and screw them into the two holes in the bearing housing as shown **(see illustration)**. Tighten the bolts until they contact the surface of the crankcase, then continue tightening them evenly and a little at a time until the bearing housing is displaced **(see illustration)**. Withdraw the input shaft from the crankcase.
6 To remove the inner input shaft bearing see *Tools and Workshop Tips* in the *Reference* section.

Installation

7 Slide the input shaft into the crankcase far enough for the left-hand end of the shaft to locate in its bearing **(see illustration)**. Obtain three 6 mm bolts, 25 mm long excluding the bolt head, and three flat washers. Insert the bolts and washers through the bearing housing screw holes and screw them into the crankcase. Tighten the bolts evenly and a little at a time to draw the bearing housing into its

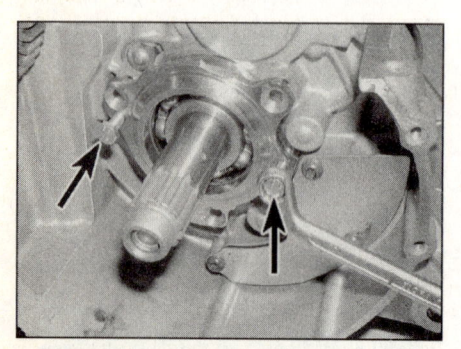

25.5a Displace the bearing housing by screwing in two bolts (arrowed) . . .

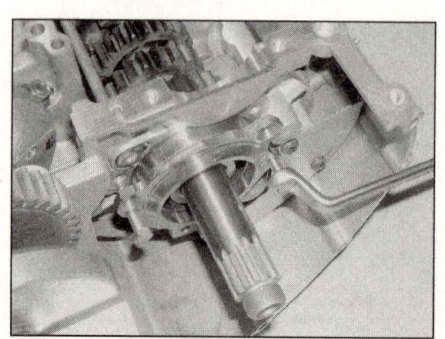

25.5b . . . and turning them against the crankcase surface

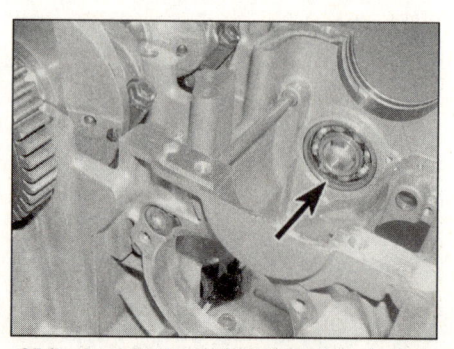

25.7a Locate the end of the input shaft in the bearing (arrowed)

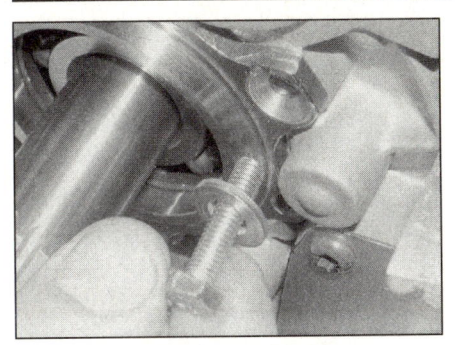

Engine, clutch and transmission 2•49

25.7b Using bolts and washers . . .

25.7c . . . draw the bearing housing into the crankcase

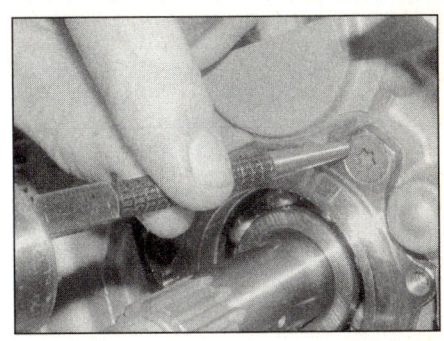

25.8 Tighten the new Torx screws as specified and then stake them in place

location in the crankcase **(see illustrations)**. When the housing is fully installed, unscrew the bolts.

8 Apply a suitable thread locking compound to the new Torx screws and tighten them to the torque setting specified at the beginning of this Chapter. Stake the edge of each screw into the indent in the housing using a suitable punch **(see illustration)**.

9 Install the selector drum and forks (see Section 27).

10 Fit the output shaft bearing half-ring retainer into its slot in the upper crankcase **(see illustration 25.3a)**. Smear the inside of the new output shaft seal with grease. Slide the seal onto the left-hand end of the shaft **(see illustration 25.3b)**.

11 Lower the output shaft into position in the upper crankcase, making sure the groove in the bearing engages correctly with the half-ring retainer and the pin on the bearing locates correctly in the crankcase **(see illustrations 25.2b and a)**.

Caution: If the half-ring retainer is not correctly engaged, the crankcase halves will not seat correctly.

12 Make sure output shaft is correctly seated and that the selector forks are located in the grooves in the appropriate gear pinions (see Section 27).

13 Position the gears in the neutral position and check the shafts are free to rotate easily and independently (i.e. the input shaft can turn whilst the output shaft is held stationary) before proceeding further.

14 Reassemble the crankcase halves (see Section 19).

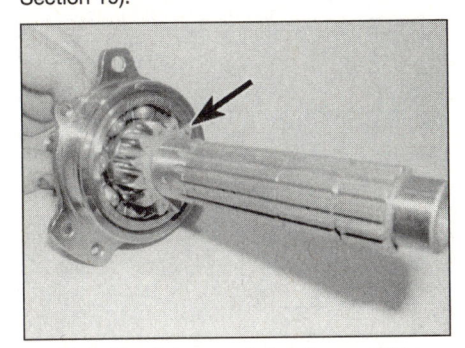

26.8 The 1st gear pinion (arrowed) is integral with the shaft

26 Transmission shaft overhaul

1 Remove the transmission shafts from the crankcase (see Section 25). Always disassemble the transmission shafts separately to avoid mixing up the components.

> **HAYNES HINT**: *When disassembling the transmission shafts, place the parts on a long rod or thread a wire through them to keep them in order and facing the proper direction.*

Input shaft disassembly

2 Slide the 2nd gear pinion off the left-hand end of the shaft, noting which way around it is fitted – mark its outer face with a marker pen as an aid to reassembly **(see illustration 26.26)**.

3 Note how the tabs on the lock washer fit into the slotted splined washer and remove the lockwasher **(see illustration 26.25)**.

4 Turn the slotted splined washer to align it with the splines on the shaft and slide it off the shaft **(see illustration 26.24)**.

5 Slide the 6th gear pinion and its splined bush off the shaft, followed by the splined washer **(see illustrations 26.23c, b and a)**.

6 Remove the circlip securing the combined 3rd/4th gear pinion, then slide the pinion off the shaft noting which way round it fits **(see illustrations 26.22b and a)**. Discard the circlip as a new one must be fitted on reassembly.

26.9 Remove the bearing and housing if required

7 Remove the circlip securing the 5th gear pinion, then slide the splined washer, the pinion and its bush off the shaft **(see illustrations 26.21b and a and 26.20b and a)**. Discard the circlip as a new one must be fitted on reassembly.

8 The 1st gear pinion is integral with the shaft **(see illustration)**.

9 If required, remove the bearing and its housing from the right-hand end of the shaft, referring to *Tools and Workshop Tips* (Section 5) in the *Reference* section **(see illustration)**.

Shaft inspection

10 Wash all the components in solvent and dry them off.

11 Check the gear teeth for cracking, chipping, pitting and other obvious wear or damage. Any pinion that is damaged must be replaced with a new one.

12 Inspect the dogs and the dog holes in the gears for cracks, chips, and excessive wear especially in the form of rounded edges. Make sure mating gears engage properly. Replace mating gears as a set if necessary.

13 Check for signs of scoring or bluing on the pinions, bushes and shaft. This could be caused by overheating due to inadequate lubrication. Check that all the oil holes and passages are clear. Replace any worn or damaged parts with new ones.

14 Check that each pinion moves freely on the shaft or bush but without undue freeplay. Check that each bush moves freely on the shaft but without undue freeplay.

15 The shaft is unlikely to sustain damage unless the engine has seized, placing an unusually high loading on the transmission, or the machine has covered a very high mileage. Check the surface of the shaft, especially where a pinion turns on it, and replace the shaft with a new one if it has scored or picked up, or if there are any cracks. Check the shaft runout using V-blocks and a dial gauge and replace the shaft with a new one if the runout exceeds the limit specified at the beginning of this Chapter.

16 Check the washers and replace any that are bent or worn with new ones.

17 Check the bearings referring to *Tools and Workshop Tips* (Section 5) in the *Reference*

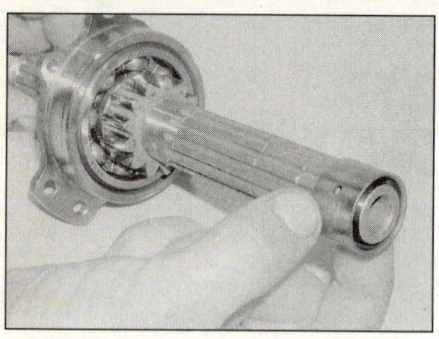

2•50 Engine, clutch and transmission

26.20a Slide the 5th gear pinion bush . . .

26.20b . . . the 5th gear pinion . . .

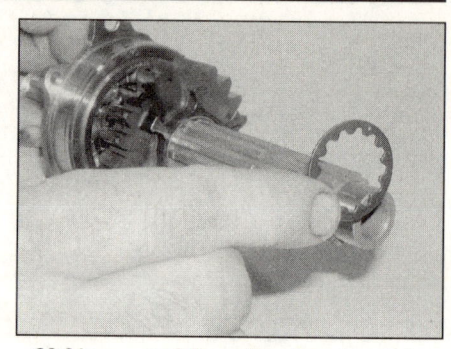

26.21a . . . and the splined washer onto the shaft . . .

section. Do not forget the input shaft left-hand bearing, which is housed in the crankcase.

Input shaft reassembly

18 During reassembly, apply clean engine oil or molybdenum disulphide oil (a 50/50 mixture of molybdenum disulphide grease and engine oil) to the mating surfaces of the shaft, pinions and bushes. Use new circlips and do not expand their ends any further than is necessary to slide them along the shaft. Install them so that their chamfered side faces the pinion they secure (see *Correct fitting of a stamped circlip* illustration in *Tools and Workshop Tips* (Section 2) in the *Reference* section). Also refer to the exploded view of the input shaft in illustration 28.1a.

19 If removed, fit the bearing and its housing onto the right-hand end of the shaft, referring to *Tools and Workshop Tips* (Section 5) in the *Reference* section **(see illustration 26.9)**.

20 Slide the 5th gear pinion bush onto the left-hand end of the shaft then fit the 5th gear pinion onto the bush with its dog holes facing away from the integral 1st gear **(see illustrations)**.

21 Slide the splined washer onto the shaft, then fit the new circlip, making sure that it locates correctly in the groove in the shaft **(see illustrations)**.

22 Slide the combined 3rd/4th gear pinion onto the shaft with the smaller 3rd gear pinion facing the 5th gear pinion. Ensure the oil hole in the pinion aligns with the oil holes in the shaft. Fit the new circlip, making sure it locates correctly in its groove in the shaft **(see illustrations)**.

23 Slide the splined washer onto the shaft, followed by the splined 6th gear pinion bush, aligning the oil hole in the bush with the hole in the shaft. Fit the 6th gear pinion, making sure its dog holes face the 3rd/4th gear pinion **(see illustrations)**.

24 Slide the slotted splined washer onto the shaft and locate it in its groove, then turn it in the groove, so that the splines on the washer locate against the splines on the shaft and secure the washer in the groove **(see illustration)**.

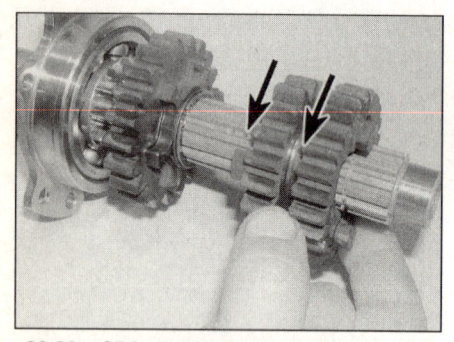

26.21b . . . and secure them with the circlip

26.22a Slide the 3rd/4th gear pinion onto the shaft . . .

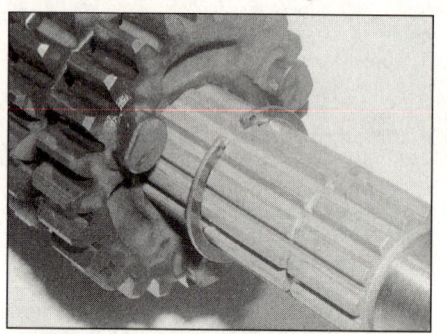

26.22b . . . and secure it with the circlip

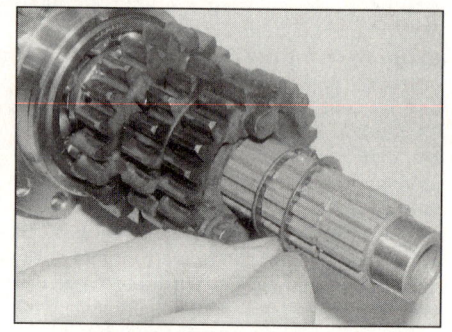

26.23a Install the splined washer . . .

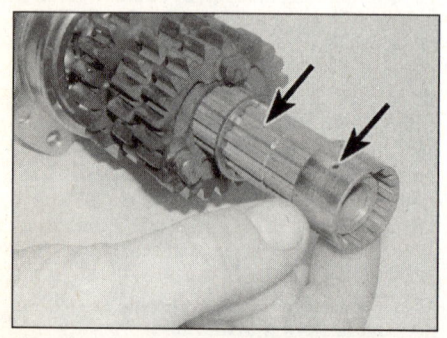

26.23b . . . align the oil holes (arrowed) and fit the 6th gear pinion bush . . .

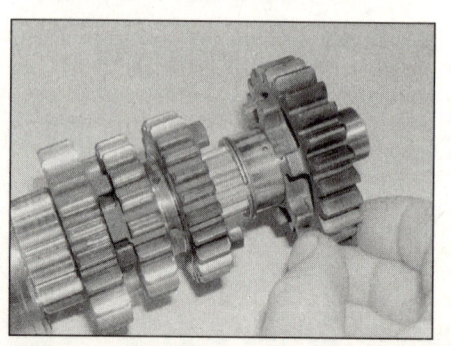

26.23c . . . and slide on the 6th gear pinion

26.24 Install the slotted splined washer as described . . .

Engine, clutch and transmission 2•51

26.25 ... then slide on the tabbed lockwasher ...

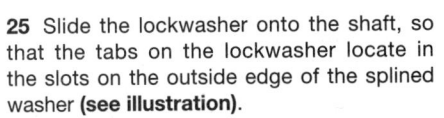

26.26 ... and the 2nd gear pinion

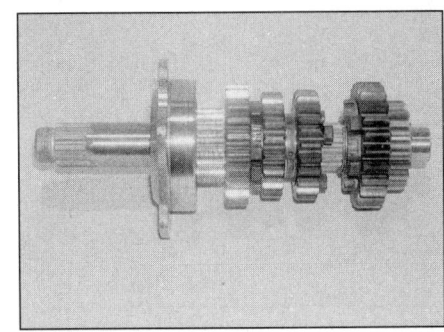

26.27 The assembled gearbox input shaft

25 Slide the lockwasher onto the shaft, so that the tabs on the lockwasher locate in the slots on the outside edge of the splined washer **(see illustration)**.
26 Slide the 2nd gear pinion onto the shaft, the correct way around as noted on removal **(see illustration)**.
27 Check that all components have been correctly installed. The assembled shaft should look as shown **(see illustration)**.

Output shaft disassembly

28 Slide the bearing off the right-hand end of the shaft **(see illustration 26.49)**.
29 Slide the thrust washer off the shaft, followed by the 1st gear pinion and its bush **(see illustrations 26.48c, b and a)**.
30 Slide the 5th gear pinion off the shaft **(see illustration 26.47)**.
31 Remove the circlip securing the 3rd gear pinion, then slide the splined washer, the pinion and its splined bush off the shaft **(see illustrations 26.46d, c, b and a)**. Discard the circlip as a new one must be fitted on reassembly.
32 Note how the tabs on the lock washer fit into the slotted splined washer and remove the lockwasher **(see illustration 26.45)**.
33 Turn the slotted splined washer to align it with the splines on the shaft and slide it off the shaft **(see illustrations 26.44)**.
34 Slide the 4th gear pinion and its splined bush, followed by the splined washer, off the shaft **(see illustrations 26.43c, b and a)**.
35 Remove the circlip securing the 6th gear pinion, then slide the pinion off the shaft **(see illustrations 26.42b and a)**. Discard the circlip as a new one must be fitted on reassembly.
36 Remove the circlip securing the 2nd gear pinion, then slide the splined washer, the pinion and its bush off the shaft **(see illustrations 26.41d, c, b and a)**.
37 If required, remove the collar and bearing from the left-hand end of the shaft, referring to *Tools and Workshop Tips* (Section 5) in the *Reference* section **(see illustration)**.

Shaft inspection

38 Refer to Steps 10 to 17 above.

Output shaft reassembly

39 During reassembly, apply engine oil or molybdenum disulphide oil (a 50/50 mixture of molybdenum disulphide grease and engine oil) to the mating surfaces of the shaft, pinions and bushes. When installing the new circlips, do not expand their ends any further than is necessary to slide them along the shaft. Install them so that their chamfered side faces the pinion they secure (see *Correct fitting of a stamped circlip* illustration in *Tools and Workshop Tips* (Section 2) in the *Reference* section). Also refer to the exploded view of the input shaft in illustration 28.1b.
40 If removed, fit the bearing and collar onto the left-hand end of the shaft, referring to *Tools and Workshop Tips* (Section 5) in the *Reference* section.
41 Slide the 2nd gear pinion bush onto the shaft, then slide on the 2nd gear pinion (dog holes facing away from the bearing) and the splined washer. Fit the new circlip, making sure it locates correctly in its groove on the shaft **(see illustrations)**.
42 Align the oil holes in the shaft and the 6th

26.37 Remove the collar (A) and bearing (B) if required

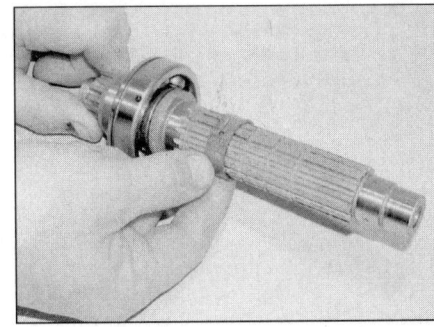

26.41a Slide the 2nd gear pinion bush ...

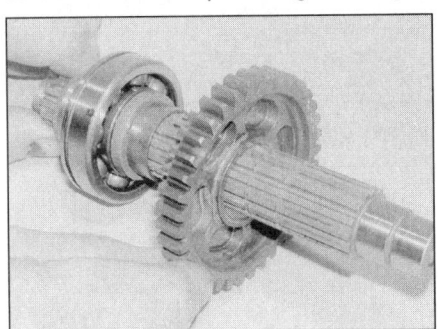

26.41b ... the 2nd gear pinion ...

26.41c ... and the splined washer onto the shaft ...

26.41d ... and secure them with the circlip

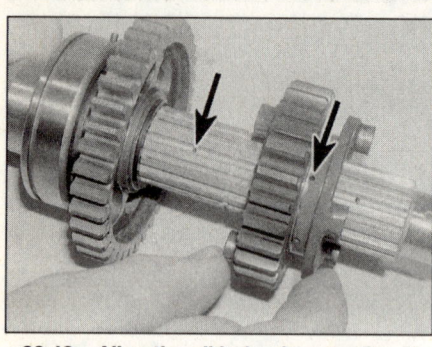

2•52 Engine, clutch and transmission

26.42a Align the oil holes (arrowed) and slide the 6th gear pinion onto the shaft . . .

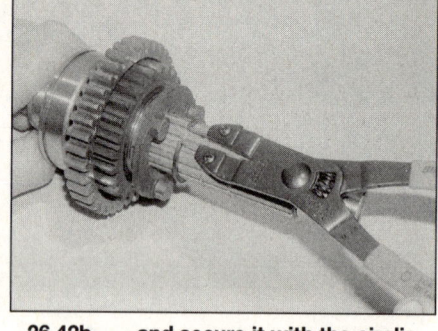

26.42b . . . and secure it with the circlip

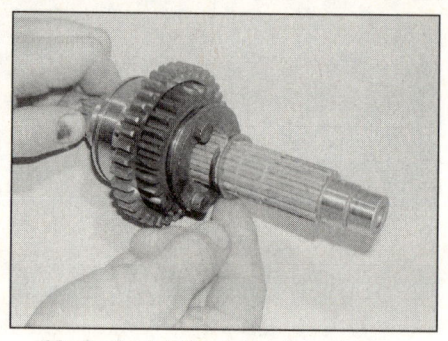

26.43a Install the splined washer . . .

gear pinion, and slide the pinion onto the shaft with its selector fork groove facing away from the 2nd gear pinion, then fit the new circlip, making sure it locates correctly in its groove on the shaft **(see illustrations)**.

43 Slide the splined washer and the splined 4th gear pinion bush onto the shaft, making sure the oil hole in the bush aligns with the hole in the shaft, then fit the 4th gear pinion so that its dished side and dog holes face the 6th gear pinion **(see illustrations)**.

44 Slide the slotted splined washer onto the shaft and locate it in its groove, then turn it in the groove so that the splines on the washer align against the splines on the shaft and secure the washer in the groove **(see illustration)**.

45 Slide the lockwasher onto the shaft, so that the tabs on the lockwasher locate into the slots in the outer rim of the splined washer **(see illustration)**.

46 Slide the splined 3rd gear pinion bush onto the shaft, making sure the oil hole in the bush aligns with the hole in the shaft, then fit the 3rd gear pinion (dished side and dog holes facing away from the 4th gear pinion) and the splined washer. Fit the new circlip, making sure it locates correctly in its groove in the shaft **(see illustrations)**.

47 Align the oil holes in the shaft and the 5th

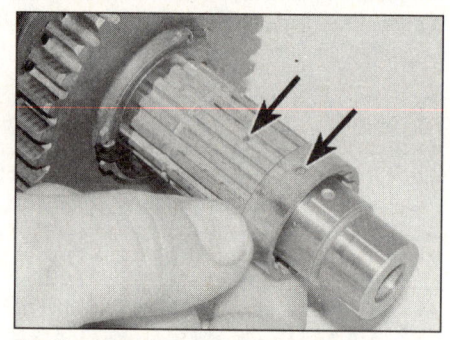

26.43b . . . then align the oil holes (arrowed) and fit the 4th gear pinion bush . . .

26.43c . . . and slide on the 4th gear pinion

26.44 Install the slotted splined washer as described . . .

26.45 . . . then slide on the tabbed lockwasher

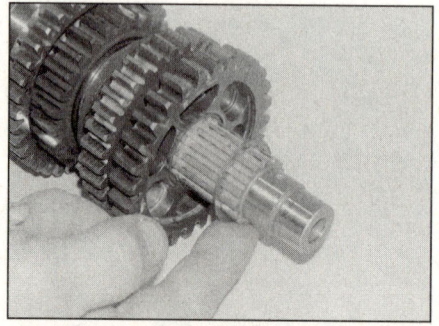

26.46a Align the oil holes (arrowed) and fit the 3rd gear pinion bush . . .

26.46b . . . then slide on the 3rd gear pinion . . .

26.46c . . . and the splined washer . . .

26.46d . . . and secure them with the circlip

Engine, clutch and transmission 2•53

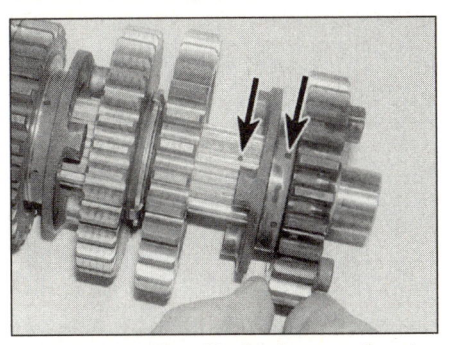

26.47 Align the oil holes (arrowed) and slide the 5th gear pinion onto the shaft

26.48a Install the 1st gear pinion bush . . .

26.48b . . . then slide the 1st gear pinion . . .

26.48c . . . and the thrust washer onto the shaft . . .

26.49 . . . and fit the bearing

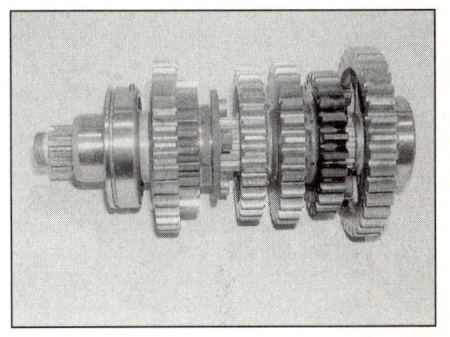

26.50 The assembled gearbox output shaft

gear pinion, and slide the pinion onto the shaft with its selector fork groove facing the 3rd gear pinion **(see illustration)**.

48 Slide the 1st gear pinion bush onto the shaft, followed by the 1st gear pinion (dished side facing the 5th gear pinion) and the thrust washer **(see illustrations)**.

49 Fit the bearing onto the end of the shaft with its open side facing the 1st gear pinion **(see illustration)**.

50 Check that all components have been correctly installed. The assembled shaft should look as shown **(see illustration)**.

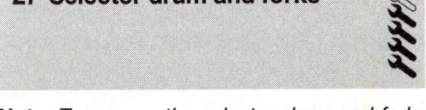

27 Selector drum and forks

Note: *To remove the selector drum and forks the engine must be removed from the frame.*

Removal

1 Position the transmission in neutral. Remove the engine from the frame (see Section 4). Remove the gearchange mechanism (see Section 15), then separate the crankcase halves (see Section 19).

2 Note how the output shaft selector forks locate in the grooves on the 5th and 6th gear pinions and how the guide pins on the forks locate in the grooves in the selector drum, then remove the output shaft (see Section 25).

3 Note the position of the selector drum as an aid for installation; note the position of the neutral detent on the left-hand end of the selector drum **(see illustration)**.

4 Note that each selector fork is lettered for identification. The right-hand fork has an 'R', the centre fork a 'C', and the left-hand fork an 'L' **(see illustration)**. These letters face the right-hand side (clutch side) of the engine. If

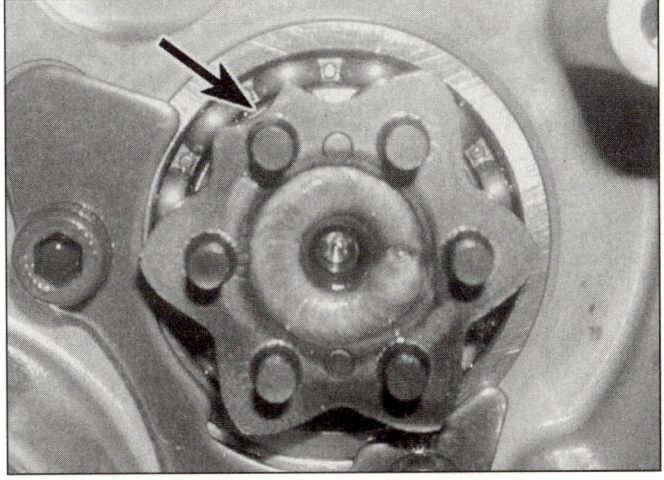

27.3 Note the position of the neutral detent (arrowed) on the end of the selector drum

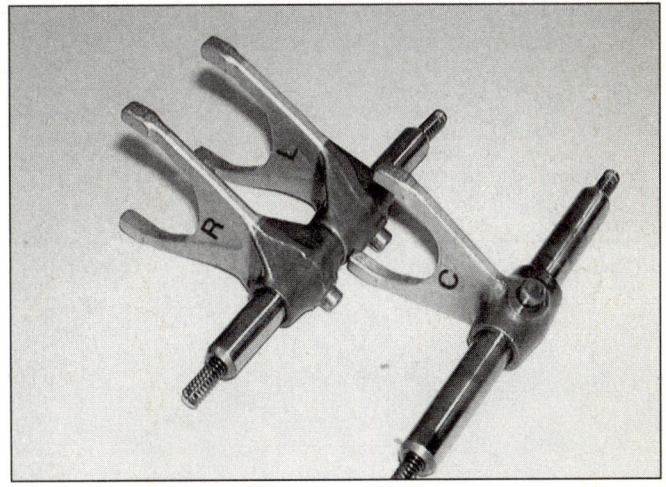

27.4 Note the letter on each fork denoting its position

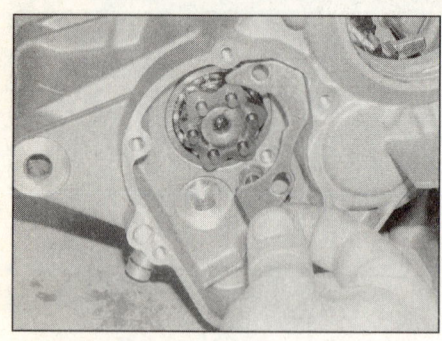

2•54 Engine, clutch and transmission

27.6a Remove the selector drum retainer plate . . .

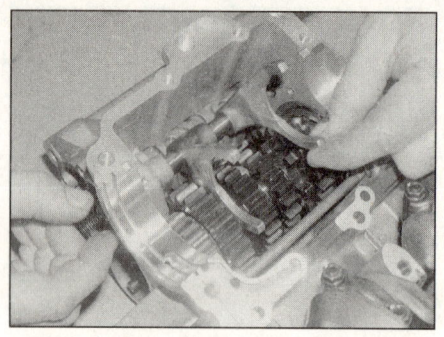

27.6b . . . then withdraw the shaft for the output shaft selector forks

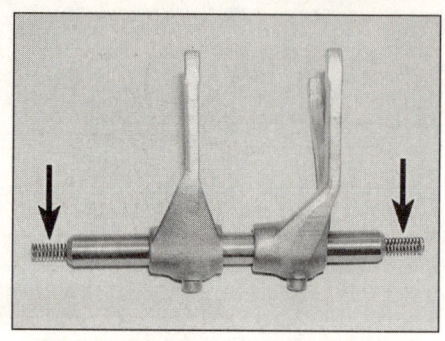

27.7 Install the forks on the shaft for safekeeping. Note the springs (arrowed)

no letters are visible, mark the forks yourself using a felt pen before removing the forks.
5 Note how the input shaft selector fork locates in the groove on the 3rd/4th gear pinion and how the guide pin on the fork locates in the groove in the selector drum.
6 Unscrew the bolts securing the selector drum retainer plate and remove the plate, noting how it fits **(see illustration)**. Support the output shaft selector forks ('L' and 'R') and withdraw the fork shaft from the crankcase **(see illustration)**. Note the springs in the ends of the shaft and remove them for safekeeping, if loose.
7 Remove the selector forks and slide them back onto the shaft in the correct order and the right way round **(see illustration)**.
8 Support the input shaft selector fork ('C') and withdraw the fork shaft from the crankcase **(see illustration)**. Remove the springs from the ends of the shaft for safekeeping, if loose. Move the fork guide pin out of its track in the selector drum, then withdraw the selector drum from the left-hand side of the casing **(see illustration)**.
9 Move the selector fork round in its groove in the 3rd/4th gear pinion and remove it **(see illustration)**. Slide the fork back onto the shaft.

Inspection

10 Inspect the selector forks for any signs of wear or damage, especially around the fork ends where they engage with the grooves in the pinions. Check that each fork fits correctly in its pinion groove. Check closely to see if the forks are bent. If the forks are in any way damaged they must be replaced with new ones.
11 Check that the forks fit correctly on their shaft. They should move freely with a light fit but no appreciable freeplay. Check that the fork shaft holes in the casing are not worn or damaged.
12 Check the selector fork shaft runout using V-blocks and a dial gauge and replace the shaft with a new one if the runout exceeds the limit specified at the beginning of this Chapter. A bent shaft will cause difficulty in selecting gears and make the gearchange action heavy.
13 Inspect the selector drum grooves and selector fork guide pins for signs of wear or damage. If either show signs of wear or damage they must be replaced with new ones.
14 Check the selector drum bearing referring to *Tools and Workshop Tips* (Section 5) in the *Reference* section. If the bearing is worn a new selector drum will have to be fitted as the bearing is not available separately. Also check that the neutral switch contact on the right-hand end of the drum is not damaged or worn away. If required, remove the contact and replace it with a new one.

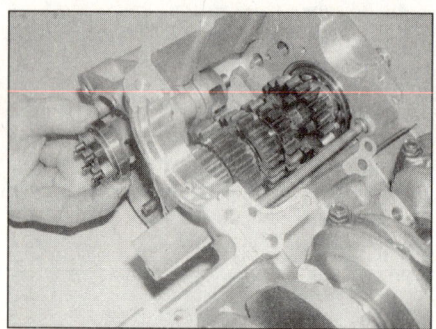

Installation

15 Locate the input shaft selector fork ('C') in its groove in the 3rd/4th gear pinion, making sure the letter faces the right-hand (clutch) side of the engine, then slide the fork round and below the input shaft so that it does not get in the way when installing the selector drum.
16 Lubricate the end of the selector drum with clean engine oil, then align the selector drum so that the neutral detent points to the upper rear engine mounting and slide the drum into the crankcase **(see illustration)**. Make sure the drum end locates in its bore in the crankcase, and that the neutral contact on the drum locates against the neutral switch contact on the inside back of the crankcase **(see illustration)**.

27.8a Withdraw the shaft for the input shaft selector fork . . .

27.8b . . . then disengage the fork guide pin and withdraw the selector drum . . .

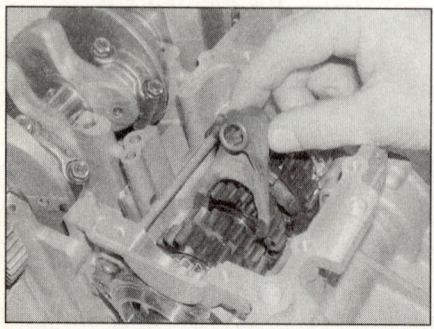

27.9 . . . and the fork

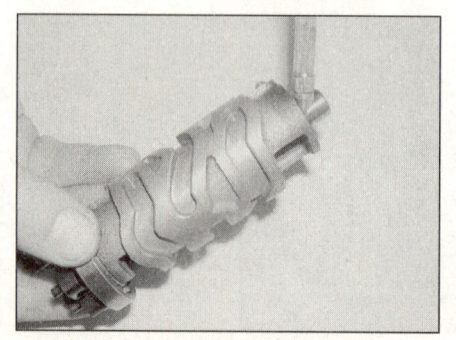

27.16a Lubricate the end of the selector drum before assembly

27.16b Neutral contact on the drum (arrowed) should align with the neutral switch

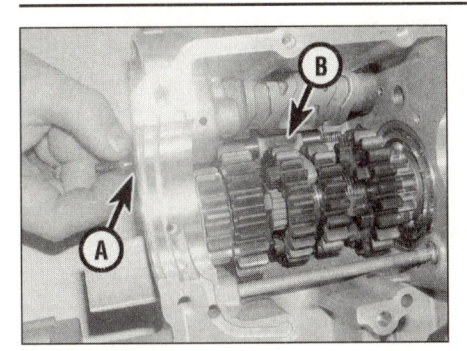

Engine, clutch and transmission 2•55

27.18 Slide the fork shaft (A) through the fork (B)

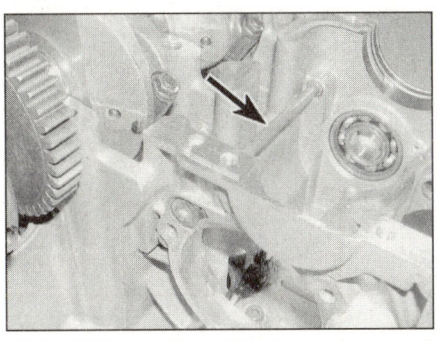

28.2a Withdraw the oil feed pipe (arrowed) from the crankcase . . .

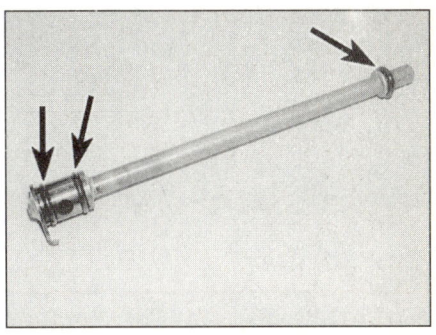

28.2b . . . and check the condition of the O-rings (arrowed)

17 If removed, fit the springs into the ends of the selector fork shafts and lubricate the shafts with clean engine oil.
18 Move the input shaft selector fork round in its groove and locate the fork guide pin into its track in the selector drum, then slide the fork shaft into the crankcase and through the fork **(see illustration)**.
19 Position the output shaft forks ('R' and 'L') in the crankcase, making sure the letters face the right-hand (clutch) side of the engine and the fork guide pins locate in their tracks in the drum. Slide the fork shaft into the crankcase and through the forks **(see illustration 27.6b)**.
20 Apply a suitable non-permanent thread locking compound to the selector drum retainer plate bolts. Install the plate and tighten the bolts to the torque setting specified at the beginning of this Chapter.
21 Lower the transmission output shaft into the crankcase. Ensure that the fork marked 'R' locates in the groove in the 5th gear pinion, and that the fork marked 'L' locates in the groove in the 6th gear pinion (see Step 2).
22 Check that the output shaft is correctly seated and that the transmission shafts rotate easily and independently (see Section 25).

28 Crankcases and cylinder bores

Crankcase halves

1 After the crankcases have been separated, remove the crankshaft, connecting rods and pistons, bearings, transmission shafts, selector drum and forks, and any other components or assemblies, referring to the relevant Sections of this and other Chapters (see Step 3 of Section 19).
2 Withdraw the oil feed pipe from the upper crankcase – it is a push-fit **(see illustration)**. Check the condition of the pipe O-rings and replace them with new ones if they are in any way damaged, deformed or deteriorated **(see illustration)**.
3 Unscrew the bolts retaining the external U-shaped oil pipe on the front of the lower crankcase and pull the pipe out of its sockets **(see illustration)**. Discard the O-rings as new ones must be fitted on reassembly.
4 Unscrew the main oil gallery plug from each side of the lower crankcase and discard the O-rings as new ones must be fitted on reassembly **(see illustration)**.
5 Unscrew the bolts securing the oil baffle plate in the clutch housing and remove it noting how it fits **(see illustrations)**. Unscrew the bolts securing the crankcase breather cover. Remove the cover and discard its gasket.
6 Clean the crankcases thoroughly with solvent and dry them with compressed air. Blow out all oil passages and pipes with compressed air **(see illustrations)**.
7 Remove all traces of old gasket sealant from the mating surfaces. Minor damage to the surfaces can be cleaned up with careful use of a fine sharpening stone.

Caution: Be very careful not to nick or gouge the crankcase mating surfaces, or oil leaks will result. Check both crankcase halves very carefully for cracks and other damage.

8 Before proceeding further, check the cylinder bores (see Steps 18 to 21).
9 Inspect the bearing seats for signs of

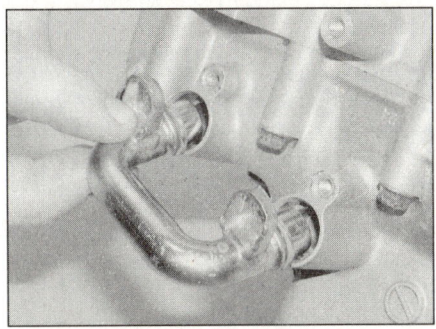

28.3 Remove the external oil pipe . . .

28.4 . . . and the oil passageway plug and discard the O-rings

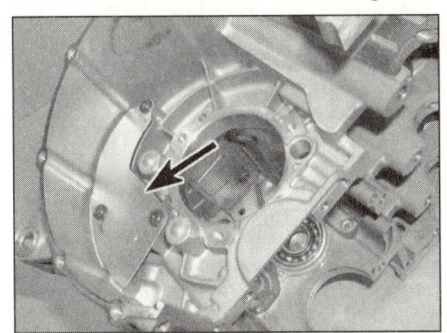

28.5 Oil baffle plate is in the back of the clutch housing (arrowed)

28.6a Clean the crankcases thoroughly . . .

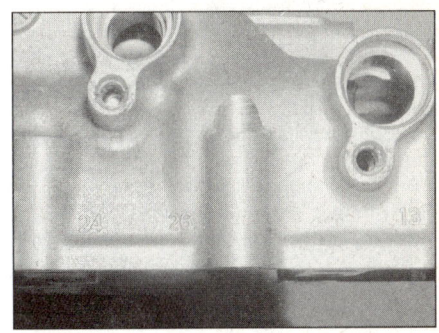

28.6b . . . and blow through the oil passageways with compressed air

2•56 Engine, clutch and transmission

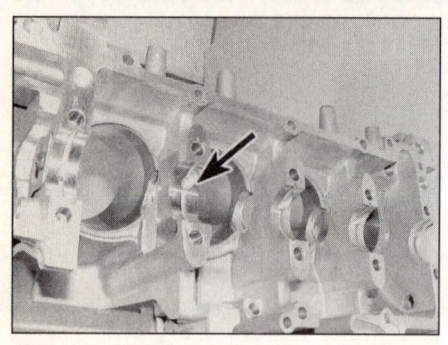

28.9 Inspect the bearing seats and oilways (arrowed)

28.18 Examine the cylinder walls carefully

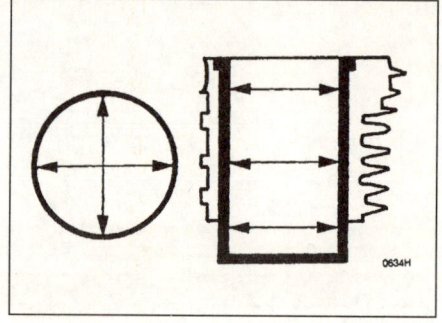

28.19 Measure the cylinder bore in the directions shown with a telescoping gauge

damage, especially if an engine or transmission bearing has overheated or seized (see Section 20) **(see illustration)**. If bearing shells or a ball bearing cage are not a precise fit in their seats, ask your Yamaha dealer for a suitable bearing locking compound which will overcome small amounts of wear. Otherwise the crankcase halves will have to be replaced with a new set.

10 Small cracks or holes in aluminium castings can be repaired with an epoxy resin adhesive as a temporary measure. Permanent repairs can only be effected by argon-arc welding, and only a specialist in this process is in a position to advise on the economy or practical aspect of such a repair. Note that low temperature aluminium welding kits are available for minor repairs. If any damage is found that can't be repaired, renew the crankcase halves as a set.

11 Damaged threads can be economically reclaimed by using a diamond section wire insert which is easily fitted after drilling and re-tapping the affected thread.

12 Sheared studs or screws can usually be removed with stud or screw extractors; if you are in any doubt consult your Yamaha dealer or specialist motorcycle engineer.

> **HAYNES HINT**: Refer to Tools and Workshop Tips (Section 2) in the Reference section for details of installing a thread insert and using screw extractors.

13 Install the oil baffle plate, then apply a suitable non-permanent thread locking compound to the threads of the bolts and tighten them to the torque setting specified at the beginning of this Chapter. Fit the crankcase breather cover using a new cover and tighten its bolts.

14 Lightly grease the new O-rings for the oil gallery plugs and install the plugs, tightening them to the specified torque setting.

15 Lightly grease the new O-rings for the external U-shaped oil pipe and install the pipe, then tighten the retaining bolts securely.

16 Lightly grease the O-rings on the oil feed pipe and install the pipe, locating the tab on the outer end in the cut-out in the crankcase. Ensure the outer end of the pipe is a flush fit with the crankcase; the pipe is retained by the lip of the input shaft bearing housing.

17 Install the remaining components in the reverse order of removal.

Cylinder bores

18 Check the cylinder walls carefully for scratches and score marks **(see illustration)**.

19 Using telescoping gauges and a micrometer (see *Tools and Workshop Tips*), check the dimensions of each cylinder to assess the amount of wear, taper and ovality. Measure near the top (but below the level of the top piston ring at TDC), the centre and bottom (but above the level of the oil ring at BDC) of the bore. Measure both parallel to and across the crankshaft axis in each case and calculate the average cylinder dimension at each point **(see illustration)**. Compare the results to the specifications at the beginning of this Chapter.

20 If the precision measuring tools are not available, take the crankcase to a Yamaha dealer or specialist motorcycle engineer for assessment and advice.

21 If the cylinders are worn beyond the service limit, or badly scratched, scuffed or scored, replace the crankcases with a new set. The cylinders cannot be rebored. If new crankcases are fitted, new pistons and rings must be used.

29 Running-in procedure

1 Make sure the engine oil and coolant levels are correct (see *Pre-ride checks*).

2 Make sure there is fuel in the tank.

3 Turn the ignition 'ON' and check that the oil level/coolant temperature warning light and the fuel indicator light come on for a few seconds and then go off. Ensure that the transmission is in neutral and that the neutral light is illuminated.

4 Start the engine, then allow it to run at a moderately fast idle until it reaches normal operating temperature.

5 As no oil pressure warning light is fitted, an oil pressure check is advised (see Section 3).

6 If a lubrication failure is suspected, stop the engine immediately and try to find the cause. If an engine is run without oil, even for a short period of time, severe damage will occur. After running the rebuilt engine for 1000 miles (1600 km), change the engine oil and filter (see Chapter 1).

7 Check carefully that there are no oil or coolant leaks and make sure the transmission and controls, especially the brakes and clutch, work properly before road testing the machine.

8 Treat the machine gently for the first few miles to allow the oil to circulate throughout the engine and any new parts installed to seat.

9 Great care is necessary if the engine has been extensively overhauled – the bike will have to be run in as when new. This means more use of the transmission and a restraining hand on the throttle until at least 600 miles (1000 km) have been covered. There is no point in keeping to any set road speed – the main idea is to keep from labouring the engine and to gradually increase performance up to the 1000 mile (1600 km) mark. These recommendations apply less when only a partial overhaul has been done, though it does depend to an extent on the nature of the work carried out and which components have been renewed. Experience is the best guide, since it is easy to tell when an engine is running freely. If in any doubt, consult a Yamaha dealer. The following maximum engine speed limitations, which Yamaha provide for new motorcycles, can be used as a guide.

Up to 600 miles (1000 km)
Do not exceed 7000 rpm

600 to 1000 miles (1000 to 1600 km)
Vary throttle position/speed. Do not exceed 9000 rpm for long periods

Over 1000 miles (1600 km)
Normal riding. Do not exceed tachometer red line

10 Upon completion of the road test, and after the engine has cooled down completely, recheck the valve clearances (see Chapter 1) and check the engine oil and coolant levels (see *Pre-ride checks*).

Chapter 3
Cooling system

Contents

	Section number		Section number
Coolant hoses, pipes and unions	8	Cooling system checks	see Chapter 1
Coolant change	see Chapter 1	General information	1
Coolant top-up	see Pre-ride checks	Oil cooler	see Chapter 2
Coolant reservoir	3	Radiator	2
Coolant temperature display, warning light and sensor	5	Thermostat	6
Cooling fan(s) and fan relay	4	Water pump	7

Degrees of difficulty

Easy, suitable for novice with little experience	Fairly easy, suitable for beginner with some experience	Fairly difficult, suitable for competent DIY mechanic	Difficult, suitable for experienced DIY mechanic	Very difficult, suitable for expert DIY or professional

Specifications

Coolant
Coolant type .... 50% distilled water, 50% ethylene glycol anti-freeze with corrosion inhibitors for aluminium engines. **Note:** *Yamaha specify that soft tap water can be used, but NOT hard water. If in doubt, boil the water first or use only distilled water.*

Coolant capacity
  Radiator .... 2.15 litres
  Reservoir .... 0.44 litre

Radiator
Cap valve opening pressure .... 16.0 to 20.3 psi (1.1 to 1.4 bars)

Coolant temperature sensor
Resistance @ 0°C .... 5.21 to 6.37 K-ohms
Resistance @ 10°C .... approx. 4 K-ohms
Resistance @ 20°C .... approx 3 K-ohms
Resistance @ 80°C .... 290 to 350 ohms

Thermostat
Opening temperature .... 71 to 85°C
Valve lift .... 8 mm @ 85°C

Water pump
Impeller shaft tilt (max.) .... 0.15 mm

Torque wrench settings
Coolant temperature sensor .... 20 Nm
Radiator mounting bolts .... 7 Nm
Thermostat cover bolts .... 12 Nm
Water pump cover/drain bolts .... 10 Nm
Water pump mounting bolts .... 12 Nm

3•2 Cooling system

1 General information

The cooling system uses a water/antifreeze mixture to carry excess heat away from the engine. The cylinders are surrounded by a water jacket, through which the coolant is circulated by thermo-syphonic action in conjunction with a water pump. The water pump drives off the oil pump which is driven by chain and sprockets off the back of the clutch.

Heated coolant rises through the system to a thermostat and then to the radiator. It flows across the radiator, where it is cooled by the air flow, then down to the water pump and back into the engine, where the cycle is repeated. The thermostat is fitted in the system to prevent the coolant flowing through the radiator when the engine is cold, therefore accelerating the speed at which the engine reaches normal operating temperature.

A coolant temperature sensor is fitted into the back of the cylinder head which provides signals for the coolant temperature display on the instrument panel and for the ECU as part of the engine management system.

A relay-controlled cooling fan (two fans on 2005 models) is fitted behind the radiator, to aid cooling in extreme conditions. The relay is controlled by a signal from the ECU.

Some coolant is routed from the engine through the fast idle unit on the throttle bodies then back to the radiator – when the coolant is cold the unit increases engine idle speed for fast warm-up.

The complete cooling system is partially sealed and pressurised, the pressure being controlled by a spring-loaded valve contained in the radiator cap. By pressurising the coolant the boiling point is raised, preventing premature boiling in adverse conditions. The overflow hose from the system is connected to a reservoir mounted inside the left-hand fairing side panel, into which excess coolant is expelled under pressure. The discharged coolant automatically returns to the radiator when the engine cools.

⚠ **Warning: Do not remove the pressure cap from the radiator when the engine is hot. Scalding hot coolant and steam may be blown out under pressure and could cause serious injury. When the engine has cooled, place a thick rag such as a towel over the pressure cap; slowly rotate the cap anti-clockwise to the first stop. This procedure allows any residual pressure to escape. When the pressure has stopped escaping, press down on the cap while turning it anti-clockwise, and remove it.**

Do not allow antifreeze to come into contact with your skin, or painted surfaces of the motorcycle. Rinse off any spills immediately with plenty of water. Antifreeze is highly toxic if ingested.

Never leave antifreeze lying around in an open container or in puddles on the floor; children and pets are attracted by its sweet smell and may drink it. Check with the local authorities about disposing of used antifreeze. Many communities will have collection centres which will see that antifreeze is disposed of safely.

Caution: At all times use the specified type of antifreeze, and always mix it with distilled water in the correct proportion. The antifreeze contains corrosion inhibitors which are essential to avoid damage to the cooling system. A lack of these inhibitors could lead to a build-up of corrosion which will block the coolant passages inside the engine, resulting in overheating and severe engine damage. Distilled water must be used as opposed to tap water to avoid a build-up of scale which would also block the passages.

Read the *Safety first!* section of this manual carefully before starting work.

2 Radiator

Removal

⚠ **Warning: The engine must be completely cool before carrying out this procedure.**

1 Remove the fairing side panels and lower fairing (see Chapter 7). Remove the air filter housing (see Chapter 4).
2 Drain the cooling system (see Chapter 1).
3 Disconnect the cooling fan motor wiring at the black connector(s) **(see illustration)**.
4 Release the clutch cable from its guides on the right-hand side of the radiator **(see illustration)**.
5 Release the trim clips securing the radiator cover – there is no need to remove the cover **(see illustration)**.
6 Unscrew the radiator lower mounting bolt and remove the bolt and washer **(see illustration)**. Note the spacer that fits in the

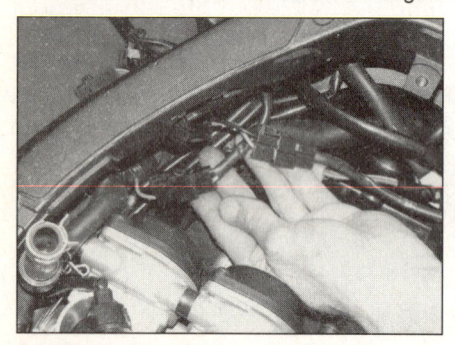

2.3 Disconnect the fan wiring connector(s)

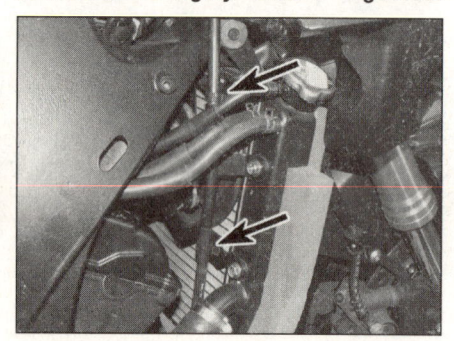

2.4 Release the cable from its guides (arrowed)

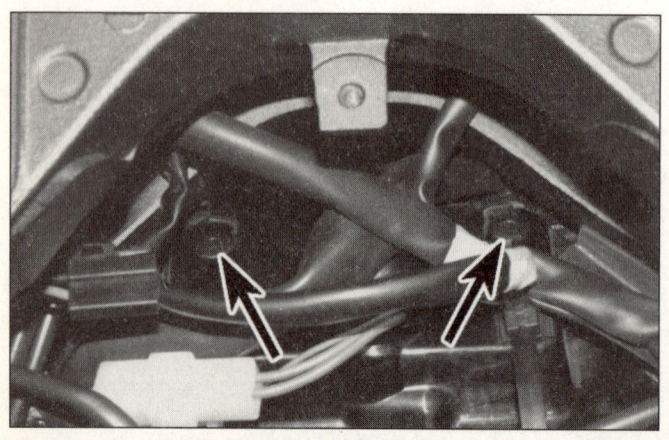

2.5 Release the trim clips (arrowed)

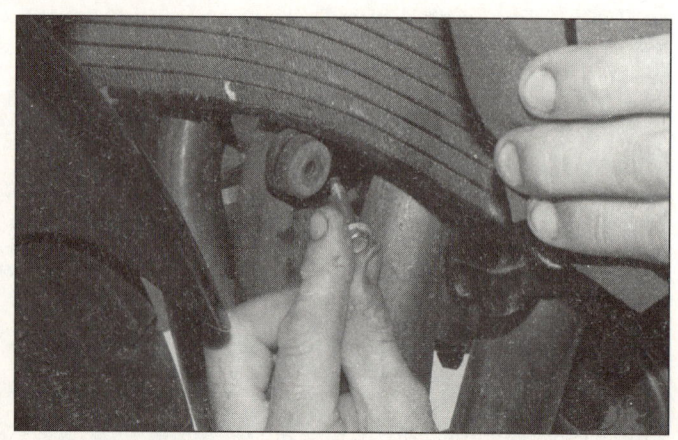

2.6 Unscrew the lower mounting bolt

Cooling system 3•3

2.7a Detach the hoses from the left-hand side . . .

2.7b . . . and from the right-hand side

2.8a Remove the upper mounting bolt . . .

2.8b . . . then displace the radiator to the right to free it from the lug

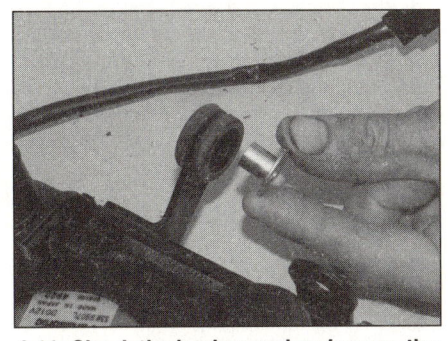

2.11 Check the bushes and make sure the collars are fitted

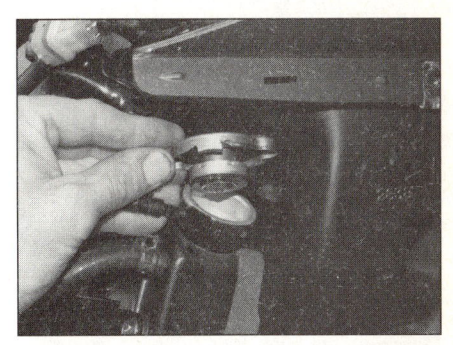

2.12 Have your cap pressure-tested if necessary

bush in the radiator mounting tab and remove it if it is loose.

7 Slacken the clamps securing the radiator inlet and outlet hoses and the oil cooler outlet hose, and detach the hoses from the radiator, noting which fits where **(see illustrations)**. **Note:** *Loosen the upper (left-hand) radiator mounting bolt and swing the radiator forward to facilitate removal of the left-hand inlet hose if required.* Release the clips securing the by-pass hose, the fast idle unit hose and the overflow hose to the reservoir and slide them back off the unions, then detach the hoses, noting which fits where.

8 Unscrew the upper (left-hand) mounting bolt and remove the bolt and washer **(see illustration)**. Note the spacer that fits in the bush in the radiator mounting tab and remove it if it is loose. Carefully manoeuvre the radiator to the right-hand side to free the upper right-hand radiator mounting tab from the frame lug, then remove the radiator **(see illustration)**.

9 If necessary, separate the cooling fan(s) from the radiator (see Section 4).

10 Check the radiator for signs of damage and clear any dirt or debris that might obstruct airflow and inhibit cooling. Radiator fins can be straightened carefully with a flat-bladed screwdriver, but if the fins are badly damaged or broken the radiator must be replaced with a new one. Also check the mounting bushes, and replace them with new ones if necessary **(see illustration 2.11)**.

Installation

11 Installation is the reverse of removal, noting the following.
- Make sure the spacers, bushes and washers are correctly installed with the mounting bolts **(see illustration)**. Tighten the bolts to the torque setting specified at the beginning of this Chapter.
- Ensure the coolant hoses are in good condition (see Chapter 1), and are securely retained by their clamps or clips, using new ones if necessary **(see illustrations 2.7a and b)**.
- Make sure that the wiring connectors are a good fit **(see illustration 2.3)**.
- Refill the cooling system as described in Chapter 1.

Radiator pressure cap

12 If problems such as overheating or loss of coolant occur, check the entire system as described in Chapter 1. The radiator cap opening pressure should be checked by a Yamaha dealer with the special tester required for the job **(see illustration)**. If the cap is defective, replace it with a new one.

3 Coolant reservoir

Removal

1 Remove the fairing left-hand side panel and the lower fairing (see Chapter 7).

2 Remove the reservoir cover, noting how the fuel tank drain and breather hoses route through the guide on its base **(see illustration)**. Remove the cap and draw out the radiator overflow hose **(see illustration)**.

3.2a Undo the screws and remove the cover

3.2b Remove the cap

3•4 Cooling system

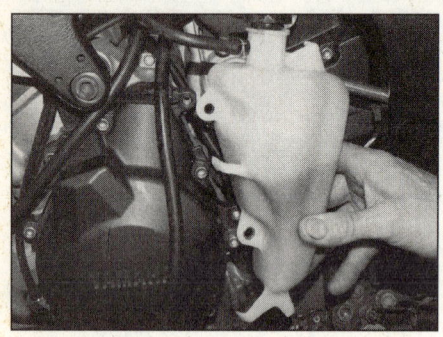

3.3a Undo the reservoir bolts...

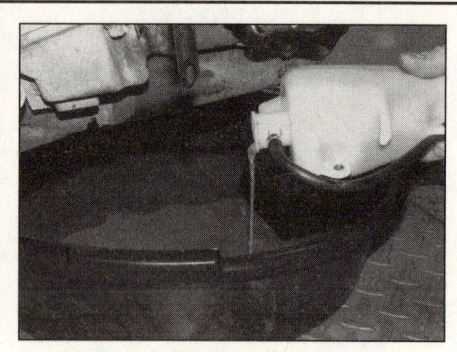

3.3b ...and drain the reservoir

3 Unscrew the reservoir mounting bolts and lift the reservoir off the motorcycle, carefully drawing the breather hose attached to the filler neck out of its guides and noting its routing **(see illustration)**. Tip the coolant out of the reservoir into a suitable container **(see illustration)**.

Installation

4 Installation is the reverse of removal, noting the following:
- Ensure the breather hose is correctly routed and secured.
- Ensure the fuel tank drain and breather hoses are correctly routed.
- Fill the reservoir with the specified coolant up to the correct level (see *Pre-ride checks*).

4 Cooling fan(s) and cooling fan relay

Cooling fan(s)

Check

1 If the engine is overheating and the coolant temperature warning light is on, yet the cooling fan isn't cutting in, first check the fan fuse (see Chapter 8). If the fuse is good make sure there is battery voltage at the red wire to the fuse with the ignition OFF.

2 If the fuse is good remove the left-hand cockpit trim panel (see Chapter 7). Check that voltage is present at the brown/green wire to the fan relay, which is mounted on the air duct, with the ignition OFF, and to the red/white wire to the relay when the ignition is ON. If there is, the fault lies in either the wiring and connectors between the relay and the fan(s), the cooling fan motor or the fan relay. If not check the circuit between the cooling fan relay and the main (ignition) switch, referring to the wiring diagram for your model (see Chapter 8).

3 To test the cooling fan motor(s), remove the left and right-hand fairing side panels (see Chapter 7), and the air filter housing (see Chapter 4). Trace the wiring from the fan motor and disconnect it at the connector **(see illustration 2.3)**. Using a 12 volt battery and two jumper wires, connect the positive (+) battery lead to the blue wire terminal on the fan side of the wiring connector and the negative (–) lead to the black wire terminal. Once connected, the fan should operate. If it does not, and the wiring is all good, then the fan motor is faulty. Replace the fan assembly with a new one – individual components are not available.

Removal and installation

⚠ **Warning: The engine must be completely cool before carrying out this procedure.**

4 Remove the radiator (see Section 2).
5 Unscrew the three bolts securing the fan assembly to the radiator and remove it **(see illustration)**.
6 Installation is the reverse of removal.

Cooling fan relay

Check

7 Remove the left-hand cockpit trim panel (see Chapter 7). Refer to Step 2 if not already done and check the power to the relay.
8 If the voltage is good, disconnect the fan relay wiring connector **(see illustration)**. Set a multimeter to the ohms x 1 scale and connect the positive (+) probe to the brown/green wire terminal on the relay on R and S (2003 and 2004) models, or one of the black wire terminals on T (2005) models, and the negative (-) probe to the blue wire terminal on the relay on R and S (2003 and 2004) models, or the other black wire terminal on T (2005) models. Using a fully-charged 12 volt battery and two insulated jumper wires, connect the positive (+) terminal of the battery to the red/white wire terminal on the relay, and the negative (–) terminal to the green/yellow wire terminal on the relay. At this point the relay should be heard to click and the multimeter read 0 ohms (continuity). If this is the case the relay is proved good. If the relay does not click when battery voltage is applied and indicates no continuity (infinite resistance) across its terminals, it is faulty and must be replaced with a new one. If the relay is good, and the wiring between the relay, the fan motor(s) and the ECU is good, test the fan motor(s) (if not already done), and the coolant temperature sensor (see Section 5).

Removal and installation

9 Remove the left-hand cockpit trim panel (see Chapter 7). The relay is mounted on the air duct **(see illustration 4.8)**.

4.5 Cooling fan mounting bolts (arrowed) – T (2005) model shown

4.8 Cooling fan relay (arrowed)

Cooling system 3•5

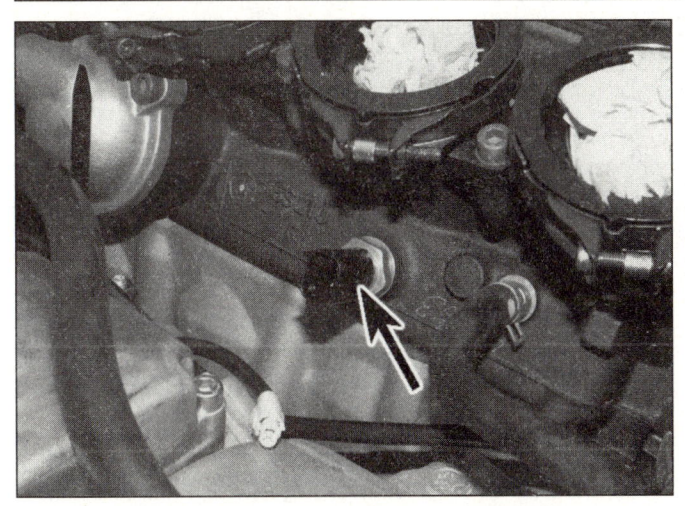

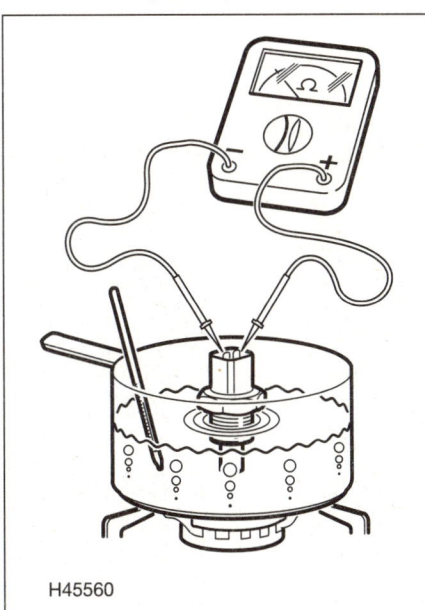

5.7 Coolant temperature sensor (arrowed)

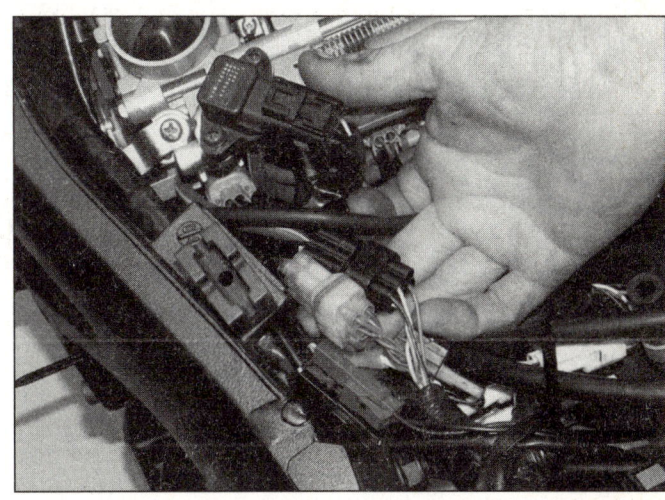

5.8 Reconnect the throttle body sub-loom wiring connectors

10 Release the relay from its mounting, then disconnect the wiring connector.
11 Install the new relay and connect the wiring connector.

5 Coolant temperature display, warning light and sensor

Temperature display and warning light

Check

1 The circuit consists of the sender mounted in the back of the cylinder head and the display and warning light mounted in the instrument cluster.
2 The temperature display should function as follows:

0 to 39°C	LO
40 to 116°C	Actual temperature of coolant
117 to 139°C	Actual temperature of coolant, temperature symbol flashing and warning light on
Above 141°C	HI, temperature symbol flashing and warning light on

3 If the system malfunctions, first check the signal fuse (see Chapter 8) and the sensor wiring and connections. Next check the temperature sensor as described below.
4 If no problems are found, take the instrument cluster to a Yamaha dealer for further assessment – Yamaha provide no specific test data for the instruments themselves. If there are any faults, even if just the warning light LED is faulty, a new cluster will have to be fitted, as no individual components are available.

Removal and installation

5 Refer to Chapter 8, Sections 16 and 17 for removal and installation details.

Coolant temperature sensor

Check

6 Remove the throttle bodies and the rubber heat shield (see Chapter 4).
7 Check for continuity between the sensor body and earth (ground) **(see illustration)**. There should be continuity. If there is no continuity, check that the sensor is tight in the cylinder head (see torque Specifications at the beginning of this Chapter).
8 Place the throttle bodies on the engine and reconnect the sub-loom wiring connectors **(see illustration)**. Using a jumper wire, connect between the terminals on the sub-loom side of the temperature sensor connector, then turn the ignition ON. The temperature display and warning light should come on. If they don't, check the wiring between the connector and the instrument cluster (see the wiring diagrams at the end of this manual). If the wiring is good, refer to Step 4 above.
9 If the display and warning light do come on, it is likely that the sensor is faulty.
10 To check the operation of the sensor, remove it from the engine as described below, then fill a small heatproof container with cold coolant (see Specifications) and place it on a stove. Using an ohmmeter, connect the probes to the terminals on the sensor. Suspend the sensor in the coolant so that just the sensing portion and the threads are submerged. Also place a thermometer capable of reading temperatures of up to 100°C in the water so that its bulb is close to the sensor **(see illustration)**. Note: *None of the components should be allowed to directly touch the container.* Check the temperature of the cold coolant and compare the reading on the meter with the resistances specified at the beginning of the Chapter according to the temperature.

⚠ **Warning: This must be done very carefully to avoid the risk of personal injury.**

11 Heat the coolant, stirring it gently and note the resistance readings at the temperatures specified at the beginning of this Chapter. If the meter readings obtained are widely different, or they are obtained at different temperatures, then the sensor is faulty and must be replaced with a new one.

Removal and installation

⚠ **Warning: The engine must be completely cool before carrying out this procedure.**

12 Remove the throttle bodies and the rubber heat shield (see Chapter 4). Partially drain the cooling system sufficient to avoid spilling coolant when the sensor is removed from the cylinder head (see Chapter 1).
13 Unscrew the sensor and remove it from the head **(see illustration 5.7)**. Discard the sealing washer and obtain a new one.

5.10 Coolant temperature sensor test set-up

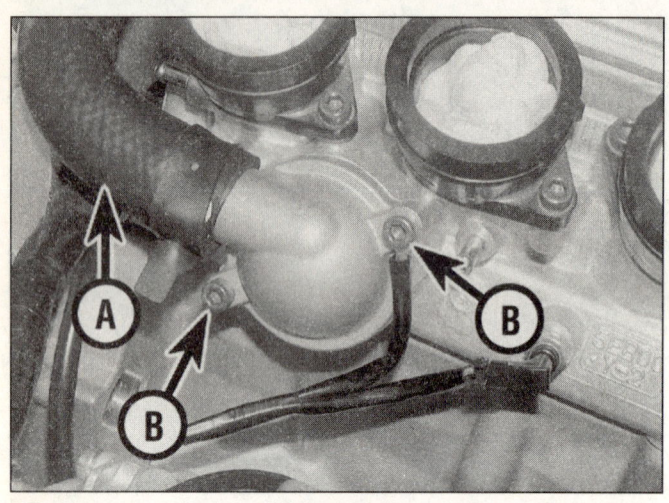

3•6 Cooling system

6.3 Disconnect the hose (A) if required, and unscrew the housing bolts (B)

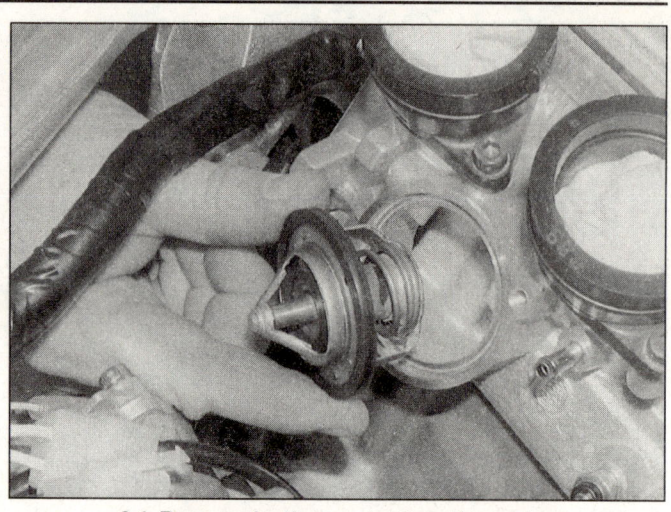

6.4 Remove the thermostat from the engine

14 On reassembly, apply a suitable sealant (Yamaha advise Three Bond Sealock 10) to the sensor threads, then install the sensor using a new sealing washer and tighten it to the torque setting specified at the beginning of this Chapter.

15 Top-up the cooling system (see Chapter 1 and *Pre-ride checks*) and install the remaining components in the reverse order of removal.

6 Thermostat

⚠️ *Warning: The engine must be completely cool before carrying out this procedure.*

1 The thermostat is automatic in operation and should give many years' service without requiring attention. In the event of a failure, the valve will probably jam open, in which case the engine will take much longer than normal to warm up. Conversely, if the valve jams shut, the coolant will be unable to circulate and the engine will overheat. Neither condition is acceptable, and the fault must be investigated promptly.

Removal

2 Remove the throttle bodies and the rubber heat shield (see Chapter 4). Partially drain the cooling system to a sufficient level to avoid spilling coolant when the thermostat housing is removed from the cylinder head (see Chapter 1).

3 If required slacken the clamp securing the radiator inlet hose to the thermostat housing and detach the hose **(see illustration)**. Unscrew the bolts securing the cover to the cylinder head and remove the cover, being prepared to catch any residual coolant.

4 Lift the thermostat out of its recess in the cylinder head, noting how it fits **(see illustration)**.

5 Inspect the cover for cracks and corrosion, especially around the hose union. Clean off any corrosion with a wire brush or steel wool.

Check

6 Examine the thermostat visually before carrying out the test. If it remains in the open position at room temperature, it should be replaced with a new one.

7 To check the operation of the thermostat, suspend it in a container of cold water. Place a thermometer capable of reading temperatures up to 100°C in the water so that the bulb is close to the thermostat **(see illustration)**. Heat the water whilst stirring it gently, noting the temperature when the thermostat opens, and compare the result with the specifications given at the beginning of this Chapter. Also check the amount the valve opens after it has been heated at 85°C for a few minutes and compare the measurement to the specifications. If the readings obtained differ from those given, the thermostat is faulty and must be replaced with a new one.

8 In the event of the thermostat jamming closed, *as an emergency measure only*, it can be removed and the machine used without it. **Note:** *Take care when starting the engine from cold, as it will take much longer than usual to warm up.* Ensure that a new unit is installed as soon as possible.

Installation

9 Smear the thermostat seal lightly with lithium-based grease and fit the thermostat into the cylinder head, making sure that it seats correctly and that the breather hole is at the top **(see illustration)**.

10 Install the cover and tighten the bolts to the specified torque setting. Make sure the radiator inlet hose is pushed fully onto its union and tighten the clamp securely **(see illustration 6.3)**.

11 Top-up the cooling system (see Chapter 1 and *Pre-ride checks*) and install the remaining components in the reverse order of removal.

7 Water pump

Check

1 Remove the fairing right-hand side panel and lower fairing (see Chapter 7).

2 The water pump is located on the right-hand side of the engine and is driven by the oil pump.

3 To prevent leakage of water from the cooling system to the lubrication system and vice versa, two seals are fitted on the pump shaft. The seal inside the water pump is of the mechanical type which bears on the rear face of the impeller **(see illustration 7.15)**. The other seal, which is located in the pump housing, is of the normal feathered lip type.

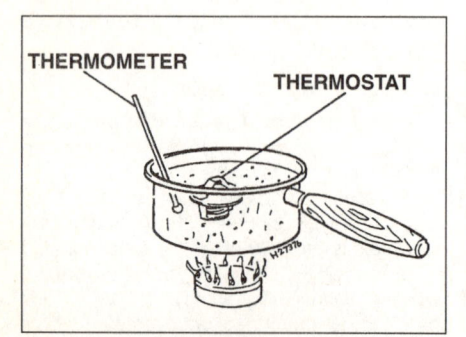

6.7 Thermostat test set-up

6.9 Fit the thermostat with the breather hole (arrowed) at the top

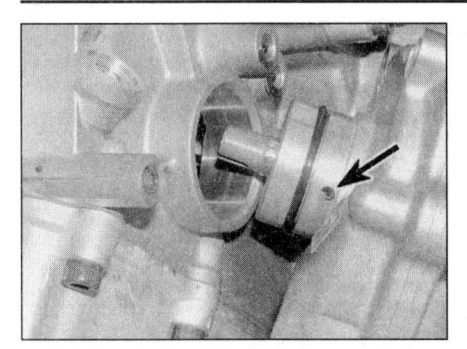

Cooling system 3•7

7.3 Check the drain hole (arrowed) for signs of leakage

7.5 Release the clamps and pull the hoses off their unions

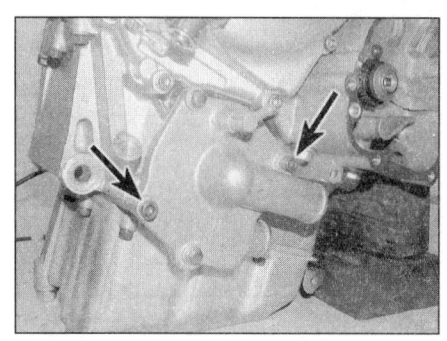

7.7a Unscrew the bolts (arrowed) . . .

If either seal fails, a drain hole in the pump body allows the coolant or oil to escape and prevents them mixing **(see illustration)**. If on inspection there are signs of leakage, the pump must be removed and new seals installed (see Steps 14 to 21). If you are not sure about the condition of the seals, remove the pump and check them visually.

Removal

4 Drain the coolant (see Chapter 1).
5 Slacken the clamps securing the large bore hoses on the pump cover and detach the hoses, noting which fits where **(see illustration)**. Release the clip securing the small by-pass hose and slide it up the hose, then pull the hose off its union.
6 Unscrew the bolts securing the clutch cable adjuster bracket to the timing rotor cover, then detach the clutch cable from the release mechanism arm and secure the cable clear of the engine (see Chapter 2).
7 Unscrew the pump mounting bolts and draw the pump out of the crankcase **(see illustration)**. Discard the O-ring on the back of the pump body as a new one must be fitted on reassembly **(see illustration)**.
8 If required unscrew the pump cover bolts and lift off the pump cover; discard the O-ring as a new one must be fitted on reassembly **(see illustration)**.

Inspection

9 To check the pump impeller bearing, wiggle the impeller back-and-forth and spin it by hand. If there is excessive movement, or the bearing is noisy or rough when turned, the bearing

7.7b . . . and withdraw the pump

must be replaced with a new one. Also check the bearing referring to *Tools and Workshop Tips* (Section 5) in the *Reference* section.
10 Withdraw the impeller from the pump body to check the condition of the impeller shaft **(see illustration)**. If there are signs of wear or other damage, the impeller must be replaced with a new one. Check that the shaft is straight – if it tilts by more than the specified limit, replace it with a new one.
11 Check the condition of the rubber damper and its holder on the rear face of the impeller. Do not remove them from the shaft unnecessarily, as they cannot be reused. If they are damaged or deteriorated, fit a new impeller – Yamaha do not list the damper and holder as being available separately, though it is worth checking first. If they are available, lever off the old ones with a flat-bladed screwdriver. Apply coolant to the new ones and press them squarely down the shaft on to the back of the impeller.

7.8 Remove and discard the cover O-ring

12 Inspect the pump body for corrosion or a build-up of scale and clean with steel wool as necessary, then rinse the pump body in running clean water.
13 Lubricate the impeller shaft with coolant and slide it into the pump body.

Seal and bearing renewal

14 Remove the pump from the engine and the cover from the pump (Steps 4 to 8), then withdraw the impeller from the pump body **(see illustration 7.10)**.
15 To remove the mechanical seal, tap it out towards the inside of the pump body from the outside using a suitable punch, noting which way round it fits **(see illustration)**. Discard it, as a new one must be fitted.
16 To remove the oil seal, first remove the mechanical seal (see Step 15) then remove the circlip retaining the bearing in the pump body **(see illustration)**. Tap the oil seal and bearing out from the inside of the body using a suitable

7.10 Withdraw the impeller from the pump

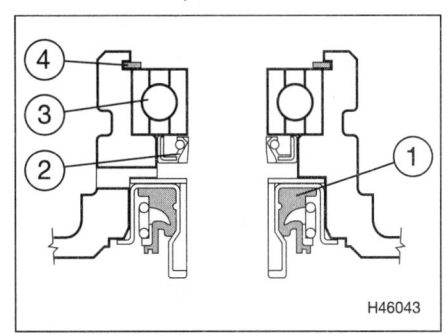

7.15 Mechanical seal (1), oil seal (2), bearing (3) and circlip (4)

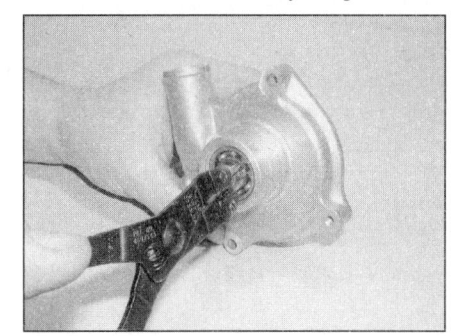

7.16 To remove the bearing, first remove the circlip

3•8 Cooling system

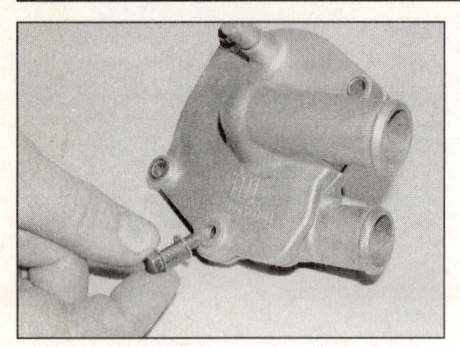

7.22 Use a new sealing washer on the drain bolt . . .

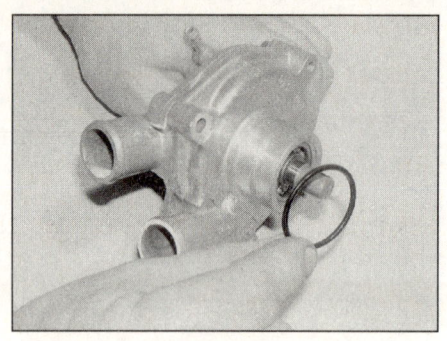

7.23 . . . and a new O-ring on the pump body

sized bearing driver or socket **(see illustration 7.15)**. Note which way round the seal fits. Discard it, as a new one must be fitted.

17 Clean any traces of sealant from around the mechanical seal seat with a suitable solvent.

18 Press or drive the bearing into the pump body until it is properly seated, then install the circlip **(see illustration 7.15)**.

19 Apply a smear of coolant to the outside of the new oil seal. Press or drive the seal into the body from the inside until it fits against the bearing. The marked side of the seal should be facing the bearing.

20 Smear Yamaha Bond 1215 or a suitable equivalent to the mechanical seal seat. Press or carefully drive the new mechanical seal into the pump body using a suitable sized socket or seal driver which bears only on the outer rim of the seal and not on the centre. Yamaha produce a special tool, Part No. 90890-04078 (European models) or YM-33221 (US models), for installing the seal if required.

21 Lubricate the impeller shaft with coolant and slide it into the pump body.

Installation

22 Fit the new cover O-ring into its groove then fit the cover and install the cover bolt and drain bolt, fitting a new sealing washer to the drain bolt, and tighten the bolts to the specified torque setting **(see illustration)**.

23 Fit a new pump body O-ring and smear it lightly with grease **(see illustration)**. Install the pump in the crankcase, ensuring that the impeller shaft engages the drive peg on the oil pump spindle, and tighten the mounting bolts to the specified torque.

24 Install the remaining components in the reverse order of removal

8 Coolant hoses, pipes and unions

Removal

1 Before removing a hose, pipe or union, drain the coolant (see Chapter 1). **Note:** *When removing components of the cooling system, be prepared to catch any residual fluids.*

2 Use a screwdriver to slacken the larger-bore hose clamps, then slide them back along the hose and clear of the union spigot. The smaller-bore hoses are secured by spring clips which can be expanded by squeezing their ears together with pliers.

Caution: The radiator unions are fragile. Do not use excessive force when attempting to remove the hoses.

3 If a hose proves stubborn, release it by rotating it on its union before working it off. If all else fails, cut the hose with a sharp knife then slit it at each union so that it can be peeled off in two pieces. Whilst this means renewing the hose, it is preferable to buying a new radiator.

4 Remove the union on the engine by detaching the hose (see above), then unscrewing the union retaining bolts. Discard the O-ring, as a new one must be fitted on reassembly **(see illustrations)**.

Installation

5 Slide the clip onto the hose and then work the hose onto its union.

6 Rotate the hose on its union to settle it in position before sliding the clip into place and tightening it securely.

7 If the union on the engine has been removed, fit a new O-ring and smear it with grease, then install the union and tighten the mounting securely.

> **HAYNES HiNT** *If the hose is difficult to push onto its union, it can be softened by soaking it in very hot water, or alternatively a little soapy water can be used as a lubricant.*

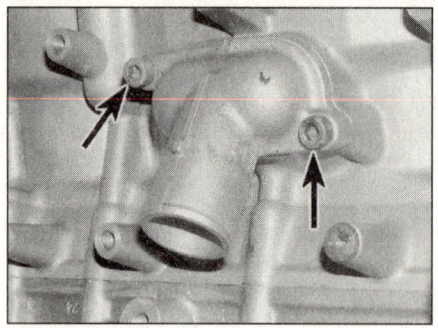

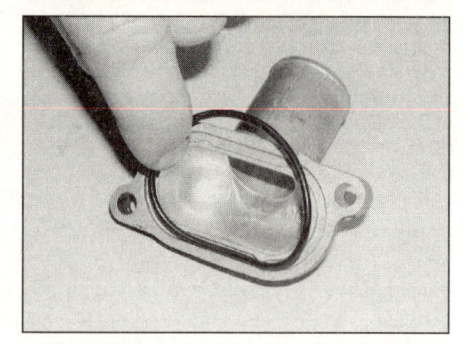

8.4a Coolant inlet union bolts (arrowed)

8.4b Use a new O-ring on installation

Chapter 4
Engine management system

Contents

	Section number		Section number
Air filter	see Chapter 1	Fuel tank	2
Air filter housing	5	General information and precautions	1
Air induction system (AIS)	15	Idle speed	see Chapter 1
Catalytic converter	16	Ignition coils	18
ECU (Engine Control Unit)	19	Ignition (main) switch	see Chapter 8
Exhaust system	14	Ignition system check	17
Fast idle system	11	Ignition timing	20
Fuel hoses	see Chapter 1	Immobiliser system	21
Fuel injection system components	8	Neutral switch	see Chapter 8
Fuel injection system description	6	Sidestand switch	see Chapter 8
Fuel injection system fault diagnosis	7	Spark plugs	see Chapter 1
Fuel level warning light and sensor	4	Starter circuit cut-off relay	see Chapter 8
Fuel rail and injectors	10	Throttle bodies	9
Fuel pressure regulator	12	Throttle body synchronisation	see Chapter 1
Fuel pump	3	Throttle cable check and adjustment	see Chapter 1
Fuel system check	see Chapter 1	Throttle cables	13

Degrees of difficulty

Easy, suitable for novice with little experience	Fairly easy, suitable for beginner with some experience	Fairly difficult, suitable for competent DIY mechanic	Difficult, suitable for experienced DIY mechanic	Very difficult, suitable for expert DIY or professional

Specifications

General information
Cylinder numbering	1 to 4 from left to right
Ignition timing	10° BTDC @ 1300 rpm
Spark plugs	see Chapter 1

Component test data
AIS cut-off valve resistance	18.0 to 22.0 ohms @ 20°C
Atmospheric pressure sensor output voltage	3.75 to 4.25V
Camshaft position sensor output voltage	
On	4.8V or more
Off	0.8V or less
Crankshaft position sensor resistance	248 to 372 ohms @ 20°C
Coolant temperature sensor	
Resistance @ 0°C	5.21 to 6.37 K-ohms
Resistance @ 80°C	290 to 350 ohms
Fuel pump resistance	0.2 to 3.0 ohms @ 20°C
Intake air pressure sensor output voltage	3.75 to 4.25V
Intake air temperature sensor resistance	2.2 to 2.7 ohms @ 20°C
Speed sensor output voltage	
On	4.8V or more
Off	0.6V or less
Throttle position sensor	
Resistance	0 to 5 (± 1.5) K-ohms @ 20°C
Maximum resistance	3.5 to 6.5 K-ohms @ 20°C
Voltage (for position adjustment)	0.63 to 0.73V
Tip-over sensor output voltage	
Sensor upright	approx. 1.0V
Sensor tilted at specified angle	approx. 4.0V

4•2 Engine management system

Fuel
Grade	Unleaded, minimum 95 RON (Research Octane Number)
Fuel tank capacity (including reserve)	17 litres
Reserve (fuel light ON)	3.5 litres

Throttle bodies
Type	
R and S (2003 and 2004) models	4 x Mikuni 38EIS
T (2005) model	4 x Mikuni 40EIS
Throttle valve size	# 100
Intake vacuum	see Chapter 1

Fuel injector
Manufacturer	Nippon
Type	INP-250/4
Operating pressure	42 psi (2.9 Bar)

Ignition HT coils
Primary resistance	0.24 to 0.32 ohms @ 20°C
Secondary resistance	5.0 to 6.8 K-ohms @ 20°C
Minimum spark gap	6 mm

Torque wrench settings
Camshaft position sensor bolt	
R and S (2003 and 2004) models	10 Nm
T (2005) models	7.5 Nm
Crankshaft position sensor bolts	10 Nm
Exhaust downpipe assembly nuts	20 Nm
Exhaust downpipe mounting bolt	20 Nm
Fuel tank mounting bolts	7 Nm
Fuel pump screws	4 Nm
Silencer clamp bolt	20 Nm
Silencer mounting bolt	23 Nm
Timing rotor cover bolts	12 Nm

1 General information and precautions

General information

All models are fitted with a fully electronic engine management system which controls both the fuelling and ignition from one engine control unit, or ECU.

Fuel system

The fuel system consists of the fuel tank with internal level sensor, fuel pump and integral filter, the fuel supply and return hoses, the fuel injectors located in the throttle bodies, and the control cables. Air is drawn into the throttle bodies via an air filter, which is housed under the fuel tank.

The fuel pump is activated initially by the ignition switch, and fuel pressure is controlled by a regulator located on the right-hand end of the fuel rail.

In the event of the machine falling over, a tip-over sensor cuts power to the fuel and ignition systems.

The fuel injection system is controlled by the engine control unit (ECU) which monitors data sent from the various system sensors and adjusts fuel delivery to the engine and ignition timing accordingly. The ECU has its own fault diagnosis function and displays fault codes and diagnostic codes on the LCD display in the instrument cluster.

The exhaust is a four-into-two-into-one design. An air induction system (AIS) introduces filtered air into the exhaust ports to promote the burning of excess fuel in the exhaust gases to reduce harmful emissions.

Many of the fuel system service procedures are considered routine maintenance items and for that reason are included in Chapter 1.

Ignition system

The ignition system comprises a timing rotor, crankshaft position sensor (CKP sensor), the engine control unit (ECU) and ignition coils. All models are fitted with four 'stick' style HT coils which are integral with the spark plug caps.

The timing rotor on the right-hand end of the crankshaft generates a signal in the CKP sensor as the crankshaft rotates. The CKP sensor sends that signal to the ECU which, in conjunction with data sent from the various other system sensors, calculates the best ignition timing and supplies the ignition coils with the power necessary to produce a spark at the plugs. There is no provision for adjusting the ignition timing.

The system incorporates a starter safety circuit which will cut the ignition if the sidestand is extended whilst the engine is running and in gear, or if a gear is selected whilst the engine is running and the sidestand is extended. It also prevents the engine from being started if the engine is in gear unless the clutch lever is pulled in and the stand is up.

Models sold in certain markets are fitted with an immobiliser system which will not allow the engine to be started unless the correct key is used. The immobiliser system has its own fault diagnosis function. An alarm system is available as an optional extra.

There is no provision for adjusting the ignition timing on these models.

Note: *Individual engine management system components can be checked but not repaired if faulty. If system troubles occur, and the faulty component can be isolated, the only cure for the problem in most cases is to replace the part with a new one. Keep in mind that most electronic parts, once purchased, cannot be returned. To avoid unnecessary expense, make very sure the faulty component has been positively identified before buying a new part.*

Engine management system 4•3

Precautions

⚠️ **Warning:** *Petrol (gasoline) is extremely flammable, so take extra precautions when you work on any part of the fuel system. Don't smoke or allow open flames or bare light bulbs near the work area, and don't work in a garage where a natural gas-type appliance is present. If you spill any fuel on your skin, rinse it off immediately with soap and water. When you perform any kind of work on the fuel system, wear safety glasses and have a fire extinguisher suitable for a class B type fire (flammable liquids) on hand.*

- Always perform service procedures in a well-ventilated area to prevent a build-up of fumes.
- Never work in a building containing a gas appliance with a pilot light, or any other form of naked flame. Ensure that there are no naked light bulbs or any sources of flame or sparks nearby.
- Do not smoke (or allow anyone else to smoke) while in the vicinity of petrol (gasoline), or of components containing petrol. Remember the possible presence of vapour from these sources and move well clear before smoking.
- Check all electrical equipment belonging to the house, garage or workshop where work is being undertaken (see the *Safety First!* section of this manual). Remember that certain electrical appliances such as drills, cutters, etc, create sparks in the normal course of operation and must not be used near petrol (gasoline) or any component containing it. Again, remember the possible presence of fumes before using electrical equipment.
- Always mop up any spilt fuel and safely dispose of the rag used.
- Any stored fuel that is drained off during servicing work must be kept in sealed containers that are suitable for holding petrol (gasoline), and clearly marked as such; the containers themselves should be kept in a safe place. Note that this last point applies equally to the fuel tank if it is removed from the machine; also remember to keep its filler cap closed at all times.
- Read the *Safety first!* section of this manual carefully before starting work.

2.2a Slacken the rear bolt (arrowed) . . .

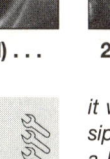

2 Fuel tank

⚠️ **Warning:** *Refer to the precautions given in Section 1 before starting work.*

Raise

1 Make sure the fuel filler cap is secure. Remove the rider's seat (see Chapter 7).
2 Loosen but do not remove the bolt securing the rear of the tank **(see illustration)**. Unscrew the bolts securing the front of the tank **(see illustration)**.
3 Raise the tank at the front and support it using a block of wood **(see illustration)**.

Removal

Note: *To reduce the weight of the tank remove*

2.3 . . . and raise and support the tank

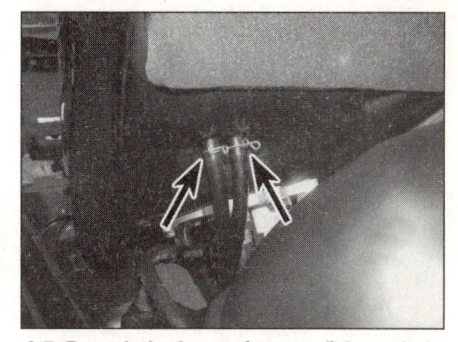

2.2b . . . then unscrew the front bolts . . .

it when it is nearly empty, or if the tank is full siphon the fuel into a suitable container using a hand pump (available from tool suppliers) before removing the tank.
4 Raise the tank (see Steps 1 to 3).
5 Release the clamps securing the overflow hose and, on all except California models, the breather hose to their unions on the underside of the tank and detach the hoses, noting which fits where **(see illustration)**. On California models, detach the EVAP hose from its union.
6 Remove the security clip on the fuel supply hose connector, then press in the two tabs on the connector and pull it off the union **(see illustrations)**. Have a rag ready to catch any residual fuel from the hose.
7 Release the clamp securing the fuel return hose and pull it off the union **(see illustration)**. Have a rag ready to catch any residual fuel from the hose.

2.5 Detach the hoses (arrowed) from their unions

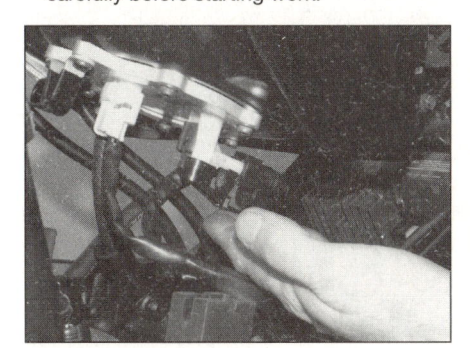

2.6a Remove the security clip . . .

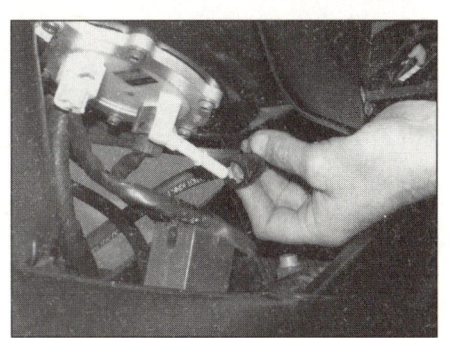

2.6b . . . and release the fuel supply hose

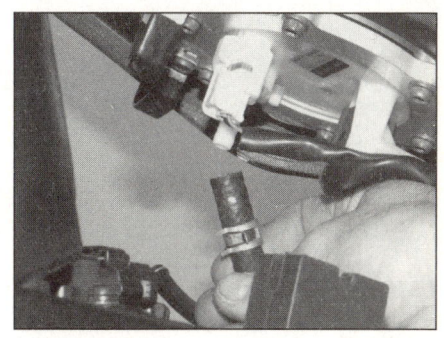

2.7 Detach the fuel return hose from its union

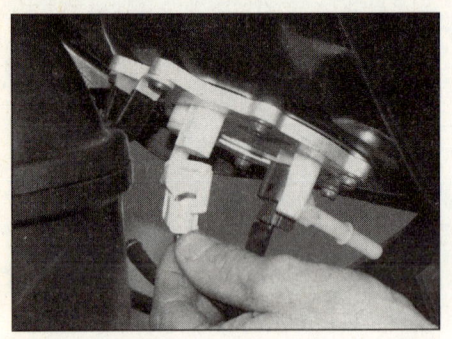

4•4 Engine management system

2.8 Disconnect the two wiring connectors

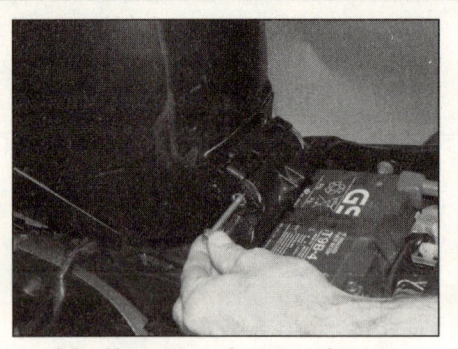

2.9a Unscrew and remove the rear mounting bolt . . .

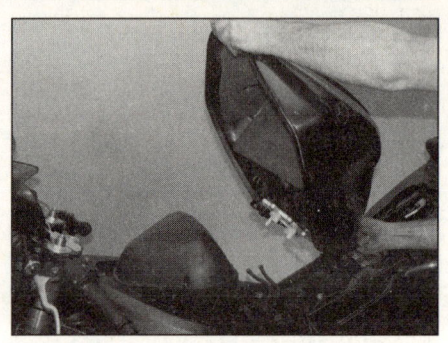

2.9b . . . and lift the tank away

8 Disconnect the fuel pump (green) and fuel level sensor (white) wiring connectors **(see illustration)**.

9 Remove the support and lower the tank. Unscrew the bolt securing the rear of the tank, then carefully lift the tank off the frame **(see illustrations)**. **Note:** *A U-shaped bracket on the fuel pump retaining ring is designed to protect the fuel unions and wiring connectors when the tank is off the bike – take care not to rest the tank on the underside of the fuel pump.*

10 Inspect the tank support and mounting bolt rubbers for signs of damage or deterioration and replace them with new ones if necessary.

Installation

11 Installation is the reverse of removal, noting the following:
- Make sure the hoses are properly attached and secured by their clamps. Make sure the wiring connectors are secure.
- Tighten the mounting bolts to the torque settings specified at the beginning of the chapter.
- Start the engine and check that there are no signs of fuel leakage. If the tank has been emptied, ensure it is refilled before turning the ignition (main) switch ON.

Repair

12 All repairs to the fuel tank should be carried out by a professional who has experience in this critical and potentially dangerous work. Even after cleaning and flushing of the fuel system, explosive fumes can remain and ignite during repair of the tank.

13 If the fuel tank is removed from the bike, it should not be placed in an area where sparks or open flames could ignite the fumes coming out of the tank. Be especially careful inside garages where a natural gas-type appliance is located, because the pilot light could cause an explosion.

3 Fuel pump

⚠ **Warning:** *Refer to the precautions given in Section 1 before starting work.*

Check

1 The fuel pump is located inside the fuel tank. When the ignition is switched ON, it should be possible to hear the pump run for a few seconds until the system is up to pressure. If you can't hear anything, first check that the battery is fully-charged, then check the main, ignition and fuel injection system fuses, the ignition and engine kill switches, and the pump relay which is contained within the relay assembly (see Chapter 8). If they are good, check the wiring and terminals in the circuit for physical damage or loose or corroded connections and rectify as necessary (see the *Wiring Diagrams* at the end of Chapter 8). If the pump still will not run, check the pump resistance as follows:

2 Make sure the ignition is OFF. Raise the fuel tank and disconnect the pump (green) wiring connector (see Section 2). Using an ohmmeter or multimeter set to the ohms scale, measure the resistance between the terminals on the pump side of the connector. Connect the positive (+) probe to the red/blue wire terminal in the connector and the negative (-) probe to the black wire terminal. Compare the result to the specification at the beginning of the Chapter; if the result is not as specified fit a new fuel pump. If it is as specified, and you are certain all the wiring and connectors are good, have the ECU checked by a Yamaha dealer.

Fuel delivery check

3 Raise the fuel tank, then disconnect the fuel supply and return hoses (see Section 2).

4 Plug the open end of the return hose and place the open end of the supply hose in a suitable container.

5 Ensure the ignition is OFF, then disconnect the fuel pump (green) wiring connector. Using a fully-charged 12 volt battery and two insulated jumper wires, connect the battery positive (+) terminal to the pump's red/blue wire terminal, and the battery negative (-) terminal to the pump's black wire terminal. Fuel should flow from the pump into the container. If fuel does not flow, the pump is defective and must be replaced with a new one. If fuel flows but you suspect the flow rate to be insufficient, make sure all hoses are in good condition and are not trapped or kinked, then check the pressure regulator (see Section 12 – special equipment is needed) and/or have the system operating pressure and the fuel pressure regulator checked by a Yamaha dealer. If the filter is blocked a new pump will have to be installed as the filter is an integral component.

Removal and installation

6 Siphon the fuel from the tank into a suitable container using a hand-pump, available from good tool and DIY stores.

7 Remove the fuel tank (see Section 2), and lay it upside down on plenty of clean rag.

8 Unscrew the bolts securing the pump retaining ring and remove the ring, noting how it fits **(see illustrations)**.

9 Carefully lift the pump and manoeuvre it out of the tank, noting that there is little clearance and delicate bits can easily catch the rim (see

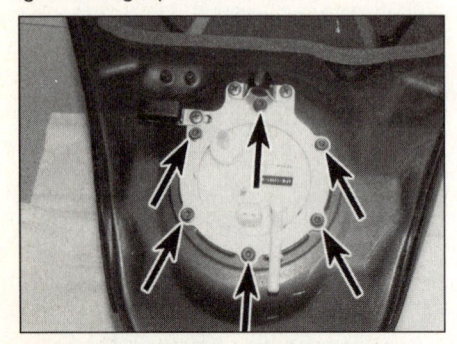

3.8a Unscrew the bolts (arrowed) . . .

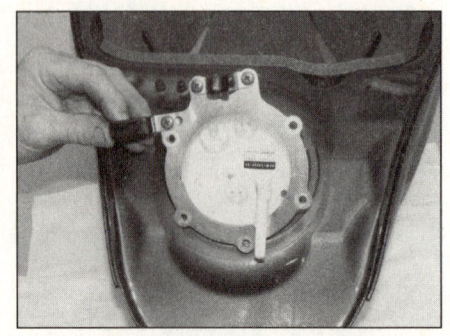

3.8b . . . and remove the ring

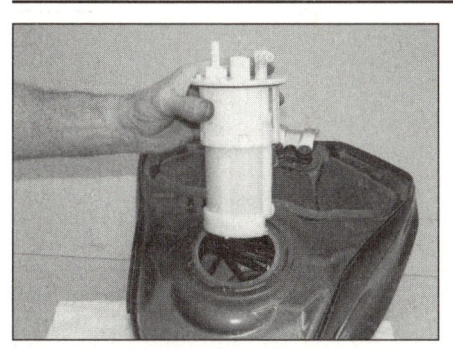

Engine management system 4•5

3.9a Carefully lift the pump out of the tank

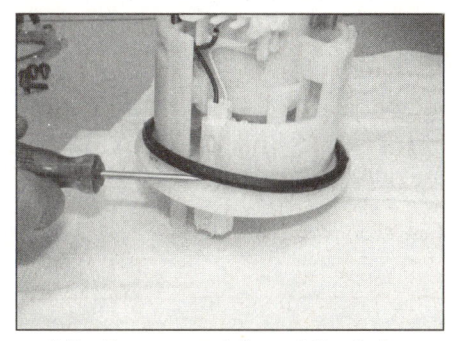

3.9b Remove and discard the O-ring

3.10a Position the pump as shown when inserting it

illustration). Remove the pump O-ring and discard it as a new one must be fitted **(see illustration)**.

10 Install the pump using a new O-ring, fitting its flat side down onto the pump base **(see illustration 3.9b)**. When inserting the pump, sit the wider diameter section of the rear on the rim of the aperture as shown so there is clearance for the protruding parts at the front **(see illustration)**. Align the pump so the fuel supply hose union points to the back, and fit the retaining ring with the U-shaped support bracket at the front **(see illustration 3.8a)**. Align the cut-out in the retaining ring with the stud on the underside of the pump **(see illustration)**. Tighten the screws evenly and in a criss-cross sequence to the torque setting specified at the beginning of the Chapter.

4 Fuel level warning light and sensor

1 The circuit consists of the sensor mounted on the fuel pump inside the tank and the warning light mounted in the instrument cluster. **Note:** *A circuit check is performed whenever the ignition (main) switch is turned ON. The warning light should come ON for a few seconds, then go OFF. If it doesn't, check the warning light LED (see Chapter 8).*

2 If a fault occurs, the warning light will be seen to flash eight times and then go out for 2.5 seconds, and this will repeat until the engine is switched OFF. If the system

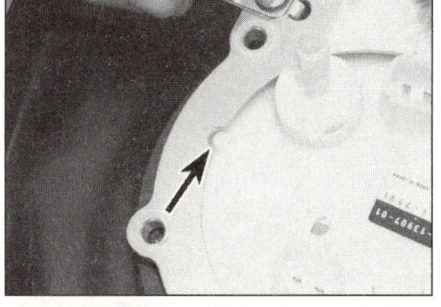

3.10b Cut-out in retaining ring must align with stud (arrowed)

malfunctions, check first that the battery is fully-charged and that the fuses are good (see Chapter 8). If they are, remove the fuel pump from the tank (see Section 3).

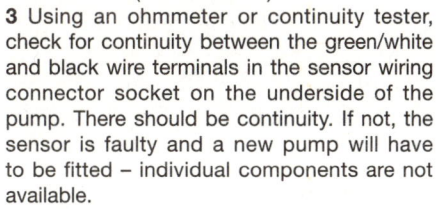

3 Using an ohmmeter or continuity tester, check for continuity between the green/white and black wire terminals in the sensor wiring connector socket on the underside of the pump. There should be continuity. If not, the sensor is faulty and a new pump will have to be fitted – individual components are not available.

4 If the sensor is good, install the pump in the fuel tank and install the tank. Disconnect the instrument cluster wiring connector (see Chapter 8). With the ignition ON, check for battery voltage (12V) at the instrument cluster wiring connector by connecting the positive (+) probe of a voltmeter to the green/white wire terminal on the loom side of the connector, and the negative (–) probe to the black wire terminal. If no voltage is present, the fault lies in the wiring. Check all the relevant wiring and wiring connectors (see Chapter 8), referring to the *Wiring Diagrams* at the end of Chapter 8.

5 If voltage is present, refer to Chapter 8 and check the fuel warning light LED in the instrument cluster. If the LED is faulty, a new cluster will have to be fitted as individual components are not available.

5 Air filter housing

Removal

1 Raise or remove the fuel tank (see Section 2).

2 Unscrew the bolt securing the front of the housing to the frame, noting the sleeve and grommet **(see illustration)**. Release the clip and pull the crankcase breather hose off its union at the rear of the housing **(see illustration)**.

3 Slacken the clamps securing the housing to the throttle body intakes on the underside **(see illustration)**. Slacken the clamps securing the air intake ducts to the front of the housing on each side.

4 Lift the housing up off the throttle bodies and out of the intake ducts, then when accessible release the clamps securing the throttle body air hoses and the AIS hose and detach them from the filter housing,

5.2a Unscrew the bolt at the front

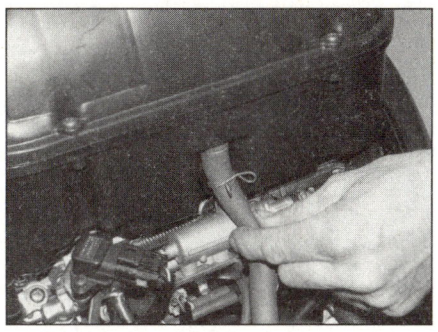

5.2b Detach the breather hose from the rear

5.3 Slacken the clamps (arrowed)

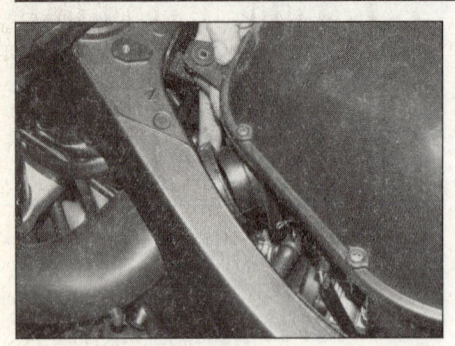

4•6 Engine management system

5.4a Lift the housing off the throttle bodies and out of the air ducts . . .

5.4b . . . and detach the hoses from the right-hand side . . .

5.4c . . . and the sensor and hose from the left-hand side

5.5 Slacken the clamp (arrowed) and remove the duct joint piece on each side

noting which fits where, and draw the intake air temperature sensor out, then remove the housing **(see illustrations)**.

5 If required slacken the clamps securing the air duct joint pieces and draw them out of the frame, noting which fits where **(see illustration)**.

Installation

6 Installation is the reverse of removal. Lubricate the housing where it fits over the throttle bodies with a squirt of WD40 or a smear of grease to aid installation. Check the condition of the various hoses and their clamps and replace them with new ones if necessary.

6 Fuel injection system description

1 The fuel injection system consists of two main component groups, the fuel circuit and the electronic control circuit **(see illustration)**.
2 The fuel circuit consists of the tank, pump and filter, pressure regulator, throttle bodies and injectors. Fuel is pumped under pressure from the tank to the fuel rail, from which the individual injectors are fed. Operating pressure is maintained by the pressure regulator. The

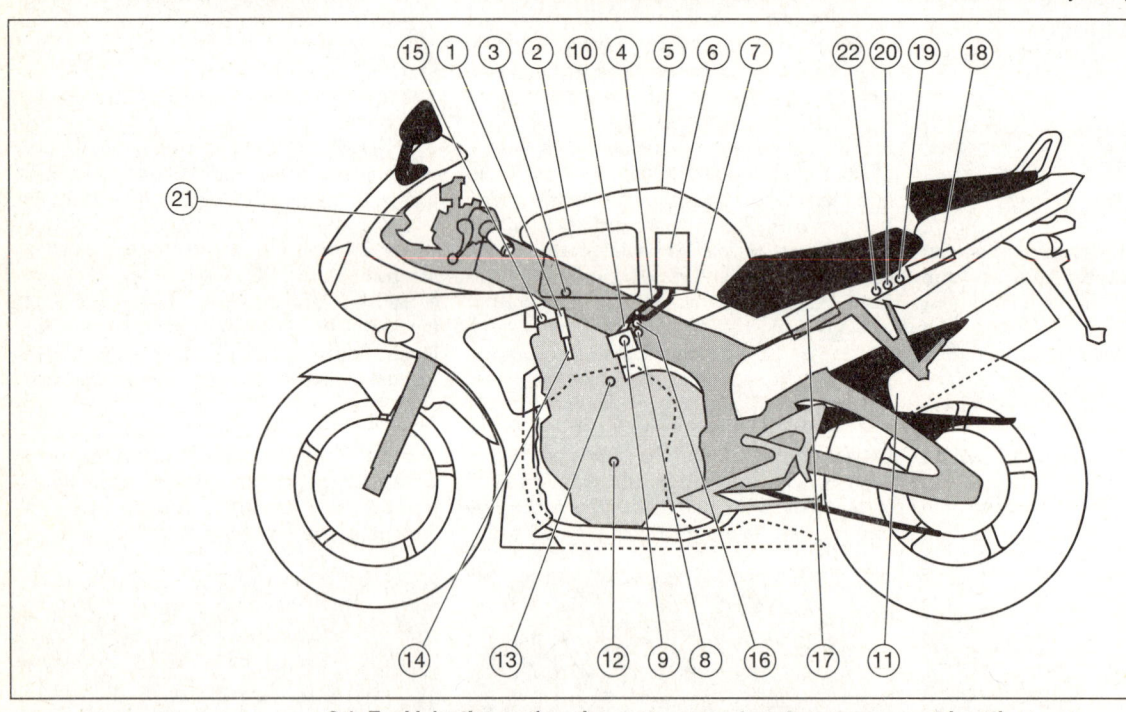

6.1 Fuel injection and engine management system component location

1 Ignition coil/plug cap
2 Air filter housing
3 Intake air temperature (IAT) sensor
4 Fuel supply hose
5 Fuel tank
6 Fuel pump
7 Fuel return hose
8 Intake air pressure (IAP) sensor
9 Throttle position (TP) sensor
10 Fuel injectors
11 Catalytic converter
12 Crankshaft position (CKP) sensor
13 Engine coolant temperature (ECT) sensor
14 Spark plug
15 Camshaft position (CMP) sensor
16 Fuel pressure regulator
17 Battery
18 Engine control unit (ECU)
19 Atmoshperic pressure (AP) sensor
20 Relay assembly
21 Engine warning light
22 Tip-over sensor

Engine management system 4•7

injectors spray pressurised fuel into the throttle bodies where it mixes with air and vaporises, before entering the cylinder where it is compressed and ignited.

3 The electronic control circuit consists of the engine control unit (ECU), which operates and co-ordinates both the fuel injection and ignition systems, and the various sensors which provide the ECU with information on engine operating conditions.

4 The ECU monitors signals from the following sensors:
   Intake air temperature sensor.
   Intake air pressure sensor.
   Throttle position sensor.
   Camshaft position sensor (cylinder identification).
   Crankshaft position sensor.
   Coolant temperature sensor.
   Atmospheric pressure sensor.
   Speed sensor.

5 Based on the information it receives, the ECU calculates the appropriate ignition and fuel requirements of the engine. By varying the length of the electronic pulse it sends to each injector, the ECU controls the length of time the injectors are held open and thereby the amount of fuel that is supplied to the engine. Fuel supply varies according to the engine's needs for starting, warming-up, idling, cruising and acceleration.

6 In the event of an abnormality in any of the sensor signals, the ECU will determine whether the engine can still be run safely. If it can, a back-up mode substitutes the sensor signal with a fixed signal, restricting performance but allowing the bike to be ridden home or to a dealer. When this occurs, the engine management warning light in the instrument cluster will come on and stay on. In some cases the engine will continue to run after the fault has been registered, but once stopped the engine will not be able to be restarted. If the fault is serious, the fuel injection system will be shut down and the engine will not run. When this occurs, the engine management warning light will flash while the start switch is being pressed. **Note:** *The warning light should come on for 1.4 seconds after the ignition (main) switch has been turned ON and while the starter switch is being pressed. If the warning light does not come on, check its LED circuit in the instrument cluster (see Chapter 8).*

7 After the engine has been stopped, the appropriate self-diagnostic fault code will appear on the clock LCD. See Section 7 for fault diagnosis.

7 Fuel injection system fault diagnosis

1 The system incorporates a self-diagnostic function whereby most faults, when they occur, are identified by a fault code which is displayed on the clock LCD after the engine has been stopped. The codes are stored in the ECU memory until a deletion operation is performed (see Step 9). In the case of a minor fault in the injection system, the engine management warning light in the instrument cluster will come on and stay on and the engine will continue to run enabling the machine to be ridden, although performance will be significantly reduced. In the case of a major fault the warning light will flash when the ignition switch is turned ON and it will not be possible to run the engine. Certain faults will not activate the warning light and are not subject to a fault code, but will be recorded as a diagnostic code. If the engine does not run correctly but no warning light and fault code are shown, enter diagnostic mode (see Step 3 onwards), check the code given and refer to the table.

2 Compare the fault code displayed with those in Table 1 to identify the faulty component and the appropriate diagnostic code (where given), then follow the procedure in Steps 3 to 5 and set the instrument cluster to diagnostic mode to confirm the appropriate test procedure and specifications. If a diagnostic code is not given for a particular fault code (i.e. 11 or 12), refer to Section 8 and check the component as described.

Table 1 Fuel system fault codes

Fault code	Faulty component – symptoms	Possible causes	Diagnostic code
11	Camshaft position sensor – engine will continue to run but will not restart once turned OFF	Faulty wiring or wiring connector Damaged or improperly installed sensor Faulty ECU	-
12	Crankshaft position sensor – engine will stop and will not restart	Faulty wiring or wiring connector Damaged or improperly installed sensor or timing rotor Faulty ECU	-
13	Intake air pressure sensor – engine will run, air pressure signal fixed at 760 mmHg	Faulty wiring or wiring connector Damaged or faulty sensor	03
14	Intake air pressure sensor hose system – engine will run, air pressure signal fixed at 760 mmHg	Hose system detached, pinched or blocked Faulty ECU	03
15	Throttle position sensor – engine will run, sensor signal fixed fully open	Faulty wiring or wiring connector Damaged or improperly installed sensor Faulty ECU	01
16	Throttle position sensor – engine will run, sensor signal fixed fully open	Throttle position sensor stuck Faulty ECU	01
19	Sidestand switch – engine will not run	Faulty wiring or wiring connector Faulty ECU	20
20	Intake air pressure sensor/atmospheric pressure sensor – engine will run, air pressure signals fixed at 760 mmHg	Damaged air pressure sensor/atmospheric pressure sensor Sensor hose pinched or blocked Faulty ECU	03/02
21	Coolant temperature sensor – engine will run, coolant temperature fixed at 60°C	Faulty wiring or wiring connector Damaged or improperly installed sensor Faulty ECU	06

4•8 Engine management system

Fault code	Faulty component – symptoms	Possible causes	Diagnostic code
22	Intake air temperature sensor – engine will run, intake temperature fixed at 20°C	Faulty wiring or wiring connector Damaged or improperly installed sensor Faulty ECU	05
23	Atmospheric pressure sensor – engine will run, air pressure signal fixed at 760 mmHg	Faulty wiring or wiring connector Damaged or improperly installed sensor Faulty ECU	02
30	Tip-over sensor – engine will not run, fuel system turned OFF	Machine overturned Faulty ECU	08
33	No 1 cylinder ignition coil – engine will run on other 3 cylinders, fuel supply to No 1 cylinder cut	Faulty wiring or wiring connector Damaged ignition coil Faulty ignition cut-off circuit Faulty ECU	30
34	No 2 cylinder ignition coil – engine will run on other 3 cylinders, fuel supply to No 2 cylinder cut	Faulty wiring or wiring connector Damaged ignition coil Faulty ignition cut-off circuit Faulty ECU	31
35	No 3 cylinder ignition coil – engine will run on other 3 cylinders, fuel supply to No 3 cylinder cut	Faulty wiring or wiring connector Damaged ignition coil Faulty ignition cut-off circuit Faulty ECU	32
36	No 4 cylinder ignition coil – engine will run on other 3 cylinders, fuel supply to No 4 cylinder cut	Faulty wiring or wiring connector Damaged ignition coil Faulty ignition cut-off circuit Faulty ECU	33
-	No 1 cylinder fuel injector	Faulty wiring or wiring connector	36
-	No 2 cylinder fuel injector	Faulty wiring or wiring connector	37
-	No 3 cylinder fuel injector	Faulty wiring or wiring connector	38
-	No 4 cylinder fuel injector	Faulty wiring or wiring connector	39
-	Air induction system	Faulty wiring or wiring connector	48
-	Starter cut-off relay	Faulty wiring or wiring connector Damaged relay	50
-	Radiator cooling fan relay	Faulty wiring or wiring connector Damaged relay	51
-	Headlight relay	Faulty wiring or wiring connector Damaged relay	52
41	Tip-over sensor – engine will not run, fuel system turned OFF	Faulty wiring or wiring connector Damaged sensor Faulty ECU	08
42	Speed sensor/neutral switch – engine will run, signal fixed in sixth gear	Damaged speed sensor/neutral switch Faulty wiring or wiring connector Faulty ECU	07/21
43	Battery voltage – engine will run, signal fixed at 12V	Faulty wiring or wiring connector Faulty ECU	09
44	Carbon monoxide density in exhaust gas incorrect – engine will run	Faulty air induction system (AIS) Error writing CO to EPROM Faulty ECU	60
46	Abnormal power supply to FI system (fuel pump/starter circuit cut-off) relay – engine will continue to run, but will not restart	Faulty wiring or wiring connector (red/blue wire) Faulty charging system	-
-	Fault code history display	Multiple codes displayed at 2 second intervals	61
-	Fault code total in ECU memory		62
50	ECU malfunction – fault code may not be displayed, engine will not run	Faulty wiring or wiring connector Damaged ECU	-
Er-1 Er-2 Er-3 Er-4	No communication or unreadable communication between ECU and instrument cluster – wiring harness, injection system component wiring connector, instrument cluster or ECU fault	Faulty wiring or wiring connector Damaged instrument cluster Damaged ECU	-

Note: *The engine will not run when two or more ignition coils or fuel injectors fail.*

Engine management system 4•9

3 To set-up the diagnostic mode, first ensure that the main (ignition) switch is OFF and that the engine stop switch is ON, then disconnect the fuel pump wiring connector (see Section 2).

4 Press the SELECT and RESET buttons on the instrument cluster simultaneously, then turn the ignition (main) switch ON, keeping the SELECT and RESET buttons pressed for at least 8 seconds.

5 Select the diagnostic mode by pressing the SELECT button until DIAG appears on the clock LCD. Confirm the selection by pressing the SELECT and RESET buttons simultaneously for 2 seconds, then turn the engine stop switch OFF.

6 Use the SELECT or RESET button to enter the appropriate diagnostic code on the clock LCD. The SELECT button displays the code numbers in ascending order, the RESET button displays the numbers in descending order. The appropriate test specifications are displayed on the trip LCD.

7 Compare the diagnostic code with Table 2 to identify the test action required. Compare the test results to any data displayed on the meter for that diagnostic code. To cancel the diagnostic mode, turn the ignition (main) switch OFF.

Table 2 Fuel system diagnostic codes and data

Diagnostic code	Action required	Data displayed
01	Check angle data displayed with throttle fully closed Check angle data displayed with throttle fully open	Fully closed – 15 to 17 Fully open – 97 to 100
02	Compare actual atmospheric pressure* with data displayed	-
03	Turn the engine stop switch ON and crank the engine using the starter motor to generate a pressure difference	10 to 200 mmHg
05	Check the temperature** in the air filter housing and compare with data displayed	-
06	Check the temperature*** of the coolant and compare with data displayed	-
07	Turn the rear wheel in the normal direction of rotation and check pulses generated are displayed	0 to 999
08	Check the operation of the tip-over sensor	Machine upright – 0.4 to 1.4V Laid over – 3.8 to 4.2V
09	Turn the engine stop switch ON and check battery voltage (see Chapter 8)	0 to 18.7V. Normally 12V
20	Select a gear position other than neutral	Stand retracted – ON Stand down – OFF
21	Check the operation of the neutral switch	Gearbox in neutral – ON In gear – OFF
30 to 33	Check the operation of the appropriate ignition coil – setting the engine kill switch from OFF to ON will generate five sparks in the appropriate coil and the engine management warning light comes on. Check for the sparks by removing the plugs and checking as described in Section 17	-
36 to 39	Check the operation of the appropriate fuel injector – setting the engine kill switch from OFF to ON will generate five pulses in the appropriate injector and the engine management warning light comes on. Check for the pulses using a sounding rod as described in Section 10	-
48	Check the operation of the air induction system solenoid – setting the engine kill switch from OFF to ON will actuate the solenoid five times and the engine management warning light comes on. You should be able to hear the solenoid – refer to Section 15 for access and further checks	-
50	Check the operation of the fuel injection system (fuel pump/starter cut-off) relays – setting the engine kill switch from OFF to ON will actuate the relay five times and the engine management warning light comes on. You should be able to hear the relay click – refer to Section 8 (fuel pump relay) and Chapter 8 (starter circuit cut-off relay) for access and further checks	-
51	Check the operation of the radiator cooling fan relay – setting the engine kill switch from OFF to ON will actuate the solenoid five times and the engine management warning light comes on. You should be able to hear the solenoid – refer to Chapter 3 for access and further checks	-
52	Check the operation of the headlight relay – setting the engine kill switch from OFF to ON will actuate the solenoid five times and the engine management warning light comes on. You should be able to hear the solenoid – refer to Chapter 8 for access and further checks	-
60	Check the carbon monoxide density in the exhaust gas Check the AIS cut-off valve	Faulty cylinder – 01 to 04
61	Once corrected, delete the fault codes	11 to 50
62	Once corrected, delete the fault codes	00 to 21
70	Programme control number displayed	00 to 255

* If an atmospheric pressure gauge is not available, use 760 mmHg as the standard
** If possible, check the temperature next to the sensor, otherwise use the ambient temperature as the standard
*** Check the temperature of the coolant as close as possible to the sensor

4•10 Engine management system

8 Once the fault has been corrected, confirm that the fault code is no longer displayed by turning the ignition (main) switch OFF and then ON again. If the code is no longer displayed on the clock LCD the repair is complete.

9 To delete the fault code from the ECU memory, follow the procedure in Steps 3 to 5 to set-up the diagnostic mode, then enter code 62 on the clock LCD. The total number of stored codes will be displayed on the trip LCD (00 to 21). Turn the engine stop switch ON to delete the stored codes – the LCD should display 00 codes.

8 Fuel injection system components

1 If a fault is indicated in any of the system components, first check the wiring and connectors between the appropriate component and the ECU (see *Wiring diagrams* at the end of Chapter 8). A continuity test of all wires will locate a break or short in any circuit. Inspect the terminals inside the wiring connectors and ensure they are not loose, bent or corroded. Spray the inside of the connectors with a proprietary electrical terminal cleaner before reconnection.

2 It is possible to undertake most checks on system components using a multimeter and comparing the results with the specifications at the beginning of the Chapter. **Note:** *Different meters may give slightly different results to those specified even though the component being tested is not faulty – do not consign a component to the bin before having it double-checked.* However, some faults will only become evident when a component is tested with specialised equipment, in which case the checks should be undertaken by a Yamaha dealer.

3 If after a thorough check the source of a fault has not been identified, it is possible that the ECU itself is faulty. Yamaha provides no test specifications for the ECU. In order to determine conclusively that the unit is defective, it should be substituted with a known good one. If the problem is rectified, the original unit is faulty.

Camshaft position sensor

Check

4 Support the machine on an auxiliary stand with the rear wheel off the ground. Make sure the ignition is OFF. Remove the air filter housing (see Section 5). Note the routing of all cables, wiring and hoses over and around the radiator cover. Release the cable ties securing the wiring **(see illustration)**. Release the trim clips securing the cover and remove it, noting how it fits **(see illustrations)**.

5 Using a voltmeter or multimeter set to the volts (DC) scale, insert the positive (+) probe of the meter into the white/black wire terminal in the back of the connector, with the connector still connected, and insert the negative (-) probe into the black/blue terminal **(see illustration)**. Turn the ignition (main) switch ON, select a high gear and rotate the rear wheel by hand in its normal direction of rotation. As the engine turns, the output voltage should fluctuate between the two levels shown in the specifications at the beginning of the Chapter. Turn the ignition OFF.

6 If the voltage is not as specified, replace the sensor with a new one.

Removal and installation

7 Disconnect the sensor wiring connector (see Step 4 for access) **(see illustration 8.5)**. Unscrew the bolt securing the sensor to the valve cover and withdraw the sensor **(see illustration)**. On installation, smear the sensor O-ring with grease and apply a suitable thread lock to the bolt threads **(see illustration)**. Tighten the bolt to the torque setting specified at the beginning of the Chapter. Install the radiator cover and air filter housing.

Crankshaft position sensor

Check

8 Remove the right-hand fairing side panel (see Chapter 7). Remove the fuel tank (see Section 2). Make sure the ignition is OFF.

9 The crankshaft position sensor is on the right-hand end of the crankshaft. Trace the wiring from the timing rotor cover and disconnect it at the connector. Referring to the wiring diagram at the end of this manual, trace the wiring from the sensor up to the connector, which is situated on the right hand side of the frame and disconnect it. Using an ohmmeter or multimeter set to the ohms x 100 scale, measure the resistance between the terminals on the sensor side of the connector. Connect

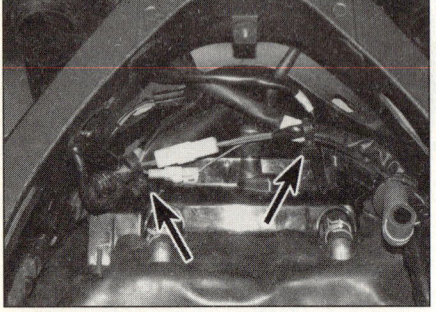

8.4a Release the cable ties (arrowed) . . .

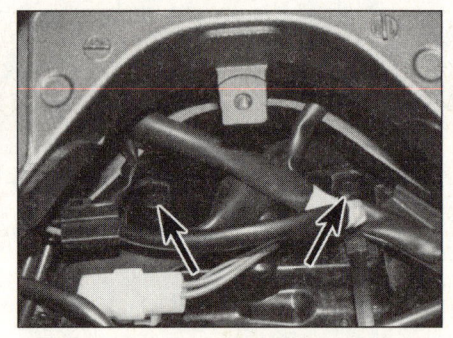

8.4b . . . then move the wiring aside and release the trim clips (arrowed) . . .

8.4c . . . and remove the cover

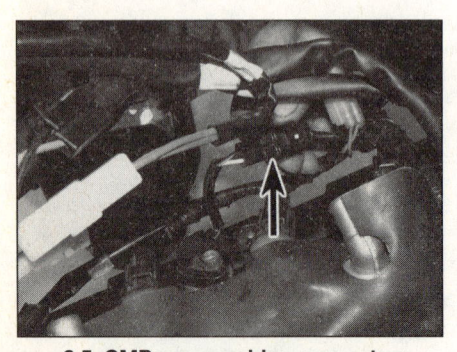

8.5 CMP sensor wiring connector (arrowed)

8.7a Unscrew the bolt (arrowed) and remove the sensor

8.7b Smear grease onto the O-ring (arrowed)

Engine management system 4•11

8.12 Unscrew the bolts (arrowed) and remove the cover

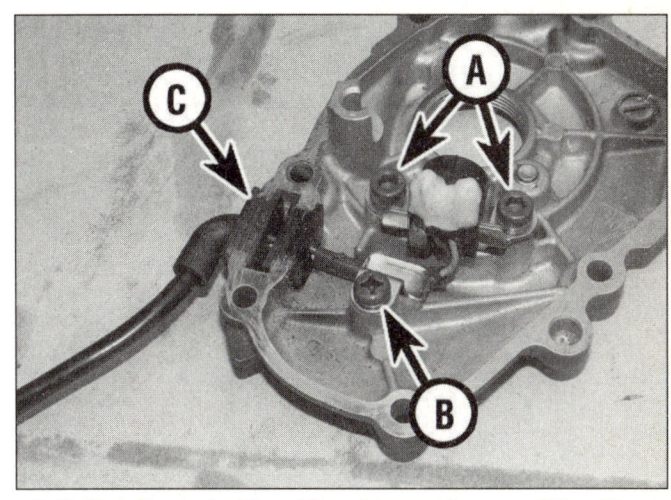

8.13 Undo the bolts (A) and the wiring guide screw (B) and free the grommet (C)

the positive (+) probe to the grey wire terminal in the connector and the negative (−) probe to the black wire terminal. If the result is not as specified, replace the sensor with a new one.

Removal and installation

10 Remove the lower fairing and the right-hand fairing side panel (see Chapter 7), and disconnect the battery negative (−) lead (Chapter 8). Remove the fuel tank (see Section 2).

11 Trace the wiring from the timing rotor cover and disconnect it at the connector. Feed the wiring back to the coil, noting its routing and releasing it from any clips.

12 Place an oil pan under the timing rotor cover on the right-hand side of the engine to catch any oil as it is removed. Unscrew the bolts and remove the cover, noting the clamp for the coolant hose and the bracket for the clutch cable **(see illustration)**. Discard the gasket, as a new one must be used and remove the dowels from either the crankcase or the cover if they are loose.

13 Unscrew the bolts securing the pick-up coil and the screw securing the wiring guide to the inside of the cover, then free the wiring grommet from the cut-out in the cover and remove the coil **(see illustration)**.

14 Apply a suitable sealant to the wiring grommet. Fit the coil and the wiring grommet into their locations in the cover and tighten the bolts to the torque setting specified at the beginning of this Chapter.

15 Ensure the dowels for the timing rotor cover are in place and that the cam chain tensioner blade pivot pin locates in the hole in the cover **(see illustrations)**. Install the cover bolts, the clamp for the coolant hose and the bracket for the clutch cable and tighten the bolts to the torque setting specified at the beginning of this Chapter – the longer bolts secure the clutch cable bracket **(see illustration 8.12)**.

16 Feed the wiring up to the connector and reconnect it.

17 Reconnect the battery negative (−) terminal and install the remaining components in the reverse order of removal.

Intake air pressure sensor

Check

18 Make sure the ignition is OFF. Raise or remove the fuel tank (see Section 2).

19 The sensor is on the fuel rail **(see illustration)**. Check the condition of the vacuum hose between the underside of the sensor and the throttle bodies. If the hose is cracked or perished replace it with a new one. Ensure the hose is a tight fit on the sensor union, the hose connectors and the throttle bodies.

20 Using a voltmeter or multimeter set to the volts (DC) scale, insert the positive (+) probe of the meter into the pink/white wire terminal in the back of the connector, with the connector still connected, and insert the negative (−) probe into the black/blue terminal. Turn the ignition ON and measure the sensor output voltage. Turn the ignition OFF.

21 If the voltage is not as specified, replace the sensor with a new one.

Removal and installation

22 Raise or remove the fuel tank (see Section 2). Disconnect the vacuum hose and the wiring connector from the sensor **(see illustration 8.19)**. Undo the screws securing the sensor to the fuel rail and remove the sensor. On installation, ensure the wiring connector terminals are clean and that the vacuum hose is a tight fit on the sensor union.

Throttle position sensor

Check

23 Check the engine idle speed and make sure it is correctly set (see Chapter 1). Make sure the ignition is OFF. Remove the air filter housing (see Section 5).

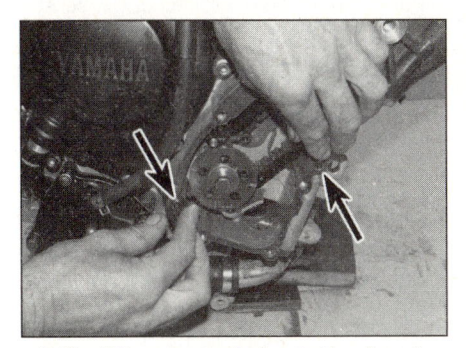

8.15a Fit a new gasket onto the dowels (arrowed) . . .

8.15b . . . then install the cover, making sure it locates correctly

8.19 Intake air pressure (IAP) sensor (arrowed)

4•12 Engine management system

8.24 Throttle position sensor (arrowed) and its wiring connector

8.26 Throttle position sensor screws (arrowed) – a security Torx bit is needed to undo them

24 The sensor is on the right-hand end of the throttle body assembly **(see illustration)**. Disconnect the sensor wiring connector. Using an ohmmeter or multimeter set to the K-ohms scale, connect the positive (+) probe to the yellow wire terminal in the connector and the negative (-) probe to the black/blue wire terminal and measure the resistance range between the terminals on the sensor side of the connector – open and close the throttle twistgrip slowly and check that the resistance changes gradually within the specified range. If the result is not as specified, if the resistance does not change or changes abruptly, replace the sensor with a new one.

25 Next, connect the ohmmeter or multimeter positive (+) probe to the blue wire terminal in the connector and the negative (-) probe to the black wire terminal and measure the sensor maximum resistance. If the result is not as specified, replace the sensor with a new one.

Removal and installation

26 Disconnect the sensor wiring connector **(see illustration 8.24)**. Displace the throttle body assembly to access the sensor fixing screws (see Section 9). The sensor is secured by two Torx security screws **(see illustration)**. Undo the Torx screws and lift off the sensor, noting how the slot in the sensor fits over the throttle shaft. If the slot is worn or broken, replace the sensor with a new one.

27 To install the sensor, position the slot in the sensor onto the throttle shaft and tighten the screws hand-tight. Connect the sensor wiring connector. Now adjust the position of the sensor. Using a voltmeter or multimeter set to the volts (DC) scale, insert the positive (+) probe of the meter into the blue wire terminal in back of the connector, with the connector still connected, and insert the negative (-) probe into the yellow terminal. Turn the ignition ON and carefully adjust the position of the sensor until the voltage is within the specified range, then tighten the fixing screws. Turn the ignition OFF. Install the throttle body assembly (see Section 9).

Sidestand switch

28 Follow the procedure in Chapter 8 to check the operation of the switch.

Atmospheric pressure sensor

29 Make sure the ignition is OFF. Remove the seat cowling (see Chapter 7). The sensor is on the right-hand side of the sub-frame **(see illustration)**.

30 Using a voltmeter or multimeter set to the volts (DC) scale, insert the positive (+) probe of the meter into the blue wire terminal in back of the connector, with the connector still connected, and insert the negative (-) probe into the black/blue terminal. Turn the ignition ON and measure the sensor output voltage. Turn the ignition OFF.

31 If the output voltage is not as specified, the sensor air passage may be clogged with dirt. Disconnect the wiring connector and undo the screws securing the sensor. Clean the outside of the sensor with a damp cloth and check the air passage for any obstruction, then install the sensor and retest the output voltage (see Step 30).

32 If the voltage is still not as specified, replace the sensor with a new one.

Coolant temperature sensor

33 Follow the procedure in Chapter 3 to check the operation of the sensor.

Intake air temperature sensor

Check

34 Raise the fuel tank (See Section 2). The sensor is mounted in the left-hand side of the air filter housing **(see illustration 5.4c)**.

35 Make sure the ignition is OFF. Disconnect the wiring connector from the sensor. Using an ohmmeter or multimeter set to the ohms x 100 scale, measure the resistance between the terminals on the sensor side of the connector. Connect the positive (+) probe to the brown/white wire terminal in the sensor and the negative (-) probe to the black/blue wire terminal. If the result is not as specified replace the sensor with a new one.

Removal and installation

36 Raise the fuel tank (See Section 2). The sensor fits into a grommet in the left-hand side of the air filter housing **(see illustration 5.4c)**. To remove the sensor, first disconnect the wiring connector, then pull the sensor out.

Tip-over sensor

Check

37 Make sure the ignition is OFF. Remove the seat cowling (see Chapter 7).

8.29 Atmospheric pressure sensor (arrowed)

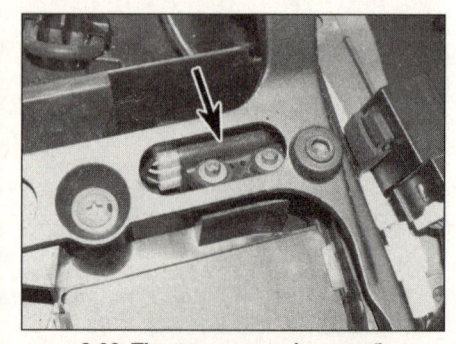

8.38 Tip-over sensor (arrowed)

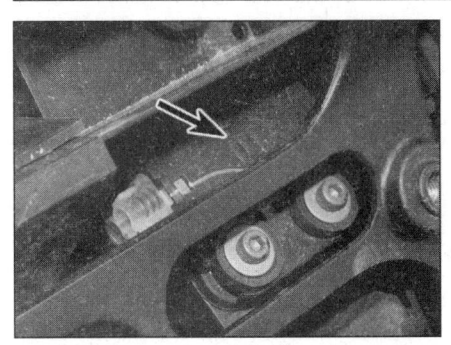

Engine management system 4•13

8.41 Note the UP marking on the sensor

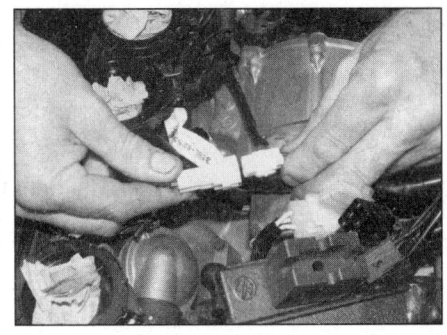

8.44 Disconnect the speed sensor wiring connector

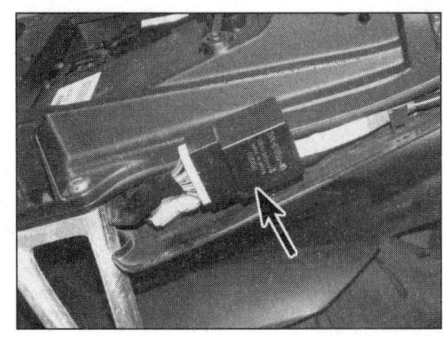

8.48 Relay assembly (arrowed)

38 The sensor is situated to the rear of the ECU **(see illustration)**. Remove the sensor (see Step 41) but do not disconnect the wiring connector.

39 Using a voltmeter or multimeter set to the volts (DC) scale, insert the positive (+) probe of the meter into the blue wire terminal in back of the connector, with the connector still connected, and insert the negative (-) probe into the yellow/green terminal. Turn the ignition ON. Hold the sensor in its normal position when the bike is upright with the UP mark facing up **(see illustration 8.41)**, then tilt it 65° to one side and then the other. Turn the ignition OFF.

40 If the voltage is not as specified when the sensor is upright and tilted over, replace the sensor with a new one. Note the top surface of the sensor is marked UP.

Removal and installation

41 Make sure the ignition is OFF. Remove the seat cowling (see Chapter 7). Undo the screws securing the sensor, noting the washers **(see illustration 8.38)**. Displace the sensor and disconnect the wiring connector. Note the top surface of the sensor is marked UP **(see illustration)** – make sure this mark is on top when installing the sensor.

Ignition coils

42 Follow the procedure in Section 18 to check the ignition coils.

Speed sensor

Check

43 Support the machine on an auxiliary stand with the rear wheel off the ground. Make sure the ignition is OFF. Raise or remove the fuel tank (see Section 2). The sensor is on the back of the crankcase.

44 Trace the wiring from the sensor to the white three-pin connector on the right-hand side **(see illustration)**. Using a voltmeter or multimeter set to the volts (DC) scale, insert the positive (+) probe of the meter into the pink wire terminal in the back of the connector, with the connector still connected, and insert the negative (-) probe into the black/white terminal. Turn the ignition (main) switch ON, select a high gear and rotate the rear wheel by hand in its normal direction of rotation. As the engine turns, the output voltage should fluctuate between the two levels shown in the specifications at the beginning of the Chapter. Turn the ignition OFF.

45 If the voltage is not as specified, replace the sensor with a new one.

Removal and installation

46 To remove the sensor, first disconnect the wiring connector **(see illustration 8.44)**. Lift the rubber heat shield. Undo the screw securing the sensor to the crankcase and withdraw the sensor. Discard the sealing washer as a new one must be fitted. On installation, ensure the wiring connector terminals are clean and that the pins are not damaged.

Neutral switch

47 Follow the procedure in Chapter 8 to check the operation of the switch.

Fuel pump relay

48 Make sure the ignition is OFF. Remove the seat cowling (see Chapter 7). The relay assembly is mounted on the left-hand side of the rear sub-frame **(see illustration)** and contains the fuel pump relay and starter circuit cut-off relay.

49 Disconnect the relay unit wiring connector. Using an ohmmeter or continuity tester, connect the positive (+) probe to the red wire terminal on the relay and the negative (-) probe to the red/blue wire terminal. There should be no continuity. Using a fully-charged 12V battery and some jumper leads, connect the positive (+) terminal of the battery to the red/black wire terminal on the relay, and the negative (-) terminal to the light green wire terminal. There should now be continuity between the red and red/blue wire terminals.

50 If the relay does not operate, replace it with a new one.

Exhaust gas CO content

51 Have the exhaust gases analysed by a Yamaha dealer.

52 Follow the procedure in Section 15 to check the AIS.

9 Throttle bodies

⚠ **Warning:** *Refer to the precautions given in Section 1 before starting work.*

Special tool: *Access to the clamp screws is extremely restricted and requires the use of a long reach 3 mm Allen key.*

Removal

1 Remove the air filter housing (see Section 5).

2 Partially drain the cooling system (see Chapter 3).

3 Disconnect the fuel injector wiring loom connectors (1 black, 1 white) **(see illustration)**.

4 Free the idle speed adjuster from its holder **(see illustration)**.

9.3 Disconnect the wiring connectors

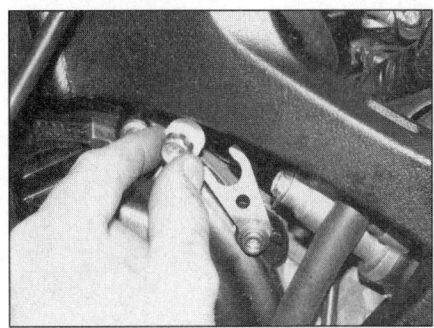

9.4 Free the idle speed adjuster

4•14 Engine management system

9.5 Release the clamps and detach the hoses

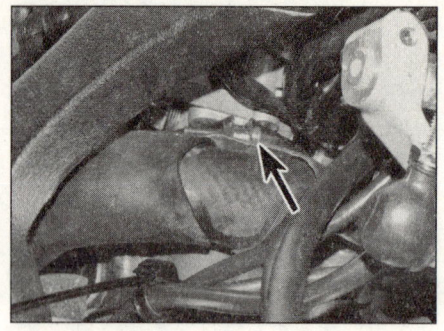

9.6a Slacken the clamp screw (arrowed) on each throttle body . . .

9.6b . . . accessing them as described

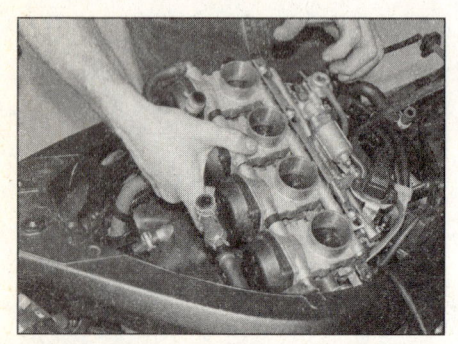

9.7a Displace the throttle bodies . . .

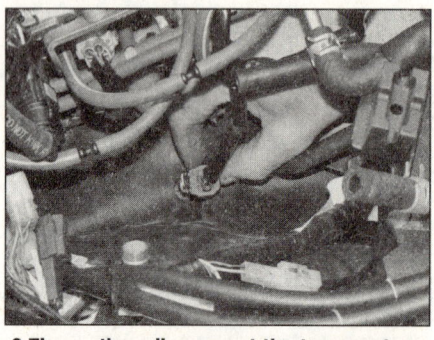

9.7b . . . then disconnect the temperature sensor wiring connector and detach the throttle cables

9.8 Note how the clamps locate on the intake rubbers, and that the rubbers are marked R or L to denote position

5 Place some rag under the fast idle unit to catch any residual coolant. Disconnect the coolant hoses from the unit, noting which fits where **(see illustration)**. Clamp or plug the hoses to prevent further loss of coolant.

6 Slacken the clamp screws on the cylinder head intake rubbers, noting their orientation – you will need a long 3 mm Allen bit and a socket extension to access them, and access the right-hand clamps from under the left-hand side of the frame and the left-hand clamps from the right-hand side **(see illustrations)**.

7 Ease the throttle body assembly off the intakes and disconnect the coolant temperature sensor wiring connector when accessible, then follow the procedure in Section 13 and detach the throttle cables **(see illustrations)**. Lift off the throttle body assembly.

8 Note how the clamps locate on the intake rubbers **(see illustration)**.

9 If required release the fuel tank drain and breather hoses from the clip on the rubber heat shield, then remove the shield, noting how it fits and how the wiring and hoses are routed **(see illustration)**.

Caution: Stuff clean rag into each cylinder head intake to prevent anything from falling inside.

Disassembly

10 Refer to Section 10 and remove the fuel rail and injectors.

11 Note the arrangement of the vacuum hoses and where they connect on the throttle body, then pull them off their unions, leaving them connected to each other, and remove them **(see illustration)**. On California models, detach the emission system hoses, noting how they fit.

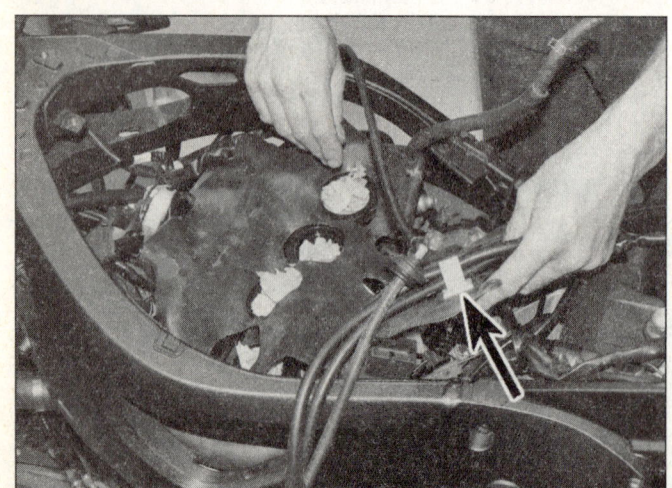

9.9 Release the hoses from the clip (arrowed) and remove the rubber shield, noting how it fits

9.11 Note the arrangement of the hoses before detaching them

Engine management system 4•15

9.12a Undo the screws and remove the cover...

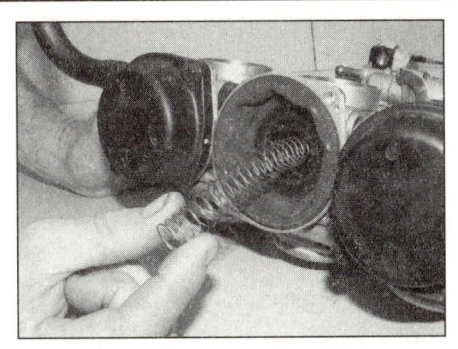

9.12b ...and the spring...

9.12c ...then withdraw the diaphragm/piston assembly

12 Unscrew and remove the top cover retaining screws and remove the cover and spring (see illustrations). Carefully peel the diaphragm away from its sealing groove in the throttle body and withdraw the diaphragm and piston (see illustration).
Caution: Do not use a sharp instrument to displace the diaphragm, as it is easily damaged.
13 The air screw should only be removed from each throttle body if absolutely necessary, but note that its setting will be disturbed (see **Haynes Hint**). Unscrew and remove the air screw along with its spring, washer and O-ring (see illustration). Discard the O-ring, as a new one must be used.

> **HAYNES HiNT** *Record the air screw's current setting by turning it in until it seats lightly, precisely counting the exact number of turns necessary to achieve this, then fully unscrew it. On installation, thread the screw all the way in then back it out the exact number of turns you've recorded.*

14 If required, remove the throttle position sensor (see Section 9).

Cleaning

Caution: Use only a petroleum-based solvent for cleaning. Do not use caustic cleaners.
15 Ensure that only metal components come into contact with the cleaning solvent and always follow manufacturer's recommendations as to cleaning time. If a spray cleaner is used, direct the spray into all passages.
16 After the cleaner has loosened and dissolved most of the varnish and other deposits, use a nylon-bristle brush to remove the stubborn deposits. Rinse the throttle bodies, then dry them with compressed air.
Caution: Never clean the jets or passages with a piece of wire or a drill bit, as they will be enlarged, causing the fuel and air metering rates to be upset.
17 Use compressed air to blow out all of the fuel and air passages.

Inspection

18 If removed, check the tapered portion of the air screw and the spring and O-ring for wear or damage. Replace the components with new ones if necessary – the O-ring is available singly, but the air screw, spring and washer come as a set.
19 Check the throttle bodies for cracks, distorted sealing surfaces and other damage. If any defects are found, fit a new throttle body assembly.
20 Check the diaphragm for splits, holes, creases and general deterioration. Holding it up to a light will help to reveal problems of this nature. Replace it with a new one if necessary.
21 Insert the piston in its throttle body and check that it moves up-and-down smoothly (see illustration 9.12c). Check the surface of the piston for wear. If it is worn excessively or doesn't move smoothly, replace it with a new one. Check the spring for distortion.
22 Operate the throttle shaft to make sure the throttle butterfly valves open and close smoothly. If they don't, clean the throttle linkage, and also check the throttle bodies for wear where butterfly valves close against them.
23 Check all the vacuum hoses for cracks, splits and kinks and replace them with new ones if necessary.

Reassembly

24 Reassemble the throttle bodies, noting the following:
● If removed the air screw must be set exactly as it was before removal.
● When installing the diaphragm in the throttle body make sure its rim is correctly located before fitting the top cover. Fit the cover with its arrow pointing forwards and locate the post in its centre in the top of the spring (see illustrations).
● After installing the piston, diaphragm, spring and top cover, make sure the piston moves smoothly up and down in its guide by lifting it with finger pressure and allowing it to drop – note that its fall will be damped by the diaphragm.

Installation

25 Installation is the reverse of removal, noting the following.
● Check for cracks or splits in the cylinder head intake rubbers, and replace them with

9.13 Only remove the air screw (arrowed) if necessary, and make sure you record its setting beforehand

9.24a Make sure the top of the spring locates over the post in the cover...

9.24b ...and that the cover is fitted so the arrow points forwards (i.e. towards the engine)

4•16 Engine management system

9.25 Make sure the rubber heat shield is correctly fitted and everything correctly routed

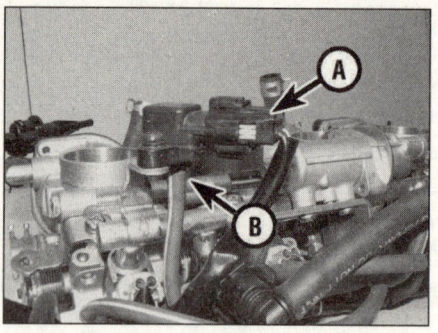

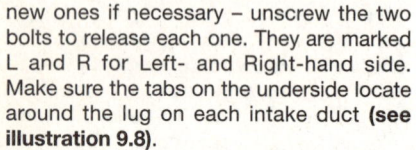

10.7a Disconnect the wiring connector (A) and detach the vacuum hose (B) . . .

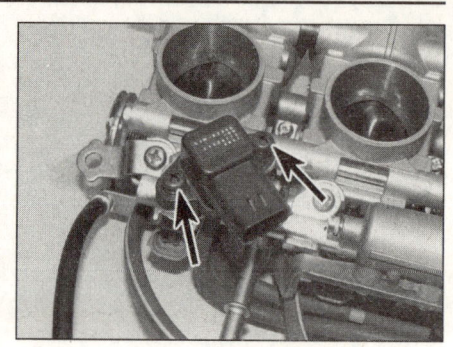

10.7b . . . then undo the screws (arrowed) and remove the sensor

new ones if necessary – unscrew the two bolts to release each one. They are marked L and R for Left- and Right-hand side. Make sure the tabs on the underside locate around the lug on each intake duct **(see illustration 9.8)**.
- Make sure the rubber heat shield is correctly positioned **(see illustration)**.
- Refer to Section 13 for installation of the throttle cables.
- Make sure the clamps on the cylinder head intake rubbers are correctly positioned **(see illustration 9.8)**. Make sure the throttle bodies are fully engage with the rubbers – they can be difficult to engage, so a squirt of WD40 or a smear of grease will ease entry. Tighten the clamps.
- Do not forget to connect the wiring loom connectors **(see illustration 9.3)**.

- Make sure all hoses are in good condition, correctly routed and secured and not trapped or kinked.
- Top-up the cooling system (see Chapter 1).
- Check idle speed and throttle body synchronisation and adjust as necessary (see Chapter 1).

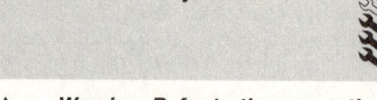

10 Fuel rail and injectors

⚠ **Warning:** *Refer to the precautions given in Section 1 before proceeding.*

Check

1 Remove the fuel tank (see Section 2).

2 If the engine runs, start it and allow it to idle. Check the operation of each injector in the throttle bodies using a stethoscope or sounding rod; an injector will emit a 'clicking' noise when functioning. If any injector is silent, either the injector or its wiring harness is faulty.
3 If the engine does not run, disconnect the wiring connector from each injector **(see illustration 10.8a)**. Connect an ohmmeter between the terminals of each injector in turn and check for a resistance – Yamaha do not specify a figure, but if there is no resistance the injector is probably faulty. Using the wiring diagrams at the end of Chapter 8 check for continuity in the wiring and connectors between the injectors and the ECU, and between the injectors and ground.

Removal

4 Remove the throttle bodies (see Section 9).
5 Remove the fast idle unit linkage bar (see Section 11, Step 10).
6 Disconnect the vacuum hose from the fuel pressure regulator **(see illustration 12.2)**. If required, undo the screws that secure the fuel pressure regulator to the fuel rail and remove it, noting the O-ring. **Note:** *Yamaha do not list the O-ring as a new part; check with a Yamaha dealer if the O-ring is leaking or damaged.*
7 Disconnect the wiring connector and the vacuum hose from the intake air pressure sensor **(see illustration)**. If required, undo the screws securing the sensor to the fuel rail and remove it **(see illustration)**.
8 Disconnect the wiring connectors from the fuel injectors and throttle position sensor, then remove the throttle body assembly wiring loom, noting its routing and releasing it from any ties **(see illustrations)**.
9 If required remove the security clip on the fuel supply hose connector, then press in the two tabs on the connector and pull it off the union **(see illustrations)**.
10 Remove the screws securing the fuel rail to the throttle bodies **(see illus-**

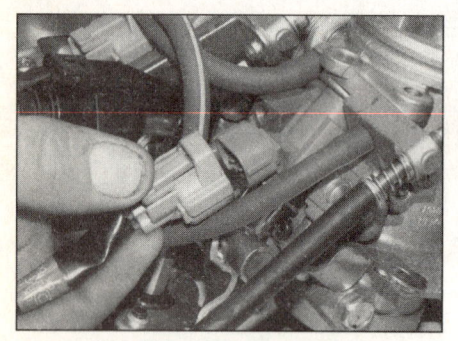

10.8a Disconnect the injector connectors . . .

10.8b . . . and the TP sensor connector

10.9a Remove the security clip . . .

10.9b . . . and release the fuel supply hose

Engine management system 4•17

10.10 Fuel rail screws (arrowed)

11.8a Unhook the spring . . .

11.8b . . . then undo the screws (arrowed) and remove the unit

tration). Carefully lift the fuel rail off the throttle bodies – the injectors will come away with the rail.

11 Pull each injector out of the fuel rail, noting how it fits. Discard the injector seals and O-ring as new ones must be fitted on reassembly. Note the cushion on each injector – these are not listed as spare parts.

12 Modern fuels contain detergents which should keep the injectors clean and free of gum or varnish from residue fuel. If an injector is suspected of being blocked, clean it through with injector cleaner. If the injector is clean but its performance is suspect, take it to a Yamaha dealer for assessment.

Installation

Note: *Apply a smear of clean engine oil to all new seals and O-rings before reassembly.*

13 Make sure the cushion is in place on each injector. Fit a new seal onto the nozzle end of each injector and a new O-ring onto the inlet end. Carefully press the injectors into the fuel rail. **Note:** *Avoid twisting the injectors as this may damage the O-rings.*

14 Fit the fuel rail and injectors onto the throttle bodies, making sure each injector is correctly aligned and its seal is correctly seated. Make sure the fuel rail is seated on its mounts with the screw holes aligned before installing the screws – do not use the screws to correctly seat and align them.

15 Install the fuel rail screws and tighten them **(see illustration 10.10)**.

16 If removed connect the fuel supply hose, making sure it clicks into place and is secure, then fit the clip **(see illustrations 10.9b and a)**.

17 Connect the individual injector wiring connectors and the TP sensor connector **(see illustrations 10.8a and b)**.

18 Install the remaining components in the reverse order of removal. Run the engine and make sure there is absolutely no fuel leakage before riding the bike.

11 Fast idle system

> **Warning:** *Refer to the precautions given in Section 1 before proceeding.*

Check

1 The fast idle unit is mounted on the upper left-hand side of the fuel rail. The wax element inside the unit expands with heat from the coolant temperature, extending the pushrod which actuates the linkage bar and the fast idle plungers on the throttle body assembly.

2 The pushrod should be fully retracted and the plungers open when the engine is cold, and the pushrod extended and the plungers closed when the engine reaches normal operating temperature, which is usually reached after 10 to 15 minutes of stop-and-go riding. If a smooth, steady idle cannot be achieved, check that the unit is operating properly.

3 With the engine cold, follow the procedure in Section 2 and raise the fuel tank. Check the position of the plunger. Install the tank and run the engine until it reaches normal operating temperature, then check the position of the plunger again.

4 If you suspect the unit is not working correctly, check the linkage bar assembly and the unit operation as follows.

Removal

Note: *With the exception of the linkage bar return spring, none of the fast idle system components are listed as being available separately, so care must be taken in handling them, and they should only be removed if necessary. If parts are worn or damaged it may be necessary to fit a complete new throttle body assembly, though check with a Yamaha dealer first.*

5 Remove the throttle bodies (see Section 9).

8 Unhook the return spring from the fast idle unit **(see illustration)**. Remove the screws securing the fast idle unit to its bracket and lift it off, noting how it fits **(see illustration)**.

9 If required undo the screw and the bolts securing the fast idle unit bracket and remove it noting how it fits **(see illustrations)**.

10 Check the action of the linkage bar and plungers (Step 12). If necessary unhook the return spring from the linkage bar, noting how it fits. Remove the screws securing the linkage bar to the throttle bodies, noting the nylon washers **(see illustration)**. Lift off the bar, noting how it fits on the ends of the

11.9a Fast idle unit bracket screw (arrowed) . . .

11.9b . . . and bolts (arrowed)

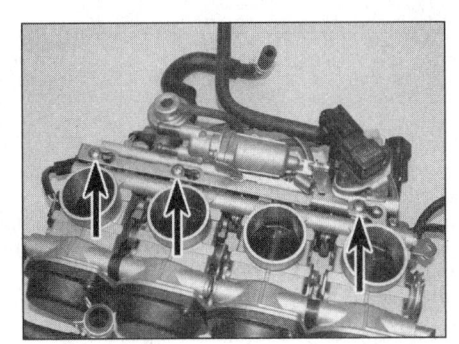

11.10a Undo the screws (arrowed) . . .

4•18 Engine management system

11.10b ... and remove the linkage bar ...

11.10c ... noting how it locates on the plungers

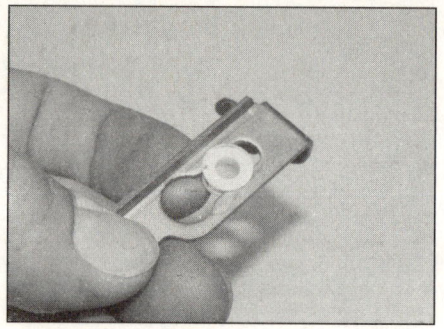

11.10d The washers can slip out of the bar, so take care not to lose them and make sure they are correctly fitted on installation

fast idle plungers with the nylon washers between the plunger ends and the bar ends **(see illustrations)**. Take care not to lose the nylon washers from the linkage bar **(see illustration)**.

11 If required, unscrew each fast idle plunger nut, using a pair of thin-nosed pliers if access is too restricted for a spanner, and withdraw the plunger assembly from each throttle body **(see illustration)**.

Inspection

12 Check the operation of the fast idle linkage bar. The bar should slide freely under tension from the return spring. Also check the operation of the fast idle plungers. If the bar sticks or there is no spring tension, remove the bar and plungers for inspection (Steps 10 and 11).

13 Yamaha gives no specifications for the fast idle unit, however its operation can be tested as follows.

14 Note the position of the pushrod when the unit is cold – it should be fully retracted. Now gently heat it using a hair dryer and check that the pushrod extends.

15 Now allow the unit to cool – as it does, the pushrod should retract.

16 If the unit does not perform as described it is faulty.

Installation

17 Installation is the reverse of removal, noting the following.
- After fitting each plunger make sure it moves in and out smoothly and freely.
- After fitting the linkage bar make sure it slides smoothly and freely **(see illustrations 11.10d, c, b and a)**.
- Make sure all hoses are in good condition, correctly routed and secured and not trapped or kinked.
- Top-up the cooling system (see Chapter 1).
- Run the engine from cold and check the fast idle system functions correctly. Make sure there is no coolant leakage.

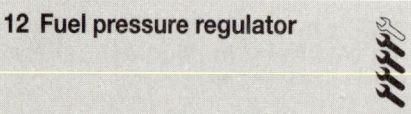

12 Fuel pressure regulator

⚠️ *Warning: Refer to the precautions given in Section 1 before proceeding.*

Removal

1 Remove the air filter housing (see Section 5).
2 Disconnect the vacuum hose from the fuel pressure regulator **(see illustration)**.
3 Release the clip securing the fuel return hose and slide it back, then pull the hose off its union **(see illustration 12.2)**.
4 Undo the screws that secure the fuel pressure regulator to the fuel rail, then carefully remove the regulator, noting the O-ring **(see illustration 12.2)**. **Note:** *Yamaha do not list the O-ring as a new part; check with a Yamaha dealer if there is leakage or if the O-ring is damaged.*

Inspection

5 A pressure gauge and adapter which fits into the fuel supply line, and a vacuum pump and gauge that attach to the regulator, are needed to check the operation of the pressure regulator. Due to cost of these items it is advised to have the regulator checked by a Yamaha dealer, or, if all other possible causes of the problem have been examined and eliminated (section 3), to substitute the suspect one with a new one and check that the problem is cured.

Installation

6 Installation is the reverse of removal, noting the following.
- Make sure the O-ring is in good condition and use a new one if necessary.

11.11 Unscrew the nut (arrowed) and remove the plunger

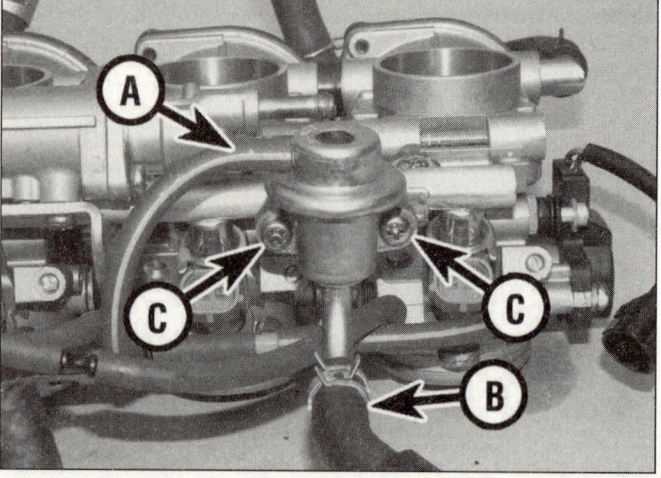

12.2 Vacuum hose (A), fuel return hose (B), fuel pressure regulator screws (C)

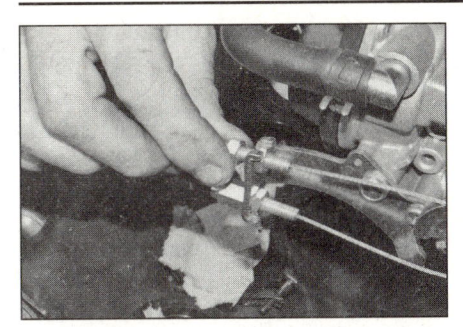

Engine management system 4•19

13.4a Slacken the locknut on the closing cable then free the adjuster from the bracket . . .

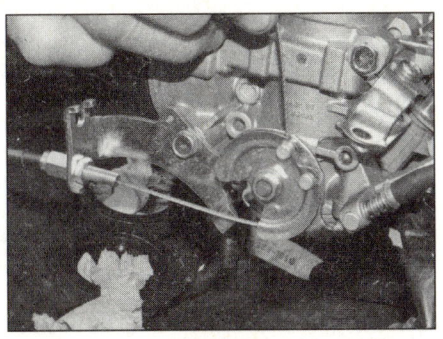

13.4b . . . and detach the cable end from the pulley

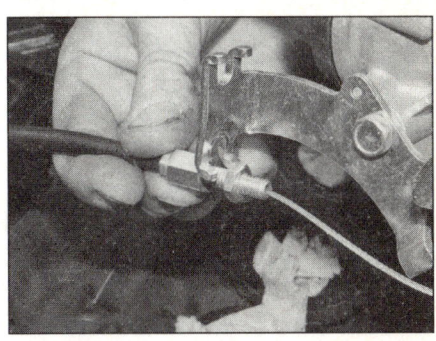

13.5a Slacken the adjuster on the opening cable then free it from the bracket . . .

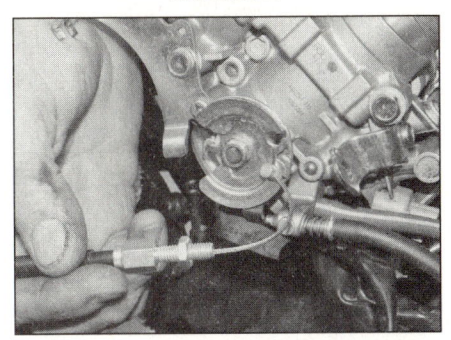

13.5b . . . and detach the cable end from the pulley

13.6a Unscrew the retaining plate bolt (arrowed) . . .

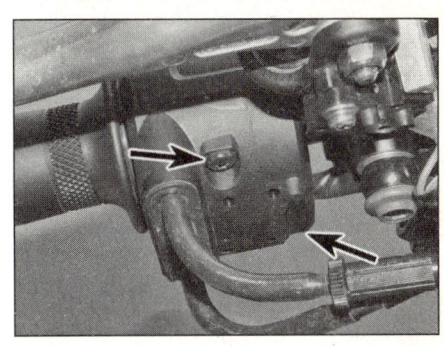

13.6b . . . then undo the housing screws (arrowed)

- Make sure the fuel return and vacuum hoses are in good condition, correctly routed and secured and not trapped or kinked **(see illustration 12.2)**.
- Run the engine and make sure there is no fuel leakage.

13 Throttle cables

⚠ **Warning: Refer to the precautions given in Section 1 before proceeding.**

Removal

1 Remove the air filter housing (see Section 5).
2 Displace the throttle bodies (See Section 9).
3 Mark each cable according to its location at both ends. If new cables are being fitted, match them to the old cables to ensure they are correctly installed.
4 Loosen the locknut on the decelerator (throttle closing) cable adjuster, then slide the adjuster out of the bracket and detach the inner cable end from the throttle pulley, noting how it fits **(see illustrations)**.
5 Unscrew the adjuster hex on the accelerator (throttle opening), then slide the adjuster out of the bracket and detach the inner cable end from the throttle pulley, noting how it fits **(see illustrations)**.
6 Unscrew the cable retaining plate bolt on the underside of the switch housing, noting how it fits **(see illustration)**. Remove the throttle housing screws and separate the halves **(see illustration)**. Detach the inner cable ends from the pulley then draw the cable elbows from the housing, noting how they fit.
7 Withdraw the cables from the machine, noting the correct routing of each cable.

Installation

8 Feed the cables from the handlebar through to the throttle bodies, making sure they are correctly routed. The cables must not interfere with any other component and should not be kinked or bent sharply.
9 Lubricate the cable ends with multi-purpose grease, then fit the cable elbows into the housing, making sure the accelerator (opening) cable fits into the front and the decelerator (closing) cable fits into the rear, and fit the ends into their sockets in the throttle twistgrip pulley. Join the housing halves, making sure the pin locates in the hole in the handlebar, then tighten the screws **(see illustration 13.6b)**. Fit the cable retaining plate and secure it with the bolt **(see illustration 13.6a)**.
10 Fit the accelerator cable end into the throttle pulley, then locate the adjuster into the lower holder on the cable bracket and tighten it against the bracket **(see illustration 13.5a)**.
11 Fit the decelerator cable end into the throttle pulley, then locate the adjuster into the upper holder on the cable bracket and secure it with the locknut **(see illustration 13.4a)**.
12 Follow the procedure in Section 9 and install the throttle body assembly, then follow the procedure in Chapter 1 to adjust the cable freeplay.
13 Install the remaining components in the reverse order of removal. Start the engine and check that the idle speed does not rise as the handlebars are turned. If it does, the throttle cables are routed incorrectly. Correct the problem before riding the motorcycle.

14 Exhaust system

⚠ **Warning: If the engine has been running the exhaust system will be very hot. Allow the system to cool before carrying out any work.**

Silencer

Removal

1 Remove the lower fairing (see Chapter 7).
2 Slacken the clamp bolt securing the silencer pipe to the downpipe assembly **(see illustration)**. Unscrew and remove the nut and washer from the silencer mounting bolt

14.2a Slacken the clamp bolt (arrowed) . . .

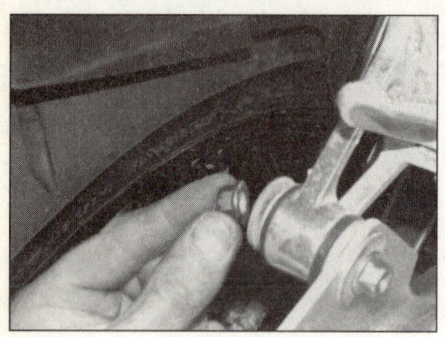

4•20 Engine management system

14.2b ... then unscrew the nut ...

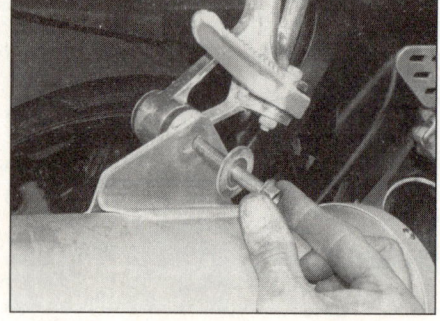

14.2c ... withdraw the bolt and remove the silencer

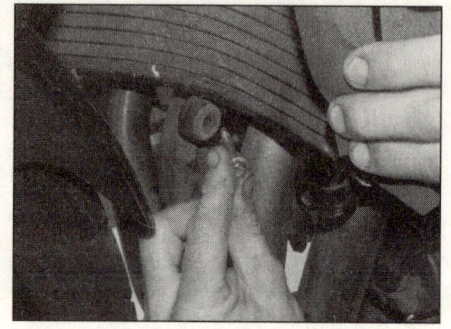

14.6 Unscrew the radiator bolt and pivot the bottom forwards

(see illustrations). Withdraw the bolt with its washer and release the silencer from the downpipe. Remove the sealing ring from the end of the silencer or downpipe assembly and discard it, as a new one should be used.

Installation

3 Check the condition of the silencer mounting rubber and replace it with a new one if it is damaged, deformed or deteriorated. Check that the collar is fitted into the inside of the rubber.
4 Fit the new sealing ring into the silencer pipe. Fit the silencer onto the downpipe assembly, making sure it is pushed fully home. Align the silencer mounting bracket at the rear and install the bolt with its washer, but do not fit the nut yet **(see illustration 14.2c)**. Tighten the clamp bolt to the torque setting specified at the beginning of the Chapter **(see illustration 14.2a)**. Fit the washer and nut onto the silencer mounting bolt and tighten it to the specified torque **(see illustration 14.2b)**.
5 Run the engine and check the system for leaks. Install the lower fairing (see Chapter 7).

Complete system

Removal

6 Remove the fairing side panels and the lower fairing (see Chapter 7). Unscrew the radiator lower mounting bolt and remove the bolt and washer **(see illustration)**. Note the spacer that fits in the bush in the radiator mounting tab and remove it if it is loose. Pivot the bottom of the radiator forwards to provide some clearance to the exhaust downpipe flange nuts. If access is still too restricted for you remove the radiator (see Chapter 3).
7 Unscrew the nut and remove the washer from the silencer mounting bolt but do not remove the bolt yet **(see illustration 14.2b)**. Unscrew the bolt securing the rear of the downpipe assembly to its bracket **(see illustration)**.
8 Unscrew the eight downpipe flange nuts and draw the flanges off the studs **(see illustration)**.
9 Supporting the system, remove the silencer mounting bolt with its washer **(see illustration 14.2c)**, then detach the downpipes from the cylinder head and remove the system **(see illustration)**.
10 Remove the gasket from each port in the cylinder head and discard them, as new ones must be fitted **(see illustration)**.

Installation

11 Check the condition of the silencer mounting rubber and replace it with a new one it if it is damaged, deformed or deteriorated. Check that the collar is fitted into the inside of the rubber.
12 Fit a new gasket into each of the cylinder head ports **(see illustration)**. If necessary, apply a smear of grease to the gaskets to keep them in place whilst fitting the downpipe.
13 Manoeuvre the assembly into position so that the head of each downpipe is located in its port in the cylinder head **(see illustration 14.9)**, then install the silencer mounting bolt with its washer **(see illustration 14.2c)**, and the downpipe assembly mounting bolt **(see illustration 14.7)**, but do not tighten it yet.
14 Locate the downpipe flanges onto the studs, then fit the nuts and tighten them to the torque setting specified at the beginning

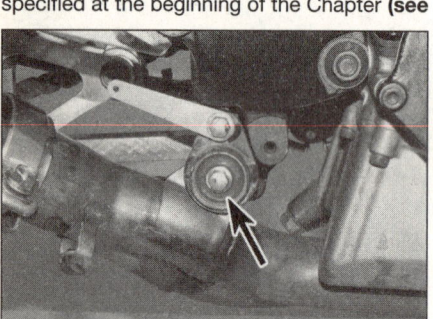

14.7 Unscrew the downpipe assembly rear mounting bolt (arrowed)

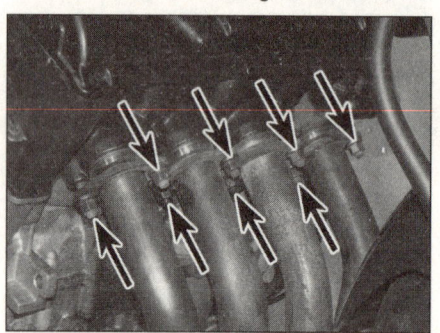

14.8 Unscrew the downpipe flange nuts (arrowed) and draw the flanges off

14.9 Detach the downpipes and remove the system

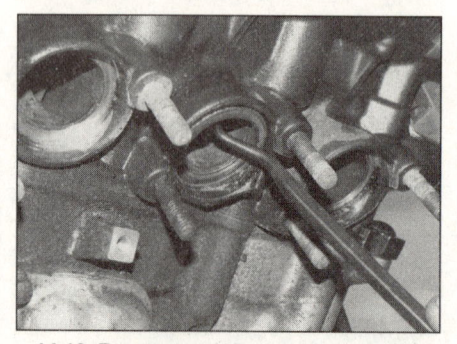

14.10 Remove and discard the gaskets

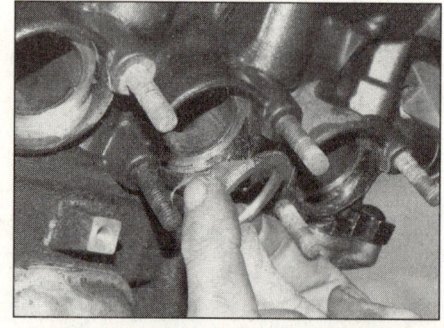

14.12 Fit a new gasket into each port, using grease to hold them in place

Engine management system 4•21

of the Chapter **(see illustration)**. Now tighten the downpipe mounting bolt to the specified torque. Fit the washer and nut onto the silencer mounting bolt and tighten it to the specified torque **(see illustration 14.2b)**.

15 Install the radiator (see Chapter 3).
16 Run the engine and check that there are no exhaust gas leaks. Install the fairing panels (see Chapter 7).

15 Air induction system (AIS)

Function

1 The air induction system uses exhaust gas pulses to suck fresh air into the exhaust ports, where it mixes with hot combustion gases. The extra oxygen causes continued combustion, allowing unburnt hydrocarbons to burn off, thereby reducing emissions. Reed valves control the flow of air into the ports, opening when there is negative pressure, and prevent exhaust gases flowing back into the AIS. An air cut-off valve controlled by signals from the ECU shuts off the flow of air from the air filter housing when the engine reaches normal operating temperature. If the coolant temperature drops, the valve opens and air is added to aid combustion and raise the gas temperature inside the exhaust system.

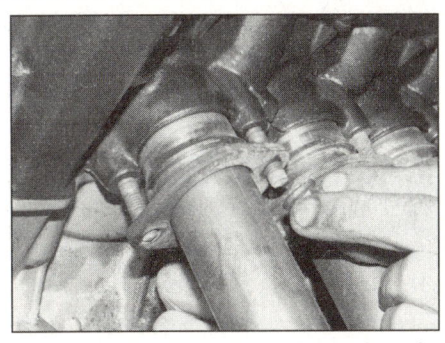

14.14 Fit the flanges over the studs and secure them with their nuts

2 Refer to Chapter 1, Section 6, for a check of the system.

Testing

Air cut-off valve

3 Remove the valve from the motorcycle (see below).
4 Check the operation of the cut-off valve by blowing through the air filter housing hose union; no air should flow through the reed valve hose unions **(see illustration)**. Now connect battery voltage (12 volts) across the valve wiring connector terminals and repeat the check; air should now flow freely through the valve if it is functioning correctly.
5 Check the resistance of the cut-off valve windings by connecting an ohmmeter between its connector terminals and compare

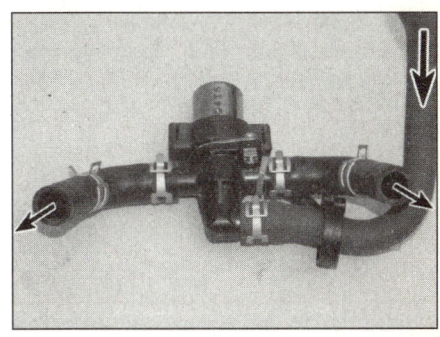

15.8a Release the cable ties (arrowed) . . .

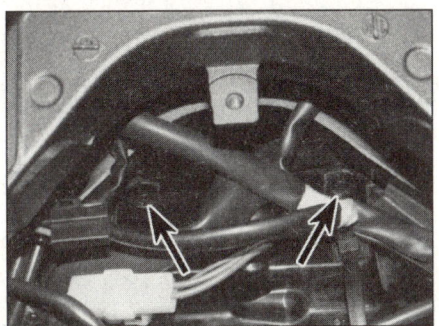

15.8b . . . then move the wiring aside and release the trim clips (arrowed) . . .

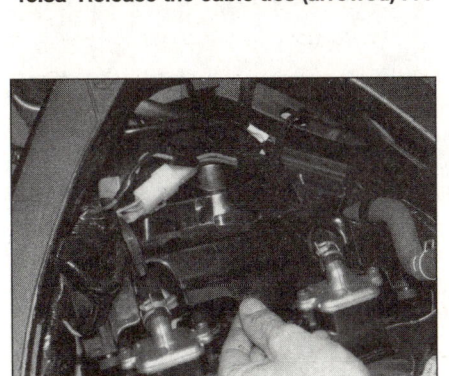

15.8c . . . and remove the cover

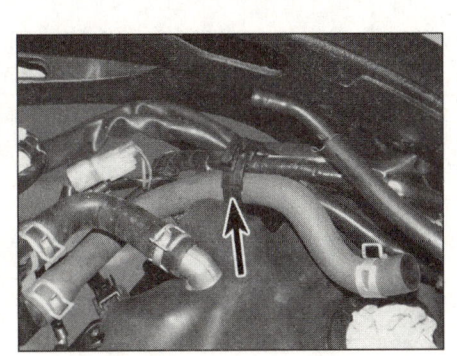

15.8d Release the cable tie (arrowed)

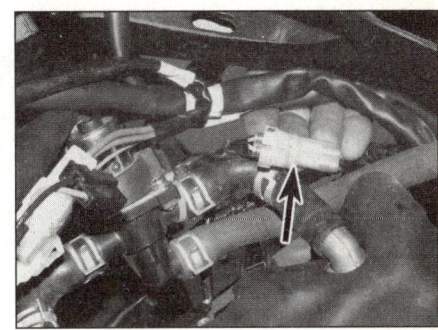

15.4 Air should flow as shown only when there is power to the solenoid

the reading obtained to that given in the Specifications. Replace the valve with a new one if faulty.

Reed valves

6 Remove the air filter housing (see Section 5). Disconnect the hose from each reed valve housing **(see illustration 15.10)**. Attach a clean auxiliary hose of the correct bore and about 12 inches long to one of the unions.
7 Check the valve by blowing and sucking on the auxiliary hose end. Air should flow through the hose only when blown down it and not when sucked back up. If this is not the case the reed valve is faulty, though it is worth removing it (see below) and cleaning it in case it is just sticking due to a build-up of debris. Check the other valve in the same way.

Removal and installation

Cut-off valve

8 Remove the air filter housing (see Section 5). Note the routing of all cables, wiring and hoses over and around the radiator cover. Release the cable ties to free the wiring. Release the trim clips securing the cover and remove it, noting how it fits. Also release the cable tie securing the wiring to the control valve air supply hose **(see illustrations)**.
9 Disconnect the cut-off valve wiring connector **(see illustration)**.

15.9 Disconnect the wiring connector (arrowed) . . .

4•22 Engine management system

10 Disconnect the hose from each reed valve housing **(see illustration)**. Remove the cut-off valve from its bracket with its hoses attached. Detach the hoses if required.
11 Installation is the reverse of removal.

Reed valves

12 Remove the air filter housing (see Section 5). Note the routing of all cables, wiring and hoses over and around the radiator cover. Release the cable ties to free the wiring **(see illustration 15.8a)**. Release the trim clips securing the cover and remove it, noting how it fits **(see illustrations 15.8b and c)**.
13 To remove either valve, first release the clamp and detach the air hose from its union **(see illustration 15.10)**. Unscrew the bolts securing the reed valve cover and remove the cover **(see illustrations)**. Remove the reed valve and the base plates, noting which way around they are fitted **(see illustrations)**.
14 Installation is the reverse of removal. Make sure the reed valve components and housings are clean and correctly fitted.

16 Catalytic converter

General information

1 A catalytic converter is incorporated in the exhaust system to minimise the level of exhaust pollutants released into the atmosphere.
2 The catalytic converter consists of a canister containing a fine mesh impregnated with a catalyst material, over which the hot exhaust gases pass. The catalyst speeds up the oxidation of harmful carbon monoxide, unburned hydrocarbons and soot, effectively reducing the quantity of harmful products released into the atmosphere via the exhaust gases.

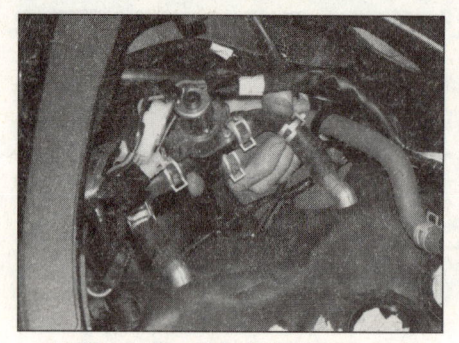

15.10 ... then detach the hoses and remove the valve

3 The catalytic converter is of the open-loop design, having no feedback to the ECU.

Precautions

4 The catalytic converter is a reliable and simple device which needs no maintenance in itself, but there are some facts of which an owner should be aware if the converter is to function properly for its full service life.
● DO NOT use leaded or lead replacement petrol (gasoline) – the additives will coat the precious metals, reducing their converting efficiency and will eventually destroy the catalytic converter.
● Always keep the ignition and fuel systems well-maintained in accordance with the manufacturer's schedule – if the fuel/air mixture is suspected of being incorrect have the exhaust gas CO content checked by a Yamaha dealer.
● If the engine develops a misfire, do not ride the bike at all (or at least as little as possible) until the fault is cured.
● DO NOT use fuel or engine oil additives – these may contain substances harmful to the catalytic converter.
● DO NOT continue to use the bike if the engine burns oil to the extent of leaving a visible trail of blue smoke.

15.13a Unscrew the bolts and remove the cover ...

● Remember that the catalytic converter is FRAGILE – handle the silencer carefully if removing it from the machine.

17 Ignition system check

Warning: *The energy levels in electronic systems can be very high. On no account should the ignition be switched on whilst the plugs or plug caps are being held. Shocks from the HT circuit can be most unpleasant. Secondly, it is vital that the engine is not turned over or run with any of the plug caps removed, and that the plugs are soundly earthed (grounded) when the system is checked for sparking. The ignition system components can be seriously damaged if the HT circuit becomes isolated.*

1 As no means of adjustment is available, any failure of the system can be traced to failure of a system component or a simple wiring fault. Of the two possibilities, the latter is by far the most likely. In the event of failure, check the system in a logical fashion, as described below.
2 Disconnect the wiring connector on the

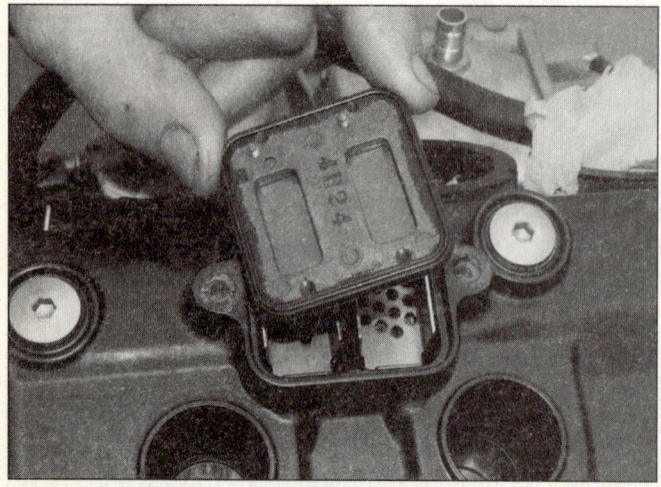

15.13b ... then remove the reed valve ...

15.13c ... and its base plates

Engine management system 4•23

17.2a Ground the plug against the reed valve housing cover . . .

17.2b . . . or use a jumper wire to connect to the crankcase earth (arrowed)

17.4 An adjustable spark gap testing tool

coil for No. 1 cylinder and pull the coil off the spark plug (see Section 18). Reconnect the wiring connector and connect the coil to a spare spark plug (preferably use a new plug, properly gapped – see Chapter 1). Lay the plug on the AIS reed valve cover with the threads contacting it so it is earthed, or alternatively as there is little slack in the wiring connect the plug to the crankcase earth using an auxiliary wire with a crocodile clip on each end **(see illustrations)**. If necessary, hold the spark plug with an insulated tool.

⚠ **Warning: Do not remove any of the spark plugs from the engine to perform this check – atomised fuel being pumped out of the open spark plug hole could ignite, causing severe injury!**

3 Check that the kill switch is in the RUN position and the transmission is in neutral, then turn the ignition switch ON and turn the engine over on the starter motor. If the system is in good condition a regular, fat blue spark should be evident at the plug electrodes. If the spark appears thin or yellowish, or is non-existent, further investigation will be necessary. Turn the ignition off and repeat the test for each coil in turn.

4 The ignition system must be able to produce a spark which is capable of jumping a particular size gap. Yamaha specify that a healthy system should produce a spark capable of jumping at least 6 mm. An ignition spark gap tester tool (which should have an adjustable gap) can be purchased to test the minimum gap across which the spark will jump **(see illustration)**.

5 Set the tool gap to 6 mm, following the manufacturer's instructions. Connect the coil of No. 1 cylinder to the test tool, and contact the tool to a good earth (ground) on the engine or frame. Check that the kill switch is in the RUN position, turn the ignition switch ON and turn the engine over on the starter motor. If the system is in good condition a regular, fat blue spark will be seen to jump the gap between the electrodes. Repeat the test for the other coils. If the test results are good the entire ignition system can be considered good. If the spark appears thin or yellowish, or is non-existent, further investigation will be necessary.

6 Ignition faults can be divided into two categories, namely those where the ignition system has failed completely, and those which are due to a partial failure. The likely faults are listed below, starting with the most probable source of failure. Work through the list systematically, referring to the appropriate Section of this Chapter and/or the specified Chapter for full details of the necessary checks and tests. **Note:** *Before checking the following items ensure that the battery is fully charged and that all fuses are in good condition.*

Loose, corroded or damaged wiring connections; broken or shorted wiring between any of the component parts of the ignition system (see Section 8 and Chapter 8).
Faulty spark plug, dirty, worn or corroded plug electrodes, or incorrect gap between electrodes (Chapter 1).
Faulty ignition (main) switch or engine kill switch (see Chapter 8).
Faulty neutral, clutch or sidestand switch (see Chapter 8).
Faulty tip-over sensor or starter cut-off relay (see Section 8 and Chapter 8).
Faulty crankshaft position sensor (Section 8) or damaged timing rotor trigger (Chapter 2).
Faulty ignition coil(s) (Section 18).
Faulty ECU (Section 19).

7 If the above checks don't reveal the cause of the problem, have the ignition system tested by a Yamaha dealer.

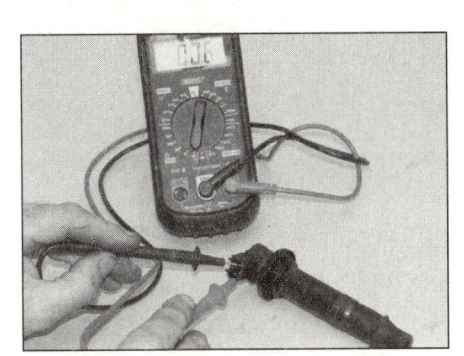

18 Ignition coils

Check

1 Remove each coil (see Steps 5 and 6) and check them visually for cracks and other damage. Inspect the wiring terminals and the spark plug terminal.

2 Measure the primary circuit resistance with a multimeter as follows. Set the meter to the ohms x 1 scale and measure the resistance between the terminals on the coil **(see illustration)**. If the reading obtained is not within the range shown in the Specifications, it is likely that the coil is defective.

3 Measure the secondary circuit resistance with a multimeter as follows. Set the meter to the K-ohm scale. Connect one meter probe to one primary circuit terminal and the other probe to the spark plug terminal **(see illustration)**. If the reading obtained is not within the range shown in the Specifications, it is likely that the coil is defective.

4 If a coil is confirmed to be faulty, it must be replaced with a new one: the coils are sealed units and cannot therefore be repaired.

Removal and installation

5 Remove the air filter housing (see Section 5). Note the routing of all cables, wiring and hoses over and around the radiator cover. Release the cable ties to free the wiring **(see**

18.2 To test the coil primary resistance, connect the multimeter leads between the connector socket terminals

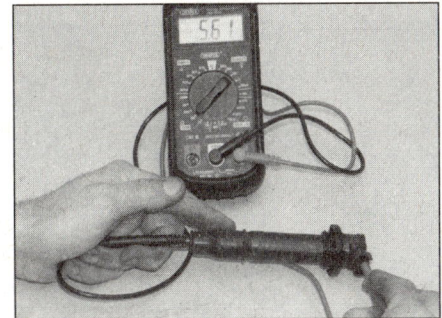

18.3 To test the coil secondary resistance, connect the multimeter leads between one terminal and the spark plug socket

4•24 Engine management system

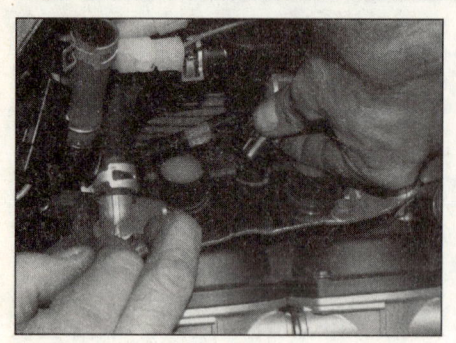

18.6a Disconnect the wiring connector . . .

18.6b . . . then pull the coil up off the spark plug and remove it

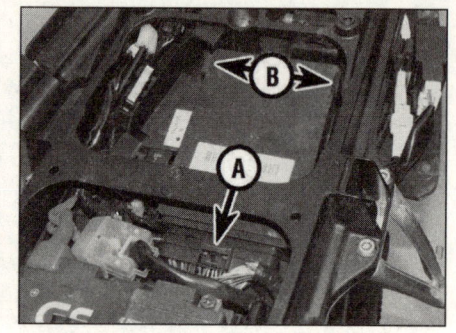

19.3 Disconnect the wiring connector (A) and release the clips (B)

illustration 15.8a). Release the trim clips securing the cover and remove it, noting how it fits **(see illustrations 15.8b and c)**.

6 Clean the area around each coil to prevent any dirt falling into the spark plug channels. Check that the cylinder location is marked on each wiring sleeve, then disconnect the coil wiring connectors **(see illustration)**. Pull the coil off each spark plug **(see illustration)**.

7 Installation is the reverse of removal. Make sure the coils are pushed down firmly onto the spark plugs and that the wiring connectors are securely connected.

19 ECU (Engine Control Unit)

Check

1 If the tests shown in the preceding Sections have failed to isolate the cause of an ignition fault, it is possible that the ECU itself is faulty. No details are available with which the unit can be tested. The best way to determine whether it is faulty or not is to substitute it with a known good one, having first checked all other components in the ignition system. Otherwise, take the unit to a Yamaha dealer for assessment.

Removal

2 Remove the rider's seat (see Chapter 7). Disconnect the battery negative (–) lead.
3 Disconnect the wiring connector from the ECU, then unclip the unit and remove it **(see illustration)**.

Installation

4 Installation is the reverse of removal. Make sure the wiring connector is correctly and securely connected.

20 Ignition timing

General information

1 Since no provision exists for adjusting the ignition timing, and since no ignition component is subject to mechanical wear, there is no need for regular checks. However, the ignition timing be checked if investigating a fault such as a loss of power or a misfire, but only after a thorough examination of all the other ignition system components and wiring.

2 The ignition timing is checked dynamically (engine running) using a stroboscopic lamp. The inexpensive neon lamps should be adequate in theory, but in practice may produce a pulse of such low intensity that the timing mark remains indistinct. If possible, one of the more precise xenon tube lamps should be used, powered by an external source of the appropriate voltage. **Note:** *Do not use the machine's own battery, as an incorrect reading may result from stray impulses within the machine's electrical system.*

Check

3 Warm the engine up to normal operating temperature, then stop it.
4 Unscrew the timing inspection bolt (the small bolt, not the large slotted plug) from the centre of the ignition rotor cover on the right-hand side of the engine **(see illustration)**.
5 The mark on the ignition rotor which indicates the firing point at idle speed for the No. 1 cylinder is an 'H' mark on its side **(see illustration)**. The static timing marks with which this should align are the cut-outs in the inspection hole.
6 Connect the timing light to the No. 1 cylinder ignition coil as described in the manufacturer's instructions.

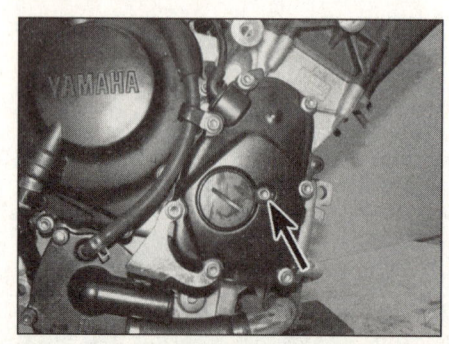

20.4 Unscrew the timing inspection bolt

> **HAYNES HINT**
> *The timing marks can be highlighted with white paint to make them more visible under the stroboscope light.*

7 Start the engine and aim the light at the inspection hole.
8 With the machine idling at the specified speed, the 'H' timing mark should appear precisely in the middle of the two static timing marks **(see illustration 20.5)**. **Note:** *It is essential that the reading is taken at the specified idling speed.* Now increase engine speed – using the idle speed adjuster will be more accurate than opening the throttle. At this point the dynamic timing mark should move anti-clockwise in relation to the static mark. This confirms the ignition is advancing.
9 If the ignition timing is incorrect, or suspected of being incorrect, one of the ignition system components is at fault, and the system must be tested as described in the preceding Sections of this Chapter.
10 When the check is complete, install the timing inspection bolt, using a new sealing washer if the old one is damaged or deformed, and tighten it securely. Install the remaining components in the reverse order of removal.

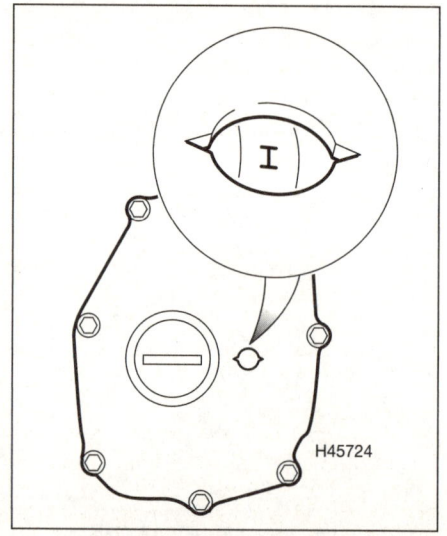

20.5 Timing mark alignment

Engine management system 4•25

21 Immobiliser system

General information

1 The immobiliser system will only allow the machine to be started if the correct registered key is used to turn the ignition ON. The system consists of a transponder which is part of the ignition key, a receiver which is fitted around the ignition switch **(see illustration 21.27c)**, and the engine control unit (ECU).
2 When the ignition is switched ON, the ECU sends power through the receiver to the transponder. The transponder sends a coded signal back through the receiver to the ECU. If the signal sent by the transponder matches the signal stored in the ECU memory, the immobiliser indicator light in the instrument cluster (marked by a key symbol and located in the tachometer face) comes on for about a second, then goes out, and the ECU allows the engine to be started. If the key code signal is not recognised, or if there is a fault in the system, the indicator light flashes. If the light flashes, refer to the fault diagnosis and troubleshooting Sections below. Likewise if the light does not come on at all.
3 The ECU can store the codes for up to three registered keys, two of which are standard use keys with black casings, and one is a code re-registering key with a red casing. They keys should be kept separately (i.e. not on the same key-ring) as the proximity of another key to the one being used in the switch can lead to the signal from it being jammed, and the bike will not start. The key has a built in transponder which can be damaged if the key is dropped or knocked, gets too hot, is too close to a magnetic object, or is submerged in water. If all the keys are lost, the ECU must be replaced with a new one, so always make sure you have one spare key. If a new key is obtained, it must be registered into the system before the bike can be started.

> **HAYNES HINT**
> *If you lose a key, or suspect it has been stolen, immediately re-register your code re-registering key and your remaining key – this will cancel the registration of the key that has been lost (or possibly stolen) which means that it will not be possible to start the bike using that key.*
> *If all three keys are lost, or if the ignition switch is faulty, a new ECU, immobiliser unit and lock set must be fitted. If either the immobiliser or ECU is faulty either unit can be replaced on its own.*

Standard key registration procedure

Note: *This must be done when a key is lost and a new one is obtained, or when a new 'code re-registering key' has been registered.*
4 Obtain a new key from a Yamaha dealer, and have it cut to match the original key.
5 Turn the ignition switch ON using the code re-registering key, then turn it OFF and within 5 seconds turn it ON with the key you wish to register. The immobiliser indicator light should flash on and off every half second. This indicates that the system is in registration mode. At this point the registration of the other existing standard key will have been cancelled, so this will also have to be registered.
6 To register the second key, turn the ignition OFF and remove the first key, placing it well away from the receiver, and within 5 seconds insert the second key into the switch and turn it ON. Turn the ignition OFF and remove the key. If the light stops flashing, more than 5 seconds have elapsed and the system is no longer in registration mode, in which case start again.
7 On completion turn the ignition OFF and remove the key. After five seconds the light will stop flashing and the system is no longer in registration mode.
8 Check that both registered keys can start the motorcycle.

Code re-registering key registration procedure

Note: *This must be done when a new ECU or immobiliser receiver is fitted.*
9 Obtain a new key from a Yamaha dealer, and have it cut to match the original key.
10 Turn the ignition switch ON using the new code re-registering key. The immobiliser light will come on for about one second, then go out, indicating that the key has been registered.
11 Check that the key can start the motorcycle.
12 Now register the standard keys as described in Steps 4 to 8.

Installing a new ECU

13 Install the ECU (see Section 19).
14 Turn the ignition switch ON using the code re-registering key. This registers the key to the new ECU.
15 Check that the key can start the motorcycle.
16 Now register the standard keys as described in Steps 4 to 8.

Installing a new immobiliser

17 Remove the old immobiliser receiver from the ignition switch and fit the new one (see Step 27).
18 Turn the ignition switch ON using the code re-registering key. This registers the key to the new immobiliser.
19 Check that the key can start the motorcycle.
20 Now register the standard keys as described in Steps 4 to 8.

Fault diagnosis

21 If there is a fault in the system, the immobiliser indicator light in the instrument cluster (marked by a key symbol and located in the tachometer face) flashes and a fault code is shown in the LCD display.

Fault code	Symptoms	Possible causes
51	Signal from key not being received by immobiliser	Interference from other keys or magnet Faulty key transponder Faulty immobiliser receiver
52	Code from key not recognised by receiver	Interference from other key Unregistered key being used
53	Signal from immobiliser not being received by ECU	Faulty wiring or wiring connector Faulty immobiliser receiver Faulty ECU
54	Code from immobiliser not recognised by ECU	Faulty wiring or wiring connector Immobiliser unregistered to ECU – code re-registering key not registered Faulty immobiliser receiver Faulty ECU
55	Key registration error	Same key being registered twice
56	Code from immobiliser not recognised by ECU	Faulty wiring or wiring connector Faulty immobiliser receiver Faulty ECU

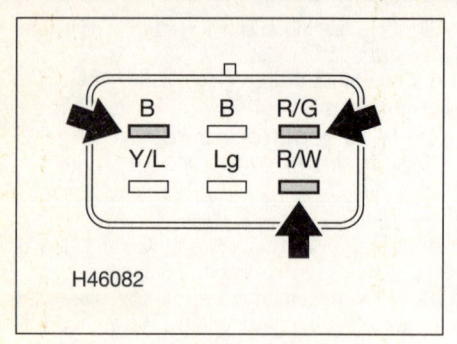

21.24 Wire terminal identification in the immobiliser 6-pin connector

Tests are made on the loom side of the connector

Troubleshooting procedure

22 If fault code 51 or 52 is shown, first check that none of the other registered keys are close to the receiver. If they are, remove them and try the ignition again.

23 If any fault code is shown, first check the fuses and the wiring and connectors between the immobiliser receiver, ignition switch and the ECU (see *Wiring diagrams* at the end of Chapter 8). A continuity test of all wires will locate a break or short in any circuit. Inspect the terminals inside the wiring connectors and ensure they are not loose, bent or corroded. Spray the inside of the connectors with a proprietary electrical terminal cleaner before reconnection. Also make sure the battery is in good condition and that the ignition switch is not faulty (see Chapter 8).

24 Remove the air filter housing (see Section 5), then release the wiring connector holder from its aperture in the frame and draw the connector out and disconnect it. Using a voltmeter, connect the positive (+) probe to the red/white (R/W) wire terminal on the loom side of the connector and the negative (−) probe to the black (B) wire terminal indicated **(see illustration)**. Turn the ignition ON – there should be battery voltage. Now repeat the test with the positive (+) probe connected to the red/green (R/G) wire terminal. If no voltage was recorded in either test refer to the wiring diagrams and check the red/white and red/green circuits to their power sources, and check the black wire for continuity to earth. If there is voltage the immobiliser receiver is probably faulty and must be replaced with a new one.

25 If the immobiliser LED or the LCD display in the instrument cluster do not come on, refer to Chapter 8 and check the instrument cluster.

26 If all indications are that either the immobiliser or the ECU are faulty, it is worth having them checked by a Yamaha dealer before buying replacements.

Replacement

27 To replace the receiver, remove the air filter housing (see Section 5), then release the wiring connector holder from its aperture in the frame and draw it out, and open to access the connector and disconnect it **(see illustrations)**. Feed the wiring back to the receiver, freeing it from any ties and noting its routing. Undo the Torx screws and remove the receiver, noting how it fits **(see illustration)**. If you don't have the correct tools to easily access the screws, removing the fairing will help (see Chapter 7), otherwise follow the procedure for removing the top yoke in the ignition switch replacement Section in Chapter 8.

28 To replace the ECU see Section 19.

21.27a Release the holder from the frame and draw it out . . .

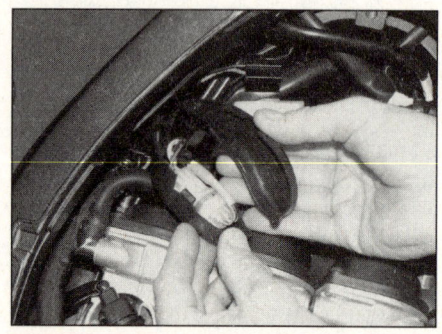

21.27b . . . and open it to access the wiring connector

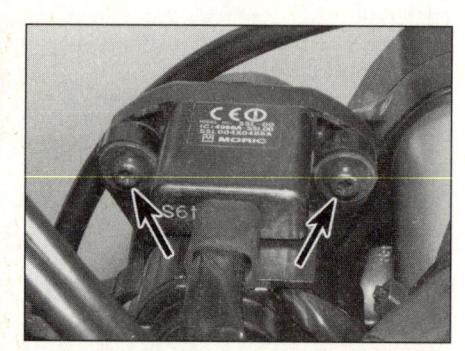

21.27c Receiver Torx screws (arrowed)

Chapter 5
Frame and suspension

Contents

	Section number		Section number
Footrests, brake pedal and gearchange lever	3	Sidestand	4
Fork overhaul	8	Sidestand lubrication	see Chapter 1
Fork oil change	7	Sidestand switch	see Chapter 8
Fork removal and installation	6	Steering head bearing check and adjustment	see Chapter 1
Frame inspection and repair	2	Steering head bearings	10
General information	1	Steering stem	9
Handlebars and levers	5	Suspension adjustment	13
Handlebar switches	see Chapter 8	Suspension check	see Chapter 1
Rear shock absorber	11	Swingarm bearings	15
Rear suspension linkage	12	Swingarm removal and installation	14

Degrees of difficulty

Easy, suitable for novice with little experience	Fairly easy, suitable for beginner with some experience	Fairly difficult, suitable for competent DIY mechanic	Difficult, suitable for experienced DIY mechanic	Very difficult, suitable for expert DIY or professional

Specifications

Front forks
Fork oil type .... Yamaha suspension oil '01' or equivalent
Fork oil capacity (per leg)
   R and S (2003 and 2004) models .... 490 cc
   T (2005) models .... 475 cc
Fork oil level*
   R and S (2003 and 2004) models .... 106 mm
   T (2005) models .... 92 mm
Fork spring free length
   R and S (2003 and 2004) models
     Standard .... 249.3 mm
     Service limit .... 244.3 mm
   T (2005) models
     Standard .... 248.8 mm
     Service limit .... 243.8 mm

*Oil level is measured from the top of the tube with the fork spring removed and the leg fully compressed.

5•2 Frame and suspension

Torque wrench settings

Clutch lever bracket clamp bolt	11 Nm
Fairing stay-to-main frame bolts	23 Nm
Footrest bracket bolts	28 Nm
Fork clamp bolts	
Bottom yoke	23 Nm
Top yoke	26 Nm
Fork damper cartridge bolt	
R and S (2003 and 2004) models	40 Nm
T (2005) models	23 Nm
Fork damper cartridge rod-to-top bolt locknut	15 Nm
Fork top bolt	23 Nm
Front brake master cylinder clamp bolts	13 Nm
Handlebar clamp bolts	
R and S (2003 and 2004) models	33 Nm
T (2005) models	32 Nm
Handlebar end weights	23 Nm
Handlebar positioning bolts	13 Nm
Rear master cylinder mounting bolts	18 Nm
Rear shock absorber nuts	44 Nm
Rear suspension linkage plate and linkage arm nuts	44 Nm
Sidestand bracket bolts	61 Nm
Steering stem nut	113 Nm
Rear sub-frame-to-main frame bolts	47 Nm
Swingarm pivot adjuster	6 Nm
Swingarm pivot bolt nut	95 Nm

1 General information

All models use a twin spar box-section Deltabox III aluminium frame, incorporating the engine as a stressed member.

Front suspension is by a pair of oil-damped, telescopic forks with internal coil springs, conventional on R and S (2003 and 2004) models and upside-down on T (2005) models. The forks have a cartridge damper and are adjustable for spring pre-load and both rebound and compression damping.

At the rear, an aluminium alloy swingarm acts on a single shock absorber via a three-way linkage. The shock absorber is adjustable for spring pre-load and for both rebound and compression damping.

2 Frame inspection and repair

1 The frame should not require attention unless accident damage has occurred. In most cases, fitting a new frame is the only satisfactory remedy for such damage. A few frame specialists have the jigs and other equipment necessary for straightening the frame to the required standard of accuracy, but even then there is no simple way of assessing to what extent the frame may have been over-stressed.

2 After the machine has covered a high mileage, the frame should be examined closely for signs of cracking or splitting at the welded joints. Loose engine mount bolts can cause ovaling or fracturing of the mounts themselves. Minor damage can often be repaired by welding, depending on the extent and nature of the damage, but this is a task for an expert.

3 Remember that a frame which is out of alignment will cause handling problems. If misalignment is suspected as the result of an accident, first check the wheel alignment (see Chapter 6). To have the frame checked thoroughly it will be necessary to strip the machine completely.

3 Footrests, brake pedal and gearchange lever

Brake pedal and rider's right-hand footrest

Removal

1 Remove the split pin and washer from the clevis pin connecting the brake pedal to the master cylinder pushrod (see illustration). Remove the clevis pin and separate the pushrod from the pedal. Discard the split pin, as a new one must be used on reassembly.

2 Unhook the pedal return spring and brake light switch spring from the lug on the back of

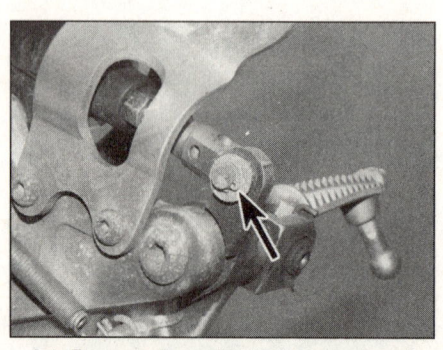

3.1 Remove the split pin (arrowed) and washer and withdraw the pivot pin

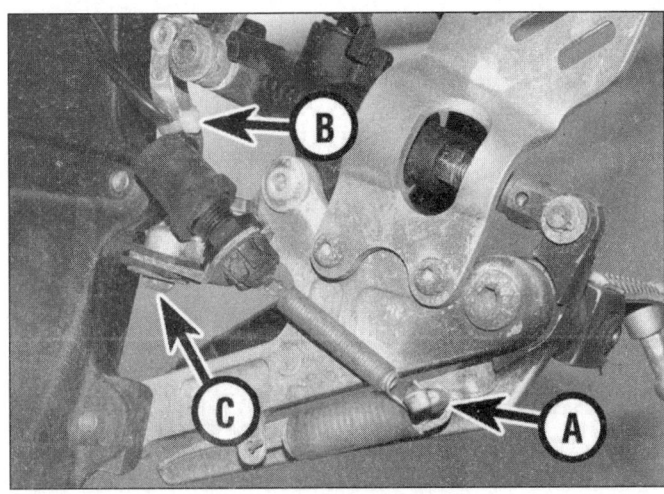

Frame and suspension 5•3

3.2 Unhook the springs from the lug (A) then cut the cable tie (B) and unscrew the bolt (C)

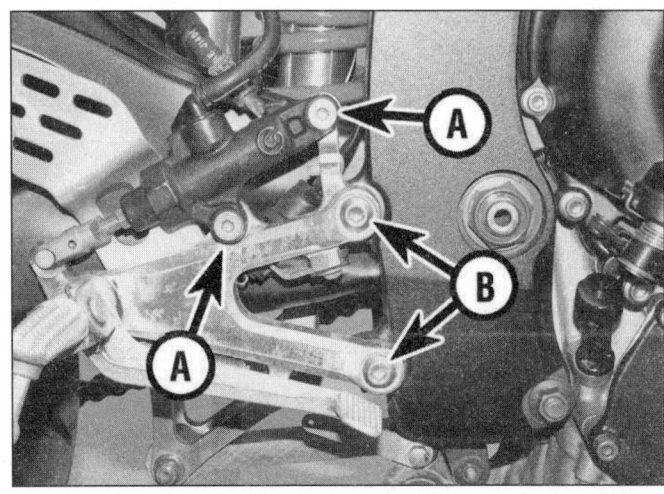

3.3 Unscrew the bolts (A) and displace the master cylinder. Footrest bracket bolts (B)

the pedal **(see illustration)**. Cut the cable tie securing the brake light switch wiring to the footrest bracket. Unscrew the bolt securing the switch to the bracket and remove the washer. Note the collar fitted in the rubber grommet and take care it doesn't drop out.

3 Unscrew the bolts securing the rear brake master cylinder to the footrest bracket and remove the bolts **(see illustration)**. To prevent straining the hydraulic hose, use a cable tie to secure the master cylinder to the frame clear of the bracket.

4 Unscrew the bolts securing the footrest bracket to the frame and remove the bracket **(see illustration 3.3)**. Unscrew the footrest bolt, then remove the footrest from the bracket and remove the pedal **(see illustration)**. Note the washer fitted between the pedal and the footrest bracket. If required unscrew the two bolts securing the heel plate and remove the plate.

Installation

5 Installation is the reverse of removal. Apply grease to the brake pedal pivot. Use a new split pin on the clevis pin securing the brake pedal to the master cylinder pushrod. **Note:** *See Chapter 1 for details of adjusting the pedal height and brake light switch setting.*

Tighten the footrest bracket bolts and the master cylinder bolts to the torque settings specified at the beginning of this Chapter.

Gearchange lever and rider's left-hand footrest

Removal

6 To remove the gearchange lever, counter-hold the gearchange linkage rod using a spanner on its flats and slacken the locknuts, then unscrew the rod and separate it from

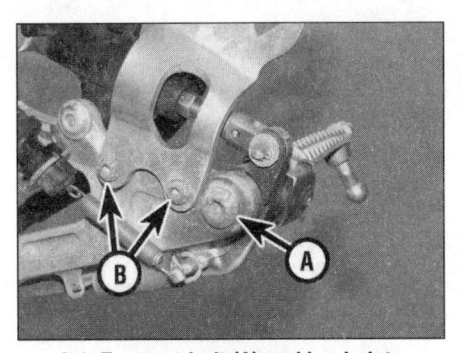

3.4 Footrest bolt (A) and heel plate bolts (B)

the lever and the arm **(see illustrations)** – the rod is reverse-threaded on the lever end, so will unscrew from both lever and arm simultaneously when turned in the one direction. Withdraw the rod from the frame **(see illustration)**. Unscrew the gearchange lever pivot bolt and remove the bolt, washers (noting their order) and lever **(see illustration)**.

7 To remove the footrest, remove the split pin and washer from the pivot pin, then withdraw the pivot and remove the footrest,

3.6a Unscrew the locknuts (arrowed) . . .

3.6b . . . counter-holding the rod

3.6c Withdraw the rod from the frame

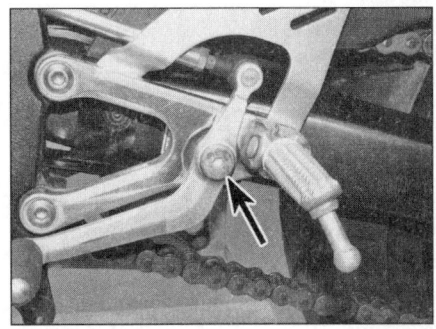

3.6d Gearchange lever pivot bolt (arrowed)

5•4 Frame and suspension

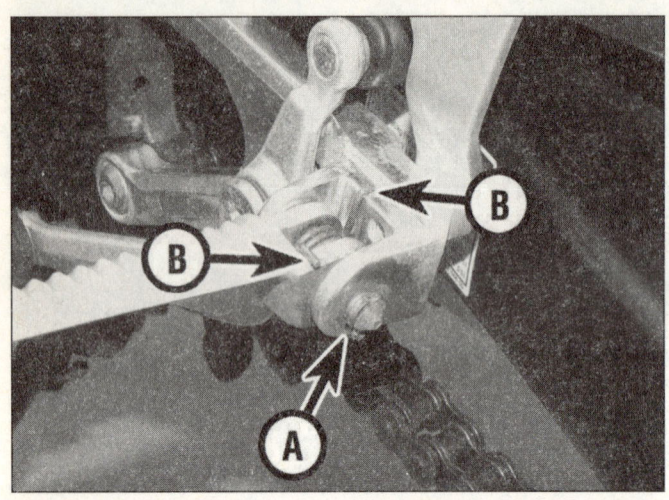

3.7 Remove the split pin and washer (A), then withdraw the pivot pin – note the fitting of the return spring ends (B)

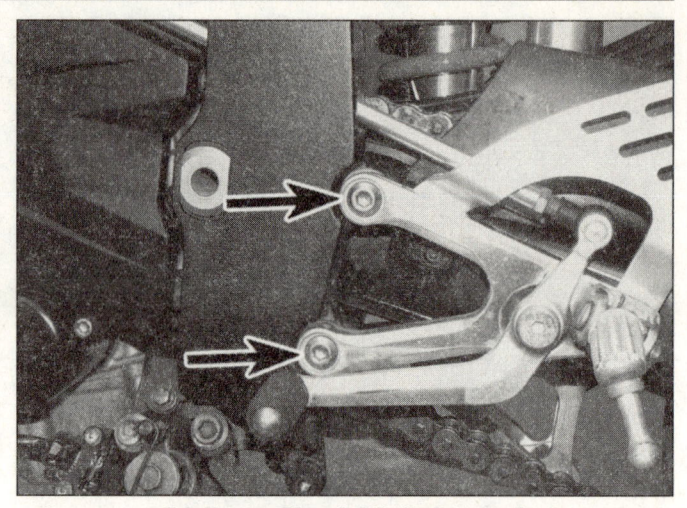

3.8 Footrest bracket bolts (arrowed)

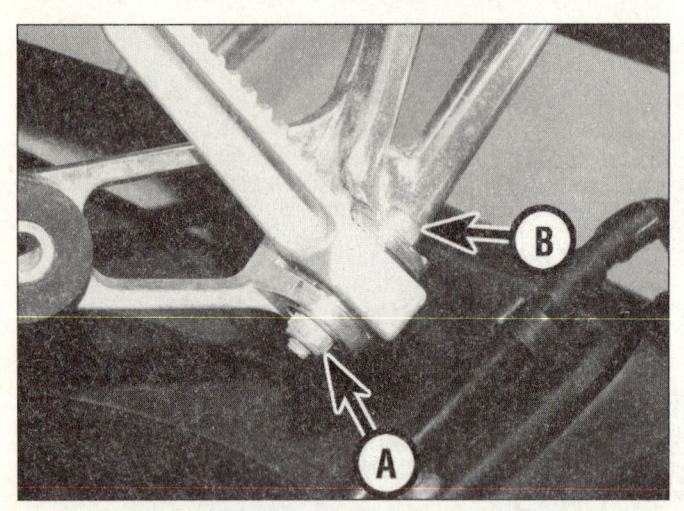

3.10 Unscrew the nut (A) then withdraw the bolt (B)

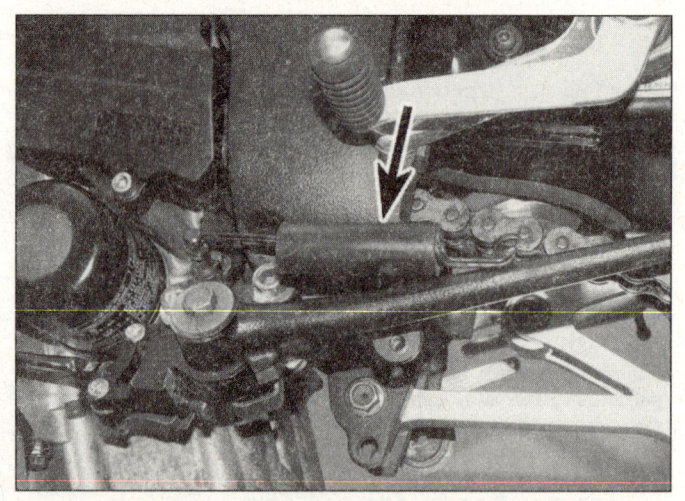

4.2 Unhook and remove the spring (arrowed)

noting how the return spring ends locate **(see illustrations)**. Discard the split pin and use a new one on installation.

8 To remove the heel plate, first follow Step 6. Unscrew the bolts securing the footrest bracket to the frame and remove the bracket **(see illustration)**. Unscrew the two bolts securing the heel plate and remove the plate.

Installation

9 Installation is the reverse of removal. Apply grease to the gearchange lever pivot and make sure the washers are correctly fitted. Tighten the footrest bracket bolts to the torque setting specified at the beginning of this Chapter. To adjust the gearchange lever position, first loosen both locknuts on the linkage rod. Rotate the rod in one direction or the other to either raise or lower the lever height. Make sure the linkage rod length is within the 242 mm specification advised by Yamaha, then tighten both locknuts securely.

Passenger footrests

10 Unscrew the footrest pivot bolt and nut, then withdraw the bolt and remove the footrest **(see illustration)**. Note the fitting of the detent plate, ball, spring and bolt spacer – take care that they do not fall out when removing the footrest.

11 To remove the footrest brackets, remove the seat cowling (see Chapter 7), and the exhaust silencer, which is supported by the right-hand bracket (see Chapter 4). Unscrew the bolts securing the footrest bracket to the frame and remove the bracket.

12 Installation is the reverse of removal. Tighten the bracket bolts to the torque setting specified at the beginning of the Chapter.

4 Sidestand

1 Support the motorcycle securely in an upright position using an auxiliary stand. Remove the lower fairing (see Chapter 7).

2 With the stand in the raised position unhook the spring, noting how it fits, and remove it **(see illustration)**.

3 Unscrew the stand centre bolt and remove the bolt, washer, spring hook, stand and washer **(see illustration)**. Note how the contact plate on the stand locates against the switch plunger when the stand is lowered.

4.3 Unscrew the bolt (arrowed)

Frame and suspension 5•5

4.4a Unscrew the nut (arrowed) on the back

4.4b Stand bracket bolts (arrowed)

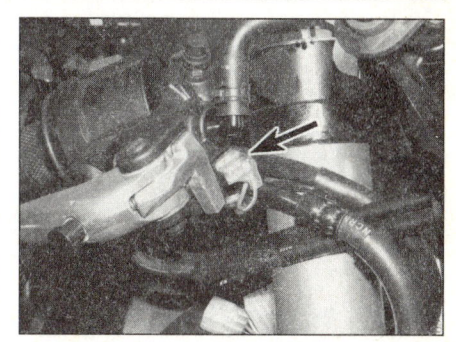

5.1a Disconnect the wiring connectors (arrowed)

4 If required, counter-hold the stand pivot stub and unscrew the nut on the back of the stand bracket; remove the nut and washer and withdraw the pivot stub from the bracket **(see illustration)**. Unscrew the bracket bolts and remove the bracket from the frame **(see illustration)**.

5 Installation is the reverse of removal, noting the following points:
- Apply a suitable thread locking compound to the bracket bolts before installation and tighten the bolts to the specified torque setting.
- Apply lithium based grease to the pivot contact areas.
- Ensure the stand contact plate actuates the switch when the stand is lowered.
- Check the spring tension – it must hold the stand up when it is not in use. If the spring has sagged, renew it.
- Check the operation of the sidestand switch (see Chapter 1).

5 Handlebars and levers

Handlebars
Removal
Note: *To displace the left-hand handlebar from the forks without having to remove the clutch lever or switch assembly follow Steps 4 to 6. The front brake master cylinder and reservoir must be removed from the right-hand handlebar before displacing the handlebar, but the throttle cables and pulley/switch housing and twistgrip can remain in place – ignore Steps 2 and 3.*

1 To remove the right handlebar, first disconnect the brake light switch wiring connectors **(see illustration)**. Remove the bolt securing the reservoir to its bracket on the top yoke **(see illustration)**. Unscrew the master cylinder clamp bolts and remove the clamp, noting how it fits, then lift the master cylinder away from the handlebar **(see illustration)**. There is no need to disconnect the hydraulic hose between the reservoir and the master cylinder. Keep the reservoir upright to prevent fluid spillage and make sure no strain is placed on the hose.

2 Displace the switch housing from the handlebar and detach both cable nipples from the throttle pulley (see Chapter 4, Section 13).
3 Unscrew the handlebar end weight and remove the weight, then slide the twistgrip off the handlebar **(see illustration)**.
4 To remove the left handlebar, disconnect the clutch switch wiring connectors **(see illustration)**. Undo the switch housing screws and detach the housing from the handlebar **(see illustration)**.
5 Unscrew the handlebar end weight and pull the grip off the bar **(see illustration 5.3)**. Push a screwdriver between the grip and the bar and blow compressed air or spray lubricant inside the grip to loosen it. If the grip has been bonded in place you may need to cut it free.
6 Detach the clutch cable from the lever (see

5.1b Unscrew the bolt (arrowed)

5.1c Unscrew the master cylinder clamp bolts (arrowed) and displace the assembly

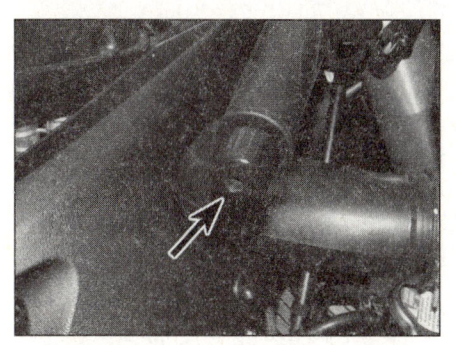

5.3 Handlebar end-weight (arrowed)

5.4a Disconnect the wiring connectors (arrowed)

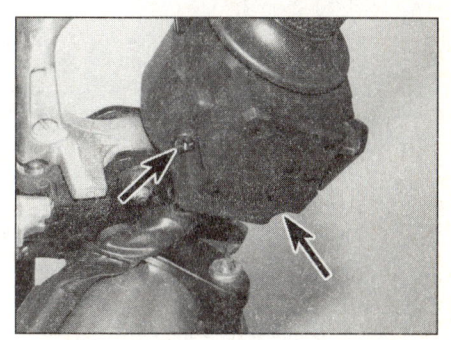

5.4b Undo the screws (arrowed) and detach the switch housing

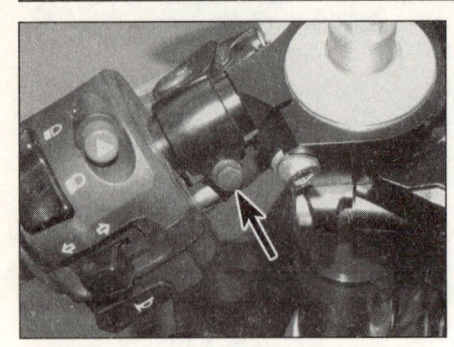

5•6 Frame and suspension

5.6 Slacken the lever bracket clamp bolt (arrowed)

5.7a Remove the blanking cap...

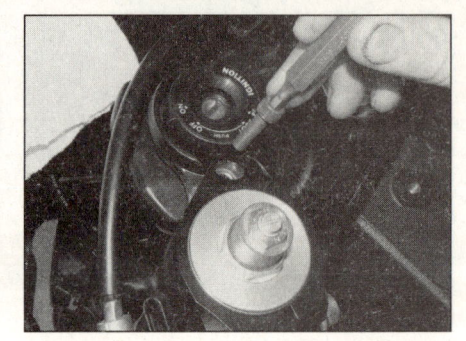

5.7b ...then unscrew the bolt

Chapter 2, Section 12), then slacken the lever bracket pinch bolt and slide the lever off the bar end **(see illustration)**.

7 Remove the blanking cap from the head of the handlebar positioning bolt using a small flat-bladed screwdriver, then unscrew the bolt **(see illustrations)**.

8 Slacken the handlebar clamp bolt and ease the handlebar up and off the fork **(see illustrations)**.

Installation

9 Installation is the reverse of removal, noting the following.

- Tighten the handlebar positioning bolts and handlebar clamp bolts, in that order, to the torque settings specified at the beginning of this Chapter.

- Lubricate the right-hand bar before sliding on the throttle twistgrip. Tighten the end weights to the specified torque.
- Align the slit in the clutch lever bracket with the punch mark on the underside of the handlebar, and tighten the clamp bolt to the specified torque.
- Align the master cylinder clamp mating surfaces with the punch mark on the top of the handlebar, and fit the clamp with the UP mark facing up **(see illustration)**. Make sure there is 8 mm between the switch housing and the master cylinder clamp. Tighten the clamp bolts to the specified torque, tightening the top bolt first. Do not forget to reconnect the front brake light switch and clutch switch wiring connectors **(see illustrations 5.1a and 5.4a)**.

- Apply grease to the clutch and throttle cable ends. Refer to Chapter 4 for the installation of the throttle cables and Chapter 2 for the clutch cable.
- Locate the peg on the switch housing in the hole in the handlebar – on the right the hole is in the top, on the left it is on the underside, of the handlebar.
- Check and adjust throttle and clutch cable freeplay (see Chapter 1).
- Check the operation of all switches and the front brake and clutch before taking the machine on the road.

Clutch lever

10 Thread the clutch cable adjuster fully into the bracket to provide maximum freeplay in the cable **(see illustration)**. Unscrew the lever pivot bolt locknut, then push the pivot bolt out of the bracket and remove the lever, detaching the cable nipple as you do so **(see illustration)**. Note the bush inside the lever and remove it if it is loose.

11 Installation is the reverse of removal. Apply grease to the pivot bolt shaft, the bush and the contact areas between the lever and its bracket, and to the clutch cable nipple. Adjust the clutch cable freeplay (see Chapter 1).

Front brake lever

12 Unscrew the lever pivot bolt locknut, then unscrew the pivot bolt and withdraw it

5.8a Slacken the bolt (arrowed)...

5.8b ...and ease the handlebar up and off the fork

5.9 Align the clamp mating surfaces with the punch mark (arrowed)

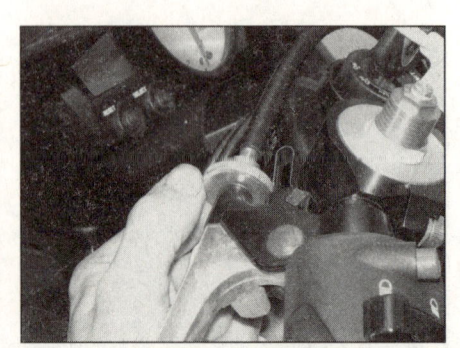

5.10a Thread the adjuster in

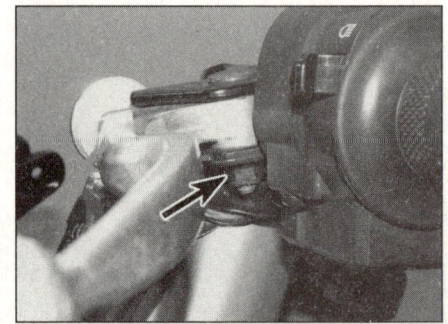

5.10b Unscrew the locknut (arrowed) then undo the pivot screw (arrowed) and remove the lever

Frame and suspension 5•7

from the bracket, and remove the lever **(see illustrations)**.
13 Installation is the reverse of removal. Apply grease to the pivot bolt shaft and the contact areas between the lever and its bracket.

6 Fork removal and installation

Removal

Note: *Although not strictly necessary, before removing the forks it is recommended that the fairing side panels and fairing are removed (see Chapter 7). This will improve access and prevent accidental damage to the paintwork should a tool slip.*

1 Support the motorcycle with an auxiliary stand so that the front wheel is off the ground. Remove the fairing side panels and the fairing (see Chapter 7).
2 Remove the front mudguard (see Chapter 7).
3 Remove the front wheel (see Chapter 6).
4 Work on each fork leg individually. Note the routing of the various cables and hoses around the forks, then release the cable tie(s) on the fork.
5 Note the amount of protrusion of the fork tube above the handlebar clamp **(see illustration 6.9)**. Displace the handlebar (see Section 5).
6 Slacken the fork clamp bolt in the top yoke **(see illustration)**. If the fork leg is to be disassembled, or if the fork oil is being changed, loosen the fork top bolt at this stage, but don't remove it **(see illustration)**.
7 Support the fork leg, then loosen the fork clamp bolts in the bottom yoke **(see illustration)**. Remove the fork leg by twisting it and pulling it downwards **(see illustration)**. Note which fork leg fits on which side.

> **HAYNES HiNT**
> *If the fork legs are seized in the yokes, spray the area with penetrating oil and allow time for it to soak in before trying again.*

Installation

8 Remove all traces of corrosion from the fork tubes and the yokes.
9 Slide the fork leg up through the bottom yoke

5.12a Undo the nut...

5.12b ...then remove the pivot screw and remove the lever

and into the top yoke, making sure the wiring, cables and hoses are the correct side of the leg as noted on removal **(see illustration 6.7b)**. Locate the handlebar over the fork and onto the top yoke and set the amount of protrusion of the fork tube above the handlebar clamp as noted on removal and equal on both sides – Yamaha specify that the tops of the tubes should be flush with the tops of the handlebar clamps when they are fitted, leaving the top bolt face above the clamp **(see illustration)**.
10 Tighten the fork clamp bolts in the bottom yoke to the torque setting specified at the beginning of this Chapter **(see illustration 6.7a)**. Now displace the handlebar again. If the fork leg has been dismantled or if the oil has been changed, tighten the top bolt to the specified torque setting **(see illustration 6.6b)**. Tighten the fork clamp bolt in the top yoke to the specified torque setting **(see illustration 6.6a)**. Install the handlebar (see Section 5).

6.6a Slacken the clamp bolt (arrowed)

11 Install the remaining components in the reverse order of removal. Do not forget to fit new cable tie(s) where removed.
12 Check the operation of the front forks and brakes before taking the machine out on the road.

7 Fork oil change

1 After a high mileage the fork oil will deteriorate and its damping and lubrication qualities will be impaired. Always change the oil in both fork legs.

R and S (2003 and 2004) models

2 Remove the fork; ensure that the top bolt is loosened while the leg is still clamped in the bottom yoke (see Section 6).

6.6b If the fork is to be disassembled slacken the fork top bolt now

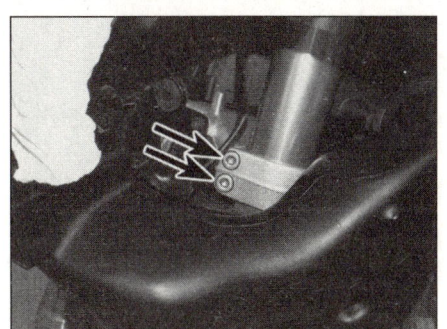

6.7a Slacken the fork clamp bolts (arrowed) in the bottom yoke...

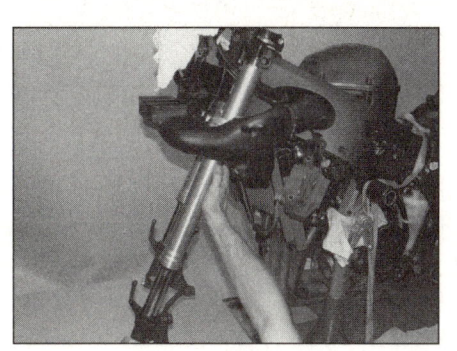

6.7b ...then draw the fork down and out of the yokes

6.9 Set the amount of fork protrusion as shown and described

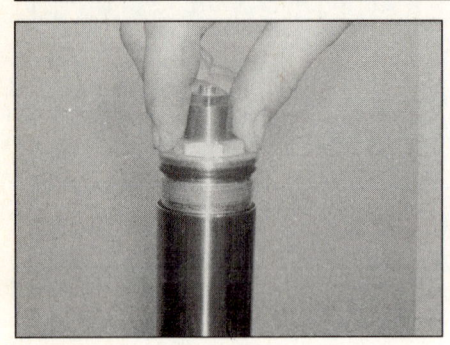

5•8 Frame and suspension

7.3 Thread the top bolt out of the tube

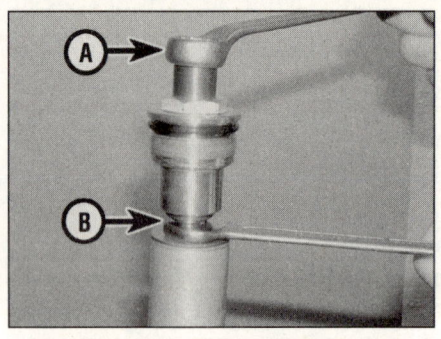

7.4a Counter-hold the adjuster using a spanner (A) and slacken the locknut (B) . . .

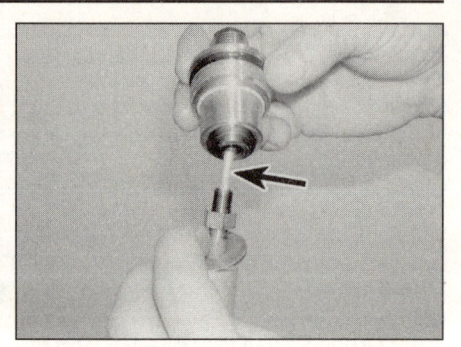

7.4b . . . then thread the top bolt off and withdraw the rebound damping adjuster rod (arrowed)

3 Unscrew the top bolt from the top of the fork tube **(see illustration)**. The bolt will remain threaded on the damper rod.

4 Counter-hold the spring pre-load hex and loosen the damper cartridge rod locknut, then unscrew the top bolt from the rod **(see illustrations)**. Withdraw the damping adjuster rod from the damper rod.

5 Remove the washer, spacer, spacer seat, and spring from the fork **(see illustrations 7.9e, d, c and b)**.

6 Invert the fork leg over a suitable container and pump the fork and damper rod vigorously to expel as much oil as possible. Support the fork upside down in the container and allow it to drain for a few minutes, then pump the fork and rod again. Wipe any excess oil off the spring and spacer. If the fork oil contains metal particles inspect the fork bushes for wear (see Section 8).

7 Fully compress the fork tube in the slider, then slowly pour in the correct quantity of the specified grade of fork oil and carefully pump the damper cartridge rod at least ten times to distribute the oil **(see illustration)**. Now pump the fork tube in the slider using short strokes no longer than 100 mm, and leave the leg upright for ten minutes to allow any air bubbles to disperse.

8 Ensure the fork tube is still fully compressed into the slider; measure the fork oil level from the top of the tube **(see illustration)**. Add or subtract fork oil until it is at the level specified at the beginning of this Chapter.

9 Pull the damper rod and fork tube out of the slider to their full extension, then install the spring with its closer wound coils at the top. Fit the spacer seat, spacer, washer and damping adjuster rod **(see illustrations)**.

10 Position the damper cartridge rod locknut

7.7 Pour the oil into the top of the tube and distribute and bleed it as described . . .

7.8 . . . then measure the level

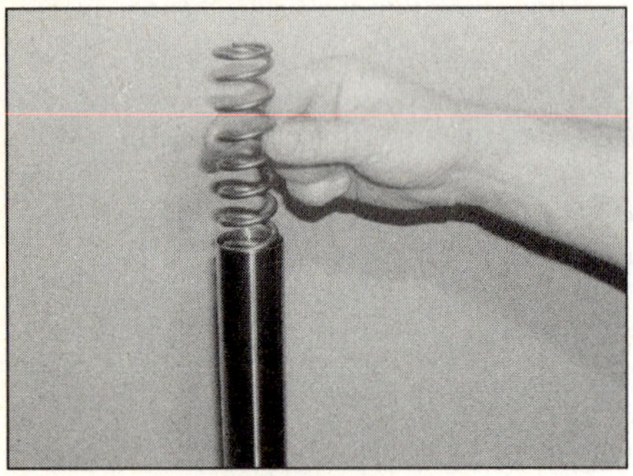

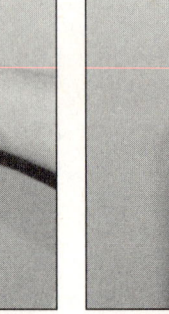

7.9a Install the spring . . .

7.9b . . . the spacer seat . . .

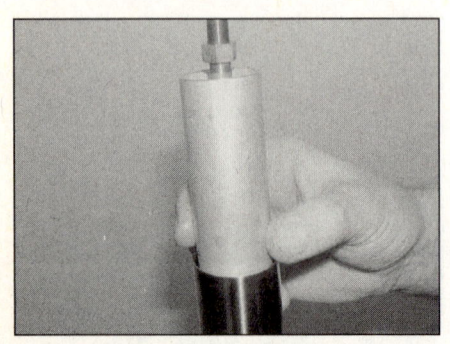

7.9c . . . the spacer . . .

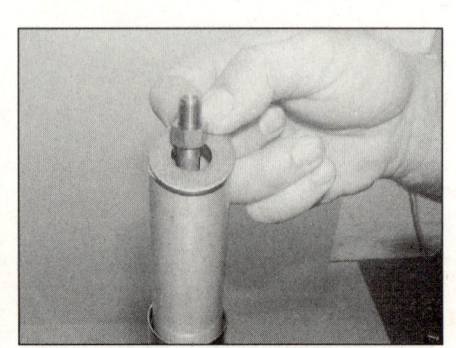

7.9d . . . the washer . . .

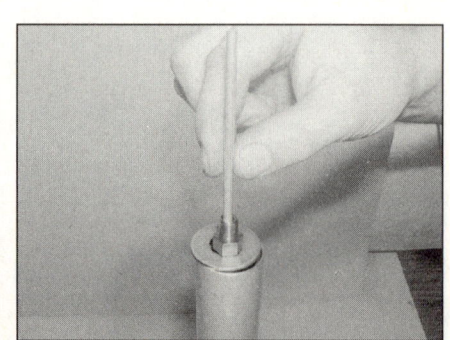

7.9e . . . and the rebound damping adjuster rod

Frame and suspension 5•9

so that the distance between the top of the nut and the top of the rod is 11 mm **(see illustration)**.

11 Lubricate the top bolt O-ring with fork oil, fitting a new one if necessary, then thread the top bolt onto the damper cartridge rod until it seats against the locknut **(see illustration 7.4b)**. Counter-hold the spring pre-load hex and tighten the locknut securely against it, to the specified torque if the correct tools are available **(see illustration 7.4a)**.

12 Fully extend the outer tube and carefully screw the top bolt into the tube, making sure it is not cross-threaded **(see illustration 7.3)**. **Note:** *The top bolt can be tightened to the specified torque setting when the fork leg has been installed and is securely held in the bottom yoke.*

13 Install the fork (see Section 6).

T (2005) models

Special Tool: *A special tool is needed to disassemble the forks – see Step 16.*

14 Remove the fork leg; ensure that the top bolt is loosened while the leg is still clamped in the bottom yoke (see Section 6).

15 Support the fork leg in an upright position and unscrew the fork top bolt from the top of the fork tube **(see illustration)**. Slide the fork tube down onto the slider.

16 With the aid of an assistant, pull up on the fork top bolt, then press down on the spacer to compress the spring and expose the locknut on the bottom of the damping adjuster. **Note:** *Yamaha produces service tools (spacer holder Pt. No. 90890-01441 and stopper plate Pt. No. 90890-01434) to do this.* Alternatively, use the home-made set-up shown using a piece of threaded rod, some nuts and some steel strap, making sure the tool is wide enough to fit over the tube **(see illustration)**. Do not insert the handle pieces too far into the spacer as they could foul the top bolt. Insert the stopper plate or slotted washer under the locknut **(see illustrations)**. Carefully release the pressure on the spacer and allow the plate or slotted washer to rest against the underside of the locknut under spring pressure.

17 Counter-hold the locknut and loosen the top bolt, then thread the top bolt assembly off the damper rod and remove it **(see illustration)**. **Note:** *The top bolt assembly should not be disassembled.*

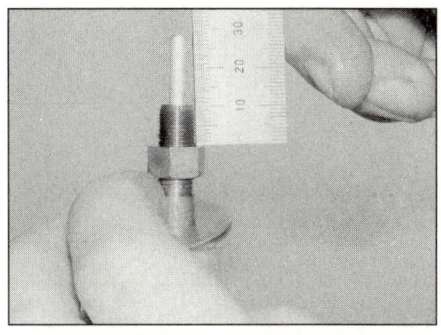

7.10 Set the locknut 11 mm below the top of the thread as shown

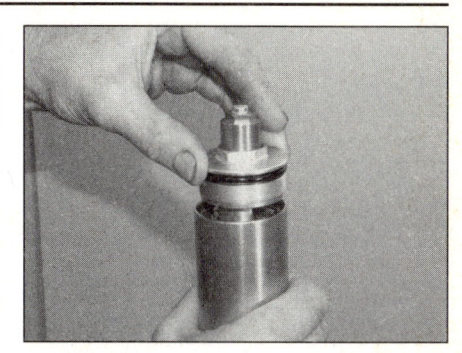

7.15 Unscrew the fork top bolt

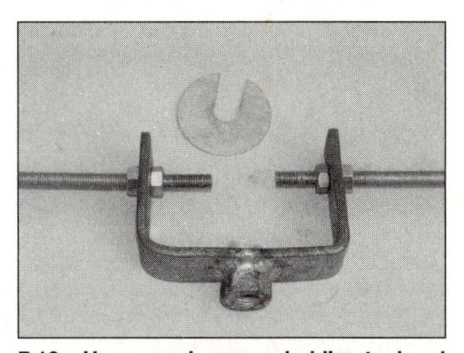

7.16a Home-made spacer holding tool and slotted washer

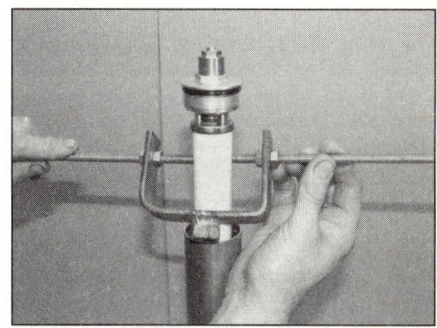

7.16b Fit the tool onto the spacer . . .

18 Withdraw the damping adjuster rod from inside the damper cartridge rod **(see illustration)**.

19 Compress the spacer and remove the plate or slotted washer, then carefully allow the spring to relax and remove the spacer with the tool still attached **(see illustration)**. Note the shaped washer on the top of the spacer and remove it. Withdraw the spring from the tube, noting which way up it fits **(see illustration)**.

7.16c . . . then compress the spring and slide the washer under the nut

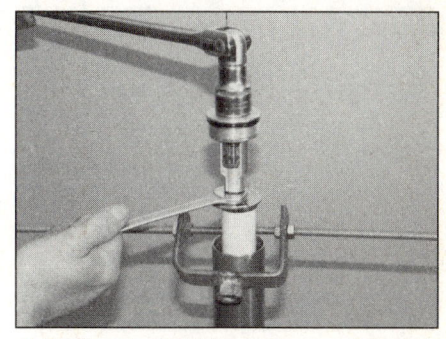

7.17 Counter-hold the locknut and thread the top bolt off the rod

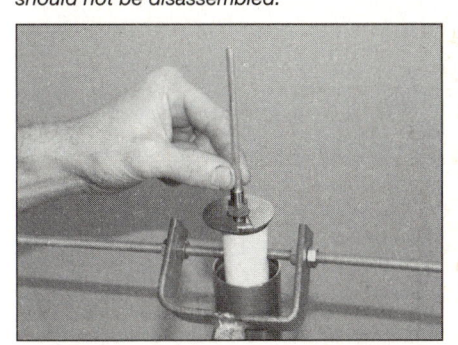

7.18 Withdraw the damping adjuster rod

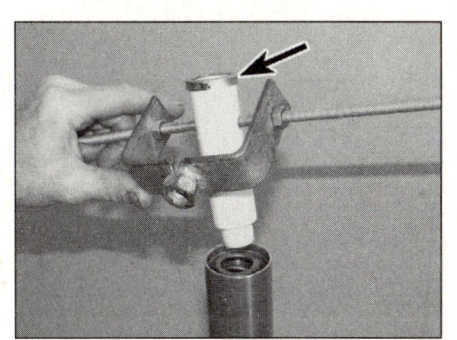

7.19a Remove the spacer, noting the washer (arrowed) on its top . . .

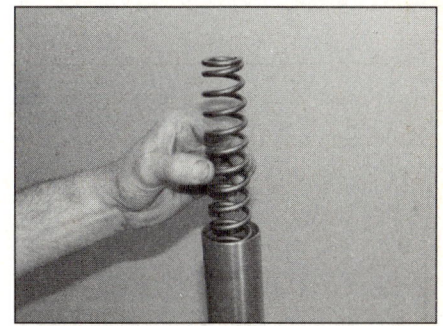

7.19b . . . then remove the spring

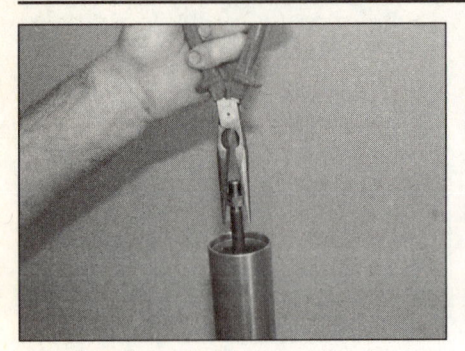

5•10 Frame and suspension

7.20a Draw the damper rod out ...

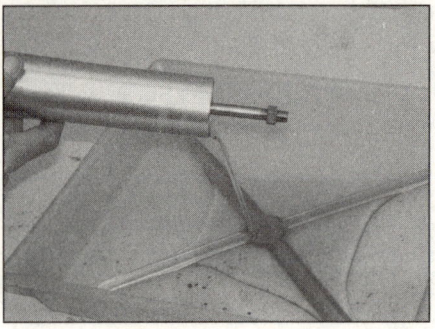

7.20b ... then drain the oil as described

7.22a Pour the oil into the top of the tube and distribute and bleed it as described ...

20 Draw the damper rod out of the tube using long nosed pliers **(see illustration)**. Invert the fork leg over a suitable container and pump the fork and damper rod to expel as much oil as possible **(see illustration)**.

21 Support the leg and allow it to drain for several minutes. Wipe any excess oil off the spring and spacer. If the fork oil contains metal particles inspect the fork components for signs of wear (see Section 8).

22 Slowly pour in the correct quantity and type of fork oil as specified at the beginning of this Chapter, keeping a hold on the damper rod to prevent it sinking **(see illustration)**. Secure the fork leg upright and if required fit a slotted washer under the locknut as shown to prevent the rod sinking into the tube, and allow it to stand for several minutes to allow all the air to escape **(see illustration)**. Now pump the rod again – once all the air is expelled you should feel stiff resistance when pumping the rod. Take great care to ensure that all air is expelled from the damper cartridge at this stage.

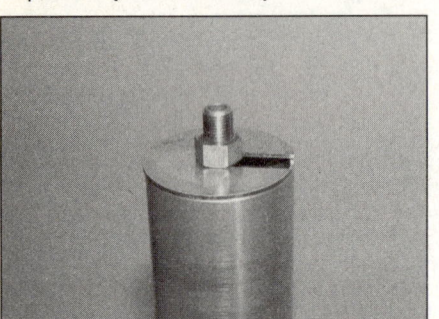

7.22b ... using the slotted washer as shown to prevent the damper rod sinking

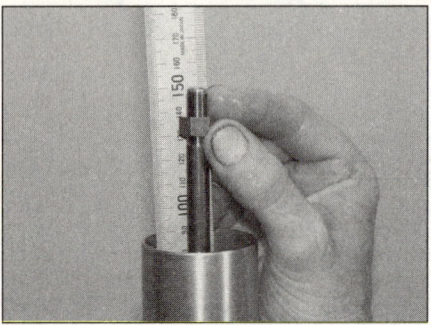

7.23 Measure the level of oil and adjust the quantity if necessary

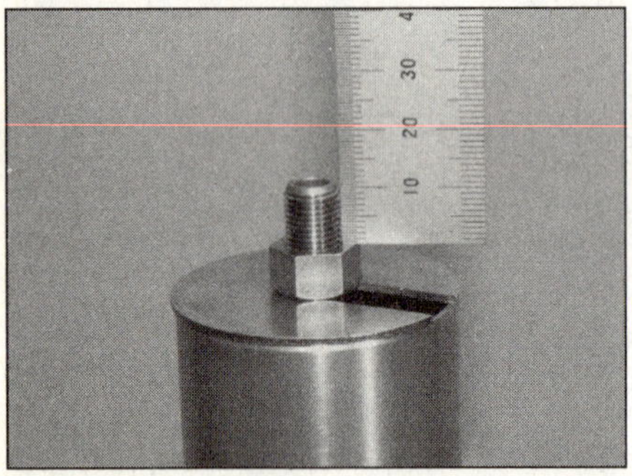

23 Fully compress the fork tube and damper rod onto the slider and measure the oil level from the top of the tube **(see illustration)**. Add or subtract oil until it is at the level specified at the beginning of this Chapter.

24 Position the damper cartridge rod locknut so that the distance between the top of the nut and the top of the rod is 11 mm **(see illustration)**.

25 Install the spring with its tapered end upwards, sliding it over the damper rod **(see illustration)**. Draw the rod out and fit a piece of thin wire around the rod under the locknut to help keep it extended **(see illustration)**. Fit the spacer and the shaped washer, sliding them over the wire or holding tool if being used **(see illustration)**.

7.24 Set the locknut in the correct position

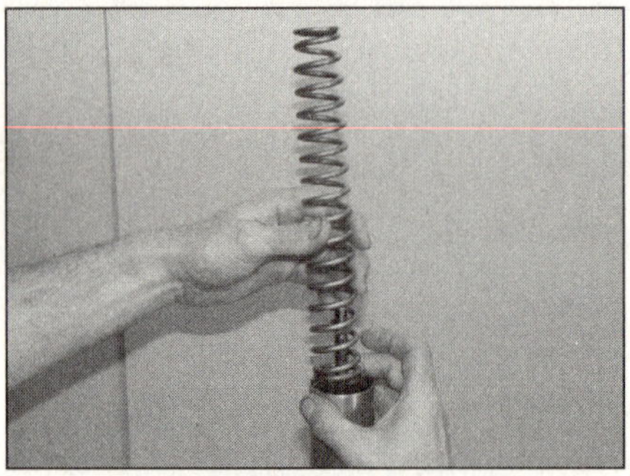

7.25a Fit the spring ...

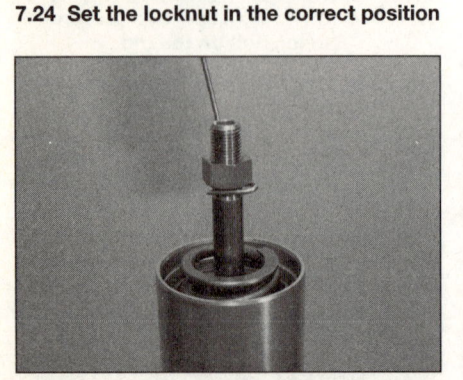

26 Keeping the damper rod fully extended, press down on the spacer to compress the spring using the holding tool (see Step 16), then insert the stopper plate or slotted washer under the locknut **(see illustration)**. Remove the wire.

7.25b ... then draw the rod out and tie some wire round to hold it up ...

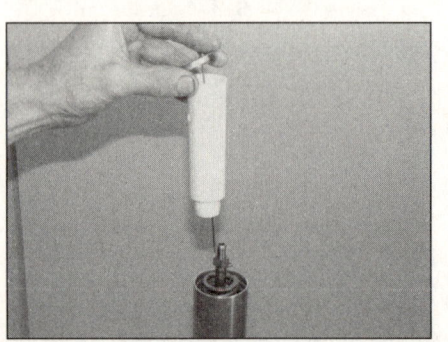

7.25c ... while fitting the spacer and the shaped washer

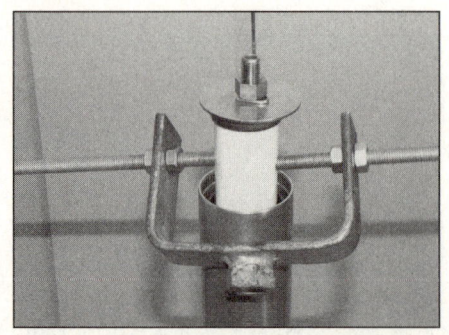

7.26 Fit the slotted washer between the spacer seat and the nut, then remove the wire

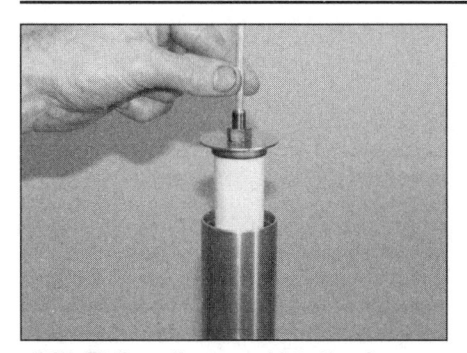

Frame and suspension 5•11

7.27 Fit the adjuster rod into the damper rod

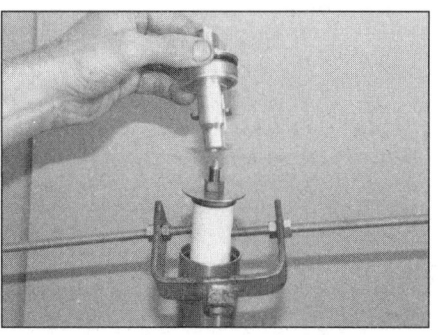

7.28 Thread the top bolt onto the damper rod

7.29 Make sure the spacer seat locates correctly over the top bolt

27 Fit the damping adjuster rod inside the damper rod **(see illustration)**.
28 Thread the top bolt onto the damper rod and screw it all the way down to the locknut **(see illustration)**. Counter-hold the top bolt and tighten the locknut securely against it, to the specified torque if the correct tools are available.
29 Press down on the spacer to compress the spring and remove the plate or slotted washer, then carefully release the spring pressure, making sure the flats in the shaped washer align with and slide over the flat sides of the top bolt assembly **(see illustration)**. Remove the holding tool.
30 Pull the slider all the way out of the fork tube and carefully screw the top bolt into the tube making sure it is not cross-threaded **(see illustration 7.15)**. Note: *The top bolt can be tightened to the specified torque setting at this stage but a better method is to tighten the top bolt when the fork leg has been installed and is securely clamped in the bottom yoke (see Section 6)*.
31 Install the forks (see Section 6).

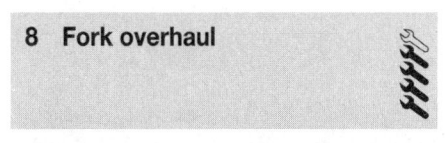

8 Fork overhaul

R and S (2003 and 2004) models

Special Tool: *Yamaha service tools are available for holding the damper cartridge and installing the fork top bush, although alternatives are discussed in the procedure.*

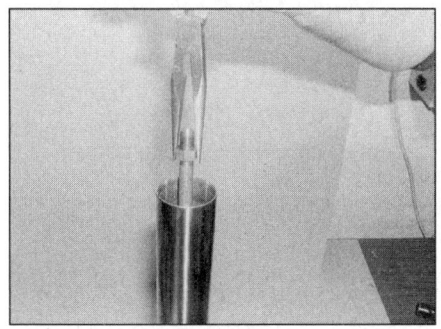

Disassembly

1 Remove the fork; ensure that the top bolt is loosened while the leg is still clamped in the bottom yoke (see Section 6). Always dismantle the fork legs separately to avoid interchanging parts and thus causing an accelerated rate of wear. Store all components in separate, clearly marked containers.
2 Remove the stone guard from the fork slider **(see illustration)**.
3 Lay the fork flat on the bench and hold it down, then slacken and lightly re-tighten (to prevent oil coming out) the damper rod bolt in the base of the fork slider **(see illustration)**. If the bolt refuses to slacken and instead the damper cartridge turns with it inside the fork, turn the leg upside down and compress the fork tube in the slider so that the spring exerts maximum pressure on the damper cartridge assembly, then loosen the bolt. If the bolt does not loosen, use an air wrench. If necessary,

Yamaha produce a service tool (Part No. 90890-01473) which passes down over the damper cartridge rod and engages the head of the cartridge body to hold it in place, and this can be applied at Step 5).
4 Refer to Section 7, Steps 3 to 6 and drain the oil form the fork.
5 Remove the previously slackened damper cartridge bolt and its copper sealing washer from the bottom of the slider **(see illustration 8.3)**. Discard the sealing washer as a new one must be used on reassembly.
6 Withdraw the damper cartridge from inside the fork tube **(see illustration)**.
7 Carefully prise out the dust seal from the top of the slider and slide it off the tube **(see illustration)**. Discard the seal as a new one must be used.
8 Carefully remove the retaining clip, taking care not to scratch the surface of the tube; compress the fork to avoid damaging its working surface **(see illustration)**.

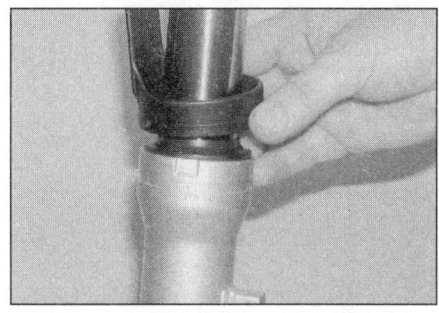

8.2 Remove the stone guard, noting how it fits

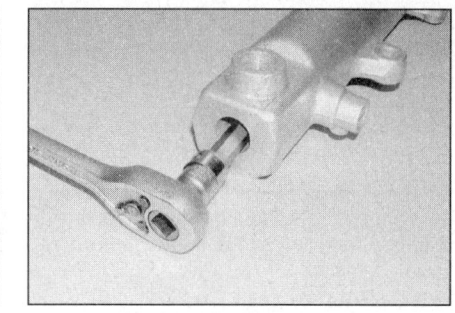

8.3 Slacken the damper rod bolt

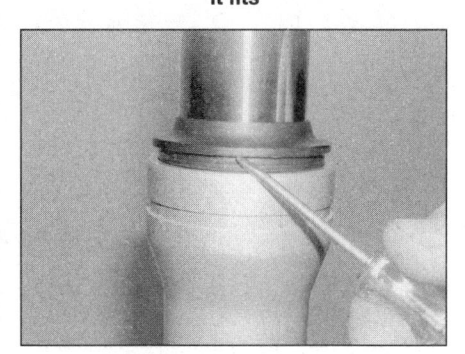

8.6 Withdraw the damper cartridge

8.7 Prise out the dust seal using a flat-bladed screwdriver

8.8 Prise out the retaining clip using a flat-bladed screwdriver

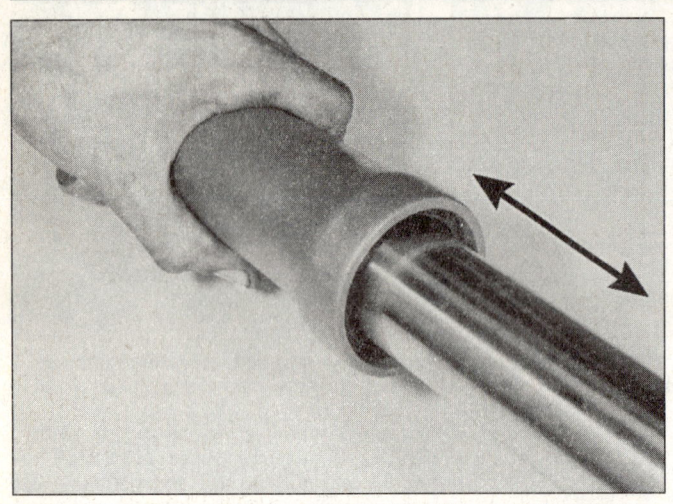

8.9a To separate the fork tube from the slider, pull them apart firmly several times . . .

8.9b . . . the slide-hammer effect of the bottom bush (4) will displace the top bush (3), washer (2), and oil seal (1)

9 To separate the tube from the slider it is necessary to displace the oil seal and top bush. The bottom bush will not pass through the top bush, and this can be used to good effect. Push the tube gently inwards until it stops against the damper cartridge seat. Take care not to do this forcibly or the seat may be damaged. Then pull the tube sharply outwards until the bottom bush strikes the top bush. Repeat this operation until the seal and top bush are tapped out of the slider and the tube can be fully withdrawn **(see illustrations)**.

10 Slide the oil seal, its washer and the top bush off the fork tube, noting which way up they fit. Discard the oil seal as a new one must be fitted on reassembly. **Note:** *Yamaha recommend that both the top and bottom bushes should be replaced with new ones when the forks are disassembled.*

11 Tip the damper cartridge seat out of the slider, noting which way up it fits.

Inspection

12 Clean all parts in solvent and blow them dry with compressed air, if available. Check the fork tube for score marks, scratches, flaking or pitted chrome finish and excessive or abnormal wear. Look for dents in the tube and replace the tubes in both forks with new ones if any are found. Check the fork seal seat for nicks, gouges and scratches. If damage is evident, leaks will occur. Also check the oil seal washer for damage or distortion; replace damaged or worn parts with new ones as necessary.

13 Check the fork tube for runout (bending) using V-blocks and a dial gauge, or have it done by a Yamaha dealer or suspension specialist **(see illustration)**. Yamaha specify a runout limit of 0.2 mm, so if the tube is bent beyond that seek the advice of a suspension specialist – straightening is sometimes possible but the best thing to do is fit a new tube.

⚠️ *Warning: If the tube is bent, it should not be straightened – replace it with a new one.*

14 Check the spring for cracks and other damage. Measure the spring free length and compare the measurement to the specifications at the beginning of this Chapter **(see illustration)**. If a spring is defective or has sagged below the service limit, replace the springs in both fork legs with new ones. Never replace only one spring.

15 Examine the working surfaces of the two bushes; if worn or scuffed (the grey Teflon surface will have worn away and the copper underneath will be visible) they must be replaced with new ones (but see Step 10). Note that separation of the fork may damage the bushes and it is advisable to fit new ones as a matter of course. The bottom bush (on the fork tube) can be removed by gently opening out its slit with a large flat-bladed screwdriver so that it can be slid off the end of the fork tube; use the same method to install the new bush.

16 Check the damper cartridge for damage and wear, and replace it with a new one if necessary. If available, blow compressed air through the oil passages.

17 Examine the damper cartridge seat and replace it with a new one if it is worn or distorted.

Reassembly

18 Fit the damper cartridge into the fork tube and slide it into place so that it projects fully from the bottom of the tube, then fit the seat onto the bottom of the cartridge.

19 Oil the fork tube and bottom bush with the specified fork oil and insert the assembly into the slider so that the damper seat is at the bottom of the slider. Fit a new copper sealing washer to the damper cartridge bolt and apply a few drops of a suitable non-permanent thread-locking compound, then thread the

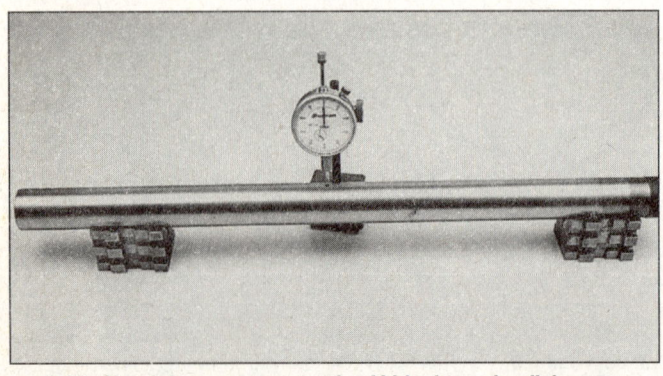

8.13 Check for any runout using V-blocks and a dial gauge

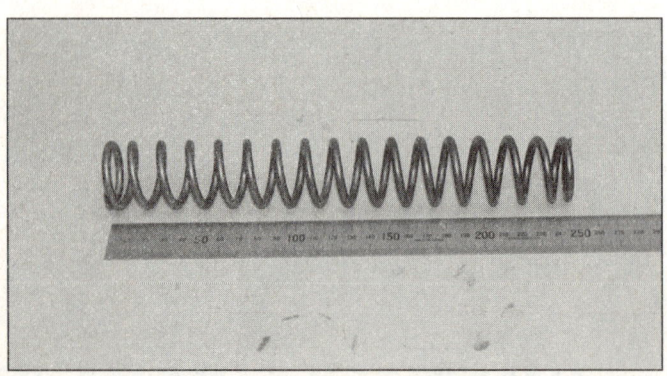

8.14 Measure the free length of the spring

Frame and suspension 5•13

8.20a Slide the top bush down the tube . . .

8.20b . . . then the washer . . .

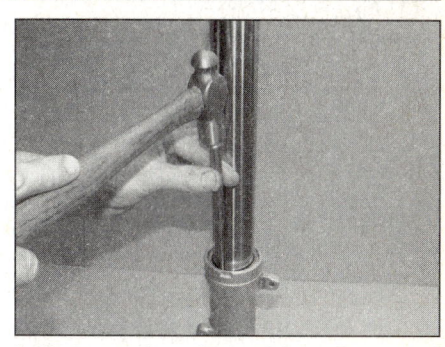

8.20c . . . and tap the bush into place using the washer as an interface

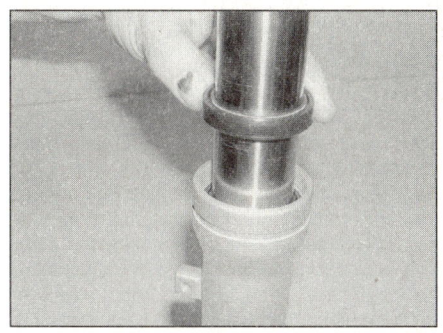

8.21 Fit the oil seal . . .

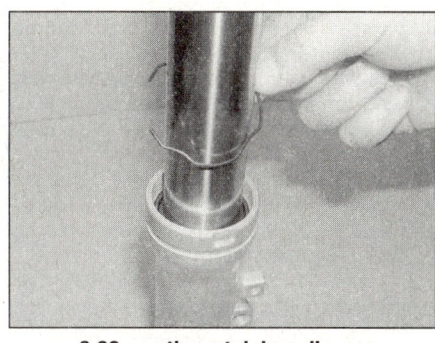

8.22 . . . the retaining clip . . .

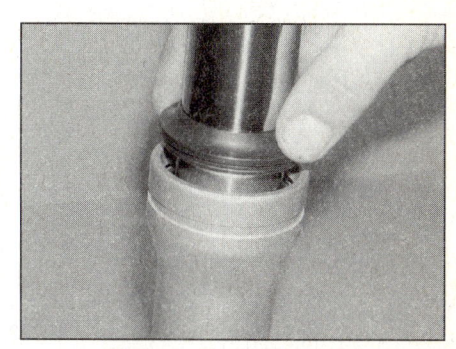

8.23 . . . and the dust seal

bolt into the bottom of the slider **(see illustration 8.3)**. Tighten the bolt to the specified torque setting. If the damper cartridge rotates inside the tube, hold the rod with spring pressure or the service tool as on disassembly.

20 Push the fork tube fully into the slider, then oil the top bush and slide it down over the tube **(see illustrations)**. Press the bush squarely into its recess in the slider, then fit the oil seal washer on top of the bush and use a hammer and a suitable piece of tubing to tap the bush into place – Yamaha produce service tools for this, part Nos. 90890-01367 and 01374 (or YM33963 and YM8020A in the US); note that excessive force should be unnecessary and will damage the bush. **Note:** *Take care not to scratch the fork tube during reassembly; if the fork tube is pushed fully into the slider any accidental scratching is confined to the area above the oil seal.*

21 Lubricate the **new** oil seal with lithium grease and slide it down over the tube with its markings facing upwards. Press the seal squarely into the slider and tap it lightly into place as described in Step 20 until the retaining clip groove is visible above the seal **(see illustration)**.

22 Fit the retaining clip, making sure it is correctly located in its groove **(see illustration)**.

23 Lubricate the inside of the new dust seal then slide it down the fork tube and press it into position **(see illustration)**.

24 Fit the stoneguard **(see illustration 8.2)**.

25 Refer to Section 7, Steps 7 to 12 and fill the fork with oil and finish reassembly.

26 Install the fork (see Section 6).

T (2005) models

Special Tool: *Yamaha service tools are available for holding the damper cartridge and installing the fork seal, although alternatives are discussed in the procedure.*

Disassembly

27 Always dismantle the fork legs separately to avoid interchanging parts. Store all components in separate, clearly marked containers.

28 Lay the fork flat on the bench with the caliper mounting lugs to the left and hold it down, then slacken and lightly re-tighten (to prevent oil coming out) the damper rod bolt in

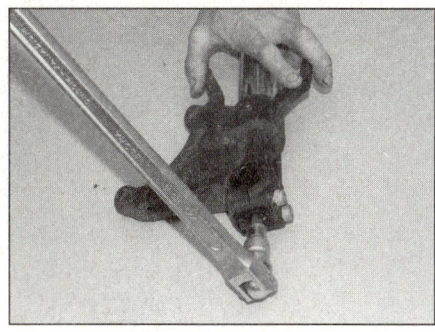

8.28 Slacken the damper rod bolt

the base of the fork slider **(see illustration)**. If the bolt refuses to slacken and instead the damper cartridge turns with it inside the fork, turn the leg upside down and compress the fork tube in the slider so that the spring exerts maximum pressure on the damper cartridge assembly, then loosen the bolt. If the bolt does not loosen, use an air wrench. If necessary, Yamaha produce a service tool (Part No. 90890-01423 (YM-01423 in the US)) which passes down over the damper cartridge rod and engages the head of the cartridge body to hold it in place, and this can be applied at Step 30).

29 Refer to Section 7, Steps 15 to 21 and drain the oil form the fork.

30 Unscrew the front axle clamp bolts **(see illustration)**. Remove the previously loosened damper cartridge bolt and its sealing washer

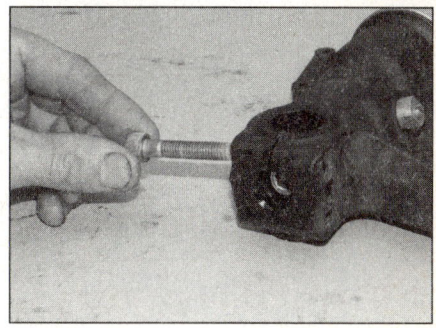

8.30a Unscrew the clamp bolts . . .

5•14 Frame and suspension

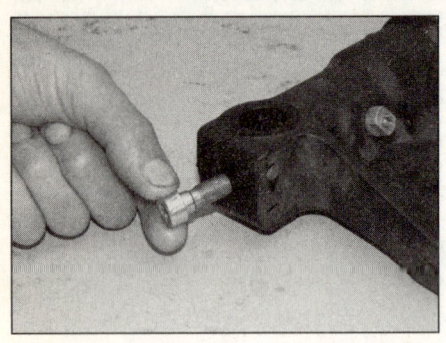

8.30b ... then unscrew the damper bolt

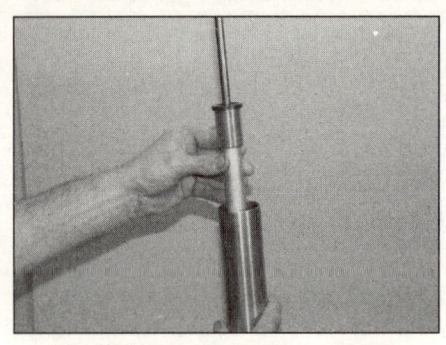

8.31 Withdraw the damper cartridge

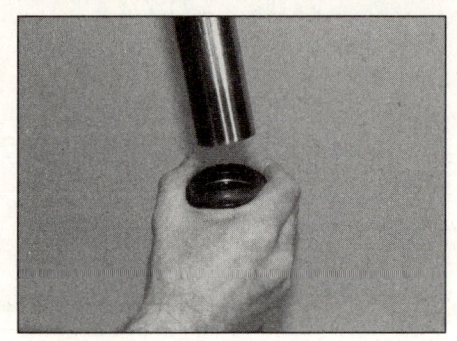

8.32 Withdraw the slider from the tube

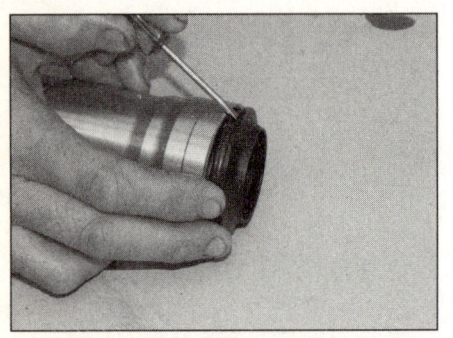

8.33a Remove the dust seal ...

from the bottom of the slider **(see illustration)**. Discard the washer as a new one must be fitted on reassembly.

31 Withdraw the damper cartridge assembly from inside the fork tube **(see illustration)**.

32 Draw the slider out of the tube **(see illustration)**.

33 Carefully prise the dust seal from the bottom of the tube to gain access to the oil seal retaining clip, then remove the retaining clip **(see illustrations)**. Carefully prise out the oil seal using either a seal hook or an internal puller with slide-hammer attachment, taking great care not to damage the rim of the tube, then remove the oil seal washer **(see illustrations)**. Discard the seals as new ones must be fitted on reassembly.

Inspection

Note: *The fork bushes cannot be replaced with new ones. If, upon inspection, the bushes are found to be worn, new fork tubes will have to be fitted.*

34 Follow Steps 12 to 17 to clean and inspect the fork components, but note that both fork bushes are integral components of the fork tube; if either or both of the bushes are worn or scuffed, the fork tube must be replaced with a new one. Do not attempt to remove the bushes. **Note:** *Do not remove the compression damping adjusters.*

8.33b ... followed by the retaining clip

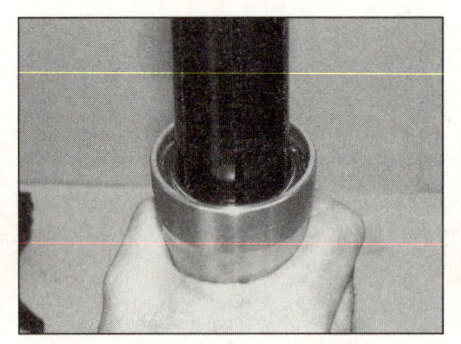

8.33c Fit the puller under the seal ...

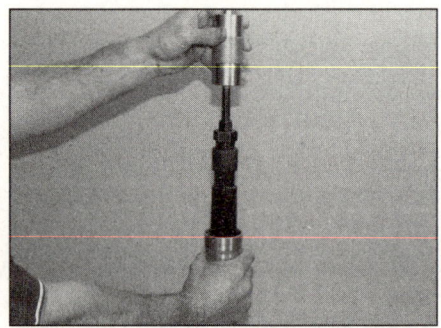

8.33d ... then attach the slide-hammer ...

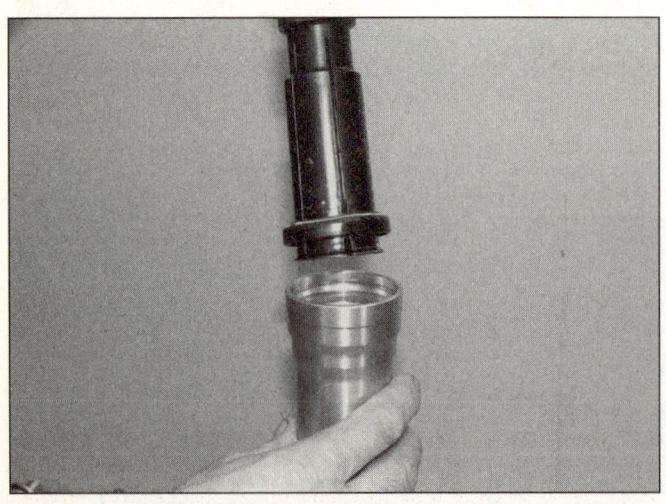

8.33e ... and use it to draw the seal out

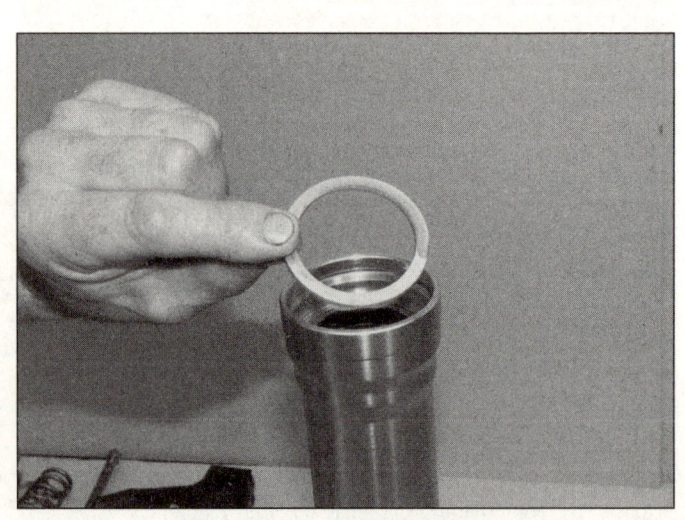

8.33f Remove the oil seal washer

Frame and suspension 5•15

8.35a Fit the new oil seal . . .

8.35b . . . using a suitable socket and the old seal . . .

8.35c . . . to drive it in if necessary

Reassembly

35 Fit the oil seal washer into the fork tube **(see illustration 8.33f)**. Fit the new oil seal into the tube and press or tap it into place until it seats and the retaining clip groove is visible – on the fork we stripped we were able to press the seal in with our fingers, but if necessary tap it in using a suitable socket with walls thin enough so it sits only on the hard outer rim of the seal and not on the spring rim on the top of the seal – you can use the old seal as an interface between the socket and the new seal, especially if the socket is not the ideal size **(see illustrations)**. Alternatively obtain the Yamaha service tool (Pt. No. 90890-01442 (YM-01442 in the US)).

36 Fit the retaining clip, making sure it locates correctly in its groove **(see illustration)**. Press the dust seal into the tube **(see illustration)**.

37 Lubricate the inner surfaces of the new seals with the specified fork oil. Lubricate the slider and bushes inside the fork tube with fork oil, then carefully insert the slider fully into the fork tube **(see illustration)**.

38 Insert the damper cartridge assembly into the fork leg until it contacts the bottom of the slider **(see illustration 8.31)**. Fit a new sealing washer onto the damper cartridge bolt and apply a few drops of a suitable non-permanent thread locking compound, then install the bolt into the bottom of the slider and tighten it to the torque setting specified at the beginning of this Chapter **(see illustrations)**. Note: *If the damper cartridge assembly rotates inside the slider, fit the slotted washer under the damper rod locknut and use it pull up on the rod which should help the bolt to tighten. Alternatively the Yamaha service tool described in Step 28 can be used to hold the head of the cartridge body, or a suitable tool that will achieve the same result can be fabricated from a piece of*

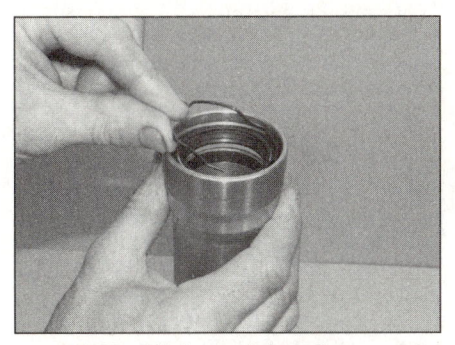

8.36a Fit the retaining clip . . .

8.36b . . . then the new dust seal

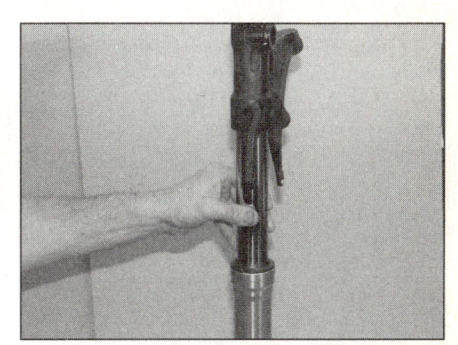

8.37 Fit the slider into the tube

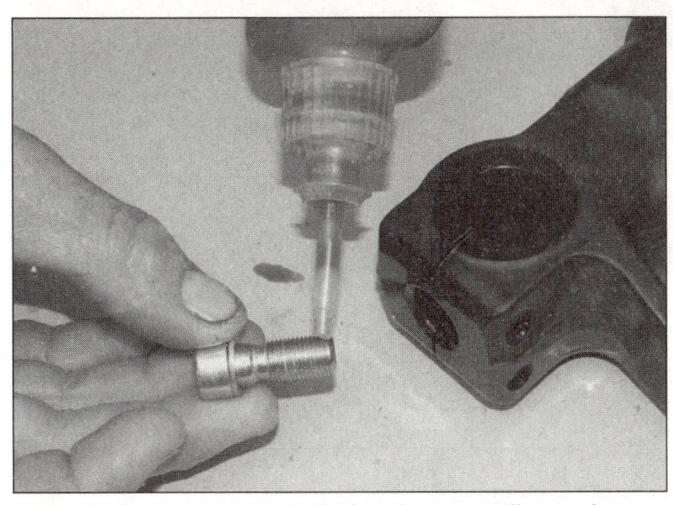

8.38a Fit the bolt using threadlock and a new sealing washer . . .

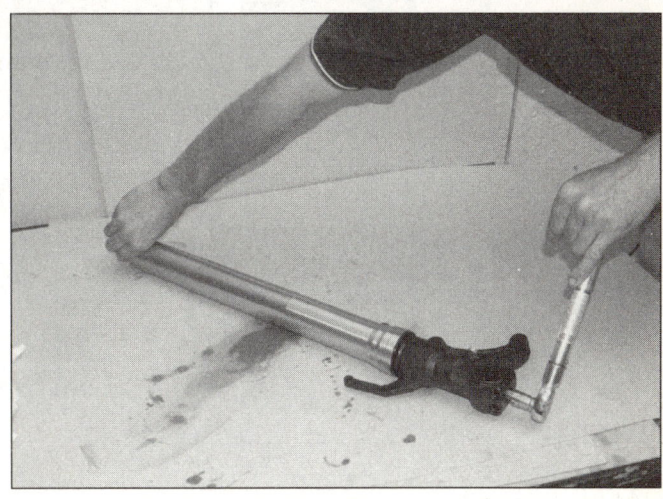

8.38b . . . and tighten it to the specified torque, pulling up on the damper rod if necessary

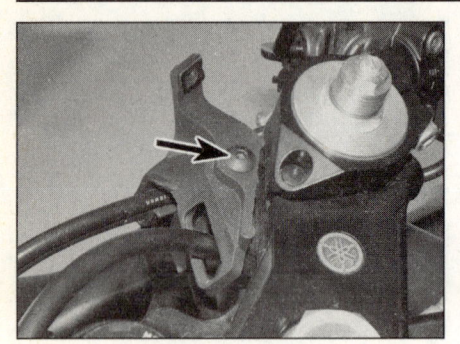

5•16 Frame and suspension

9.2 Unscrew the cable guide bolt (arrowed)

9.3a Disconnect the ignition switch wiring connectors (arrowed)

9.3b To access the immobiliser connectors unclip the connector holder and draw it out of the frame . . .

tubing. Thread the axle clamp bolts in finger-tight **(see illustration 8.30a)**.
39 Refer to Section 7, Steps 22 to 30 and fill the fork with oil and finish reassembly.
40 Install the fork (see Section 6).

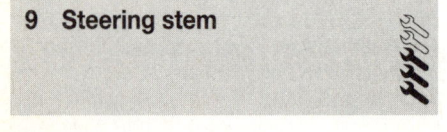

9 Steering stem

Removal

1 Remove the fairing side panels and fairing, and for best access the air intake ducting (see Chapter 7). It is also advisable to raise the fuel tank to avoid the possibility of scratching it (see Chapter 4).
2 Displace the handlebars and lay them aside, making sure they are adequately supported and cushioned on some rag (see Section 5). Remove the front forks (see Section 6). Unscrew the bolt securing the cable holder/brake fluid reservoir bracket to the top yoke **(see illustration)**.
3 If you prefer to remove the top yoke completely rather than just lay it aside on some rag, trace the wiring from the ignition switch, and where fitted the immobiliser receiver, and disconnect it at the connector(s) – to access the connectors remove the air filter housing (see Chapter 4) **(see illustrations)**.
4 Unscrew the bolts securing the bracket for the horn and the brake hoses to the bottom yoke and displace the bracket with everything attached **(see illustration)**.
5 Unscrew the steering stem nut and remove it and its washer, then lift the top yoke up off the steering stem **(see illustrations)**.
6 Remove the tabbed lockwasher, noting how it fits, then unscrew and remove the locknut using, if necessary, either a C-spanner, a peg spanner or a drift located in one of the notches (though it shouldn't be tight and can probably be undone with your fingers) **(see illustrations)**. Remove the rubber washer **(see illustration)**.
7 Supporting the bottom yoke, unscrew the adjuster nut using either a C-spanner, a peg-spanner or a drift located in one of the notches, then remove the adjuster nut and

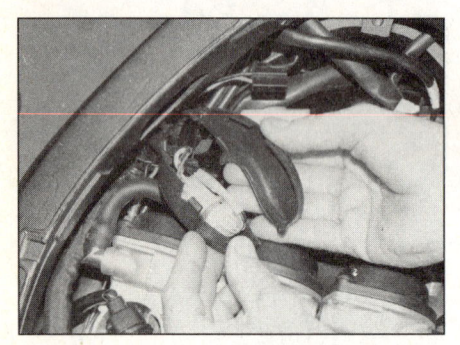

9.3c . . . then unclip the holder lid

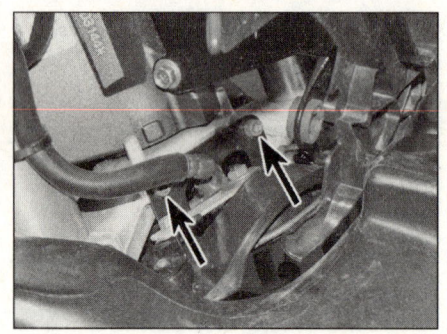

9.4 Unscrew the bolts (arrowed) and displace the bracket

9.5 Unscrew the nut and remove the washer then lift off the top yoke

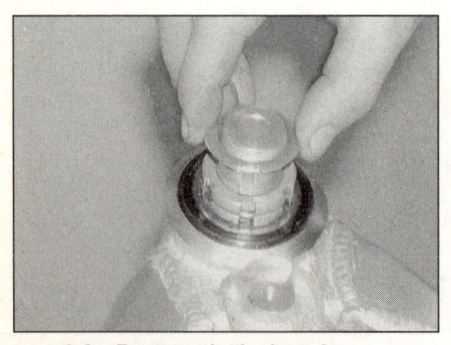

9.6a Remove the lockwasher . . .

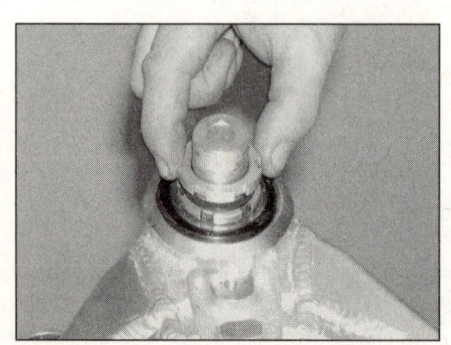

9.6b . . . then unscrew the locknut . . .

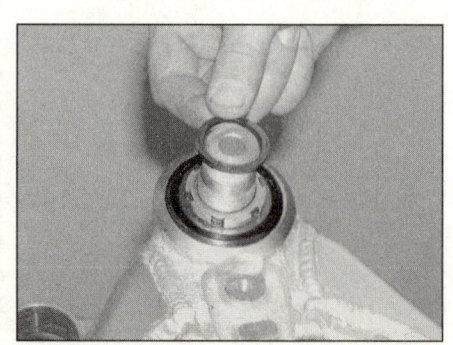

9.6c . . . and remove the rubber washer

Frame and suspension 5•17

9.7a Unscrew the adjuster nut . . .

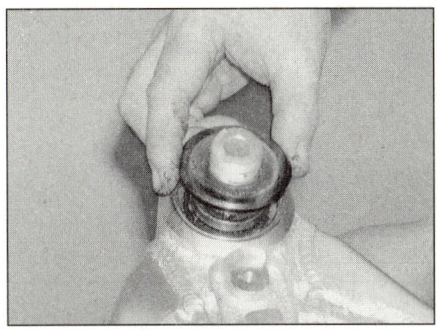

9.7b . . . and remove the bearing cover . . .

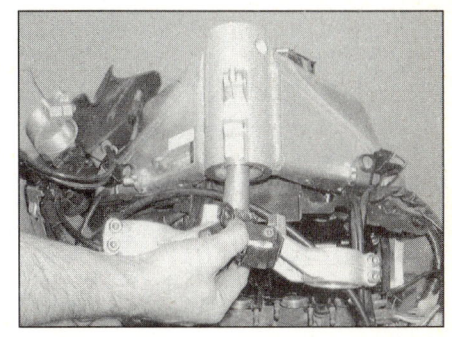

9.8 . . . then draw the bottom yoke/steering stem out of the steering head

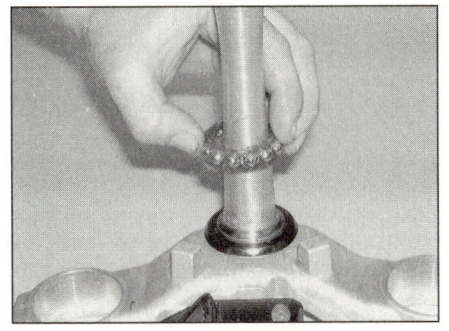

9.10a Remove the lower bearing . . .

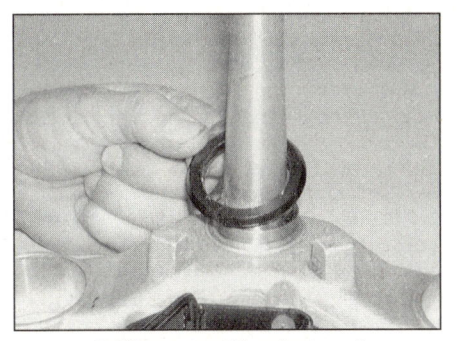

9.10b . . . and the dust seal

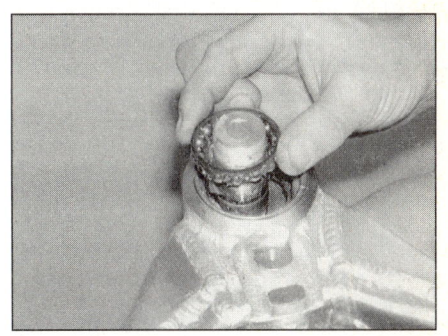

9.12a Fit the upper bearing . . .

the bearing cover from the steering stem **(see illustrations)**.

8 Gently lower the bottom yoke and steering stem out of the frame **(see illustration)**.

9 Remove the inner race and bearing from the top of the steering head **(see illustrations 9.12b and a)**.

10 Remove the bearing and dust seal from the base of the steering stem **(see illustrations)**. Discard the dust seal as a new one must be fitted on reassembly. Use a suitable solvent to remove all traces of old grease from the bearings and races and check them for wear or damage as described in Section 10. **Note:** *Do not remove the races from the steering head or the steering stem unless they are to be replaced with new ones – do not re-use the races if they have been removed.*

Installation

11 Smear a liberal quantity of lithium-based grease onto the bearing races and work some grease well into both the upper and lower bearings. Fit the new dust seal over the lower bearing inner race on the steering stem, then fit the bearing **(see illustration 9.10b and a)**.

12 Carefully lift the bottom yoke and steering stem up through the steering head **(see illustration 9.8)**. Install the upper bearing and the inner race into the top of the steering head **(see illustrations)**. Fit the bearing cover then thread the adjuster nut onto the steering stem making sure it is tight enough to hold the stem in the head without any play **(see illustrations 9.7b and a)**. Install the forks and wheel, as their leverage and inertia need to be taken into account to properly set the bearings, then refer to the procedure in Chapter 1, Section 15, and adjust the bearings as described, noting that you may need to carry out the procedure several times if new bearings have been fitted to allow them to settle.

13 Install the rubber washer and the locknut **(see illustrations 9.6c and b)**. Tighten the locknut finger-tight, then tighten it further until its notches align with those in the adjuster nut. If necessary, counter-hold the adjuster nut to prevent it turning. Install the tabbed lockwasher so that the tabs fit into the notches in both the locknut and adjuster nut **(see illustration)**.

14 Fit the top yoke onto the steering stem, then install the washer and steering stem nut and tighten it to the torque setting specified at the beginning of this Chapter **(see illustration)**.

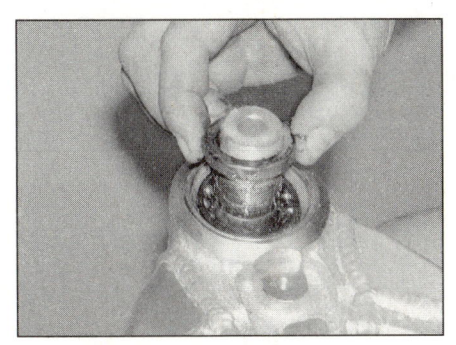

9.12b . . . and the inner race

9.13 Align the notches and fit the tabbed lockwasher

9.14 Tighten the steering stem nut to the specified torque

5•18 Frame and suspension

10.3a Locate the end of the drift in the cutout (arrowed) . . .

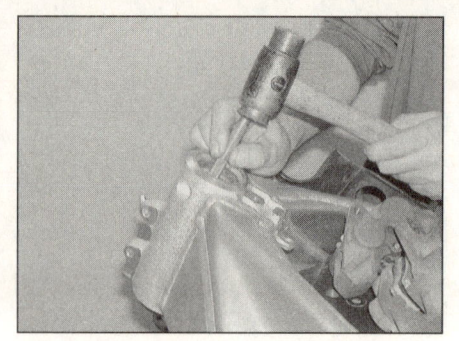

10.3b . . . and drive the race out

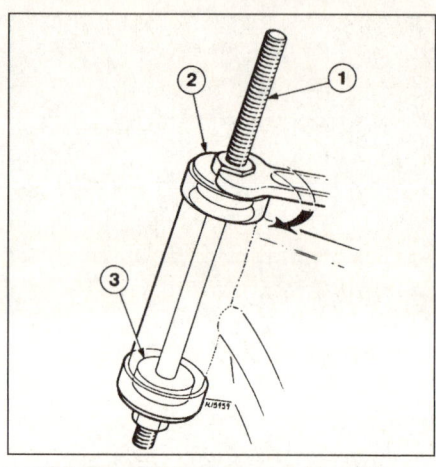

15 Install the remaining components in the reverse order of removal. Carry out a check of the steering head bearing freeplay as described in Chapter 1, and if necessary re-adjust.

10 Steering head bearings

Inspection

1 Remove the steering stem (see Section 9). Using a suitable solvent remove all traces of old grease from the bearings and races.
2 Check for wear or damage – the races should be polished and free from indentations. Inspect the bearing balls for signs of wear, damage or discoloration, and examine the retainer cages for cracks or splits. Spin the bearing balls by hand. They should spin freely and smoothly. If there are signs of wear on any of the above components, both upper and lower bearing assemblies must be replaced with a new set. **Note:** *Do not remove the races from the steering head or the steering stem unless they are to be replaced with new ones – do not re-use the races if they have been removed.*

Renewal

3 The outer races are an interference fit in the steering head and can be tapped out with a suitable drift located in the cut-outs in the head **(see illustrations)**. Alternate between the left and right-hand cut-outs so that the race is driven out squarely. It may prove advantageous to curve the end of the drift slightly to improve access.
4 Alternatively, the races can be removed using a slide-hammer type bearing extractor – these can often be hired from tool shops.
5 The new outer races can be installed in the head using a drawbolt arrangement **(see illustration)**, or by using a large diameter tubular drift. Ensure that the drawbolt washer or drift (as applicable) bears only on the outer edge of the race and does not contact the bearing surface.

> **HAYNES HiNT** *Installation of new bearing outer races is made much easier if the races are left overnight in the freezer. This causes them to contract slightly making them a looser fit. Alternatively, use a freeze spray.*

6 To remove the lower bearing race from the steering stem, first thread the steering stem nut onto the top of the stem to protect the threads, they lay the stem over and drive a chisel between the base of the race and the bottom yoke. Work the chisel around the race to ensure it lifts squarely. Once there is clearance beneath the race, use two levers placed on opposite sides of the race to work it free, using blocks of wood to improve leverage and protect the yoke **(see illustration)**. If the race is firmly in place it will be necessary to use a bearing puller **(see illustration)**. Alternatively, take the steering stem to a Yamaha dealer.
7 Fit the new lower race onto the steering

10.5 Drawbolt arrangement for fitting steering stem bearing races
1 Long bolt or threaded bar
2 Thick washer
3 Guide for lower race

stem. A length of tubing with an internal diameter slightly larger than the steering stem will be needed to tap the new race into position **(see illustration)**.
8 Install the steering stem (see Section 9).

11 Rear shock absorber

⚠ **Warning: Do not attempt to disassemble the shock absorber. It is nitrogen-charged under high pressure. Improper disassembly could result in serious injury. Take the shock to a Yamaha dealer or suspension specialist for servicing and disposal.**

Removal

1 Support the motorcycle so that no weight is transmitted through any part of the rear suspension – tie the front brake lever to the handlebar to ensure the bike can't roll forward. Position a support under the swingarm so that it does not drop when the shock absorber is removed.
2 Remove the lower fairing (see Chapter 7) and the rear wheel (see Chapter 6).

10.6a Remove the lower bearing race as described . . .

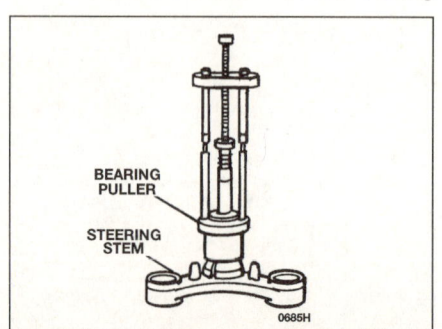

10.6b . . . or using a puller if necessary

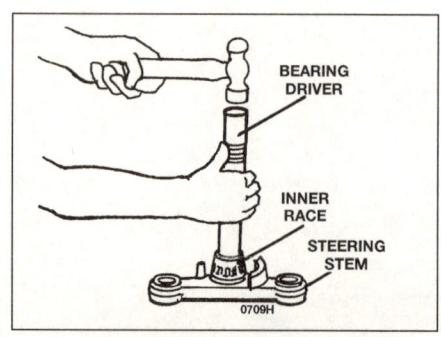

10.7 Drive the new race on using a suitable driver or a length of tubing

Frame and suspension 5•19

11.3a Unscrew the nut . . .

11.3b . . . and withdraw the shock absorber bottom bolt

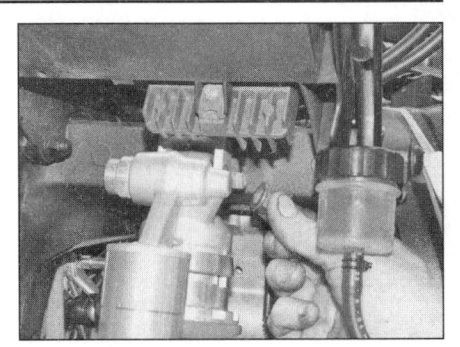

11.4 Unscrew the nut . . .

11.5a . . . then withdraw the bolt . . .

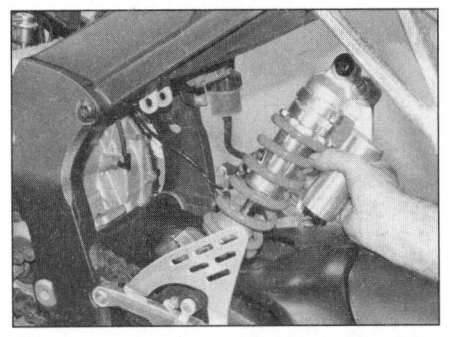

11.5b . . . and remove the shock absorber from the top

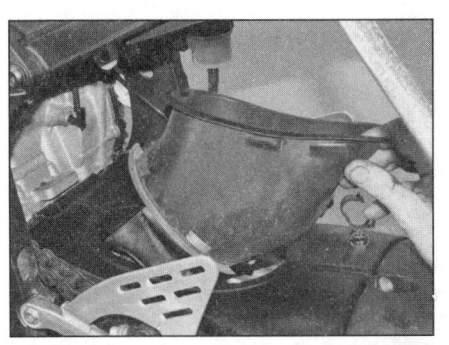

11.5c Remove the boot if required, noting how it locates

3 Unscrew the nut and withdraw the bolt securing the linkage plates to the bottom of the shock **(see illustration)**.
4 Unscrew the nut on the shock absorber upper mounting bolt **(see illustration)**.
5 Support the shock absorber and withdraw the upper mounting bolt **(see illustration)**. Lower the swingarm and remove the shock from the top of the swingarm **(see illustration)**. If required remove the rubber boot from the swingarm, noting how it fits **(see illustration)**.

Inspection

6 Inspect the body of the shock absorber for obvious physical damage and the coil spring for looseness, cracks or signs of fatigue.
7 Inspect the shock damper rod for signs of bending, pitting and oil leakage **(see illustration)**.
8 Inspect the gas cylinder for damage.
9 Inspect the pivot bush in the upper mounting for wear – it is not available as a spare part so if worn a new shock absorber must be fitted **(see illustration)**.
10 Withdraw the collar from the lower mounting and inspect the bearing seals and needle bearing **(see illustration)**. If necessary, lever out the seals and discard them **(see illustration)**. The bearing can be pressed out with a suitably sized socket if a new one has to be fitted (see *Tools and Workshop Tips* in the *Reference* section) **(see illustration)**. Clean and grease the bearing. Grease the lips of new

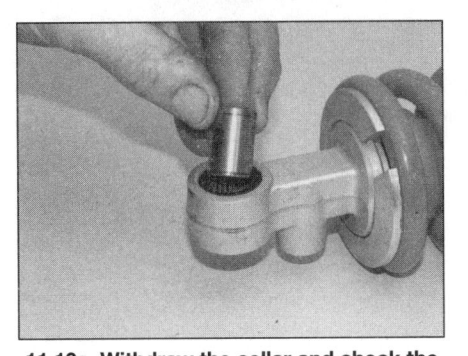

11.7 Check around the rod for signs of oil and pitting (arrowed)

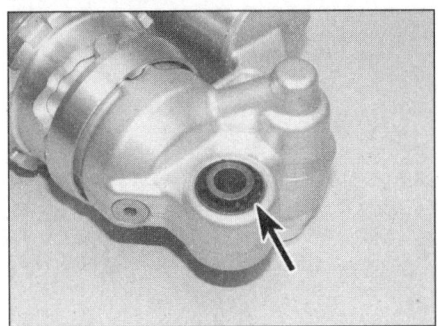

11.9 Check the condition of the upper mounting bush (arrowed)

11.10a Withdraw the collar and check the seals bearing

11.10b Lever the seals out and discard them

11.10c Replace the bearing (arrowed) with a new one if necessary

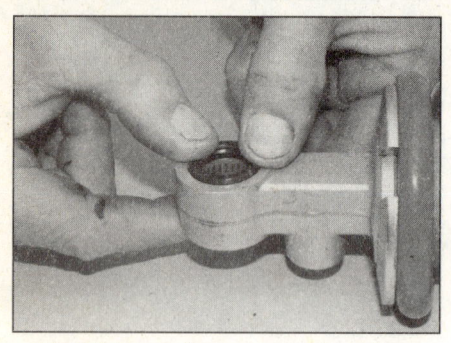

5•20 Frame and suspension

11.10d Press the new seals into place

12.4a Unscrew the nut . . .

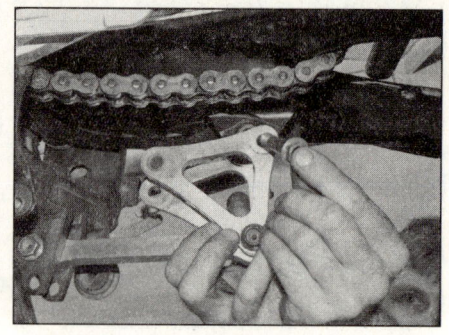

12.4b . . . then withdraw the bolt and swing the linkage down

bearing seals and press them into place with the marked side facing out **(see illustration)**.
11 Ensure that the spring pre-load adjusting ring is clean and free to rotate; inspect the indents on the ring for wear.
12 Ensure that the rebound damping and compression damping adjusters are clean and free to rotate.
13 With the exception of the lower mounting components the shock cannot be dismantled for the replacement of parts. If it is worn or damaged, it must be replaced with a new one.

Installation

14 Installation is the reverse of removal. If not already done, withdraw the collar from the lower mounting then clean the seals and needle bearing and apply lithium-based grease **(see illustration 11.10a)**. Also clean and grease the upper mounting bush **(see illustration 11.9)**.

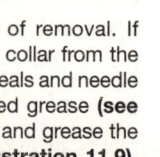

Make sure the rubber boot is correctly located. Install the bolts and nuts finger-tight only until all components are in position, then tighten the nuts to the torque settings specified at the beginning of this Chapter.

12 Rear suspension linkage

Removal

1 Support the motorcycle so that no weight is transmitted through any part of the rear suspension – tie the front brake lever to the handlebar to ensure the bike can't roll forward. Position a support under the rear wheel or swingarm so that it does not drop when the linkage is removed.
2 Remove the lower fairing (see Chapter 7).

3 Unscrew the nut and withdraw the bolt securing the linkage plates to the bottom of the shock absorber **(see illustrations 11.3a and b)**.
4 Note the position of the markings on the left-hand face of each linkage plate. Unscrew the nut and withdraw the bolt securing the plates to the swingarm **(see illustrations)**.
5 Unscrew the nut and withdraw the bolt securing the linkage plates to the linkage arm and remove the plates **(see illustration)**.
6 Unscrew the nut and withdraw the bolt securing the linkage arm to the frame and remove the arm, noting which way round it fits **(see illustrations)**.

Inspection

7 Withdraw the collars from the bearings in each end of the linkage arm and from the linkage plate mounting in the swingarm **(see illustrations)**. Lever out the bearing seals **(see illustration)**. Thoroughly clean all components

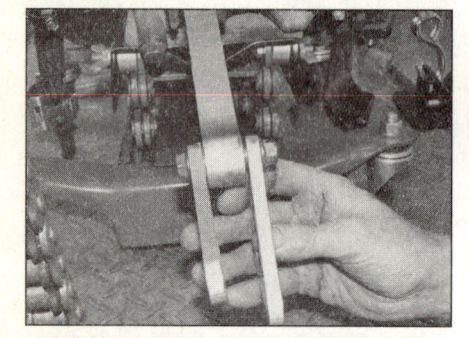

12.5 Unscrew the nut then withdraw the bolt and remove the plates

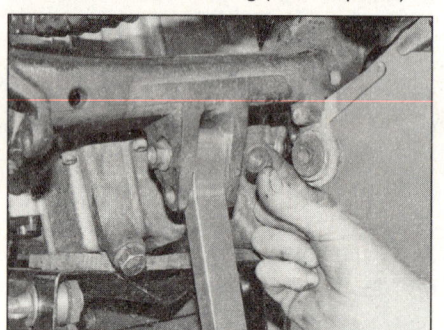

12.6a Unscrew the nut . . .

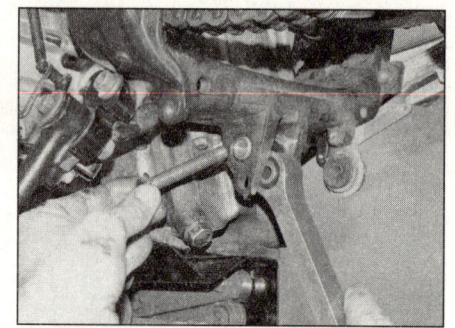

12.6b . . . then withdraw the bolt and remove the arm

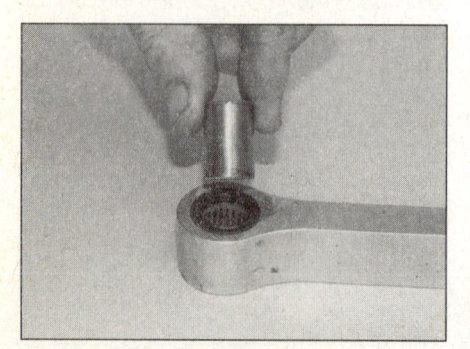

12.7a Withdraw the collars from the linkage arm . . .

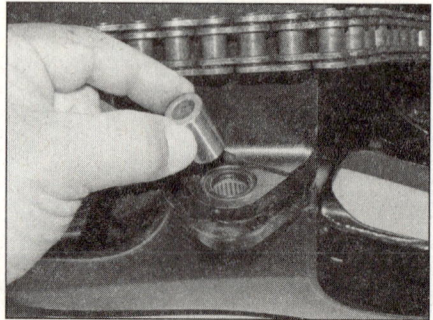

12.7b . . . and the swingarm . . .

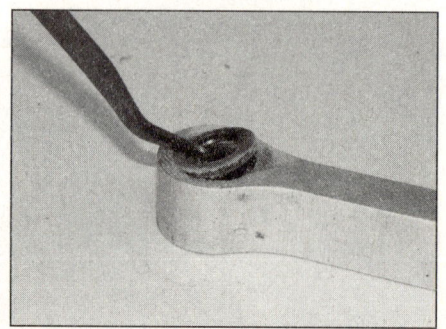

12.7c . . . and lever out the seals

Frame and suspension 5•21

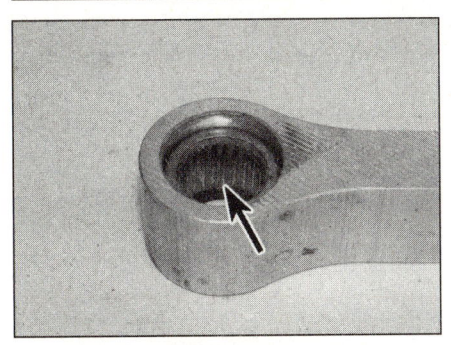

12.9a Check the needle bearings (arrowed) in the linkage arm . . .

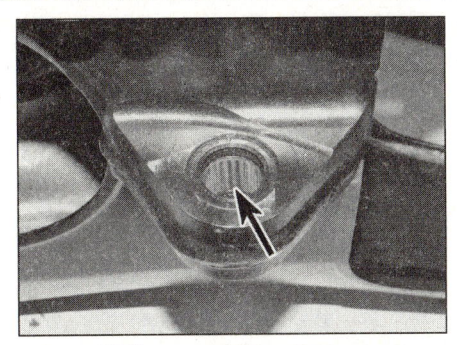

12.9b . . . and the swingarm

12.12a Press the new seals into place . . .

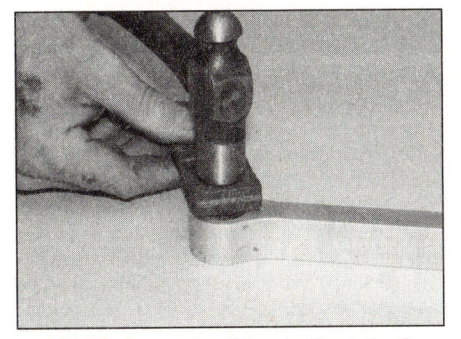

12.12b . . . or tap them in if required

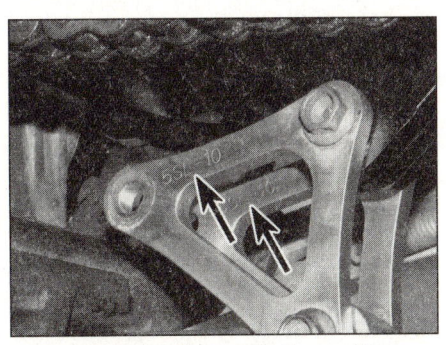

12.13 Install the plates with the markings on the upper left-hand edge (arrowed)

with a suitable solvent, removing all traces of dirt, corrosion and grease.
8 Inspect all components closely, looking for obvious signs of wear such as heavy scoring, or for damage such as cracks or distortion. Inspect the bolt holes in the linkage plates for elongation.
9 Check the condition of the needle roller bearings in the linkage arm and in the linkage plate mounting in the swingarm **(see illustrations)**. Refer to *Tools and Workshop Tips* (Section 5) in the Reference section for more information on bearings. Slip each collar back into its bearing and check that there is not an excessive amount of freeplay between the two components.
10 Worn bearings can be driven or drawn out of their bores, but note that removal will destroy them; new bearings should be obtained before work commences. The new bearings should be pressed or drawn into their bores rather than driven into position. In the absence of a press, a suitable drawbolt tool can be made up as described in *Tools and Workshop Tips* in the Reference section. When fitting the new bearings make sure they are central in their bores.
11 Lubricate the needle bearings, collars and seals with grease.
12 Press the new seals squarely into place with the marked side facing out **(see illustration)**. Install the collars **(see illustrations 12.7b and a)**.

Installation

13 Installation is the reverse of removal, noting the following:
● If not already done, withdraw the collars from the arm and the linkage plate mounting in the swingarm then clean the seals and needle bearings and apply lithium-based grease **(see illustrations 12.7a and b)**.
● Assemble the linkage plates with the markings on the left-hand side and on the upper edge **(see illustration)**.
● Install the nuts and bolts finger-tight only until all components are in position, then tighten the nuts to the torque settings specified at the beginning of the Chapter.

13 Suspension adjustment

Note: *Refer to the Owner's Manual supplied with the machine for recommended front and rear suspension settings to suit loading.*
Caution: *Never attempt to turn an adjuster beyond the minimum or maximum setting.*

Front forks

1 The front forks are adjustable for spring pre-load, rebound damping, and compression damping.
2 **Spring pre-load** is adjusted using a suitable spanner on the adjuster hex flats on the top of the forks; the amount of pre-load is indicated by lines on the adjuster **(see illustrations)**. There are eight lines. The standard position is with the 7th line just visible above the fork top bolt hex. Turn the adjuster clockwise

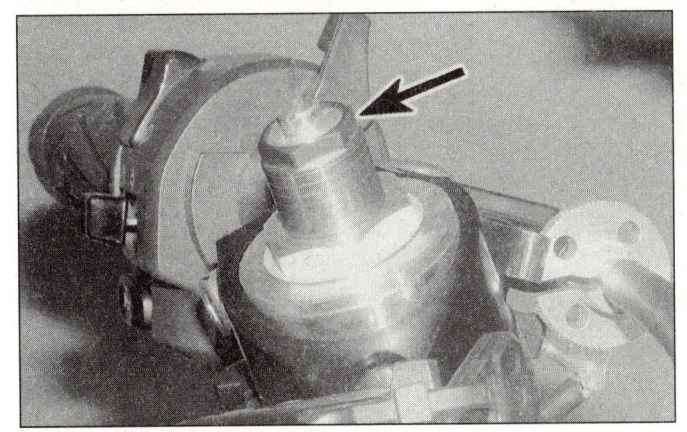

13.2a Spring pre-load adjuster (arrowed) on R and S models

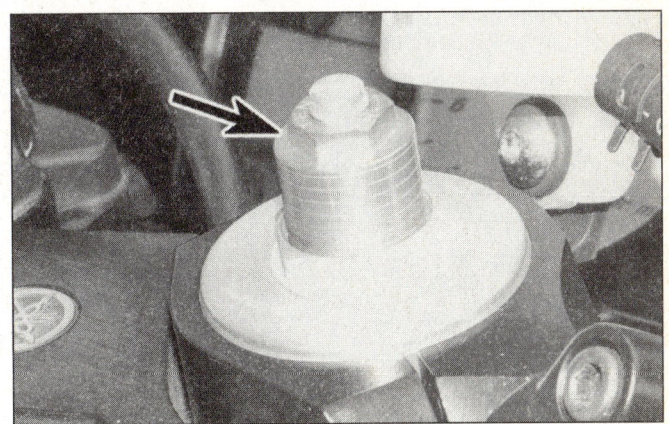

13.2b Spring pre-load adjuster (arrowed) on T model

5•22 Frame and suspension

13.3a Adjusting rebound damping on R and S models

13.3b Rebound damping adjuster (arrowed) on T model

13.5a Adjusting compression damping on R and S models

to increase pre-load, and anti-clockwise to decrease it. Always make sure both adjusters are set equally.

3 Rebound damping is adjusted using a screwdriver in the slot in the adjuster protruding from the spring pre-load adjuster **(see illustrations)**. Turn the adjuster clockwise to increase damping and anti-clockwise to decrease it. There are ten positions. To establish the current setting, turn the adjuster in (clockwise) until it stops, counting the number of clicks, then reset it as required by turning it out (anti-clockwise).

4 On R and S (2003 and 2004 models), the standard position is nine clicks out. On T (2005) models, the standard position is six clicks out. On all models, the maximum position is one click out and the minimum setting is ten clicks out. Always make sure both adjusters are set equally.

5 Compression damping is adjusted using a screwdriver in the slot in the adjuster on the base of each fork slider **(see illustrations)**. Turn the adjuster clockwise to increase damping and anti-clockwise to decrease it. There are nine positions. To establish the current setting, turn the adjuster in (clockwise) until it stops, counting the number of clicks, then reset it as required by turning it out (anti-clockwise).

6 On R and S (2003 and 2004 models), the standard position is seven clicks out. The maximum position is one click out. The minimum setting is nine clicks out. Always make sure both adjusters are set equally.

7 On T (2005) models, the standard position is six clicks out. The maximum position is one click out. The minimum setting is thirteen clicks out. Always make sure both adjusters are set equally.

Rear shock absorber

8 The rear shock absorber is adjustable for spring pre-load, rebound damping, and compression damping.

9 Spring pre-load is adjusted using a suitable C-spanner (one is provided in the bike's toolkit) to turn the adjuster ring on the top of the shock absorber **(see illustration)**. There are nine positions. Position 1 is the softest setting, position 4 is the standard, position 9 is the hardest. Align the setting required with the adjustment stopper. Turn the spring seat anti-clockwise to increase pre-load and clockwise to decrease it.

10 Rebound damping is adjusted by turning the adjuster on the base of the shock absorber **(see illustration)**. Turn the adjuster clockwise to increase damping and anti-clockwise to decrease it. There are twenty positions. To establish the current setting, turn the adjuster clockwise until it stops, counting the number of clicks, then reset it as required by turning it anti-clockwise. The standard position is ten clicks anti-clockwise on R and S (2003 and 2004) models and six clicks anti-clockwise on T (2005) models, the maximum position is five clicks anti-clockwise and the minimum is twenty clicks anti-clockwise.

11 Compression damping is adjusted using a screwdriver in the slot in the adjuster on the top of the shock absorber **(see illustration)**. Turn the adjuster clockwise to increase damping and anti-clockwise to decrease it. There are twenty positions. To establish the current setting, turn the adjuster in (clockwise) until it stops, counting the number of clicks, then reset it as required by turning it out (anti-clockwise). The standard position is ten clicks out on R and S (2003 and 2004) models and five clicks out on T (2005) models, the maximum position is one click out and the minimum is twenty clicks out.

13.5b Compression damping adjuster (arrowed) on T model

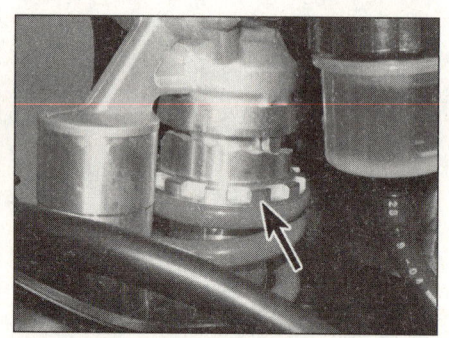

13.9 Spring pre-load adjuster (arrowed)

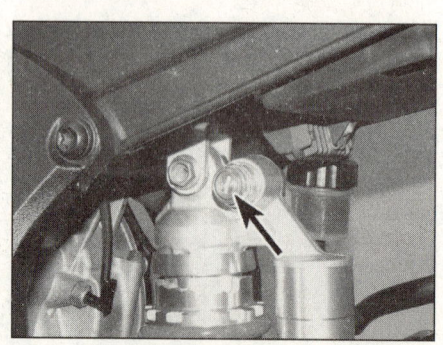

13.10 Rebound damping adjuster (arrowed)

13.11 Compression damping adjuster (arrowed)

14 Swingarm removal and installation

Removal

Special Tool: A special tool is needed to unscrew the swingarm pivot adjuster bolt (see Step 6).

Frame and suspension 5•23

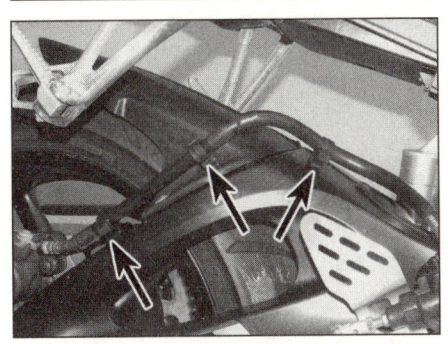

14.3 Free the brake hose from its guides (arrowed)

14.5 Unscrew the nut and remove the washer

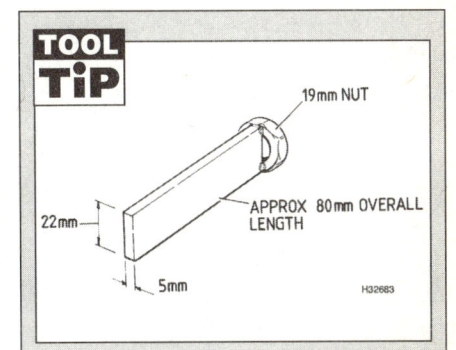

A tool can be made from a piece of steel bar dimensioned as shown and a 19 mm nut

14.6a Slacken the adjuster bolt using a tool as described

14.6b Withdraw the pivot bolt and remove the swingarm

1 Support the motorcycle so that no weight is transmitted through any part of the rear suspension – tie the front brake lever to the handlebar to ensure the bike can't roll forward. Position a support under the rear wheel or swingarm so that it does not drop when the shock absorber is removed.

2 Remove the exhaust silencer (see Chapter 4), the shock absorber (see Section 11) and the front sprocket cover and chain guide (see Chapter 6).

3 Release the brake hose from its guides on the swingarm and hugger **(see illustration)**.

4 Before removing the swingarm it is advisable to check for play in the bearings (see Chapter 1). Any problems which were not evident with the other suspension components attached may now show up.

5 Unscrew the nut on the end of the swingarm pivot bolt and remove the washer **(see illustration)**. Push the pivot bolt in slightly so the slots in the adjuster bolt are accessible.

6 Loosen the swingarm pivot adjuster **(see illustration)**. Yamaha provide a shaft wrench and socket adapter for this purpose (part Nos. 90890-01471 (US – YM-01471) and 01476), or alternatively a suitable tool for use with a socket can be made (see **Tool Tip**). Support the swingarm, then withdraw the pivot bolt and remove the swingarm, disengaging the chain from the sprocket and bringing it with the swingarm **(see illustration)**. Knock the pivot bolt through using a large drift if required, but be careful not to damage the threaded end; note how the flat sides on the bolt head locate in the recess in the frame.

7 If required unscrew the bolts securing the chainguard and the chain slider to the swingarm and remove them, noting how they fit **(see illustrations)**. Note the collars in the mounts. If the slider is badly worn or damaged, it should be replaced with a new one.

8 If required unscrew the bolts securing the

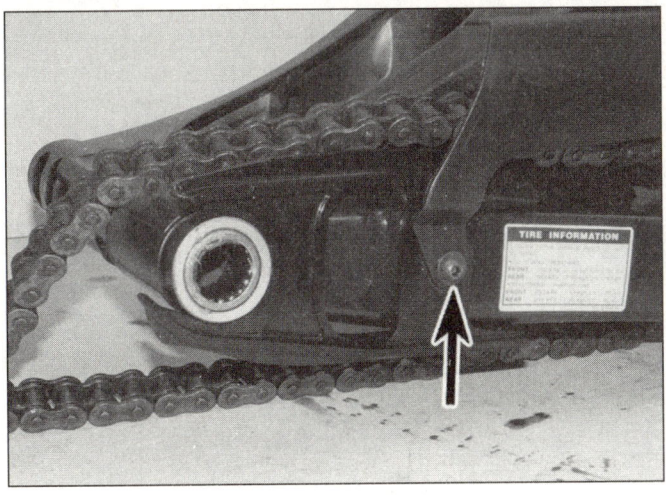

14.7a Unscrew the bolt (arrowed) at the front . . .

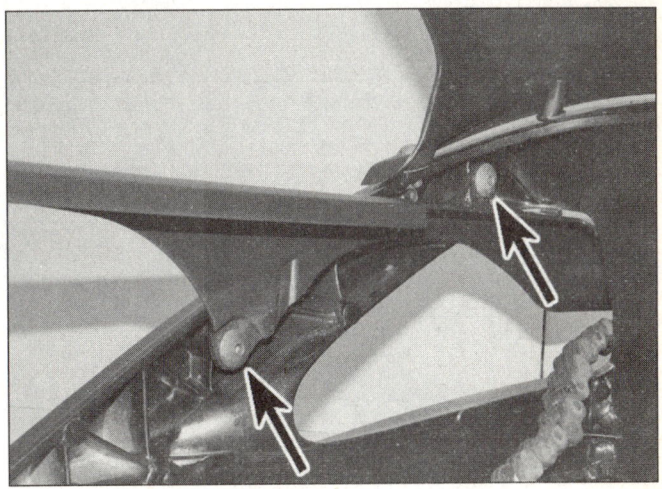

14.7b . . . and the two (arrowed) on the inside

5•24 Frame and suspension

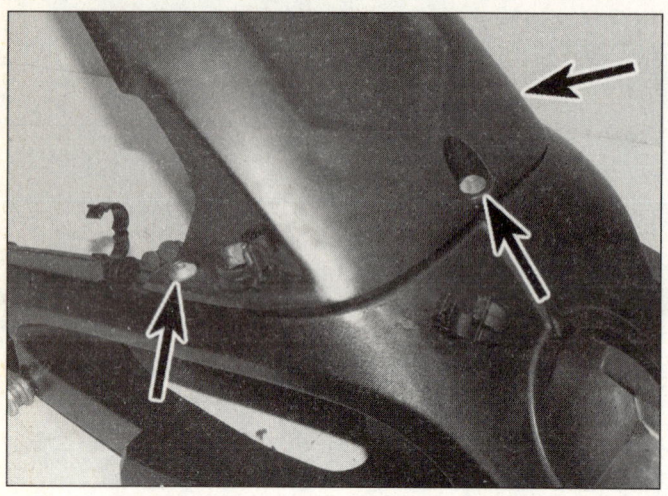

14.8 Unscrew the bolts and remove the hugger

14.10 Remove the cover from each side...

mudguard (hugger) to the swingarm and remove it **(see illustration)**.
9 Inspect all components for wear and damage as described in Section 15.

Installation
10 Remove the bearing cover from each side of the swingarm and check the condition of the seal inside the cover **(see illustration)**. If the seal is in good condition, the covers can be reused, otherwise discard them and fit new ones.
11 Withdraw the long inner sleeve **(see illustration)**. Wipe all old grease from the inner sleeve and bearings, then apply fresh lithium-based grease to their surfaces **(see illustration)**. Slide the sleeve back through the bearings. Grease the suspension linkage bearing on the underside of the swingarm (see Section 12).
12 If removed, install the chain slider and chainguard, making sure the collars are in the mounts, and the hugger **(see illustrations 14.7a and b)**.
13 Grease the inside of the bearing covers and fit them **(see illustration 14.10)**. Grease the swingarm pivot bolt.
14 Ensure the pivot adjuster is threaded far enough into the inside of the frame to allow easy installation of the swingarm **(see illustration)**. Loop the drive chain over the slider at the front, then manoeuvre the swingarm into a position that allows the chain to be engaged over the front sprocket **(see illustration)**. Slide the pivot bolt through from the left-hand side so that its right-hand end enters the pivot adjuster, but does not protrude from it, thus allowing the tool to be located in its slots **(see illustration 14.6b)**.
15 Tighten the swingarm pivot adjuster to the torque setting specified at the beginning of the Chapter using the special tool **(see illustration)**. Slide the pivot bolt all the way through, locating the flats on its head in the flats in the frame **(see illustration)**. Fit the

14.11a ... then withdraw the sleeve ...

14.11b ... and apply fresh grease to all pivot components

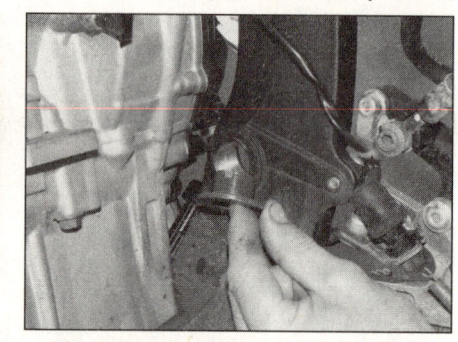

14.14a Make sure the pivot adjuster is threaded all the way into the frame

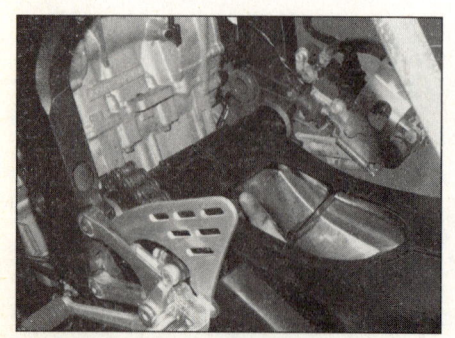

14.14b Manoeuvre the swingarm into place

14.15a Tighten the adjuster bolt to the specified torque ...

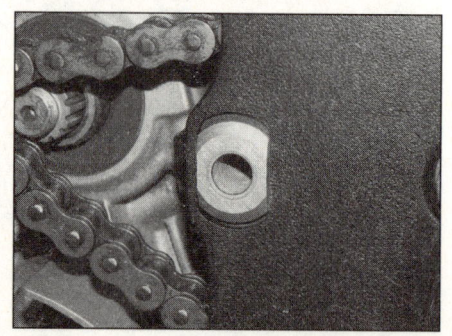

14.15b ... then slide the pivot bolt all the way through locating it in the frame as shown

Frame and suspension 5•25

washer and nut onto the pivot bolt and tighten the nut to the specified torque setting **(see illustration 14.5)**.

16 Install the remaining components in the reverse order of removal. Check and adjust the drive chain slack (see Chapter 1), and check the operation of the rear suspension before taking the machine on the road.

15 Swingarm bearings

Inspection

1 Remove the swingarm (see Section 14).
2 Thoroughly clean the swingarm, removing all traces of dirt, corrosion and grease. Pay particular attention to the area covered by the chain slider and the slots for the rear axle and the chain adjuster plates. Unscrew the chain adjusters and check the condition of the threads in the swingarm; if they are damaged consult a specialist engineer or a Yamaha dealer to have them repaired. Note that if the chain is to be separated from the swingarm it must be split at it's soft link (see Chapter 6).
3 If not already done, remove the bearing cover from each side of the swingarm and withdraw the long inner sleeve **(see illustrations 14.10 and 11a)**. Clean all old grease off the bearings.
4 Inspect all components for signs of wear such as heavy scoring, and cracks or distortion due to accident damage. Any damaged or worn component must be replaced with a new one.
5 Remove any corrosion from the swingarm pivot bolt and the inner sleeve with steel wool. Check they are straight by rolling them on a flat surface such as a piece of plate glass. If available, measure the runout with V-blocks and replace either component with a new one if it is bent.

Bearing check and replacement

6 Remove the swingarm (see Section 14). Remove the bearing cover from each side of the swingarm and withdraw the long inner sleeve **(see illustrations 14.10 and 11a)**. Clean all old grease off the bearings.
7 Refer to Tools and Workshop Tips in the Reference section and check the bearings – there is a needle bearing in each side **(see illustration)**. Clean them and inspect them for wear or damage. If the bearings do not run smoothly and freely or if there is excessive freeplay in them or between them and the sleeve, they must be replaced with new ones

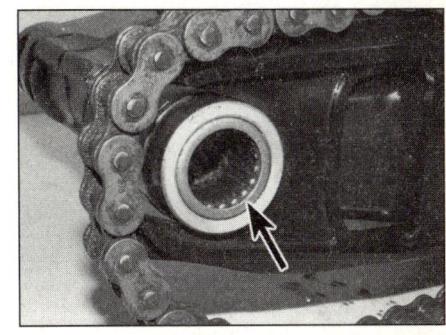

15.7 Check the bearing (arrowed) in each pivot

– refer to the Reference Section for removal and installation methods. The needle bearings must be replaced with new ones if removed – they cannot be reused.
8 Inspect the bearing seats and remove any scoring or corrosion carefully with steel wool or a suitable scraper.
9 The new bearings must be pressed or drawn into their bores, rather than driven into position. In the absence of a press, a suitable drawbolt arrangement can be made up as described in Tools and Workshop Tips (Section 5) in the Reference section. Lubricate the bearings with lithium-based grease.

Notes

Chapter 6
Brakes, wheels and final drive

Contents

	Section number		Section number
Brake fluid level check	see *Pre-ride checks*	Rear brake caliper	7
Brake hoses and unions	10	Rear brake disc	8
Brake light switches	see Chapter 8	Rear brake master cylinder	9
Brake pad wear check	see Chapter 1	Rear brake pads	6
Brake system bleeding and fluid change	11	Rear sprocket coupling/rubber dampers	20
Brake system check	see Chapter 1	Rear wheel	15
Drive chain replacement	18	Sprockets	19
Drive chain maintenance	see Chapter 1	Tyre pressure, tread depth and condition	see *Pre-ride checks*
Front brake calipers	3	Tyre fitting	17
Front brake discs	4	Wheel alignment check	13
Front brake master cylinder	5	Wheel and sprocket coupling bearings	16
Front brake pads	2	Wheel bearing check	see Chapter 1
Front wheel	14	Wheel check	see Chapter 1
General information	1	Wheel inspection and repair	12

Degrees of difficulty

Easy, suitable for novice with little experience	Fairly easy, suitable for beginner with some experience	Fairly difficult, suitable for competent DIY mechanic	Difficult, suitable for experienced DIY mechanic	Very difficult, suitable for expert DIY or professional

Specifications

Brakes

Brake fluid type	DOT 4
Brake pad friction material wear limit	see Chapter 1
Front caliper bore ID	
Upper bore	30.2 mm
Lower bore	27.0 mm
Front disc thickness	
R and S (2003 and 2004) models	
Standard	5.0 mm
Service limit	4.5 mm
T (2005) models	
Standard	4.5 mm
Service limit	4.0 mm
Front disc maximum runout	0.1 mm
Front master cylinder bore ID	14.0 mm
Rear caliper bore ID	38.1 mm
Rear disc thickness	
Standard	5.0 mm
Service limit	4.5 mm
Rear disc maximum runout	0.15 mm
Rear master cylinder bore ID	12.7 mm

Wheels

Rim size	
Front	17 x MT3.50
Rear	17 x MT5.50
Wheel runout (max)	
Axial (side-to-side)	0.5 mm
Radial (out-of-round)	1.0 mm

6•2 Brakes, wheels and final drive

Tyres

Tyre pressures	see *Pre-ride checks*
Tyre sizes*	
Front	
R and S (2003 and 2004) models	120/60-ZR17 (55W)
T (2005) model	120/70-ZR17 (55W)
Rear	180/55-ZR17 (73W)

*Refer to the owners manual or your Yamaha dealer for approved tyre brands.

Final drive

Chain type	DAIDO 532ZLV (116 links)
Chain freeplay and stretch limit	see Chapter 1
Sprocket sizes	Front 16T, Rear 48T (46T on later California models)

Torque wrench settings

Brake caliper bleed valves	
R and S (2003 and 2004) models	6 Nm
T (2005) model	
Front caliper	5 Nm
Front master cylinder	6 Nm
Rear caliper	6 Nm
Brake hose banjo bolts	30 Nm
Front brake caliper mounting bolts	
R and S (2003 and 2004) models	40 Nm
T (2005) models	35 Nm
Front brake disc bolts	18 Nm
Front brake hose guide	
R and S (2003 and 2004) models	7 Nm
T (2005) model	6 Nm
Front brake master cylinder clamp bolts	13 Nm
Front sprocket cover bolts	10 Nm
Front sprocket nut	90 Nm
Front wheel axle bolt	91 Nm
Front wheel axle pinch bolts	
R and S (2003 and 2004) models	18 Nm
T (2005) model	21 Nm
Rear brake caliper front slider pin	28 Nm
Rear brake caliper rear mounting bolt/slider pin	23 Nm
Rear brake pad retaining pin	18 Nm
Rear brake disc bolts	30 Nm
Rear brake master cylinder mounting bolts	
R and S (2003 and 2004) models	18 Nm
T (2005) models	13 Nm
Rear sprocket nuts	100 Nm
Rear wheel axle nut	110 Nm

1 General information

All models are fitted with cast alloy wheels designed for tubeless tyres only.

Both front and rear brakes are hydraulically-operated disc brakes.

The front brakes are twin floating discs with twin, opposed-piston calipers, radially mounted on T (2005) models. The rear brake is a single disc with a single-piston sliding caliper.

Drive from the gearbox to the rear wheel is by chain and sprockets.

Caution: Disc brake components rarely require disassembly. Do not disassemble components unless absolutely necessary. If a hydraulic brake line is loosened, the entire system must be disassembled, drained, cleaned and then properly filled and bled upon reassembly. Do not use solvents on internal brake components. Solvents will cause the seals to swell and distort. Use only clean brake fluid or denatured alcohol for cleaning. Use care when working with brake fluid as it can injure your eyes and it will damage painted surfaces and plastic parts.

2 Front brake pads

Warning: *The dust created by the brake system may contain asbestos, which is harmful to your health. Never blow it out with compressed air and don't inhale any of it. An approved filtering mask should be worn when working on the brakes.*

1 If new pads are being installed, displace the calipers from the discs (see Section 3) – this makes it easier to push the pistons back into

Brakes, wheels and final drive 6•3

2.2 Remove the R-clips . . .

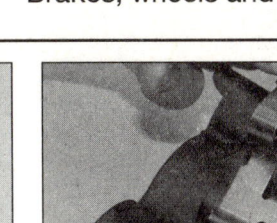

2.3a . . . then pull out the pin . . .

2.3b . . . remove the pad spring . . .

the caliper to allow for the extra thickness of new pads. Otherwise, the pads can be removed with the caliper in place. **Note:** *Yamaha recommend that a new pad spring is fitted whenever new pads are fitted.*

2 Remove the R-clip from each end of the pad retaining pin **(see illustration)**. If the clips are distorted or corroded, discard them and fit new ones on reassembly.

3 Withdraw the pin, noting how it fits through the pad spring and remove the pad spring, noting which way round it fits **(see illustrations)**. Withdraw the pads from the top of the caliper, noting how they fit **(see illustration)**. **Note:** *Do not operate the brake lever while the pads are out of the caliper.*

4 Inspect the surface of each pad for contamination and check that the friction material has not worn to or beyond its wear limit (see Chapter 1, Section 12). If either pad is worn down to or beyond the limit, is fouled with oil or grease, or is heavily scored or damaged by dirt and debris,

both pads in each caliper must be replaced with new ones. Note that it is not possible to degrease the friction material; if the pads are contaminated in any way, new ones must be fitted.

5 Check that each pad has worn evenly at each end, and that each has the same amount of wear as the other. If uneven wear is noticed, one of the pistons is probably sticking in the caliper, in which case the caliper must be overhauled (see Section 3).

6 If the pads are in good condition clean them carefully, using a fine wire brush which is completely free of oil and grease, to remove all traces of road dirt and corrosion. Using a pointed instrument, clean out the groove in the friction material and dig out any embedded particles of foreign matter. Spray the caliper with a dedicated brake cleaner to remove any dust and remove any traces of corrosion which might cause sticking of the caliper/pad operation.

7 Check the condition of the brake disc (see Section 4).

8 Remove all traces of corrosion from the pad retaining pin. Check it for signs of wear and replace it with a new one if necessary.

9 Clean around the exposed section of each piston to remove any dirt or debris that could cause the seals to be damaged. If new pads are being fitted, now push the pistons all the way back into the caliper to create room for them; if the old pads are still serviceable push the pistons in a little way. To push the pistons back use finger pressure or a piece of wood as leverage, or place the old pads back in the caliper and use a metal bar or a screwdriver inserted between them, or use grips and a piece of wood, with rag or card to protect the caliper body **(see illustration)**. Alternatively obtain a proper piston-pushing tool from a good tool supplier **(see illustration)**. As the pistons are pushed in brake fluid will be displaced back into the hydraulic reservoir so depending on the initial level it may be necessary to remove the master cylinder reservoir cap, plate and diaphragm and siphon out some fluid (see *Pre-ride checks*). If the pistons are difficult to push back, remove the bleed valve cap, then attach a length of clear hose to the bleed valve and place the open end in a suitable container, then open the valve and try again (see Section 11). Take great care not to draw any air into the system. If in doubt, bleed the brake afterwards.

10 If any of the pistons appear seized, first block or hold the other pistons using wood or cable ties, then apply the brake lever and check whether the piston in question moves at all. If it moves out but can't be pushed back in the chances are there is some hidden corrosion stopping it. If it doesn't move at all, or to fully clean and inspect the pistons, disassemble the caliper and overhaul it (see Section 3).

11 Smear the backs of the pads and the pad pin lightly with copper-based grease, making sure that none gets on the front or sides of the pads.

12 Insert the pads into the caliper so that the friction material faces the disc **(see illustration 2.3c)**. Fit the new pad spring onto the pads, making sure the arrow points in the direction of normal disc rotation **(see illustration 2.3b)**. Insert the pad retaining pin through the hole in the outer pad, then press down on the pad spring and push the pin through the spring and the hole in the inner pad **(see illustration)**. Install the R-clips, using new ones if necessary **(see illustration 2.2)**.

2.3c . . . and lift the pads out

2.9a Press the pistons in as described to make clearance for new pads

2.9b This is a commercially available piston pushing tool

2.12 Make sure the pin locates correctly

6•4 Brakes, wheels and final drive

3.2a Brake hose guide bolt (arrowed) – R and S models

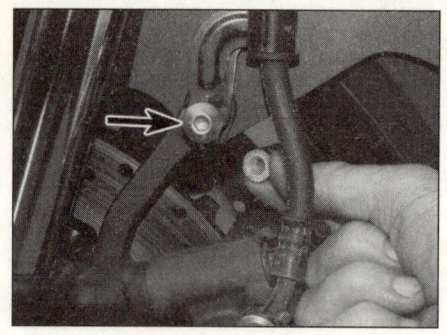

3.2b Brake hose guide bolt (arrowed) and nut – T model

3.3a Brake hose banjo bolt (arrowed)

13 If displaced, install the calipers (see Section 3). Check the fluid level in the reservoir (see *Pre-ride checks*).

14 Operate the brake lever several times to bring the pads into contact with the discs. Check the operation of the brake before riding the motorcycle.

3 Front brake calipers

Warning: *If a caliper is in need of an overhaul all old brake fluid should be flushed from the system. Also, the dust created by the brake system may contain asbestos, which is harmful to your health. Never blow it out with compressed air and do not inhale any of it. An approved filtering mask should be worn when working on the brakes. Disassembly,* overhaul and reassembly of the brake caliper must be done in a spotlessly clean work area to avoid contamination and possible failure of the brake hydraulic system components. Do not, under any circumstances, use petroleum-based solvents to clean brake parts. Use clean brake fluid of the type specified, dedicated brake cleaner or denatured alcohol only, as described. To prevent damage from spilled brake fluid, always cover paintwork when working on the braking system.

Note: *If the caliper is being overhauled (usually due to sticking pistons or fluid leaks) read through the entire procedure first and make sure that you have obtained all the new parts required, including some new DOT 4 brake fluid.*

Removal

1 If the caliper is just being displaced (e.g. for wheel removal) the pads can be left in place.

If the caliper is being overhauled, remove the brake pads (see Section 2).

2 Unscrew and remove the bolt securing the brake hose guide, on T (2005) models noting it threads into a nut on the inside of the mudguard **(see illustrations)**.

3 If the caliper is just being displaced, do not disconnect the brake hose. If the caliper is being completely removed or overhauled, unscrew the brake hose banjo bolt and detach the banjo fitting, noting its alignment with the caliper – if available, and if standard brake hoses are fitted, a hose clamp can be used to prevent fluid loss, but be prepared with a rag to catch any drops **(see illustrations)**. If a clamp is not used wrap plastic foodwrap around the banjo union and secure the hose in an upright position to minimise fluid loss. Discard the sealing washers as new ones must be used on reassembly.

4 Unscrew the caliper mounting bolts and slide the caliper off the disc **(see illustrations)**.

3.3b Fit a hose clamp to prevent fluid loss . . .

3.3c . . . then unscrew the bolt . . .

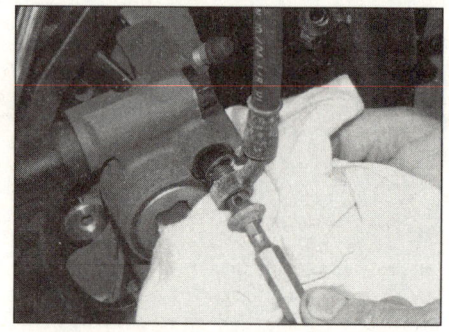

3.3d . . . and detach the hose, catching any fluid with a rag

3.4a Brake caliper mounting bolts (arrowed) on R and S models

3.4b Unscrew the caliper bolts . . .

3.4c . . . and slide the caliper off the disc – T model shown

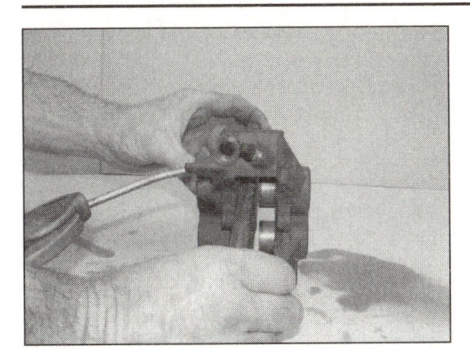

Brakes, wheels and final drive 6•5

3.6a Using a piece of wood to block the pistons on one side while applying compressed air to expel the opposite pistons

3.6b Using a tool and brake pad to block the pistons on one side while applying compressed air to expel the opposite pistons

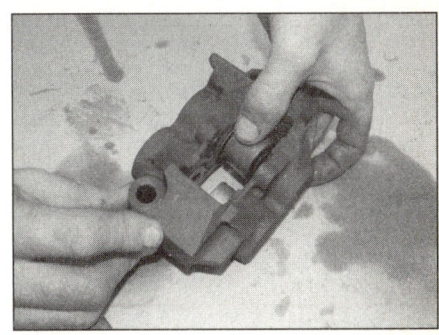

3.6c Remove each piston from its bore

If the caliper is just being displaced, secure it to the motorcycle with a cable tie to avoid straining the hydraulic hose. **Note:** *Do not operate the brake lever while either caliper is off its disc.*

Overhaul

5 Clean the exterior of the caliper with denatured alcohol or brake system cleaner. **Note:** *The pistons are of two different sizes (differing in diameter by 3 mm). Mark each piston head and the caliper body with a suitable marker to ensure that the pistons can be matched to their original bores on reassembly.*

6 Due to the construction of these calipers it is easier to overhaul one side of the caliper completely and refit the components and then do the other side, rather than removing all components in both sides. Push the pistons on one side of the caliper fully into their bores until they are flush with the body **(see illustration 2.9a or b)**. Hold the pistons in place using a piece of wood that is between 10 and 14 mm thick, or use a retracting tool as shown and one of the brake pads to provide the extra thickness **(see illustrations)**. Apply compressed air to the brake fluid inlet until the pistons on the other side contact the piece of wood or tool. Remove the wood or tool, then remove the pistons from their bores **(see illustration)**. Have some clean rag ready to catch the shower of hydraulic fluid. **Note:** *Use only low pressure air to ease the pistons out – if the air pressure is too high and the pistons are forced out, the caliper and/or pistons may be damaged.*

⚠ **Warning:** *Never place your fingers in front of the pistons in an attempt to catch or protect them when applying compressed air, as injury could result.*

7 If a piston sticks in its bore and cannot be displaced, the caliper will have to be replaced with a new one.

Caution: *Do not try to remove the pistons by levering them out, or by using pliers or any other grips. Do not attempt to remove the coloured caliper bore plugs on the outside of the caliper.*

8 Remove the dust seals and the piston seals from the piston bores, preferably using a soft wooden or plastic tool to avoid scratching the bores **(see illustrations)**. Discard the seals as new ones must be fitted on reassembly.

9 Clean the pistons and bores with clean DOT 4 brake fluid. If compressed air is available, blow it through the fluid galleries in the caliper to ensure they are clear and use it to dry the parts thoroughly (make sure it is filtered and unlubricated).

Caution: *Do not, under any circumstances, use a petroleum-based solvent to clean brake parts.*

10 Inspect the caliper bores and pistons for signs of corrosion, nicks and burrs and loss of plating. If surface defects are present, the caliper assembly must be replaced with a new one. If the caliper is in bad shape the master cylinder should also be checked.

11 Lubricate the new piston seals with the brake grease supplied in the rebuild kit, or with clean DOT 4 brake fluid if none was supplied, and carefully fit them into the lower grooves in the caliper bores. Compare the seals and measure them if necessary to ensure that the correct seals are fitted in the correct bores (see Specifications). The same applies when fitting the new dust seals and pistons.

12 Lubricate the new dust seals and fit them into the upper grooves in the caliper bores.

13 Lubricate the pistons and fit them, closed-end first, into the caliper bores **(see illustration)**. Using your thumbs, push the pistons all the way in, making sure they enter the bores squarely and do not displace the seals **(see illustration)**. Wipe away any excess lubricant as it will attract dirt.

14 Now block the side of the caliper that has been overhauled and displace the pistons from the other side, repeating steps 6 to 13.

3.8a Remove the dust seals . . .

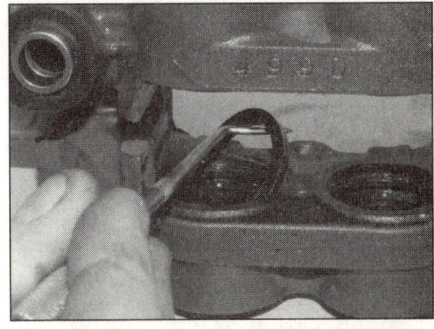

3.8b . . . and the piston seals

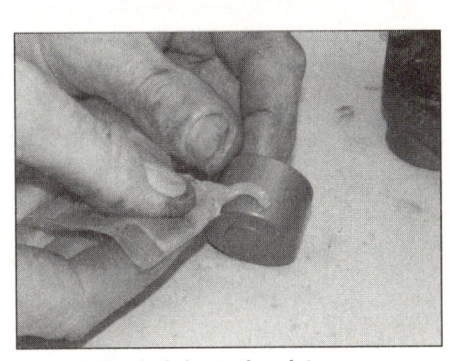

3.13a Lubricate the pistons . . .

3.13b . . . and fit them into their bores

6•6 Brakes, wheels and final drive

3.17 Always use new sealing washers

Installation

15 Slide the caliper onto the brake disc **(see illustration 3.4c)**. If the pads weren't removed, make sure they sit squarely each side of the disc.
16 Install the caliper mounting bolts and tighten them to the torque setting specified at the beginning of this Chapter **(see illustration 3.4b or a)**.
17 If removed, connect the brake hose to the caliper, using **new** sealing washers on each side of the banjo fitting **(see illustration)**. Align the fitting as noted on removal. Tighten the banjo bolt to the torque setting specified at the beginning of this Chapter.
18 Secure the brake hose guide in its guide and tighten the bolt to the specified torque **(see illustration 3.2a or b)**.
19 If removed, install the brake pads (see Section 2).
20 Top-up the hydraulic reservoir with new DOT 4 brake fluid (see *Pre-ride checks*) and bleed the system as described in Section 11. Check that there are no fluid leaks and thoroughly test the operation of the brake before riding the motorcycle.

4 Front brake discs

Inspection

1 Inspect the surface of the disc for score marks and other damage. Light scratches are normal after use and will not affect brake operation, but deep grooves and heavy score marks will reduce braking efficiency and accelerate pad wear. If a disc is badly grooved it must be replaced with a new one.
2 The disc must not be allowed to wear down to a thickness less than the service limit listed in this Chapter's Specifications. The thickness of the disc can be checked with a micrometer or Vernier caliper **(see illustration)**. If the thickness of the disc is less than the service limit, a new one must be fitted.
3 To check disc runout, position the bike on an auxiliary stand and support it so that the front wheel is raised off the ground. Mount a dial gauge to a fork leg, with the plunger on the gauge touching the surface of the disc about 10 mm (1/2 in) from the outer edge **(see illustration)**. Rotate the wheel and watch the gauge needle, comparing the reading with the limit listed in the Specifications at the beginning of this Chapter. If the runout is greater than the service limit, check the wheel bearings for play (see Chapter 1). If the bearings are worn, install new ones (see Section 16) and repeat this check. If the disc runout is still excessive, a new disc will have to be fitted.

Removal

4 Remove the wheel (see Section 14).
Caution: Don't lay the wheel down and allow it to rest on the disc – the disc could become warped. Set the wheel on wood blocks so the wheel rim supports the weight of the wheel.
5 If you are not replacing the disc with a new one, mark the relationship of the disc to the wheel so that it can be installed in the same position. Unscrew the disc retaining bolts, loosening them evenly and a little at a time in a criss-cross pattern to avoid distorting the disc, then remove the disc from the wheel **(see illustration)**.

Installation

6 Before installing the disc, make sure there is no dirt or corrosion where the disc seats on the hub, particularly right in the angle of the seat. If the disc does not sit flat when it is bolted down, it will appear to be warped when checked or when the front brake is used.
7 Install the disc on the wheel; align the previously applied register marks if you are reinstalling the original disc.
8 Clean the threads of the disc mounting bolts, then apply a suitable non-permanent thread locking compound. Install the bolts and tighten them evenly and a little at a time in a criss-cross pattern to the torque setting specified at the beginning of this Chapter. Clean the brake disc using acetone or brake system cleaner. If a new brake disc has been installed, remove any protective coating from its working surfaces. **Note:** *If new discs have been fitted, also fit new brake pads.*
9 Install the front wheel (see Section 14).
10 Operate the brake lever several times to bring the pads into contact with the disc. Check the operation of the brake carefully before riding the motorcycle.

5 Front brake master cylinder

Warning: If the brake master cylinder is in need of an overhaul all old brake fluid should be flushed from the system. Overhaul of the brake master cylinder must be done in a spotlessly clean work area to avoid contamination and possible failure of the brake hydraulic system components. Do not, under any circumstances, use petroleum-based solvents to clean brake parts. Use clean DOT 4 brake fluid, dedicated brake cleaner or denatured alcohol only, as described. To prevent damage from spilled brake fluid, always cover paintwork when working on the braking system.

Note: *If the master cylinder is being overhauled (usually due to sticking or poor action, or fluid leaks) read through the entire procedure first and make sure that you have obtained all the new parts required, including some new DOT 4 brake fluid.*

Removal

Note: *If the master cylinder is just being displaced and not completely removed from the motorcycle, unscrew the bolt securing the hydraulic reservoir to its bracket on the top yoke and follow Step 5. Secure the master cylinder to the motorcycle with a cable tie to avoid straining the hydraulic hose.*

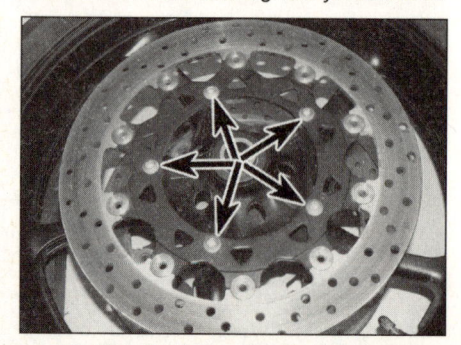

4.2 Checking disc thickness

4.3 Checking disc runout with a dial gauge

4.5 The disc is secured by five bolts

Brakes, wheels and final drive 6•7

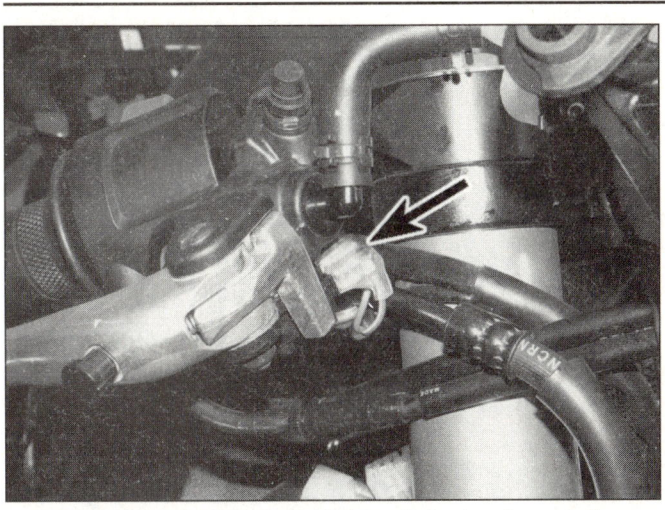

5.1 Disconnect the brake light switch wires (arrowed)

5.2 Remove the clamp (A), then slacken the cap (B) before unscrewing the bolt (C)

Keep the reservoir upright to prevent air entering the system.

1 Disconnect the brake light switch wiring connectors **(see illustration)**. Remove the front brake lever (see Chapter 5).
2 Remove the fluid reservoir cap clamp and loosen the cap, then unscrew the bolt securing the reservoir to its bracket on the top yoke **(see illustration)**.
3 Remove the reservoir cap and lift off the diaphragm plate and the diaphragm **(see illustration)**. Drain the brake fluid into a suitable container. Release the clip securing the reservoir hose to the union on the master cylinder and detach the hose **(see illustration)**. Wipe any remaining fluid out of the reservoir with a clean rag and replace the diaphragm, diaphragm plate and cap temporarily.
4 On T (2005) models slacken the master cylinder clamp bolts and swivel the master cylinder around the handlebar until the brake hose banjo bolt is better positioned for tool fitment **(see illustration 5.5)**. On all models, unscrew the brake hose banjo bolt and separate the hose banjo fitting(s) from the master cylinder, noting the alignment **(see illustration)**. Discard the sealing washers as new ones must be used on reassembly. Wrap some plastic foodwrap tightly around the end(s) of the hose(s) to prevent dirt entering the system and secure the hose(s) in an upright position and catch any fluid from the master cylinder with rag – the objective is to prevent fluid spills and system contamination.
5 Unscrew the master cylinder clamp bolts and remove the clamp, noting how it fits, then lift the master cylinder away from the handlebar **(see illustration)**.
6 If required, remove the screw securing the brake light switch and remove the switch **(see illustration)**.

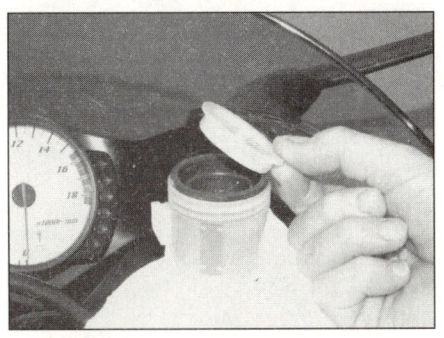

5.3a Remove the cap, plate and diaphragm and drain the reservoir

5.3b Detach the hose from its union and remove the reservoir

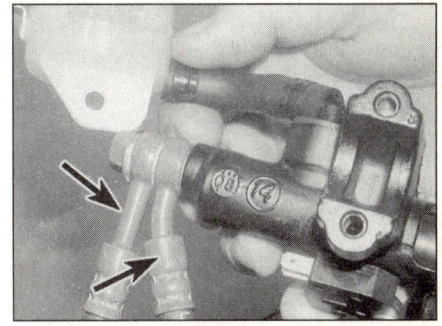

5.4a Brake hose alignment – R and S models

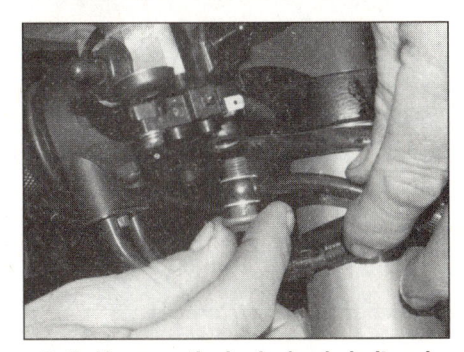

5.4b Unscrew the brake banjo bolt and detach the hose – T model shown

5.5 Unscrew the bolts (arrowed) and remove the master cylinder and its clamp

5.6 Front brake light switch screw (arrowed) – T model shown

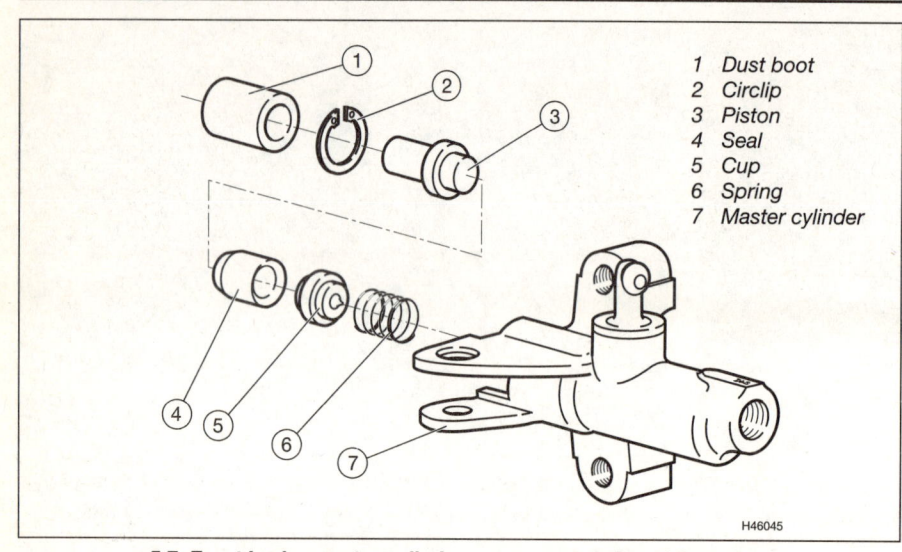

6•8 Brakes, wheels and final drive

1	Dust boot
2	Circlip
3	Piston
4	Seal
5	Cup
6	Spring
7	Master cylinder

5.7 Front brake master cylinder components – R and S models

5.8a Remove the pushrod and boot . . .

5.8b . . . then release the circlip . . .

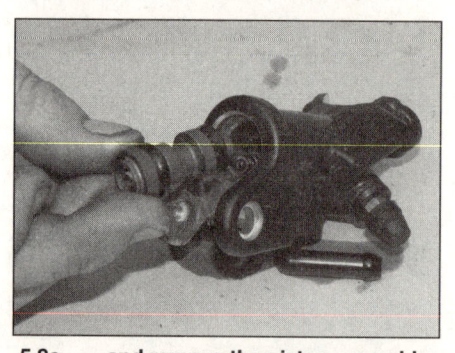

5.8c . . . and remove the piston assembly, spring and guide

Overhaul

7 On R and S (2003 and 2004) models, carefully remove the dust boot from the master cylinder to reveal the pushrod retaining circlip **(see illustration)**. Depress the pushrod and use circlip pliers to remove the circlip, then slide out the piston assembly and the spring, noting how they fit. Lay the parts out in order as they are removed to prevent confusion during reassembly. If required remove the reservoir hose union dust cover, then remove the circlip and detach the union from the master cylinder. Discard the O-ring as a new one must be used on reassembly. Inspect the reservoir hose for cracks or splits and replace it with a new one if necessary. Check the hose clips and replace them with new ones if they are distorted or corroded.

8 On T (2005) models remove the pushrod and rubber boot, then release the circlip and remove the piston assembly, spring and spring guide **(see illustrations)**. Lay the parts out in order as they are removed to prevent confusion during reassembly.

9 Clean all parts with clean DOT 4 brake fluid. If compressed air is available, blow it through the fluid galleries to ensure they are clear and use it to dry the parts thoroughly (make sure the air is filtered and unlubricated).

Caution: Do not, under any circumstances, use a petroleum-based solvent to clean brake parts.

10 Check the master cylinder bore for corrosion, scratches, nicks and score marks **(see illustration)**. If damage or wear is evident, the master cylinder must be replaced with a new one. If the master cylinder is in poor condition, then the calipers should be checked as well.

11 The dust boot, circlip, piston assembly (including the seal and cup) and spring are included in the master cylinder rebuild kit. Use all of the new parts, regardless of the apparent condition of the old ones. Fit them according to the layout of the old piston assembly.

12 On R and S (2003 and 2004) models, fit the spring into the master cylinder. Lubricate the piston assembly with brake grease or clean brake fluid and fit the assembly into the master cylinder, making sure it is the correct way round. Make sure the lips on the cup do not turn inside out when they are slipped into the bore. Depress the piston and install the new circlip, making sure it is properly located in the groove. Fit the dust boot, making sure it seats correctly in the master cylinder and the outer lips locate in the groove in the end of the piston. If removed fit a new O-ring onto the reservoir hose union, then press the union into the master cylinder and secure it with the circlip. Fit the dust cover over the union.

13 On T (2005) models fit the guide into the inner end of the spring, then fit them into the master cylinder, locating the end of the guide into the well in the end of the cylinder **(see illustrations)**. Lubricate the cup and seal on

5.10 Check the bore for damage

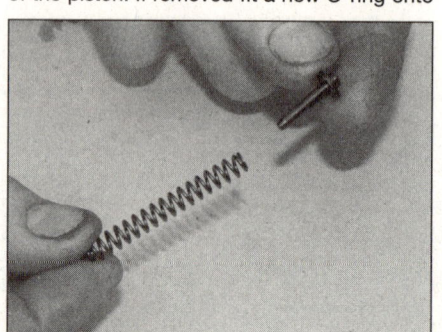

5.13a Fit the guide into the spring . . .

5.13b . . . then fit them into the master cylinder so the end of the guide locates in the well (arrowed)

Brakes, wheels and final drive 6•9

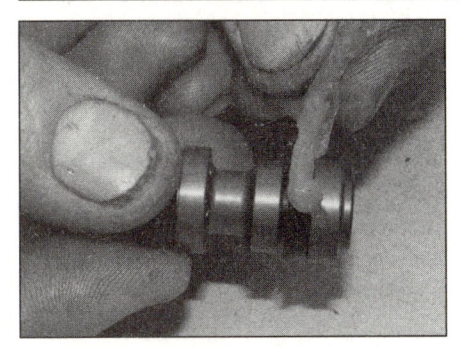

5.13c Lubricate the cup and seal . . .

5.13d . . . then slide the piston into the bore . . .

5.13e . . . and secure it with the circlip

the piston with brake grease or clean brake fluid and fit the assembly into the master cylinder, making sure it is the correct way round **(see illustrations)**. Make sure the lips on the cup do not turn inside out when they are slipped into the bore. Depress the piston and install the new circlip, making sure it is properly located in the groove **(see illustration)**. Fit the pushrod into the dust boot if not already assembled, locating the boot lips in the groove, then locate the pushrod against the outer end of the piston and press the boot into place **(see illustration 5.8a)**.

14 Inspect the fluid reservoir cap, diaphragm plate and diaphragm and replace them with new ones if they are damaged or deteriorated. Inspect the reservoir hose for cracks or splits and replace it with a new one if necessary. Check the hose clips and replace them with new ones if they are distorted or corroded.

Installation

15 If removed, fit the brake light switch onto the bottom of the master cylinder, making sure the pin locates in the hole, and tighten the screw **(see illustration 5.6)**.

16 On R and S (2003 and 2004) models attach the master cylinder to the handlebar, aligning the clamp joint with the punch mark on the top of the handlebar clamp, then fit the back of the clamp with its UP mark facing up **(see illustration)** – there should be a gap of 8.2 mm between the clamp joint and the right-hand switch assembly. Tighten the upper bolt to the torque setting specified at the beginning of this Chapter, followed by the lower bolt. Connect the brake hose banjo fittings to the master cylinder, using new sealing washers on each side of, and between, the fittings, and aligning the fittings as noted on removal **(see illustration 5.4a)**. Tighten the banjo bolt to the torque setting specified at the beginning of this Chapter.

17 On T (2005) models attach the master cylinder to the handlebar then fit the back of the clamp with its UP mark facing up, and lightly tighten the screws, allowing the assembly to swivel on the handlebar **(see illustration)**. Connect the brake hose to the master cylinder, using new sealing washers on each side of the banjo fitting **(see illustration 5.4b)**. Align the hose as noted on removal. Tighten the banjo bolt to the torque setting specified at the beginning of this Chapter. Swivel the master cylinder to align the clamp mating surfaces with the punch mark in the handlebar, then tighten the upper bolt to the torque setting specified at the beginning of this Chapter, followed by the lower bolt **(see illustration)**.

18 Install the brake lever (see Chapter 5).

19 Connect the brake light switch wiring **(see illustration 5.1)**.

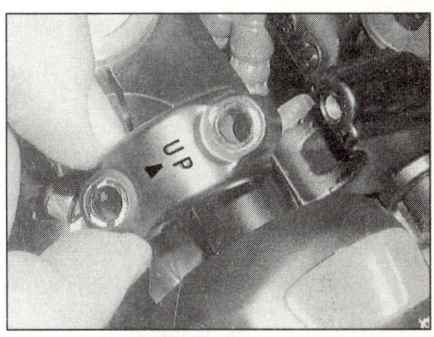

5.16 Fit the clamp with the UP mark facing up – R and S models

20 Fill the fluid reservoir with new DOT 4 brake fluid (see *Pre-ride) checks*). Refer to Section 11 and bleed the air from the system.

21 Check the operation of the brake before riding the motorcycle.

6 Rear brake pads

Warning: The dust created by the brake system may contain asbestos, which is harmful to your health. Never blow it out with compressed air and don't inhale any of it. An approved

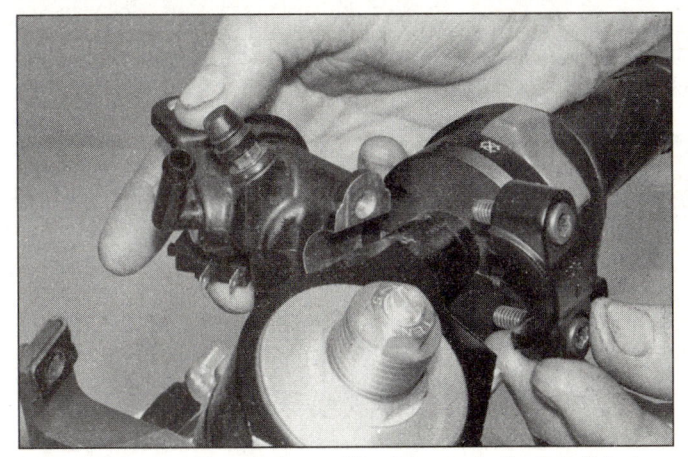

5.17a Fit the master cylinder and its clamp onto the handlebar . . .

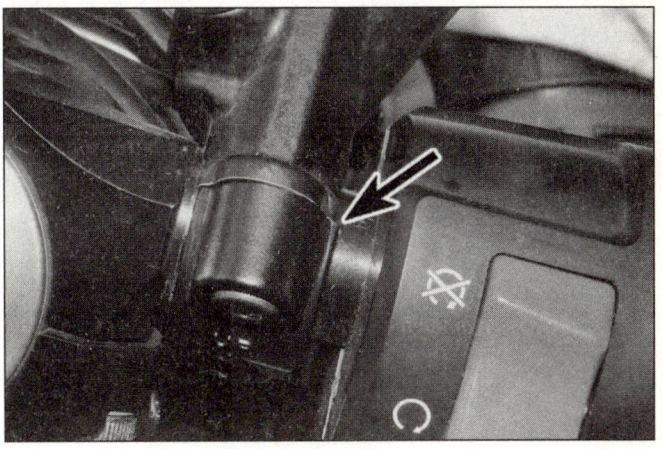

5.17b . . . and align the clamp mating surfaces (arrowed) with the punch mark on T models

6•10 Brakes, wheels and final drive

6.1a Unscrew the plug (arrowed) . . .

6.1b . . . then slacken the pin

6.1c Unscrew the rear bolt/slider pin

filtering mask should be worn when working on the brakes.

1 Unscrew the pad retaining pin plug, then slacken the pin **(see illustrations)**. Unscrew the caliper rear mounting bolt/slider pin **(see illustration)**.

2 Unscrew the pad retaining pin **(see illustration)**. Pivot the back of the caliper up off the disc and remove the pads, noting how they fit **(see illustration)**. Note the pad spring in the top of the caliper and the pad guide on the caliper bracket and remove them if required for cleaning or replacement, noting how they fit. **Note:** *Do not operate the brake pedal while the pads are out of the caliper.*

3 Where fitted and if required remove the shim from the back of each pad, noting how they fit – note that new pads should come with new shims where applicable, but make sure they do, especially if fitting after-market pads, before discarding the old ones.

4 Inspect the surface of each pad for contamination and check that the friction material has not worn beyond its service limit (see Chapter 1, Section 12). If either pad is worn down to, or beyond, the service limit, is fouled with oil or grease, or heavily scored or damaged, fit a set of new pads. **Note:** *It is not possible to degrease the friction material; if the pads are contaminated in any way they must be replaced with new ones.*

5 If the pads are in good condition clean them carefully, using a fine wire brush which is completely free of oil and grease to remove all traces of road dirt and corrosion. Using a pointed instrument, dig out any embedded particles of foreign matter. If required, spray with a dedicated brake cleaner to remove any dust.

6 Check the condition of the brake disc (see Section 8).

7 Remove all traces of corrosion from the pad pin and check it for wear and damage. Also check the slider pins and boots (see Section 7, Step 10) – slide the caliper off its bracket to do this.

8 Clean around the exposed section of the piston to remove any dirt or debris that could cause the seals to be damaged. If new pads are being fitted, now push the piston all the way back into the caliper to create room for them; if the old pads are still serviceable push the piston in a little way. To push the piston back use finger pressure or a piece of wood as leverage, or place the old pads back in the caliper and use a metal bar or a screwdriver inserted between them, or use grips and a piece of wood, with rag or card to protect the caliper body **(see illustration)**. Alternatively obtain a proper piston-pushing tool from a good tool supplier **(see illustration 2.9b)**. As the piston is pushed in brake fluid will be displaced back into the hydraulic reservoir so depending on the initial level it may be necessary to remove the master cylinder reservoir cover, plate and diaphragm and siphon out some fluid (see *Pre-ride* checks). If the piston is difficult to push back, remove the bleed valve cap, then attach a length of clear hose to the bleed valve and place the open end in a suitable container, then open the valve and try again (see Section 11). Take great care not to draw any air into the system. If in doubt, bleed the brakes afterwards.

9 If the piston appears seized, apply the brake pedal and check whether the piston moves at all. If it moves out but can't be pushed back in the chances are there is some hidden corrosion stopping it. If it doesn't move at all, or to fully clean and inspect the piston, disassemble the caliper and overhaul it (see Section 7).

10 Where applicable fit the shim onto the back of each pad **(see illustration)**. Lightly smear the back of the pad backing material or shim and the edges of the backing material where it contacts the caliper body with copper-based grease, making sure that none gets on the friction material. Also smear the pad pins.

11 Seat the pads in the caliper bracket so that the friction material of each pad faces the

6.2a Unscrew and remove the pin . . .

6.2b . . . then pivot the caliper up and remove the pads

6.8 Push the piston back into its bore

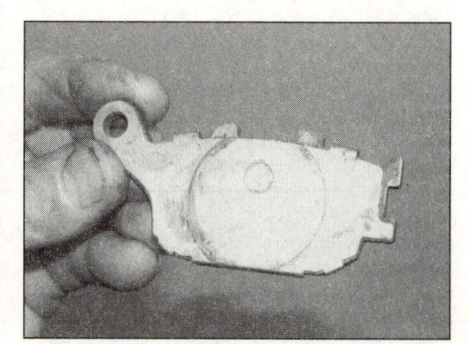

6.10 Make sure the shim tabs locate correctly all round

Brakes, wheels and final drive 6•11

6.11a Seat the pads against the disc and bracket ...

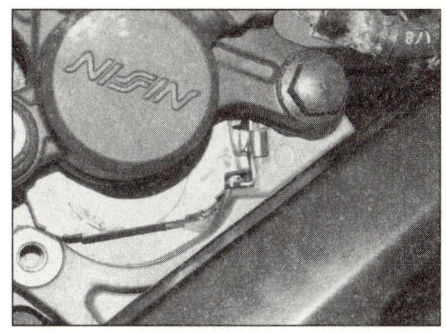

6.11b ... then pivot the caliper down, making sure the pads stay correctly located

6.12 Fit the pad pin plug

disc, making sure the leading edges locate correctly against the guide **(see illustration)**. Pivot the caliper down over the pads and onto the disc, making sure the pads stay in position **(see illustration)**.

12 Push up on the end of each pad so the pads compress the spring and insert the pad pin when the holes are aligned **(see illustration 6.2a)**. Tighten the pad pin to the specified torque setting, then fit the pin plug **(see illustration)**.

13 Clean the rear mounting bolt/slider pin and apply some lithium based grease to the section of the shank the caliper slides on, then tighten it to the torque setting specified at the beginning of the Chapter **(see illustration 6.1c)**.

14 Operate the brake pedal until the pads contact with the disc. Check the level of fluid in the hydraulic reservoir and top-up if necessary (see *Pre-ride checks*).

15 Check the operation of the rear brake before riding the motorcycle.

7 Rear brake caliper

⚠️ **Warning:** *If a caliper is in need of an overhaul all old brake fluid should be flushed from the system. Also, the dust created by the brake system may contain asbestos, which is harmful to your health. Never blow it out with compressed air and do not inhale any of it. An approved filtering mask should be worn when working on the brakes. Overhaul of the brake caliper must be done in a spotlessly clean work area to avoid contamination and possible failure of the brake hydraulic system components. Do not, under any circumstances, use petroleum-based solvents to clean brake parts. Use clean brake fluid of the type specified, dedicated brake cleaner or denatured alcohol only, as described. To prevent damage from spilled brake fluid, always cover paintwork when working on the braking system.*

Removal

Note: *If the caliper is being overhauled (usually due to sticking pistons or fluid leaks) read through the entire procedure first and make sure that you have obtained all the new parts required, including some new DOT 4 brake fluid.*

1 If the caliper is being completely removed or overhauled, unscrew the brake hose banjo bolt and detach the banjo union, noting its alignment with the caliper – if standard brake hoses are fitted a hose clamp can be used to prevent fluid loss **(see illustration)**. If a clamp is not used wrap plastic foodwrap around the banjo union and secure the hose in an upright position to minimise fluid loss. Discard the sealing washers as new ones must be fitted on reassembly.

2 If the caliper is being overhauled, remove the brake pads (see Section 6). Pivot the caliper up and draw it away from the bike so the front slider pin comes out of the bracket. If required remove the pad spring from the caliper and the guide from the bracket, noting how they fit **(see illustrations 7.15a and b)**.

3 If the caliper is just being displaced, free the brake hose from its guide or guides (as required) on the swingarm **(see illustration)**. Unscrew the caliper rear mounting bolt/slider pin and the front slider pin, then lift the caliper off its bracket and the disc **(see illustrations)**. If required, remove the pad spring from the caliper and the guide from the bracket, noting how they fit **(see illustrations 7.15a and b)**.

Overhaul

4 Clean the exterior of the caliper with denatured alcohol or brake system cleaner. Have some clean rag ready to catch any spilled brake fluid.

5 Place a piece of wood between the piston and the caliper body – it should be just thick enough to stop the piston leaving the bore

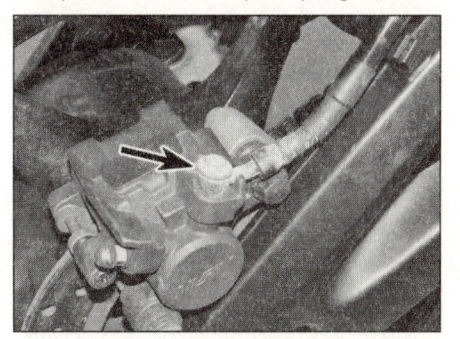

7.1 Brake hose banjo bolt (arrowed)

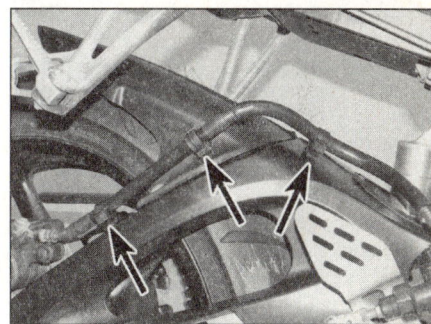

7.3a Release the hose from its guides (arrowed) as required

7.3b Unscrew the bolts ...

7.3c ... and lift the caliper off

6•12 Brakes, wheels and final drive

7.5a Fit the wood, then apply the compressed air as described . . .

7.5b . . . until the piston is displaced

7.7 Remove the seals and discard them

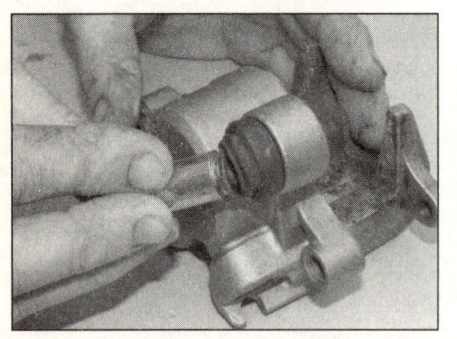

7.10a Remove the collar

7.10b The boot for the front pin will be in the bracket if it wasn't on the pin

7.11a Lubricate the new piston seal with brake fluid . . .

entirely **(see illustration)**. Apply compressed air gradually and progressively, starting with a fairly low pressure, to the fluid inlet on the caliper body and allow the piston to ease out of its bore, controlling it with the wood **(see illustration)**.

6 If the piston is stuck in its bore due to corrosion the caliper should be replaced with a new one. Do not try to remove a piston by levering it out or by using pliers or other grips.

7 Remove the dust seal and the piston seal from the piston bore preferably using a soft wooden or plastic tool to avoid scratching the bores **(see illustration)**. Discard the seals as new ones must be fitted on reassembly.

8 Clean the piston and bore with clean brake fluid of the specified type. Blow compressed air through the fluid passages in the caliper to ensure they are clear (make sure it is filtered and unlubricated).

Caution: Do not, under any circumstances, use a petroleum-based solvent to clean brake parts.

9 Inspect the caliper bore and piston for signs of corrosion, nicks and burrs and loss of plating. If surface defects are present, the piston and/or the caliper assembly must be replaced with new ones. If the caliper is in poor condition, the master cylinder should also be checked.

10 Remove the collar from the rear rubber boot in the caliper **(see illustration)**. Clean off all traces of corrosion and hardened grease from the collar, boots and pins – the boot for the front pin may be on the pin but could have stayed in the bracket **(see illustration)**.

Replace the rubber boots with new ones if they are damaged, deformed or deteriorated, making sure they locate correctly. Apply a smear of silicone based grease to the collar, boots and slider pins. Fit the collar into the rear boot.

11 Lubricate the new piston seal with brake grease or clean DOT 4 brake fluid and fit it into the lower groove in the caliper bore **(see illustrations)**.

12 Lubricate the new dust seal with brake grease or clean DOT 4 brake fluid and fit it into the upper groove in the caliper bore **(see illustration)**.

13 Lubricate the piston with clean DOT 4 brake fluid and fit it, closed-end first, into the caliper bore, taking care not to displace the seals **(see illustration)**. Using your thumbs,

7.11b . . . then fit it into its groove . . .

7.12 . . . followed by the new dust seal

7.13a Fit the piston . . .

Brakes, wheels and final drive 6•13

7.13b ... and push it all the way in

7.15a Make sure the spring (arrowed) in the caliper ...

push the piston all the way in, making sure it enters the bore squarely **(see illustration)**.

Installation

14 If the caliper has not been overhauled, refer to Step 10 and clean, check and re-grease the slider pin boots and collar.
15 Make sure that the pad spring and pad guide are correctly fitted **(see illustrations)**.
16 If the caliper was overhauled, slide it onto the bracket and leave it with the rear pivoted up, then install the brake pads (see Section 6).
17 If the caliper was just displaced, fit it onto the disc and bracket **(see illustration 7.3c)**, making sure the pads locate on each side of the disc, and the front edges locate correctly against the guide. Install the rear mounting bolt/slider pin and the front slider pin and tighten them to the torque settings specified at the beginning of the Chapter **(see illustration 7.3b)**. Fit the brake hose into its guide(s) **(see illustration 7.3a)**.
18 If detached, connect the brake hose to the caliper, using new sealing washers on each side of the fitting **(see illustration 7.1)**. Align the hose as noted on removal. Tighten the banjo bolt to the torque setting specified at the beginning of the Chapter.
19 Top up the hydraulic reservoir with DOT 4 brake fluid (see *Pre-ride checks*) and bleed the system as described in Section 11. Check that there are no fluid leaks and test the operation of the rear brake before riding the motorcycle.

8 Rear brake disc

Inspection

1 Refer to Section 4 of this Chapter, noting that the dial gauge should be attached to the swingarm.

Removal

2 Remove the rear wheel (see Section 15).
Caution: Don't lay the wheel down and allow it to rest on the disc or the sprocket – they could become warped. Set the wheel on wood blocks so the wheel rim supports the weight of the wheel.
3 If you are not replacing the disc with a new one, mark the relationship of the disc to the wheel so that it can be installed in the same position. Unscrew the disc retaining bolts, loosening them evenly and a little at a time in a criss-cross pattern to avoid distorting the disc, then remove the disc from the wheel **(see illustration)**.

Installation

4 Before installing the disc, make sure there is no dirt or corrosion where the disc seats on the hub, particularly right in the angle of the seat. If the disc does not sit flat when it is bolted down, it will appear to be warped when checked or when the rear brake is used.
5 Install the disc on the wheel; align the previously applied register marks if you are reinstalling the original disc.
6 Clean the threads of the disc mounting bolts, then apply a suitable non-permanent thread locking compound. Install the bolts and tighten them evenly and a little at a time in a criss-cross pattern to the torque setting specified at the beginning of this Chapter **(see illustration 8.3)**. Clean the brake disc using acetone or brake system cleaner. If a new brake disc has been installed, remove any protective coating from its working surfaces.
Note: *If a new disc is fitted, also fit new brake pads.*
7 Install the rear wheel (see Section 15).
8 Operate the brake pedal several times to bring the pads into contact with the disc. Check the operation of the rear brake carefully before riding the motorcycle.

9 Rear brake master cylinder

Warning: If the brake master cylinder is in need of an overhaul all old brake fluid should be flushed from the system. Overhaul of the brake master cylinder must be done in a spotlessly clean work area to avoid contamination and possible failure of the brake hydraulic system components. Do not, under any circumstances, use petroleum-based solvents to clean brake parts. Use clean DOT 4 brake fluid of the type specified, dedicated brake cleaner or

7.15b ... and the guide (arrowed) on the bracket are correctly fitted

8.3 The disc is secured by five bolts

6•14 Brakes, wheels and final drive

9.1a Undo the screw . . .

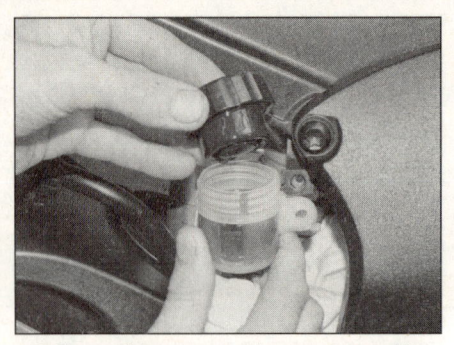

9.1b . . . then remove the cap assembly and drain the reservoir

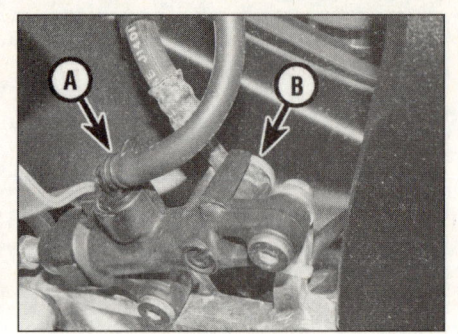

9.1c Reservoir hose clamp (A) and brake hose banjo bolt (B)

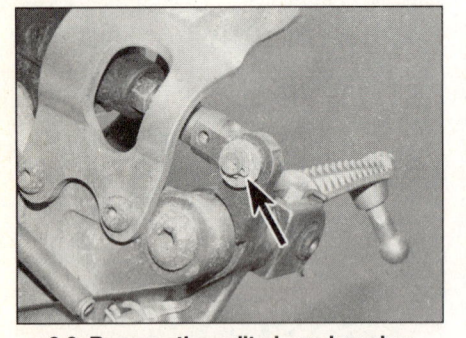

9.3 Remove the split pin and washer (arrowed) and withdraw the pin

9.4 Master cylinder bolts (arrowed)

denatured alcohol only, as described. To prevent damage from spilled brake fluid, always cover paintwork when working on the braking system.

Note: *If the master cylinder is being overhauled (usually due to sticking or poor action, or fluid leaks) read through the entire procedure first and make sure that you have obtained all the new parts required, including some new DOT 4 brake fluid.*

Removal

Note: *If the master cylinder is just being displaced and not completely removed from the motorcycle, remove the screw securing the fluid reservoir to the frame and follow Steps 3 and 4. Secure the master cylinder to the frame with a cable tie to avoid straining the hydraulic hose and keep the reservoir upright to prevent air entering the system.*

1 Undo the screw securing the fluid reservoir to the frame, then remove the reservoir cap, diaphragm plate and diaphragm **(see illustrations)**. Drain the brake fluid into a suitable container. Release the clip securing the reservoir hose to the union on the master cylinder and detach the hose, catching any residual fluid in a rag **(see illustration)**. Wipe any remaining fluid out of the reservoir with a clean rag and refit the diaphragm, diaphragm plate and cap temporarily.

2 Unscrew the brake hose banjo bolt and separate the hose banjo fitting from the master cylinder, noting its alignment – if standard brake hoses are fitted a hose clamp can be used to prevent fluid loss **(see illustration 9.1c**. If you haven't got the correct tools to access the bolt with the master cylinder mounted on its bracket, follow Steps 3 and 4 then unscrew the bolt. Discard the sealing washers, as new ones must be used on reassembly. If a clamp is not used wrap plastic foodwrap tightly around the end of the hose to prevent dirt entering the system and secure it in an upright position. The objective is to prevent excessive loss of brake fluid, fluid spills and system contamination.

3 Remove the split pin and washer from the clevis pin connecting the brake pedal to the master cylinder pushrod **(see illustration)**. Remove the clevis pin and separate the pushrod from the pedal. Discard the split pin, as a new one must be used on reassembly.

4 Unscrew the two bolts securing the master cylinder to the footrest bracket and remove the master cylinder **(see illustration)**.

Overhaul

5 Carefully remove the reservoir hose union from the master cylinder **(see illustration)**. Discard the O-ring as a new one must be used on reassembly.

6 Measure the position of the clevis on the pushrod, then slacken the locknut and thread the clevis and nut off the pushrod.

7 Carefully remove the dust boot from the end of the master cylinder to reveal the pushrod retaining circlip. Depress the pushrod and use

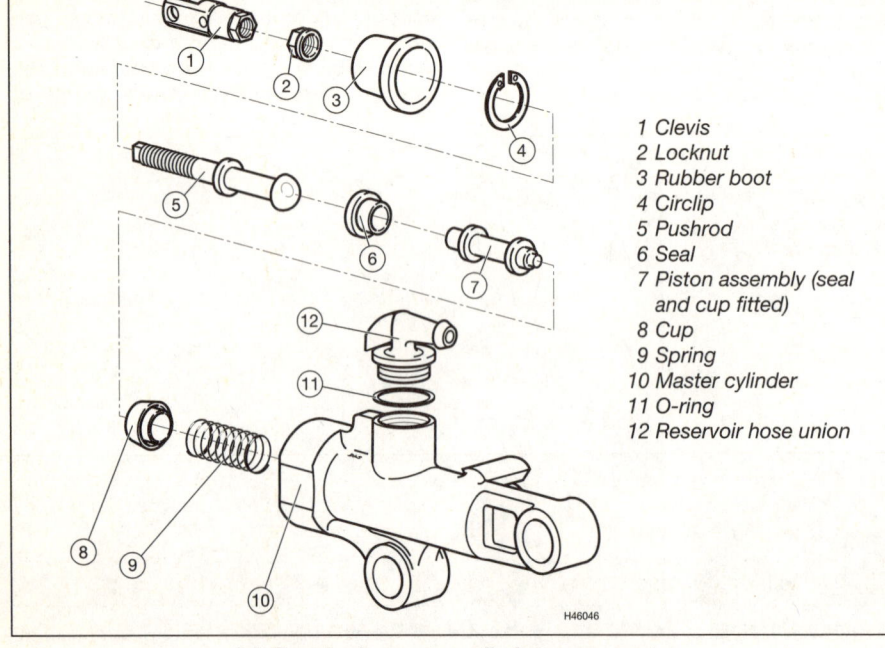

1 Clevis
2 Locknut
3 Rubber boot
4 Circlip
5 Pushrod
6 Seal
7 Piston assembly (seal and cup fitted)
8 Cup
9 Spring
10 Master cylinder
11 O-ring
12 Reservoir hose union

9.5 Rear brake master cylinder components

Brakes, wheels and final drive 6•15

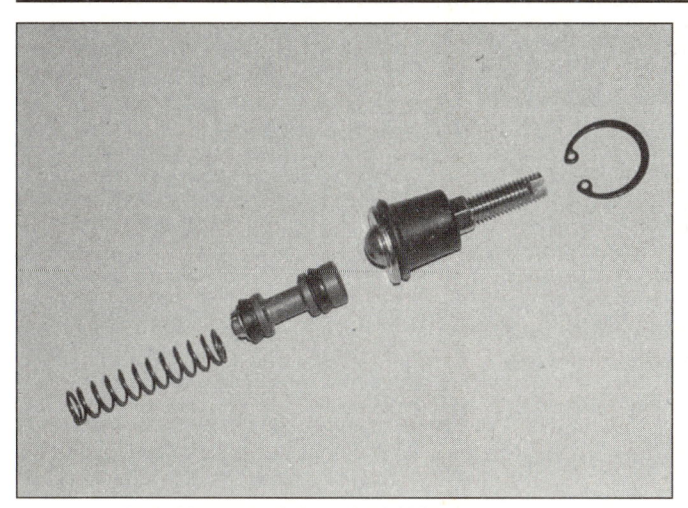

9.10 Master cylinder rebuild kit components

9.17 Make sure the banjo fitting locates between the lugs (arrowed)

circlip pliers to remove the circlip, then slide out the pushrod, piston assembly and spring, noting how they fit. Lay the parts out in order to prevent confusion during reassembly **(see illustration 9.10)**.

8 Clean all of the parts with clean DOT 4 brake fluid. If compressed air is available, blow it through the fluid galleries to ensure they are clear and use it to dry the parts thoroughly (make sure the air is filtered and unlubricated).

Caution: Do not, under any circumstances, use a petroleum-based solvent to clean brake parts.

9 Check the master cylinder bore for corrosion, scratches, nicks and score marks. If damage or wear is evident, the master cylinder must be replaced with a new one. If the master cylinder is in poor condition, then the caliper should be checked as well.

10 The dust boot, circlip, pushrod, piston assembly including the cup and seal) and spring are included in the master cylinder rebuild kit **(see illustration)**. Use all of the new parts, regardless of the apparent condition of the old ones. Fit them according to the layout of the old piston assembly. If the cup and seal are not already on the piston lubricate them with brake grease or clean brake fluid before fitting them to make it easier, and fit them with their wider sides facing the inner end of the piston.

11 Fit the spring into the master cylinder. Lubricate the piston assembly with brake grease or clean brake fluid and fit the assembly into the master cylinder, making sure it is the correct way round. Make sure the lips on the cup and seal do not turn inside out when they are slipped into the bore.

12 Fit the pushrod, then push it in to compress the spring and fit the new circlip, making sure it is properly located in its groove.

13 Fit the dust boot, making sure it seats correctly in the master cylinder and locates correctly around the pushrod.

14 If removed, thread the clevis locknut and the clevis onto the pushrod. Position the clevis as noted on removal (see Step 6), then tighten the locknut securely. Note that the clevis position controls brake pedal height and can be set after installation as described in Chapter 1.

15 If removed fit a new O-ring onto the reservoir hose union, then press the union into the master cylinder, making sure it is positioned correctly so the locating butt is on the inside of the tab on the cylinder **(see illustration 9.17)**.

16 Inspect the fluid reservoir cap, diaphragm plate and diaphragm and renew any parts if they are damaged or deteriorated. Inspect the reservoir hose for cracks or splits and replace it with a new one if necessary. Check the hose clips and replace them if they are strained or corroded.

Installation

17 Installation is the reverse of removal, noting the following points:
● Fit the master cylinder onto the footrest bracket and tighten its mounting bolts to the torque setting specified at the beginning of this Chapter **(see illustration 9.4)**.
● Secure the master cylinder pushrod clevis pin with a new split pin **(see illustration 9.3)**.
● Connect the brake hose banjo fitting to the master cylinder, using new sealing washers on each side of the banjo fitting, and aligning the fitting so it locates between the two lugs **(see illustration)**. Tighten the banjo bolt to the specified torque setting.
● Attach the fluid reservoir in position temporarily; ensure that the hose is correctly routed, then connect it to the union on the master cylinder and secure it with the clip **(see illustration 9.1a and c)**.
● Fill the fluid reservoir with new DOT 4 brake fluid (see *Pre-ride checks*). Refer to Section 11 of this Chapter and bleed the air from the system.
● Ensure the reservoir diaphragm is correctly seated, and that the cap is tightened securely **(see illustration 9.1b)**.
● Set the brake pedal height and check the rear brake light switch setting as described in Chapter 1.
● Check the operation of the rear brake before riding the motorcycle.

10 Brake hoses and unions

Inspection

1 Brake hose condition should be checked regularly and the hoses replaced with new ones at the specified interval (see Chapter 1).

2 Twist and flex the hoses while looking for cracks, bulges and seeping hydraulic fluid. Check extra carefully around the areas where the hoses connect with the banjo fittings, as these are common areas for hose failure.

3 Check the banjo fittings connected to the brake hoses. If the fittings are rusted, scratched or cracked, fit new hoses.

Renewal

4 The brake hoses have banjo fittings on each end. Cover the surrounding area with plenty of rags and unscrew the banjo bolt at each end of the hose, noting the alignment of the fitting with the master cylinder or brake caliper **(see illustrations 3.3a, 5.4a or b, 7.1 and 9.1c)** – on T (2005) models slacken the master cylinder clamp bolts and swivel the master cylinder around the handlebar until the brake hose banjo bolt is better positioned for tool fitment. Free the hose from any clips or guides and remove it, noting its routing. Discard the sealing washers.

5 Position the new hose, making sure it is not twisted or otherwise strained, and ensure that it is correctly routed through any clips or guides and is clear of all moving components.

6 Check that the fittings align correctly, then

6•16 Brakes, wheels and final drive

install the banjo bolts, using new sealing washers on both sides of the fittings **(see illustrations 3.17 and 5.4b)**. Tighten the banjo bolts to the torque setting specified at the beginning of this Chapter.

7 Flush the old brake fluid from the system, refill with new DOT 4 brake fluid (see *Pre-ride checks*) and bleed the air from the system (see Section 11).

8 Check the operation of the brakes before riding the motorcycle.

11 Brake system bleeding and fluid change

Special Tool: *In its simplest form, the brake bleeding equipment described in Step 2 will be required. A quicker alternative would be a 'one-man' brake bleeding kit consisting of a non-return valve in the pipe which prevents air being drawn back into the caliper. If, however, either set-up fails to bleed the brake effectively, use of a vacuum-type brake bleeding tool (see illustration 11.18) is advised.*

Bleeding air from the system

1 Bleeding the brakes is simply the process of removing air from the brake fluid reservoirs, the hoses and the brake calipers. Bleeding is necessary whenever a brake system hydraulic connection is loosened, after a component or hose is removed, or when the master cylinder or caliper is overhauled. Leaks in the system may also allow air to enter, but leaking brake fluid will reveal their presence and warn you of the need for repair.

2 To bleed the brakes, you will need some new DOT 4 brake fluid, a length of clear vinyl or plastic hose, a small container partially filled with clean brake fluid, some rags and a spanner to fit the brake caliper bleed valve **(see illustration)**.

3 Cover the fuel tank and other painted components to prevent damage in the event that brake fluid is spilled.

4 When bleeding the rear brake, slacken the screw securing the fluid reservoir to the frame to allow it to be tilted for topping up **(see illustration 9.1a)**.

5 Refer to *Pre-ride checks* at the start of this manual and remove the reservoir cap,

11.2 Set-up for bleeding the brakes

diaphragm plate and diaphragm. Slowly pump the brake lever (front brake) or pedal (rear brake) a few times, until no air bubbles can be seen floating up from the holes in the bottom of the reservoir. This bleeds the air from the master cylinder end of the line. Temporarily refit the reservoir cap. On T (2005) models the front master cylinder is fitted with a bleed valve – if there is evidence of air in the system bleed the master cylinder as well, both before and after bleeding the calipers, as described below.

6 Pull the dust cap off the bleed valve **(see illustrations)**. Attach one end of the clear vinyl or plastic hose to the bleed valve and submerge the other end in the clean brake fluid in the container **(see illustration)**. *Note: To avoid damaging the bleed valve during the procedure, loosen it and then tighten it temporarily with a ring spanner before attaching the hose. With the hose attached, the valve can then be opened and closed with an open-ended spanner.*

7 Remove the reservoir cap and check the fluid level. Do not allow the fluid level to drop below the lower mark during the procedure.

8 Carefully pump the brake lever or pedal three or four times and hold it in (front) or down (rear) while opening the bleed valve. When the valve is opened, brake fluid will flow out into the clear tubing, and the lever will move toward the handlebar, or the pedal will move down. If there is air in the system you will see air bubbles in the brake fluid coming out.

9 Retighten the bleed valve, then release the brake lever or pedal gradually. Top-up the reservoir as required and repeat the process until no air bubbles are visible in the brake fluid, and the lever or pedal is firm when applied. On completion, disconnect the hose, then tighten the bleed valve to the torque setting specified at the beginning of this Chapter and fit the dust cap. When bleeding the front brake system, both calipers must be bled.

> **HAYNES HiNT**
> *If it is not possible to produce a firm feel to the lever or pedal, the fluid may be aerated. Let the brake fluid in the system stabilise for a few hours and then repeat the procedure when the tiny bubbles in the system have settled out.*

10 Top-up the reservoir, install the diaphragm, diaphragm plate and cap, and wipe up any spilled brake fluid. Tighten the rear brake fluid reservoir screw. Check the entire system for fluid leaks.

11 Check the operation of the brakes before riding the motorcycle.

Changing the fluid

12 Changing the brake fluid is a similar process to bleeding the brakes and requires the same materials plus a suitable tool for siphoning the fluid out of the hydraulic reservoir. Also ensure that the container is large enough to take all the old fluid when it is flushed out of the system.

13 Follow Steps 3, 4 and 6, then remove the reservoir cap, diaphragm plate and diaphragm and siphon the old fluid out of the reservoir. Fill the reservoir with new brake fluid, then follow Step 8.

14 Retighten the bleed valve, then release the brake lever or pedal gradually. Keep the reservoir topped-up with new fluid to above the LOWER level at all times or air may enter the system and greatly increase the length of the task. Repeat the process until new fluid can be seen emerging from the bleed valve.

> **HAYNES HiNT**
> *Old brake fluid is invariably much darker in colour than new fluid, making it easy to see when all old fluid has been expelled from the system.*

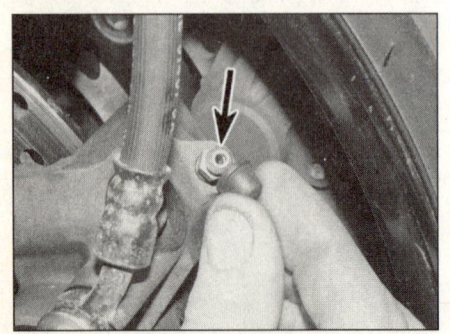

11.6a Front brake caliper bleed valve (arrowed)

11.6b Front master cylinder bleed valve (arrowed) – T model

11.6c Rear brake caliper bleed valve (arrowed)

Brakes, wheels and final drive 6•17

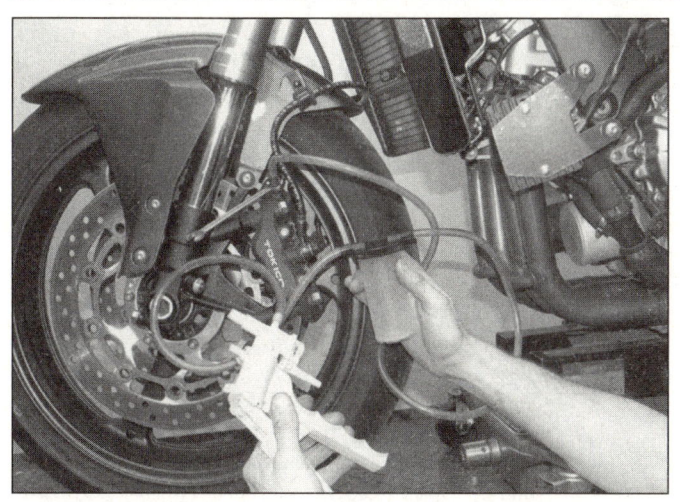

11.18 Sucking out brake fluid using a vacuum-operated bleeding tool

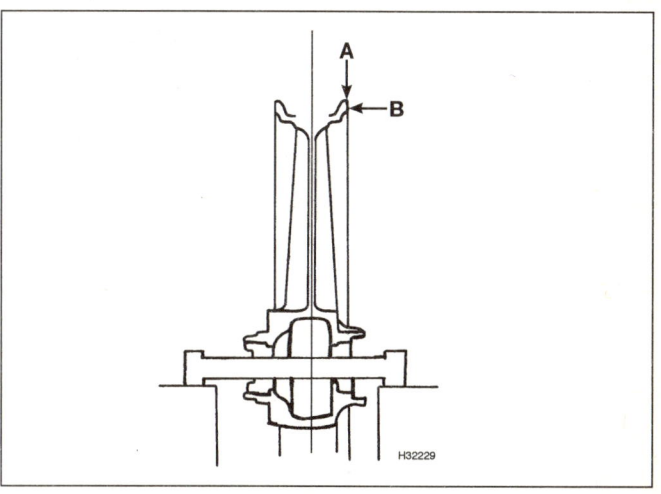

12.2 Check the wheel for radial (out-of-round) runout (A) and axial (side-to-side) runout (B)

15 Disconnect the hose, then tighten the bleed valve to the specified torque setting and install the dust cap.
16 Top-up the reservoir, install the diaphragm, diaphragm plate and cap, and wipe up any spilled brake fluid. Attach the rear brake fluid reservoir to the frame and tighten the retaining screw securely. Check the entire system for fluid leaks.
17 Check the operation of the brakes before riding the motorcycle.

Draining the system for overhaul

18 Draining the brake fluid is again a similar process to bleeding the brakes. The quickest and easiest way is to use a commercially available vacuum-type brake bleeding tool **(see illustration)** – follow the manufacturer's instructions. Otherwise follow the procedure described above for changing the fluid, but quite simply do not put any new fluid into the reservoir – the system fills itself with air instead.

12 Wheel inspection and repair

1 In order to carry out a proper inspection of the wheels, it is necessary to support the bike upright so that the wheel being inspected is raised off the ground. Position the motorcycle on an auxiliary stand. Clean the wheels thoroughly to remove mud and dirt that may interfere with the inspection procedure or mask defects. Make a general check of the wheels (see Chapter 1) and tyres (see *Pre-ride checks*).
2 Attach a dial gauge to the fork or the swingarm and position its tip against the side of the wheel rim **(see illustration)**. Spin the wheel slowly and check the axial (side-to-side) runout at the rim.
3 In order to accurately check radial (out of round) runout with the dial gauge, remove the wheel from the machine, and the tyre from the wheel. With the axle clamped in a vice and the dial gauge positioned on the top of the rim, the wheel can be rotated to check the runout.
4 An easier, though slightly less accurate, method is to attach a stiff wire pointer to the fork or the swingarm and position the end a fraction of an inch from the edge of the wheel rim where the wheel and tyre join. If the wheel is true, the distance from the pointer to the rim will be constant as the wheel is rotated. **Note:** *If wheel runout is excessive, check the wheel bearings very carefully before renewing the wheel.*
5 The wheels should also be inspected for cracks, flat spots on the rim and other damage. Look very closely for dents in the area where the tyre bead contacts the rim. Dents in this area may prevent complete sealing of the tyre against the rim, which leads to deflation of the tyre over a period of time. If damage is evident, or if runout in either direction is excessive, the wheel will have to be replaced with a new one. Never attempt to repair a damaged cast alloy wheel.

13 Wheel alignment check

1 Misalignment of the wheels due to a bent frame or forks can cause strange and possibly serious handling problems. If the frame or forks are at fault, repair by a frame specialist or replacement with new parts are the only options.
2 To check wheel alignment you will need an assistant, a length of string or a perfectly straight piece of wood and a ruler. A plumb bob or spirit level for checking that the wheels are vertical will also be required.
3 In order to make a proper check of the wheels it is necessary to support the bike in an upright position, using an auxiliary stand. First ensure that the chain adjuster markings coincide on each side of the swingarm (see Chapter 1, Section 1). Next, measure the width of both tyres at their widest points. Subtract the smaller measurement from the larger measurement, then divide the difference by two. The result is the amount of offset that should exist between the front and rear tyres on both sides of the machine.
4 If a string is used, have your assistant hold one end of it about halfway between the floor and the rear axle, with the string touching the back edge of the rear tyre sidewall.
5 Run the other end of the string forward and pull it tight so that it is roughly parallel to the floor **(see illustration)**. Slowly bring the string into contact with the front edge of the rear tyre sidewall, then turn the front wheel until it is parallel with the string. Measure the distance from the front tyre sidewall to the string.

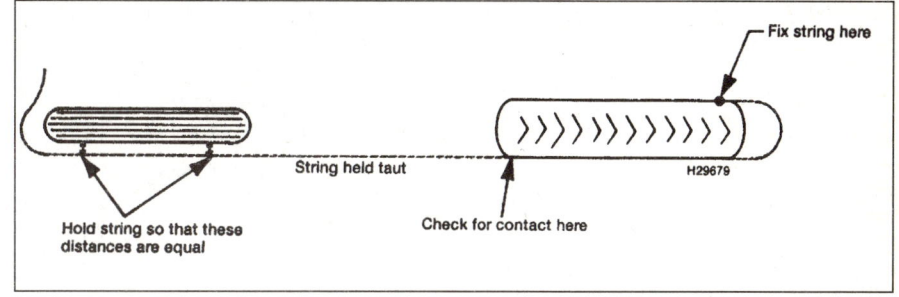

13.5 Wheel alignment check using string

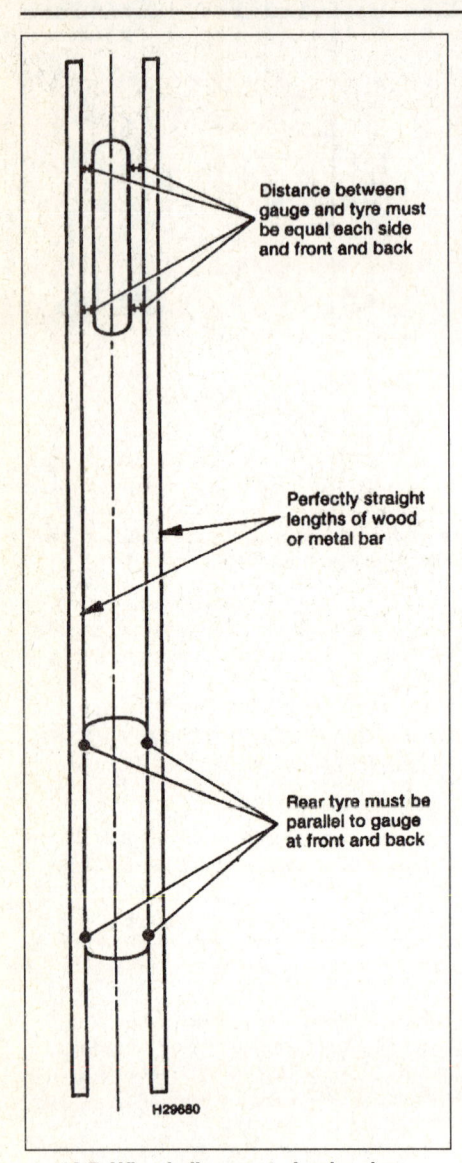

6•18 Brakes, wheels and final drive

13.7 Wheel alignment check using a straight-edge

6 Repeat the procedure on the other side of the motorcycle. The distance from the front tyre sidewall to the string should be equal on both sides.

7 As previously mentioned, a perfectly straight length of wood or metal bar may be substituted for the string **(see illustration)**.

8 If the distance between the string and tyre is greater on one side, or if the rear wheel appears to be out of alignment, have your machine checked by a Yamaha dealer.

9 If the front-to-back alignment is correct, the wheels still may be out of alignment vertically.

10 Using a plumb bob or spirit level, check the rear wheel to make sure it is vertical. To do this, hold the string of the plumb bob against the tyre upper sidewall and allow the weight to settle just off the floor. If the string touches both the upper and lower tyre sidewalls and is perfectly straight, the wheel is vertical. If it is not, adjust the stand until it is.

14.3a Slacken the axle clamp bolts (arrowed) on each side . . .

14.3b . . . then unscrew the axle bolt

11 Once the rear wheel is vertical, check the front wheel in the same manner. If both wheels are not perfectly vertical, the frame and/or major suspension components are bent.

14 Front wheel

Removal

1 Remove the lower fairing (see Chapter 7). Using an auxiliary stand, support the motorcycle securely in an upright position with the front wheel off the ground.

2 Displace the front brake calipers (see Section 3).

3 Slacken the axle clamp bolts on the bottom of each fork slider, then unscrew the axle bolt, which is on the right-hand end of the axle on R and S (2003 and 2004) models and on the left-hand end on T (2005) models **(see illustrations)**.

4 Drive the axle out from the bolt side, making sure the internal threads are not damaged, until you can grasp it from the other side, then support the wheel, withdraw the axle, and remove the wheel from between the forks **(see illustration)**.

5 Remove the shouldered spacers with the dust covers from both sides of the wheel, noting how the spacers fit inside the bearing seals **(see illustration)**.

Caution: Don't lay the wheel down and allow it to rest on the brake disc – the disc could become warped. Set the wheel on wood blocks so the wheel rim supports the weight of the wheel, or keep the wheel upright. Don't operate the brake lever with the wheel removed.

6 Clean the axle and remove any corrosion using steel wool. Check the axle for straightness by rolling it on a flat surface such as a piece of plate glass. If available, place the axle in V-blocks and check for runout using a dial gauge. If the axle is bent, replace it with a new one.

7 Wipe any old grease off the bearing seals and check the condition of the seals and the wheel bearings (see Section 16).

8 Clean the axle spacers and remove any corrosion with steel wool. The spacers should be perfectly smooth where they locate in the seals.

Installation

9 Apply lithium-based grease to the insides of the bearing seals, then fit the spacers with the dust covers into the seals so that the shouldered end of the spacers faces out **(see illustration 14.5)**.

10 Apply a thin coat of lithium-based grease to the axle, then lift the wheel into position between the forks, making sure the spacers remain in place, and slide the axle in from the left-hand side on R and S (2003 and 2004) models and from the right-hand side on T (2005) models **(see illustration 14.4)**.

11 Check that the axle is correctly located

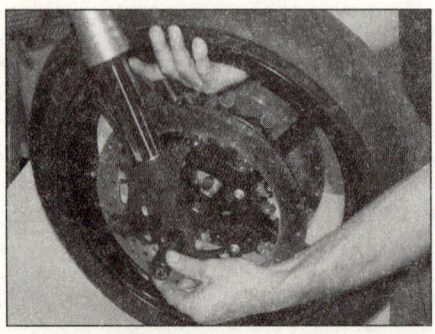

14.4 Withdraw the axle and remove the wheel

14.5 Remove the shouldered spacer and dust seal from each side

Brakes, wheels and final drive 6•19

15.4a Unscrew the axle nut and remove the washer . . .

15.4b . . . then remove the adjuster plate

15.5a Withdraw the axle and lower the wheel . . .

then fit the axle bolt and tighten it to the torque setting specified at the beginning of the Chapter **(see illustration 14.3b)**.
12 Install the brake calipers, making sure the pads sit squarely on each side of the discs (see Section 3). Apply the front brake to bring the pads back into contact with the discs. Take the bike off its auxiliary stand and compress the forks by applying the brake and pressing down on the handlebars to align the wheel and the suspension.
13 Tighten the pinch bolts on the bottom of the each fork slider to the specified torque setting **(see illustration 14.3a)**.
14 Install the lower fairing (see Chapter 7).
15 Check the operation of the front brake before riding the motorcycle.

15 Rear wheel

Removal

1 Using an auxiliary stand, support the motorcycle securely in an upright position with the rear wheel off the ground.
2 Displace the rear brake caliper (see Section 7).
3 Loosen the chain adjuster locknuts and turn the adjusters fully in to provide some slack in the chain (see Chapter 1).
4 Unscrew the axle nut and remove the nut, washer and right-hand chain adjuster plate **(see illustrations)**.
5 Support the wheel, then withdraw the axle along with the left-hand chain adjuster plate and lower the wheel to the ground **(see illustration)**. Note how the caliper bracket locates between the wheel and the swingarm and remove the bracket **(see illustration)**.
6 Disengage the chain from the rear wheel sprocket and remove the wheel from the swingarm **(see illustration)**.
7 Remove the plain spacer from the right-hand side of the wheel and the shouldered spacer with the dust cover from the left-hand side, noting how the spacers fit inside the bearing seals **(see illustrations)**.
Caution: Don't lay the wheel down and allow it to rest on the disc or the sprocket – *they could become warped. Set the wheel on wood blocks so the wheel rim supports the weight of the wheel, or keep the wheel upright. Don't operate the brake pedal with the wheel removed.*
8 Slide the adjuster plate off the axle, noting how it fits. **Note:** *The left and right-hand adjuster plates are different and must not be swapped around on reassembly.*
9 Clean the axle and remove any corrosion using steel wool. Check the axle for straightness by rolling it on a flat surface such as a piece of plate glass. If available, place the axle in V-blocks and check for runout using a dial gauge. If the axle is bent, replace it with a new one.
10 Wipe any old grease off the bearing seals and check the condition of the seals and the wheel bearings (see Section 16). Lift the sprocket coupling out of the hub to check the left-hand side wheel bearing **(see illustration 16.22)**.
11 Clean the axle spacers and remove any corrosion with steel wool. The spacers should be perfectly smooth where they locate in the seals.

Installation

12 If removed fit the sprocket coupling **(see illustration 16.22)**. Apply lithium-based grease to the insides of the bearing seals, then fit the plain spacer into the right-hand side of the wheel and the shouldered spacer with the dust cover into the left-hand side **(see illustrations 15.7a and b)**.
13 Manoeuvre the wheel into place in the swingarm and engage the drive chain on the sprocket **(see illustration 15.6)**.

15.5b . . . then remove the caliper bracket

15.6 Disengage the chain and draw the wheel out the back

15.7a Remove the plain spacer from the right-hand side . . .

15.7b . . . and the shouldered spacer and seal from the left

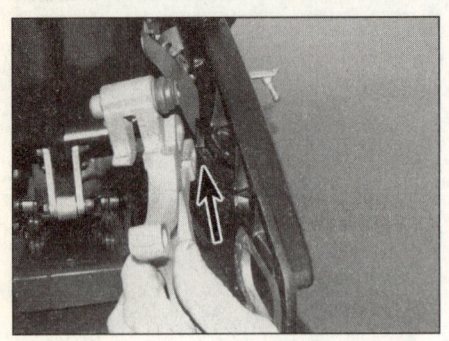

6•20 Brakes, wheels and final drive

15.14 Make sure the sliding section at the front of the bracket locates correctly in the cut-out in the swingarm (arrowed)

15.17 Locate the axle head and adjustment marker as shown

14 Locate the brake caliper bracket on the swingarm **(see illustration)**.
15 Slide the left-hand chain adjuster plate onto the axle and align the flats on the axle head with the plate. Apply a thin coat of lithium-based grease to the axle.
16 Lift the wheel into position, making sure the spacers and caliper bracket remain in place, and slide the axle through from the left-hand side **(see illustration 15.5a)**. Ensure the axle passes through the caliper bracket.
17 Locate the left-hand chain adjuster plate in the slot in the swingarm with the raised sections on the plate vertical, and make sure the flats in the axle head locate against the raised sections **(see illustration)**.
18 Fit the right-hand chain adjuster plate with its chamfered edges horizontal, then fit the washer and the axle nut **(see illustrations 15.4b and a)**.
19 Adjust the chain tension as described in Chapter 1, then tighten the axle nut to the torque setting specified at the beginning of this Chapter.
20 Install the brake caliper (see Section 7).
21 Apply the rear brake to bring the pads into contact with the disc. Check the operation of the rear brake before riding the motorcycle.

16 Wheel and sprocket coupling bearings

Front wheel bearings

Note: *Always fit the wheel bearings in sets, never individually. Avoid using a high pressure cleaner on the wheel bearing area.*

1 Remove the wheel (see Section 14).
2 Lever out the bearing seals from both sides of the hub using a seal hook or a large, flat-bladed screwdriver and a piece of wood, taking care not to damage the hub **(see illustration)**. Discard the seals as new ones must be fitted on reassembly.
3 Inspect the bearings (see *Tools and Workshop Tips (Section 5)* in the Reference Section) – a caged ball bearing is fitted in each side of the hub. **Note:** *Do not remove the bearings unless they are going to be replaced with new ones.*
4 If the bearings are worn, remove them using an internal expanding puller with slide-hammer attachment, which can be obtained commercially (see *Tools and Workshop Tips*) **(see illustration and 16.15a)**. Remove the spacer which fits between the bearings.
5 Turn the wheel over and remove the remaining bearing using the same procedure.
6 Thoroughly clean the hub area of the wheel with a suitable solvent and inspect the bearing seats for scoring and wear. If the seats are damaged, consult a Yamaha dealer before reassembling the wheel.
7 The new bearings can be installed in the hub using a drawbolt arrangement or by using a bearing driver or suitable socket (see *Tools and Workshop Tips*) **(see illustration)**. Ensure that the drawbolt washer or driver (as applicable) bears only on the outer edge of the race and does not contact the bearing seat.
8 Install the bearings with the marked or sealed side facing outwards. Ensure the bearing is fitted squarely and all the way into its seat. Turn the wheel over then install the bearing spacer and the other new bearing.
9 Apply a smear of grease to the new seals, then press them into the hub **(see illustration)**. Level the seals with the rim of the hub using a hammer and a small block of wood if necessary.
10 Clean the brake discs using acetone or brake system cleaner, then install the wheel (see Section 14).

Rear wheel bearings

11 Remove the rear wheel (see Section 15) and lift the sprocket coupling out of the hub **(see illustration 16.22)**.
12 Set the wheel on wooden blocks with the disc (right-hand side) facing up, then lever out the bearing seal using a seal hook or a large flat-bladed screwdriver and a piece of wood, taking care not to damage the hub **(see illustration)**. Discard the seal as a new one must be fitted on reassembly.

16.2 Lever out the bearing seals

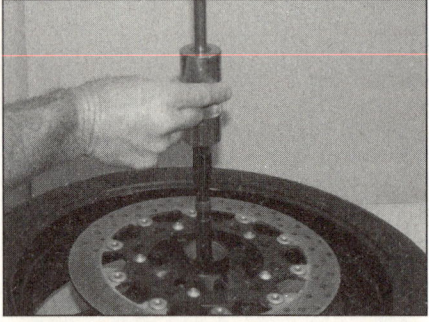

16.4 Using an expanding puller with slide-hammer attachment to remove the bearings

16.7 Using a socket to drive the bearing in

16.9 Press the seal into place

16.12 Lever out the bearing seal

Brakes, wheels and final drive 6•21

13 Inspect the bearings (see Tools and Workshop Tips (Section 5) in the Reference Section) – a caged ball bearing is fitted in the right-hand side of the hub and a needle roller bearing is fitted in the left-hand side. **Note:** *Do not remove the bearings unless they are going to be replaced with new ones – they will be destroyed by the removal method.*

14 If the bearings are worn, remove the circlip securing the caged ball bearing **(see illustration)**. Turn the wheel over and rest it on the wooden blocks. Remove the collar from inside the needle bearing, then withdraw the bearing spacer **(see illustrations)**. Using a metal rod (preferably a brass punch) inserted through the centre of the needle bearing, tap evenly around the outer race of the caged ball bearing to drive it from the hub **(see illustration)**.

15 Turn the wheel over and drive the needle bearing out of the hub using the same procedure. Alternatively use a bearing puller as shown **(see illustrations)**.

16 Thoroughly clean the hub area of the wheel with a suitable solvent and inspect the bearing seats for scoring and wear. If the seats are damaged, consult a Yamaha dealer before reassembling the wheel.

17 First install the caged ball bearing into its recess in the right-hand side of the hub, with its marked side facing outwards. Using an old bearing (if new ones are being fitted), a bearing driver or a socket large enough to contact the outer race of the bearing, drive it in squarely until it is completely seated **(see illustration)**. Fit the circlip, making sure it locates correctly in its groove **(see illustration 16.14a)**.

18 Lubricate the right-hand bearing seal with lithium-based grease and press it into the hub, using a bearing driver or a suitable socket with a small block of wood to level the seal with the inner rim of the hub if necessary **(see illustration)**.

19 Turn the wheel over and install the bearing spacer **(see illustration 16.14c)**. Fit the new needle bearing, which must be pressed or drawn (not driven) into position **(see illustration)**. In the absence of a press, a suitable drawbolt arrangement can be made up as described in Tools and Workshop Tips (Section 5) in the Reference section.

16.14a Remove the circlip (arrowed) from the right-hand side . . .

16.14c . . . and spacer from the left

Fit the collar into the needle bearing **(see illustration 16.14b)**.

20 Clean the brake disc using acetone or brake system cleaner,

16.15a Locate the knife-edged puller attachment under the lower edge of the bearing and tighten the tool so it expands . . .

16.14b . . . and the collar . . .

16.14d Drive the bearing out using a drift

21 Check the sprocket coupling/rubber dampers (see Section 20). Fit the sprocket coupling then install the wheel (see Section 15).

16.15b . . . then pull the bearing out

16.17 Using a socket to drive the bearing in

16.18 Press the seal into place

16.19 Needle bearings must be drawn or pressed and not driven into place

6•22 Brakes, wheels and final drive

16.22 Lift the sprocket coupling off the wheel

16.23 Lever out the bearing seal

16.25 Drive the bearing out from the inside

16.27 Using a socket to drive the bearings in

16.28 Fit the grease seal and press or tap it into place

Sprocket coupling bearing

22 Remove the rear wheel (see Section 15) and lift the sprocket coupling out of the hub **(see illustration)**.
23 Lever out the bearing seal using a seal hook or a large flat-bladed screwdriver and a piece of wood, taking care not to damage the rim of the coupling **(see illustration)**. Discard the seal as a new one must be fitted on reassembly.
24 Inspect the bearing (see Tools and Workshop Tips (Section 5) in the Reference Section). **Note:** *Do not remove the bearing unless it is going to be replaced with a new one.*
25 Support the coupling on blocks of wood and drive the bearing out from the inside using a bearing driver or socket **(see illustration)**.
26 Thoroughly clean the bearing seat with a suitable solvent and inspect the seat for scoring and wear. If the seat is damaged, consult a Yamaha dealer before reassembling the wheel.
27 Fit the bearing into the coupling with its marked side facing out. Using the old bearing (if a new one is being fitted), a bearing driver or a socket large enough to contact the outer race of the bearing, drive it in until it is completely seated **(see illustration)**.
28 Lubricate the new seal with lithium-base grease and press it into the coupling, using a bearing driver or a suitable socket to tap it in if necessary **(see illustration)**.

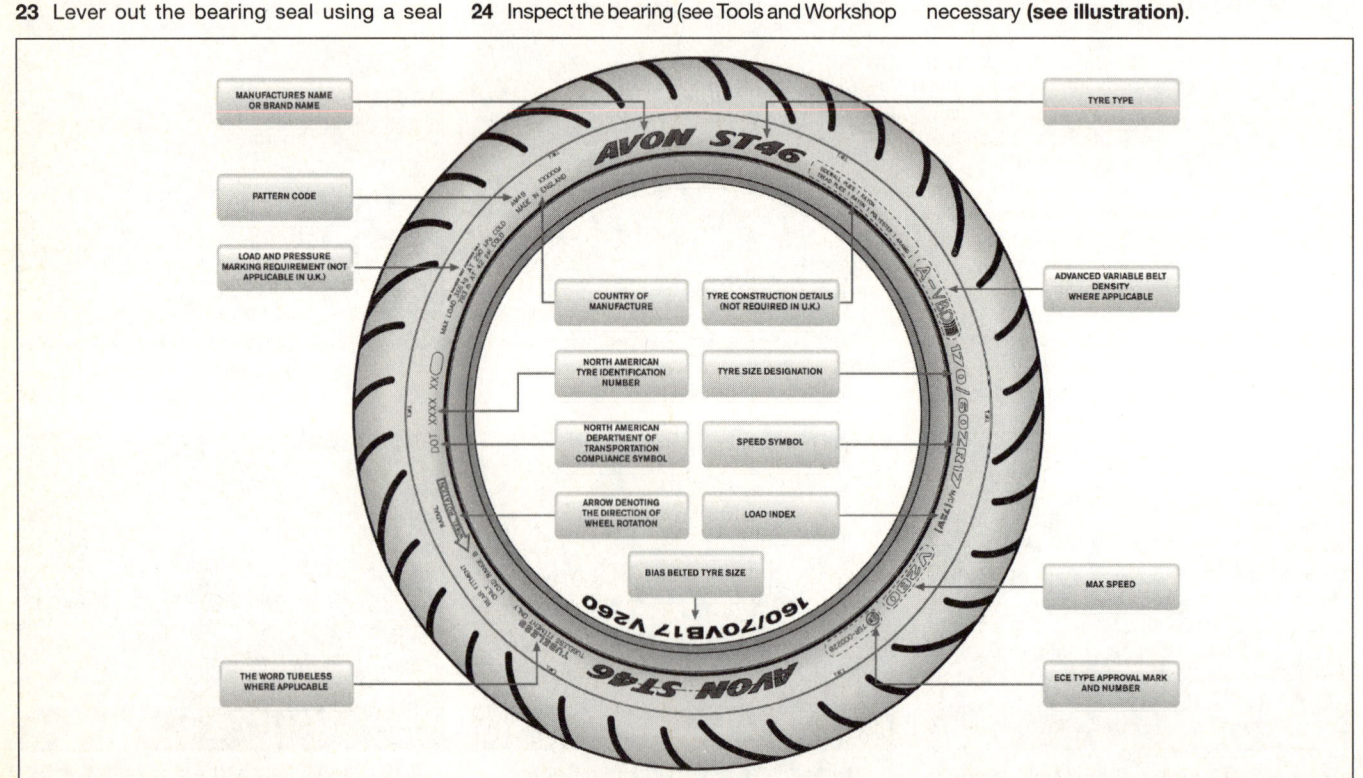

17.3 Common tyre sidewall markings

Brakes, wheels and final drive 6•23

29 Check the sprocket coupling rubber dampers (see Section 20).
30 Clean the brake disc using acetone or brake system cleaner, then install the sprocket coupling assembly and install the wheel (see Section 15).

17 Tyres

General information

1 The wheels fitted on all models are designed to take tubeless tyres only. Tyre sizes are given in the Specifications at the beginning of this chapter.
2 Refer to *Pre-ride checks* at the beginning of this manual for tyre maintenance and pressures.

Fitting new tyres

3 When selecting new tyres, refer to the tyre information in the Owner's Manual. Ensure that front and rear tyre types are compatible, and of the correct size and speed rating; if necessary, seek advice from a Yamaha dealer or motorcycle tyre specialist **(see illustration)**.
4 It is recommended that tyres are fitted by a motorcycle tyre specialist and that this is not attempted in the home workshop. This is particularly relevant in the case of tubeless tyres because the force required to break the seal between the wheel rim and tyre bead is substantial, and is usually beyond the capabilities of an individual working with normal tyre levers. Additionally, the specialist will be able to balance the wheels after tyre fitting.
5 Note that punctured tubeless tyres can in some cases be repaired. Seek the advice of a Yamaha dealer or a motorcycle tyre specialist concerning tyre repairs.

18 Drive chain

Removal

Note: *All models are fitted with a riveted soft (joining) link which can be disassembled using one of several commercially-available drive chain cutting/staking tools. Such chains can be recognised by the soft link side plate's identification marks (and usually its different colour), as well as by the riveted ends of the link's two pins which look as if they have been deeply centre-punched, instead of peened over as with all the other pins.*

⚠ **Warning: Use ONLY the correct service tools to disassemble and assemble the riveted-type of soft link – if you do not have access to such tools or do not have the skill to operate them correctly, have the old chain removed and a new one fitted by a Yamaha dealer.**

1 Remove the front sprocket cover (see Section 19).
2 Place the soft link in a suitable position for working on, by rotating the back wheel **(see illustration)**.
3 Slacken the drive chain as described in Chapter 1.
4 Split the chain at the soft link using the chain cutter, following the manufacturer's operating instructions carefully (see also Section 8 in *Tools and Workshop Tips* in the *Reference* Section). Remove the chain from the bike, noting its routing through the swingarm.

Installation

⚠ **Warning: NEVER install a drive chain which uses a clip-type master (split) link.**

5 Route the drive chain through the swingarm sections and around the front and rear sprockets, leaving the two ends in a convenient position to work on.
6 Refer to Section 8 in *Tools and Workshop Tips* in the *Reference* Section. Fit an O-ring onto each pin of the **new** soft link, then slide the link through from the inside and fit the other two O-rings. Install the new side plate with its identification marks facing out and use the chain tool to press the sideplate into position. Rivet the link pin ends using the chain tool, following the instructions of both the chain manufacturer and the tool manufacturer carefully. DO NOT re-use old soft link components.
7 After riveting, check the soft link and pin ends for any signs of cracking. If there is any evidence of cracking, the soft link, O-rings and side plate must be replaced with new ones.
8 Install the sprocket cover (see Section 19).
9 On completion, adjust and lubricate the chain following the procedures described in Chapter 1.

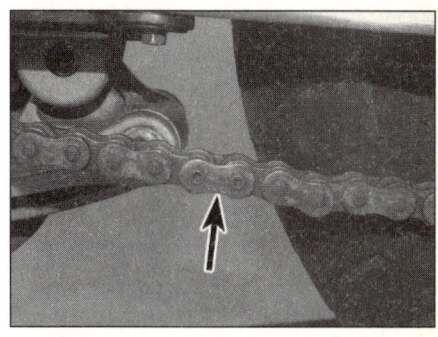

18.2 The soft link is identified by its different pin ends (arrowed)

19 Sprockets

Front sprocket cover

1 Remove the fairing left-hand side panel (see Chapter 7).
2 Unscrew the bolts securing the coolant reservoir and drain it or place it aside, supporting it upright using cable ties **(see illustration)**.
3 Unscrew the bolts securing the front sprocket cover and remove it **(see**

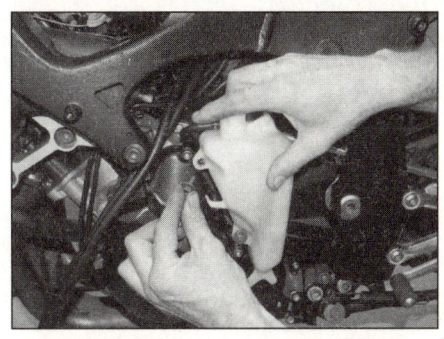

19.2 Displace the coolant reservoir for access to the sprocket cover

19.3a Unscrew the bolts (arrowed) . . .

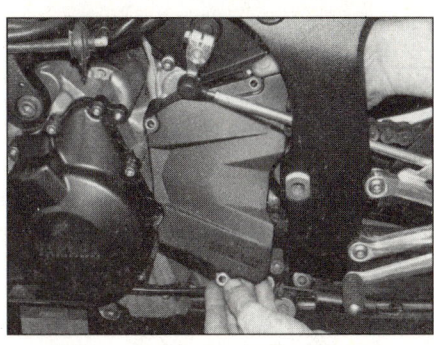

19.3b . . . and remove the cover . . .

19.3c . . . and the guide

6•24 Brakes, wheels and final drive

19.6a Bend the tabs down . . .

19.6b . . . then unscrew the nut . . .

19.6c . . . and remove the washer

illustrations). Remove the chain guide, noting how it fits **(see illustration)**.

4 Installation is the reverse of removal. If the reservoir has been drained, refer to *Pre-ride checks* or Chapter 1 and add the specified coolant mix.

Front sprocket

5 Remove the front sprocket cover (see Steps 1 to 3).
6 Bend back the tabs on the sprocket nut lockwasher **(see illustration)**. Have an assistant apply the rear brake hard, then unscrew the nut and remove the washer **(see illustrations)**. Discard the washer, as a new one must be used on reassembly. Adjust the chain so that it is fully slack (see Chapter 1, Section 1).
7 Slide the sprocket and chain off the shaft and slip the sprocket out of the chain **(see illustration)**. If there is not enough slack in the chain to disengage the sprocket, slip the

19.7 Draw the sprocket off the shaft and disengage the chain

19.9 Lock the nut by bending the washer tabs against it

chain off the rear wheel sprocket. **Note:** *If the sprocket is not being replaced with a new one, mark its outside face with a scratch, or dab of paint, so that it can be installed the same way round.*

8 Engage the new sprocket with the chain and slide it on the shaft. If removed, install the chain on the rear sprocket and take up the slack in the chain (see Chapter 1).
9 Install the **new** lockwasher, then fit the nut with its shouldered side facing in and tighten it to the torque setting specified at the beginning of this Chapter, applying the rear brake to prevent the sprocket from turning **(see illustrations 19.6c and b)**. Bend the tabs of the lockwasher up against the nut flats **(see illustration)**.
10 Install the front sprocket cover.
11 Install the remaining components in the reverse order of removal.

Rear sprocket

12 Remove the rear wheel (see Section 15).
Caution: *Don't lay the wheel down and allow it to rest on the disc or the sprocket – they could become warped. Set the wheel on wood blocks so the wheel rim supports the weight of the wheel. Don't operate the brake pedal with the wheel removed.*
13 Unscrew the nuts securing the sprocket to the hub assembly **(see illustration)**. Remove the sprocket, noting which way round it fits. **Note:** *The size of the sprocket (i.e. its number of teeth) is stamped on the outside face of the sprocket.*
14 Install the sprocket onto the hub with the

19.13 Rear sprocket nuts

stamped mark facing out. Tighten the nuts evenly and in a criss-cross sequence to the torque setting specified at the beginning of this Chapter.
15 Install the rear wheel (see Section 15).

20 Rear sprocket coupling/ rubber dampers

1 Remove the rear wheel (see Section 15). Set the wheel on wooden blocks with the sprocket facing up
Caution: *Don't lay the wheel down and allow it to rest on the disc– it could become warped. Set the wheel on wood blocks so the wheel rim supports the weight of the wheel. Don't operate the brake pedal with the wheel removed.*
2 Lift the sprocket coupling out of the hub, leaving the rubber dampers in position **(see illustration 16.22)**. Check the coupling for cracks or any obvious signs of damage. Also check the sprocket studs for looseness, wear or damage.
3 Lift the rubber damper segments from the hub and check them for cracks, hardening, wear and general deterioration **(see illustration)**. Replace the rubber dampers as a set, if necessary.
4 Checking and replacement procedures for the sprocket coupling bearing are described in Section 16.
5 Installation is the reverse of removal.
6 Install the rear wheel (see Section 15).

20.3 Check the rubber dampers as described

Chapter 7
Bodywork

Contents

	Section number		Section number
Fairing and body panels	3	Mirrors	4
Front mudguard	6	Seats	2
General information	1	Windshield	5

Degrees of difficulty

Easy, suitable for novice with little experience	**Fairly easy,** suitable for beginner with some experience	**Fairly difficult,** suitable for competent DIY mechanic	**Difficult,** suitable for experienced DIY mechanic	**Very difficult,** suitable for expert DIY or professional

1 General information

1 This Chapter covers the procedures necessary to remove and install the body parts. Since many service and repair operations on these motorcycles require the removal of the body parts, the procedures are grouped here and referred to from other Chapters.

2 In the case of damage to the body parts, it is usually necessary to remove the broken component and replace it with a new (or used) one. The material from which the body panels are made does not lend itself to conventional repair techniques. There are, however, some shops that specialise in 'plastic welding', so it may be worthwhile seeking the advice of one of these specialists before consigning an expensive component to the bin. There are also fairing repair kits available for DIY use.

3 When attempting to remove any body panel, first study it closely, noting any fasteners and associated fittings, to be sure of returning everything to its correct place on installation. In some cases the aid of an assistant will be required when removing panels, to help avoid the risk of damage to paintwork. Once the evident fasteners have been removed, try to withdraw the panel as described but DO NOT FORCE IT – if it will not release, check that all fasteners have been removed and try again. Where a panel engages another by means of tabs, be careful not to break the tab or its mating slot or to damage the paintwork. Remember that a few moments of patience at this stage will save you a lot of money in replacing broken fairing panels! To remove trim clips, push the centre into the body, then draw the clip out of the panel **(see illustration)**. To undo quick-release screws, turn them 90° anti-clockwise.

4 When installing a body panel, first study it closely, noting any fasteners and associated fittings removed with it, to be sure of returning everything to its correct place. Check that all fasteners are in good condition, including all trim clips and rubber mounts; any of these that are faulty must be replaced with new ones before the panel is reassembled. Check also that all mounting brackets are straight, and repair or renew them if necessary before attempting to install the panel. Where assistance was required to remove a panel, make sure your assistant is on hand to install it. To install trim clips, first push the centre back out so that it protrudes from the top of the clip. Fit the clip into its hole, then push the centre in so that it is flush with the top of the clip. To install quick-release screws, turn them 90° clockwise.

5 Tighten the fasteners securely, but be careful not to overtighten any of them or the panel may break (not always immediately) due to the uneven stress.

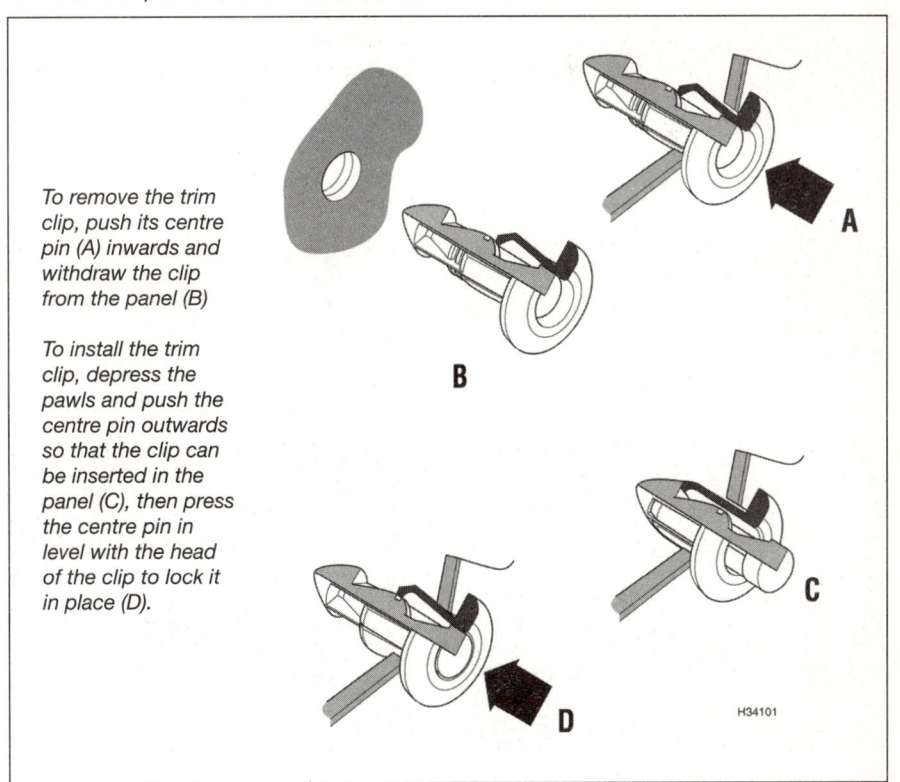

To remove the trim clip, push its centre pin (A) inwards and withdraw the clip from the panel (B)

To install the trim clip, depress the pawls and push the centre pin outwards so that the clip can be inserted in the panel (C), then press the centre pin in level with the head of the clip to lock it in place (D).

1.3 Trim clip removal

7•2 Bodywork

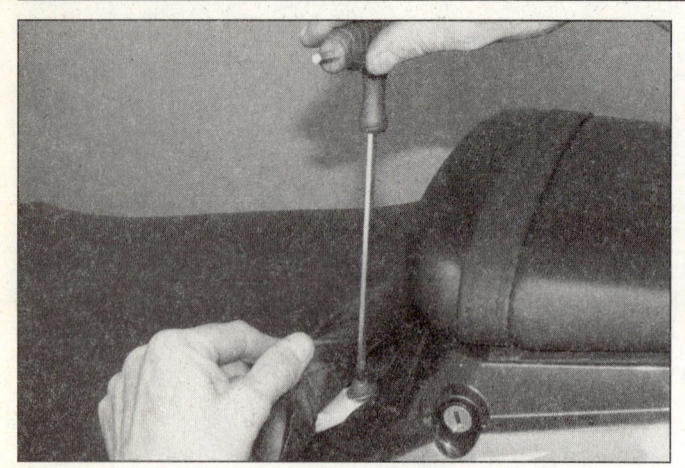

2.1a Unscrew the bolt on each side . . .

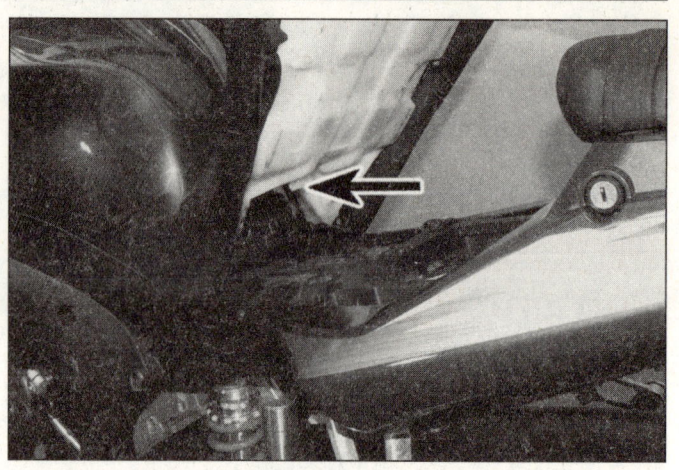

2.1b . . . and remove the seat, noting how its tab (arrowed) locates

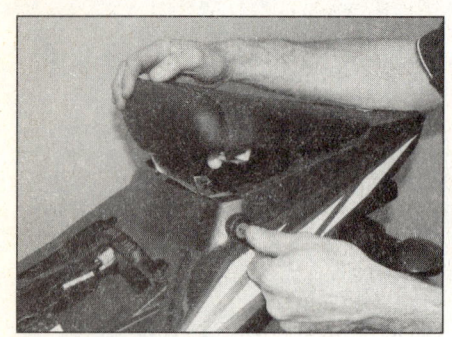

2.2a Unlock the seat and lift it up

2.2b Note how the tab (arrowed) locates

2 Seats

1 To remove the rider's seat, pull up each rear corner of the seat to access the bolts that retain it, then unscrew the bolts and remove the seat, noting how the tab at the front locates under the tank bracket **(see illustrations)**.
2 To remove the passenger seat, insert the ignition key into the seat lock located on the left-hand side of the bike, and turn it anti-clockwise to unlock the seat **(see illustration)**. Lift up the front of the seat and draw it forwards, noting how the tab at the back locates **(see illustration)**.
3 Installation is the reverse of removal. Push down on the front of the passenger seat to engage the latch.

3 Fairing and body panels

Seat cowling

1 Remove the seats (see Section 2).
2 Release and remove the six trim clips on the underside of the seat cowling (three on each side) **(see illustration)**.
3 Release the trim clip on each side at the front of the cowling **(see illustration)**. Remove the screw on the top of the cowling at the back, then carefully draw the cowling back and off the bike **(see illustration)**.
4 Installation is the reverse of removal.

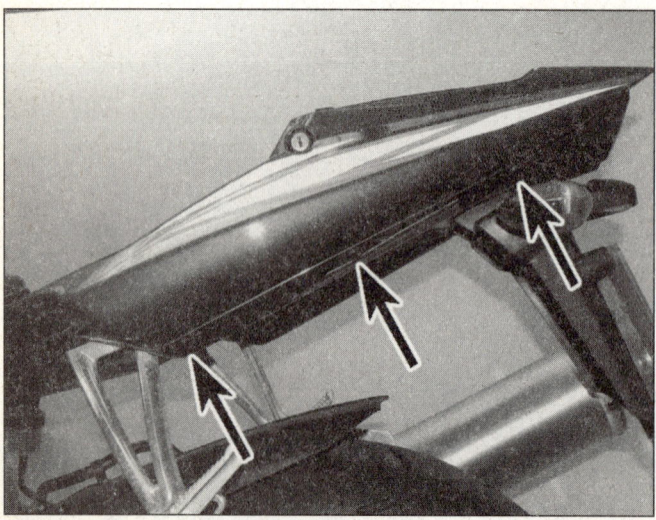

3.2 Release the trim clips (arrowed) on each side

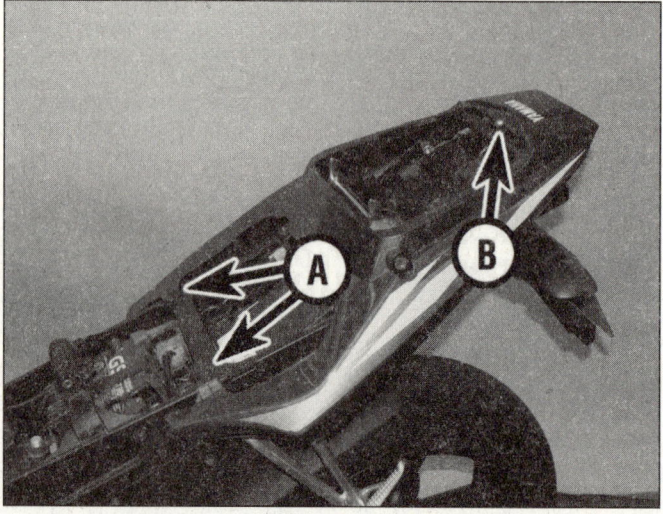

3.3a Release the trim clips (A) and undo the screw (B) . . .

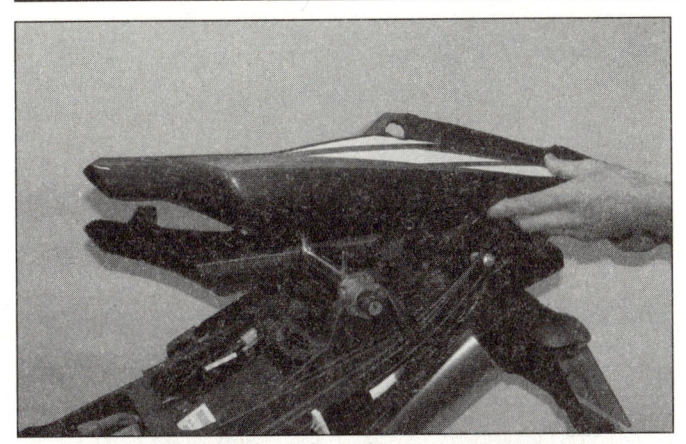

Bodywork 7•3

3.3b ... then carefully draw the cowling off the bike

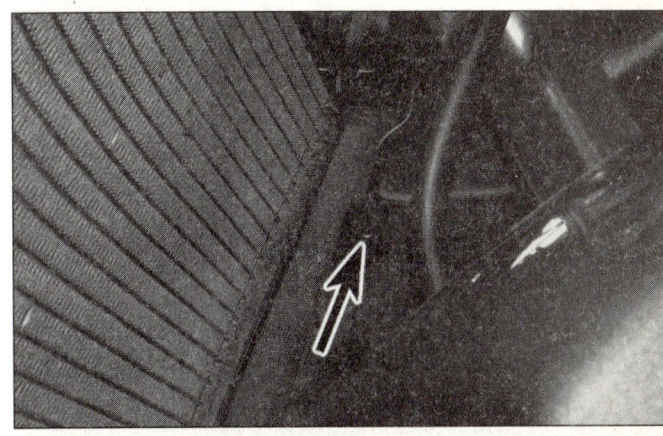

3.6 Release the trim clip (arrowed)

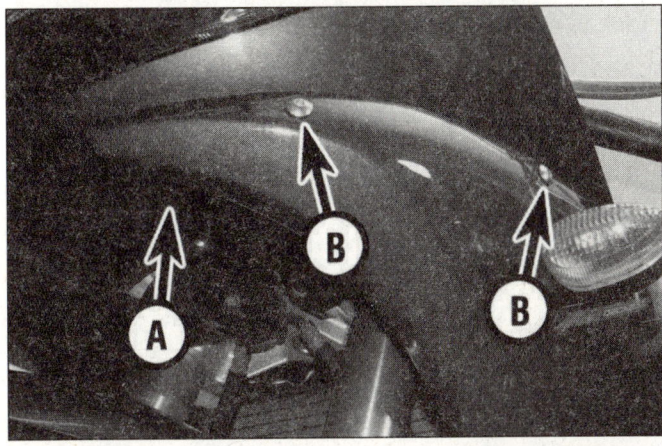

3.7 Release the trim clip (A) and undo the screws (B)

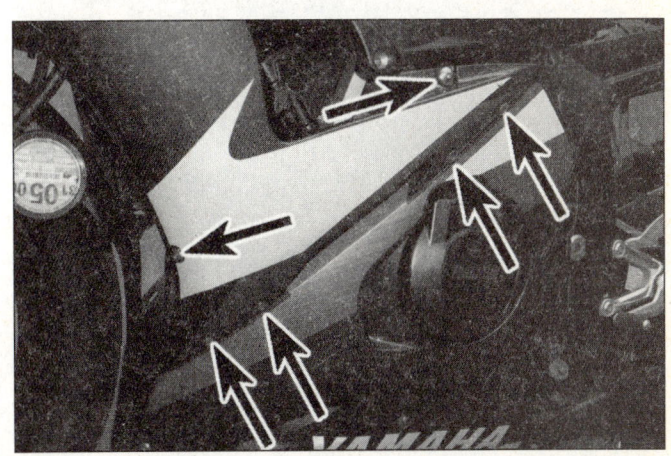

3.8 Undo the screws (arrowed) ...

Fairing side panels

5 Remove the cockpit trim panel (Step 16).
6 Remove the trim clip on the inside of the side panel, forward of the radiator, that secures the panel to the lower edge of the air intake duct **(see illustration)**.
7 Undo the two screws and release the trim clip along the top edge of the panel at the front **(see illustration)**.
8 Undo the six screws along the bottom edge of the panel **(see illustration)**.
9 Carefully draw the top rear of the panel away to release the peg from the grommet **(see illustration)**. Release the panel from the fairing and the lower fairing and displace it, noting how it engages, then disconnect the turn signal wiring connector when accessible and remove the panel **(see illustrations)**. Note the foam cushion on the inside of the panel.
10 If required undo the screws securing the inner trim section – on the left-hand side first displace the cooling fan relay and the fusebox

3.9a ... then release the peg from its grommet ...

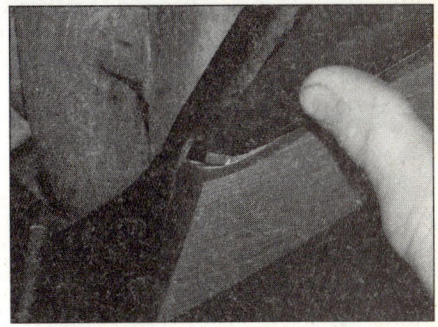

3.9b ... and displace the panel ...

3.9c ... noting how it locates ...

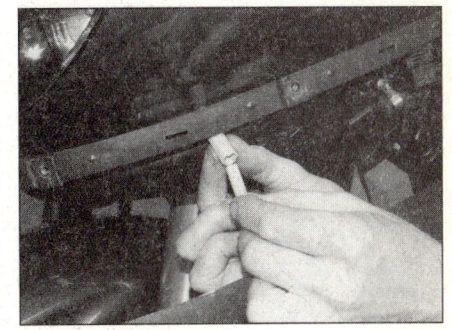

3.9d ... and disconnect the turn signal wiring connector

7•4 Bodywork

3.10a Displace the relay and fusebox (arrowed) . . .

3.10b . . . then undo the screws (arrowed) and remove the panel

from the front of it, noting how they locate **(see illustrations)**.

11 Installation is the reverse of removal.

Lower fairing

12 If required, and to make the procedure easier, remove the fairing side panels (Steps 5 to 9). If you leave the panels in place, undo the six screws along the bottom edge of the panel **(see illustration 3.8)**.

13 Release the trim clip on each side at the front securing the lower fairing to the bottom of the radiator **(see illustration)**.

14 Undo the two screws on each side, one in the middle and one at the back, then carefully lower the fairing and remove it, noting how it engages with the side panels along its top edge if not removed **(see illustrations)**. *Note: The lower fairing is a three-piece assembly – if required, the left and right-hand sections and the front section can be separated.*

15 Installation is the reverse of removal.

Cockpit trim panels

16 Undo the two screws securing the trim panel to the fairing side panel **(see illustration)**.

Ease the panel forwards to release the tabs on the outer edge from the hooks on the fairing side panel **(see illustration)**.

17 Installation is the reverse of removal. Make sure the panel locates correctly with the fairing and fairing side panel.

Fairing

18 Remove both cockpit trim panels (Step 16) and fairing side panels (Steps 5 to 9).

19 Remove the mirrors (see Section 4).

20 Disconnect the front wiring loom connectors **(see illustration)**.

3.13 Release the trim clip (arrowed) on each side

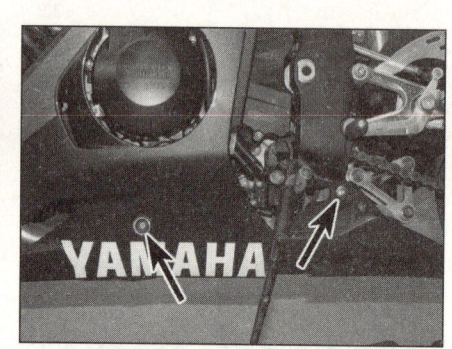

3.14a Undo the screws (arrowed) . . .

3.14b . . . and manoeuvre the lower fairing out from under the bike

3.16a Undo the screws (arrowed) . . .

3.16b . . . then move the panel forwards to release the tabs (arrowed)

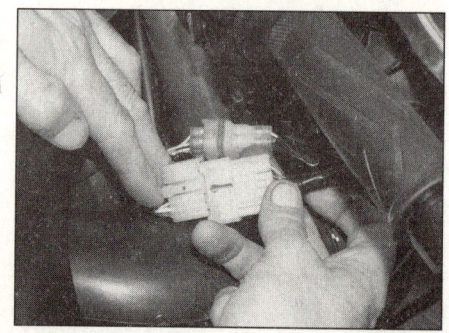

3.20 Disconnect the wiring connectors

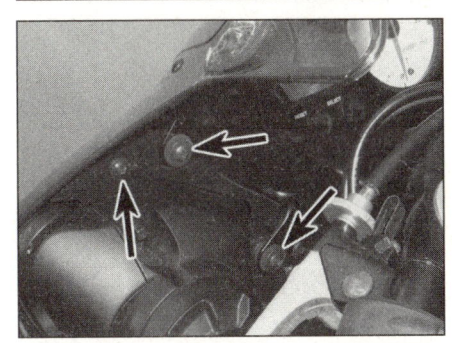

Bodywork 7•5

3.21a Undo the screws (arrowed) on each side . . .

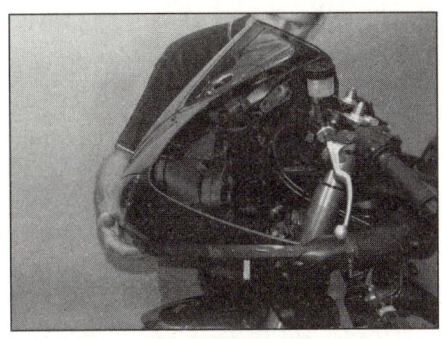

3.21b . . . then displace the fairing forwards . . .

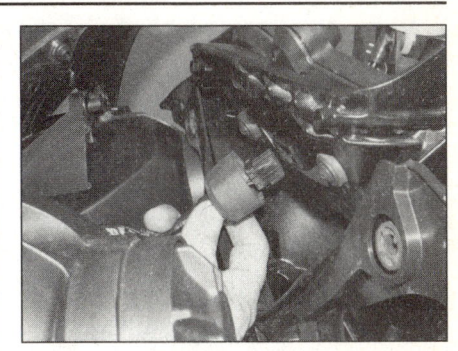

3.21c . . . and disconnect the instrument wiring connector

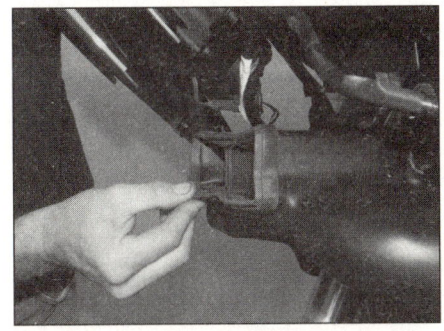

3.21d Ensure the rubber surround is correctly fitted

3.23a Slacken the clamp screw (arrowed) . . .

3.23b . . . then undo the screws (arrowed) and remove the intakes

21 Undo the three screws on each side **(see illustration)**. Carefully draw the fairing forwards and disconnect the instrument cluster wiring connector when accessible, then remove the fairing **(see illustrations)** – the headlight comes away with the fairing, but the instrument cluster and air ducts stay in place. Note the rubber surround for the intake ducts and make sure it is correctly located before installing the fairing as it can easily become dislodged **(see illustration)**.
22 Note the rubber pads with collars for the mirror bolts and remove them from the fairing stay if required.
23 If required slacken the clip securing each air duct intake piece to the joint piece that runs into the frame, then undo the screws securing the front of the intake piece and remove them **(see illustrations)**.
24 If required, remove the headlight unit (see Chapter 8).
25 Installation is the reverse of removal. Make sure the instrument cluster and front loom wiring connectors are connected.

4 Mirrors

1 Unscrew the two nuts securing each mirror and remove the mirror **(see illustrations)**. Note the rubber pad with collars for the mirror bolts fixed between the fairing and fairing stay **(see illustration)**.
2 Installation is the reverse of removal.

5 Windshield

1 Remove the mirrors (see Section 4).
2 Undo the four screws securing the windshield to the fairing and remove the windshield, noting how it fits. Note that the screws thread into rubber-bodied wellnuts set in the screen.
3 Installation is the reverse of removal. Do not overtighten the screws.

4.1a Unscrew the nuts (arrowed) . . .

4.1b . . . and remove the mirror

4.1c Note the collars in the rubber pad

7•6 Bodywork

6.1a Front mudguard bolts (arrowed) – T model shown

6.1b Collect the nut from the end of the rear bolt

6.2 Carefully draw the mudguard from between the forks

6 Front mudguard

1 Unscrew the bolts securing the mudguard to the fork slider noting that there is a nut on the inside of the rear bolt **(see illustrations)**.

2 Draw the mudguard forward from between the forks and remove it from the motorcycle **(see illustration)**.

3 Note the collars and bushes in the mudguard mounting holes and remove them if they are loose. The bushes should be a tight fit in the mudguard; replace them with new ones if they are worn or perished.

4 Installation is the reverse of removal.

Chapter 8
Electrical system

Contents

	Section number		Section number
Alternator rotor and stator	31	Ignition (main) switch	18
Battery charging	4	Ignition system components	see Chapter 4
Battery	3	Instrument and warning lights	17
Brake light switches	14	Instrument check and replacement	16
Brake/tail light LEDs and licence plate bulb	9	Instrument cluster removal and installation	15
Charging system testing	30	Lighting system check	6
Clutch switch	23	Neutral switch	21
Coolant temperature display, warning light and sensor	see Chapter 3	Oil level sensor	26
Cooling fan(s) and fan relay	see Chapter 3	Regulator/rectifier	32
Electrical system fault finding	2	Relay assembly	24
Fuel pump and relay	see Chapter 4	Sidestand switch	22
Fuses	5	Starter motor overhaul	29
General information	1	Starter motor removal and installation	28
Handlebar switch check	19	Starter relay	27
Handlebar switch removal and installation	20	Tail light unit	10
Headlight and headlight aim	8	Turn signal assemblies	13
Headlight bulbs and sidelight bulbs	7	Turn signal bulbs	12
Horn	25	Turn signal circuit check	11

Degrees of difficulty

Easy, suitable for novice with little experience	Fairly easy, suitable for beginner with some experience	Fairly difficult, suitable for competent DIY mechanic	Difficult, suitable for experienced DIY mechanic	Very difficult, suitable for expert DIY or professional

Specifications

Battery
Capacity	12V, 8Ah
Type	GT9B-4
Charge condition	
Fully charged	12.8V
Half-charged	12.4V
Discharged	12V or less
Charging time	Until fully charged (12.8V) (see Section 4)
Current leakage	1mA (max)

Oil level sensor
Resistance	
Upright	484 to 536 ohms @ 20°C
Upside down	114 to 126 ohms @ 20°C

Starter relay
Resistance	4.18 to 4.62 ohms @ 20°C

Starter motor
Brush length
- Standard.. 10 mm
- Service limit (min).................................. 3.5 mm

Commutator diameter
- Standard.. 28 mm
- Service limit (min).................................. 27 mm

Mica undercut... 0.7 mm
Commutator resistance.................................. 0.012 to 0.022 ohms

Alternator
Nominal output... 14V, 300W @ 5000 rpm
Stator coil resistance................................. 0.18 to 0.26 ohms @ 20°C

Regulator/rectifier
Regulated voltage output (no load)..................... 14.1 to 14.9V @ 5000 rpm

Fuses
R and S (2003 and 2004) Europe models
- Main.. 40A
- Headlight... 20A
- Fan... 15A
- Ignition.. 15A
- Brake light, horn..................................... 15A
- Instruments (clock), immobiliser...................... 10A
- Turn signals, sidelight, tail light................... 10A
- Fuel injection system................................. 15A

R and S (2003 and 2004) US and Canada models
- Main.. 40A
- Headlight, tail light................................. 20A
- Fan... 15A
- Ignition.. 15A
- Brake light, horn, turn signals....................... 15A
- Instruments (clock)................................... 10A
- Fuel injection system................................. 15A

T (2005) Europe models
- Main.. 40A
- Headlight... 20A
- Fuel injection system................................. 15A
- Ignition.. 15A
- Brake light, horn..................................... 15A
- Instruments (clock), immobiliser...................... 10A
- Turn signals, sidelight, tail light................... 10A
- Cooling fans.. 15A x 2

T (2005) US and Canada models
- Main.. 40A
- Headlight, tail light................................. 20A
- Ignition.. 15A
- Brake light, horn, turn signals....................... 15A
- Instruments (clock)................................... 10A
- Fuel injection system................................. 15A
- Cooling fans.. 15A x 2

Bulbs
Headlight.. 55W halogen x 2
Sidelight.. 5W x 2
Brake/tail light....................................... LED
Turn signal lights
- UK models... 21W x 4
- US models... 21/5W x 2 (front with running light), 21W x 2 (rear)

Instrument cluster illumination lights................. 1.4W x 2
Instrument warning lights.............................. LED

Torque wrench settings
Alternator cover bolts................................. 12 Nm
Alternator rotor bolt.................................. 75 Nm
Alternator stator bolts................................ 10 Nm
Neutral switch... 20 Nm
Oil level sensor bolts................................. 10 Nm
Starter motor long bolts............................... 3.4 Nm
Starter motor mounting bolts........................... 10 Nm

Electrical system 8•3

1 General information

All models have a 12 volt electrical system charged by a three-phase alternator with a separate regulator/rectifier.

The regulator maintains the charging system output within the specified range to prevent overcharging, and the rectifier converts the ac (alternating current) output of the alternator to dc (direct current) to power the lights and other components and to charge the battery. The alternator rotor is mounted on the left-hand end of the crankshaft.

The starting system includes the starter motor, the battery, the relay and the various wires and switches. If the engine kill switch is in the RUN position and the ignition (main) switch is ON, the starter relay allows the starter motor to operate only if the transmission is in neutral (neutral switch on) or, if the transmission is in gear, if the clutch lever is pulled into the handlebar and the sidestand is up. The starter motor is mounted on the top of the crankcase.

Note: *Keep in mind that electrical parts, once purchased, cannot be returned. To avoid unnecessary expense, make very sure the faulty component has been positively identified before buying a replacement part.*

2 Electrical system fault finding

⚠ **Warning:** *To prevent the risk of short circuits, the ignition (main) switch must always be OFF and the battery negative (–) terminal should be disconnected before any of the bike's other electrical components are disturbed. Don't forget to reconnect the terminal securely once work is finished or if battery power is needed for circuit testing.*

1 A typical electrical circuit consists of an electrical component, the fuse, switches, relays, etc. related to that component and the wiring and connectors that link the component to both the battery and the frame. To aid in locating a problem in any electrical circuit, refer to *Wiring Diagrams* at the end of this Chapter.

2 Before tackling any troublesome electrical circuit, first study the wiring diagram (see end of Chapter) thoroughly to get a complete picture of what makes up that individual circuit. Faults can often be tracked down by noting if other components related to that circuit are operating properly or not. If several components or circuits fail at one time, it may be that the fault lies in the fuse or earth (ground) connection, as several circuits are often routed through the same fuse and earth (ground) connections.

3 Electrical problems often stem from simple causes, such as loose or corroded connections or a blown fuse. Prior to any electrical fault finding, always check the condition of the fuse, wires and connections in the problem circuit visually. Intermittent failures can be especially frustrating, since you cannot always duplicate the failure when it is convenient to do a test. In such situations, it is good practice to clean all connections and terminals in the affected circuit, whether or not they appear to be good, and ensure that the connectors fit together tightly.

4 If testing instruments are going to be used, study the wiring diagram to plan where you will make the necessary connections in order to pinpoint the trouble spot accurately.

5 The basic tools needed for electrical fault finding include a battery and bulb test circuit, a continuity tester, a test light, and jumper wires. A multimeter capable of reading volts, ohms and amps is also very useful as an alternative to the above, and is necessary for performing more extensive tests and checks.

⚠ *If the ignition is switched ON for any checks, remember to switch it OFF again before proceeding further or removing any electrical component from the system.*

> **HAYNES HiNT** *Refer to Fault Finding Equipment in the Reference section for details of how to use electrical test equipment.*

3 Battery

Caution: *Be extremely careful when handling or working around the battery. The electrolyte is very caustic and an explosive gas (hydrogen) is given off when the battery is charging.*

Removal and installation

1 Remove the rider's seat (see Chapter 7).
2 Unscrew the negative (–) terminal bolt first and disconnect the lead from the battery **(see illustration)**. Lift up the insulating cover to access the positive (+) terminal, then unscrew the bolt and disconnect the lead. Release the battery strap and remove the battery from the bike **(see illustration)**.
3 On installation, ensure the battery terminals and lead ends are clean, then reconnect the leads, connecting the positive (+) terminal first.
4 Install the seat (see Chapter 7).

> **HAYNES HiNT** *Battery corrosion can be kept to a minimum by applying a layer of petroleum jelly to the terminals after the leads have been connected.*

Inspection and maintenance

5 The battery is of the maintenance-free (sealed) gel type, therefore requiring no specific

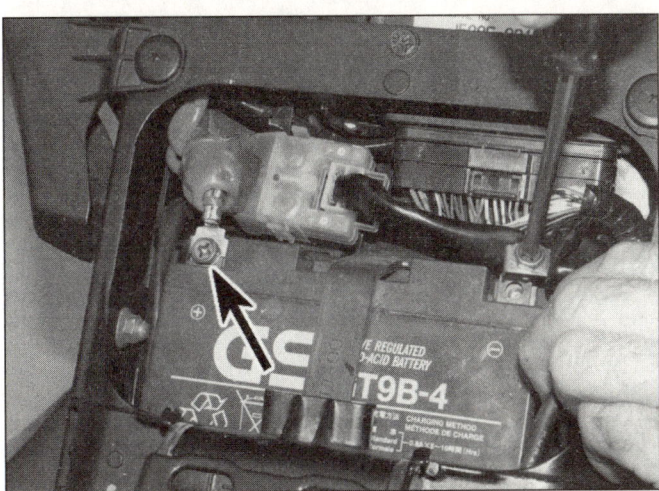

3.2a Disconnect the negative lead first, followed by the positive lead (arrowed)

3.2b Release the strap (arrowed) and remove the battery

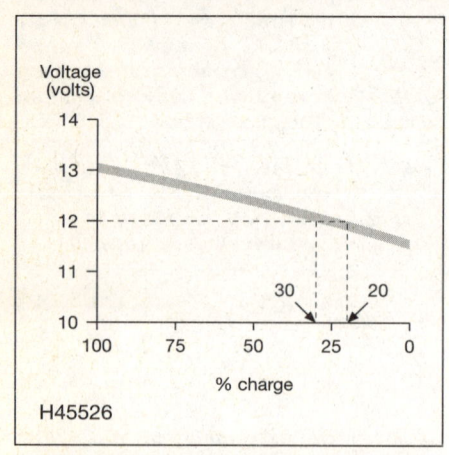

8•4 Electrical system

3.10 Measure the terminal voltage and assess the condition of the battery using the chart

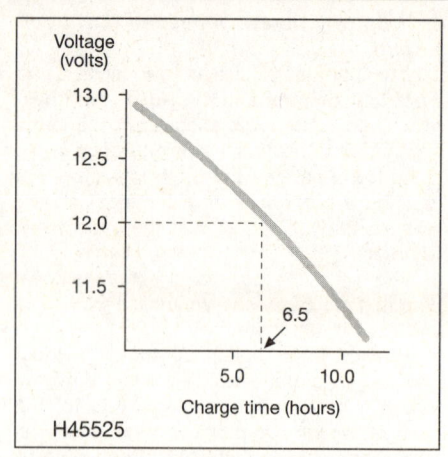

4.2 Measure the voltage to determine the required charging time

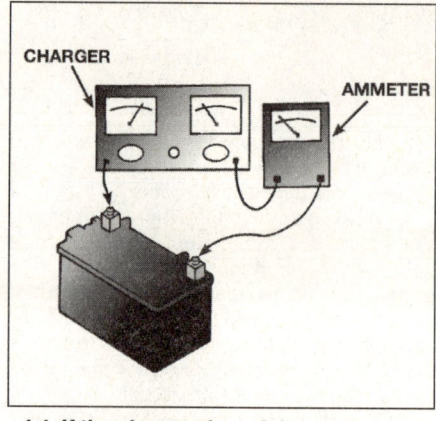

4.4 If the charger doesn't have ammeter built in, connect one in series as shown. DO NOT connect the ammeter between the battery terminals or it will be ruined

maintenance. Do not attempt to open the battery as resulting damage will mean it will be unfit for further use. However, the following checks should still be regularly performed.

6 Check the battery terminals and leads for tightness and corrosion. If corrosion is evident, unscrew the terminal bolts and disconnect the leads from the battery, disconnecting the negative (–) terminal first. Clean the terminals and lead ends with a wire brush or penknife and steel wool. Reconnect the leads, connecting the negative (–) terminal last, and apply a thin coat of petroleum jelly to the connections to slow further corrosion.

7 The battery case should be kept clean to prevent current leakage, which can discharge the battery over a period of time (especially when it sits unused). Remove the battery from the motorcycle and wash the outside of the case with a solution of baking soda and water. Rinse the battery thoroughly, then dry it.

8 Look for cracks in the case and replace the battery with a new one if any are found.

9 If the motorcycle sits unused for long periods of time, disconnect the leads from the battery terminals, negative (–) terminal first. Refer to Section 4 and charge the battery once every month to six weeks.

10 The condition of the battery can be assessed by measuring the voltage present at the battery terminals, and comparing the figure against the chart **(see illustration)**. Connect the voltmeter positive (+) probe to the battery positive (+) terminal, and the negative (–) probe to the battery negative (–) terminal. When fully charged, there should be 12.8 volts (or more) present. If the voltage falls below 12.0 volts the battery must be removed, disconnecting the negative (–) terminal first, and recharged as described in Section 4.

4 Battery charging

Caution: Be extremely careful when handling or working around the battery. The electrolyte is very caustic and an explosive gas (hydrogen) is given off when the battery is charging.

1 Ensure the charger is suitable for charging a 12V battery.

2 Remove the battery from the motorcycle (see Section 3). If not already done, refer to Section 3, Step 10, and check the open circuit voltage of the battery. Refer to the chart **(see illustration)** and read off the charging time required according to the voltage reading taken.

3 Connect the charger to the battery BEFORE switching the charger ON. Make sure that the positive (+) lead on the charger is connected to the positive (+) terminal on the battery, and the negative (–) lead is connected to the negative (–) terminal. The battery should be charged for the specified time, or until the voltage across the terminals reaches 12.8V (allow the battery to stabilise for 30 minutes after charging, before taking a voltage reading). Note that exceeding this charging time can cause the battery to overheat, buckling the plates and rendering it useless.

4 Charge the battery at the rate marked on its casing, i.e. 0.8A for 5 to 10 hours. Few owners will have access to an expensive current controlled charger, so if a normal domestic charger is used check that after a possible initial peak, the charge rate falls to a safe level **(see illustration)**. If the battery becomes hot during charging **STOP**. Further charging will cause damage. **Note:** *In emergencies the battery can be charged at a higher rate of around 3.0 amps for a period of 1 hour. However, this is not recommended and the low amp charge is by far the safer method of charging the battery.*

5 If the recharged battery discharges rapidly when left disconnected it is likely that an internal short caused by physical damage or sulphation has occurred. A new battery will be required. A sound battery will tend to lose its charge at about 1% per day.

6 Install the battery (see Section 3).

7 If the motorcycle sits unused for long periods of time, charge the battery once every month to six weeks and leave it disconnected. Alternatively purchase a trickle charger which allows the battery to remain connected.

5 Fuses

1 The electrical system is protected by fuses of different ratings.

- On Europe R and S (2003 and 2004) models the fuel injection system fuse and the turn signal, sidelight, tail light fuse are housed in the secondary fusebox under the rider's seat, and all others except the main fuse are housed in the primary fusebox, which is located under the left-hand cockpit trim panel.
- On US R and S (2003 and 2004) models all except the main fuse are held in the fusebox (primary) located under the left-hand cockpit trim panel.
- On T (2005) models the cooling fan fuses are housed in the secondary fusebox under the rider's seat, and all others except the main fuse are housed in the primary fusebox, which is located under the left-hand cockpit trim panel **(see illustrations)**.

5.1a The secondary fusebox (arrowed) is under the rider's seat

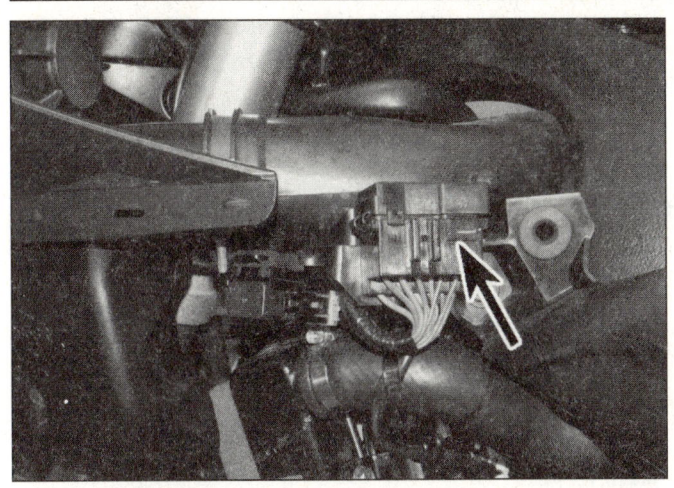

Electrical system 8•5

5.1b The primary fusebox (arrowed) is under the left-hand cockpit trim panel

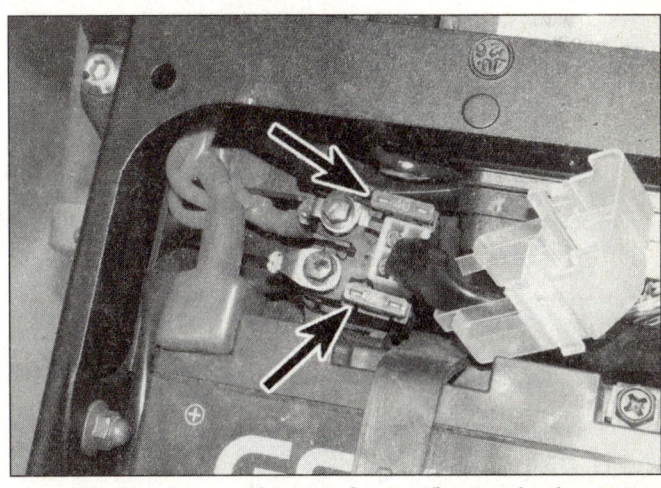

5.1c The main fuse and its spare (arrowed) are under the starter relay cover

- On all models the main fuse is integral with the starter relay, which is located under the rider's seat **(see illustration)**.

2 To access the primary fusebox fuses, remove the left-hand cockpit trim panel (see Chapter 7) and unclip the fusebox lid. To access the secondary fusebox fuses remove the rider's seat and unclip the fusebox lid. To access the main fuse, remove the rider's seat and unclip the starter relay cover.

3 The fuses can be removed and checked visually. If you can't pull the fuse out with your fingertips, use a suitable pair of pliers. A blown fuse is easily identified by a break in the element **(see illustration)**, or the fuse can be tested for continuity using an ohmmeter or continuity tester – if there is no continuity, it has blown. Each fuse is clearly marked with its rating and must only be replaced by a fuse of the same rating. Spare fuses are housed in the relevant fusebox, and a spare main fuse is housed in the starter relay. If a spare fuse is used, always replace it with a new one so that a spare of each rating is carried on the bike at all times.

⚠ **Warning: Never put in a fuse of a higher rating or bridge the terminals with any other substitute, however temporary it may be. Serious damage may be done to the circuit, or a fire may start.**

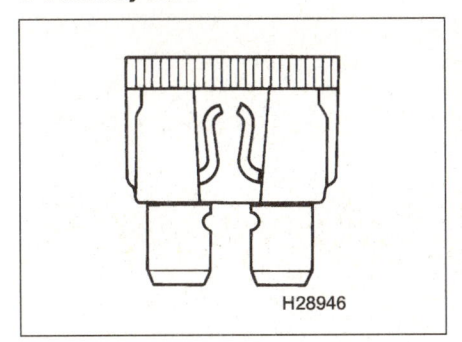

4 If a fuse blows, be sure to check the wiring circuit very carefully for evidence of a short-circuit. Look for bare wires and chafed, melted or burned insulation. If the fuse is renewed before the cause is located, the new fuse will blow immediately.

5 Occasionally a fuse will blow or cause an open-circuit for no obvious reason. Corrosion of the fuse ends and fusebox terminals may occur and cause poor fuse contact. If this happens, remove the corrosion with a penknife or steel wool, then spray the fuse end and terminals with electrical contact cleaner.

6 Lighting system check

Note: *If the ignition is switched ON for any checks, remember to switch it OFF again before proceeding further or removing any electrical component from the system.*

1 The battery provides power for operation of the headlight, tail light, brake light, turn signals and instrument cluster lights. If none of the lights operate, always check battery condition before proceeding. Low battery voltage indicates either a faulty battery or a defective charging system. Refer to Section 3 for battery checks and Section 30 for charging system tests. Also, check the condition of the fuses (see Section 5). When checking for a blown filament in a bulb, it is advisable to back up a visual check with a continuity test of the filament as it is not always apparent that a bulb has blown. When testing for continuity, remember that on tail light and turn signal bulbs it is often the metal body of the bulb that is the ground or earth.

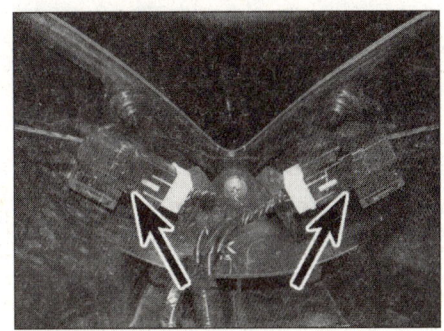

Headlight and relays

2 If the headlight fails to work, check the bulb first (see Section 7), and then the main fuse and headlight fuse. Next disconnect the headlight wiring connector **(see illustration 7.2b)** and check for battery voltage on the supply side of the wiring connector with a test light or multimeter – connect the negative probe of the multimeter to earth (black wire) and the positive probe to first the high beam terminal (black/yellow wire) and then the low beam terminal (black/blue wire) with the ignition switch ON. Don't forget to select either high or low beam as appropriate at the handlebar switch while conducting this test.

3 If no voltage is indicated at either terminal, check the wiring between the headlight connector, relays, dimmer switch and the ignition switch, referring to *Wiring Diagrams* at the end of the chapter, then check the switches themselves.

4 If voltage is indicated, check for continuity between the black wire connector terminal and earth (ground). If there is no continuity, check the earth (ground) circuit for an open or poor connection.

5 To check the headlight relays (one is the main ON/OFF relay, the other is the dimmer relay), first remove the windshield (see Chapter 7); the relays are mounted on top of the headlight unit **(see illustration)**. Disconnect the relevant relay wiring connector and make the checks on the relay side of the connector. Use a continuity tester (or a multimeter set to the resistance range) and a 12V battery with insulated jumper wires according to the relevant procedure below.

5.3 A blown fuse can be identified by a break in its element

6.5 Headlight relays (arrowed)

8•6 Electrical system

6 Test the ON/OFF relay by connecting the multimeter probes between the red/yellow and black/blue wire terminals on the relay; there should be no continuity. Leaving the meter in place, use the jumper wires to connect the battery positive (+) terminal to the blue/black wire terminal and the battery negative (−) terminal to the yellow/white wire terminal. The relay should now close and continuity (0 ohms) should be shown on the meter.

7 Test the dimmer relay by connecting the meter probes between the black/blue and black/yellow wire terminals on the relay; there should be no continuity. Leaving the meter in place, use the jumper wires to connect the battery positive (+) terminal to the yellow wire terminal and the battery negative (-) terminal to the black wire terminal. The relay should now close and continuity (0 ohms) should be shown on the meter.

Tail light

8 The tail light consists of a number of LEDs in a sealed unit. When a single LED fails it cannot be replaced with a new one, however the failure of one LED will not affect the function of the others. If enough LEDs have failed so as to impair the safe operation of the motorcycle, replace the tail light unit with a new one (Section 10).

9 If the tail light fails to work completely, first check the battery, main fuse and circuit fuse, then the wiring connector **(see illustration 10.2)**. Next check for battery voltage at the blue/red wire terminal on the supply side of the tail light wiring connector, with the ignition switch ON.

10 If no voltage is indicated, check the wiring between the tail light, fusebox and the ignition switch, then check the switch itself.

11 If voltage is indicated, check for continuity between the black wire terminal and earth (ground). If there is no continuity, check the earth (ground) circuit for a broken or poor connection.

Sidelight (European models)

12 If the sidelight fails to work with the ignition switch either in the ON position or in the P position check the battery, main fuse and circuit fuse, then check each bulb and the bulb terminals and wiring connector (see Section 7). Next check for battery voltage at the blue/red wire terminal on the supply side of the sidelight wiring connector, with the ignition switch first in the ON position, then in the P position.

13 If no voltage is indicated in either position, check the wiring between the sidelight, fusebox and the ignition switch, then check the switch (Section 18).

14 If voltage is indicated, check for continuity between the wiring connector terminals on the bulb side of the wiring connector and the corresponding terminals in the bulbholder; no continuity indicates a break in the circuit. If continuity is present, check for continuity between the black wire terminal and earth (ground). If there is no continuity, check the earth (ground) circuit for a broken or poor connection.

15 If the sidelight bulbs work with the ignition switch in one position (ON or P) but not the other then switch is faulty.

Brake light

16 The brake light consists of a number of LEDs in a sealed unit. When a single LED fails it cannot be replaced with a new one, however the failure of one LED will not affect the function of the others. If enough LEDs have failed so as to impair the safe operation of the motorcycle, replace the tail light unit with a new one (Section 10).

17 If the brake light fails to work completely, first check the battery, main fuse and circuit fuse, then the wiring connector **(see illustration 10.2)**. Next check for battery voltage at the yellow wire terminal on the supply side of the tail light wiring connector, with the ignition switch ON and the brake lever or pedal applied.

18 If no voltage is indicated, check the brake light switches (see Section 14), then the wiring between the tail light and the switches.

19 If voltage is indicated, check for continuity between the black wire terminal and earth (ground). If there is no continuity, check the earth (ground) circuit for a broken or poor connection.

Turn signal lights

20 If one light fails to work, check the bulb and the bulb terminals (see Section 12), then the wiring connector. If none of the turn signals work, first check the battery, main fuse and circuit fuse.

21 If the fuse is good, check the turn signal relay (see Section 11).

Instrument cluster lights

22 See Section 17.

7 Headlight bulbs and sidelight bulbs

Note: *The headlight bulbs are of the quartz-halogen type. Do not touch the bulb glass as skin acids will shorten the bulb's service life. If the bulb is accidentally touched, it should be wiped carefully when cold with a rag soaked in methylated spirit and dried before fitting.*

⚠️ **Warning: Allow the bulb time to cool before removing it if the headlight has been on.**

Headlight

1 Remove the relevant cockpit trim panel (see Chapter 7).

2 Remove the cover by turning it anti-clockwise, then disconnect the wiring connector from the back of the headlight bulb **(see illustrations)**.

3 Release the bulb retaining clip, noting how it fits, then remove the bulb from the back of the reflector **(see illustrations)**.

4 Fit the new bulb, bearing in mind the information in the **Note** above. Make sure the tabs on the bulb flange are aligned with the slots in the back of the reflector, and secure the bulb in position with the retaining clip.

5 Connect the wiring connector then fit the cover, turning it clockwise to lock it in place.

6 Check the operation of the headlight, then install the cockpit trim panel.

7.2a Remove the cover . . .

7.2b . . . and disconnect the wiring connector

7.3a Release the clip . . .

7.3b . . . and remove the bulb

Electrical system 8•7

> **HAYNES HINT:** *Always use a paper towel or dry cloth when handling new bulbs to prevent injury if the bulb should break, and to increase bulb life.*

Sidelight (European models)

7 Remove the relevant cockpit trim panel (see Chapter 7). Release the trim clip securing the side light cover by pushing its centre in then drawing the whole clip out – see Chapter 7 for illustration **(see illustration)**. Remove the cover **(see illustration)**.

8 Pull the bulbholder out of the back of the headlight unit, then carefully pull the bulb out of the holder **(see illustrations)**.

9 Fit the new bulb and check the operation of the light, then fit the bulbholder into the back of the headlight unit.

10 Reset the trim clip by drawing the centre out of the body. Fit the cover and push the centre of the trim clip in to lock it. Fit the cockpit trim panel (see Chapter 7).

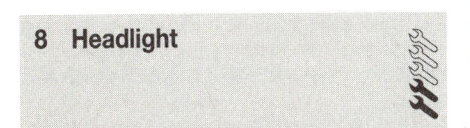

8 Headlight

7.7a Release the trim clip . . .

7.7b . . . then remove the cover

7.8a Draw the bulbholder out . . .

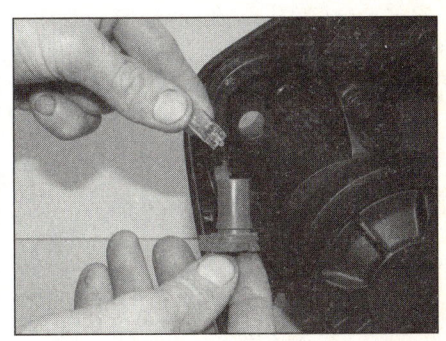

7.8b . . . and replace the bulb with a new one

Removal and installation

1 Remove the fairing (see Chapter 7).
2 Remove the screws securing the headlight unit and lift it out of the fairing **(see illustration)**.
3 Remove the headlight bulbs and the sidelight bulbholders, then unclip the relays from the front of the headlight unit **(see illustration 6.5)** and remove the wiring sub-loom, noting how it fits.
4 Installation is the reverse of removal. Make sure all the wiring is correctly connected and secured. Check the operation of the headlight and sidelight. Check the headlight aim.

Headlight aim

Note: *An improperly adjusted headlight may cause problems for oncoming traffic or provide poor, unsafe illumination of the road ahead. Before adjusting the headlight aim, be sure to consult with local traffic laws and regulations – for UK models refer to MOT Test Checks in the Reference section.*

5 The headlight beams can adjusted both horizontally and vertically. Before making any adjustment, check that the tyre pressures are correct and the suspension is adjusted as required. Make any adjustments to the headlight aim with the machine on level ground, with the fuel tank half full and with an assistant sitting on the seat. If the bike is usually ridden with a passenger on the back, have a second assistant to do this.

6 Remove the cockpit trim panels to access the beam adjusters (see Chapter 7).
7 Vertical adjustment is made by turning the adjuster screw on the top of the relevant beam unit **(see illustration)**. Turn it clockwise to move the beam up, and anti-clockwise to move it down.
8 Horizontal adjustment is made by turning the adjuster screw on the inner side of the relevant beam unit **(see illustration 8.7)**. For the left-hand beam turn the adjuster clockwise

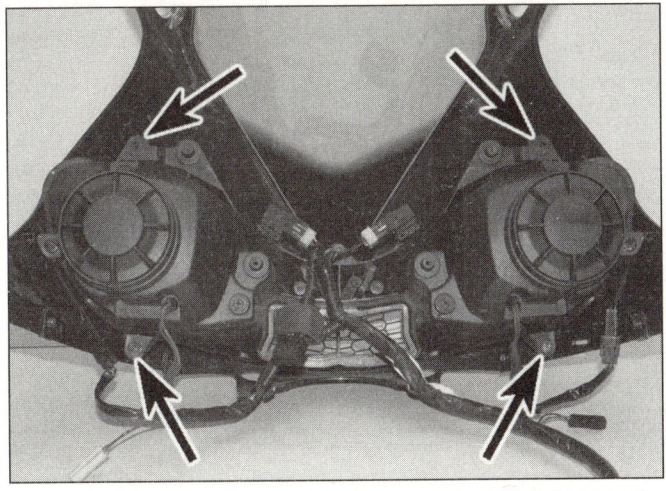

8.2 Undo the screws (arrowed) and remove the headlight from the fairing

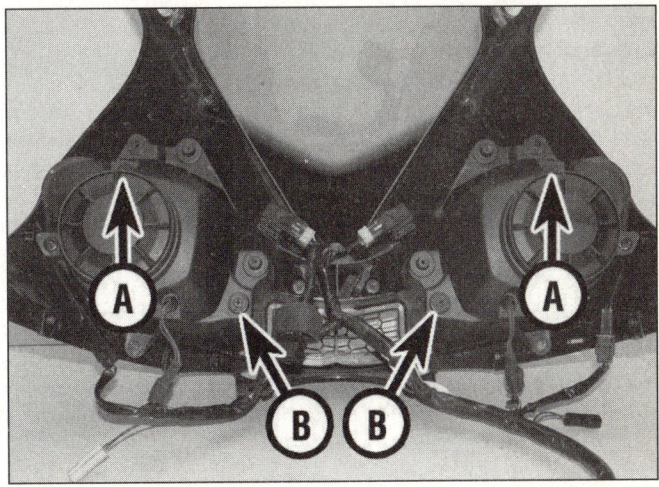

8.7 Vertical alignment adjusters (A), horizontal alignment adjusters (B)

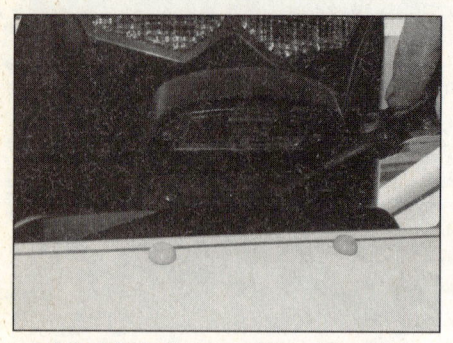

8•8 Electrical system

9.2a Undo the screws securing the light . . .

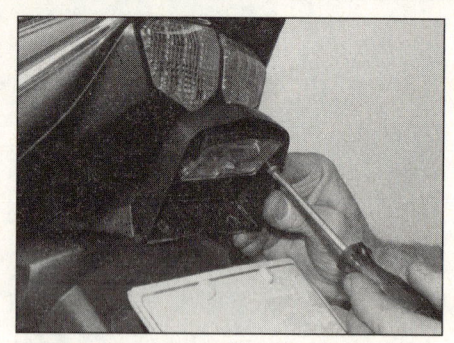

9.2b . . . then undo the screws securing the lens

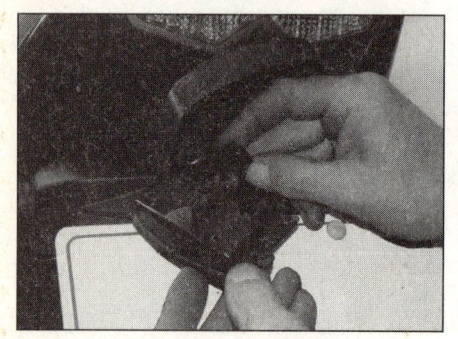

9.3a Remove the bulbholder . . .

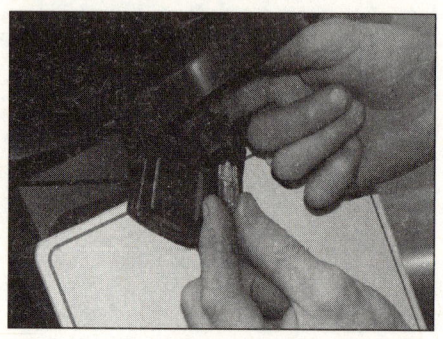

9.3b . . . then remove the bulb from the holder

to move the beam to the right, and anti-clockwise to move it to the left. For the right-hand beam turn the adjuster clockwise to move the beam to the left, and anti-clockwise to move it to the right.

9 Brake/tail light LEDs and licence plate bulb

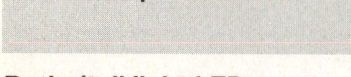

Brake/tail light LEDs

1 If one or more of the LEDs within the brake or tail light unit has failed, replace the entire tail light assembly with a new one – individual LEDs are not available (see Section 10).

Licence plate light bulb

Note: *It is a good idea to use a paper towel or dry cloth when handling a new bulb to prevent injury if it breaks, and to increase bulb life.*

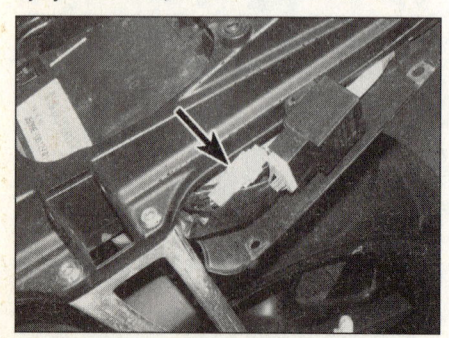

2 Undo the screws securing the licence plate light unit to the rear mudguard and displace it to access the lens screws **(see illustration)**. Undo the lens screws and remove the lens **(see illustration)**.
3 Release the bulbholder **(see illustration)**. Carefully pull the bulb out of its socket and replace it with a new one **(see illustration)**.
4 Fit the bulbholder and check the light works, then fit the lens and the light unit

10 Tail light unit

1 Remove the seat cowling (see Chapter 7).
2 Disconnect the tail light wiring connector and feed the wiring back to the light noting its routing **(see illustration)**.
3 Release the trim clips securing the light unit and remove it **(see illustration)**. Refer to Chapter 7, Section 1 for details on how to release the trim clips, if required.
4 Installation is the reverse of removal. Check the operation of the tail light and the brake light, then replace the seat cowling.

11 Turn signal circuit check

1 Most turn signal problems are the result of a burned-out bulb or corroded socket. This is especially true when the turn signals function properly in one direction, but fail to flash in the other direction. Check the bulbs and the sockets (see Section 12) and the wiring connectors. Also, check the main fuse and circuit fuse (see Section 5) and the switch (see Section 19).
2 The battery provides power for operation of the turn signals, so if they do not operate, check the battery voltage. Low battery voltage indicates either a faulty battery or a defective charging system. Refer to Section 3 for battery checks and Section 30 for charging system tests.
3 If the bulbs, sockets, connectors, fuses, switch and battery are good, remove the rider's seat (see Chapter 7) and check the turn signal relay as follows **(see illustration)**.
4 Disconnect the relay connector and check for voltage at the blue/red wire terminal in the connector with the ignition ON. If no voltage is indicated, refer to the appropriate wiring diagram at the end of this Chapter and check the wiring between the relay, fusebox and the ignition (main) switch for continuity.
5 If voltage is indicated, reconnect the relay connector and check for voltage at the brown/white wire terminal in the connector with the ignition ON, and with the signal switch turned to either LEFT or RIGHT.
6 If no voltage is indicated, replace the relay with a new one.
7 If voltage is indicated, check the wiring between the relay, turn signal switch and turn signal lights for continuity.

10.2 Disconnect the wiring connector (arrowed)

10.3 Release the trim clips (arrowed) and remove the tail light

11.3 Turn signal relay (arrowed)

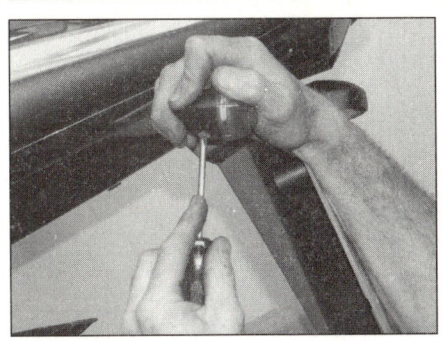

Electrical system 8•9

12.1 Undo the screw and remove the lens

12.2 Release the bulb and replace it with a new one

12.3 Make sure the lens locates correctly

12 Turn signal bulbs

1 Remove the screw securing the turn signal lens and remove the lens, noting how it fits **(see illustration)**.
2 Push the bulb into the holder and twist it anti-clockwise to remove it **(see illustration)**. Check the socket terminals for corrosion and clean them, if necessary. Line up the pins of the new bulb with the slots in the socket, then push the bulb in and turn it clockwise until it locks into place. **Note:** *US models fitted with front running lights, use dual filament bulbs which have offset pins and can only be fitted one way in their holders.*
3 Fit the lens onto the holder, making sure the tab locates correctly **(see illustration)**. Do not overtighten the screw as the lens or threads could be damaged.

13 Turn signal assemblies

Front

1 Remove the fairing side panel from the side concerned (see Chapter 7)
2 Unclip the turn signal mounting plate and draw it off the wiring **(see illustration)**. Push the turn signal stem through the panel, noting how it fits and remove the turn signal **(see illustrations)**. Take care not to snag the wiring as you pull it through the panel.
3 Installation is the reverse of removal. Make sure the wiring is correctly routed and securely connected. Check the operation of the turn signals.

Rear

4 Remove the seat cowling (see Chapter 7).
5 Trace the wiring back from the turn signal and disconnect it at the connectors **(see illustration)**. Feed it through to the turn signal, noting its routing.
6 Unclip the turn signal mounting plate and draw it off the wiring **(see illustration)**. Push the turn signal stem through the mudguard, noting how it fits and remove the turn signal.

Take care not to snag the wiring as you pull it through the panel.
7 Installation is the reverse of removal. Make sure the wiring is correctly routed and securely connected. Check the operation of the turn signals.

14 Brake light switches

Circuit check

1 Before checking the switches, check the brake light circuit (see Section 6).
2 The front brake light switch is mounted on the underside of the brake master cylinder. Disconnect the wiring connectors from the

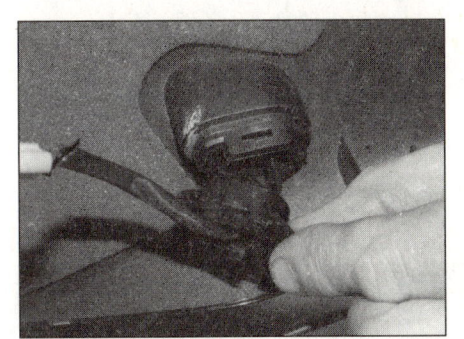

13.2a Release the mounting plate . . .

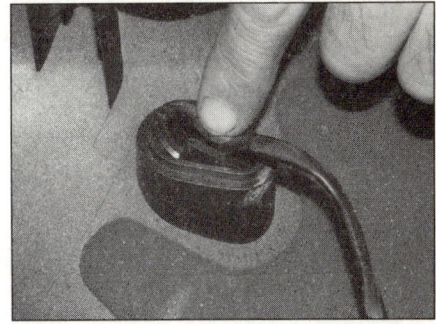

13.2b . . . then push the stem through . . .

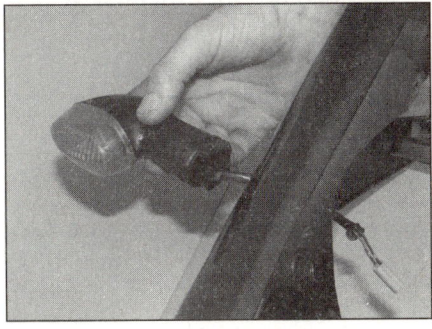

13.2c . . . and remove the turn signal

13.5 Disconnect the relevant wiring connector

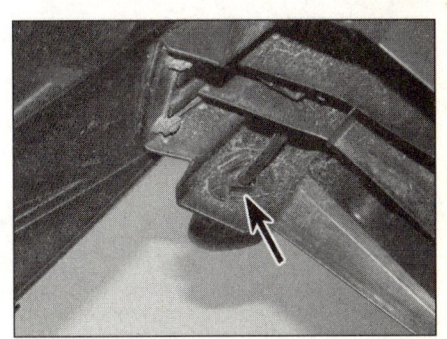

13.6 Release the mounting plate (arrowed) and push the stem through

8•10 Electrical system

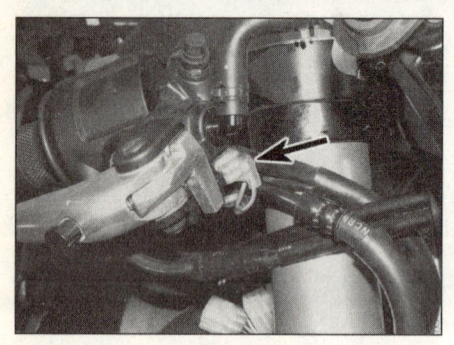

14.2 Front brake switch wiring connectors (arrowed)

14.3 Rear brake switch wiring connector

14.8 Note the routing of the wiring . . .

switch **(see illustration)**. Using a continuity tester, connect its probes to the terminals of the switch. With the brake lever at rest, there should be no continuity. With the brake lever applied, there should be continuity. If the switch does not behave as described, replace it with a new one.

3 The rear brake light switch is mounted on the inside of the rider's right-hand footrest bracket, above the brake pedal. Raise and support the fuel tank (see Chapter 4) to access its 2-pin brown wiring connector **(see illustration)**. Trace the wiring from the switch and disconnect it at the connector. Using a continuity tester, connect the probes to the two terminals on the switch side of the wiring connector. With the brake pedal at rest, there should be no continuity. With the brake pedal applied, there should be continuity. If the switch does not behave as described, replace it with a new one.

4 If the switches are good, connect the wiring and check for voltage at the brown wire terminal on the supply side of the connector with the ignition switch ON. If no voltage is indicated, check the wiring between the switch, fusebox and the ignition switch (see *Wiring Diagrams* at the end of this Chapter).

Switch removal and installation

Front brake light switch

5 The switch is mounted on the underside of the brake master cylinder. Disconnect the wiring connectors from the switch **(see illustration 14.2)**.
6 Undo the single screw securing the switch to the bottom of the master cylinder and remove the switch.
7 Installation is the reverse of removal. The switch is not adjustable.

Rear brake light switch

8 The switch is mounted on the inside of the rider's right-hand footrest bracket. Raise and support the fuel tank (see Chapter 4) to access the 2-pin brown wiring connector, then trace the wiring from the switch and disconnect it at the connector **(see illustration 14.3)**. Feed it through to the switch, noting its routing, and cut the cable tie on the footrest bracket **(see illustration)**.
9 Detach the lower end of the switch spring from the pin on the back of the brake pedal **(see illustration)**. Unscrew the bolt and remove the washer securing the switch bracket to the footrest bracket and remove the switch assembly.

10 Thread the switch out of it's adjuster nut in the bracket, then press the nut ears in and draw it out of the bracket – note the bush and spacer in the switch bracket and remove them if they are loose.
11 Installation is the reverse of removal, noting the following:
● Replace the switch bracket bush with a new one if it is worn or perished.
● Ensure the end of the switch spring is correctly located in the groove on the brake pedal pin.
● Secure the wiring to the footrest bracket with a new cable tie.
● Adjust the switch as necessary (see Chapter 1, Section 12).

15 Instrument cluster removal and installation

1 Remove the fairing (see Chapter 7).
2 Undo the screws securing the instrument cluster to the fairing stay **(see illustration)**. Pull the cluster off the fairing stay, noting how the three pins on the back locate in three bushes on the stay.

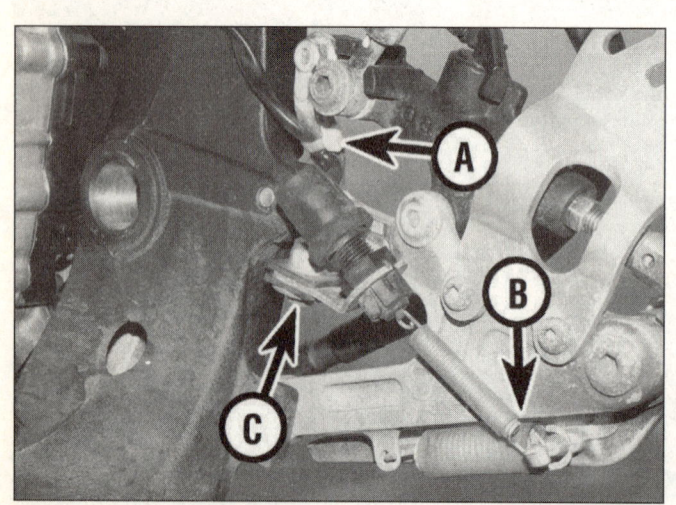

14.9 . . . and release it from the cable tie (A). Unhook the springs (B), then unscrew the bolt (C) and remove the switch

15.2 Undo the screws (arrowed) and remove the instrument cluster

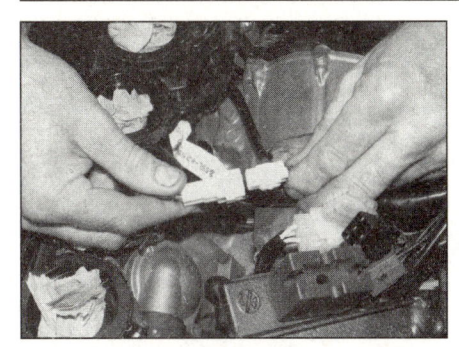

Electrical system 8•11

16.6 Disconnect the speed sensor wiring connector

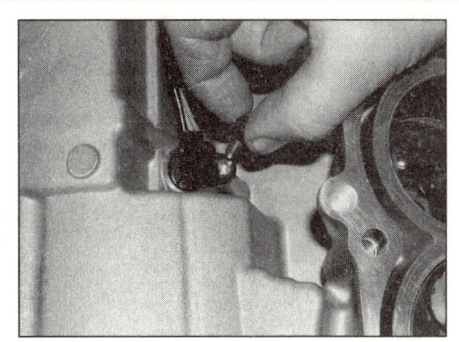

16.8 Undo the screw and remove the sensor

3 Installation is the reverse of removal. If the bushes in the stay are worn or perished replace them with new ones.

16 Instrument check and replacement

Check

1 If all instrument and display functions fail at the same time, check the circuit fuse and the wiring and connectors, referring to the *Wiring Diagrams* at the end of the Chapter.

Tachometer

2 No test details are available for the tachometer. If it fails a new printed circuit board must be installed (see Steps 10 and 11).

Oil level display

3 The oil level display is controlled by the oil level sensor – refer to Section 26 for test details.

Coolant temperature display

4 The coolant temperature display is controlled by the coolant temperature sensor – refer to Chapter 3 for test details.

Speedometer

5 The speedometer is controlled by the speed sensor, which is mounted in the top of the crankcase underneath the starter motor. To test the output from the sensor, place the motorcycle on an auxiliary stand so the rear wheel is off the ground. Make sure the transmission is in neutral.

6 Raise or remove the fuel tank (see Chapter 4). Disconnect the sensor wiring connector **(see illustration)**. Connect the positive (+) probe of a multimeter set to the DC20V scale to the white/yellow wire terminal on the wiring loom side of the connector, and connect the negative (–) probe to the blue wire terminal. Turn the ignition ON. Turn the rear wheel in its normal direction of rotation and check the reading on the multimeter – it should be seen to fluctuate between 0.6 and 4.8 volts as the wheel is turned. If not, and if the wiring between the speed sensor and the connector is good, replace the speed sensor with a new one (Steps 8 and 9).

7 If the multimeter reading is correct, refer to *Wiring Diagrams* at the end of this Chapter and check the wiring and connectors between the sensor, ECU and the instrument cluster for continuity. If no fault can be found, the instrument cluster printed circuit board is faulty and must be replaced with a new one (Steps 10 and 11).

8 To fit a new sensor, first remove the starter motor (see Section 28). Trace the wiring from the sensor and disconnect it at the wiring connector **(see illustration 16.6)**. Remove the screw and withdraw the sensor from the crankcase **(see illustration)**. Discard the O-ring.

9 Install the sensor using a new O-ring, and tighten the fixing screw. Connect the sensor wiring connector, then install the starter motor (see Section 28).

Replacement

10 The tachometer and LCD display, along with the select and reset buttons and all LEDs are part of the instrument cluster printed circuit board inside the cluster housing.

11 In the event of an instrument or display failure undo the six screws on the rear cover, then remove the cover and carefully lift the circuit board/instrument assembly out and replace it with a new one **(see illustrations)**.

17 Instrument and warning lights

1 The warning and indicator functions (neutral, high beam, turn signals, fuel level, oil level and coolant temperature) are all illuminated by LEDs on the instrument cluster circuit board.

2 The fuel level indicator light should come on for a few seconds when the ignition is switched ON as a check of the LED, and then go off. If the light does not go off, first check the fuel level, and if the level is good check the LED circuit (see Step 4). If the light does not come on, test the LED as described below.

3 The combined warning LED for the engine oil level and coolant temperature should also come on as a check of the LED, and then go off. Refer to Chapter 26 of this Chapter and Section 5 of Chapter 3 for checking of the circuits.

4 To test whether an LED has failed, remove the instrument cluster (see Section 15). Using a fully charged 12V battery and two suitable jumper wires, refer to *Wiring Diagrams* at the end of this Chapter and connect the positive (+) and negative (-) battery terminals to the relevant terminals on the instrument cluster for the LED being tested.

5 If the LED comes on, the fault lies elsewhere in the electrical circuit for the LED in question. Check the signal fuse and wiring, and the operation of the component linked to the LED.

6 If the LED has failed a new instrument circuit board must be installed (see Section 16).

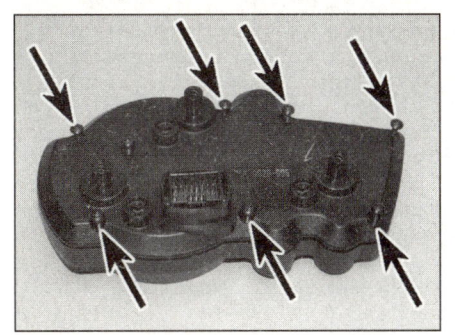

16.11a Undo the screws (arrowed) . . .

16.11b . . . and remove the cover

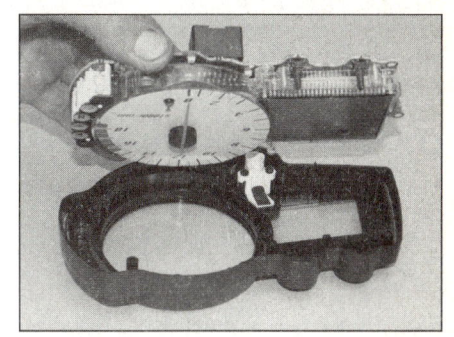

16.11c Remove the PCB, noting how it locates

8•12 Electrical system

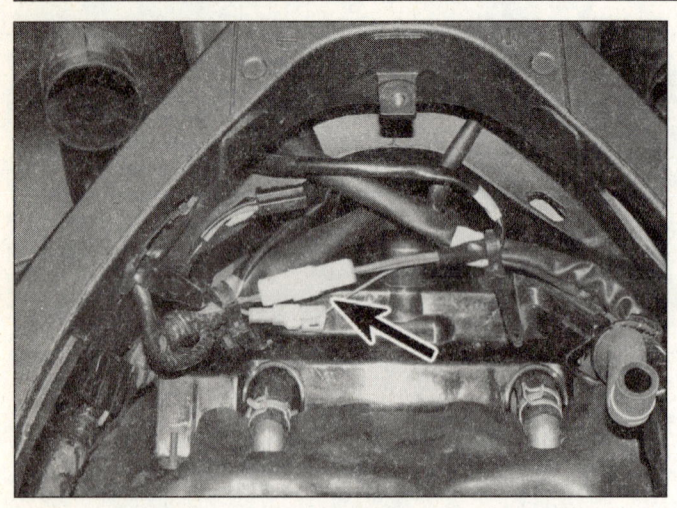

18.1 Ignition switch wiring connectors (arrowed)

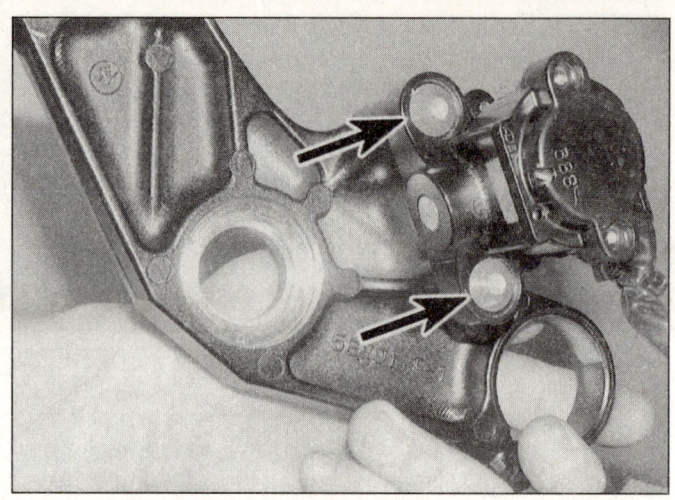

18.7 Remove the shear-head bolts (arrowed) as described

18 Ignition (main) switch

⚠️ **Warning: To prevent the risk of short circuits, disconnect the battery negative (–) lead before making any ignition (main) switch checks.**

Check

1 Remove the air filter housing (see Chapter 4). Trace the ignition (main) switch wiring back from the switch and disconnect it at the white connectors **(see illustration)**. Make the checks on the switch side of the connector.
2 Using a multimeter or a continuity tester, check the continuity of the connector terminal pairs (see *Wiring Diagrams* at the end of this Chapter). Continuity should exist between the terminals connected by a solid line on the diagram when the switch key is turned to the indicated position.
3 If the switch fails any of the tests, replace it with a new one.

Removal

4 Disconnect the battery negative (–) lead. Remove the air filter housing (see Chapter 4), trace the ignition (main) switch wiring back from the switch and disconnect it at the connectors **(see illustration 18.1)**. Release the wiring from any cable ties and feed it back to the switch noting the correct routing. Where an immobiliser is fitted, disconnect its wiring at the connector **(see illustration 21.27b in Chapter 4)**.
5 Remove the fairing (see Chapter 7), then displace the handlebars and remove the top yoke (see Chapter 5, Sections 5 and 9).
6 Where an immobiliser is fitted, detach the receiver from the top yoke as described in Chapter 4, Section 27.
7 Two shear-head security bolts mount the switch to the underside of the top yoke **(see illustration)**. The heads of the bolts must be tapped around using a suitable punch or drift, or drilled off, before the switch can be removed. To do this, mount the yoke in a vice equipped with soft jaws to avoid damaging the yoke.
8 Remove the bolts and discard them as new ones must be used on reassembly, then withdraw the switch from the top yoke.

Installation

9 Installation is the reverse of removal, noting the following:
● Ensure the switch is installed in the yoke the correct way round before tightening the shear-head bolts.
● Obtain the correct type shear-head bolts from a Yamaha dealer – do not use another type of bolt. Tighten the bolts until their heads shear off.
● Ensure the wiring is securely connected and correctly routed.
● Ensure all top yoke and handlebar nuts and bolts are tightened to the torque settings specified in Chapter 5.

19 Handlebar switch check

1 Generally speaking, the handlebar switch units are reliable and trouble-free. Most problems, when they do occur, are caused by dirty or corroded contacts, but wear and breakage of internal parts is a possibility that should not be overlooked. If breakage does occur, the entire switch unit and related wiring harness will have to be replaced with a new one, as individual parts are not available.
2 The switches can be checked for continuity using an multimeter or a continuity tester.
3 Remove the right-hand fairing side panel and its inner trim section to access the switch wiring connectors (see Chapter 7). Trace the wiring harness of the switch in question back to its connector (either blue or off-white) and disconnect it **(see illustration)**.
4 Check for continuity between the terminals of the switch harness with the switch in the various positions (i.e. switch OFF – no continuity, switch ON – continuity) – see *Wiring Diagrams* at the end of this Chapter.
5 If the continuity check indicates a problem exists, refer to Section 20, displace the switch from the handlebar and spray the switch contacts with electrical contact cleaner. If they are accessible, the contacts can be scraped clean with a penknife or polished with steel wool **(see illustration)**. If switch components are damaged or broken, it should be obvious when the switch is disassembled.

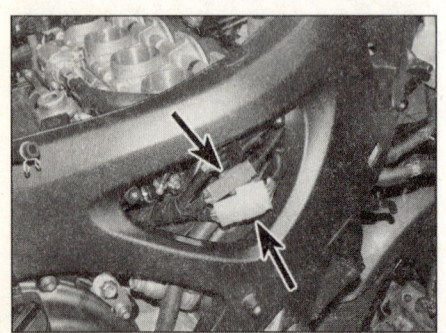

19.3 Handlebar switch wiring connectors (arrowed)

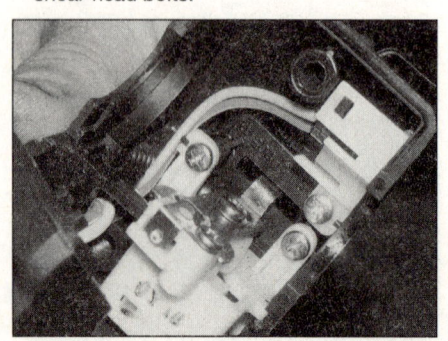

19.5 Keep the switch internals clean and corrosion-free

Electrical system 8•13

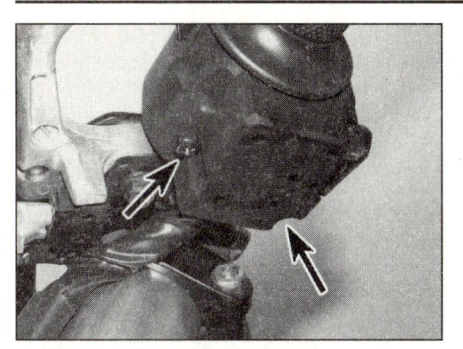

20.4 Left-hand switch housing screws (arrowed)

21.2 Pull the wiring connector off the switch (arrowed)

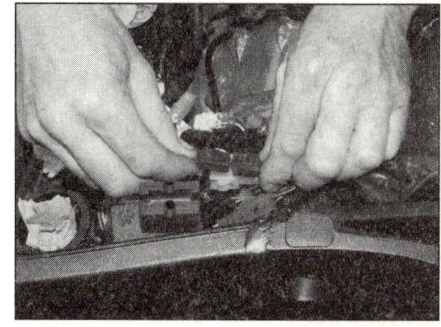

22.2 Disconnect the sidestand switch wiring connector

20 Handlebar switch removal and installation

Removal

1 If the switch unit is to be removed from the motorcycle, rather than just displaced from the handlebar, remove the right-hand fairing side panel and its trim section (see Chapter 7) and trace the wiring harness of the switch in question back to its connector (either blue or off-white) and disconnect it **(see illustration 19.3)**. Feed the wiring back to the switch, freeing it from any clips and ties and noting its correct routing.
2 Disconnect the wiring connectors from the brake light switch (if removing the right-hand switch unit) or the clutch switch (if removing the left-hand switch unit) **(see illustration 14.2 or 23.2)**.
3 To remove the right-hand switch, refer to Chapter 4 for details on detaching the throttle cables, which involves separating the switch unit halves and detaching them from the handlebar.
4 To remove the left-hand switch unscrew the switch unit screws and free the unit from the handlebar by separating the halves **(see illustration)**.

Installation

5 Installation is the reverse of removal. Refer to Chapter 4 for installation of the throttle cables. Make sure the locating pin in the switch unit locates in the hole in the handlebar. Make sure the wiring is securely connected and correctly routed and tied to the frame.

21 Neutral switch

Check

1 Before checking the electrical circuit, check the circuit fuse (see Section 5).
2 The switch is located on the back of the engine in front of the rear shock absorber. Make sure the transmission is in neutral. Disconnect the wiring connector from the switch **(see illustration)**.
3 With the connector disconnected and the ignition switched ON, the neutral light should be out. If not, the wire between the connector and instrument cluster must be earthed (grounded) at some point.
4 Check for continuity between the terminal on the switch and the crankcase – with the transmission in neutral, there should be continuity; with the transmission in gear, there should be no continuity. If there is continuity when in gear or no continuity when in neutral, remove the switch (see below), and check that the contact plunger is not damaged or seized in the switch body.
5 If the switch is good, check the wire between the connector, relay assembly and the instrument cluster for continuity. Refer to Section 24 for details of checking the diode in the relay assembly.
6 Check for battery voltage at the brown wire terminal on the wiring loom side of the instrument cluster connector with the ignition ON. If no voltage is indicated, refer to the wiring diagram at the end of this Chapter and check for continuity between the connector and the circuit fuse.
7 If voltage is indicated, check the LED in the instrument cluster (see Section 17), then check the starter circuit cut-off relay (Section 24) and other components in the starter circuit as described in the relevant Sections of this Chapter. If all components are good, check the wiring between the various components (see *Wiring Diagrams* at the end of this Chapter).

Removal and installation

8 The switch is located on the back of the engine. Pull the wire connector off the switch terminal, then unscrew the switch and withdraw it from the casing **(see illustration 21.2)**. Discard the sealing washer as a new one must be used on reassembly.
9 Install the switch using a new sealing washer and tighten it to the torque setting specified at the beginning of this Chapter.
10 Connect the wire to the switch terminal and check the operation of the neutral light.

22 Sidestand switch

Check

1 The sidestand switch is mounted on the back of the sidestand bracket. The switch is part of the safety circuit which prevents or stops the engine running if the transmission is in gear whilst the sidestand is down, and prevents the engine from starting if the transmission is in gear unless the sidestand is up and the clutch lever is pulled in. Before checking the electrical circuit, check the main and ignition fuses (see Section 5).
2 To access the wiring connector, raise or remove the fuel tank (see Chapter 4). Trace the wiring from the switch and disconnect it at the 2-pin blue connector **(see illustration)**.
3 Check the operation of the switch using a multimeter or continuity tester. Connect the meter probes to the terminals on the switch side of the connector. With the sidestand up there should be continuity (zero resistance) between the terminals, and with the stand down there should be no continuity (infinite resistance).
4 If the switch does not perform as expected, check the plunger is not seized in the switch body. If the plunger is fine replace the switch with a new one.
5 If the switch is good, check the starter circuit cut-off relay (Section 24) and other components in the starter circuit as described in the relevant Sections of this Chapter. If all components are good, check the wiring between the various components (see *Wiring Diagrams* at the end of this Chapter).

Renewal

6 The sidestand switch is mounted on the back of the sidestand bracket. Raise or remove the fuel tank (see Chapter 4), then trace the wiring from the switch and disconnect it at the connector **(see illustration 22.2)**. Release the wiring from any cable ties and feed it back to the switch noting its routing.
7 Remove the lower fairing (see Chapter 7), then unscrew the nuts and remove the bolts securing

8•14 Electrical system

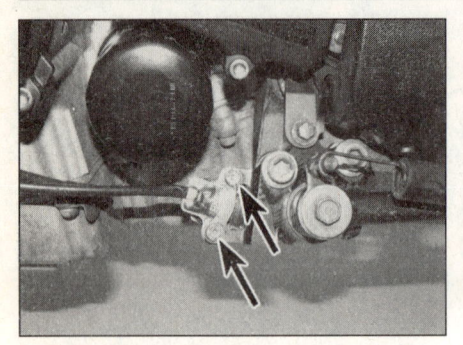

22.7 Sidestand switch mounting bolts (arrowed)

the switch to the bracket and remove the switch **(see illustration)**.

8 Install the new switch and tighten the bolts/nuts. Ensure the tab on the sidestand engages the switch plunger correctly.

9 Make sure the wiring is correctly routed up to the connector and retained by all the necessary clips and ties. Reconnect the wiring connector and check the operation of the switch, then install the fuel tank and lower fairing.

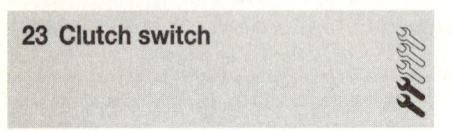

23 Clutch switch

Check

1 The clutch switch is mounted on the underside of the clutch lever bracket. The switch is part of the safety circuit which prevents or stops the engine running if the transmission is in gear whilst the sidestand is down, and prevents the engine from starting if the transmission is in gear unless the sidestand is up and the clutch lever is pulled in. The switch is not adjustable.

2 To check the switch, disconnect the wiring connectors **(see illustration)**. Connect the probes of a multimeter or a continuity tester to the two switch terminals. There should be continuity (zero resistance) with the clutch lever pulled in, and no continuity (infinite resistance) with the clutch lever out.

3 If the switch is good, check the starter circuit cut-off relay (Section 24) and other components in the starter circuit as described in the relevant Sections of this Chapter. If

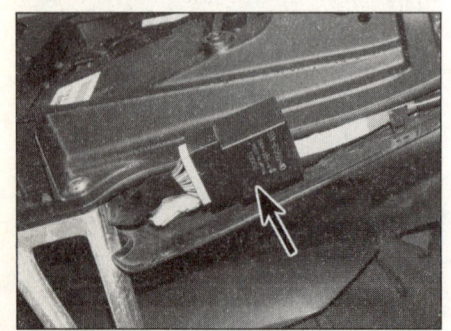

24.2 Relay assembly (arrowed)

23.2 Clutch switch wiring connectors (arrowed)

all components are good, check the wiring between the various components (see *Wiring Diagrams* at the end of this Chapter).

Renewal

4 The clutch switch is mounted on the underside of the clutch lever bracket.
5 Disconnect the wiring connectors **(see illustration 23.2)**, then undo the screw and remove the switch.
6 Installation is the reverse of removal.

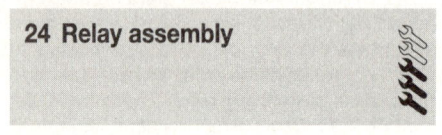

24 Relay assembly

Starter circuit cut-off relay and diodes

1 The starter circuit cut-off relay and its associated diodes are contained within the relay assembly. They are part of the safety circuit which prevents or stops the engine running if the transmission is in gear whilst the sidestand is down, and prevents the engine from starting if the transmission is in gear unless the sidestand is up and the clutch lever is pulled in.

2 The relay assembly is mounted on the left-hand side of the rear sub-frame **(see illustration)**. Remove the seat cowling for access (see Chapter 7).

3 Disconnect the battery negative (–) lead, then displace the relay and disconnect the wiring connector. Move the relay assembly to the bench for testing. Refer to the wiring diagram for your model (see end of Chapter) and the following procedures:

4 To check the operation of the relay, first connect a multimeter set to the ohms x 1 scale, or a continuity tester, between the two blue/white wire terminals of the relay. There should be no continuity.

5 Leave the multimeter or continuity tester connected to the relay. Now, using a fully charged 12V battery and two suitable jumper wires, connect the battery positive (+) terminal to the relay's red/black wire terminal and the battery negative (–) terminal to the relay's black/yellow wire terminal. With voltage applied, the test equipment should show continuity. If it doesn't, replace the relay assembly with a new one.

6 The diodes contained within the relay assembly can be checked by performing a continuity test – diodes should show continuity in one direction and no continuity when the meter or tester probes are reversed. Connect the multimeter (set to ohms) or continuity tester across the wire terminals for the diode being tested – refer to the appropriate wiring diagram at the end of this Chapter if necessary, and perform the following tests. If any diode shows the same condition in both directions it is faulty, and the relay assembly must be replaced with a new one.

Positive probe (+)	Negative probe (-)	Result
Light blue	Black/yellow	No continuity
Black/yellow	Light blue	Continuity
Light blue	Blue/yellow	No continuity
Blue/yellow	Light blue	Continuity
Blue/black	Blue/yellow	No continuity
Blue/yellow	Blue/black	Continuity
Light blue	Light blue/white	No continuity
Light blue/white	Light blue	Continuity
Black/red	Black/yellow	No continuity
Black/yellow	Black/red	Continuity

7 If the cut-out relay and diodes are good, but the starting system fault still exists, check all other components in the starting circuit (i.e. the neutral switch, side stand switch, clutch switch, starter switch and starter relay) as described in the relevant Sections of this Chapter. If all components are good, check the wiring between the various components (see *Wiring Diagrams* at the end of this Chapter).

8 Installation is the reverse of removal.

Fuel pump relay

9 Refer to Chapter 4, Section 8.

25 Horn

Check

1 If the horn doesn't work, first check the circuit fuse (see Section 5) and the battery (see Section 3).

2 The horn is mounted on the bottom yoke. Remove either the left or right-hand fairing side panel for best access to it (see Chapter 7).

3 Pull the wiring connectors off the horn terminals. Using two jumper wires, apply battery voltage directly to the terminals on the horn. If the horn sounds, check the switch (see Section 19) and the wiring between the switch and the horn (see *Wiring Diagrams* at the end of this Chapter).

Electrical system 8•15

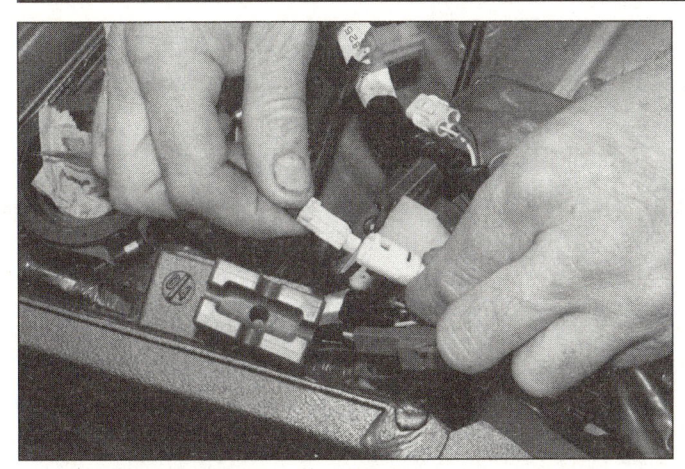

26.5 Disconnect the oil level sensor wiring connector

26.6 Unscrew the bolt to free the wiring from the clamp (A), then unscrew the bolts (B) and withdraw the sensor

4 If the horn doesn't sound, replace it with a new one.

Removal and installation

5 Remove either the left or right-hand fairing side panel (see Chapter 7) for best access to the horn and pull the wiring connectors off the horn terminals.

6 Unscrew the bolt securing the horn and remove it from the bike.

7 Install the horn and tighten the bolt securely. Connect the wiring connectors and check the operation of the horn, then install the fairing panel.

26 Oil level sensor

Check

1 The oil level warning light will come on for a few seconds when the ignition is switched ON as a check of the warning light LED. It should then go out and the motorcycle can be started. If the warning light remains on and/or the oil level symbol in the digital display remains illuminated, check the oil level as described in *Pre-ride checks*. If the oil level is correct, check the sensor as described below. Equally if the warning light comes on (and/or flashes) whilst the motorcycle is being ridden, stop the engine and check the oil level immediately.

2 If the warning light does not come on when the ignition is switched ON, check the LED as described in Section 17. If there is a fault in the wiring circuit it will be detected by a self diagnosis function and the warning light will flash ten times, then go out for 2.5 seconds, and this will be repeated until the fault is repaired.

3 To check the sensor, remove it from the sump (see Steps 4 to 6). Connect one probe of a multimeter set to the ohms x 100 scale to the sensor wire and the other probe to the base of the sensor. With the sensor upright (i.e. in its normal installed position with the wiring at the bottom), the resistance should be as specified at the beginning of the Chapter. Turn the sensor upside down and check the resistance – it should be as specified. If either condition does not occur, replace the sensor with a new one.

HAYNES HINT: *On all models the warning light may flicker during sudden acceleration or deceleration or when riding up or down hill. Note that this is a characteristic of the system and provided the oil level is correct, does not indicate a fault.*

Removal

4 Drain the engine oil (see Chapter 1).

5 Raise or remove the fuel tank (see Chapter 4), then trace the wire back from the sensor and disconnect it at the connector (see illustration). Release the wire from any cable ties and the clamp secured by one sump bolt (see illustration 26.6), and feed it back to the sensor noting the correct routing.

6 Unscrew the two bolts securing the sensor to the bottom of the sump and withdraw it from the sump, being prepared to catch any residual oil (see illustration). Check the condition of the O-ring and replace it with a new one if it is damaged, deformed or deteriorated – the O-ring is not listed as a spare part by Yamaha, but they or an O-ring supplier should be able to match the size to avoid having to fit a new sensor.

Installation

7 Smear the sensor O-ring with lithium grease, then fit the sensor into the sump. Tighten its bolts to the torque setting specified at the beginning of this Chapter.

8 Feed the wiring to the connector (see illustration 26.5) and secure it with the cable ties. Don't forget to install the clamp and sump bolt (see illustration 26.6).

9 Fill the engine with the specified amount of oil (see Chapter 1) and check the operation of the sensor. Install the fuel tank.

27 Starter relay

Check

1 If the starter circuit is faulty, first check the main fuse and ignition fuse (see Section 5).

2 Remove the rider's seat (see Chapter 7). The starter relay is located behind the battery (see illustration). Lift the terminal cover and unscrew the bolt securing the thick black starter motor lead to its terminal; position the lead away from the relay terminal (see illustration). With the ignition switch ON, the engine kill switch in the

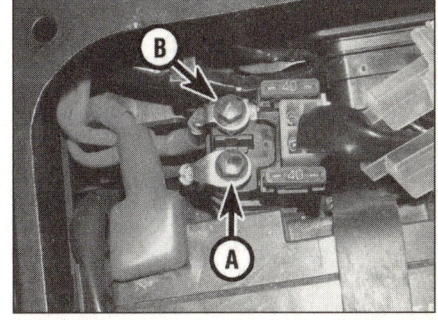

27.2a Starter relay (arrowed)

27.2b Remove the cover and disconnect the black starter lead (A). Red battery lead (B)

8•16 Electrical system

27.9 Remove the cover and disconnect the wiring connector

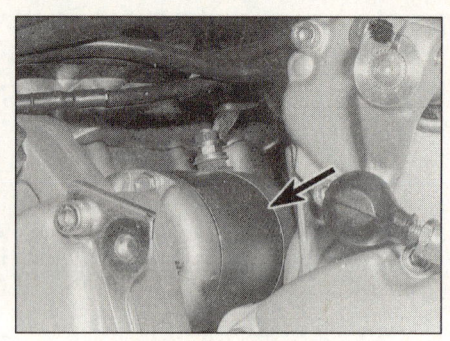

28.1 Starter motor (arrowed)

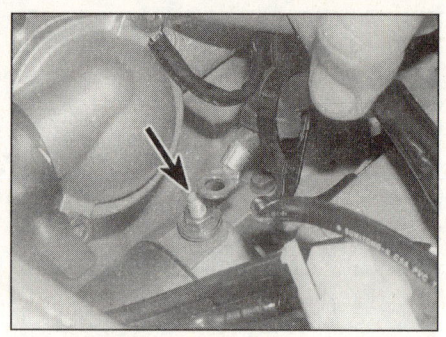

28.2 Pull back the terminal cover then unscrew the nut and detach the lead

RUN position, and the transmission in neutral, press the starter switch. The relay should be heard to click.

3 If the relay doesn't click, switch the ignition OFF, remove the relay (see Steps 8 and 9) and test it as follows.

4 Connect a multimeter set to the ohms x 1 scale, or a continuity tester, between the relay's starter motor (black) and battery (red) lead terminals. There should be no continuity.

5 Leave the multimeter or continuity tester connected to the relay. Now, using a fully-charged 12V battery and two suitable jumper wires, connect the battery positive (+) terminal to the relay's red/white wire terminal, and the battery negative (–) terminal to the relay's blue/white wire terminal. With voltage applied, the relay should be heard to click and the test equipment should show continuity. Disconnect the battery and test meter.

6 If the relay does not click when battery voltage is applied and indicates no continuity (infinite resistance) across its terminals, it is faulty and must be replaced with a new one. The relay coil resistance can be checked by connecting a multimeter set to the ohms x 1 range across the red-white and blue-white terminals of the relay wire connector; the value should be as specified at the beginning of this Chapter.

7 If the relay is good, check for battery voltage at the red/white wire terminal on the loom side of the relay wiring connector when the starter button is pressed with the ignition switched ON. If voltage is present, check the other components in the starter circuit as described in the relevant Sections of this Chapter. If no voltage is present, check the wiring between the various components (see *Wiring Diagrams* at the end of this Chapter).

Renewal

8 Remove the rider's seat (see Chapter 7). The starter relay is located behind the battery **(see illustration 27.2a)**. Disconnect the battery negative (–) lead before removing the relay.

9 Remove the terminal cover and disconnect the relay wiring connector **(see illustration)**. Unscrew the two bolts securing the starter motor and battery leads to the relay and detach the leads, noting which fits where **(see illustration 27.2b)**. Remove the relay with its rubber sleeve from its mounting lug on the frame.

10 Installation is the reverse of removal. The black starter motor lead connects to the front terminal, and the red battery lead to the rear terminal **(see illustration 27.2b)**. Make sure the terminal bolts are tightened securely. Connect the negative (–) lead last when reconnecting the battery.

28 Starter motor removal and installation

28.3a Unscrew the two bolts . . .

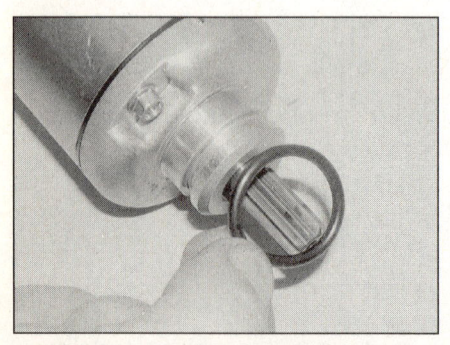

28.3b . . . and remove the starter motor

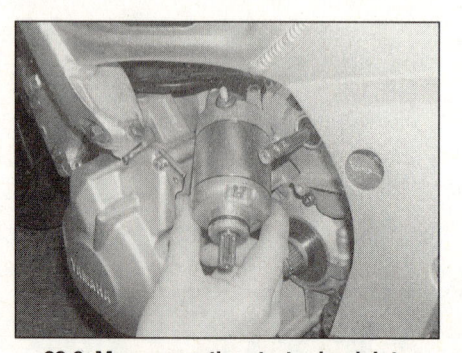

28.5 Fit a new O-ring and lubricate it

28.6 Manoeuvre the starter back into position

Removal

1 Remove the left-hand fairing side panel (see Chapter 7). Remove the fuel tank (see Chapter 4). Disconnect the battery negative (–) lead (see Section 3). The starter motor is mounted on the crankcase, behind the cylinder block **(see illustration)**.

2 Peel back the terminal boot and unscrew the nut securing the lead to the starter motor terminal and detach the lead **(see illustration)**.

3 Unscrew the two bolts securing the starter motor and draw the starter motor out of the crankcase and remove it from the machine **(see illustrations)**.

4 Remove the O-ring on the end of the starter motor and discard it, as a new one must be used.

Installation

5 Fit a new O-ring onto the end of the starter motor, making sure it is seated in its groove, and smear it with grease **(see illustration)**.

6 Manoeuvre the motor into position and slide it into the crankcase **(see illustration)**.

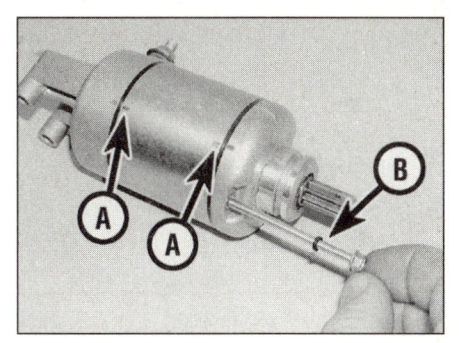

Electrical system 8•17

29.2 Note the alignment marks (A) then unscrew the two bolts, noting the O-rings (B)

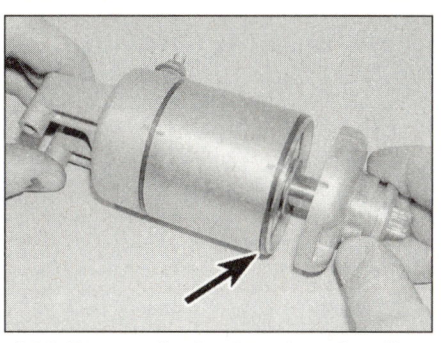

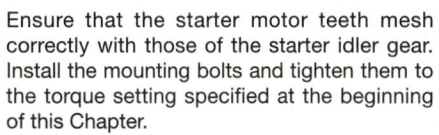

29.3 Remove the front cover and sealing ring (arrowed)

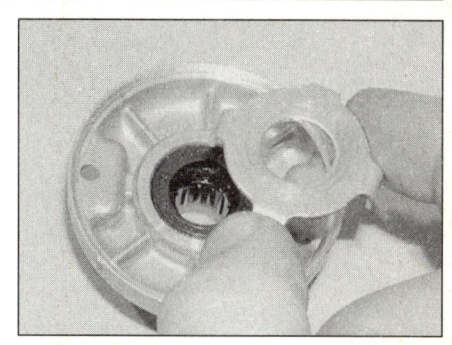

29.4a Remove the tabbed washer . . .

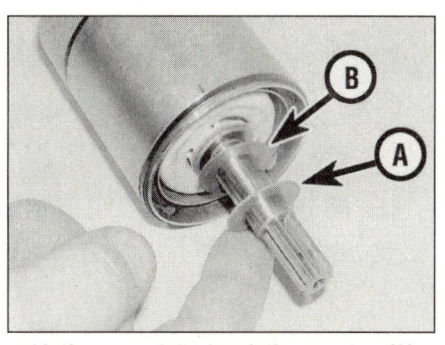

29.4b . . . and the insulating washer (A) and shim(s) (B)

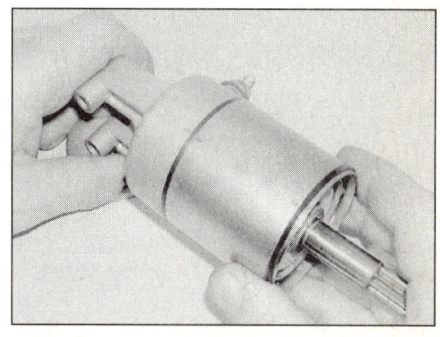

29.5 Carefully draw the main housing off the armature

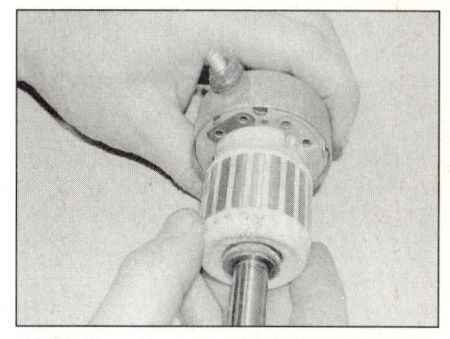

29.6a Draw the rear cover and brushplate off . . .

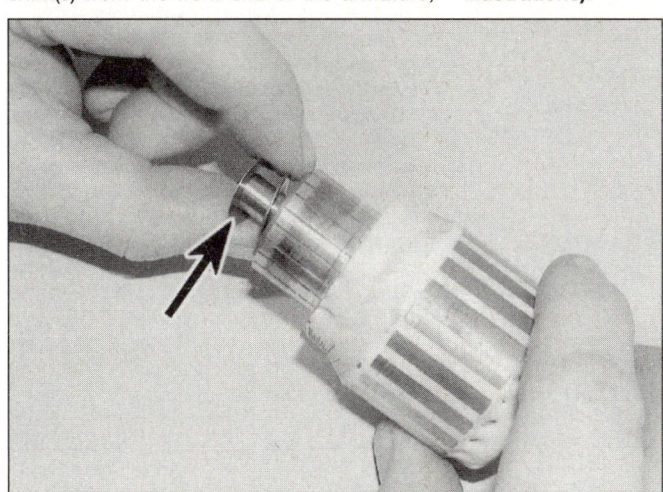

29.6b . . . and remove the shims from the end of the shaft

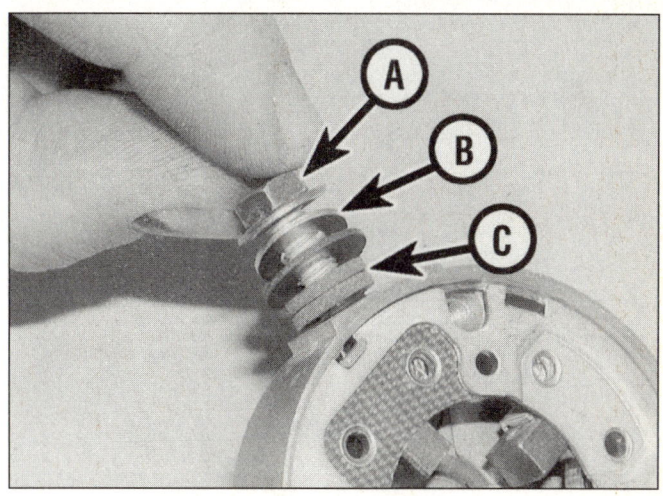

29.7 Unscrew the nut (A) and remove the plain washer (B) and the large and small insulating washers (C)

Ensure that the starter motor teeth mesh correctly with those of the starter idler gear. Install the mounting bolts and tighten them to the torque setting specified at the beginning of this Chapter.

7 Connect the lead to the starter motor terminal and secure it with the nut **(see illustration 28.2)**. Make sure the boot is correctly seated over the terminal.

8 Connect the battery negative (–) lead and install the fuel tank (see Chapter 4) and the fairing side panel (see Chapter 7).

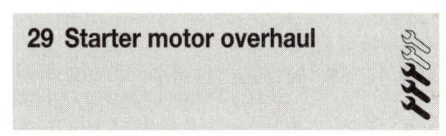

29 Starter motor overhaul

Disassembly

1 Remove the starter motor (see Section 28).
2 Note the alignment marks between the main housing and the front and rear covers, or make your own if they are unclear, then unscrew and remove the two long bolts **(see illustration)**.
3 Remove the front cover from the motor **(see illustration)**.
4 Remove the tabbed washer from inside the cover and slide the insulating washer and shim(s) from the front end of the armature, noting the order in which they are fitted **(see illustrations)**.
5 Holding the armature in place, draw the main housing off, noting that the attraction of the magnets will have to be overcome. Remove the sealing rings and discard them as new ones must be fitted on reassembly **(see illustration)**.
6 Remove the rear cover and brushplate assembly from the armature commutator **(see illustration)**. Remove the shim(s) from the rear end of the armature shaft **(see illustration)**.
7 Noting the order in which they are fitted, unscrew the terminal nut and remove it along with its washer and insulating washers **(see illustrations)**.

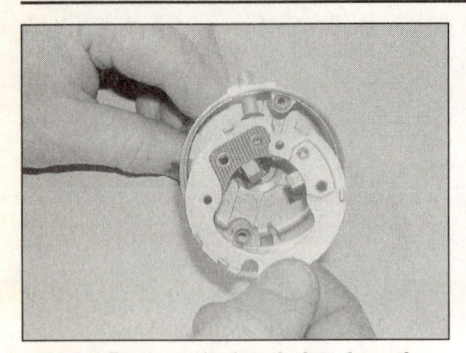

8•18 Electrical system

29.8a Remove the brushplate from the cover ...

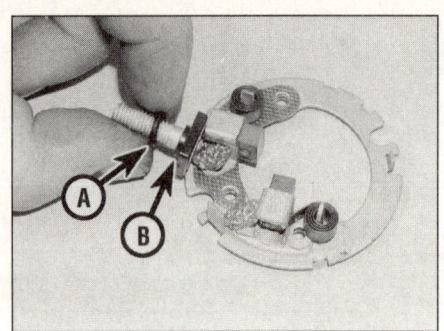

29.8b ... then remove the O-ring (A) and insulating washer (B) from the terminal

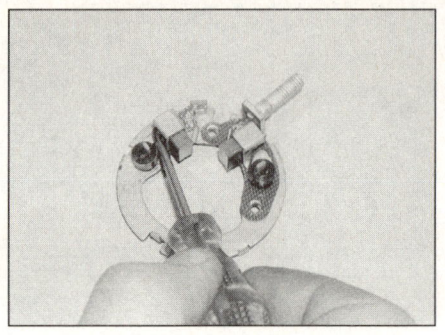

29.9 Move the brush springs aside and slide the brushes out

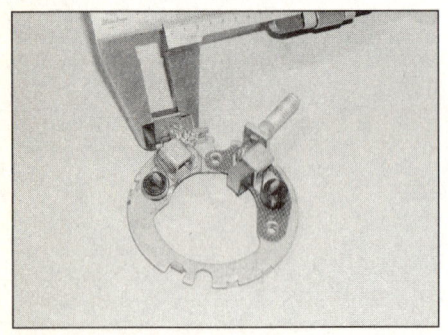

29.10 Measure the length of each brush

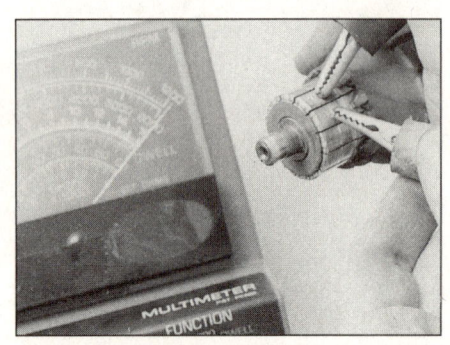

29.12 Continuity should exist between the commutator bars

29.13 There should be no continuity between the bars and the armature shaft

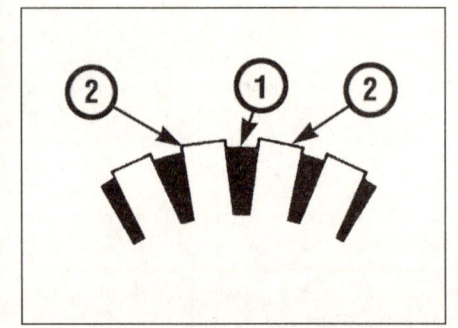

29.14 Mica (1) must be the specified depth below the commutator bars (2)

8 Withdraw the terminal and brushplate assembly from the rear cover and remove the O-ring and square insulating washer from the terminal **(see illustrations)**.

9 Lift the brush springs and slide the brushes out from their holders, noting that one brush is attached to the terminal and the other is attached to the brushplate **(see illustration)**.

Inspection

10 Check the general condition of all the starter motor components. The parts that are most likely to require attention are the brushes. Measure the length of the brushes and compare the results to the brush length listed in this Chapter's Specifications **(see illustration)**. If either of the brushes are worn beyond the service limit, renew the brushplate assembly. If the brushes are not worn excessively, cracked, chipped, or otherwise damaged, they may be re-used.

11 Inspect the commutator bars on the armature for scoring, scratches and discoloration. The commutator can be cleaned and polished with steel wool, but do not use sandpaper or emery paper. After cleaning, wipe away any residue with a cloth soaked in electrical system cleaner or denatured alcohol.

12 Using a multimeter or a continuity tester, check for continuity between the commutator bars **(see illustration)**. Continuity should exist (Yamaha specify 0.0012 to 0.0022 ohms) between each bar and all of the others.

13 Check for continuity between the commutator bars and the armature shaft **(see illustration)**. There should be no continuity (infinite resistance – Yamaha specify a resistance of over 1 M-ohm); if the checks indicate otherwise, the armature is defective.

14 Check the depth of the insulating mica undercut between the commutator bars **(see illustration)** – if it is less than the amount specified at the beginning of this Chapter, scrape the mica away using a suitably shaped hacksaw blade until it is correct.

15 Measure the diameter of the commutator and replace the starter motor with a new one if it has worn below the minimum diameter specified.

16 Check the starter pinion gear for worn, cracked, chipped and broken teeth. If the gear is damaged or worn, replace the starter motor with a new one.

17 Inspect the end covers for signs of cracks or wear. Check the oil seal and needle bearing in the front cover and the bush in the rear cover for wear and damage. Inspect the magnets in the main housing and the housing itself for cracks.

18 Inspect the terminal insulating washers, the O-ring and square insulating washer for signs of damage, and renew them if necessary.

Reassembly

19 Slide the brushes back into their holders and place the brush spring ends onto the brushes **(see illustration 29.9)**.

20 Fit the square insulating washer and O-ring onto the terminal and fit the terminal and brushplate assembly into the rear cover **(see illustrations 29.8b and a)**.

21 Fit the insulating washers onto the terminal, followed by the plain washer and nut, and tighten the nut **(see illustration 29.7)**.

22 Slide the shims onto the rear end of the armature shaft **(see illustration 29.6b)**. Lubricate the shaft with a smear of grease, then insert the shaft into the rear cover, locating the brushes on the commutator as you do, taking care not to damage the brushes **(see illustration 29.6a)**. Check that each brush is securely pressed against the commutator by its spring and is free to move easily in its holder.

23 Fit new O-rings onto the main housing, then fit the housing over the armature and onto the rear cover, aligning the marks made on removal – hold the armature to prevent it being drawn out of the rear cover by the attraction of the magnets, and make sure

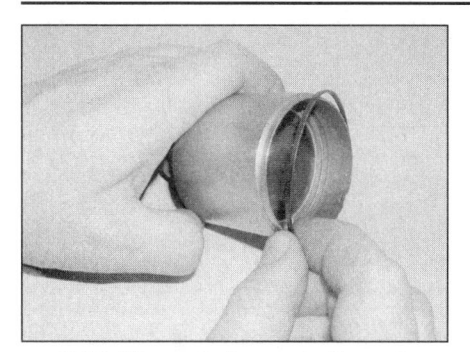

Electrical system 8•19

29.23 Fit new O-rings onto the main housing

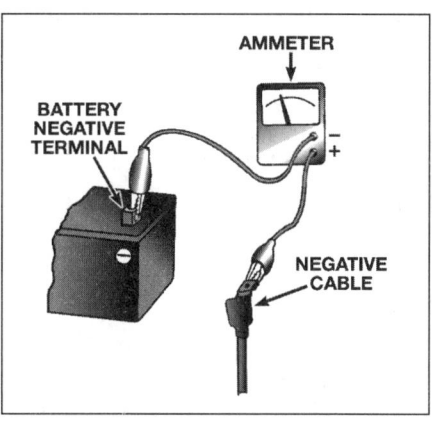

30.5 Checking the charging system leakage rate - connect the meter as shown

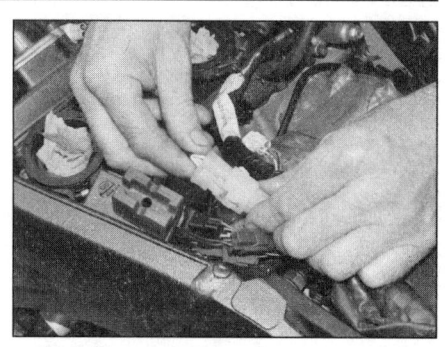

31.2 Disconnect the alternator wiring connector

you do not get your fingers caught between the housing and the rear cover as the housing is drawn on **(see illustration and 29.5 and 29.2)**.

24 Slide the shims and then the insulating washer onto the front end of the armature shaft and lubricate the shaft with a smear of grease **(see illustration 29.4b)**. Apply a smear of grease to the inside of the front cover oil seal. Fit the tabbed washer into the cover, making sure the tabs locate correctly **(see illustrations 29.4a)**. Fit the cover onto the main housing, aligning the marks made on removal **(see illustration 29.3)**.

25 Check that the marks on the rear cover, main housing and front cover are correctly aligned, then install the bolts and tighten them to the specified torque setting **(see illustration 29.2)**.

26 Install the starter motor (see Section 28).

30 Charging system testing

1 If the performance of the charging system is suspect, the system as a whole should be checked first, followed by testing of the individual components. *Note: Before beginning the checks, make sure the battery is fully charged and that all system connections are clean and tight.*

2 Checking the output of the charging system and the performance of the various components within the charging system requires the use of a multimeter (with voltage, current and resistance checking facilities). If a multimeter is not available, the job of checking the charging system should be left to a Yamaha dealer or automotive electrician.

3 When making the checks, follow the procedures carefully to prevent incorrect connections or short circuits, as irreparable damage to electrical system components may result if short circuits occur.

Leakage test

Caution: Always connect an ammeter in series, never in parallel with the battery, otherwise it will be damaged. Do not turn the ignition ON or operate the starter motor when the ammeter is connected – a sudden surge in current will blow the meter's fuse.

4 Turn the ignition switch OFF. Remove the rider's seat (see Chapter 7) and disconnect the lead from the battery negative (–) terminal (see Section 3).

5 Set the multimeter to the Amps function and connect its negative (–) probe to the battery negative (–) terminal, and positive (+) probe to the disconnected negative (–) lead **(see illustration)**. Always set the meter to a high amps range initially and then bring it down to the mA (milli Amps) range; if there is a high current flow in the circuit it may blow the meter's fuse.

6 No current flow should be indicated. If current leakage is indicated (generally greater than 1mA, but may be more if an alarm is fitted), there is a short circuit in the wiring. Using the wiring diagrams at the end of this Chapter, systematically disconnect individual electrical components, checking the meter each time until the source is identified.

7 If no leakage is indicated, disconnect the meter and connect the negative (–) lead to the battery, tightening it securely.

Output test

8 Start the engine and warm it up to normal operating temperature. Remove the rider's seat (see Chapter 7).

9 To check the regulated voltage output, allow the engine to idle and connect a multimeter set to the 0 to 20 volts DC scale (voltmeter) across the terminals of the battery, positive (+) lead to battery positive (+) terminal, negative (–) lead to battery negative (–) terminal **(see illustration 3.2a)**. Slowly increase the engine speed to 5000 rpm and note the reading obtained.

10 The regulated voltage should be as specified at the beginning of the Chapter. If the voltage is outside these limits, check the alternator, then the regulator/rectifier (see Sections 31 and 32).

11 Stop the engine and disconnect the test meter.

31 Alternator rotor and stator

Check

1 Raise or remove the fuel tank (see Chapter 4).

2 Trace the wiring back from the alternator cover on the left-hand side of the engine and disconnect it at the white connector containing the three white wires **(see illustration)**.

3 Using a multimeter set to the ohms x 1 (ohmmeter) scale, measure the resistance between the centre wire and each of the other two on the alternator side of the connector, then between the outer two wires, taking a total of three readings, then check for continuity between each terminal and ground (earth). If the stator coil windings are in good condition the resistance readings should be within the range shown in the Specifications at the beginning of this Chapter and there should be no continuity (infinite resistance) between the terminals and ground (earth). If not, check the fault is not due to damaged wiring between the connector and coils. If the wiring is good, the alternator stator coil assembly is at fault and should be replaced with a new one.

Removal

Special Tool: *A centre-bolt type puller is essential for removal of the alternator rotor from the crankshaft.*

4 Drain the engine oil (see Chapter 1). Raise or remove the fuel tank (see Chapter 4). Remove the left-hand fairing side panel and the lower fairing (see Chapter 7). Remove the coolant reservoir (see Chapter 3).

5 Trace the wiring back from the alternator cover on the left-hand side of the engine and disconnect it at the white connector containing the three white wires **(see illustration 31.2)**. Free the wiring from any clips or guides and feed it through to the alternator cover.

6 Working in a criss-cross pattern, unscrew the bolts securing the alternator cover and remove the cover, and the wiring guide **(see**

8•20 Electrical system

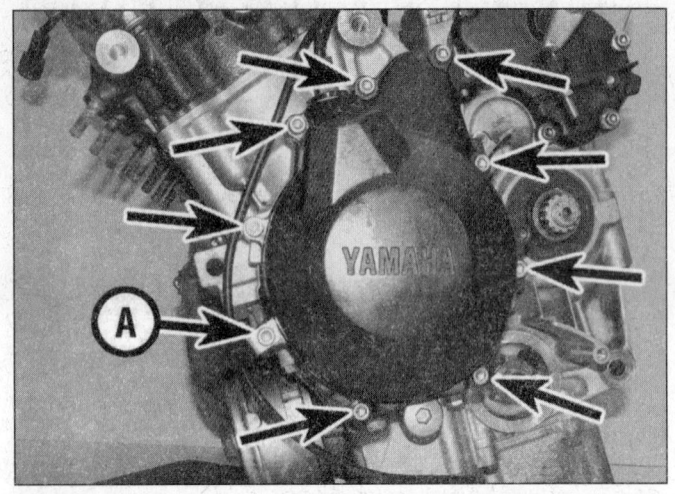

31.6a Alternator cover bolts (arrowed) – note the wiring clamp (A)

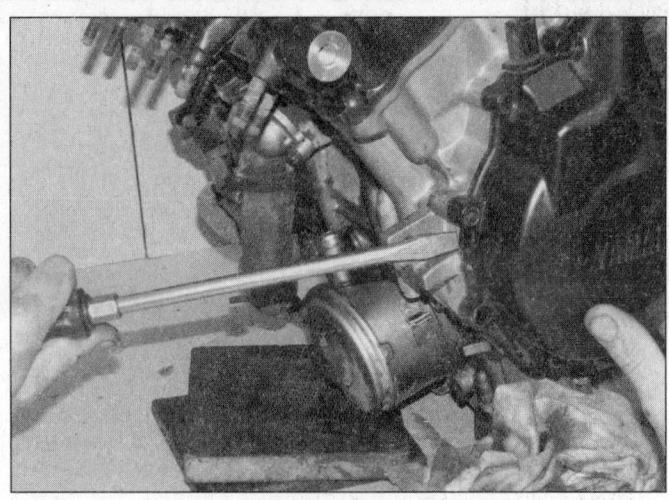

31.6b Remove the cover, using the leverage point as shown if necessary

31.8 Removing the rotor using a commercially available puller

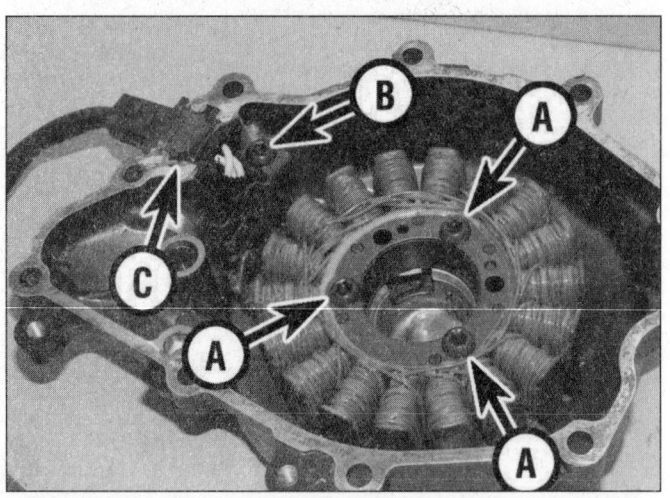

31.9 Unscrew the stator bolts (A) and the wiring clamp bolt (B) and free the grommet (C)

illustrations). Note the dowels in the cover or the crankcase, and remove them if they are loose. Discard the gasket, as a new one must be used on reassembly.

7 To remove the rotor bolt it is necessary to stop the rotor from turning, which is best achieved using a rotor holding tool (Yamaha part No. 90890-01701 or YS-01880-A, or alternatively there are several commercially available types – keep the tool strap away from any raised projections on the rotor) **(see illustration 31.13b)**. If a rotor holding strap or tool is not available, and if the engine is still in the frame, place the transmission in gear and have an assistant apply the rear brake, then unscrew the bolt and remove the washer. Discard the washer as a new one should be used.

8 To remove the rotor from the shaft it is necessary to use a rotor puller. Yamaha provide a special tool (Part Nos. 90890-01362 and 90890-04089 or YU-33270 and YM-33282), or alternatively a similar tool can be obtained commercially **(see illustration)**. **Note:** *The rotor has three threaded holes designed to accept the bolts of the puller.*

9 To remove the stator, undo the screw securing the wiring clamp and the three screws securing the stator to the inside of the cover, then remove the assembly, noting how the wiring grommet locates in the edge of the cover **(see illustration)**.

Installation

10 Install the stator, aligning the wiring grommet with the recess in the cover **(see illustration 31.9)**. Apply a suitable non-permanent thread locking compound to the stator screw threads, then install the screws and tighten them to the torque setting specified at the beginning of this Chapter.

11 Apply a suitable sealant to the wiring grommet, then press it into the recess in the cover and secure the wiring with the clamp.

12 Clean the tapered end of the crankshaft and the corresponding mating surface on the inside of the rotor with a suitable solvent. Make sure that no metal objects have attached themselves to the magnet on the inside of the rotor, then slide the rotor onto the shaft **(see illustration)**.

13 Apply some clean engine oil to the rotor

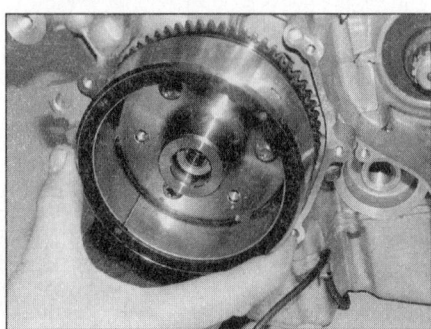

31.12 Slide the rotor onto the shaft

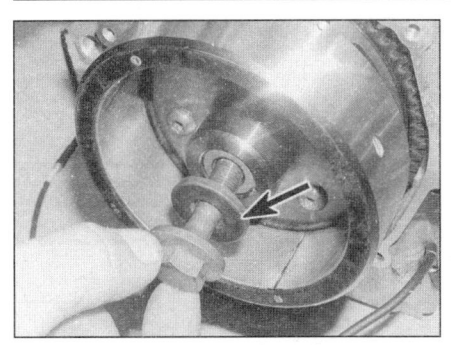

Electrical system 8•21

31.13a Fit the lubricated bolt with a new washer ...

31.13b ... and tighten it to the specified torque

31.14a Locate the new gasket onto the dowels (arrowed) ...

bolt threads, fit the new washer onto the bolt and tighten the bolt to the torque setting specified at the beginning of this Chapter **(see illustration)**. Use the method employed on removal to prevent the rotor from turning **(see illustration)**.

14 If removed, install the dowels in the crankcase and fit the new gasket, making sure it locates onto the dowels **(see illustration)**. Install the cover, making sure the starter idle gear shaft locates in its bore **(see illustration)**. Tighten the bolts evenly in a criss-cross pattern to the specified torque setting, not forgetting the wiring clamp **(see illustration 31.6a)**.

15 Feed the wiring to the connector, making sure it is correctly routed and secured by any cable ties **(see illustration 31.2)**.

16 Install the coolant reservoir (see Chapter 3). Install the lower fairing and left-hand side panel (see Chapter 7), and the fuel tank (see Chapter 4). Fill the engine up to the specified level with oil and the reservoir with coolant (see Pre-ride checks and Chapter 1).

32 Regulator/rectifier

Check

1 Yamaha provide no test specifications for the regulator/rectifier other than the charging system output test (see Section 30). If the regulator/rectifier is suspected of being faulty, first check all other components and the wiring and connectors in the charging circuit, referring to the relevant Sections in this Chapter and to the wiring diagrams at the end.

2 If all other components and the wiring are good, remove the unit (see below) and take it to a Yamaha dealer for testing. Alternatively, substitute the suspect unit with a known good one and see if the fault is cured.

> **HAYNES HINT** *Clues to a faulty regulator are constantly blowing bulbs, with brightness varying considerably with engine speed, and battery overheating.*

Renewal

3 The regulator/rectifier is mounted to the frame underneath the rear mounting for the fuel tank – remove the tank for access (see Chapter 4). Disconnect the wiring connector **(see illustration)**.

4 Unscrew the two bolts securing the regulator/rectifier and remove it, noting there are two washers that fit on the bolts behind the regulator/rectifier – take care not to let them drop.

5 Install the new unit and tighten its bolts, not forgetting the washers. Connect the wiring connector. Install the fuel tank (see Chapter 4).

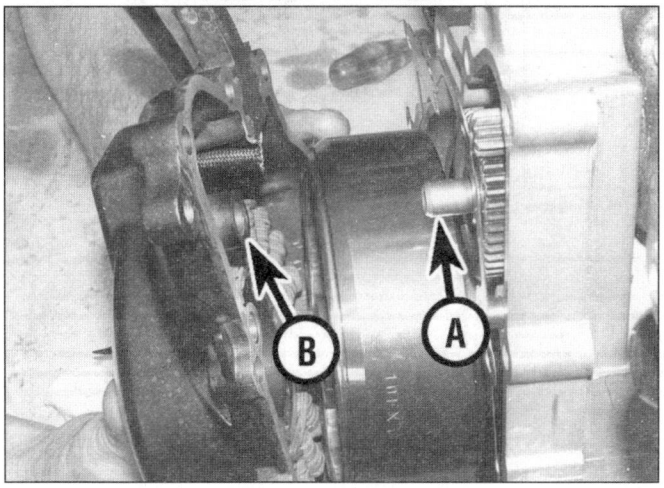

31.14b ... then fit the cover, locating the shaft (A) in the bore (B)

32.3 Regulator/rectifier (arrowed)

8•22 Wiring diagrams

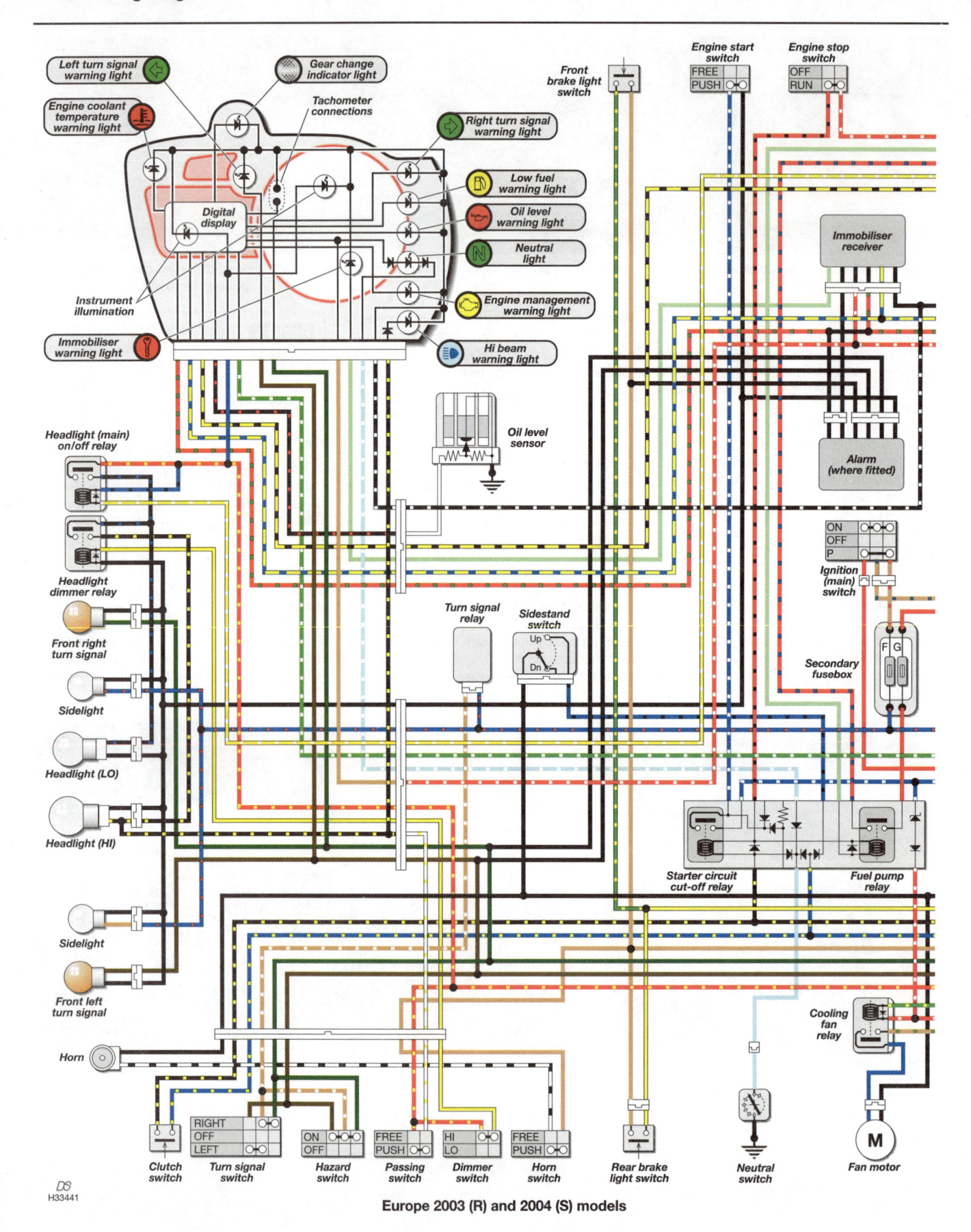

Europe 2003 (R) and 2004 (S) models

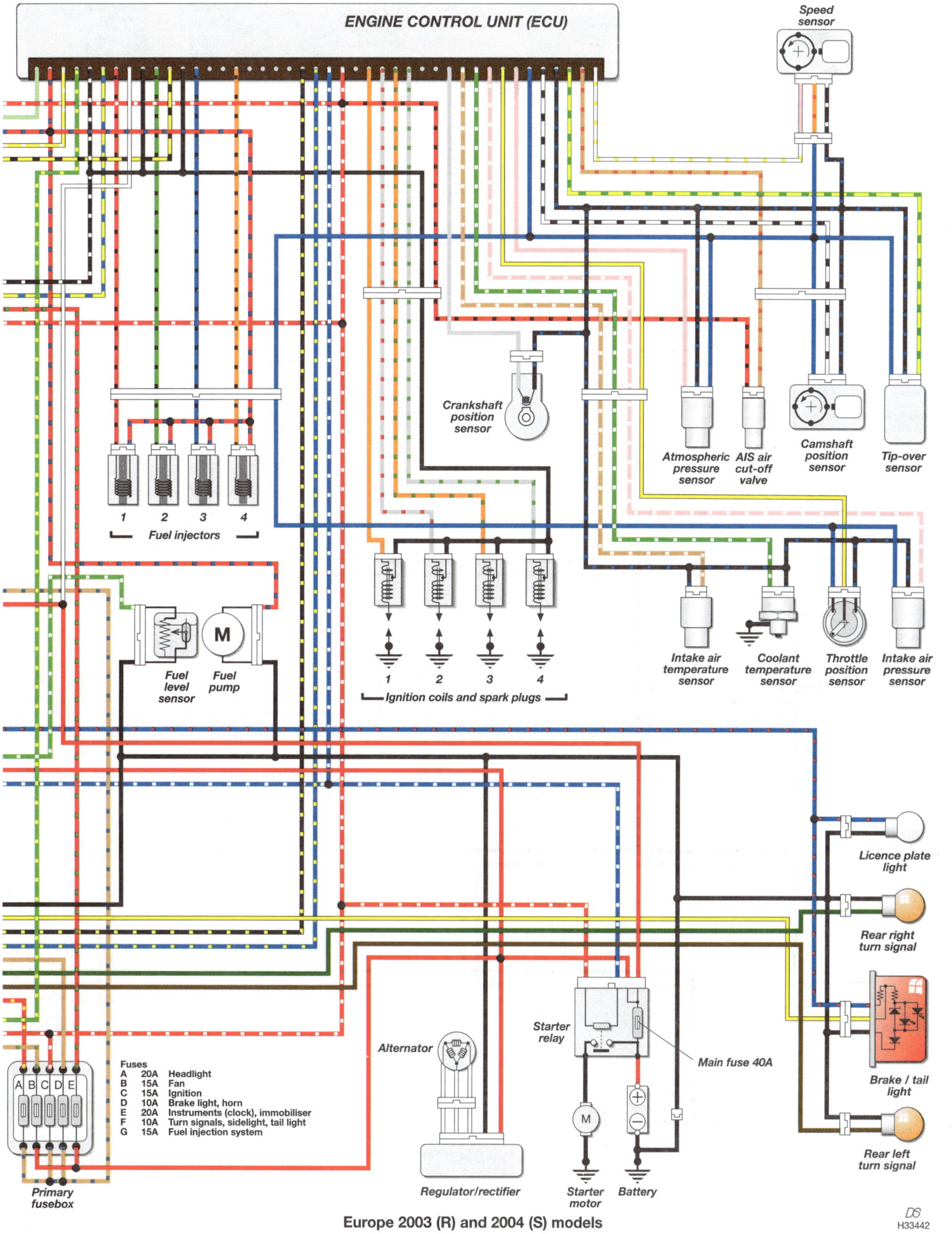

Europe 2003 (R) and 2004 (S) models

8•24 Wiring diagrams

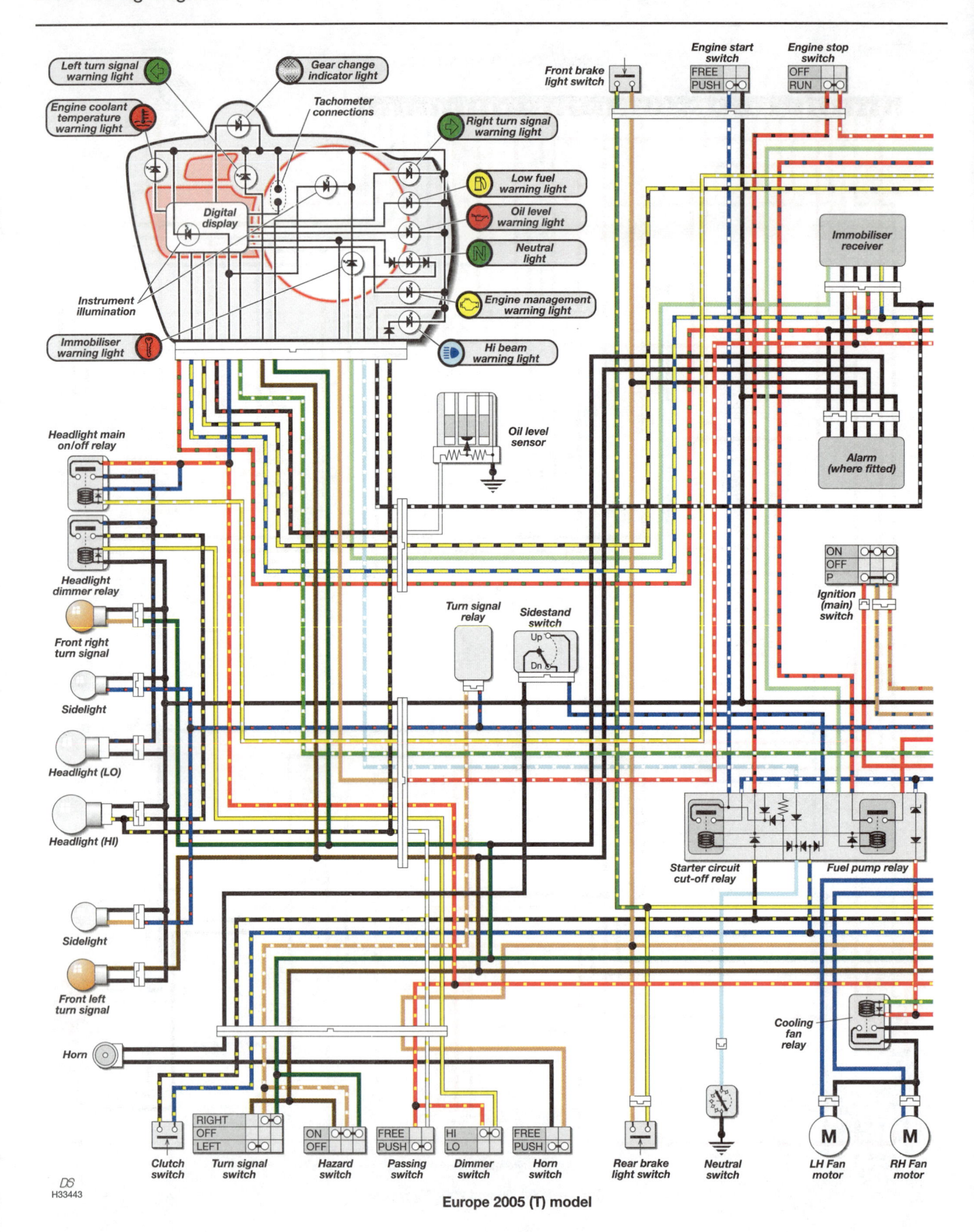

Europe 2005 (T) model

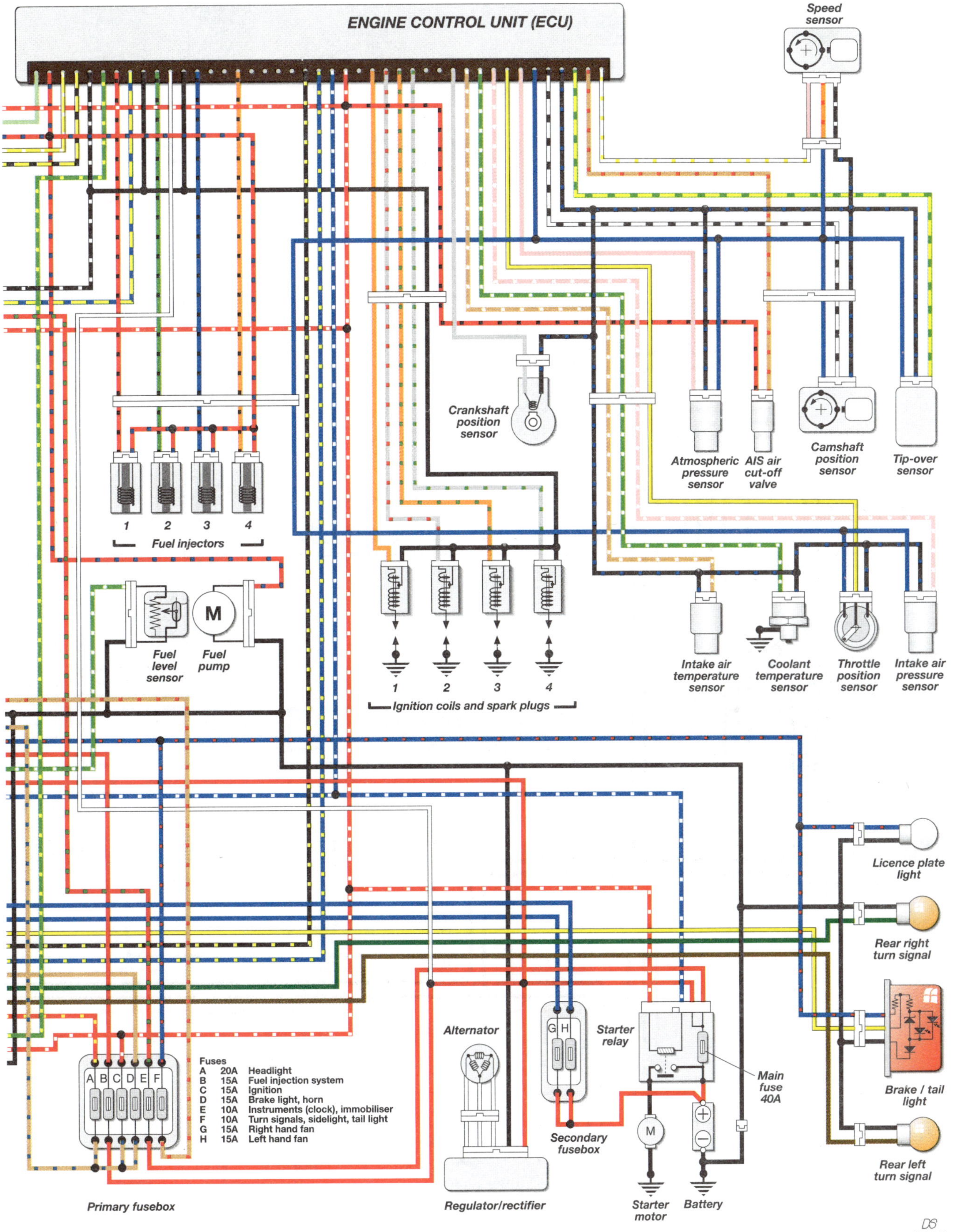

Europe 2005 (T) model

8•26 Wiring diagrams

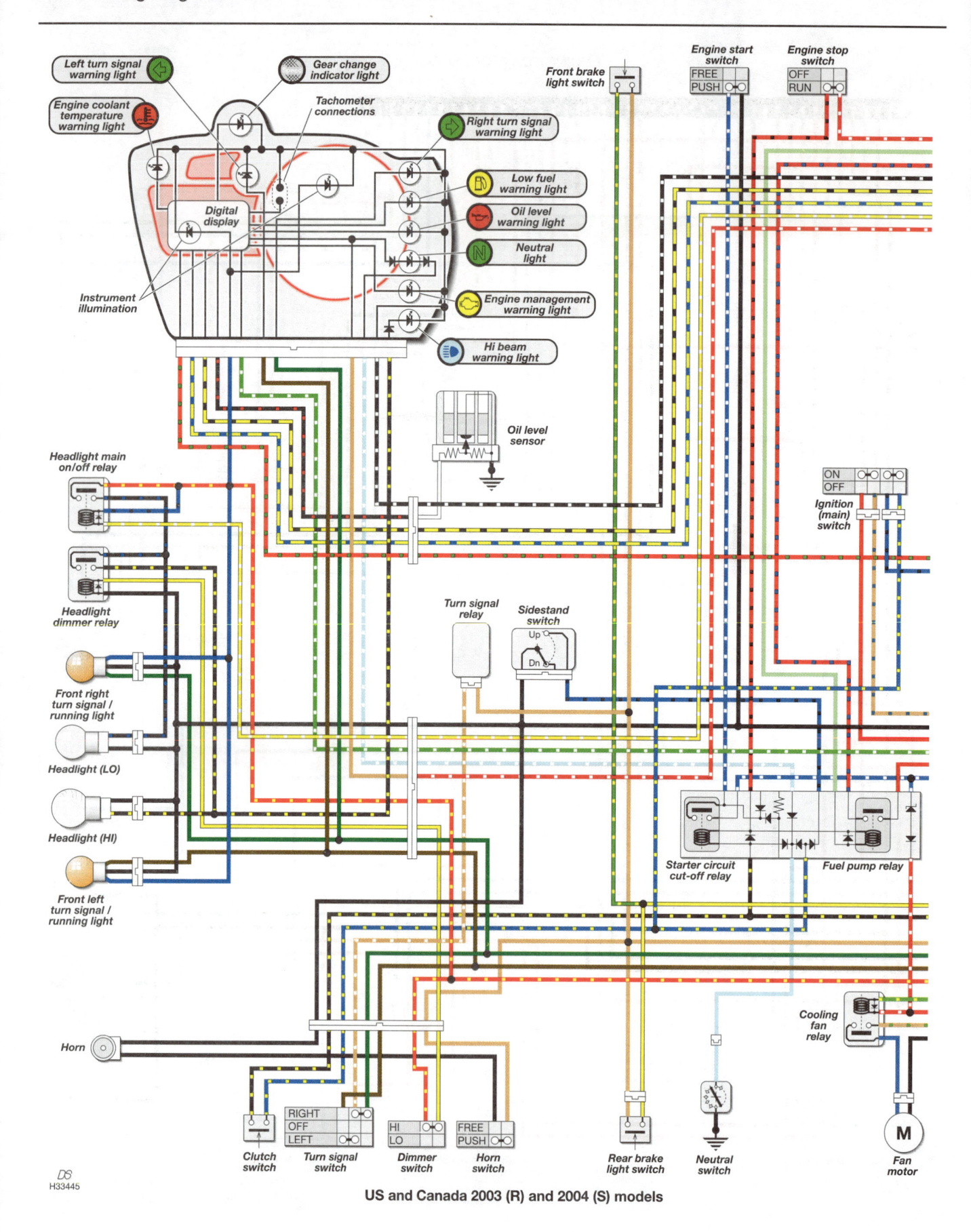

US and Canada 2003 (R) and 2004 (S) models

Wiring diagrams 8•27

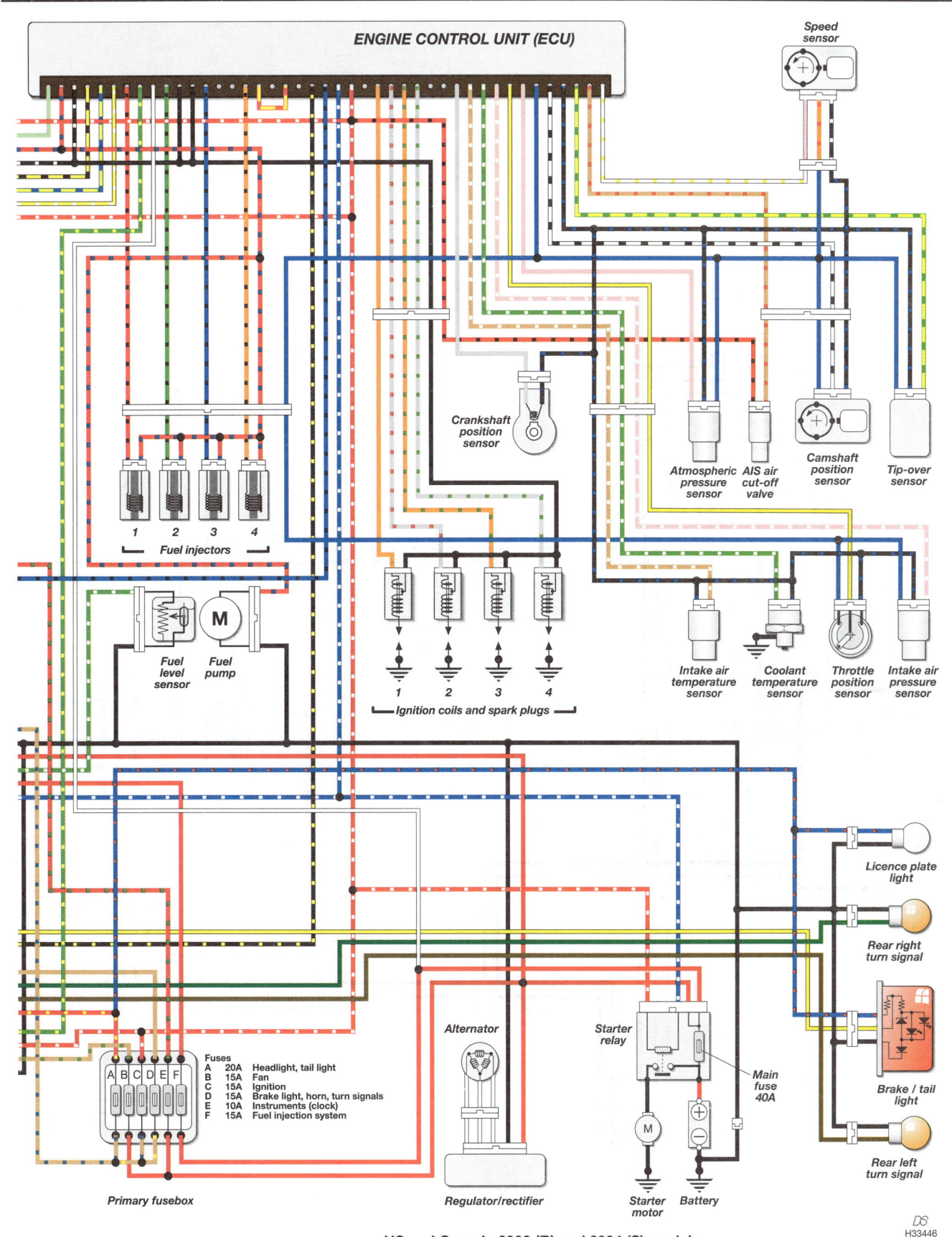

US and Canada 2003 (R) and 2004 (S) models

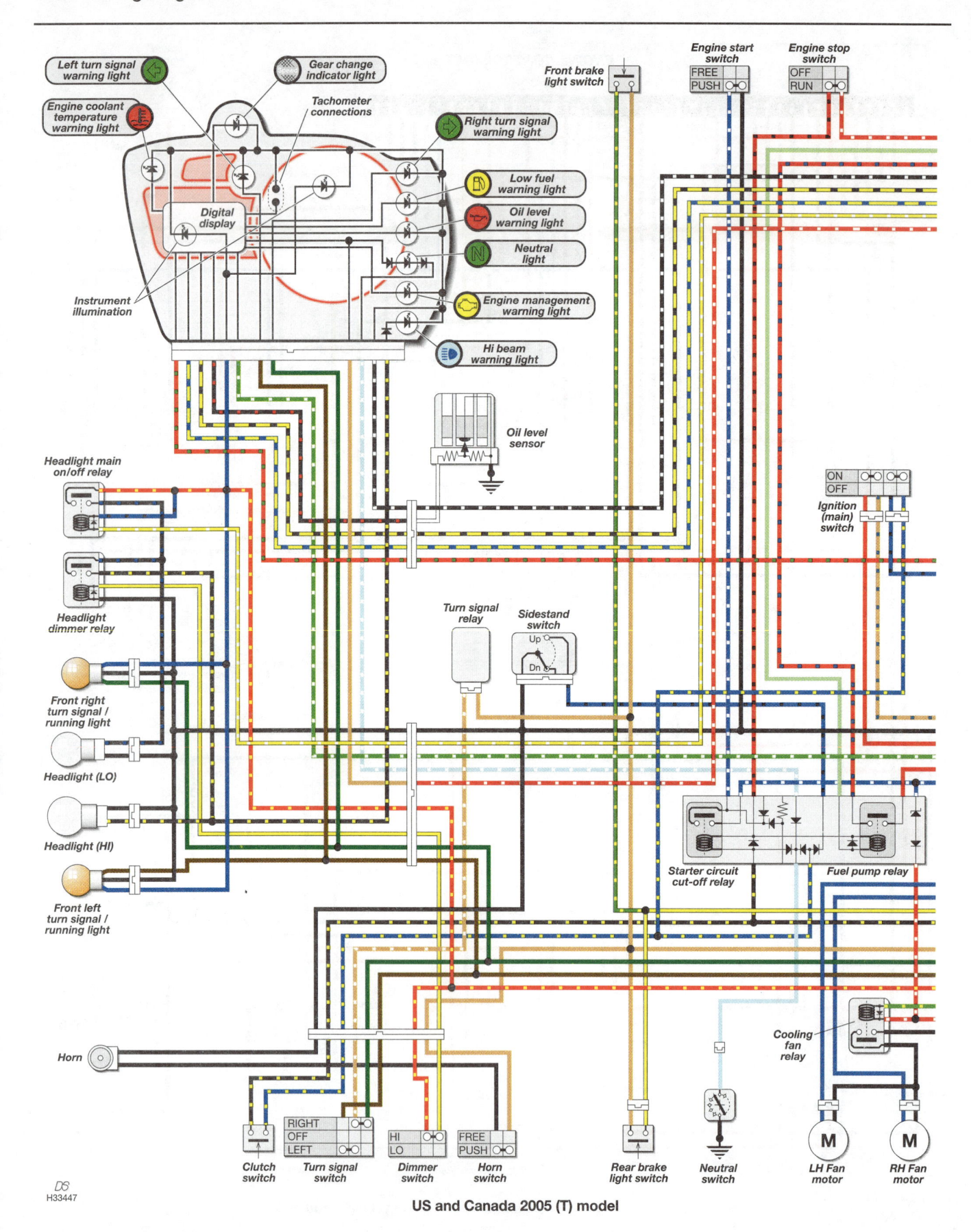

8•28 Wiring diagrams

US and Canada 2005 (T) model

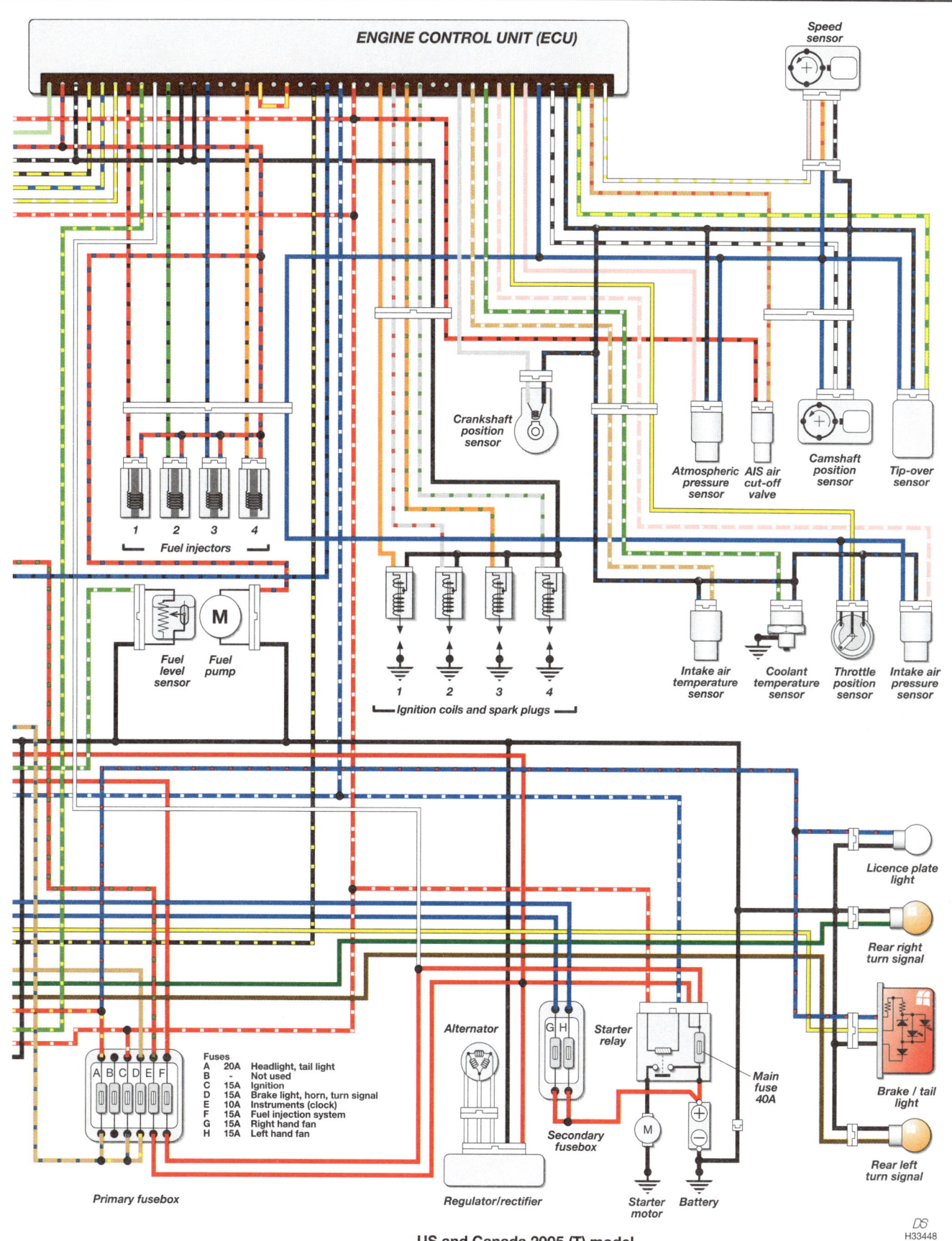

Wiring diagrams 8•29

Engine Control Unit (ECU)

Speed sensor

Crankshaft position sensor

Fuel injectors 1 2 3 4

Fuel level sensor

Fuel pump

Ignition coils and spark plugs 1 2 3 4

Atmospheric pressure sensor

AIS air cut-off valve

Camshaft position sensor

Tip-over sensor

Intake air temperature sensor

Coolant temperature sensor

Throttle position sensor

Intake air pressure sensor

Fuses
- A 20A Headlight, tail light
- B -   Not used
- C 15A Ignition
- D 15A Brake light, horn, turn signal
- E 10A Instruments (clock)
- F 15A Fuel injection system
- G 15A Right hand fan
- H 15A Left hand fan

Primary fusebox

Alternator

Regulator/rectifier

Starter relay

Secondary fusebox

Main fuse 40A

Starter motor

Battery

Licence plate light

Rear right turn signal

Brake / tail light

Rear left turn signal

US and Canada 2005 (T) model

H33448

Notes

Reference REF•1

Reference

Tools and Workshop Tips — REF•2
- Building up a tool kit and equipping your workshop
- Using tools
- Understanding bearing, seal, fastener and chain sizes and markings
- Repair techniques

Security — REF•20
- Locks and chains
- U-locks
- Disc locks
- Alarms and immobilisers
- Security marking systems
- Tips on how to prevent bike theft

Lubricants and fluids — REF•23
- Engine oils
- Transmission (gear) oils
- Coolant/anti-freeze
- Fork oils and suspension fluids
- Brake/clutch fluids
- Spray lubes, degreasers and solvents

Conversion Factors — REF•26

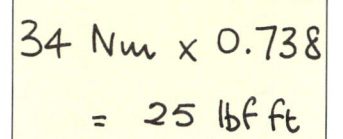

$34\ Nm \times 0.738 = 25\ lbf\ ft$

- Formulae for conversion of the metric (SI) units used throughout the manual into Imperial measures

MOT Test Checks — REF•27
- A guide to the UK MOT test
- Which items are tested
- How to prepare your motorcycle for the test and perform a pre-test check

Storage — REF•32
- How to prepare your motorcycle for going into storage and protect essential systems
- How to get the motorcycle back on the road

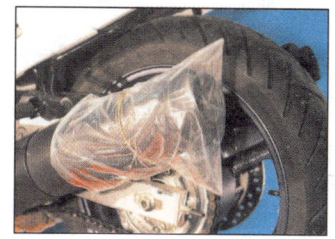

Fault Finding — REF•35
- Common faults and their likely causes
- How to check engine cylinder compression
- How to make electrical tests and use test meters

Technical Terms Explained — REF•47
- Component names, technical terms and common abbreviations explained

Index — REF•51

REF•2 Tools and Workshop Tips

Buying tools

A toolkit is a fundamental requirement for servicing and repairing a motorcycle. Although there will be an initial expense in building up enough tools for servicing, this will soon be offset by the savings made by doing the job yourself. As experience and confidence grow, additional tools can be added to enable the repair and overhaul of the motorcycle. Many of the specialist tools are expensive and not often used so it may be preferable to hire them, or for a group of friends or motorcycle club to join in the purchase.

As a rule, it is better to buy more expensive, good quality tools. Cheaper tools are likely to wear out faster and need to be renewed more often, nullifying the original saving.

Warning: To avoid the risk of a poor quality tool breaking in use, causing injury or damage to the component being worked on, always aim to purchase tools which meet the relevant national safety standards.

The following lists of tools do not represent the manufacturer's service tools, but serve as a guide to help the owner decide which tools are needed for this level of work. In addition, items such as an electric drill, hacksaw, files, soldering iron and a workbench equipped with a vice, may be needed. Although not classed as tools, a selection of bolts, screws, nuts, washers and pieces of tubing always come in useful.

For more information about tools, refer to the Haynes *Motorcycle Workshop Practice Techbook* (Bk. No. 3470).

Manufacturer's service tools

Inevitably certain tasks require the use of a service tool. Where possible an alternative tool or method of approach is recommended, but sometimes there is no option if personal injury or damage to the component is to be avoided. Where required, service tools are referred to in the relevant procedure.

Service tools can usually only be purchased from a motorcycle dealer and are identified by a part number. Some of the commonly-used tools, such as rotor pullers, are available in aftermarket form from mail-order motorcycle tool and accessory suppliers.

Maintenance and minor repair tools

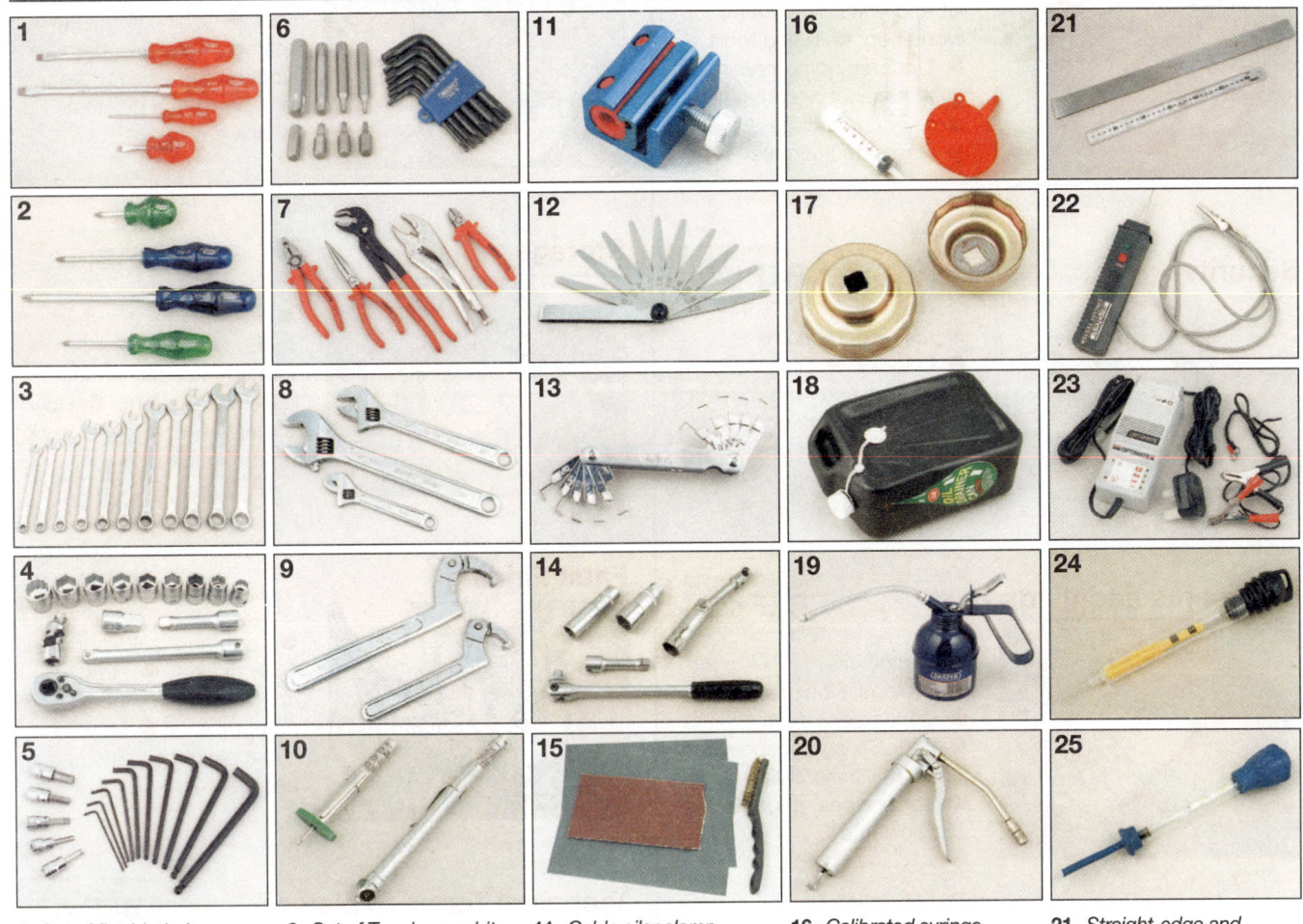

1 Set of flat-bladed screwdrivers
2 Set of Phillips head screwdrivers
3 Combination open-end and ring spanners
4 Socket set (3/8 inch or 1/2 inch drive)
5 Set of Allen keys or bits
6 Set of Torx keys or bits
7 Pliers, cutters and self-locking grips (Mole grips)
8 Adjustable spanners
9 C-spanners
10 Tread depth gauge and tyre pressure gauge
11 Cable oiler clamp
12 Feeler gauges
13 Spark plug gap measuring tool
14 Spark plug spanner or deep plug sockets
15 Wire brush and emery paper
16 Calibrated syringe, measuring vessel and funnel
17 Oil filter adapters
18 Oil drainer can or tray
19 Pump type oil can
20 Grease gun
21 Straight-edge and steel rule
22 Continuity tester
23 Battery charger
24 Hydrometer (for battery specific gravity check)
25 Anti-freeze tester (for liquid-cooled engines)

Tools and Workshop Tips REF•3

Repair and overhaul tools

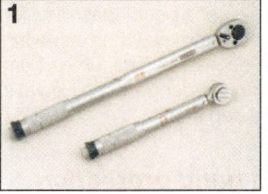

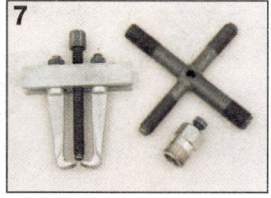

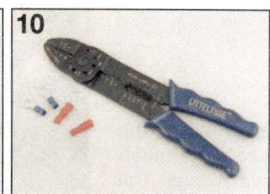

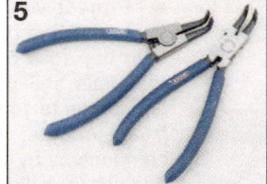

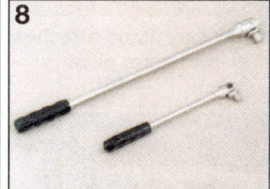

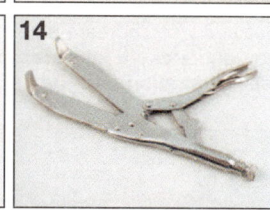

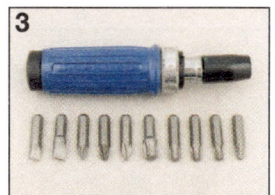

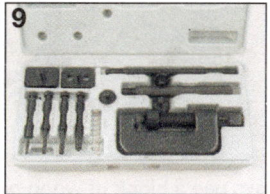

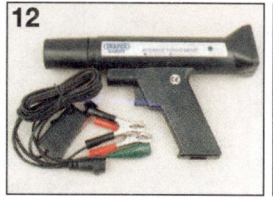

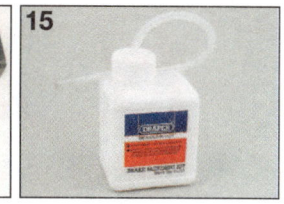

1 Torque wrench
   (small and mid-ranges)
2 Conventional, plastic or
   soft-faced hammers
3 Impact driver set
4 Vernier gauge
5 Circlip pliers (internal and
   external, or combination)
6 Set of cold chisels
   and punches
7 Selection of pullers
8 Breaker bars
9 Chain breaking/
   riveting tool set
10 Wire stripper and
   crimper tool
11 Multimeter (measures
   amps, volts and ohms)
12 Stroboscope (for
   dynamic timing checks)
13 Hose clamp
   (wingnut type shown)
14 Clutch holding tool
15 One-man brake/clutch
   bleeder kit

Specialist tools

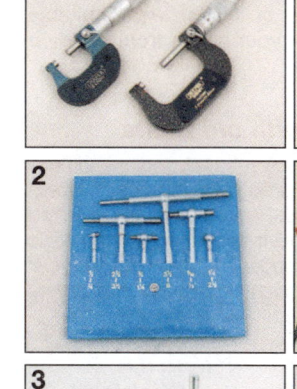

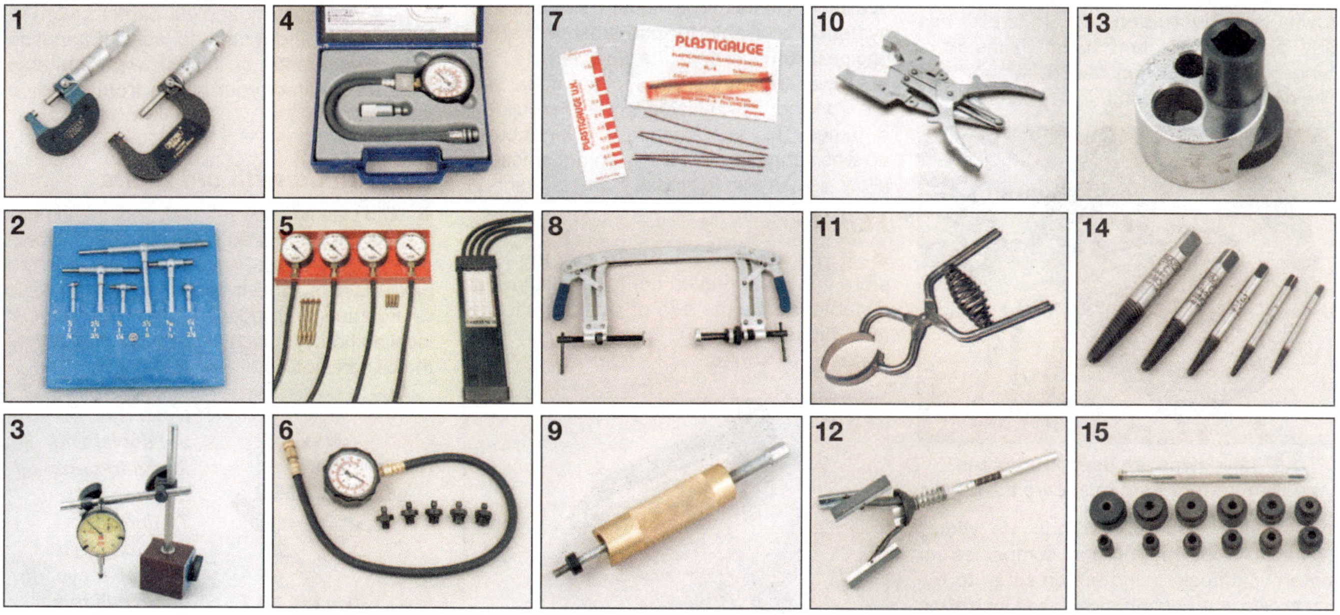

1 Micrometers
   (external type)
2 Telescoping gauges
3 Dial gauge
4 Cylinder
   compression gauge
5 Vacuum gauges (left) or
   manometer (right)
6 Oil pressure gauge
7 Plastigauge kit
8 Valve spring compressor
   (4-stroke engines)
9 Piston pin drawbolt tool
10 Piston ring removal and
   installation tool
11 Piston ring clamp
12 Cylinder bore hone
   (stone type shown)
13 Stud extractor
14 Screw extractor set
15 Bearing driver set

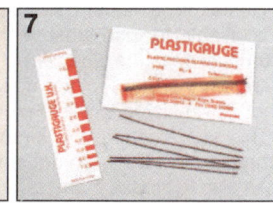

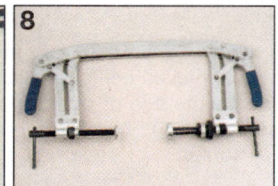

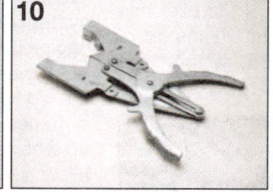

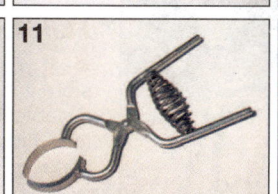

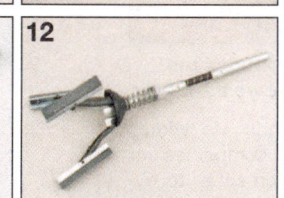

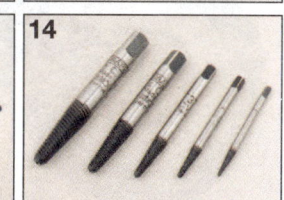

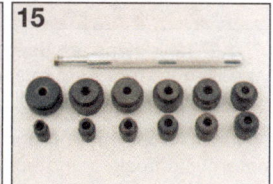

REF•4 Tools and Workshop Tips

1 Workshop equipment and facilities

The workbench

- Work is made much easier by raising the bike up on a ramp - components are much more accessible if raised to waist level. The hydraulic or pneumatic types seen in the dealer's workshop are a sound investment if you undertake a lot of repairs or overhauls **(see illustration 1.1)**.

1.1 Hydraulic motorcycle ramp

- If raised off ground level, the bike must be supported on the ramp to avoid it falling. Most ramps incorporate a front wheel locating clamp which can be adjusted to suit different diameter wheels. When tightening the clamp, take care not to mark the wheel rim or damage the tyre - use wood blocks on each side to prevent this.
- Secure the bike to the ramp using tie-downs **(see illustration 1.2)**. If the bike has only a sidestand, and hence leans at a dangerous angle when raised, support the bike on an auxiliary stand.

1.2 Tie-downs are used around the passenger footrests to secure the bike

- Auxiliary (paddock) stands are widely available from mail order companies or motorcycle dealers and attach either to the wheel axle or swingarm pivot **(see illustration 1.3)**. If the motorcycle has a centrestand, you can support it under the crankcase to prevent it toppling whilst either wheel is removed **(see illustration 1.4)**.

1.3 This auxiliary stand attaches to the swingarm pivot

1.4 Always use a block of wood between the engine and jack head when supporting the engine in this way

Fumes and fire

- Refer to the Safety first! page at the beginning of the manual for full details. Make sure your workshop is equipped with a fire extinguisher suitable for fuel-related fires (Class B fire - flammable liquids) - it is not sufficient to have a water-filled extinguisher.
- Always ensure adequate ventilation is available. Unless an exhaust gas extraction system is available for use, ensure that the engine is run outside of the workshop.
- If working on the fuel system, make sure the workshop is ventilated to avoid a build-up of fumes. This applies equally to fume build-up when charging a battery. Do not smoke or allow anyone else to smoke in the workshop.

Fluids

- If you need to drain fuel from the tank, store it in an approved container marked as suitable for the storage of petrol (gasoline) **(see illustration 1.5)**. Do not store fuel in glass jars or bottles.

1.5 Use an approved can only for storing petrol (gasoline)

- Use proprietary engine degreasers or solvents which have a high flash-point, such as paraffin (kerosene), for cleaning off oil, grease and dirt - never use petrol (gasoline) for cleaning. Wear rubber gloves when handling solvent and engine degreaser. The fumes from certain solvents can be dangerous - always work in a well-ventilated area.

Dust, eye and hand protection

- Protect your lungs from inhalation of dust particles by wearing a filtering mask over the nose and mouth. Many frictional materials still contain asbestos which is dangerous to your health. Protect your eyes from spouts of liquid and sprung components by wearing a pair of protective goggles **(see illustration 1.6)**.

1.6 A fire extinguisher, goggles, mask and protective gloves should be at hand in the workshop

- Protect your hands from contact with solvents, fuel and oils by wearing rubber gloves. Alternatively apply a barrier cream to your hands before starting work. If handling hot components or fluids, wear suitable gloves to protect your hands from scalding and burns.

What to do with old fluids

- Old cleaning solvent, fuel, coolant and oils should not be poured down domestic drains or onto the ground. Package the fluid up in old oil containers, label it accordingly, and take it to a garage or disposal facility. Contact your local authority for location of such sites or ring the oil care hotline.

Note: It is antisocial and illegal to dump oil down the drain. To find the location of your local oil recycling bank, call this number free.

OIL CARE — FOLLOW THE CODE
OIL BANK LINE
0800 66 33 66
www.oilbankline.org.uk

In the USA, note that any oil supplier must accept used oil for recycling.

2 Fasteners -
screws, bolts and nuts

Fastener types and applications

Bolts and screws

● Fastener head types are either of hexagonal, Torx or splined design, with internal and external versions of each type **(see illustrations 2.1 and 2.2)**; splined head fasteners are not in common use on motorcycles. The conventional slotted or Phillips head design is used for certain screws. Bolt or screw length is always measured from the underside of the head to the end of the item **(see illustration 2.11)**.

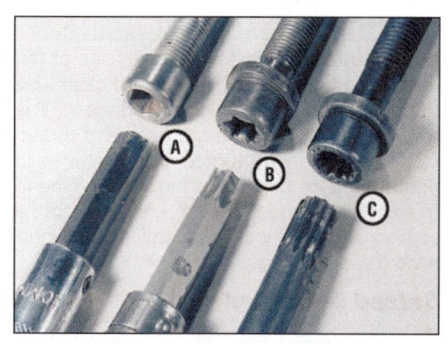

2.1 Internal hexagon/Allen (A), Torx (B) and splined (C) fasteners, with corresponding bits

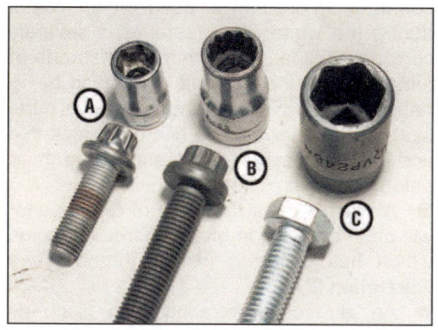

2.2 External Torx (A), splined (B) and hexagon (C) fasteners, with corresponding sockets

● Certain fasteners on the motorcycle have a tensile marking on their heads, the higher the marking the stronger the fastener. High tensile fasteners generally carry a 10 or higher marking. Never replace a high tensile fastener with one of a lower tensile strength.

Washers (see illustration 2.3)

● Plain washers are used between a fastener head and a component to prevent damage to the component or to spread the load when torque is applied. Plain washers can also be used as spacers or shims in certain assemblies. Copper or aluminium plain washers are often used as sealing washers on drain plugs.

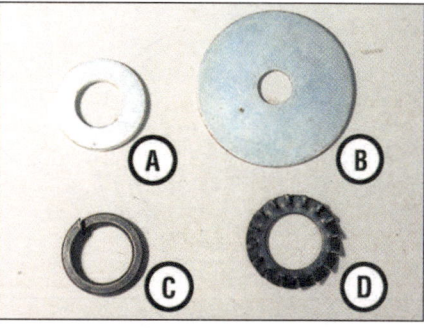

2.3 Plain washer (A), penny washer (B), spring washer (C) and serrated washer (D)

● The split-ring spring washer works by applying axial tension between the fastener head and component. If flattened, it is fatigued and must be renewed. If a plain (flat) washer is used on the fastener, position the spring washer between the fastener and the plain washer.

● Serrated star type washers dig into the fastener and component faces, preventing loosening. They are often used on electrical earth (ground) connections to the frame.

● Cone type washers (sometimes called Belleville) are conical and when tightened apply axial tension between the fastener head and component. They must be installed with the dished side against the component and often carry an OUTSIDE marking on their outer face. If flattened, they are fatigued and must be renewed.

● Tab washers are used to lock plain nuts or bolts on a shaft. A portion of the tab washer is bent up hard against one flat of the nut or bolt to prevent it loosening. Due to the tab washer being deformed in use, a new tab washer should be used every time it is disturbed.

● Wave washers are used to take up endfloat on a shaft. They provide light springing and prevent excessive side-to-side play of a component. Can be found on rocker arm shafts.

Nuts and split pins

● Conventional plain nuts are usually six-sided **(see illustration 2.4)**. They are sized by thread diameter and pitch. High tensile nuts carry a number on one end to denote their tensile strength.

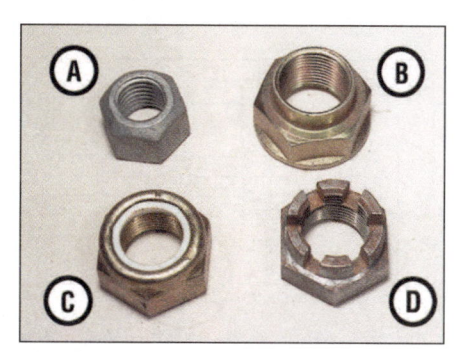

2.4 Plain nut (A), shouldered locknut (B), nylon insert nut (C) and castellated nut (D)

● Self-locking nuts either have a nylon insert, or two spring metal tabs, or a shoulder which is staked into a groove in the shaft - their advantage over conventional plain nuts is a resistance to loosening due to vibration. The nylon insert type can be used a number of times, but must be renewed when the friction of the nylon insert is reduced, ie when the nut spins freely on the shaft. The spring tab type can be reused unless the tabs are damaged. The shouldered type must be renewed every time it is disturbed.

● Split pins (cotter pins) are used to lock a castellated nut to a shaft or to prevent slackening of a plain nut. Common applications are wheel axles and brake torque arms. Because the split pin arms are deformed to lock around the nut a new split pin must always be used on installation - always fit the correct size split pin which will fit snugly in the shaft hole. Make sure the split pin arms are correctly located around the nut **(see illustrations 2.5 and 2.6)**.

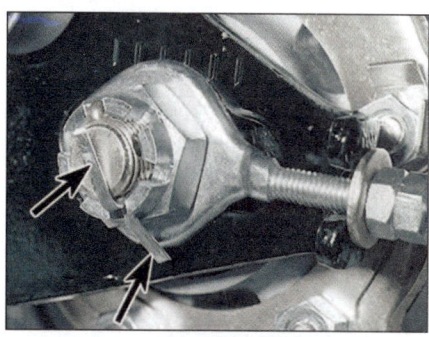

2.5 Bend split pin (cotter pin) arms as shown (arrows) to secure a castellated nut

2.6 Bend split pin (cotter pin) arms as shown to secure a plain nut

Caution: If the castellated nut slots do not align with the shaft hole after tightening to the torque setting, tighten the nut until the next slot aligns with the hole - never slacken the nut to align its slot.

● R-pins (shaped like the letter R), or slip pins as they are sometimes called, are sprung and can be reused if they are otherwise in good condition. Always install R-pins with their closed end facing forwards **(see illustration 2.7)**.

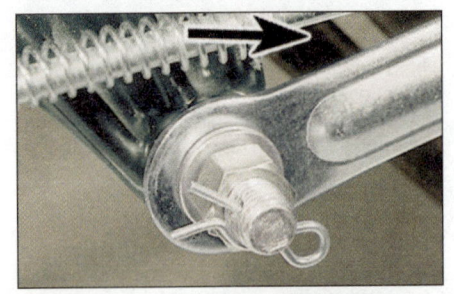

Tools and Workshop Tips

2.7 Correct fitting of R-pin. Arrow indicates forward direction

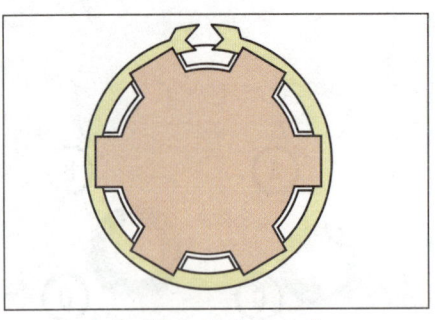

2.10 Align circlip opening with shaft channel

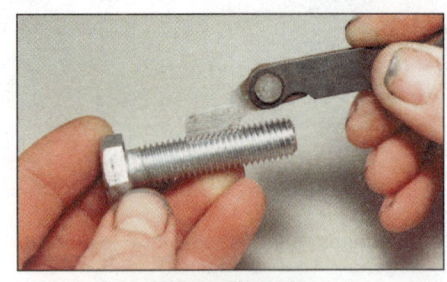

2.12 Using a thread gauge to measure pitch

Circlips (see illustration 2.8)

- Circlips (sometimes called snap-rings) are used to retain components on a shaft or in a housing and have corresponding external or internal ears to permit removal. Parallel-sided (machined) circlips can be installed either way round in their groove, whereas stamped circlips (which have a chamfered edge on one face) must be installed with the chamfer facing away from the direction of thrust load **(see illustration 2.9)**.

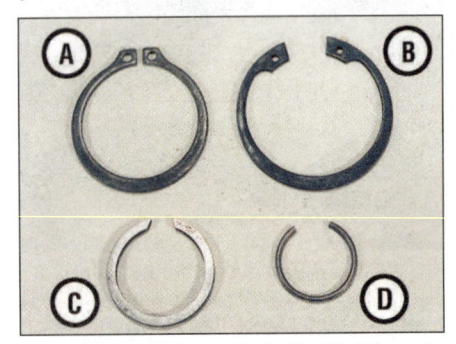

2.8 External stamped circlip (A), internal stamped circlip (B), machined circlip (C) and wire circlip (D)

- Always use circlip pliers to remove and install circlips; expand or compress them just enough to remove them. After installation, rotate the circlip in its groove to ensure it is securely seated. If installing a circlip on a splined shaft, always align its opening with a shaft channel to ensure the circlip ends are well supported and unlikely to catch **(see illustration 2.10)**.

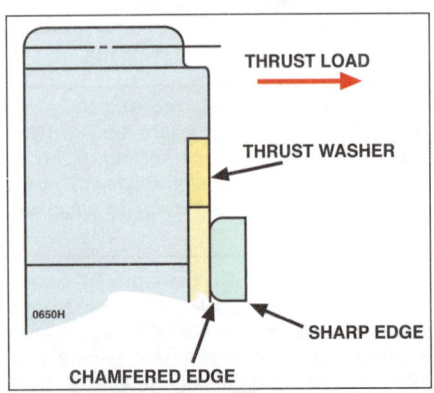

2.9 Correct fitting of a stamped circlip

- Circlips can wear due to the thrust of components and become loose in their grooves, with the subsequent danger of becoming dislodged in operation. For this reason, renewal is advised every time a circlip is disturbed.
- Wire circlips are commonly used as piston pin retaining clips. If a removal tang is provided, long-nosed pliers can be used to dislodge them, otherwise careful use of a small flat-bladed screwdriver is necessary. Wire circlips should be renewed every time they are disturbed.

Thread diameter and pitch

- Diameter of a male thread (screw, bolt or stud) is the outside diameter of the threaded portion **(see illustration 2.11)**. Most motorcycle manufacturers use the ISO (International Standards Organisation) metric system expressed in millimetres, eg M6 refers to a 6 mm diameter thread. Sizing is the same for nuts, except that the thread diameter is measured across the valleys of the nut.
- Pitch is the distance between the peaks of the thread **(see illustration 2.11)**. It is expressed in millimetres, thus a common bolt size may be expressed as 6.0 x 1.0 mm (6 mm thread diameter and 1 mm pitch). Generally pitch increases in proportion to thread diameter, although there are always exceptions.
- Thread diameter and pitch are related for conventional fastener applications and the accompanying table can be used as a guide. Additionally, the AF (Across Flats), spanner or socket size dimension of the bolt or nut **(see illustration 2.11)** is linked to thread and pitch specification. Thread pitch can be measured with a thread gauge **(see illustration 2.12)**.

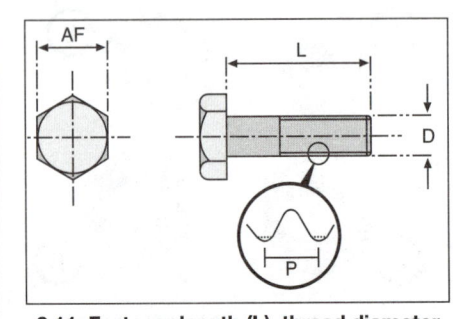

2.11 Fastener length (L), thread diameter (D), thread pitch (P) and head size (AF)

AF size	Thread diameter x pitch (mm)
8 mm	M5 x 0.8
8 mm	M6 x 1.0
10 mm	M6 x 1.0
12 mm	M8 x 1.25
14 mm	M10 x 1.25
17 mm	M12 x 1.25

- The threads of most fasteners are of the right-hand type, ie they are turned clockwise to tighten and anti-clockwise to loosen. The reverse situation applies to left-hand thread fasteners, which are turned anti-clockwise to tighten and clockwise to loosen. Left-hand threads are used where rotation of a component might loosen a conventional right-hand thread fastener.

Seized fasteners

- Corrosion of external fasteners due to water or reaction between two dissimilar metals can occur over a period of time. It will build up sooner in wet conditions or in countries where salt is used on the roads during the winter. If a fastener is severely corroded it is likely that normal methods of removal will fail and result in its head being ruined. When you attempt removal, the fastener thread should be heard to crack free and unscrew easily - if it doesn't, stop there before damaging something.
- A smart tap on the head of the fastener will often succeed in breaking free corrosion which has occurred in the threads **(see illustration 2.13)**.
- An aerosol penetrating fluid (such as WD-40) applied the night beforehand may work its way down into the thread and ease removal. Depending on the location, you may be able to make up a Plasticine well around the fastener head and fill it with penetrating fluid.

2.13 A sharp tap on the head of a fastener will often break free a corroded thread

Tools and Workshop Tips REF•7

- If you are working on an engine internal component, corrosion will most likely not be a problem due to the well lubricated environment. However, components can be very tight and an impact driver is a useful tool in freeing them (see illustration 2.14).

2.14 Using an impact driver to free a fastener

- Where corrosion has occurred between dissimilar metals (eg steel and aluminium alloy), the application of heat to the fastener head will create a disproportionate expansion rate between the two metals and break the seizure caused by the corrosion. Whether heat can be applied depends on the location of the fastener - any surrounding components likely to be damaged must first be removed (see illustration 2.15). Heat can be applied using a paint stripper heat gun or clothes iron, or by immersing the component in boiling water - wear protective gloves to prevent scalding or burns to the hands.

2.15 Using heat to free a seized fastener

- As a last resort, it is possible to use a hammer and cold chisel to work the fastener head unscrewed (see illustration 2.16). This will damage the fastener, but more importantly extreme care must be taken not to damage the surrounding component.

Caution: Remember that the component being secured is generally of more value than the bolt, nut or screw - when the fastener is freed, do not unscrew it with force, instead work the fastener back and forth when resistance is felt to prevent thread damage.

2.16 Using a hammer and chisel to free a seized fastener

Broken fasteners and damaged heads

- If the shank of a broken bolt or screw is accessible you can grip it with self-locking grips. The knurled wheel type stud extractor tool or self-gripping stud puller tool is particularly useful for removing the long studs which screw into the cylinder mouth surface of the crankcase or bolts and screws from which the head has broken off (see illustration 2.17). Studs can also be removed by locking two nuts together on the threaded end of the stud and using a spanner on the lower nut (see illustration 2.18).

2.17 Using a stud extractor tool to remove a broken crankcase stud

2.18 Two nuts can be locked together to unscrew a stud from a component

- A bolt or screw which has broken off below or level with the casing must be extracted using a screw extractor set. Centre punch the fastener to centralise the drill bit, then drill a hole in the fastener (see illustration 2.19). Select a drill bit which is approximately half to three-quarters the

2.19 When using a screw extractor, first drill a hole in the fastener . . .

diameter of the fastener and drill to a depth which will accommodate the extractor. Use the largest size extractor possible, but avoid leaving too small a wall thickness otherwise the extractor will merely force the fastener walls outwards wedging it in the casing thread.

- If a spiral type extractor is used, thread it anti-clockwise into the fastener. As it is screwed in, it will grip the fastener and unscrew it from the casing (see illustration 2.20).

2.20 . . . then thread the extractor anti-clockwise into the fastener

- If a taper type extractor is used, tap it into the fastener so that it is firmly wedged in place. Unscrew the extractor (anti-clockwise) to draw the fastener out.

⚠️ **Warning: Stud extractors are very hard and may break off in the fastener if care is not taken - ask an engineer about spark erosion if this happens.**

- Alternatively, the broken bolt/screw can be drilled out and the hole retapped for an oversize bolt/screw or a diamond-section thread insert. It is essential that the drilling is carried out squarely and to the correct depth, otherwise the casing may be ruined - if in doubt, entrust the work to an engineer.
- Bolts and nuts with rounded corners cause the correct size spanner or socket to slip when force is applied. Of the types of spanner/socket available always use a six-point type rather than an eight or twelve-point type - better grip

REF•8 Tools and Workshop Tips

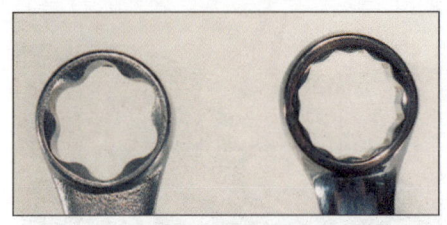

2.21 Comparison of surface drive ring spanner (left) with 12-point type (right)

is obtained. Surface drive spanners grip the middle of the hex flats, rather than the corners, and are thus good in cases of damaged heads **(see illustration 2.21)**.

• Slotted-head or Phillips-head screws are often damaged by the use of the wrong size screwdriver. Allen-head and Torx-head screws are much less likely to sustain damage. If enough of the screw head is exposed you can use a hacksaw to cut a slot in its head and then use a conventional flat-bladed screwdriver to remove it. Alternatively use a hammer and cold chisel to tap the head of the fastener around to slacken it. Always replace damaged fasteners with new ones, preferably Torx or Allen-head type.

HAYNES HiNT

A dab of valve grinding compound between the screw head and screwdriver tip will often give a good grip.

Thread repair

• Threads (particularly those in aluminium alloy components) can be damaged by overtightening, being assembled with dirt in the threads, or from a component working loose and vibrating. Eventually the thread will fail completely, and it will be impossible to tighten the fastener.

• If a thread is damaged or clogged with old locking compound it can be renovated with a thread repair tool (thread chaser) **(see illustrations 2.22 and 2.23)**; special thread

2.22 A thread repair tool being used to correct an internal thread

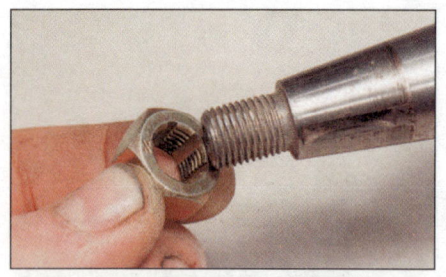

2.23 A thread repair tool being used to correct an external thread

chasers are available for spark plug hole threads. The tool will not cut a new thread, but clean and true the original thread. Make sure that you use the correct diameter and pitch tool. Similarly, external threads can be cleaned up with a die or a thread restorer file **(see illustration 2.24)**.

2.24 Using a thread restorer file

• It is possible to drill out the old thread and retap the component to the next thread size. This will work where there is enough surrounding material and a new bolt or screw can be obtained. Sometimes, however, this is not possible - such as where the bolt/screw passes through another component which must also be suitably modified, also in cases where a spark plug or oil drain plug cannot be obtained in a larger diameter thread size.

• The diamond-section thread insert (often known by its popular trade name of Heli-Coil) is a simple and effective method of renewing the thread and retaining the original size. A kit can be purchased which contains the tap, insert and installing tool **(see illustration 2.25)**. Drill out the damaged thread with the size drill specified **(see illustration 2.26)**. Carefully retap the thread **(see illustration 2.27)**. Install the

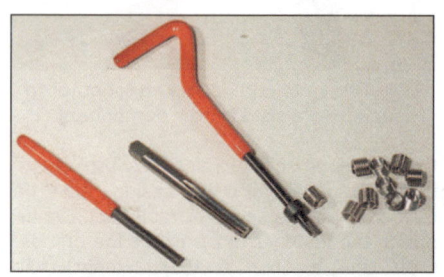

2.25 Obtain a thread insert kit to suit the thread diameter and pitch required

2.26 To install a thread insert, first drill out the original thread . . .

2.27 . . . tap a new thread . . .

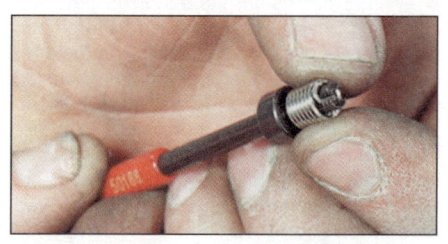

2.28 . . . fit insert on the installing tool . . .

2.29 . . . and thread into the component . . .

2.30 . . . break off the tang when complete

insert on the installing tool and thread it slowly into place using a light downward pressure **(see illustrations 2.28 and 2.29)**. When positioned between a 1/4 and 1/2 turn below the surface withdraw the installing tool and use the break-off tool to press down on the tang, breaking it off **(see illustration 2.30)**.

• There are epoxy thread repair kits on the market which can rebuild stripped internal threads, although this repair should not be used on high load-bearing components.

Tools and Workshop Tips REF•9

Thread locking and sealing compounds

● Locking compounds are used in locations where the fastener is prone to loosening due to vibration or on important safety-related items which might cause loss of control of the motorcycle if they fail. It is also used where important fasteners cannot be secured by other means such as lockwashers or split pins.

● Before applying locking compound, make sure that the threads (internal and external) are clean and dry with all old compound removed. Select a compound to suit the component being secured - a non-permanent general locking and sealing type is suitable for most applications, but a high strength type is needed for permanent fixing of studs in castings. Apply a drop or two of the compound to the first few threads of the fastener, then thread it into place and tighten to the specified torque. Do not apply excessive thread locking compound otherwise the thread may be damaged on subsequent removal.

● Certain fasteners are impregnated with a dry film type coating of locking compound on their threads. Always renew this type of fastener if disturbed.

● Anti-seize compounds, such as copper-based greases, can be applied to protect threads from seizure due to extreme heat and corrosion. A common instance is spark plug threads and exhaust system fasteners.

3 Measuring tools and gauges

Feeler gauges

● Feeler gauges (or blades) are used for measuring small gaps and clearances **(see illustration 3.1)**. They can also be used to measure endfloat (sideplay) of a component on a shaft where access is not possible with a dial gauge.

● Feeler gauge sets should be treated with care and not bent or damaged. They are etched with their size on one face. Keep them clean and very lightly oiled to prevent corrosion build-up.

3.1 Feeler gauges are used for measuring small gaps and clearances - thickness is marked on one face of gauge

● When measuring a clearance, select a gauge which is a light sliding fit between the two components. You may need to use two gauges together to measure the clearance accurately.

Micrometers

● A micrometer is a precision tool capable of measuring to 0.01 or 0.001 of a millimetre. It should always be stored in its case and not in the general toolbox. It must be kept clean and never dropped, otherwise its frame or measuring anvils could be distorted resulting in inaccurate readings.

● External micrometers are used for measuring outside diameters of components and have many more applications than internal micrometers. Micrometers are available in different size ranges, eg 0 to 25 mm, 25 to 50 mm, and upwards in 25 mm steps; some large micrometers have interchangeable anvils to allow a range of measurements to be taken. Generally the largest precision measurement you are likely to take on a motorcycle is the piston diameter.

● Internal micrometers (or bore micrometers) are used for measuring inside diameters, such as valve guides and cylinder bores. Telescoping gauges and small hole gauges are used in conjunction with an external micrometer, whereas the more expensive internal micrometers have their own measuring device.

External micrometer

Note: *The conventional analogue type instrument is described. Although much easier to read, digital micrometers are considerably more expensive.*

● Always check the calibration of the micrometer before use. With the anvils closed (0 to 25 mm type) or set over a test gauge (for

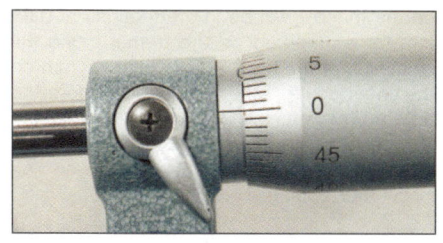

3.2 Check micrometer calibration before use

the larger types) the scale should read zero **(see illustration 3.2)**; make sure that the anvils (and test piece) are clean first. Any discrepancy can be adjusted by referring to the instructions supplied with the tool. Remember that the micrometer is a precision measuring tool - don't force the anvils closed, use the ratchet (4) on the end of the micrometer to close it. In this way, a measured force is always applied.

● To use, first make sure that the item being measured is clean. Place the anvil of the micrometer (1) against the item and use the thimble (2) to bring the spindle (3) lightly into contact with the other side of the item **(see illustration 3.3)**. Don't tighten the thimble down because this will damage the micrometer - instead use the ratchet (4) on the end of the micrometer. The ratchet mechanism applies a measured force preventing damage to the instrument.

● The micrometer is read by referring to the linear scale on the sleeve and the annular scale on the thimble. Read off the sleeve first to obtain the base measurement, then add the fine measurement from the thimble to obtain the overall reading. The linear scale on the sleeve represents the measuring range of the micrometer (eg 0 to 25 mm). The annular scale

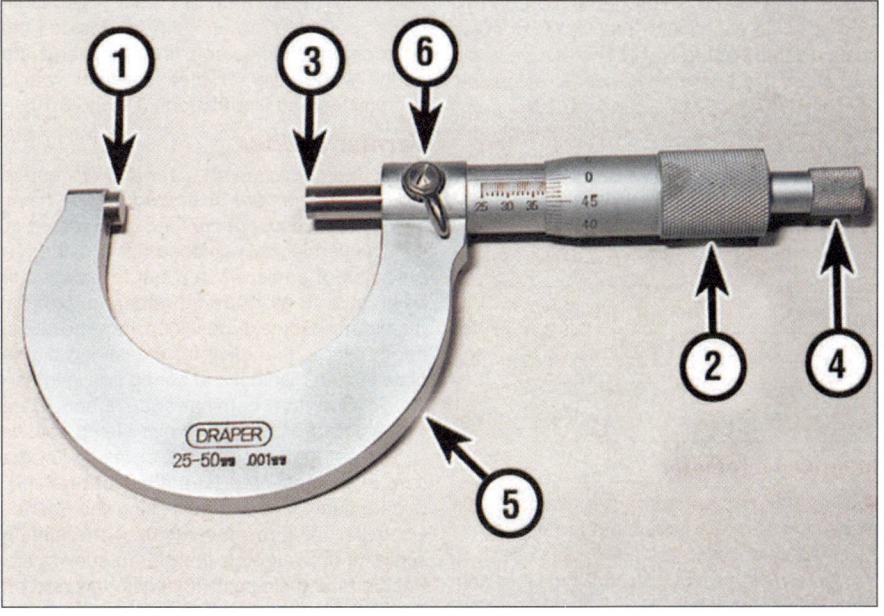

3.3 Micrometer component parts

1 Anvil	3 Spindle	5 Frame
2 Thimble	4 Ratchet	6 Locking lever

REF•10 Tools and Workshop Tips

on the thimble will be in graduations of 0.01 mm (or as marked on the frame) - one full revolution of the thimble will move 0.5 mm on the linear scale. Take the reading where the datum line on the sleeve intersects the thimble's scale. Always position the eye directly above the scale otherwise an inaccurate reading will result.

In the example shown the item measures 2.95 mm (see illustration 3.4):

Linear scale	2.00 mm
Linear scale	0.50 mm
Annular scale	0.45 mm
Total figure	**2.95 mm**

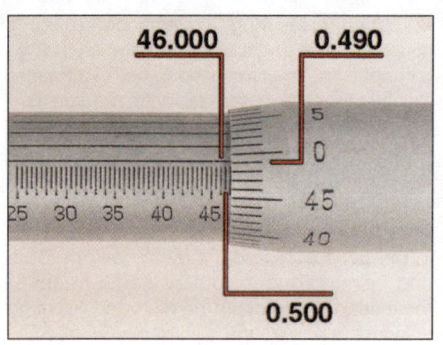

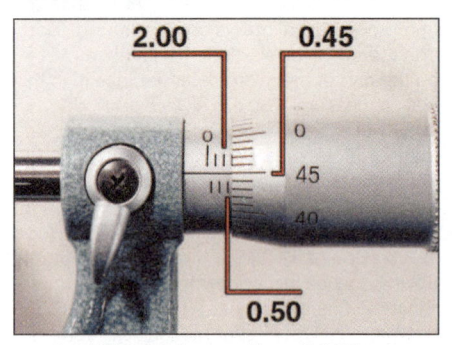

3.4 Micrometer reading of 2.95 mm

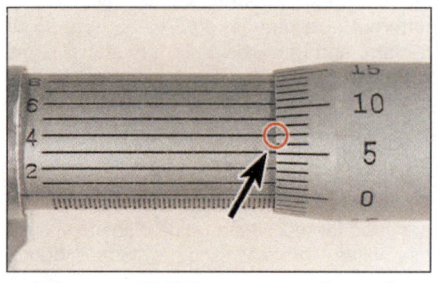

3.5 Micrometer reading of 46.99 mm on linear and annular scales . . .

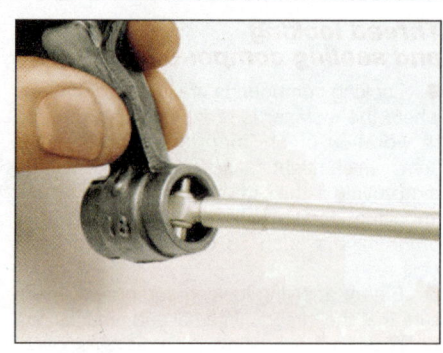

3.6 . . . and 0.004 mm on vernier scale

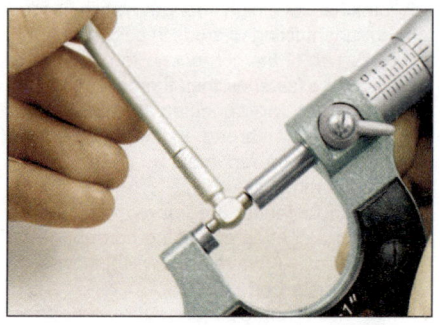

3.7 Expand the telescoping gauge in the bore, lock its position . . .

3.8 . . . then measure the gauge with a micrometer

Most micrometers have a locking lever (6) on the frame to hold the setting in place, allowing the item to be removed from the micrometer.
- Some micrometers have a vernier scale on their sleeve, providing an even finer measurement to be taken, in 0.001 increments of a millimetre. Take the sleeve and thimble measurement as described above, then check which graduation on the vernier scale aligns with that of the annular scale on the thimble **Note:** *The eye must be perpendicular to the scale when taking the vernier reading - if necessary rotate the body of the micrometer to ensure this.* Multiply the vernier scale figure by 0.001 and add it to the base and fine measurement figures.

In the example shown the item measures 46.994 mm (see illustrations 3.5 and 3.6):

Linear scale (base)	46.000 mm
Linear scale (base)	00.500 mm
Annular scale (fine)	00.490 mm
Vernier scale	00.004 mm
Total figure	**46.994 mm**

Internal micrometer

- Internal micrometers are available for measuring bore diameters, but are expensive and unlikely to be available for home use. It is suggested that a set of telescoping gauges and small hole gauges, both of which must be used with an external micrometer, will suffice for taking internal measurements on a motorcycle.
- Telescoping gauges can be used to measure internal diameters of components. Select a gauge with the correct size range, make sure its ends are clean and insert it into the bore. Expand the gauge, then lock its position and withdraw it from the bore **(see illustration 3.7)**. Measure across the gauge ends with a micrometer **(see illustration 3.8)**.
- Very small diameter bores (such as valve guides) are measured with a small hole gauge. Once adjusted to a slip-fit inside the component, its position is locked and the gauge withdrawn for measurement with a micrometer **(see illustrations 3.9 and 3.10)**.

Vernier caliper

Note: *The conventional linear and dial gauge type instruments are described. Digital types are easier to read, but are far more expensive.*
- The vernier caliper does not provide the precision of a micrometer, but is versatile in being able to measure internal and external diameters. Some types also incorporate a depth gauge. It is ideal for measuring clutch plate friction material and spring free lengths.
- To use the conventional linear scale vernier, slacken off the vernier clamp screws (1) and set its jaws over (2), or inside (3), the item to be measured **(see illustration 3.11)**. Slide the jaw into contact, using the thumbwheel (4) for fine movement of the sliding scale (5) then tighten the clamp screws (1). Read off the main scale (6) where the zero on the sliding scale (5) intersects it, taking the whole number to the left of the zero; this provides the base measurement. View along the sliding scale and select the division which

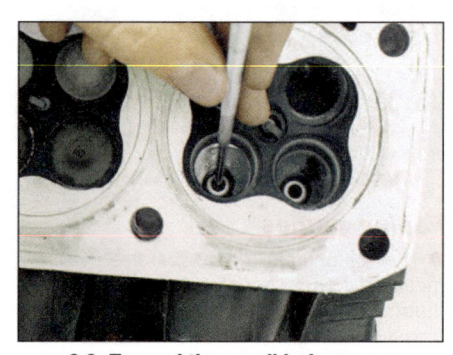

3.9 Expand the small hole gauge in the bore, lock its position . . .

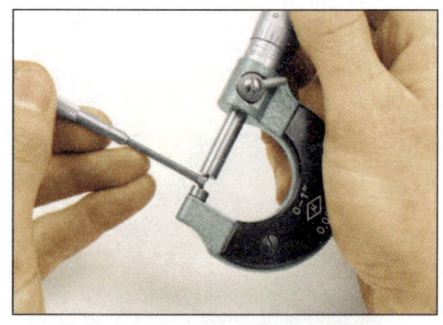

3.10 . . . then measure the gauge with a micrometer

lines up exactly with any of the divisions on the main scale, noting that the divisions usually represents 0.02 of a millimetre. Add this fine measurement to the base measurement to obtain the total reading.

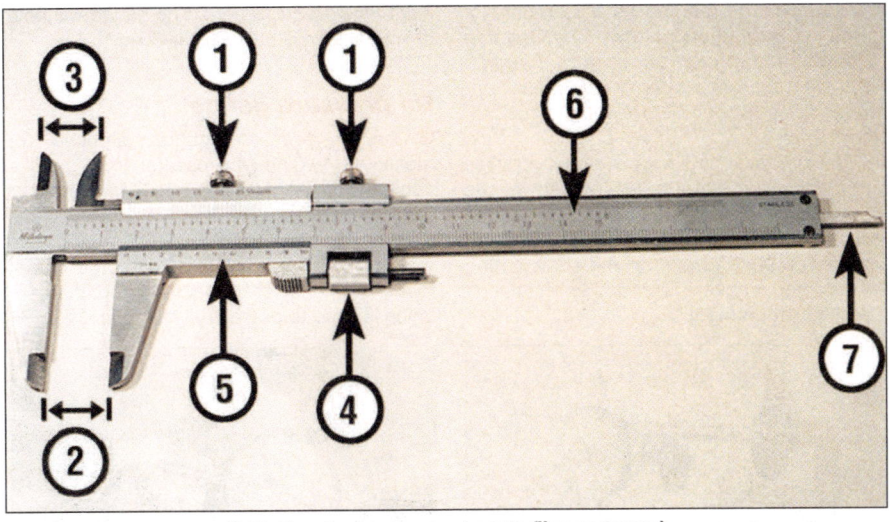

Tools and Workshop Tips REF•11

3.11 Vernier component parts (linear gauge)

1 Clamp screws
2 External jaws
3 Internal jaws
4 Thumbwheel
5 Sliding scale
6 Main scale
7 Depth gauge

In the example shown the item measures 55.92 mm (see illustration 3.12):

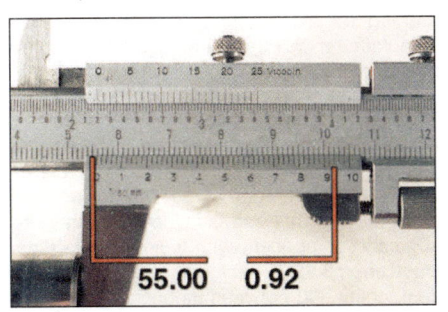

3.12 Vernier gauge reading of 55.92 mm

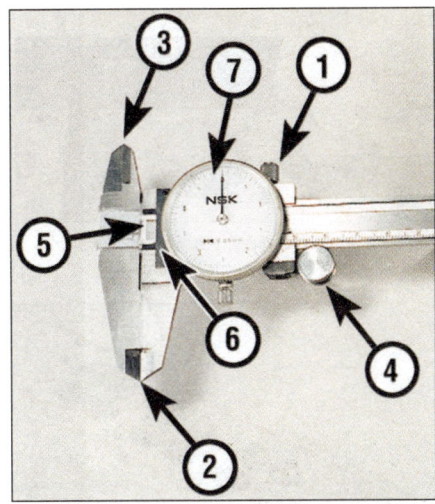

Base measurement	55.00 mm
Fine measurement	00.92 mm
Total figure	**55.92 mm**

● Some vernier calipers are equipped with a dial gauge for fine measurement. Before use, check that the jaws are clean, then close them fully and check that the dial gauge reads zero. If necessary adjust the gauge ring accordingly. Slacken the vernier clamp screw (1) and set its jaws over (2), or inside (3), the item to be measured (see illustration 3.13). Slide the jaws into contact, using the thumbwheel (4) for fine movement. Read off the main scale (5) where the edge of the sliding scale (6) intersects it, taking the whole number to the left of the zero; this provides the base measurement. Read off the needle position on the dial gauge (7) scale to provide the fine measurement; each division represents 0.05 of a millimetre. Add this fine measurement to the base measurement to obtain the total reading.

In the example shown the item measures 55.95 mm (see illustration 3.14):

Base measurement	55.00 mm
Fine measurement	00.95 mm
Total figure	**55.95 mm**

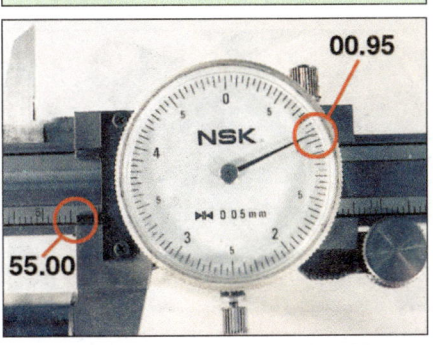

3.13 Vernier component parts (dial gauge)

1 Clamp screw
2 External jaws
3 Internal jaws
4 Thumbwheel
5 Main scale
6 Sliding scale
7 Dial gauge

3.14 Vernier gauge reading of 55.95 mm

Plastigauge

● Plastigauge is a plastic material which can be compressed between two surfaces to measure the oil clearance between them. The width of the compressed Plastigauge is measured against a calibrated scale to determine the clearance.

● Common uses of Plastigauge are for measuring the clearance between crankshaft journal and main bearing inserts, between crankshaft journal and big-end bearing inserts, and between camshaft and bearing surfaces. The following example describes big-end oil clearance measurement.

● Handle the Plastigauge material carefully to prevent distortion. Using a sharp knife, cut a length which corresponds with the width of the bearing being measured and place it carefully across the journal so that it is parallel with the shaft (see illustration 3.15). Carefully install both bearing shells and the connecting rod. Without rotating the rod on the journal tighten its bolts or nuts (as applicable) to the specified torque. The connecting rod and bearings are then disassembled and the crushed Plastigauge examined.

3.15 Plastigauge placed across shaft journal

● Using the scale provided in the Plastigauge kit, measure the width of the material to determine the oil clearance (see illustration 3.16). Always remove all traces of Plastigauge after use using your fingernails.

Caution: Arriving at the correct clearance demands that the assembly is torqued correctly, according to the settings and sequence (where applicable) provided by the motorcycle manufacturer.

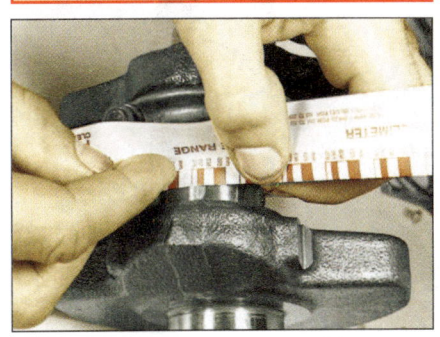

3.16 Measuring the width of the crushed Plastigauge

Tools and Workshop Tips

Dial gauge or DTI (Dial Test Indicator)

- A dial gauge can be used to accurately measure small amounts of movement. Typical uses are measuring shaft runout or shaft endfloat (sideplay) and setting piston position for ignition timing on two-strokes. A dial gauge set usually comes with a range of different probes and adapters and mounting equipment.
- The gauge needle must point to zero when at rest. Rotate the ring around its periphery to zero the gauge.
- Check that the gauge is capable of reading the extent of movement in the work. Most gauges have a small dial set in the face which records whole millimetres of movement as well as the fine scale around the face periphery which is calibrated in 0.01 mm divisions. Read off the small dial first to obtain the base measurement, then add the measurement from the fine scale to obtain the total reading.

In the example shown the gauge reads 1.48 mm (see illustration 3.17):

Base measurement	1.00 mm
Fine measurement	0.48 mm
Total figure	**1.48 mm**

3.17 Dial gauge reading of 1.48 mm

- If measuring shaft runout, the shaft must be supported in vee-blocks and the gauge mounted on a stand perpendicular to the shaft. Rest the tip of the gauge against the centre of the shaft and rotate the shaft slowly whilst watching the gauge reading (see illustration 3.18). Take several measurements along the length of the shaft and record the maximum gauge reading as the amount of runout in the shaft. **Note:** *The reading obtained will be total runout at that point - some manufacturers specify that the runout figure is halved to compare with their specified runout limit.*
- Endfloat (sideplay) measurement requires that the gauge is mounted securely to the surrounding component with its probe touching the end of the shaft. Using hand pressure, push and pull on the shaft noting the maximum endfloat recorded on the gauge (see illustration 3.19).

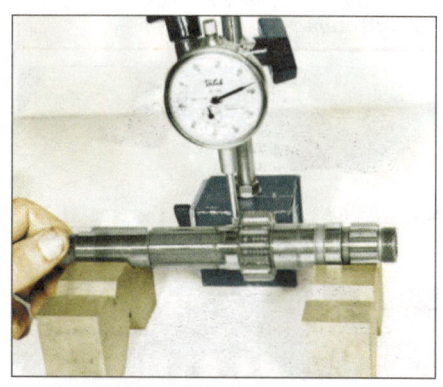

3.19 Using a dial gauge to measure shaft endfloat

- A dial gauge with suitable adapters can be used to determine piston position BTDC on two-stroke engines for the purposes of ignition timing. The gauge, adapter and suitable length probe are installed in the place of the spark plug and the gauge zeroed at TDC. If the piston position is specified as 1.14 mm BTDC, rotate the engine back to 2.00 mm BTDC, then slowly forwards to 1.14 mm BTDC.

Cylinder compression gauges

- A compression gauge is used for measuring cylinder compression. Either the rubber-cone type or the threaded adapter type can be used. The latter is preferred to ensure a perfect seal against the cylinder head. A 0 to 300 psi (0 to 20 Bar) type gauge (for petrol/gasoline engines) will be suitable for motorcycles.
- The spark plug is removed and the gauge either held hard against the cylinder head (cone type) or the gauge adapter screwed into the cylinder head (threaded type) (see illustration 3.20). Cylinder compression is measured with the engine turning over, but not running - carry out the compression test as described in *Fault Finding Equipment*. The gauge will hold the reading until manually released.

Oil pressure gauge

- An oil pressure gauge is used for measuring engine oil pressure. Most gauges come with a set of adapters to fit the thread of the take-off point (see illustration 3.21). If the take-off point specified by the motorcycle manufacturer is an external oil pipe union, make sure that the specified replacement union is used to prevent oil starvation.

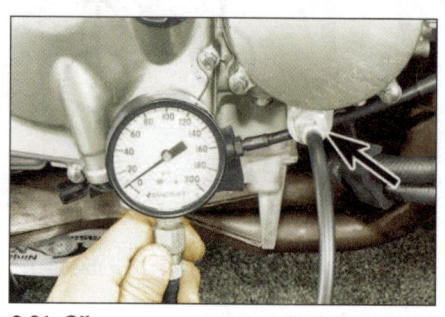

3.21 Oil pressure gauge and take-off point adapter (arrow)

- Oil pressure is measured with the engine running (at a specific rpm) and often the manufacturer will specify pressure limits for a cold and hot engine.

Straight-edge and surface plate

- If checking the gasket face of a component for warpage, place a steel rule or precision straight-edge across the gasket face and measure any gap between the straight-edge and component with feeler gauges (see illustration 3.22). Check diagonally across the component and between mounting holes (see illustration 3.23).

3.22 Use a straight-edge and feeler gauges to check for warpage

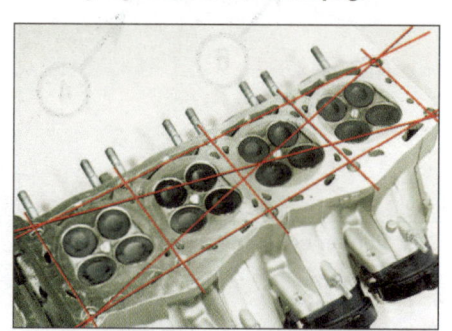

3.18 Using a dial gauge to measure shaft runout

3.20 Using a rubber-cone type cylinder compression gauge

3.23 Check for warpage in these directions

Tools and Workshop Tips REF•13

● Checking individual components for warpage, such as clutch plain (metal) plates, requires a perfectly flat plate or piece or plate glass and feeler gauges.

4 Torque and leverage

What is torque?

● Torque describes the twisting force about a shaft. The amount of torque applied is determined by the distance from the centre of the shaft to the end of the lever and the amount of force being applied to the end of the lever; distance multiplied by force equals torque.

● The manufacturer applies a measured torque to a bolt or nut to ensure that it will not slacken in use and to hold two components securely together without movement in the joint. The actual torque setting depends on the thread size, bolt or nut material and the composition of the components being held.

● Too little torque may cause the fastener to loosen due to vibration, whereas too much torque will distort the joint faces of the component or cause the fastener to shear off. Always stick to the specified torque setting.

Using a torque wrench

● Check the calibration of the torque wrench and make sure it has a suitable range for the job. Torque wrenches are available in Nm (Newton-metres), kgf m (kilograms-force metre), lbf ft (pounds-feet), lbf in (inch-pounds). Do not confuse lbf ft with lbf in.

● Adjust the tool to the desired torque on the scale (see illustration 4.1). If your torque wrench is not calibrated in the units specified, carefully convert the figure (see *Conversion Factors*). A manufacturer sometimes gives a torque setting as a range (8 to 10 Nm) rather than a single figure - in this case set the tool midway between the two settings. The same torque may be expressed as 9 Nm ± 1 Nm. Some torque wrenches have a method of locking the setting so that it isn't inadvertently altered during use.

● Install the bolts/nuts in their correct location and secure them lightly. Their threads must be clean and free of any old locking compound. Unless specified the threads and flange should be dry - oiled threads are necessary in certain circumstances and the manufacturer will take this into account in the specified torque figure. Similarly, the manufacturer may also specify the application of thread-locking compound.

● Tighten the fasteners in the specified sequence until the torque wrench clicks, indicating that the torque setting has been reached. Apply the torque again to double-check the setting. Where different thread diameter fasteners secure the component, as a rule tighten the larger diameter ones first.

● When the torque wrench has been finished with, release the lock (where applicable) and fully back off its setting to zero - do not leave the torque wrench tensioned. Also, do not use a torque wrench for slackening a fastener.

Angle-tightening

● Manufacturers often specify a figure in degrees for final tightening of a fastener. This usually follows tightening to a specific torque setting.

● A degree disc can be set and attached to the socket (see illustration 4.2) or a protractor can be used to mark the angle of movement on the bolt/nut head and the surrounding casting (see illustration 4.3).

4.2 Angle tightening can be accomplished with a torque-angle gauge . . .

4.3 . . . or by marking the angle on the surrounding component

Loosening sequences

● Where more than one bolt/nut secures a component, loosen each fastener evenly a little at a time. In this way, not all the stress of the joint is held by one fastener and the components are not likely to distort.

● If a tightening sequence is provided, work in the REVERSE of this, but if not, work from the outside in, in a criss-cross sequence (see illustration 4.4).

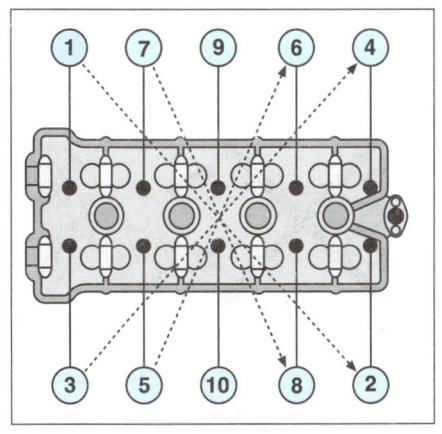

4.4 When slackening, work from the outside inwards

Tightening sequences

● If a component is held by more than one fastener it is important that the retaining bolts/nuts are tightened evenly to prevent uneven stress build-up and distortion of sealing faces. This is especially important on high-compression joints such as the cylinder head.

● A sequence is usually provided by the manufacturer, either in a diagram or actually marked in the casting. If not, always start in the centre and work outwards in a criss-cross pattern (see illustration 4.5). Start off by securing all bolts/nuts finger-tight, then set the torque wrench and tighten each fastener by a small amount in sequence until the final torque is reached. By following this practice,

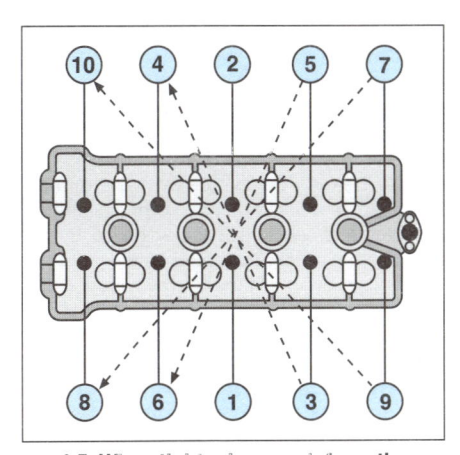

4.1 Set the torque wrench index mark to the setting required, in this case 12 Nm

4.5 When tightening, work from the inside outwards

Tools and Workshop Tips

the joint will be held evenly and will not be distorted. Important joints, such as the cylinder head and big-end fasteners often have two- or three-stage torque settings.

Applying leverage

● Use tools at the correct angle. Position a socket wrench or spanner on the bolt/nut so that you pull it towards you when loosening. If this can't be done, push the spanner without curling your fingers around it **(see illustration 4.6)** - the spanner may slip or the fastener loosen suddenly, resulting in your fingers being crushed against a component.

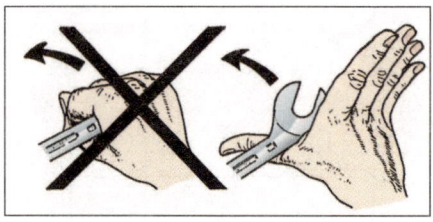

4.6 If you can't pull on the spanner to loosen a fastener, push with your hand open

● Additional leverage is gained by extending the length of the lever. The best way to do this is to use a breaker bar instead of the regular length tool, or to slip a length of tubing over the end of the spanner or socket wrench.
● If additional leverage will not work, the fastener head is either damaged or firmly corroded in place (see *Fasteners*).

5 Bearings

Bearing removal and installation

Drivers and sockets

● Before removing a bearing, always inspect the casing to see which way it must be driven out - some casings will have retaining plates or a cast step. Also check for any identifying markings on the bearing and if installed to a certain depth, measure this at this stage. Some roller bearings are sealed on one side - take note of the original fitted position.
● Bearings can be driven out of a casing using a bearing driver tool (with the correct size head) or a socket of the correct diameter. Select the driver head or socket so that it contacts the outer race of the bearing, not the balls/rollers or inner race. Always support the casing around the bearing housing with wood blocks, otherwise there is a risk of fracture. The bearing is driven out with a few blows on the driver or socket from a heavy mallet. Unless access is severely restricted (as with wheel bearings), a pin-punch is not recommended unless it is moved around the bearing to keep it square in its housing.

● The same equipment can be used to install bearings. Make sure the bearing housing is supported on wood blocks and line up the bearing in its housing. Fit the bearing as noted on removal - generally they are installed with their marked side facing outwards. Tap the bearing squarely into its housing using a driver or socket which bears only on the bearing's outer race - contact with the bearing balls/rollers or inner race will destroy it **(see illustrations 5.1 and 5.2)**.
● Check that the bearing inner race and balls/rollers rotate freely.

5.1 Using a bearing driver against the bearing's outer race

5.2 Using a large socket against the bearing's outer race

Pullers and slide-hammers

● Where a bearing is pressed on a shaft a puller will be required to extract it **(see illustration 5.3)**. Make sure that the puller clamp or legs fit securely behind the bearing and are unlikely to slip out. If pulling a bearing

5.3 This bearing puller clamps behind the bearing and pressure is applied to the shaft end to draw the bearing off

off a gear shaft for example, you may have to locate the puller behind a gear pinion if there is no access to the race and draw the gear pinion off the shaft as well **(see illustration 5.4)**.

Caution: Ensure that the puller's centre bolt locates securely against the end of the shaft and will not slip when pressure is applied. Also ensure that puller does not damage the shaft end.

5.4 Where no access is available to the rear of the bearing, it is sometimes possible to draw off the adjacent component

● Operate the puller so that its centre bolt exerts pressure on the shaft end and draws the bearing off the shaft.
● When installing the bearing on the shaft, tap only on the bearing's inner race - contact with the balls/rollers or outer race with destroy the bearing. Use a socket or length of tubing as a drift which fits over the shaft end **(see illustration 5.5)**.

5.5 When installing a bearing on a shaft use a piece of tubing which bears only on the bearing's inner race

● Where a bearing locates in a blind hole in a casing, it cannot be driven or pulled out as described above. A slide-hammer with knife-edged bearing puller attachment will be required. The puller attachment passes through the bearing and when tightened expands to fit firmly behind the bearing **(see illustration 5.6)**. By operating the slide-hammer part of the tool the bearing is jarred out of its housing **(see illustration 5.7)**.
● It is possible, if the bearing is of reasonable weight, for it to drop out of its housing if the casing is heated as described opposite. If this

Tools and Workshop Tips REF•15

5.6 Expand the bearing puller so that it locks behind the bearing . . .

5.7 . . . attach the slide hammer to the bearing puller

method is attempted, first prepare a work surface which will enable the casing to be tapped face down to help dislodge the bearing - a wood surface is ideal since it will not damage the casing's gasket surface. Wearing protective gloves, tap the heated casing several times against the work surface to dislodge the bearing under its own weight **(see illustration 5.8)**.

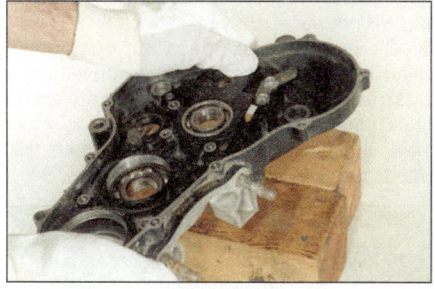

5.8 Tapping a casing face down on wood blocks can often dislodge a bearing

● Bearings can be installed in blind holes using the driver or socket method described above.

Drawbolts

● Where a bearing or bush is set in the eye of a component, such as a suspension linkage arm or connecting rod small-end, removal by drift may damage the component. Furthermore, a rubber bushing in a shock absorber eye cannot successfully be driven out of position. If access is available to a engineering press, the task is straightforward. If not, a drawbolt can be fabricated to extract the bearing or bush.

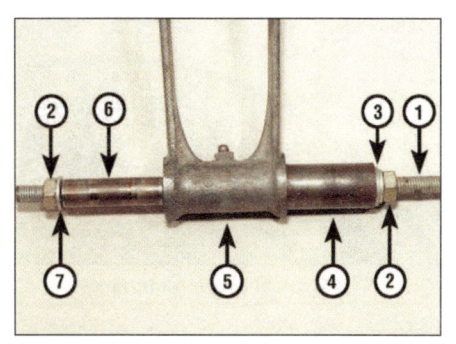

5.9 Drawbolt component parts assembled on a suspension arm

1. Bolt or length of threaded bar
2. Nuts
3. Washer (external diameter greater than tubing internal diameter)
4. Tubing (internal diameter sufficient to accommodate bearing)
5. Suspension arm with bearing
6. Tubing (external diameter slightly smaller than bearing)
7. Washer (external diameter slightly smaller than bearing)

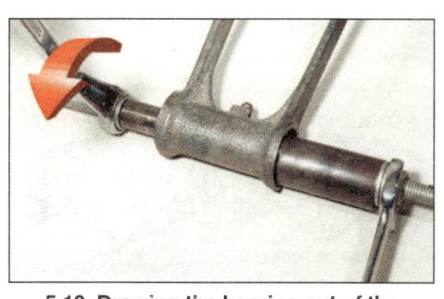

5.10 Drawing the bearing out of the suspension arm

● To extract the bearing/bush you will need a long bolt with nut (or piece of threaded bar with two nuts), a piece of tubing which has an internal diameter larger than the bearing/bush, another piece of tubing which has an external diameter slightly smaller than the bearing/bush, and a selection of washers **(see illustrations 5.9 and 5.10)**. Note that the pieces of tubing must be of the same length, or longer, than the bearing/bush.
● The same kit (without the pieces of tubing) can be used to draw the new bearing/bush back into place **(see illustration 5.11)**.

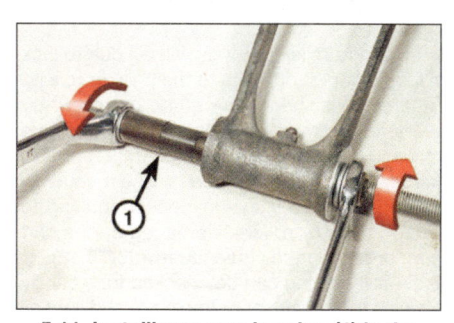

5.11 Installing a new bearing (1) in the suspension arm

Temperature change

● If the bearing's outer race is a tight fit in the casing, the aluminium casing can be heated to release its grip on the bearing. Aluminium will expand at a greater rate than the steel bearing outer race. There are several ways to do this, but avoid any localised extreme heat (such as a blow torch) - aluminium alloy has a low melting point.
● Approved methods of heating a casing are using a domestic oven (heated to 100°C) or immersing the casing in boiling water **(see illustration 5.12)**. Low temperature range localised heat sources such as a paint stripper heat gun or clothes iron can also be used **(see illustration 5.13)**. Alternatively, soak a rag in boiling water, wring it out and wrap it around the bearing housing.

> ⚠ **Warning: All of these methods require care in use to prevent scalding and burns to the hands. Wear protective gloves when handling hot components.**

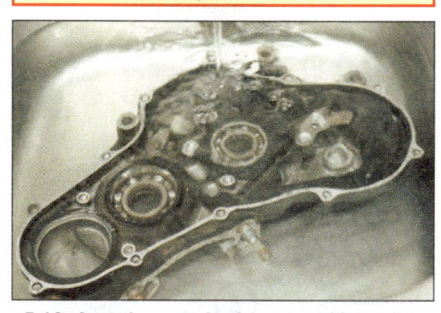

5.12 A casing can be immersed in a sink of boiling water to aid bearing removal

5.13 Using a localised heat source to aid bearing removal

● If heating the whole casing note that plastic components, such as the neutral switch, may suffer - remove them beforehand.
● After heating, remove the bearing as described above. You may find that the expansion is sufficient for the bearing to fall out of the casing under its own weight or with a light tap on the driver or socket.
● If necessary, the casing can be heated to aid bearing installation, and this is sometimes the recommended procedure if the motorcycle manufacturer has designed the housing and bearing fit with this intention.

REF•16 Tools and Workshop Tips

● Installation of bearings can be eased by placing them in a freezer the night before installation. The steel bearing will contract slightly, allowing easy insertion in its housing. This is often useful when installing steering head outer races in the frame.

Bearing types and markings

● Plain shell bearings, ball bearings, needle roller bearings and tapered roller bearings will all be found on motorcycles **(see illustrations 5.14 and 5.15)**. The ball and roller types are usually caged between an inner and outer race, but uncaged variations may be found.

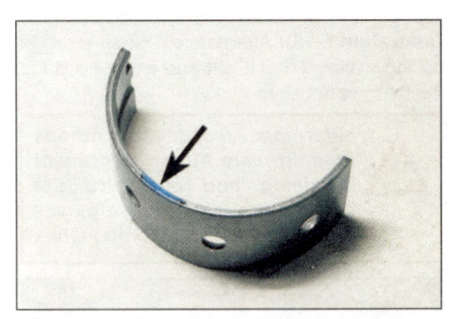

5.14 Shell bearings are either plain or grooved. They are usually identified by colour code (arrow)

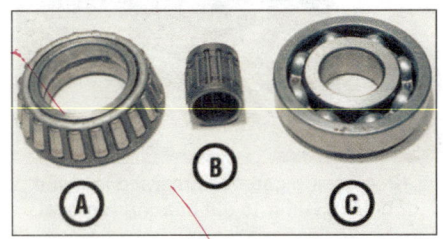

5.15 Tapered roller bearing (A), needle roller bearing (B) and ball journal bearing (C)

● Shell bearings (often called inserts) are usually found at the crankshaft main and connecting rod big-end where they are good at coping with high loads. They are made of a phosphor-bronze material and are impregnated with self-lubricating properties.

● Ball bearings and needle roller bearings consist of a steel inner and outer race with the balls or rollers between the races. They require constant lubrication by oil or grease and are good at coping with axial loads. Taper roller bearings consist of rollers set in a tapered cage set on the inner race; the outer race is separate. They are good at coping with axial loads and prevent movement along the shaft - a typical application is in the steering head.

● Bearing manufacturers produce bearings to ISO size standards and stamp one face of the bearing to indicate its internal and external diameter, load capacity and type **(see illustration 5.16)**.

● Metal bushes are usually of phosphor-bronze material. Rubber bushes are used in suspension mounting eyes. Fibre bushes have also been used in suspension pivots.

5.16 Typical bearing marking

Bearing fault finding

● If a bearing outer race has spun in its housing, the housing material will be damaged. You can use a bearing locking compound to bond the outer race in place if damage is not too severe.

● Shell bearings will fail due to damage of their working surface, as a result of lack of lubrication, corrosion or abrasive particles in the oil **(see illustration 5.17)**. Small particles of dirt in the oil may embed in the bearing material whereas larger particles will score the bearing and shaft journal. If a number of short journeys are made, insufficient heat will be generated to drive off condensation which has built up on the bearings.

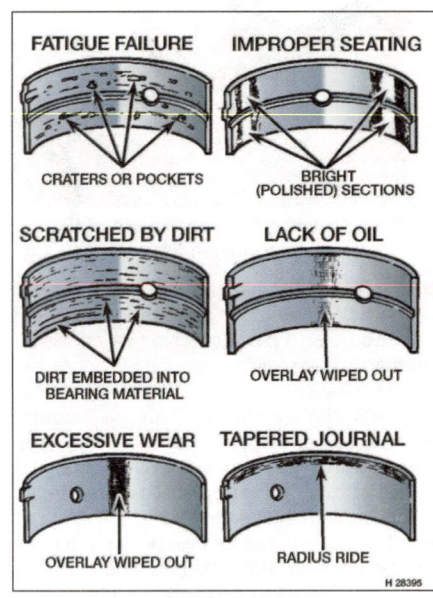

5.17 Typical bearing failures

● Ball and roller bearings will fail due to lack of lubrication or damage to the balls or rollers. Tapered-roller bearings can be damaged by overloading them. Unless the bearing is sealed on both sides, wash it in paraffin (kerosene) to remove all old grease then allow it to dry. Make a visual inspection looking to dented balls or rollers, damaged cages and worn or pitted races **(see illustration 5.18)**.

● A ball bearing can be checked for wear by listening to it when spun. Apply a film of light oil to the bearing and hold it close to the ear - hold the outer race with one hand and spin the inner race with the other hand **(see illustration 5.19)**. The bearing should be almost silent when spun; if it grates or rattles it is worn.

5.18 Example of ball journal bearing with damaged balls and cages

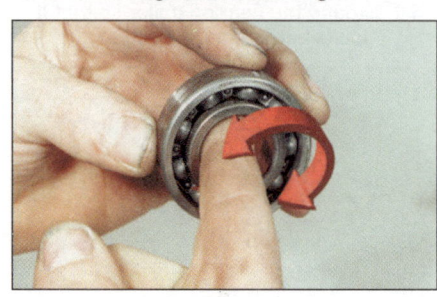

5.19 Hold outer race and listen to inner race when spun

6 Oil seals

Oil seal removal and installation

● Oil seals should be renewed every time a component is dismantled. This is because the seal lips will become set to the sealing surface and will not necessarily reseal.

● Oil seals can be prised out of position using a large flat-bladed screwdriver **(see illustration 6.1)**. In the case of crankcase seals, check first that the seal is not lipped on the inside, preventing its removal with the crankcases joined.

6.1 Prise out oil seals with a large flat-bladed screwdriver

● New seals are usually installed with their marked face (containing the seal reference code) outwards and the spring side towards the fluid being retained. In certain cases, such as a two-stroke engine crankshaft seal, a double lipped seal may be used due to there being fluid or gas on each side of the joint.

Tools and Workshop Tips REF•17

- Use a bearing driver or socket which bears only on the outer hard edge of the seal to install it in the casing - tapping on the inner edge will damage the sealing lip.

Oil seal types and markings

- Oil seals are usually of the single-lipped type. Double-lipped seals are found where a liquid or gas is on both sides of the joint.
- Oil seals can harden and lose their sealing ability if the motorcycle has been in storage for a long period - renewal is the only solution.
- Oil seal manufacturers also conform to the ISO markings for seal size - these are moulded into the outer face of the seal **(see illustration 6.2)**.

6.2 These oil seal markings indicate inside diameter, outside diameter and seal thickness

7 Gaskets and sealants

Types of gasket and sealant

- Gaskets are used to seal the mating surfaces between components and keep lubricants, fluids, vacuum or pressure contained within the assembly. Aluminium gaskets are sometimes found at the cylinder joints, but most gaskets are paper-based. If the mating surfaces of the components being joined are undamaged the gasket can be installed dry, although a dab of sealant or grease will be useful to hold it in place during assembly.
- RTV (Room Temperature Vulcanising) silicone rubber sealants cure when exposed to moisture in the atmosphere. These sealants are good at filling pits or irregular gasket faces, but will tend to be forced out of the joint under very high torque. They can be used to replace a paper gasket, but first make sure that the width of the paper gasket is not essential to the shimming of internal components. RTV sealants should not be used on components containing petrol (gasoline).
- Non-hardening, semi-hardening and hard setting liquid gasket compounds can be used with a gasket or between a metal-to-metal joint. Select the sealant to suit the application: universal non-hardening sealant can be used on virtually all joints; semi-hardening on joint faces which are rough or damaged; hard setting sealant on joints which require a permanent bond and are subjected to high temperature and pressure. **Note:** *Check first if the paper gasket has a bead of sealant impregnated in its surface before applying additional sealant.*
- When choosing a sealant, make sure it is suitable for the application, particularly if being applied in a high-temperature area or in the vicinity of fuel. Certain manufacturers produce sealants in either clear, silver or black colours to match the finish of the engine. This has a particular application on motorcycles where much of the engine is exposed.
- Do not over-apply sealant. That which is squeezed out on the outside of the joint can be wiped off, whereas an excess of sealant on the inside can break off and clog oilways.

Breaking a sealed joint

- Age, heat, pressure and the use of hard setting sealant can cause two components to stick together so tightly that they are difficult to separate using finger pressure alone. Do not resort to using levers unless there is a pry point provided for this purpose **(see illustration 7.1)** or else the gasket surfaces will be damaged.
- Use a soft-faced hammer **(see illustration 7.2)** or a wood block and conventional hammer to strike the component near the mating surface. Avoid hammering against cast extremities since they may break off. If this method fails, try using a wood wedge between the two components.

Caution: If the joint will not separate, double-check that you have removed all the fasteners.

7.1 If a pry point is provided, apply gently pressure with a flat-bladed screwdriver

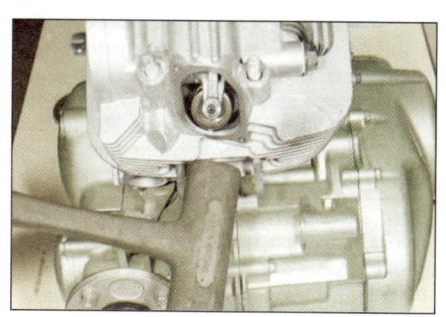

7.2 Tap around the joint with a soft-faced mallet if necessary - don't strike cooling fins

Removal of old gasket and sealant

- Paper gaskets will most likely come away complete, leaving only a few traces stuck on

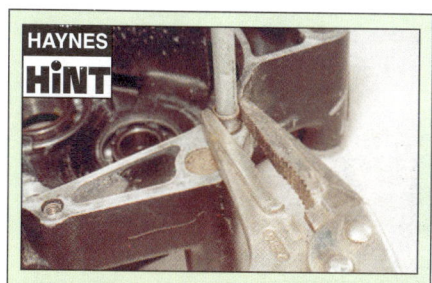

HAYNES HiNT

Most components have one or two hollow locating dowels between the two gasket faces. If a dowel cannot be removed, do not resort to gripping it with pliers - it will almost certainly be distorted. Install a close-fitting socket or Phillips screwdriver into the dowel and then grip the outer edge of the dowel to free it.

the sealing faces of the components. It is imperative that all traces are removed to ensure correct sealing of the new gasket.

- Very carefully scrape all traces of gasket away making sure that the sealing surfaces are not gouged or scored by the scraper **(see illustrations 7.3, 7.4 and 7.5)**. Stubborn deposits can be removed by spraying with an aerosol gasket remover. Final preparation of

7.3 Paper gaskets can be scraped off with a gasket scraper tool . . .

7.4 . . . a knife blade . . .

7.5 . . . or a household scraper

Tools and Workshop Tips

7.6 Fine abrasive paper is wrapped around a flat file to clean up the gasket face

7.7 A kitchen scourer can be used on stubborn deposits

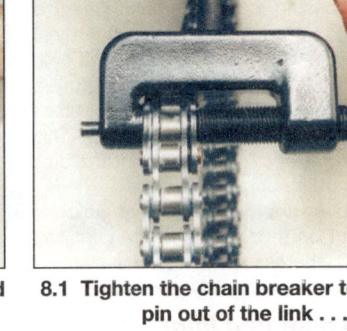

8.1 Tighten the chain breaker to push the pin out of the link . . .

8.2 . . . withdraw the pin, remove the tool . . .

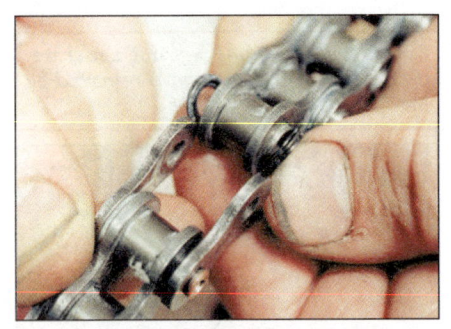

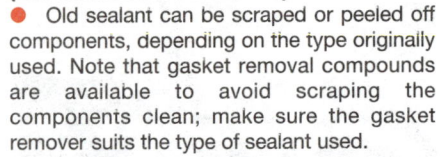

8.3 . . . and separate the chain link

8.4 Insert the new soft link, with O-rings, through the chain ends . . .

8.5 . . . install the O-rings over the pin ends . . .

8.6 . . . followed by the sideplate

8.7 Push the sideplate into position using a clamp

the gasket surface can be made with very fine abrasive paper or a plastic kitchen scourer **(see illustrations 7.6 and 7.7)**.
● Old sealant can be scraped or peeled off components, depending on the type originally used. Note that gasket removal compounds are available to avoid scraping the components clean; make sure the gasket remover suits the type of sealant used.

8 Chains

Breaking and joining final drive chains

● Drive chains for all but small bikes are continuous and do not have a clip-type connecting link. The chain must be broken using a chain breaker tool and the new chain securely riveted together using a new soft rivet-type link. Never use a clip-type connecting link instead of a rivet-type link, except in an emergency. Various chain breaking and riveting tools are available, either as separate tools or combined as illustrated in the accompanying photographs - read the instructions supplied with the tool carefully.

Warning: The need to rivet the new link pins correctly cannot be overstressed - loss of control of the motorcycle is very likely to result if the chain breaks in use.

● Rotate the chain and look for the soft link. The soft link pins look like they have been deeply centre-punched instead of peened over like all the other pins **(see illustration 8.9)** and its sideplate may be a different colour. Position the soft link midway between the sprockets and assemble the chain breaker tool over one of the soft link pins **(see illustration 8.1)**. Operate the tool to push the pin out through the chain **(see illustration 8.2)**. On an O-ring chain, remove the O-rings **(see illustration 8.3)**. Carry out the same procedure on the other soft link pin.

Caution: Certain soft link pins (particularly on the larger chains) may require their ends to be filed or ground off before they can be pressed out using the tool.

● Check that you have the correct size and strength (standard or heavy duty) new soft link - do not reuse the old link. Look for the size marking on the chain sideplates **(see illustration 8.10)**.
● Position the chain ends so that they are engaged over the rear sprocket. On an O-ring chain, install a new O-ring over each pin of the link and insert the link through the two chain ends **(see illustration 8.4)**. Install a new O-ring over the end of each pin, followed by the sideplate (with the chain manufacturer's marking facing outwards) **(see illustrations 8.5 and 8.6)**. On an unsealed chain, insert the link through the two chain ends, then install the sideplate with the chain manufacturer's marking facing outwards.
● Note that it may not be possible to install the sideplate using finger pressure alone. If using a joining tool, assemble it so that the plates of the tool clamp the link and press the sideplate over the pins **(see illustration 8.7)**. Otherwise, use two small sockets placed over

Tools and Workshop Tips REF•19

8.8 Assemble the chain riveting tool over one pin at a time and tighten it fully

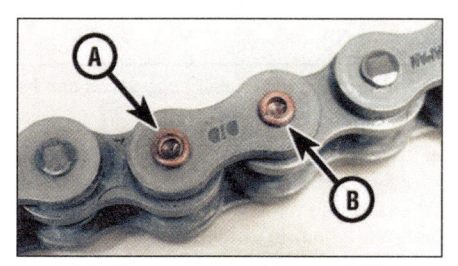

8.9 Pin end correctly riveted (A), pin end unriveted (B)

the rivet ends and two pieces of the wood between a G-clamp. Operate the clamp to press the sideplate over the pins.

● Assemble the joining tool over one pin (following the maker's instructions) and tighten the tool down to spread the pin end securely **(see illustrations 8.8 and 8.9)**. Do the same on the other pin.

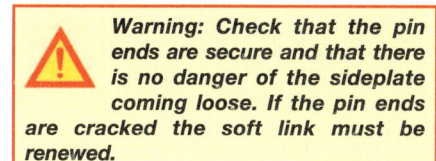

> ⚠ **Warning: Check that the pin ends are secure and that there is no danger of the sideplate coming loose. If the pin ends are cracked the soft link must be renewed.**

Final drive chain sizing

● Chains are sized using a three digit number, followed by a suffix to denote the chain type **(see illustration 8.10)**. Chain type is either standard or heavy duty (thicker sideplates), and also unsealed or O-ring/X-ring type.

● The first digit of the number relates to the pitch of the chain, ie the distance from the centre of one pin to the centre of the next pin **(see illustration 8.11)**. Pitch is expressed in eighths of an inch, as follows:

8.10 Typical chain size and type marking

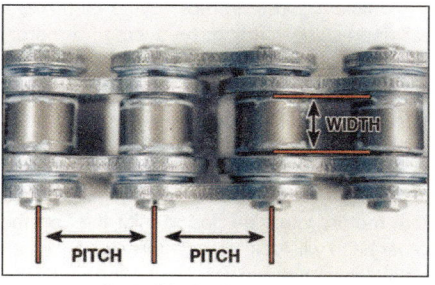

8.11 Chain dimensions

Sizes commencing with a 4 (eg 428) have a pitch of 1/2 inch (12.7 mm)

Sizes commencing with a 5 (eg 520) have a pitch of 5/8 inch (15.9 mm)

Sizes commencing with a 6 (eg 630) have a pitch of 3/4 inch (19.1 mm)

● The second and third digits of the chain size relate to the width of the rollers, again in imperial units, eg the 525 shown has 5/16 inch (7.94 mm) rollers **(see illustration 8.11)**.

9 Hoses

Clamping to prevent flow

● Small-bore flexible hoses can be clamped to prevent fluid flow whilst a component is worked on. Whichever method is used, ensure that the hose material is not permanently distorted or damaged by the clamp.

a) A brake hose clamp available from auto accessory shops **(see illustration 9.1)**.
b) A wingnut type hose clamp **(see illustration 9.2)**.
c) Two sockets placed each side of the hose and held with straight-jawed self-locking grips **(see illustration 9.3)**.
d) Thick card each side of the hose held between straight-jawed self-locking grips **(see illustration 9.4)**.

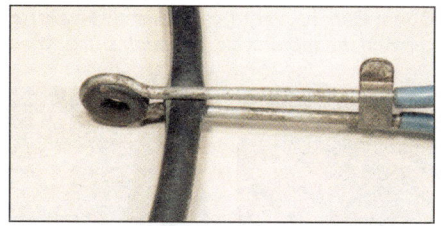

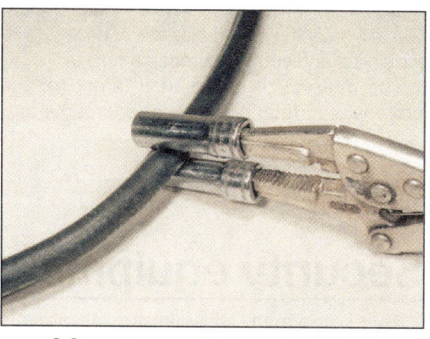

9.1 Hoses can be clamped with an automotive brake hose clamp . . .

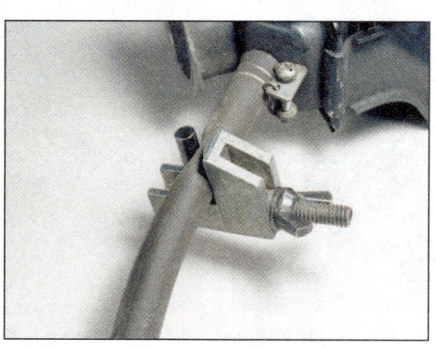

9.2 . . . a wingnut type hose clamp . . .

9.3 . . . two sockets and a pair of self-locking grips . . .

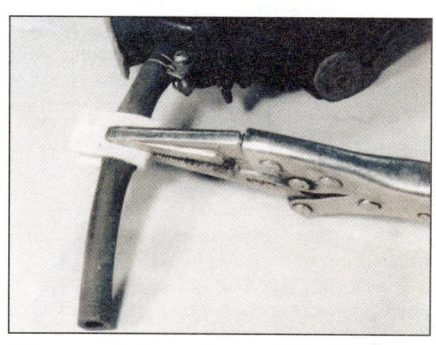

9.4 . . . or thick card and self-locking grips

Freeing and fitting hoses

● Always make sure the hose clamp is moved well clear of the hose end. Grip the hose with your hand and rotate it whilst pulling it off the union. If the hose has hardened due to age and will not move, slit it with a sharp knife and peel its ends off the union **(see illustration 9.5)**.

● Resist the temptation to use grease or soap on the unions to aid installation; although it helps the hose slip over the union it will equally aid the escape of fluid from the joint. It is preferable to soften the hose ends in hot water and wet the inside surface of the hose with water or a fluid which will evaporate.

9.5 Cutting a coolant hose free with a sharp knife

Security

Introduction

In less time than it takes to read this introduction, a thief could steal your motorcycle. Returning only to find your bike has gone is one of the worst feelings in the world. Even if the motorcycle is insured against theft, once you've got over the initial shock, you will have the inconvenience of dealing with the police and your insurance company.

The motorcycle is an easy target for the professional thief and the joyrider alike and the official figures on motorcycle theft make for depressing reading; on average a motorcycle is stolen every 16 minutes in the UK!

Motorcycle thefts fall into two categories, those stolen 'to order' and those taken by opportunists. The thief stealing to order will be on the look out for a specific make and model and will go to extraordinary lengths to obtain that motorcycle. The opportunist thief on the other hand will look for easy targets which can be stolen with the minimum of effort and risk.

Whilst it is never going to be possible to make your machine 100% secure, it is estimated that around half of all stolen motorcycles are taken by opportunist thieves. Remember that the opportunist thief is always on the look out for the easy option: if there are two similar motorcycles parked side-by-side, they will target the one with the lowest level of security. By taking a few precautions, you can reduce the chances of your motorcycle being stolen.

Security equipment

There are many specialised motorcycle security devices available and the following text summarises their applications and their good and bad points.

Once you have decided on the type of security equipment which best suits your needs, we recommended that you read one of the many equipment tests regularly carried out by the motorcycle press. These tests compare the products from all the major manufacturers and give impartial ratings on their effectiveness, value-for-money and ease of use.

No one item of security equipment can provide complete protection. It is highly recommended that two or more of the items described below are combined to increase the security of your motorcycle (a lock and chain plus an alarm system is just about ideal). The more security measures fitted to the bike, the less likely it is to be stolen.

Lock and chain

Pros: *Very flexible to use; can be used to secure the motorcycle to almost any immovable object. On some locks and chains, the lock can be used on its own as a disc lock (see below).*

Cons: *Can be very heavy and awkward to carry on the motorcycle, although some types will be supplied with a carry bag which can be strapped to the pillion seat.*

● Heavy-duty chains and locks are an excellent security measure **(see illustration 1)**. Whenever the motorcycle is parked, use the lock and chain to secure the machine to a solid, immovable object such as a post or railings. This will prevent the machine from being ridden away or being lifted into the back of a van.

● When fitting the chain, always ensure the chain is routed around the motorcycle frame or swingarm **(see illustrations 2 and 3)**. Never merely pass the chain around one of the wheel rims; a thief may unbolt the wheel and lift the rest of the machine into a van, leaving you with just the wheel! Try to avoid having excess chain free, thus making it difficult to use cutting tools, and keep the chain and lock off the ground to prevent thieves attacking it with a cold chisel. Position the lock so that its lock barrel is facing downwards; this will make it harder for the thief to attack the lock mechanism.

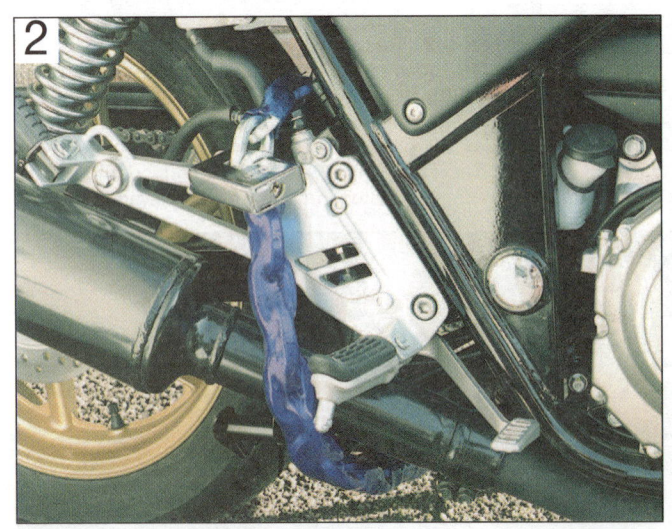

1 Ensure the lock and chain you buy is of good quality and long enough to shackle your bike to a solid object

2 Pass the chain through the bike's frame, rather than just through a wheel . . .

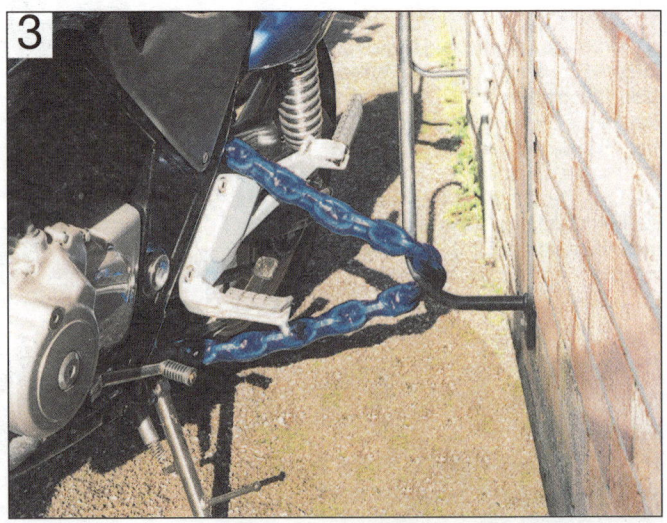

3 . . . and loop it around a solid object

Security REF•21

U-locks

Pros: *Highly effective deterrent which can be used to secure the bike to a post or railings. Most U-locks come with a carrier which allows the lock to be easily carried on the bike.*

Cons: *Not as flexible to use as a lock and chain.*

● These are solid locks which are similar in use to a lock and chain. U-locks are lighter than a lock and chain but not so flexible to use. The length and shape of the lock shackle limit the objects to which the bike can be secured **(see illustration 4)**.

Disc locks

Pros: *Small, light and very easy to carry; most can be stored underneath the seat.*

Cons: *Does not prevent the motorcycle being lifted into a van. Can be very embarrassing if you forget to remove the lock before attempting to ride off!*

● Disc locks are designed to be attached to the front brake disc. The lock passes through one of the holes in the disc and prevents the wheel rotating by jamming against the fork/brake caliper **(see illustration 5)**. Some are equipped with an alarm siren which sounds if the disc lock is moved; this not only acts as a theft deterrent but also as a handy reminder if you try to move the bike with the lock still fitted.

● Combining the disc lock with a length of cable which can be looped around a post or railings provides an additional measure of security **(see illustration 6)**.

Alarms and immobilisers

Pros: *Once installed it is completely hassle-free to use. If the system is 'Thatcham' or 'Sold Secure-approved', insurance companies may give you a discount.*

Cons: *Can be expensive to buy and complex to install. No system will prevent the motorcycle from being lifted into a van and taken away.*

● Electronic alarms and immobilisers are available to suit a variety of budgets. There are three different types of system available: pure alarms, pure immobilisers, and the more expensive systems which are combined alarm/immobilisers **(see illustration 7)**.

● An alarm system is designed to emit an audible warning if the motorcycle is being tampered with.

● An immobiliser prevents the motorcycle being started and ridden away by disabling its electrical systems.

● When purchasing an alarm/immobiliser system, check the cost of installing the system unless you are able to do it yourself. If the motorcycle is not used regularly, another consideration is the current drain of the system. All alarm/immobiliser systems are powered by the motorcycle's battery; purchasing a system with a very low current drain could prevent the battery losing its charge whilst the motorcycle is not being used.

4 U-locks can be used to secure the bike to a solid object – ensure you purchase one which is long enough

5 A typical disc lock attached through one of the holes in the disc

6 A disc lock combined with a security cable provides additional protection

7 A typical alarm/immobiliser system

REF•22 Security

Indelible markings can be applied to most areas of the bike – always apply the manufacturer's sticker to warn off thieves

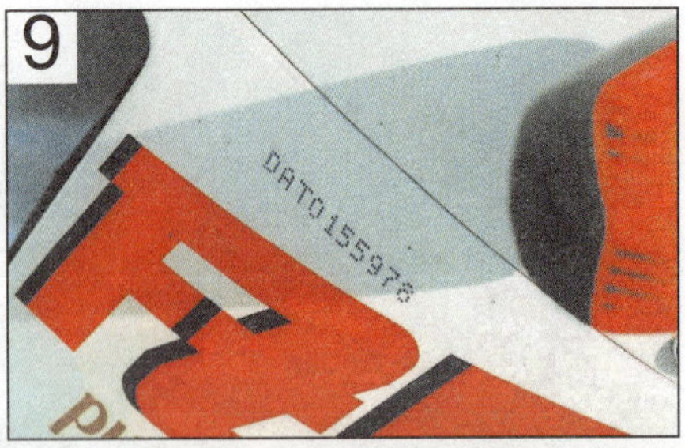

Chemically-etched code numbers can be applied to main body panels . . .

. . . again, always ensure that the kit manufacturer's sticker is applied in a prominent position

Security marking kits

Pros: Very cheap and effective deterrent. Many insurance companies will give you a discount on your insurance premium if a recognised security marking kit is used on your motorcycle.

Cons: Does not prevent the motorcycle being stolen by joyriders.

● There are many different types of security marking kits available. The idea is to mark as many parts of the motorcycle as possible with a unique security number **(see illustrations 8, 9 and 10)**. A form will be included with the kit to register your personal details and those of the motorcycle with the kit manufacturer. This register is made available to the police to help them trace the rightful owner of any motorcycle or components which they recover should all other forms of identification have been removed. Always apply the warning stickers provided with the kit to deter thieves.

Ground anchors, wheel clamps and security posts

Pros: An excellent form of security which will deter all but the most determined of thieves.

Cons: Awkward to install and can be expensive.

● Whilst the motorcycle is at home, it is a good idea to attach it securely to the floor or a solid wall, even if it is kept in a securely locked garage. Various types of ground anchors, security posts and wheel clamps are available for this purpose **(see illustration 11)**. These security devices are either bolted to a solid concrete or brick structure or can be cemented into the ground.

Permanent ground anchors provide an excellent level of security when the bike is at home

Security at home

A high percentage of motorcycle thefts are from the owner's home. Here are some things to consider whenever your motorcycle is at home:

✔ Where possible, always keep the motorcycle in a securely locked garage. Never rely solely on the standard lock on the garage door, these are usual hopelessly inadequate. Fit an additional locking mechanism to the door and consider having the garage alarmed. A security light, activated by a movement sensor, is also a good investment.

✔ Always secure the motorcycle to the ground or a wall, even if it is inside a securely locked garage.

✔ Do not regularly leave the motorcycle outside your home, try to keep it out of sight wherever possible. If a garage is not available, fit a motorcycle cover over the bike to disguise its true identity.

✔ It is not uncommon for thieves to follow a motorcyclist home to find out where the bike is kept. They will then return at a later date. Be aware of this whenever you are returning home on your motorcycle. If you suspect you are being followed, do not return home, instead ride to a garage or shop and stop as a precaution.

✔ When selling a motorcycle, do not provide your home address or the location where the bike is normally kept. Arrange to meet the buyer at a location away from your home. Thieves have been known to pose as potential buyers to find out where motorcycles are kept and then return later to steal them.

Security away from the home

As well as fitting security equipment to your motorcycle here are a few general rules to follow whenever you park your motorcycle.

✔ Park in a busy, public place.
✔ Use car parks which incorporate security features, such as CCTV.

✔ At night, park in a well-lit area, preferably directly underneath a street light.
✔ Engage the steering lock.
✔ Secure the motorcycle to a solid, immovable object such as a post or railings with an additional lock. If this is not possible, secure the bike to a friend's motorcycle. Some public parking places provide security loops for motorcycles.

✔ Never leave your helmet or luggage attached to the motorcycle. Take them with you at all times.

Lubricants and fluids

A wide range of lubricants, fluids and cleaning agents is available for motor-cycles. This is a guide as to what is available, its applications and properties.

Four-stroke engine oil

● Engine oil is without doubt the most important component of any four-stroke engine. Modern motorcycle engines place a lot of demands on their oil and choosing the right type is essential. Using an unsuitable oil will lead to an increased rate of engine wear and could result in serious engine damage. Before purchasing oil, always check the recommended oil specification given by the manufacturer. The manufacturer will state a recommended 'type or classification' and also a specific 'viscosity' range for engine oil.

● The oil 'type or classification' is identified by its API (American Petroleum Institute) rating. The API rating will be in the form of two letters, e.g. SG. The S identifies the oil as being suitable for use in a petrol (gasoline) engine (S stands for spark ignition) and the second letter, ranging from A to J, identifies the oil's performance rating. The later this letter, the higher the specification of the oil; for example API SG oil exceeds the requirements of API SF oil. **Note:** *On some oils there may also be a second rating consisting of another two letters, the first letter being C, e.g. API SF/CD. This rating indicates the oil is also suitable for use in a diesel engines (the C stands for compression ignition) and is thus of no relevance for motorcycle use.*

● The 'viscosity' of the oil is identified by its SAE (Society of Automotive Engineers) rating. All modern engines require multigrade oils and the SAE rating will consist of two numbers, the first followed by a W, e.g. 10W/40. The first number indicates the viscosity rating of the oil at low temperatures (W stands for winter – tested at –20°C) and the second number represents the viscosity of the oil at high temperatures (tested at 100°C). The lower the number, the thinner the oil. For example an oil with an SAE 10W/40 rating will give better cold starting and running than an SAE 15W/40 oil.

● As well as ensuring the 'type' and 'viscosity' of the oil match the recommendations, another consideration to make when buying engine oil is whether to purchase a standard mineral-based oil, a semi-synthetic oil (also known as a synthetic blend or synthetic-based oil) or a fully-synthetic oil. Although all oils will have a similar rating and viscosity, their cost will vary considerably; mineral-based oils are the cheapest, the fully-synthetic oils the most expensive with the semi-synthetic oils falling somewhere in-between. This decision is very much up to the owner, but it should be noted that modern synthetic oils have far better lubricating and cleaning qualities than traditional mineral-based oils and tend to retain these properties for far longer. Bearing in mind the operating conditions inside a modern, high-revving motorcycle engine it is highly recommended that a fully synthetic oil is used. The extra expense at each service could save you money in the long term by preventing premature engine wear.

● As a final note always ensure that the oil is specifically designed for use in motorcycle engines. Engine oils designed primarily for use in car engines sometimes contain additives or friction modifiers which could cause clutch slip on a motorcycle fitted with a wet-clutch.

Two-stroke engine oil

● Modern two-stroke engines, with their high power outputs, place high demands on their oil. If engine seizure is to be avoided it is essential that a high-quality oil is used. Two-stroke oils differ hugely from four-stroke oils. The oil lubricates only the crankshaft and piston(s) (the transmission has its own lubricating oil) and is used on a total-loss basis where it is burnt completely during the combustion process.

● The Japanese have recently introduced a classification system for two-stroke oils, the JASO rating. This rating is in the form of two letters, either FA, FB or FC – FA is the lowest classification and FC the highest. Ensure the oil being used meets or exceeds the recommended rating specified by the manufacturer.

● As well as ensuring the oil rating matches the recommendation, another consideration to make when buying engine oil is whether to purchase a standard mineral-based oil, a semi-synthetic oil (also known as a synthetic blend or synthetic-based oil) or a fully-synthetic oil. The cost of each type of oil varies considerably; mineral-based oils are the cheapest, the fully-synthetic oils the most expensive with the semi-synthetic oils falling somewhere in-between. This decision is very much up to the owner, but it should be noted that modern synthetic oils have far better lubricating properties and burn cleaner than traditional mineral-based oils. It is therefore recommended that a fully synthetic oil is used. The extra expense could save you money in the long term by preventing premature engine wear, engine performance will be improved, carbon deposits and exhaust smoke will be reduced.

REF•24 Lubricants and fluids

● Always ensure that the oil is specifically designed for use in an injector system. Many high quality two-stroke oils are designed for competition use and need to be pre-mixed with fuel. These oils are of a much higher viscosity and are not designed to flow through the injector pumps used on road-going two-stroke motorcycles.

Transmission (gear) oil

● On a two-stroke engine, the transmission and clutch are lubricated by their own separate oil bath which must be changed in accordance with the Maintenance Schedule.
● Although the engine and transmission units of most four-strokes use a common lubrication supply, there are some exceptions where the engine and gearbox have separate oil reservoirs and a dry clutch is used.
● Motorcycle manufacturers will either recommend a monograde transmission oil or a four-stroke multigrade engine oil to lubricate the transmission.
● Transmission oils, or gear oils as they are often called, are designed specifically for use in transmission systems. The viscosity of these oils is represented by an SAE number, but the scale of measurement applied is different to that used to grade engine oils. As a rough guide a SAE90 gear oil will be of the same viscosity as an SAE50 engine oil.

Shaft drive oil

● On models equipped with shaft final drive, the shaft drive gears are will have their own oil supply. The manufacturer will state a recommended 'type or classification' and also a specific 'viscosity' range in the same manner as for four-stroke engine oil.
● Gear oil classification is given by the number which follows the API GL (GL standing for gear lubricant) rating, the higher the number, the higher the specification of the oil, e.g. API GL5 oil is a higher specification than API GL4 oil. Ensure the oil meets or exceeds the classification specified and is of the correct viscosity. The viscosity of gear oils is also represented by an SAE number but the scale of measurement used is different to that used to grade engine oils. As a rough guide an SAE90 gear oil will be of the same viscosity as an SAE50 engine oil.
● If the use of an EP (Extreme Pressure) gear oil is specified, ensure the oil purchased is suitable.

Fork oil and suspension fluid

● Conventional telescopic front forks are hydraulic and require fork oil to work. To ensure the forks function correctly, the fork oil must be changed in accordance with the Maintenance Schedule.
● Fork oil is available in a variety of viscosities, identified by their SAE rating; fork oil ratings vary from light (SAE 5) to heavy (SAE 30). When purchasing fork oil, ensure the viscosity rating matches that specified by the manufacturer.
● Some lubricant manufacturers also produce a range of high-quality suspension fluids which are very similar to fork oil but are designed mainly for competition use. These fluids may have a different viscosity rating system which is not to be confused with the SAE rating of normal fork oil. Refer to the manufacturer's instructions if in any doubt.

Brake and clutch fluid

● All disc brake systems and some clutch systems are hydraulically operated. To ensure correct operation, the hydraulic fluid must be changed in accordance with the Maintenance Schedule.
● Brake and clutch fluid is classified by its DOT rating with most motorcycle manufacturers specifying DOT 3 or 4 fluid. Both fluid types are glycol-based and can be mixed together without adverse effect; DOT 4 fluid exceeds the requirements of DOT 3 fluid. Although it is safe to use DOT 4 fluid in a system designed for use with DOT 3 fluid, never use DOT 3 fluid in a system which specifies the use of DOT 4 as this will adversely affect the system's performance. The type required for the system will be marked on the fluid reservoir cap.
● Some manufacturers also produce a DOT 5 hydraulic fluid. DOT 5 hydraulic fluid is silicone-based and is not compatible with the glycol-based DOT 3 and 4 fluids. Never mix DOT 5 fluid with DOT 3 or 4 fluid as this will seriously affect the performance of the hydraulic system.

Coolant/antifreeze

● When purchasing coolant/antifreeze, always ensure it is suitable for use in an aluminium engine and contains corrosion inhibitors to prevent possible blockages of the internal coolant passages of the system. As a general rule, most coolants are designed to be used neat and should not be diluted whereas antifreeze can be mixed with distilled water to provide a coolant solution of the required strength. Refer to the manufacturer's instructions on the bottle.
● Ensure the coolant is changed in accordance with the Maintenance Schedule.

Chain lube

● Chain lube is an aerosol-type spray lubricant specifically designed for use on motorcycle final drive chains. Chain lube has two functions, to minimise friction between the final drive chain and sprockets and to prevent corrosion of the chain. Regular use of a good-quality chain lube will extend the life of the drive chain and sprockets and thus maximise the power being transmitted from the transmission to the rear wheel.
● When using chain lube, always allow some time for the solvents in the lube to evaporate before riding the motorcycle. This will minimise the amount of lube which will

Lubricants and fluids REF•25

'fling' off from the chain when the motorcycle is used. If the motorcycle is equipped with an 'O-ring' chain, ensure the chain lube is labelled as being suitable for use on 'O-ring' chains.

Degreasers and solvents

● There are many different types of solvents and degreasers available to remove the grime and grease which accumulate around the motorcycle during normal use. Degreasers and solvents are usually available as an aerosol-type spray or as a liquid which you apply with a brush. Always closely follow the manufacturer's instructions and wear eye protection during use. Be aware that many solvents are flammable and may give off noxious fumes; take adequate precautions when using them (see Safety First!).

● For general cleaning, use one of the many solvents or degreasers available from most motorcycle accessory shops. These solvents are usually applied then left for a certain time before being washed off with water.

Brake cleaner is a solvent specifically designed to remove all traces of oil, grease and dust from braking system components. Brake cleaner is designed to evaporate quickly and leaves behind no residue.

Carburettor cleaner is an aerosol-type solvent specifically designed to clear carburettor blockages and break down the hard deposits and gum often found inside carburettors during overhaul.

Contact cleaner is an aerosol-type solvent designed for cleaning electrical components. The cleaner will remove all traces of oil and dirt from components such as switch contacts or fouled spark plugs and then dry, leaving behind no residue.

Gasket remover is an aerosol-type solvent designed for removing stubborn gaskets from engine components during overhaul. Gasket remover will minimise the amount of scraping required to remove the gasket and therefore reduce the risk of damage to the mating surface.

Spray lubricants

● Aerosol-based spray lubricants are widely available and are excellent for lubricating lever pivots and exposed cables and switches. Try to use a lubricant which is of the dry-film type as the fluid evaporates, leaving behind a dry-film of lubricant. Lubricants which leave behind an oily residue will attract dust and dirt which will increase the rate of wear of the cable/lever.

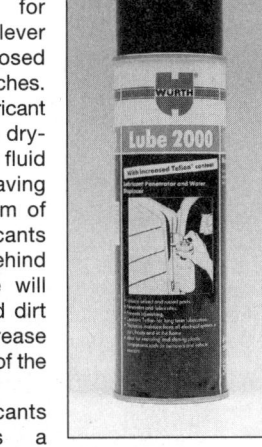

● Most lubricants also act as a moisture dispersant and a penetrating fluid. This means they can also be used to 'dry out' electrical components such as wiring connectors or switches as well as helping to free seized fasteners.

Greases

● Grease is used to lubricate many of the pivot-points. A good-quality multi-purpose grease is suitable for most applications but some manufacturers will specify the use of specialist greases for use on components such as swingarm and suspension linkage bushes. These specialist greases can be purchased from most motorcycle (or car) accessory shops; commonly specified types include molybdenum disulphide grease, lithium-based grease, graphite-based grease, silicone-based grease and high-temperature copper-based grease.

Gasket sealing compounds

● Gasket sealing compounds can be used in conjunction with gaskets, to improve their sealing capabilities, or on their own to seal metal-to-metal joints. Depending on their type, sealing compounds either set hard or stay relatively soft and pliable.

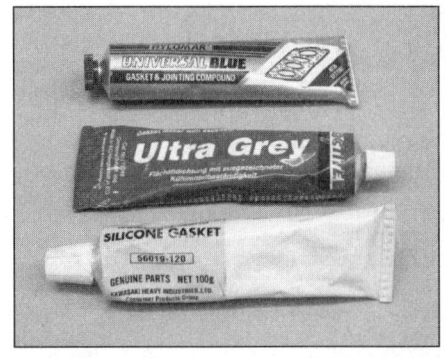

● When purchasing a gasket sealing compound, ensure that it is designed specifically for use on an internal combustion engine. General multi-purpose sealants available from DIY stores may appear visibly similar but they are not designed to withstand the extreme heat or contact with fuel and oil encountered when used on an engine (see 'Tools and Workshop Tips' for further information).

Thread locking compound

● Thread locking compounds are used to secure certain threaded fasteners in position to prevent them from loosening due to vibration. Thread locking compounds can be purchased from most motorcycle (and car) accessory shops. Ensure the threads of the both components are completely clean and dry before sparingly applying the locking compound (see 'Tools and Workshop Tips' for further information).

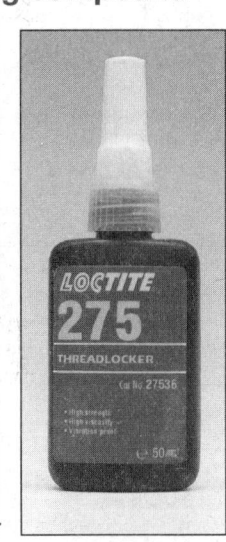

Fuel additives

● Fuel additives which protect and clean the fuel system components are widely available. These additives are designed to remove all traces of deposits that build up on the carburettors/injectors and prevent wear, helping the fuel system to operate more efficiently. If a fuel additive is being used, check that it is suitable for use with your motorcycle, especially if your motorcycle is equipped with a catalytic converter.

● Octane boosters are also available. These additives are designed to improve the performance of highly-tuned engines being run on normal pump-fuel and are of no real use on standard motorcycles.

REF•26 Conversion factors

Length (distance)
Inches (in)	x 25.4	= Millimetres (mm)	x 0.0394	=	Inches (in)
Feet (ft)	x 0.305	= Metres (m)	x 3.281	=	Feet (ft)
Miles	x 1.609	= Kilometres (km)	x 0.621	=	Miles

Volume (capacity)
Cubic inches (cu in; in³)	x 16.387	= Cubic centimetres (cc; cm³)	x 0.061	=	Cubic inches (cu in; in³)
Imperial pints (Imp pt)	x 0.568	= Litres (l)	x 1.76	=	Imperial pints (Imp pt)
Imperial quarts (Imp qt)	x 1.137	= Litres (l)	x 0.88	=	Imperial quarts (Imp qt)
Imperial quarts (Imp qt)	x 1.201	= US quarts (US qt)	x 0.833	=	Imperial quarts (Imp qt)
US quarts (US qt)	x 0.946	= Litres (l)	x 1.057	=	US quarts (US qt)
Imperial gallons (Imp gal)	x 4.546	= Litres (l)	x 0.22	=	Imperial gallons (Imp gal)
Imperial gallons (Imp gal)	x 1.201	= US gallons (US gal)	x 0.833	=	Imperial gallons (Imp gal)
US gallons (US gal)	x 3.785	= Litres (l)	x 0.264	=	US gallons (US gal)

Mass (weight)
Ounces (oz)	x 28.35	= Grams (g)	x 0.035	=	Ounces (oz)
Pounds (lb)	x 0.454	= Kilograms (kg)	x 2.205	=	Pounds (lb)

Force
Ounces-force (ozf; oz)	x 0.278	= Newtons (N)	x 3.6	=	Ounces-force (ozf; oz)
Pounds-force (lbf; lb)	x 4.448	= Newtons (N)	x 0.225	=	Pounds-force (lbf; lb)
Newtons (N)	x 0.1	= Kilograms-force (kgf; kg)	x 9.81	=	Newtons (N)

Pressure
Pounds-force per square inch (psi; lbf/in²; lb/in²)	x 0.070	= Kilograms-force per square centimetre (kgf/cm²; kg/cm²)	x 14.223	=	Pounds-force per square inch (psi; lbf/in²; lb/in²)
Pounds-force per square inch (psi; lbf/in²; lb/in²)	x 0.068	= Atmospheres (atm)	x 14.696	=	Pounds-force per square inch (psi; lbf/in²; lb/in²)
Pounds-force per square inch (psi; lbf/in²; lb/in²)	x 0.069	= Bars	x 14.5	=	Pounds-force per square inch (psi; lbf/in²; lb/in²)
Pounds-force per square inch (psi; lbf/in²; lb/in²)	x 6.895	= Kilopascals (kPa)	x 0.145	=	Pounds-force per square inch (psi; lbf/in²; lb/in²)
Kilopascals (kPa)	x 0.01	= Kilograms-force per square centimetre (kgf/cm²; kg/cm²)	x 98.1	=	Kilopascals (kPa)
Millibar (mbar)	x 100	= Pascals (Pa)	x 0.01	=	Millibar (mbar)
Millibar (mbar)	x 0.0145	= Pounds-force per square inch (psi; lbf/in²; lb/in²)	x 68.947	=	Millibar (mbar)
Millibar (mbar)	x 0.75	= Millimetres of mercury (mmHg)	x 1.333	=	Millibar (mbar)
Millibar (mbar)	x 0.401	= Inches of water (inH$_2$O)	x 2.491	=	Millibar (mbar)
Millimetres of mercury (mmHg)	x 0.535	= Inches of water (inH$_2$O)	x 1.868	=	Millimetres of mercury (mmHg)
Inches of water (inH$_2$O)	x 0.036	= Pounds-force per square inch (psi; lbf/in²; lb/in²)	x 27.68	=	Inches of water (inH$_2$O)

Torque (moment of force)
Pounds-force inches (lbf in; lb in)	x 1.152	= Kilograms-force centimetre (kgf cm; kg cm)	x 0.868	=	Pounds-force inches (lbf in; lb in)
Pounds-force inches (lbf in; lb in)	x 0.113	= Newton metres (Nm)	x 8.85	=	Pounds-force inches (lbf in; lb in)
Pounds-force inches (lbf in; lb in)	x 0.083	= Pounds-force feet (lbf ft; lb ft)	x 12	=	Pounds-force inches (lbf in; lb in)
Pounds-force feet (lbf ft; lb ft)	x 0.138	= Kilograms-force metres (kgf m; kg m)	x 7.233	=	Pounds-force feet (lbf ft; lb ft)
Pounds-force feet (lbf ft; lb ft)	x 1.356	= Newton metres (Nm)	x 0.738	=	Pounds-force feet (lbf ft; lb ft)
Newton metres (Nm)	x 0.102	= Kilograms-force metres (kgf m; kg m)	x 9.804	=	Newton metres (Nm)

Power
Horsepower (hp)	x 745.7	= Watts (W)	x 0.0013	=	Horsepower (hp)

Velocity (speed)
Miles per hour (miles/hr; mph)	x 1.609	= Kilometres per hour (km/hr; kph)	x 0.621	=	Miles per hour (miles/hr; mph)

Fuel consumption*
Miles per gallon (mpg)	x 0.354	= Kilometres per litre (km/l)	x 2.825	=	Miles per gallon (mpg)

Temperature
Degrees Fahrenheit = (°C x 1.8) + 32   Degrees Celsius (Degrees Centigrade; °C) = (°F - 32) x 0.56

It is common practice to convert from miles per gallon (mpg) to litres/100 kilometres (l/100km), where mpg x l/100 km = 282

MOT Test Checks REF•27

About the MOT Test

In the UK, all vehicles more than three years old are subject to an annual test to ensure that they meet minimum safety requirements. A current test certificate must be issued before a machine can be used on public roads, and is required before a road fund licence can be issued. Riding without a current test certificate will also invalidate your insurance.

For most owners, the MOT test is an annual cause for anxiety, and this is largely due to owners not being sure what needs to be checked prior to submitting the motorcycle for testing. The simple answer is that a fully roadworthy motorcycle will have no difficulty in passing the test.

This is a guide to getting your motorcycle through the MOT test. Obviously it will not be possible to examine the motorcycle to the same standard as the professional MOT tester, particularly in view of the equipment required for some of the checks. However, working through the following procedures will enable you to identify any problem areas before submitting the motorcycle for the test.

It has only been possible to summarise the test requirements here, based on the regulations in force at the time of printing. Test standards are becoming increasingly stringent, although there are some exemptions for older vehicles. More information about the MOT test can be obtained from the TSO publications, *How Safe is your Motorcycle* and *The MOT Inspection Manual for Motorcycle Testing*.

Many of the checks require that one of the wheels is raised off the ground. If the motorcycle doesn't have a centre stand, note that an auxiliary stand will be required. Additionally, the help of an assistant may prove useful.

Certain exceptions apply to machines under 50 cc, machines without a lighting system, and Classic bikes - if in doubt about any of the requirements listed below seek confirmation from an MOT tester prior to submitting the motorcycle for the test.

Check that the frame number is clearly visible.

> **HAYNES HiNT** *If a component is in borderline condition, the tester has discretion in deciding whether to pass or fail it. If the motorcycle presented is clean and evidently well cared for, the tester may be more inclined to pass a borderline component than if the motorcycle is scruffy and apparently neglected.*

Electrical System

Lights, turn signals, horn and reflector

✔ With the ignition on, check the operation of the following electrical components. **Note:** *The electrical components on certain small-capacity machines are powered by the generator, requiring that the engine is run for this check.*

a) Headlight and tail light. Check that both illuminate in the low and high beam switch positions.
b) Position lights. Check that the front position (or sidelight) and tail light illuminate in this switch position.
c) Turn signals. Check that all flash at the correct rate, and that the warning light(s) function correctly. Check that the turn signal switch works correctly.
d) Hazard warning system (where fitted). Check that all four turn signals flash in this switch position.
e) Brake stop light. Check that the light comes on when the front and rear brakes are independently applied. Models first used on or after 1st April 1986 must have a brake light switch on each brake.
f) Horn. Check that the sound is continuous and of reasonable volume.

✔ Check that there is a red reflector on the rear of the machine, either mounted separately or as part of the tail light lens.

✔ Check the condition of the headlight, tail light and turn signal lenses.

Headlight beam height

✔ The MOT tester will perform a headlight beam height check using specialised beam setting equipment **(see illustration 1)**. This equipment will not be available to the home mechanic, but if you suspect that the headlight is incorrectly set or may have been maladjusted in the past, you can perform a rough test as follows.

✔ Position the bike in a straight line facing a brick wall. The bike must be off its stand, upright and with a rider seated. Measure the height from the ground to the centre of the headlight and mark a horizontal line on the wall at this height. Position the motorcycle 3.8 metres from the wall and draw a vertical line up the wall central to the centreline of the motorcycle. Switch to dipped beam and check that the beam pattern falls slightly lower than the horizontal line and to the left of the vertical line **(see illustration 2)**.

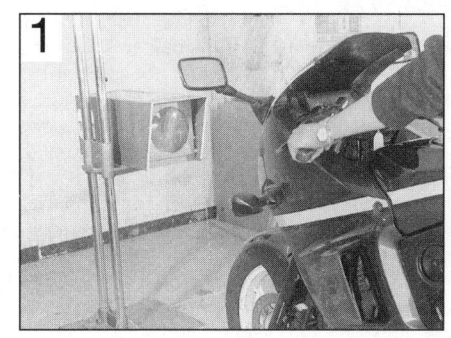

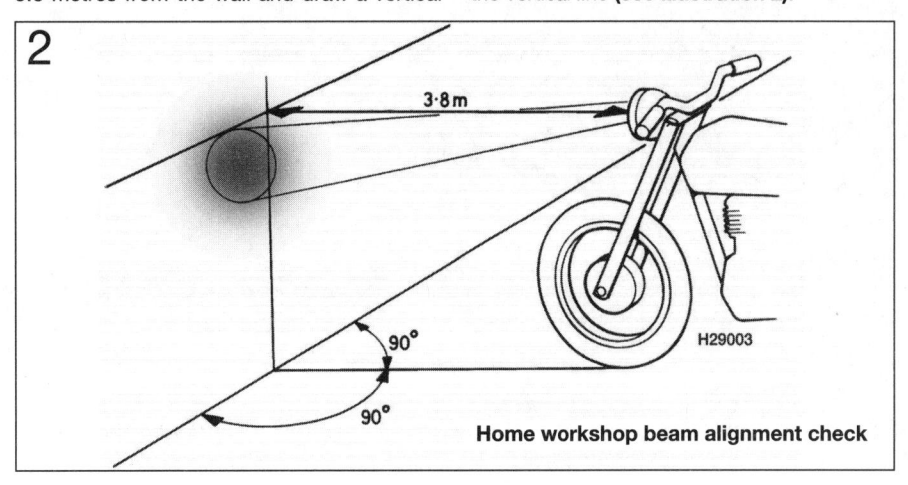

Headlight beam height checking equipment

Home workshop beam alignment check

REF•28 MOT Test Checks

Exhaust System and Final Drive

Exhaust

✔ Check that the exhaust mountings are secure and that the system does not foul any of the rear suspension components.
✔ Start the motorcycle. When the revs are increased, check that the exhaust is neither holed nor leaking from any of its joints. On a linked system, check that the collector box is not leaking due to corrosion.

✔ Note that the exhaust decibel level ("loudness" of the exhaust) is assessed at the discretion of the tester. If the motorcycle was first used on or after 1st January 1985 the silencer must carry the BSAU 193 stamp, or a marking relating to its make and model, or be of OE (original equipment) manufacture. If the silencer is marked NOT FOR ROAD USE, RACING USE ONLY or similar, it will fail the MOT.

Final drive

✔ On chain or belt drive machines, check that the chain/belt is in good condition and does not have excessive slack. Also check that the sprocket is securely mounted on the rear wheel hub. Check that the chain/belt guard is in place.
✔ On shaft drive bikes, check for oil leaking from the drive unit and fouling the rear tyre.

Steering and Suspension

Steering

✔ With the front wheel raised off the ground, rotate the steering from lock to lock. The handlebar or switches must not contact the fuel tank or be close enough to trap the rider's hand. Problems can be caused by damaged lock stops on the lower yoke and frame, or by the fitting of non-standard handlebars.
✔ When performing the lock to lock check, also ensure that the steering moves freely without drag or notchiness. Steering movement can be impaired by poorly routed cables, or by overtight head bearings or worn bearings. The tester will perform a check of the steering head bearing lower race by mounting the front wheel on a surface plate, then performing a lock to lock check with the weight of the machine on the lower bearing (see illustration 3).
✔ Grasp the fork sliders (lower legs) and attempt to push and pull on the forks (see illustration 4). Any play in the steering head bearings will be felt. Note that in extreme cases, wear of the front fork bushes can be misinterpreted for head bearing play.
✔ Check that the handlebars are securely mounted.
✔ Check that the handlebar grip rubbers are secure. They should by bonded to the bar left end and to the throttle cable pulley on the right end.

Front wheel mounted on a surface plate for steering head bearing lower race check

Front suspension

✔ With the motorcycle off the stand, hold the front brake on and pump the front forks up and down (see illustration 5). Check that they are adequately damped.

Checking the steering head bearings for freeplay

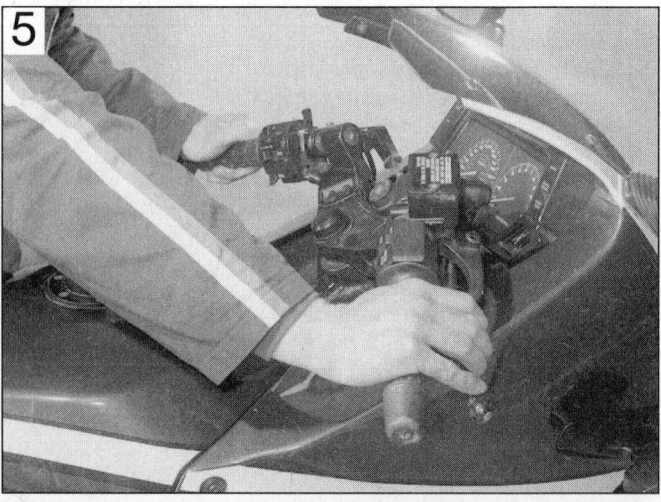

Hold the front brake on and pump the front forks up and down to check operation

MOT Test Checks REF•29

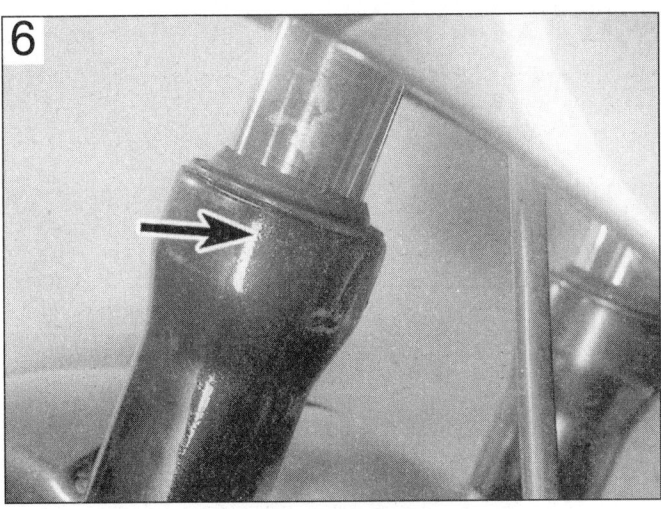

Inspect the area around the fork dust seal for oil leakage (arrow)

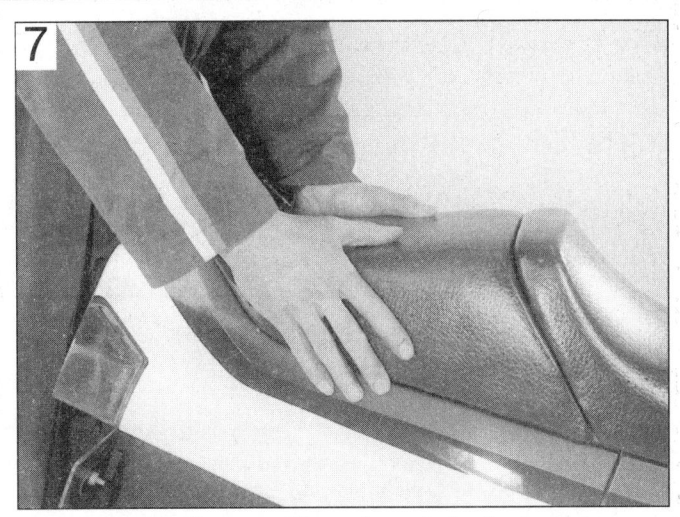

Bounce the rear of the motorcycle to check rear suspension operation

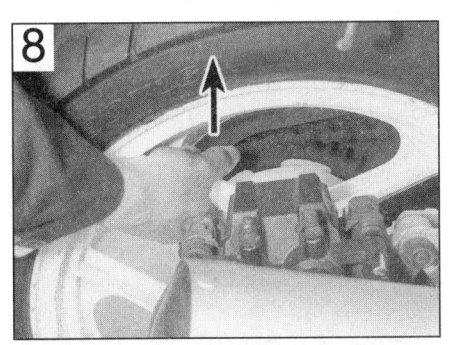

Checking for rear suspension linkage play

✔ Inspect the area above and around the front fork oil seals **(see illustration 6)**. There should be no sign of oil on the fork tube (stanchion) nor leaking down the slider (lower leg). On models so equipped, check that there is no oil leaking from the anti-dive units.

✔ On models with swingarm front suspension, check that there is no freeplay in the linkage when moved from side to side.

Rear suspension

✔ With the motorcycle off the stand and an assistant supporting the motorcycle by its handlebars, bounce the rear suspension **(see illustration 7)**. Check that the suspension components do not foul on any of the cycle parts and check that the shock absorber(s) provide adequate damping.

✔ Visually inspect the shock absorber(s) and check that there is no sign of oil leakage from its damper. This is somewhat restricted on certain single shock models due to the location of the shock absorber.

✔ With the rear wheel raised off the ground, grasp the wheel at the highest point and attempt to pull it up **(see illustration 8)**. Any play in the swingarm pivot or suspension linkage bearings will be felt as movement. **Note:** *Do not confuse play with actual suspension movement.* Failure to lubricate suspension linkage bearings can lead to bearing failure **(see illustration 9)**.

✔ With the rear wheel raised off the ground, grasp the swingarm ends and attempt to move the swingarm from side to side and forwards and backwards - any play indicates wear of the swingarm pivot bearings **(see illustration 10)**.

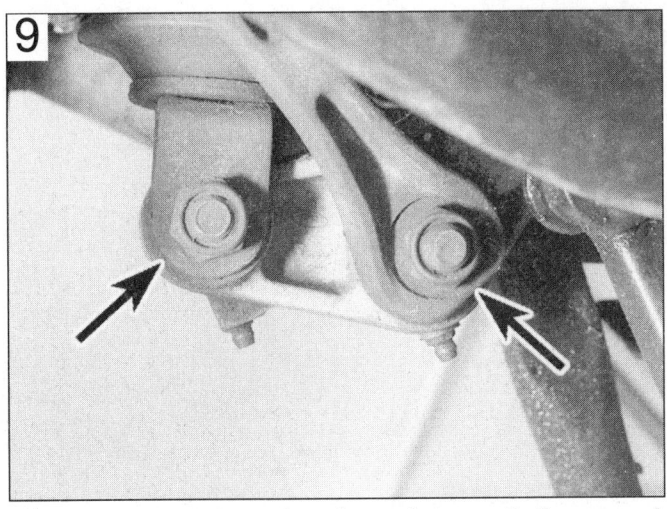

Worn suspension linkage pivots (arrows) are usually the cause of play in the rear suspension

Grasp the swingarm at the ends to check for play in its pivot bearings

REF•30 MOT Test Checks

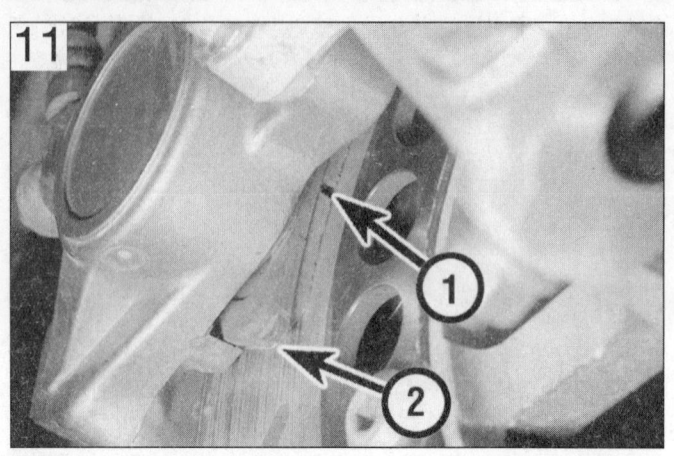

Brake pad wear can usually be viewed without removing the caliper. Most pads have wear indicator grooves (1) and some also have indicator tangs (2)

On drum brakes, check the angle of the operating lever with the brake fully applied. Most drum brakes have a wear indicator pointer and scale.

Brakes, Wheels and Tyres

Brakes

✔ With the wheel raised off the ground, apply the brake then free it off, and check that the wheel is about to revolve freely without brake drag.
✔ On disc brakes, examine the disc itself. Check that it is securely mounted and not cracked.
✔ On disc brakes, view the pad material through the caliper mouth and check that the pads are not worn down beyond the limit **(see illustration 11)**.
✔ On drum brakes, check that when the brake is applied the angle between the operating lever and cable or rod is not too great **(see illustration 12)**. Check also that the operating lever doesn't foul any other components.
✔ On disc brakes, examine the flexible hoses from top to bottom. Have an assistant hold the brake on so that the fluid in the hose is under pressure, and check that there is no sign of fluid leakage, bulges or cracking. If there are any metal brake pipes or unions, check that these are free from corrosion and damage. Where a brake-linked anti-dive system is fitted, check the hoses to the anti-dive in a similar manner.
✔ Check that the rear brake torque arm is secure and that its fasteners are secured by self-locking nuts or castellated nuts with split-pins or R-pins **(see illustration 13)**.
✔ On models with ABS, check that the self-check warning light in the instrument panel works.
✔ The MOT tester will perform a test of the motorcycle's braking efficiency based on a calculation of rider and motorcycle weight. Although this cannot be carried out at home, you can at least ensure that the braking systems are properly maintained. For hydraulic disc brakes, check the fluid level, lever/pedal feel (bleed of air if its spongy) and pad material. For drum brakes, check adjustment, cable or rod operation and shoe lining thickness.

Wheels and tyres

✔ Check the wheel condition. Cast wheels should be free from cracks and if of the built-up design, all fasteners should be secure. Spoked wheels should be checked for broken, corroded, loose or bent spokes.
✔ With the wheel raised off the ground, spin the wheel and visually check that the tyre and wheel run true. Check that the tyre does not foul the suspension or mudguards.
✔ With the wheel raised off the ground, grasp the wheel and attempt to move it about the axle (spindle) **(see illustration 14)**. Any play felt here indicates wheel bearing failure.

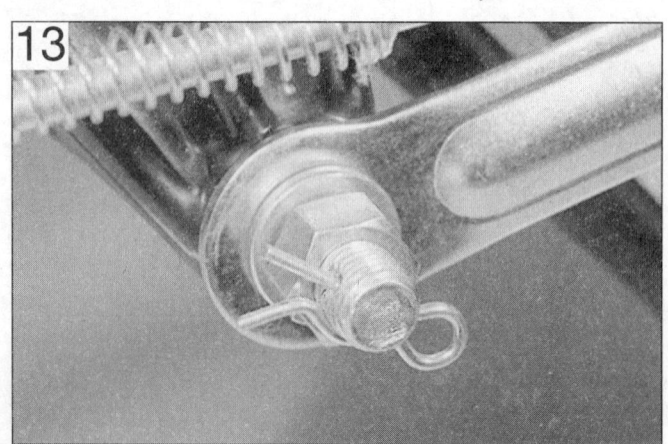

Brake torque arm must be properly secured at both ends

Check for wheel bearing play by trying to move the wheel about the axle (spindle)

MOT Test Checks REF•31

Checking the tyre tread depth

Tyre direction of rotation arrow can be found on tyre sidewall

Castellated type wheel axle (spindle) nut must be secured by a split pin or R-pin

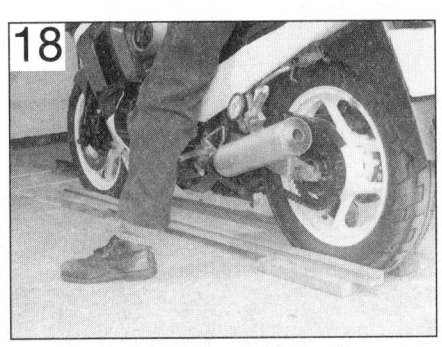

Two straightedges are used to check wheel alignment

✔ Check the tyre tread depth, tread condition and sidewall condition **(see illustration 15)**.
✔ Check the tyre type. Front and rear tyre types must be compatible and be suitable for road use. Tyres marked NOT FOR ROAD USE, COMPETITION USE ONLY or similar, will fail the MOT.

✔ If the tyre sidewall carries a direction of rotation arrow, this must be pointing in the direction of normal wheel rotation **(see illustration 16)**.
✔ Check that the wheel axle (spindle) nuts (where applicable) are properly secured. A self-locking nut or castellated nut with a split-pin or R-pin can be used **(see illustration 17)**.
✔ Wheel alignment is checked with the motorcycle off the stand and a rider seated. With the front wheel pointing straight ahead, two perfectly straight lengths of metal or wood and placed against the sidewalls of both tyres **(see illustration 18)**. The gap each side of the front tyre must be equidistant on both sides. Incorrect wheel alignment may be due to a cocked rear wheel (often as the result of poor chain adjustment) or in extreme cases, a bent frame.

General checks and condition

✔ Check the security of all major fasteners, bodypanels, seat, fairings (where fitted) and mudguards.

✔ Check that the rider and pillion footrests, handlebar levers and brake pedal are securely mounted.

✔ Check for corrosion on the frame or any load-bearing components. If severe, this may affect the structure, particularly under stress.

Sidecars

A motorcycle fitted with a sidecar requires additional checks relating to the stability of the machine and security of attachment and swivel joints, plus specific wheel alignment (toe-in) requirements. Additionally, tyre and lighting requirements differ from conventional motorcycle use. Owners are advised to check MOT test requirements with an official test centre.

# REF•32 Storage

Preparing for storage

Before you start

If repairs or an overhaul is needed, see that this is carried out now rather than left until you want to ride the bike again.

Give the bike a good wash and scrub all dirt from its underside. Make sure the bike dries completely before preparing for storage.

Engine

● Remove the spark plug(s) and lubricate the cylinder bores with approximately a teaspoon of motor oil using a spout-type oil can **(see illustration 1)**. Reinstall the spark plug(s). Crank the engine over a couple of times to coat the piston rings and bores with oil. If the bike has a kickstart, use this to turn the engine over. If not, flick the kill switch to the OFF position and crank the engine over on the starter **(see illustration 2)**. If the nature on the ignition system prevents the starter operating with the kill switch in the OFF position, remove the spark plugs and fit them back in their caps; ensure that the plugs are earthed (grounded) against the cylinder head when the starter is operated **(see illustration 3)**.

Warning: It is important that the plugs are earthed (grounded) away from the spark plug holes otherwise there is a risk of atomised fuel from the cylinders igniting.

HAYNES HINT: On a single cylinder four-stroke engine, you can seal the combustion chamber completely by positioning the piston at TDC on the compression stroke.

● Drain the carburettor(s) otherwise there is a risk of jets becoming blocked by gum deposits from the fuel **(see illustration 4)**.

● If the bike is going into long-term storage, consider adding a fuel stabiliser to the fuel in the tank. If the tank is drained completely, corrosion of its internal surfaces may occur if left unprotected for a long period. The tank can be treated with a rust preventative especially for this purpose. Alternatively, remove the tank and pour half a litre of motor oil into it, install the filler cap and shake the tank to coat its internals with oil before draining off the excess. The same effect can also be achieved by spraying WD40 or a similar water-dispersant around the inside of the tank via its flexible nozzle.

● Make sure the cooling system contains the correct mix of antifreeze. Antifreeze also contains important corrosion inhibitors.

● The air intakes and exhaust can be sealed off by covering or plugging the openings. Ensure that you do not seal in any condensation; run the engine until it is hot,

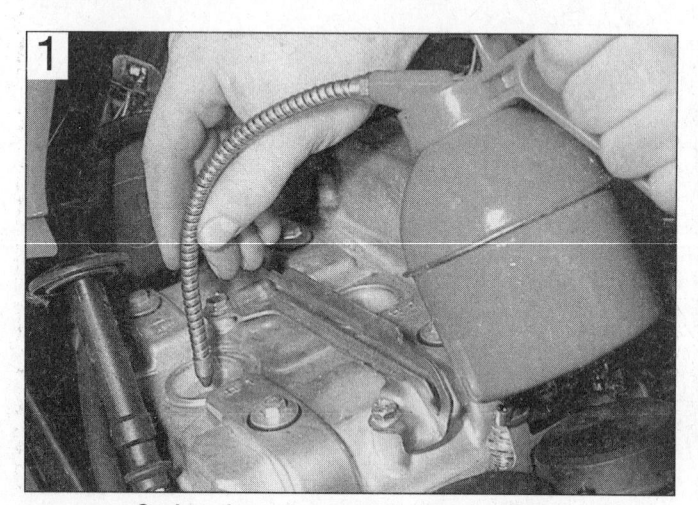

1 Squirt a drop of motor oil into each cylinder

2 Flick the kill switch to OFF . . .

3 . . . and ensure that the metal bodies of the plugs (arrows) are earthed against the cylinder head

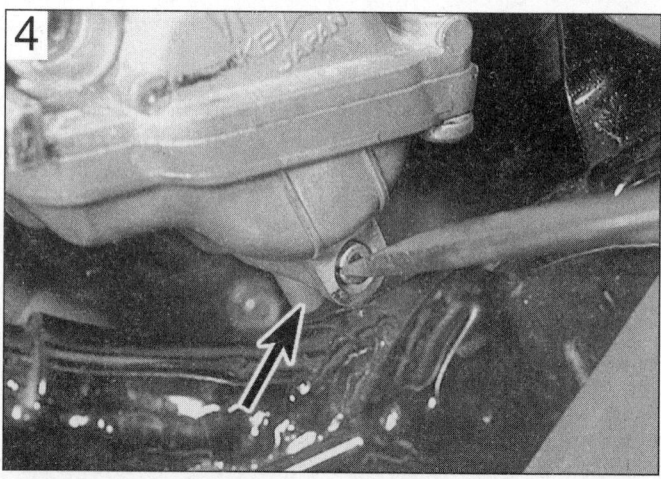

4 Connect a hose to the carburettor float chamber drain stub (arrow) and unscrew the drain screw

Storage REF•33

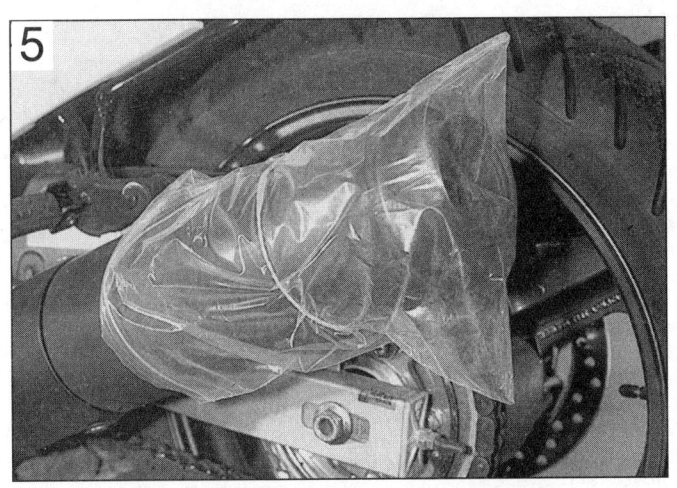

Exhausts can be sealed off with a plastic bag

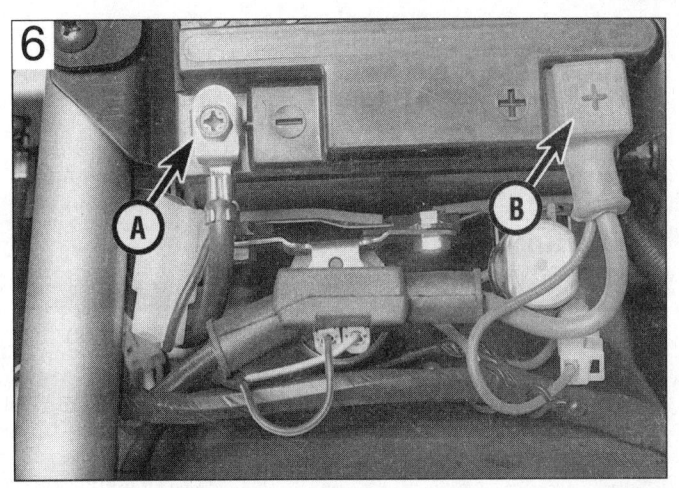

Disconnect the negative lead (A) first, followed by the positive lead (B)

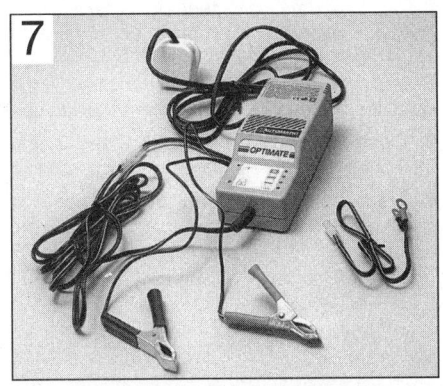

Use a suitable battery charger - this kit also assess battery condition

then switch off and allow to cool. Tape a piece of thick plastic over the silencer end(s) **(see illustration 5)**. Note that some advocate pouring a tablespoon of motor oil into the silencer(s) before sealing them off.

Battery

● Remove it from the bike - in extreme cases of cold the battery may freeze and crack its case **(see illustration 6)**.

● Check the electrolyte level and top up if necessary (conventional refillable batteries). Clean the terminals.
● Store the battery off the motorcycle and away from any sources of fire. Position a wooden block under the battery if it is to sit on the ground.
● Give the battery a trickle charge for a few hours every month **(see illustration 7)**.

Tyres

● Place the bike on its centrestand or an auxiliary stand which will support the motorcycle in an upright position. Position wood blocks under the tyres to keep them off the ground and to provide insulation from damp. If the bike is being put into long-term storage, ideally both tyres should be off the ground; not only will this protect the tyres, but will also ensure that no load is placed on the steering head or wheel bearings.
● Deflate each tyre by 5 to 10 psi, no more or the beads may unseat from the rim, making subsequent inflation difficult on tubeless tyres.

Pivots and controls

● Lubricate all lever, pedal, stand and footrest pivot points. If grease nipples are fitted to the rear suspension components, apply lubricant to the pivots.
● Lubricate all control cables.

Cycle components

● Apply a wax protectant to all painted and plastic components. Wipe off any excess, but don't polish to a shine. Where fitted, clean the screen with soap and water.
● Coat metal parts with Vaseline (petroleum jelly). When applying this to the fork tubes, do not compress the forks otherwise the seals will rot from contact with the Vaseline.
● Apply a vinyl cleaner to the seat.

Storage conditions

● Aim to store the bike in a shed or garage which does not leak and is free from damp.
● Drape an old blanket or bedspread over the bike to protect it from dust and direct contact with sunlight (which will fade paint). This also hides the bike from prying eyes. Beware of tight-fitting plastic covers which may allow condensation to form and settle on the bike.

Getting back on the road

Engine and transmission

● Change the oil and replace the oil filter. If this was done prior to storage, check that the oil hasn't emulsified - a thick whitish substance which occurs through condensation.
● Remove the spark plugs. Using a spout-type oil can, squirt a few drops of oil into the cylinder(s). This will provide initial lubrication as the piston rings and bores comes back into contact. Service the spark plugs, or fit new ones, and install them in the engine.

● Check that the clutch isn't stuck on. The plates can stick together if left standing for some time, preventing clutch operation. Engage a gear and try rocking the bike back and forth with the clutch lever held against the handlebar. If this doesn't work on cable-operated clutches, hold the clutch lever back against the handlebar with a strong elastic band or cable tie for a couple of hours **(see illustration 8)**.
● If the air intakes or silencer end(s) were blocked off, remove the bung or cover used.
● If the fuel tank was coated with a rust

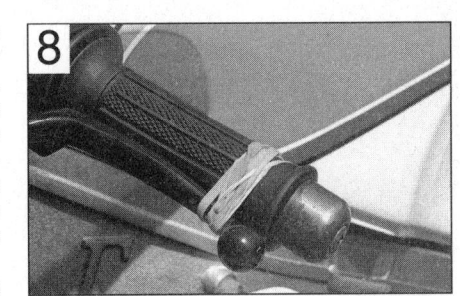

Hold clutch lever back against the handlebar with elastic bands or a cable tie

Storage

preventative, oil or a stabiliser added to the fuel, drain and flush the tank and dispose of the fuel sensibly. If no action was taken with the fuel tank prior to storage, it is advised that the old fuel is disposed of since it will go off over a period of time. Refill the fuel tank with fresh fuel.

Frame and running gear

- Oil all pivot points and cables.
- Check the tyre pressures. They will definitely need inflating if pressures were reduced for storage.
- Lubricate the final drive chain (where applicable).
- Remove any protective coating applied to the fork tubes (stanchions) since this may well destroy the fork seals. If the fork tubes weren't protected and have picked up rust spots, remove them with very fine abrasive paper and refinish with metal polish.
- Check that both brakes operate correctly. Apply each brake hard and check that it's not possible to move the motorcycle forwards, then check that the brake frees off again once released. Brake caliper pistons can stick due to corrosion around the piston head, or on the sliding caliper types, due to corrosion of the slider pins. If the brake doesn't free after repeated operation, take the caliper off for examination. Similarly drum brakes can stick due to a seized operating cam, cable or rod linkage.
- If the motorcycle has been in long-term storage, renew the brake fluid and clutch fluid (where applicable).
- Depending on where the bike has been stored, the wiring, cables and hoses may have been nibbled by rodents. Make a visual check and investigate disturbed wiring loom tape.

Battery

- If the battery has been previously removal and given top up charges it can simply be reconnected. Remember to connect the positive cable first and the negative cable last.
- On conventional refillable batteries, if the battery has not received any attention, remove it from the motorcycle and check its electrolyte level. Top up if necessary then charge the battery. If the battery fails to hold a charge and a visual checks show heavy white sulphation of the plates, the battery is probably defective and must be renewed. This is particularly likely if the battery is old. Confirm battery condition with a specific gravity check.
- On sealed (MF) batteries, if the battery has not received any attention, remove it from the motorcycle and charge it according to the information on the battery case - if the battery fails to hold a charge it must be renewed.

Starting procedure

- If a kickstart is fitted, turn the engine over a couple of times with the ignition OFF to distribute oil around the engine. If no kickstart is fitted, flick the engine kill switch OFF and the ignition ON and crank the engine over a couple of times to work oil around the upper cylinder components. If the nature of the ignition system is such that the starter won't work with the kill switch OFF, remove the spark plugs, fit them back into their caps and earth (ground) their bodies on the cylinder head. Reinstall the spark plugs afterwards.
- Switch the kill switch to RUN, operate the choke and start the engine. If the engine won't start don't continue cranking the engine - not only will this flatten the battery, but the starter motor will overheat. Switch the ignition off and try again later. If the engine refuses to start, go through the fault finding procedures in this manual. **Note:** *If the bike has been in storage for a long time, old fuel or a carburettor blockage may be the problem. Gum deposits in carburettors can block jets - if a carburettor cleaner doesn't prove successful the carburettors must be dismantled for cleaning.*
- Once the engine has started, check that the lights, turn signals and horn work properly.
- Treat the bike gently for the first ride and check all fluid levels on completion. Settle the bike back into the maintenance schedule.

Fault Finding REF•35

This Section provides an easy reference-guide to the more common faults that are likely to afflict your machine. Obviously, the opportunities are almost limitless for faults to occur as a result of obscure failures, and to try and cover all eventualities would require a book. Indeed, a number have been written on the subject.

Successful troubleshooting is not a mysterious 'black art' but the application of a bit of knowledge combined with a systematic and logical approach to the problem. Approach any troubleshooting by first accurately identifying the symptom and then checking through the list of possible causes, starting with the simplest or most obvious and progressing in stages to the most complex.

Take nothing for granted, but above all apply liberal quantities of common sense.

The main symptom of a fault is given in the text as a major heading below which are listed the various systems or areas which may contain the fault. Details of each possible cause for a fault and the remedial action to be taken are given, in brief, in the paragraphs below each heading. Further information should be sought in the relevant Chapter.

1 Engine doesn't start or is difficult to start
- [ ] Starter motor doesn't rotate
- [ ] Starter motor rotates but engine does not turn over
- [ ] Starter works but engine won't turn over (seized)
- [ ] No fuel flow
- [ ] Engine flooded
- [ ] No spark or weak spark
- [ ] Compression low
- [ ] Stalls after starting
- [ ] Rough idle

2 Poor running at low speed
- [ ] Spark weak
- [ ] Fuel/air mixture incorrect
- [ ] Compression low
- [ ] Poor acceleration

3 Poor running or no power at high speed
- [ ] Firing incorrect
- [ ] Fuel/air mixture incorrect
- [ ] Compression low
- [ ] Knocking or pinking
- [ ] Miscellaneous causes

4 Overheating
- [ ] Engine overheats
- [ ] Firing incorrect
- [ ] Fuel/air mixture incorrect
- [ ] Compression too high
- [ ] Engine load excessive
- [ ] Lubrication inadequate
- [ ] Miscellaneous causes

5 Clutch problems
- [ ] Clutch slipping
- [ ] Clutch not disengaging completely

6 Gearchanging problems
- [ ] Doesn't go into gear, or lever doesn't return
- [ ] Jumps out of gear
- [ ] Overselects

7 Abnormal engine noise
- [ ] Knocking or pinking
- [ ] Piston slap or rattling
- [ ] Valve noise
- [ ] Other noise

8 Abnormal driveline noise
- [ ] Clutch noise
- [ ] Transmission noise
- [ ] Final drive noise

9 Abnormal frame and suspension noise
- [ ] Front end noise
- [ ] Shock absorber noise
- [ ] Brake noise

10 Oil level warning light comes on
- [ ] Engine lubrication system
- [ ] Electrical system

11 Excessive exhaust smoke
- [ ] White smoke
- [ ] Black smoke
- [ ] Brown smoke

12 Poor handling or stability
- [ ] Handlebar hard to turn
- [ ] Handlebar shakes or vibrates excessively
- [ ] Handlebar pulls to one side
- [ ] Poor shock absorbing qualities

13 Braking problems
- [ ] Brakes are spongy, don't hold
- [ ] Brake lever or pedal pulsates
- [ ] Brakes drag

14 Electrical problems
- [ ] Battery dead or weak
- [ ] Battery overcharged

Fault Finding

1 Engine doesn't start or is difficult to start

Starter motor doesn't rotate
- [ ] Engine kill switch OFF.
- [ ] Main fuse blown (Chapter 8).
- [ ] Battery voltage low. Check and recharge battery (Chapter 8).
- [ ] Starter motor defective. Make sure the wiring to the starter is secure. Make sure the starter relay clicks when the start button is pushed. If the relay clicks, then the fault is in the wiring or motor (see Chapter 8).
- [ ] Starter switch not contacting. The contacts could be wet, corroded or dirty. Disassemble and clean the switch (Chapter 8).
- [ ] Wiring open or shorted. Check all wiring connections and harnesses to make sure that they are dry, tight and not corroded. Also check for broken or frayed wires that can cause a short to ground (earth) (see Wiring diagrams, Chapter 8).
- [ ] Ignition (main) switch defective. Check the switch and replace with a new one if it is defective (see Chapter 8).
- [ ] Engine kill switch defective. Check for wet, dirty or corroded contacts. Clean or replace the switch with a new one as necessary (see Chapter 8).
- [ ] Faulty neutral switch, sidestand switch or clutch switch. Check the wiring to each switch and the switch itself (see Chapter 8).
- [ ] Faulty starter circuit cut-off relay or diode (Chapter 8).
- [ ] Fuel injection system shutdown due to system fault (Chapter 4).

Starter motor rotates but engine does not turn over
- [ ] Starter clutch defective. Inspect and repair or replace with a new one (see Chapter 2).
- [ ] Damaged idler or starter gears. Inspect and replace the damaged parts (see Chapter 2).

Starter works but engine won't turn over (seized)
- [ ] Seized engine caused by one or more internally damaged components. Failure due to wear, abuse or lack of lubrication. Damage can include seized valves, followers, camshafts, pistons, crankshaft, connecting rod bearings, or transmission gears or bearings. Refer to Chapter 2 for engine disassembly.

No fuel flow
- [ ] No fuel in tank.
- [ ] Fuel tank breather hose obstructed.
- [ ] Faulty fuel pump relay. Check the relay (see Chapter 4).
- [ ] Fuel pump faulty, or the fuel filter is blocked (see Chapter 4).
- [ ] Fuel hose clogged. Remove the fuel hose and carefully blow through it. Check the fuel filter for damage.
- [ ] Fuel rail or injector clogged. For all of the injectors to be clogged, either a very bad batch of fuel with an unusual additive has been used, or some other foreign material has entered the tank. Check the fuel filter. In some cases, if a machine has been unused for several months, the fuel turns to a varnish-like liquid which can cause an injector needle to stick to its seat. Drain the tank and fuel system (Chapter 4).

Engine flooded
- [ ] Injector needle valve worn or stuck open. A piece of dirt, rust or other debris can cause the needle to seat improperly, causing excess fuel to be admitted to the throttle body. In this case, the injector should be cleaned and the needle and seat inspected (see Chapter 4). If the needle and seat are worn, then the leaking will persist and the parts should be renewed.
- [ ] Starting technique incorrect. Under normal circumstances (i.e. if all the components of the fuel injection system are good) the machine should start with the throttle closed.

No spark or weak spark
- [ ] Ignition switch OFF.
- [ ] Engine kill switch turned to the OFF position.
- [ ] Ignition or kill switch shorted. This is usually caused by water, corrosion, damage or excessive wear. The switches can be disassembled and cleaned with electrical contact cleaner. If cleaning does not help, replace the switches (see Chapter 8).
- [ ] Battery voltage low. Check and recharge the battery as necessary (Chapter 8).
- [ ] Ignition coil not making good contact. Make sure that the coils fit snugly over the plug ends.
- [ ] Spark plugs dirty, defective or worn out. Locate reason for fouled plugs using spark plug condition chart on the inside back cover and follow the plug maintenance procedures (see Chapter 1).
- [ ] Incorrect spark plugs. Wrong type or heat range. Check and install correct plugs (see Chapter 1).
- [ ] Ignition coil defective. Test and renew if necessary (Chapter 4).
- [ ] Fuel injection system shutdown due to system fault (Chapter 4).
- [ ] Camshaft position (CMP) sensor defective (see Chapter 4).
- [ ] Crankshaft position (CKP) sensor defective (see Chapter 4).
- [ ] Engine control unit (ECU) defective (see Chapter 4).
- [ ] Wiring shorted or broken between:
    a) Ignition (main) switch and engine kill switch (or blown fuse)
    b) ECU and engine kill switch
    c) ECU and ignition coils
    d) ECU and CKP sensor
- [ ] Make sure that all wiring connections are clean, dry and tight. Look for chafed and broken wires (see Chapters 4 and 8).

Compression low
- [ ] Spark plugs loose. Remove the plugs and inspect their threads. Reinstall and tighten securely (see Chapter 1).
- [ ] Cylinder head not sufficiently tightened down. If a cylinder head is suspected of being loose, then there's a chance that the gasket or head is damaged if the problem has persisted for any length of time. The head bolts should be tightened to the proper torque and in the correct sequence (Chapter 2).
- [ ] Improper valve clearance. This means that the valve is not closing completely and compression pressure is leaking past the valve. Check and adjust the valve clearances (Chapter 1).
- [ ] Cylinder and/or piston worn. Excessive wear will cause compression pressure to leak past the rings. This is usually accompanied by worn rings as well. A top-end overhaul is necessary (Chapter 2).
- [ ] Piston rings worn, weak, broken, or sticking. Broken or sticking piston rings usually indicate a lubrication or fuelling problem that causes excess carbon deposits to form on the pistons and rings. Top-end overhaul is necessary (Chapter 2).
- [ ] Piston ring-to-groove clearance excessive. This is caused by excessive wear of the piston ring lands. Piston renewal is necessary (Chapter 2).
- [ ] Cylinder head gasket damaged. If a head is allowed to become loose, or if excessive carbon build-up on the piston crown and combustion chamber causes extremely high compression, the head gasket may leak. Retorquing the head is not always sufficient to restore the seal, so a new gasket is necessary (Chapter 2).
- [ ] Cylinder head warped. This is caused by overheating or improperly tightened head bolts. Machine shop resurfacing or head renewal is necessary (Chapter 2).
- [ ] Valve spring broken or weak. Caused by component failure or wear; the springs must be renewed (Chapter 2).
- [ ] Valve not seating properly. This is caused by a bent valve (from over-revving or improper valve adjustment), burned valve or seat (incorrect air/fuel mixture) or an accumulation of carbon deposits on the seat. The valves must be cleaned and/or renewed and the seats serviced (Chapter 2).

Fault Finding

1 Engine doesn't start or is difficult to start (continued)

Stalls after starting

- ☐ Faulty fast idle system. Check the operation of the wax unit (see Chapter 4).
- ☐ Engine idle speed incorrect. Turn idle adjusting screw until the engine idles at the specified rpm (Chapter 1).
- ☐ Ignition malfunction (see Chapter 4).
- ☐ Fuel injection system malfunction (see Chapter 4).
- ☐ Fuel contaminated. The fuel can be contaminated with either dirt or water, or can change chemically if the machine has been unused for several months. Drain the tank and fuel system (Chapter 4).
- ☐ Intake air leak. Check for loose throttle body-to-intake manifold connections, loose or damaged AIS vacuum hose or throttle body vacuum hoses (Chapter 4).

Rough idle

- ☐ Idle speed incorrect (see Chapter 1).
- ☐ Ignition fault (see Chapter 4).
- ☐ Throttle body air screws not synchronised. Adjust them as described in Chapter 1.
- ☐ Fuel injection system malfunction (see Chapter 4).
- ☐ Fuel contaminated. The fuel can be contaminated with either dirt or water, or can change chemically if the machine has been unused for several months. Drain the tank and the fuel system (Chapter 4).
- ☐ Intake air leak. Check for loose throttle body-to-intake manifold connections, loose or damaged AIS vacuum hose or throttle body vacuum hoses (Chapter 4).
- ☐ Air filter clogged. Clean the air filter element or replace it with a new one (Chapter 1).

2 Poor running at low speeds

Spark weak

- ☐ Battery voltage low. Check and recharge battery (see Chapter 8).
- ☐ Ignition coils not making good contact. Make sure that the coils fit snugly over the plug ends.
- ☐ Spark plugs dirty, defective or worn out. Locate reason for fouled plugs using spark plug condition chart on the inside back cover and follow the plug maintenance procedures (see Chapter 1).
- ☐ Incorrect spark plugs. Wrong type or heat range. Check and install correct plugs (see Chapter 1).
- ☐ Ignition coil defective. Test and renew if necessary (see Chapter 4).

Fuel/air mixture incorrect

- ☐ Fuel tank breather hose obstructed.
- ☐ Fuel pump faulty, or the fuel filter is blocked (see Chapter 4).
- ☐ Fuel hose clogged. Remove the fuel hose and carefully blow through it. Check the fuel filter for damage.
- ☐ Fuel rail or injector clogged. For all of the injectors to be clogged, either a very bad batch of fuel with an unusual additive has been used, or some other foreign material has entered the tank. Check the fuel filter. In some cases, if a machine has been unused for several months, the fuel turns to a varnish-like liquid which can cause an injector needle to stick to its seat. Drain the tank and fuel system (Chapter 4).
- ☐ Intake air leak. Check for loose throttle body-to-intake manifold connections, loose or damaged AIS vacuum hose or throttle body vacuum hoses (Chapter 4).
- ☐ Air filter clogged. Clean the air filter element or replace it with a new one (Chapter 1).

Compression low

Check by performing a compression test (see Chapter 2).

- ☐ Spark plugs loose. Remove the plugs and inspect their threads. Reinstall and tighten securely (see Chapter 1).
- ☐ Cylinder head not sufficiently tightened down. If a cylinder head is suspected of being loose, then there's a chance that the gasket or head is damaged if the problem has persisted for any length of time. The head bolts should be tightened to the proper torque and in the correct sequence (Chapter 2).
- ☐ Improper valve clearance. This means that the valve is not closing completely and compression pressure is leaking past the valve. Check and adjust the valve clearances (Chapter 1).
- ☐ Cylinder and/or piston worn. Excessive wear will cause compression pressure to leak past the rings. This is usually accompanied by worn rings as well. A top-end overhaul is necessary (Chapter 2).
- ☐ Piston rings worn, weak, broken, or sticking. Broken or sticking piston rings usually indicate a lubrication or fuelling problem that causes excess carbon deposits to form on the pistons and rings. Top-end overhaul is necessary (Chapter 2).
- ☐ Piston ring-to-groove clearance excessive. This is caused by excessive wear of the piston ring lands. Piston renewal is necessary (Chapter 2).
- ☐ Cylinder head gasket damaged. If the head is allowed to become loose, or if excessive carbon build-up on the piston crown and combustion chamber causes extremely high compression, the head gasket may leak. Retorquing the head is not always sufficient to restore the seal, so a new gasket is necessary (Chapter 2).
- ☐ Cylinder head warped. This is caused by overheating or improperly tightened head bolts. Machine shop resurfacing or head renewal is necessary (Chapter 2).
- ☐ Valve spring broken or weak. Caused by component failure or wear; the springs must be renewed (Chapter 2).
- ☐ Valve not seating properly. This is caused by a bent valve (from over-revving or improper valve adjustment), burned valve or seat (improper fuelling) or an accumulation of carbon deposits on the seat (from fuelling or lubrication problems). The valves must be cleaned and/or renewed and the seats serviced (Chapter 2).

Poor acceleration

- ☐ Timing not advancing. The crankshaft position sensor (CKP) or the engine control unit (ECU) may be defective (see Chapter 4). If so, they must be renewed.
- ☐ Engine oil viscosity too high. Using a heavier oil than that recommended in Chapter 1 can damage the oil pump or lubrication system and cause drag on the engine.
- ☐ Brakes dragging. Usually caused by debris which has entered the brake caliper piston seals, or from a warped disc or bent axle (see Chapter 6).

REF•38 Fault Finding

3 Poor running or no power at high speed

Firing incorrect
- [ ] Ignition coils not making good contact. Make sure that the coils fit snugly over the plug ends and that the wiring is secure.
- [ ] Spark plugs dirty, defective or worn out. Locate reason for fouled plugs using spark plug condition chart on the inside back cover and follow the plug maintenance procedures (see Chapter 1).
- [ ] Incorrect spark plugs. Wrong type or heat range. Check and install correct plugs (see Chapter 1).
- [ ] Ignition coil defective. Test and renew if necessary (see Chapter 4).
- [ ] Faulty ECU (engine control unit) (see Chapter 4).

Fuel/air mixture incorrect
- [ ] Fuel tank breather hose obstructed.
- [ ] Fuel pump faulty, or the fuel filter is blocked (see Chapter 4).
- [ ] Fuel hose clogged. Remove the fuel hose and carefully blow through it. Check the fuel filter for damage.
- [ ] Fuel rail or injector clogged. For all of the injectors to be clogged, either a very bad batch of fuel with an unusual additive has been used, or some other foreign material has entered the tank. Check the fuel filter. In some cases, if a machine has been unused for several months, the fuel turns to a varnish-like liquid which can cause an injector needle to stick to its seat. Drain the tank and fuel system (Chapter 4).
- [ ] Intake air leak. Check for loose throttle body-to-intake manifold connections, loose or damaged AIS vacuum hose or throttle body vacuum hoses (Chapter 4).
- [ ] Air filter clogged. Clean the air filter element or replace it with a new one (Chapter 1).

Compression low
Check by performing a compression test (see Chapter 2).
- [ ] Spark plugs loose. Remove the plugs and inspect their threads. Reinstall and tighten securely (see Chapter 1).
- [ ] Cylinder head not sufficiently tightened down. If a cylinder head is suspected of being loose, then there's a chance that the gasket or head is damaged if the problem has persisted for any length of time. The head bolts should be tightened to the proper torque and in the correct sequence (Chapter 2).
- [ ] Improper valve clearance. This means that the valve is not closing completely and compression pressure is leaking past the valve. Check and adjust the valve clearances (Chapter 1).
- [ ] Cylinder and/or piston worn. Excessive wear will cause compression pressure to leak past the rings. This is usually accompanied by worn rings as well. A top-end overhaul is necessary (Chapter 2).
- [ ] Piston rings worn, weak, broken, or sticking. Broken or sticking piston rings usually indicate a lubrication or fuelling problem that causes excess carbon deposits to form on the pistons and rings. Top-end overhaul is necessary (Chapter 2).
- [ ] Piston ring-to-groove clearance excessive. This is caused by excessive wear of the piston ring lands. Piston renewal is necessary (Chapter 2).
- [ ] Cylinder head gasket damaged. If a head is allowed to become loose, or if excessive carbon build-up on the piston crown and combustion chamber causes extremely high compression, the head gasket may leak. Retorquing the head is not always sufficient to restore the seal, so a new gasket is necessary (Chapter 2).
- [ ] Cylinder head warped. This is caused by overheating or improperly tightened head bolts. Machine shop resurfacing or head renewal is necessary (Chapter 2).
- [ ] Valve spring broken or weak. Caused by component failure or wear; the springs must be replaced with new ones (Chapter 2).
- [ ] Valve not seating properly. This is caused by a bent valve (from over-revving or improper valve adjustment), burned valve or seat (improper fuelling) or an accumulation of carbon deposits on the seat (from fuelling or lubrication problems). The valves must be cleaned and/or renewed and the seats serviced (Chapter 2).

Knocking or pinking
- [ ] Carbon build-up in combustion chamber. Use of a fuel additive that will dissolve the adhesive bonding the carbon particles to the piston crown and chamber is the easiest way to remove the build-up. Otherwise, the cylinder head will have to be removed and decarbonised (Chapter 2).
- [ ] Incorrect or poor quality fuel. Old or improper grades of fuel can cause detonation. This causes the piston to rattle, thus the knocking or pinking sound. Drain old fuel and always use the recommended fuel grade.
- [ ] Spark plug heat range incorrect. Uncontrolled detonation indicates the plug heat range is too hot. The plug in effect becomes a glow plug, raising cylinder temperatures. Install the proper heat range plug (Chapter 1).
- [ ] Improper air/fuel mixture. This will cause the cylinders to run hot, which leads to detonation. A blockage in the fuel system or an air leak can cause this imbalance (see Chapter 4).

Miscellaneous causes
- [ ] Throttle valve doesn't open fully. Adjust the throttle twistgrip freeplay (see Chapter 1).
- [ ] Clutch slipping due loose or worn clutch components (see Chapter 2).
- [ ] Timing not advancing. The crankshaft position sensor (CKP) or the engine control unit (ECU) may be defective (see Chapter 4). If so, they must be replaced with new ones.
- [ ] Engine oil viscosity too high. Using a heavier oil than the one recommended in Chapter 1 can damage the oil pump or lubrication system and cause drag on the engine.
- [ ] Brakes dragging. Usually caused by debris which has entered the brake caliper piston seals, or from a warped disc or bent axle (see Chapter 6).

Fault Finding REF•39

4 Overheating

Engine overheats
- ☐ Coolant level low. Check and add coolant (see *Pre-ride checks*).
- ☐ Leak in cooling system. Check cooling system hoses and radiator for leaks and other damage. Repair or renew parts as necessary (see Chapter 3).
- ☐ Faulty thermostat. Check and renew as described in Chapter 3.
- ☐ Faulty radiator cap. Remove the cap and have it pressure tested.
- ☐ Coolant passages clogged. Drain, flush and refill with fresh coolant (Chapter 1).
- ☐ Water pump defective. Remove the pump and check the components (see Chapter 3).
- ☐ Clogged or damaged radiator fins (see Chapter 3).
- ☐ Faulty cooling fan or fan switch (see Chapter 3).

Firing incorrect
- ☐ Wrongly connected ignition coil wiring.
- ☐ Spark plugs dirty, defective or worn out. Locate reason for fouled plugs using spark plug condition chart on the inside back cover and follow the plug maintenance procedures (see Chapter 1).
- ☐ Incorrect spark plugs. Wrong type or heat range. Check and install correct plugs (see Chapter 1).
- ☐ Ignition coil defective. Test and replace with a new one if necessary (see Chapter 4).
- ☐ Faulty ECU (engine control unit) (see Chapter 4).

Fuel/air mixture incorrect
- ☐ Fuel tank breather hose obstructed.
- ☐ Fuel pump faulty, or the fuel filter is blocked (see Chapter 4).
- ☐ Fuel hose clogged. Remove the fuel hose and carefully blow through it. Check the fuel filter for damage.
- ☐ Fuel rail or injector clogged. For all of the injectors to be clogged, either a very bad batch of fuel with an unusual additive has been used, or some other foreign material has entered the tank. Check the fuel filter. In some cases, if a machine has been unused for several months, the fuel turns to a varnish-like liquid which can cause an injector needle to stick to its seat. Drain the tank and fuel system (Chapter 4).
- ☐ Intake air leak. Check for loose throttle body-to-intake manifold connections, loose or damaged AIS vacuum hose or throttle body vacuum hoses (Chapter 4).
- ☐ Air filter clogged. Clean the air filter element or replace it with a new one (Chapter 1).

Compression too high
Check by performing a compression test (see Chapter 2).
- ☐ Carbon build-up in combustion chamber. Use of a fuel additive that will dissolve the adhesive bonding the carbon particles to the piston crown and chamber is the easiest way to remove the build-up. Otherwise, the cylinder head will have to be removed and decarbonised (Chapter 2).
- ☐ Improperly machined head surface or installation of incorrect gasket during engine assembly.

Engine load excessive
- ☐ Clutch slipping due loose or worn clutch components (see Chapter 2).
- ☐ Engine oil level too high. Too much oil will cause pressurisation of the crankcase and inefficient engine operation. Check Specifications and drain to proper level (Chapter 1 and *Pre-ride checks*).
- ☐ Engine oil viscosity too high. Using a heavier oil than the one recommended in Chapter 1 can damage the oil pump or lubrication system as well as cause drag on the engine.
- ☐ Brakes dragging. Usually caused by debris which has entered the brake caliper piston seals, or from a warped disc or bent axle (see Chapter 6).

Lubrication inadequate
- ☐ Engine oil level too low. Friction caused by intermittent lack of lubrication or from oil that is overworked can cause overheating. The oil provides a definite cooling function in the engine. Check the oil level (see *Pre-ride checks*).
- ☐ Low engine oil pressure. Check the pressure (see Chapter 2).
- ☐ Blocked oil filter or oil cooler (see Chapter 2).

Miscellaneous causes
- ☐ Modification to exhaust system. Most aftermarket exhaust systems cause the engine to run leaner, which make them run hotter. When installing an accessory exhaust system, always check with the manufacturer/supplier as to whether the fuel system requires adjustment.

5 Clutch problems

Clutch slipping
- ☐ Insufficient clutch cable freeplay. Check and adjust (see Chapter 1).
- ☐ Clutch plates worn or warped. Overhaul the clutch assembly (see Chapter 2).
- ☐ Clutch springs broken or weak. Old or heat-damaged (from slipping clutch) springs should be renewed (Chapter 2).
- ☐ Faulty clutch release mechanism. Replace any defective parts with new ones (see Chapter 2).
- ☐ Clutch centre or housing unevenly worn. This causes improper engagement of the plates. Replace the damaged or worn parts (see Chapter 2).
- ☐ Incorrect oil used in engine. Oils designed for car engines often contain friction modifiers which if used in an engine with a wet clutch can promote clutch slip. Always use an oil designed for motorcycle engines (see *Pre-ride checks*).

Clutch not disengaging completely
- ☐ Excessive clutch cable freeplay. Check and adjust (see Chapter 1).
- ☐ Clutch plates warped or damaged. This will cause clutch drag, which in turn will cause the machine to creep. Overhaul the clutch assembly (see Chapter 2).
- ☐ Clutch springs fatigued or broken. Check and renew the springs (see Chapter 2).
- ☐ Engine oil deteriorated. Old, thin oil will not provide proper lubrication for the plates, causing the clutch to drag. Renew the oil and filter (see Chapter 1).
- ☐ Engine oil viscosity too high. Using a heavier oil than recommended in Chapter 1 can cause the plates to stick together. Change to the correct weight oil.
- ☐ Clutch housing bearing seized on the transmission input shaft. Lack of lubrication, severe wear or damage can cause the bearing to seize. Overhaul of the clutch, and perhaps transmission, may be necessary to repair the damage (see Chapter 2).
- ☐ Faulty clutch release mechanism. Renew any defective parts (see Chapter 2).
- ☐ Loose clutch centre nut. Causes housing and centre misalignment putting a drag on the engine. Engagement adjustment continually varies. Overhaul the clutch assembly (see Chapter 2).

Fault Finding

6 Gearchanging problems

Doesn't go into gear or lever doesn't return
- [ ] Clutch not disengaging (see above).
- [ ] Gearchange mechanism stopper arm spring weak or broken, or arm roller broken or worn. Replace the spring or arm with a new one (see Chapter 2).
- [ ] Selector fork(s) bent, worn or seized. Overhaul the transmission (see Chapter 2).
- [ ] Gear(s) stuck on shaft. Most often caused by a lack of lubrication or excessive wear in transmission bearings and bushes. Overhaul the transmission (see Chapter 2).
- [ ] Selector drum binding. Caused by lubrication failure or excessive wear. Replace the drum and/or its bearing with a new one (see Chapter 2).
- [ ] Gearchange mechanism return spring weak or broken (see Chapter 2).
- [ ] Gearchange linkage arm broken. Splines stripped out of arm or shaft, caused by a loose linkage arm pinch bolt or from dropping the machine (see Chapter 2).

Jumps out of gear
- [ ] Selector fork(s) worn (see Chapter 2).
- [ ] Selector fork groove(s) in selector drum worn (see Chapter 2).
- [ ] Gear pinion dogs or dog slots worn or damaged. The gear pinions should be inspected and renewed. No attempt should be made to repair the worn parts.

Overselects
- [ ] Gearchange mechanism stopper arm spring weak or broken, or arm roller broken or worn. Renew the spring or arm (see Chapter 2).
- [ ] Gearchange mechanism return spring weak or broken (see Chapter 2).

7 Abnormal engine noise

Knocking or pinking
- [ ] Carbon build-up in combustion chamber. Use of a fuel additive that will dissolve the adhesive bonding the carbon particles to the piston crown and chamber is the easiest way to remove the build-up. Otherwise, the cylinder head will have to be removed and decarbonised (Chapter 2).
- [ ] Incorrect or poor quality fuel. Old or improper grades of fuel can cause detonation. This causes the piston to rattle, thus the knocking or pinking sound. Drain old fuel and always use the recommended fuel grade.
- [ ] Spark plug heat range incorrect. Uncontrolled detonation indicates the plug heat range is too hot. The plug in effect becomes a glow plug, raising cylinder temperatures. Install the proper heat range plug (Chapter 1).
- [ ] Improper air/fuel mixture. This will cause the cylinders to run hot, which leads to detonation. A blockage in the fuel system or an air leak can cause this imbalance (see Chapter 4).

Piston slap or rattling
- [ ] Cylinder-to-piston clearance excessive. Cylinder and/or piston worn, usually accompanied by worn rings as well. A top-end overhaul is necessary (see Chapter 2).
- [ ] Piston ring(s) worn, broken or sticking. Overhaul the top-end (see Chapter 2).
- [ ] Piston pin, piston pin bore or connecting rod small-end worn from high mileage or seized due to lack of lubrication (see Chapter 2).
- [ ] Piston seizure damage. Usually from lack of lubrication or overheating. Replace the pistons and upper crankcase, as necessary (see Chapter 2).
- [ ] Connecting rod big-end clearance excessive. Caused by excessive wear or lack of lubrication. Replace worn parts.
- [ ] Connecting rod bent. Caused by over-revving, trying to start a badly flooded engine or from ingesting a foreign object into the combustion chamber. Replace the damaged parts (Chapter 2).

Valve noise
- [ ] Incorrect valve clearances – check and adjust (see Chapter 1).
- [ ] Valve spring broken or weak. Check and replace weak valve springs with new ones (see Chapter 2).
- [ ] Camshaft or camshaft journals in the cylinder head worn or damaged. Lubrication failure at high rpm is usually the cause of damage due to insufficient oil or failure to change the oil at the recommended intervals. Since there are no replaceable bearings in the head, the head itself will have to be replaced with a new one (see Chapter 2).

Other noise
- [ ] Cylinder head gasket leaking. Check around the joint for blowing with the engine running.
- [ ] Exhaust pipe leaking at cylinder head connection. Caused by incorrect fit of pipe(s), loose exhaust flange or damaged gasket. All exhaust system fasteners should be tightened evenly and carefully to avoid leaks (see Chapter 4).
- [ ] Crankshaft runout excessive. Caused by a bent crankshaft (from over-revving) or damage from an upper cylinder component failure. Can also be attributed to dropping the machine on either of the crankshaft ends.
- [ ] Engine mounting bolts loose – ensure all the bolts are tightened to the specified torque settings (see Chapter 2).
- [ ] Crankshaft bearings worn (see Chapter 2).
- [ ] Cam chain rattle, due to worn chain or defective tensioner. Also worn chain tensioner/guide blades (see Chapter 2).

8 Abnormal driveline noise

Clutch noise
- [ ] Clutch housing/friction plate clearance excessive (Chapter 2).
- [ ] Wear between the clutch housing splines and input shaft splines (Chapter 2).
- [ ] Worn release bearing (Chapter 2).

Transmission noise
- [ ] Bearings worn. Also includes the possibility that the shafts are worn. Overhaul the transmission (Chapter 2).
- [ ] Gears worn or chipped (Chapter 2).
- [ ] Metal chips jammed in gear teeth. Probably pieces from a broken clutch, gear or selector mechanism that were picked up by the gears. This will cause early bearing failure (Chapter 2).
- [ ] Engine oil level too low. Causes a howl from transmission. Also affects engine power and clutch operation (Pre-ride checks).

Final drive noise
- [ ] Chain not adjusted properly (Chapter 1).
- [ ] Front or rear sprocket loose. Tighten fasteners (Chapter 6).
- [ ] Sprockets and/or chain worn. Fit new sprockets and chain (Chapter 6).
- [ ] Rear sprocket warped. Fit a new sprocket (Chapter 6).
- [ ] Rubber dampers in rear wheel worn (Chapter 6).

Fault Finding REF•41

9 Abnormal frame and suspension noise

Front end noise
☐ Low fluid level or improper viscosity oil in forks. This can sound like spurting and is usually accompanied by irregular fork action (Chapter 5).
☐ Spring weak or broken. Makes a clicking or scraping sound. Fork oil, when drained, will have a lot of metal particles in it (Chapter 5).
☐ Steering head bearings loose or damaged. Clicks when braking. Check and adjust or replace with new ones as necessary (Chapters 1 and 5).
☐ Fork yoke clamp bolts loose – ensure all the bolts are tightened to the specified torque (Chapter 6).
☐ Forks bent. Good possibility if machine has been dropped. Replace the sliders or tubes with new ones as required (Chapter 5).
☐ Front axle or axle pinch bolts loose. Tighten them to the specified torque (Chapter 6).
☐ Loose or worn wheel bearings. Check and replace with new ones as needed (Chapters 1 and 6).

Shock absorber noise
☐ Fluid level incorrect. Indicates a leak caused by defective seal. Shock will be covered with oil. Replace shock with a new one or seek advice on repair from a suspension specialist (Chapter 5).
☐ Defective shock absorber with internal damage. This is in the body of the shock and can't be remedied. The shock must be replaced with a new one or rebuilt (Chapter 5).
☐ Bent or damaged shock body. Replace the shock with a new one (Chapter 5).
☐ Loose or worn suspension linkage components. Check and replace with new ones as necessary (Chapter 5).

Brake noise
☐ Squeal caused by pad shim not installed or positioned correctly (where fitted) (Chapter 6).
☐ Squeal caused by dust on brake pads. Usually found in combination with glazed pads. Clean using brake cleaning solvent (Chapter 6).
☐ Pads glazed. Caused by excessive heat from prolonged hard use or from contamination. DO NOT use sandpaper, emery cloth, carborundum cloth or any other abrasive to roughen the pad surfaces as abrasives will stay in the pad material and damage the disc. A very fine flat file can be used, but new pads is the best remedy (Chapter 6).
☐ Contamination of brake pads. Oil or brake fluid can cause the brake pads to chatter or squeal. Fit new pads. Identify the cause of the contamination, especially check the caliper piston seals for leaking fluid. Clean disc thoroughly with brake system cleaner (Chapter 6).
☐ Disc warped. Can cause a chattering, clicking or intermittent squeal. Usually accompanied by a pulsating lever and uneven braking. Replace the disc with new one (Chapter 6).
☐ Loose or worn wheel bearings. Check and replace with new ones as needed (Chapters 1 and 6).

10 Oil level warning light comes on

Engine lubrication system
☐ Engine oil level low. Inspect for leak or other problem causing low oil level and add recommended oil (see *Pre-ride checks*).
☐ Engine oil pump defective, blocked oil strainer gauze or failed pressure regulator. Carry out an oil pressure check (Chapter 2).
☐ Engine oil viscosity too low. Very old, thin oil or an improper weight of oil used in the engine. Change to correct oil (Chapter 1).
☐ Camshaft or crankshaft journals worn. Excessive wear causing drop in oil pressure. Abnormal wear could be caused by oil starvation at high rpm from low oil level or improper weight or type of oil (Chapter 1).

Electrical system
☐ Oil level switch defective. Check the switch according to the procedure in Chapter 8. Replace it with a new one it if is defective.
☐ Oil level warning LED or symbol defective. Check for pinched, shorted, disconnected or damaged wiring (Chapter 8).

11 Excessive exhaust smoke

White smoke
☐ Piston rings worn or broken, causing oil from the crankcase to be pulled past the piston into the combustion chamber. Replace the rings with new ones (Chapter 2).
☐ Cylinders worn or scored. Caused by overheating or oil starvation. Install a new upper crankcase (Chapter 2).
☐ Valve stem oil seal damaged or worn. Replace the oil seals with new ones (Chapter 2).
☐ Valve guide worn. Perform a complete valve job (Chapter 2).
☐ Engine oil level too high, which causes the oil to be forced past the rings. Drain oil to the proper level (see Chapter 1 and *Pre-ride checks*).
☐ Head gasket broken between oil return and cylinder. Causes oil to be pulled into the combustion chamber. Replace the head gasket with a new one and check the head for warpage (Chapter 2).
☐ Abnormal crankcase pressurisation which forces oil past the rings, usually caused by a clogged breather.

Black smoke
☐ Air filter clogged. Clean the air filter element or replace it with a new one (Chapter 1).
☐ Fuel injection system malfunction (Chapter 4).

Brown smoke
☐ Air filter poorly sealed or not installed (Chapter 1).
☐ Fuel injection system malfunction (Chapter 4).

12 Poor handling or stability

Handlebars hard to turn
☐ Steering head bearing adjuster nut too tight. Check adjustment as described in Chapter 1.
☐ Bearings damaged. Roughness can be felt as the bars are turned from side-to-side. Replace the bearings with new ones (Chapter 5).
☐ Races dented or worn. Denting results from wear in only one position (e.g., straight ahead), from a collision or hitting a pothole or from dropping the machine. Replace the bearings with new ones (Chapter 5).
☐ Steering stem lubrication inadequate. Causes are grease getting hard from age or being washed out by high pressure car washes. Disassemble steering head and repack bearings (Chapter 5).
☐ Steering stem bent. Caused by a collision, hitting a pothole or by dropping the machine. Replace damaged part. Don't try to straighten the steering stem (Chapter 5).
☐ Front tyre air pressure too low (*Pre-ride checks*).

REF•42 Fault Finding

12 Poor handling or stability (continued)

Handlebar shakes or vibrates excessively
- [ ] Tyres worn or out of balance (Chapter 6).
- [ ] Swingarm bearings worn. Replace the bearings with new ones (Chapter 5).
- [ ] Wheel rim(s) warped or damaged. Inspect wheels for runout (Chapter 6).
- [ ] Wheel bearings worn. Worn front or rear wheel bearings can cause poor tracking. Worn front bearings will cause wobble (Chapters 1 and 6).
- [ ] Fork yoke clamp bolts or handlebar clamp bolts loose. Tighten them to the specified torque (Chapter 5).
- [ ] Engine mounting bolts loose. Will cause excessive vibration with increased engine rpm – ensure all the bolts are tightened to the specified torque settings (see Chapter 2).

Machine pulls to one side
- [ ] Frame bent. Definitely suspect this if the machine has been dropped. May or may not be accompanied by cracking near the steering head, swingarm mountings or engine mountings. Replace the frame with a new one (Chapter 5).
- [ ] Wheels out of alignment. Caused by improper location of axle spacers or from bent steering stem or frame (Chapter 5).
- [ ] Forks bent. Disassemble the forks and replace the damaged parts (Chapter 5).
- [ ] Swingarm bent or twisted. Replace the arm with a new one (Chapter 5).
- [ ] Fork oil level uneven. Check and add or drain as necessary (Chapter 5).

Poor shock absorbing qualities
- [ ] Too hard:
    a) Suspension settings incorrect.
    b) Fork oil level excessive (Chapter 5).
    c) Fork oil viscosity too high. Use a lighter oil (see the Specifications in Chapter 5).
    d) Fork tube bent. Causes a harsh, sticking feeling (Chapter 5).
    e) Fork internal damage (Chapter 5).
    f) Shock shaft or body bent or damaged (Chapter 5).
    g) Shock internal damage.
    h) Tyre pressure too high (Pre-ride checks).
- [ ] Too soft:
    a) Suspension settings incorrect.
    b) Fork oil level too low (Chapter 5).
    c) Fork oil viscosity too light (Chapter 5).
    d) Fork springs weak or broken (Chapter 5).
    e) Fork or shock oil leaking (Chapter 5).
    f) Shock internal damage (Chapter 5).

13 Braking problems

Brakes are spongy, don't hold
- [ ] Low brake fluid level (see Pre-ride checks).
- [ ] Air in hydraulic system. Caused by inattention to master cylinder fluid level or by leakage. Locate problem and bleed brakes (Chapter 6).
- [ ] Pad or disc worn (Chapters 1 and 6).
- [ ] Contaminated pads. Caused by contamination with oil, grease, brake fluid, etc. Fit new pads. Identify the cause of the contamination, especially check the caliper piston seals for leaking fluid. Clean disc thoroughly with brake system cleaner (Chapter 6).
- [ ] Brake fluid deteriorated. Fluid is old or contaminated. Drain system, replenish with new fluid and bleed the system (Chapter 6).
- [ ] Master cylinder internal seals worn or damaged causing fluid to bypass (Chapter 6).
- [ ] Master cylinder bore scratched by foreign material or broken spring. Fit a new master cylinder (Chapter 6).
- [ ] Disc warped. Replace disc with new one (Chapter 6).

Brake lever or pedal pulsates
- [ ] Disc warped. Replace disc with new one (Chapter 6).
- [ ] Axle bent. Replace axle with new one (Chapter 6).
- [ ] Brake caliper bolts loose – tighten the bolts to the specified torque (Chapter 6).
- [ ] Wheel warped or otherwise damaged (Chapter 6).
- [ ] Wheel bearings damaged or worn (Chapters 1 and 6).

Brakes drag
- [ ] Master cylinder piston seized. Caused by wear or damage to piston or cylinder bore (Chapter 6).
- [ ] Lever balky or stuck. Check pivot and lubricate (Chapter 6).
- [ ] Brake caliper piston seized in bore. Caused by corrosion or ingestion of dirt past deteriorated seal (Chapter 6).
- [ ] Caliper sticking on slider pins due to corrosion (rear caliper). Clean and lubricate pins and check dust boots (Chapter 6).
- [ ] Brake pad damaged. Pad material separated from backing plate. Usually caused by faulty manufacturing process or from contact with chemicals. Fit new pads (Chapter 6).
- [ ] Pads improperly installed (Chapter 6).
- [ ] Brake caliper incorrectly installed (Chapter 6).

14 Electrical problems

Battery dead or weak
- [ ] Battery faulty. Caused by sulphated plates which are shorted through sedimentation. Confirm by terminal voltage check (Chapter 8).
- [ ] Broken battery terminal making only occasional contact.
- [ ] Battery leads making poor contact (Chapter 8).
- [ ] Load excessive. Caused by addition of high wattage lights or other electrical accessories.
- [ ] Ignition (main) switch defective. Switch either grounds (earths) internally or fails to shut off system. Renew the switch (Chapter 8).
- [ ] Regulator/rectifier defective (Chapter 8).
- [ ] Alternator stator coil open or shorted (Chapter 8).
- [ ] Charging system fault. Check for excessive current leakage (Chapter 8).
- [ ] Wiring faulty. Wiring grounded (earthed) or connections loose in ignition, charging or lighting circuits (Chapter 8).

Battery overcharged
- [ ] Regulator/rectifier defective. Overcharging is noticed when battery gets excessively warm (Chapter 8).
- [ ] Battery faulty. Confirm with battery terminal voltage check (Chapter 8).
- [ ] Battery amperage too low, wrong type or size of battery. Install manufacturer's specified amp-hour battery to handle charging load (Chapter 8).

Fault Finding Equipment REF•43

Checking engine compression

● Low compression will result in exhaust smoke, heavy oil consumption, poor starting and poor performance. A compression test will provide useful information about an engine's condition and if performed regularly, can give warning of trouble before any other symptoms become apparent.
● A compression gauge will be required, along with an adapter to suit the spark plug hole thread size. Note that the screw-in type gauge/adapter set up is preferable to the rubber cone type.
● Before carrying out the test, first check the valve clearances as described in Chapter 1.

1 Run the engine until it reaches normal operating temperature, then stop it and remove the spark plug(s), taking care not to scald your hands on the hot components.
2 Install the gauge adapter and compression gauge in No. 1 cylinder spark plug hole **(see illustration 1)**.

Screw the compression gauge adapter into the spark plug hole, then screw the gauge into the adapter

3 On kickstart-equipped motorcycles, make sure the ignition switch is OFF, then open the throttle fully and kick the engine over a couple of times until the gauge reading stabilises.
4 On motorcycles with electric start only, the procedure will differ depending on the nature of the ignition system. Flick the engine kill switch (engine stop switch) to OFF and turn the ignition switch ON; open the throttle fully and crank the engine over on the starter motor for a couple of revolutions until the gauge reading stabilises. If the starter will not operate with the kill switch OFF, turn the ignition switch OFF and refer to the next paragraph.
5 Install the plugs back in their coils. Lay the plugs on the AIS reed valve cover with their threads earthed against it, or alternatively as there is little slack in the wiring connect the plugs to the crankcase earth using an auxiliary wire with a crocodile clip on each end; this is essential to prevent damage to the ignition

All spark plugs must be earthed (grounded) against the cylinder head

system **(see illustration 2)**. Position the plugs well away from the plug holes otherwise there is a risk of atomised fuel escaping from the plug holes and igniting. As a safety precaution, cover the cylinder head cover with rag. Turn the ignition switch and kill switch ON, open the throttle fully and crank the engine over on the starter motor for a couple of revolutions until the gauge reading stabilises.
6 After one or two revolutions the pressure should build up to a maximum figure and then stabilise. Take a note of this reading and on multi-cylinder engines repeat the test on the remaining cylinders.
7 The correct pressures are given in Chapter 2 Specifications. If the results fall within the specified range and on multi-cylinder engines all are relatively equal, the engine is in good condition. If there is a marked difference between the readings, or if the readings are lower than specified, inspection of the top-end components will be required.
8 Low compression pressure may be due to worn cylinder bores, pistons or rings, failure of the cylinder head gasket, worn valve seals, or poor valve seating.
9 To distinguish between cylinder/piston wear and valve leakage, pour a small quantity of oil into the bore to temporarily seal the piston rings, then repeat the compression tests **(see illustration 3)**. If the readings show

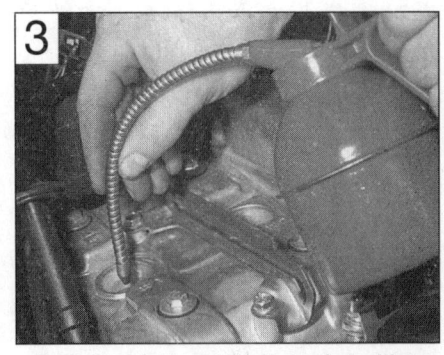

Bores can be temporarily sealed with a squirt of motor oil

a noticeable increase in pressure this confirms that the cylinder bore, piston, or rings are worn. If, however, no change is indicated, the cylinder head gasket or valves should be examined.
10 High compression pressure indicates excessive carbon build-up in the combustion chamber and on the piston crown. If this is the case the cylinder head should be removed and the deposits removed. Note that excessive carbon build-up is less likely with the used on modern fuels.

Checking battery open-circuit voltage

⚠ *Warning: The gases produced by the battery are explosive - never smoke or create any sparks in the vicinity of the battery. Never allow the electrolyte to contact your skin or clothing - if it does, wash it off and seek immediate medical attention.*

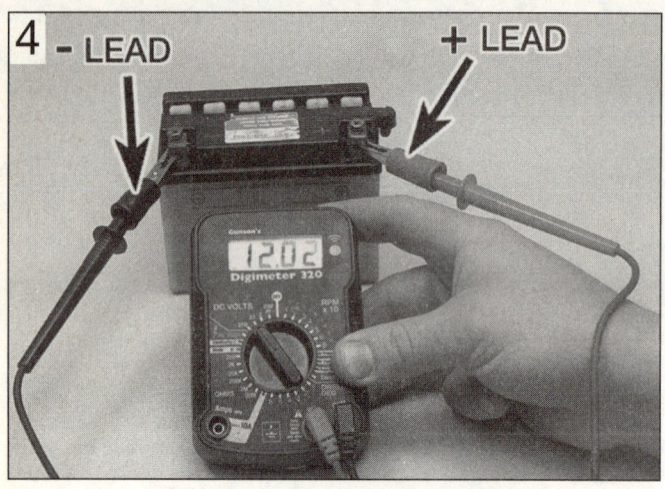

REF•44 Fault Finding Equipment

Measuring open-circuit battery voltage

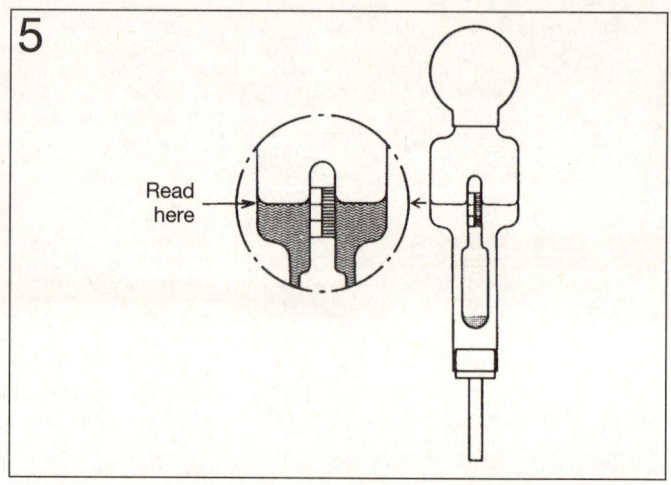

Float-type hydrometer for measuring battery specific gravity

- Before any electrical fault is investigated the battery should be checked.
- You'll need a dc voltmeter or multimeter to check battery voltage. Check that the leads are inserted in the correct terminals on the meter, red lead to positive (+ve), black lead to negative (-ve). Incorrect connections can damage the meter.
- A sound fully-charged 12 volt battery should produce between 12.3 and 12.6 volts across its terminals (12.8 volts for a maintenance-free battery). On machines with a 6 volt battery, voltage should be between 6.1 and 6.3 volts.

1 Set a multimeter to the 0 to 20 volts dc range and connect its probes across the battery terminals. Connect the meter's positive (+ve) probe, usually red, to the battery positive (+ve) terminal, followed by the meter's negative (-ve) probe, usually black, to the battery negative terminal (-ve) **(see illustration 4)**.

2 If battery voltage is low (below 10 volts on a 12 volt battery or below 4 volts on a six volt battery), charge the battery and test the voltage again. If the battery repeatedly goes flat, investigate the motorcycle's charging system.

Checking battery specific gravity (SG)

⚠️ *Warning: The gases produced by the battery are explosive - never smoke or create any sparks in the vicinity of the battery. Never allow the electrolyte to contact your skin or clothing - if it does, wash it off and seek immediate medical attention.*

- The specific gravity check gives an indication of a battery's state of charge.
- A hydrometer is used for measuring specific gravity. Make sure you purchase one which has a small enough hose to insert in the aperture of a motorcycle battery.
- Specific gravity is simply a measure of the electrolyte's density compared with that of water. Water has an SG of 1.000 and fully-charged battery electrolyte is about 26% heavier, at 1.260.
- Specific gravity checks are not possible on maintenance-free batteries. Testing the open-circuit voltage is the only means of determining their state of charge.

1 To measure SG, remove the battery from the motorcycle and remove the first cell cap. Draw some electrolyte into the hydrometer and note the reading **(see illustration 5)**. Return the electrolyte to the cell and install the cap.

2 The reading should be in the region of 1.260 to 1.280. If SG is below 1.200 the battery needs charging. Note that SG will vary with temperature; it should be measured at 20°C (68°F). Add 0.007 to the reading for every 10°C above 20°C, and subtract 0.007 from the reading for every 10°C below 20°C. Add 0.004 to the reading for every 10°F above 68°F, and subtract 0.004 from the reading for every 10°F below 68°F.

3 When the check is complete, rinse the hydrometer thoroughly with clean water.

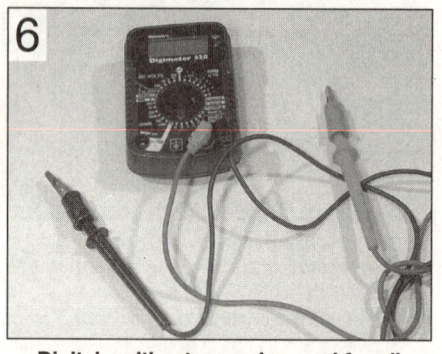

Checking for continuity

- The term continuity describes the uninterrupted flow of electricity through an electrical circuit. A continuity check will determine whether an **open-circuit** situation exists.
- Continuity can be checked with an ohmmeter, multimeter, continuity tester or battery and bulb test circuit **(see illustrations 6, 7 and 8)**.

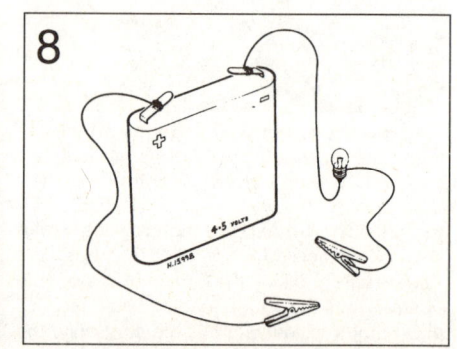

Digital multimeter can be used for all electrical tests

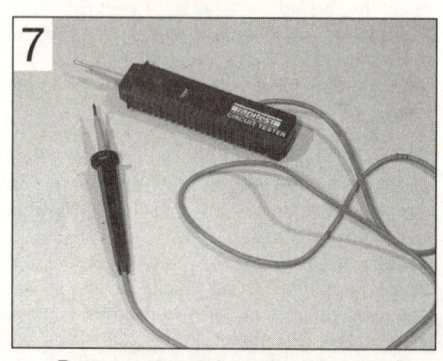

Battery-powered continuity tester

Battery and bulb test circuit

Fault Finding Equipment REF•45

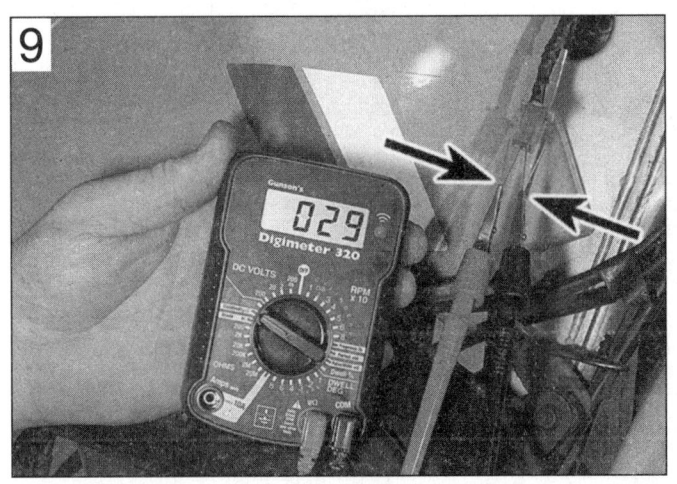

Continuity check of front brake light switch using a meter - note split pins used to access connector terminals

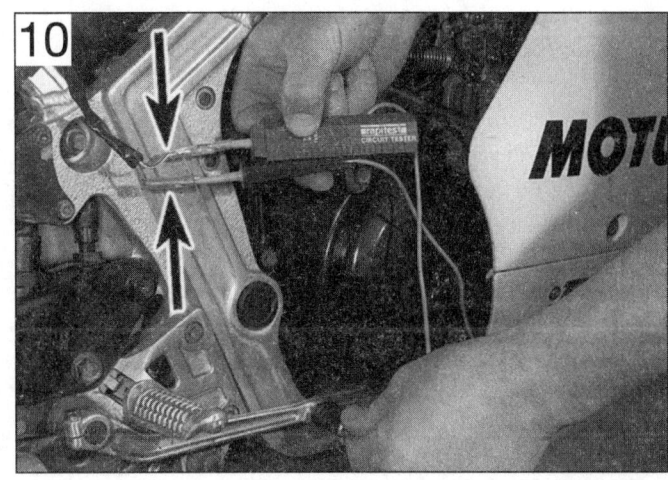

Continuity check of rear brake light switch using a continuity tester

● All of these instruments are self-powered by a battery, therefore the checks are made with the ignition OFF.
● As a safety precaution, always disconnect the battery negative (-ve) lead before making checks, particularly if ignition switch checks are being made.
● If using a meter, select the appropriate ohms scale and check that the meter reads infinity (∞). Touch the meter probes together and check that meter reads zero; where necessary adjust the meter so that it reads zero.
● After using a meter, always switch it OFF to conserve its battery.

Switch checks

1 If a switch is at fault, trace its wiring up to the wiring connectors. Separate the wire connectors and inspect them for security and condition. A build-up of dirt or corrosion here will most likely be the cause of the problem - clean up and apply a water dispersant such as WD40.
2 If using a test meter, set the meter to the ohms x 10 scale and connect its probes across the wires from the switch **(see illustration 9)**. Simple ON/OFF type switches, such as brake light switches, only have two wires whereas combination switches, like the ignition switch, have many internal links. Study the wiring diagram to ensure that you are connecting across the correct pair of wires. Continuity (low or no measurable resistance - 0 ohms) should be indicated with the switch ON and no continuity (high resistance) with it OFF.
3 Note that the polarity of the test probes doesn't matter for continuity checks, although care should be taken to follow specific test procedures if a diode or solid-state component is being checked.
4 A continuity tester or battery and bulb circuit can be used in the same way. Connect its probes as described above **(see illustration 10)**. The light should come on to indicate continuity in the ON switch position, but should extinguish in the OFF position.

Wiring checks

● Many electrical faults are caused by damaged wiring, often due to incorrect routing or chaffing on frame components.
● Loose, wet or corroded wire connectors can also be the cause of electrical problems, especially in exposed locations.

1 A continuity check can be made on a single length of wire by disconnecting it at each end and connecting a meter or continuity tester across both ends of the wire **(see illustration 11)**.
2 Continuity (low or no resistance - 0 ohms) should be indicated if the wire is good. If no continuity (high resistance) is shown, suspect a broken wire.

Checking for voltage

● A voltage check can determine whether current is reaching a component.
● Voltage can be checked with a dc voltmeter, multimeter set on the dc volts scale, test light or buzzer **(see illustrations 12 and 13)**. A meter has the advantage of being able to measure actual voltage.
● When using a meter, check that its leads are inserted in the correct terminals on the meter, red to positive (+ve), black to negative (-ve). Incorrect connections can damage the meter.
● A voltmeter (or multimeter set to the dc volts scale) should always be connected in parallel (across the load). Connecting it in series will not harm the meter, but the reading will not be meaningful.
● Voltage checks are made with the ignition ON.

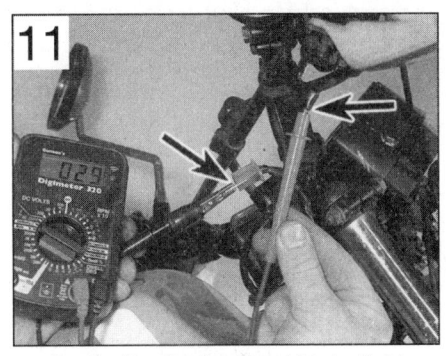

Continuity check of front brake light switch sub-harness

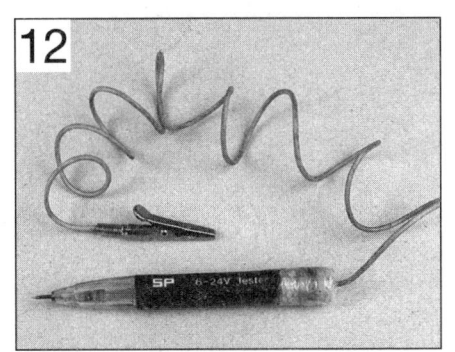

A simple test light can be used for voltage checks

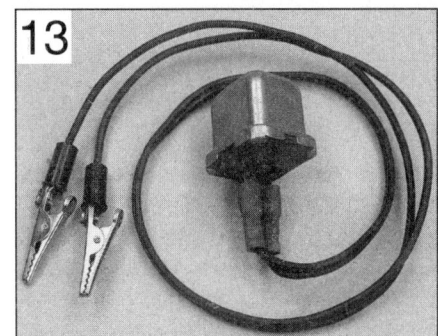

A buzzer is useful for voltage checks

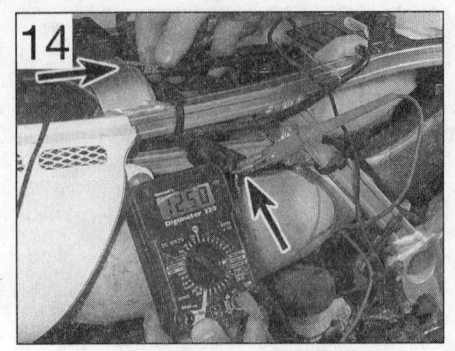

REF•46 Fault Finding Equipment

Checking for voltage at the rear brake light power supply wire using a meter...

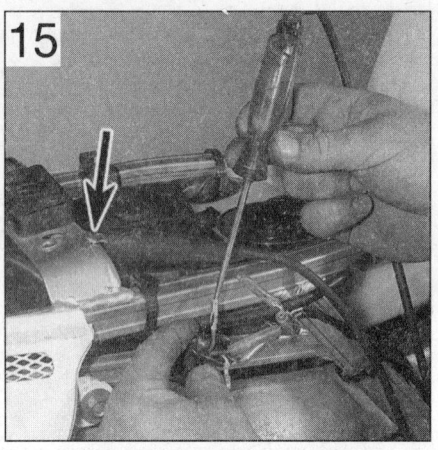

1 First identify the relevant wiring circuit by referring to the wiring diagram at the end of this manual. If other electrical components share the same power supply (ie are fed from the same fuse), take note whether they are working correctly - this is useful information in deciding where to start checking the circuit.

2 If using a meter, check first that the meter leads are plugged into the correct terminals on the meter (see above). Set the meter to the dc volts function, at a range suitable for the battery voltage. Connect the meter red probe (+ve) to the power supply wire and the black probe to a good metal earth (ground) on the motorcycle's frame or directly to the battery negative (-ve) terminal **(see illustration 14)**. Battery voltage should be shown on the meter

... or a test light - note the earth connection to the frame (arrow)

with the ignition switched ON.

3 If using a test light or buzzer, connect its positive (+ve) probe to the power supply terminal and its negative (-ve) probe to a good earth (ground) on the motorcycle's frame or directly to the battery negative (-ve) terminal **(see illustration 15)**. With the ignition ON, the test light should illuminate or the buzzer sound.

4 If no voltage is indicated, work back towards the fuse continuing to check for voltage. When you reach a point where there is voltage, you know the problem lies between that point and your last check point.

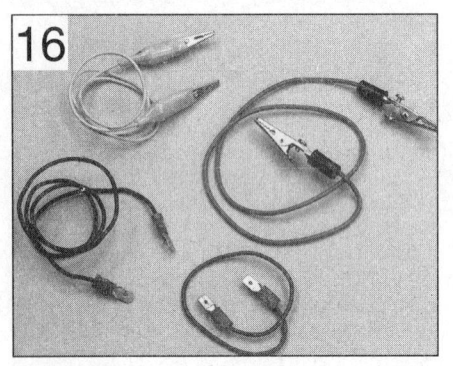

Checking the earth (ground)

● Earth connections are made either directly to the engine or frame (such as sensors, neutral switch etc. which only have a positive feed) or by a separate wire into the earth circuit of the wiring harness. Alternatively a short earth wire is sometimes run directly from the component to the motorcycle's frame.
● Corrosion is often the cause of a poor earth connection.
● If total failure is experienced, check the security of the main earth lead from the negative (-ve) terminal of the battery and also the main earth (ground) point on the wiring harness. If corroded, dismantle the connection and clean all surfaces back to bare metal.

1 To check the earth on a component, use an insulated jumper wire to temporarily bypass its earth connection **(see illustration 16)**. Connect one end of the jumper wire between the earth terminal or metal body of the component and the other end to the motorcycle's frame.

2 If the circuit works with the jumper wire installed, the original earth circuit is faulty. Check the wiring for open-circuits or poor connections. Clean up direct earth connections, removing all traces of corrosion and remake the joint. Apply petroleum jelly to the joint to prevent future corrosion.

Tracing a short-circuit

● A short-circuit occurs where current shorts to earth (ground) bypassing the circuit components. This usually results in a blown fuse.

● A short-circuit is most likely to occur where the insulation has worn through due to wiring chafing on a component, allowing a direct path to earth (ground) on the frame.

1 Remove any bodypanels necessary to access the circuit wiring.
2 Check that all electrical switches in the circuit are OFF, then remove the circuit fuse and connect a test light, buzzer or voltmeter (set to the dc scale) across the fuse terminals. No voltage should be shown.
3 Move the wiring from side to side whilst observing the test light or meter. When the test light comes on, buzzer sounds or meter shows voltage, you have found the cause of the short. It will usually shown up as damaged or burned insulation.
4 Note that the same test can be performed on each component in the circuit, even the switch.

A selection of jumper wires for making earth (ground) checks

Technical Terms Explained REF•47

A

ABS (Anti-lock braking system) A system, usually electronically controlled, that senses incipient wheel lockup during braking and relieves hydraulic pressure at wheel which is about to skid.
Aftermarket Components suitable for the motorcycle, but not produced by the motorcycle manufacturer.
Allen key A hexagonal wrench which fits into a recessed hexagonal hole.
Alternating current (ac) Current produced by an alternator. Requires converting to direct current by a rectifier for charging purposes.
Alternator Converts mechanical energy from the engine into electrical energy to charge the battery and power the electrical system.
Ampere (amp) A unit of measurement for the flow of electrical current. Current = Volts ÷ Ohms.
Ampere-hour (Ah) Measure of battery capacity.
Angle-tightening A torque expressed in degrees. Often follows a conventional tightening torque for cylinder head or main bearing fasteners **(see illustration)**.

Angle-tightening cylinder head bolts

Antifreeze A substance (usually ethylene glycol) mixed with water, and added to the cooling system, to prevent freezing of the coolant in winter. Antifreeze also contains chemicals to inhibit corrosion and the formation of rust and other deposits that would tend to clog the radiator and coolant passages and reduce cooling efficiency.
Anti-dive System attached to the fork lower leg (slider) to prevent fork dive when braking hard.
Anti-seize compound A coating that reduces the risk of seizing on fasteners that are subjected to high temperatures, such as exhaust clamp bolts and nuts.
API American Petroleum Institute. A quality standard for 4-stroke motor oils.
Asbestos A natural fibrous mineral with great heat resistance, commonly used in the composition of brake friction materials. Asbestos is a health hazard and the dust created by brake systems should never be inhaled or ingested.
ATF Automatic Transmission Fluid. Often used in front forks.
ATU Automatic Timing Unit. Mechanical device for advancing the ignition timing on early engines.
ATV All Terrain Vehicle. Often called a Quad.
Axial play Side-to-side movement.
Axle A shaft on which a wheel revolves. Also known as a spindle.

B

Backlash The amount of movement between meshed components when one component is held still. Usually applies to gear teeth.
Ball bearing A bearing consisting of a hardened inner and outer race with hardened steel balls between the two races.
Bearings Used between two working surfaces to prevent wear of the components and a build-up of heat. Four types of bearing are commonly used on motorcycles: plain shell bearings, ball bearings, tapered roller bearings and needle roller bearings.
Bevel gears Used to turn the drive through 90°. Typical applications are shaft final drive and camshaft drive **(see illustration)**.

Bevel gears are used to turn the drive through 90°

BHP Brake Horsepower. The British measurement for engine power output. Power output is now usually expressed in kilowatts (kW).
Bias-belted tyre Similar construction to radial tyre, but with outer belt running at an angle to the wheel rim.
Big-end bearing The bearing in the end of the connecting rod that's attached to the crankshaft.
Bleeding The process of removing air from an hydraulic system via a bleed nipple or bleed screw.
Bottom-end A description of an engine's crankcase components and all components contained there-in.
BTDC Before Top Dead Centre in terms of piston position. Ignition timing is often expressed in terms of degrees or millimetres BTDC.
Bush A cylindrical metal or rubber component used between two moving parts.
Burr Rough edge left on a component after machining or as a result of excessive wear.

C

Cam chain The chain which takes drive from the crankshaft to the camshaft(s).
Canister The main component in an evaporative emission control system (California market only); contains activated charcoal granules to trap vapours from the fuel system rather than allowing them to vent to the atmosphere.
Castellated Resembling the parapets along the top of a castle wall. For example, a castellated wheel axle or spindle nut.
Catalytic converter A device in the exhaust system of some machines which converts certain pollutants in the exhaust gases into less harmful substances.
Charging system Description of the components which charge the battery, ie the alternator, rectifier and regulator.
Circlip A ring-shaped clip used to prevent endwise movement of cylindrical parts and shafts. An internal circlip is installed in a groove in a housing; an external circlip fits into a groove on the outside of a cylindrical piece such as a shaft. Also known as a snap-ring.
Clearance The amount of space between two parts. For example, between a piston and a cylinder, between a bearing and a journal, etc.
Coil spring A spiral of elastic steel found in various sizes throughout a vehicle, for example as a springing medium in the suspension and in the valve train.
Compression Reduction in volume, and increase in pressure and temperature, of a gas, caused by squeezing it into a smaller space.
Compression damping Controls the speed the suspension compresses when hitting a bump.
Compression ratio The relationship between cylinder volume when the piston is at top dead centre and cylinder volume when the piston is at bottom dead centre.
Continuity The uninterrupted path in the flow of electricity. Little or no measurable resistance.
Continuity tester Self-powered bleeper or test light which indicates continuity.
Cp Candlepower. Bulb rating commonly found on US motorcycles.
Crossply tyre Tyre plies arranged in a criss-cross pattern. Usually four or six plies used, hence 4PR or 6PR in tyre size codes.
Cush drive Rubber damper segments fitted between the rear wheel and final drive sprocket to absorb transmission shocks **(see illustration)**.

Cush drive rubbers dampen out transmission shocks

D

Degree disc Calibrated disc for measuring piston position. Expressed in degrees.
Dial gauge Clock-type gauge with adapters for measuring runout and piston position. Expressed in mm or inches.
Diaphragm The rubber membrane in a master cylinder or carburettor which seals the upper chamber.
Diaphragm spring A single sprung plate often used in clutches.
Direct current (dc) Current produced by a dc generator.

Technical Terms Explained

Decarbonisation The process of removing carbon deposits - typically from the combustion chamber, valves and exhaust port/system.
Detonation Destructive and damaging explosion of fuel/air mixture in combustion chamber instead of controlled burning.
Diode An electrical valve which only allows current to flow in one direction. Commonly used in rectifiers and starter interlock systems.
Disc valve (or rotary valve) A induction system used on some two-stroke engines.
Double-overhead camshaft (DOHC) An engine that uses two overhead camshafts, one for the intake valves and one for the exhaust valves.
Drivebelt A toothed belt used to transmit drive to the rear wheel on some motorcycles. A drivebelt has also been used to drive the camshafts. Drivebelts are usually made of Kevlar.
Driveshaft Any shaft used to transmit motion. Commonly used when referring to the final driveshaft on shaft drive motorcycles.

E

Earth return The return path of an electrical circuit, utilising the motorcycle's frame.
ECU (Electronic Control Unit) A computer which controls (for instance) an ignition system, or an anti-lock braking system.
EGO Exhaust Gas Oxygen sensor. Sometimes called a Lambda sensor.
Electrolyte The fluid in a lead-acid battery.
EMS (Engine Management System) A computer controlled system which manages the fuel injection and the ignition systems in an integrated fashion.
Endfloat The amount of lengthways movement between two parts. As applied to a crankshaft, the distance that the crankshaft can move side-to-side in the crankcase.
Endless chain A chain having no joining link. Common use for cam chains and final drive chains.
EP (Extreme Pressure) Oil type used in locations where high loads are applied, such as between gear teeth.
Evaporative emission control system Describes a charcoal filled canister which stores fuel vapours from the tank rather than allowing them to vent to the atmosphere. Usually only fitted to California models and referred to as an EVAP system.
Expansion chamber Section of two-stroke engine exhaust system so designed to improve engine efficiency and boost power.

F

Feeler blade or gauge A thin strip or blade of hardened steel, ground to an exact thickness, used to check or measure clearances between parts.
Final drive Description of the drive from the transmission to the rear wheel. Usually by chain or shaft, but sometimes by belt.
Firing order The order in which the engine cylinders fire, or deliver their power strokes, beginning with the number one cylinder.
Flooding Term used to describe a high fuel level in the carburettor float chambers, leading to fuel overflow. Also refers to excess fuel in the combustion chamber due to incorrect starting technique.

Free length The no-load state of a component when measured. Clutch, valve and fork spring lengths are measured at rest, without any preload.
Freeplay The amount of travel before any action takes place. The looseness in a linkage, or an assembly of parts, between the initial application of force and actual movement. For example, the distance the rear brake pedal moves before the rear brake is actuated.
Fuel injection The fuel/air mixture is metered electronically and directed into the engine intake ports (indirect injection) or into the cylinders (direct injection). Sensors supply information on engine speed and conditions.
Fuel/air mixture The charge of fuel and air going into the engine. See **Stoichiometric ratio**.
Fuse An electrical device which protects a circuit against accidental overload. The typical fuse contains a soft piece of metal which is calibrated to melt at a predetermined current flow (expressed as amps) and break the circuit.

G

Gap The distance the spark must travel in jumping from the centre electrode to the side electrode in a spark plug. Also refers to the distance between the ignition rotor and the pickup coil in an electronic ignition system.
Gasket Any thin, soft material - usually cork, cardboard, asbestos or soft metal - installed between two metal surfaces to ensure a good seal. For instance, the cylinder head gasket seals the joint between the block and the cylinder head.
Gauge An instrument panel display used to monitor engine conditions. A gauge with a movable pointer on a dial or a fixed scale is an analogue gauge. A gauge with a numerical readout is called a digital gauge.
Gear ratios The drive ratio of a pair of gears in a gearbox, calculated on their number of teeth.
Glaze-busting see **Honing**
Grinding Process for renovating the valve face and valve seat contact area in the cylinder head.
Gudgeon pin The shaft which connects the connecting rod small-end with the piston. Often called a piston pin or wrist pin.

H

Helical gears Gear teeth are slightly curved and produce less gear noise that straight-cut gears. Often used for primary drives.

Installing a Helicoil thread insert in a cylinder head

Helicoil A thread insert repair system. Commonly used as a repair for stripped spark plug threads **(see illustration)**.
Honing A process used to break down the glaze on a cylinder bore (also called glaze-busting). Can also be carried out to roughen a rebored cylinder to aid ring bedding-in.
HT (High Tension) Description of the electrical circuit from the secondary winding of the ignition coil to the spark plug.
Hydraulic A liquid filled system used to transmit pressure from one component to another. Common uses on motorcycles are brakes and clutches.
Hydrometer An instrument for measuring the specific gravity of a lead-acid battery.
Hygroscopic Water absorbing. In motorcycle applications, braking efficiency will be reduced if DOT 3 or 4 hydraulic fluid absorbs water from the air - care must be taken to keep new brake fluid in tightly sealed containers.

I

lbf ft Pounds-force feet. An imperial unit of torque. Sometimes written as ft-lbs.
lbf in Pound-force inch. An imperial unit of torque, applied to components where a very low torque is required. Sometimes written as in-lbs.
IC Abbreviation for Integrated Circuit.
Ignition advance Means of increasing the timing of the spark at higher engine speeds. Done by mechanical means (ATU) on early engines or electronically by the ignition control unit on later engines.
Ignition timing The moment at which the spark plug fires, expressed in the number of crankshaft degrees before the piston reaches the top of its stroke, or in the number of millimetres before the piston reaches the top of its stroke.
Infinity (∞) Description of an open-circuit electrical state, where no continuity exists.
Inverted forks (upside down forks) The sliders or lower legs are held in the yokes and the fork tubes or stanchions are connected to the wheel axle (spindle). Less unsprung weight and stiffer construction than conventional forks.

J

JASO Quality standard for 2-stroke oils.
Joule The unit of electrical energy.
Journal The bearing surface of a shaft.

K

Kickstart Mechanical means of turning the engine over for starting purposes. Only usually fitted to mopeds, small capacity motorcycles and off-road motorcycles.
Kill switch Handebar-mounted switch for emergency ignition cut-out. Cuts the ignition circuit on all models, and additionally prevent starter motor operation on others.
km Symbol for kilometre.
kmh Abbreviation for kilometres per hour.

L

Lambda (λ) sensor A sensor fitted in the exhaust system to measure the exhaust gas oxygen content (excess air factor).

Technical Terms Explained   REF•49

Lapping see **Grinding**.
LCD Abbreviation for Liquid Crystal Display.
LED Abbreviation for Light Emitting Diode.
Liner A steel cylinder liner inserted in a aluminium alloy cylinder block.
Locknut A nut used to lock an adjustment nut, or other threaded component, in place.
Lockstops The lugs on the lower triple clamp (yoke) which abut those on the frame, preventing handlebar-to-fuel tank contact.
Lockwasher A form of washer designed to prevent an attaching nut from working loose.
LT Low Tension Description of the electrical circuit from the power supply to the primary winding of the ignition coil.

M

Main bearings The bearings between the crankshaft and crankcase.
Maintenance-free (MF) battery A sealed battery which cannot be topped up.
Manometer Mercury-filled calibrated tubes used to measure intake tract vacuum. Used to synchronise carburettors on multi-cylinder engines.
Micrometer A precision measuring instrument that measures component outside diameters **(see illustration)**.

Tappet shims are measured with a micrometer

MON (Motor Octane Number) A measure of a fuel's resistance to knock.
Monograde oil An oil with a single viscosity, eg SAE80W.
Monoshock A single suspension unit linking the swingarm or suspension linkage to the frame.
mph Abbreviation for miles per hour.
Multigrade oil Having a wide viscosity range (eg 10W40). The W stands for Winter, thus the viscosity ranges from SAE10 when cold to SAE40 when hot.
Multimeter An electrical test instrument with the capability to measure voltage, current and resistance. Some meters also incorporate a continuity tester and buzzer.

N

Needle roller bearing Inner race of caged needle rollers and hardened outer race. Examples of uncaged needle rollers can be found on some engines. Commonly used in rear suspension applications and in two-stroke engines.
Nm Newton metres.
NOx Oxides of Nitrogen. A common toxic pollutant emitted by petrol engines at higher temperatures.

O

Octane The measure of a fuel's resistance to knock.
OE (Original Equipment) Relates to components fitted to a motorcycle as standard or replacement parts supplied by the motorcycle manufacturer.
Ohm The unit of electrical resistance. Ohms = Volts ÷ Current.
Ohmmeter An instrument for measuring electrical resistance.
Oil cooler System for diverting engine oil outside of the engine to a radiator for cooling purposes.
Oil injection A system of two-stroke engine lubrication where oil is pump-fed to the engine in accordance with throttle position.
Open-circuit An electrical condition where there is a break in the flow of electricity - no continuity (high resistance).
O-ring A type of sealing ring made of a special rubber-like material; in use, the O-ring is compressed into a groove to provide the sealing action.
Oversize (OS) Term used for piston and ring size options fitted to a rebored cylinder.
Overhead cam (sohc) engine An engine with single camshaft located on top of the cylinder head.
Overhead valve (ohv) engine An engine with the valves located in the cylinder head, but with the camshaft located in the engine block or crankcase.
Oxygen sensor A device installed in the exhaust system which senses the oxygen content in the exhaust and converts this information into an electric current. Also called a Lambda sensor.

P

Plastigauge A thin strip of plastic thread, available in different sizes, used for measuring clearances. For example, a strip of Plastigauge is laid across a bearing journal. The parts are assembled and dismantled; the width of the crushed strip indicates the clearance between journal and bearing.
Polarity Either negative or positive earth (ground), determined by which battery lead is connected to the frame (earth return). Modern motorcycles are usually negative earth.
Pre-ignition A situation where the fuel/air mixture ignites before the spark plug fires. Often due to a hot spot in the combustion chamber caused by carbon build-up. Engine has a tendency to 'run-on'.
Pre-load (suspension) The amount a spring is compressed when in the unloaded state. Preload can be applied by gas, spacer or mechanical adjuster.
Premix The method of engine lubrication on older two-stroke engines. Engine oil is mixed with the petrol in the fuel tank in a specific ratio. The fuel/oil mix is sometimes referred to as "petroil".
Primary drive Description of the drive from the crankshaft to the clutch. Usually by gear or chain.
PS Pfedestärke - a German interpretation of BHP.
PSI Pounds-force per square inch. Imperial measurement of tyre pressure and cylinder pressure measurement.
PTFE Polytetrafluroethylene. A low friction substance.
Pulse secondary air injection system A process of promoting the burning of excess fuel present in the exhaust gases by routing fresh air into the exhaust ports.

Q

Quartz halogen bulb Tungsten filament surrounded by a halogen gas. Typically used for the headlight **(see illustration)**.

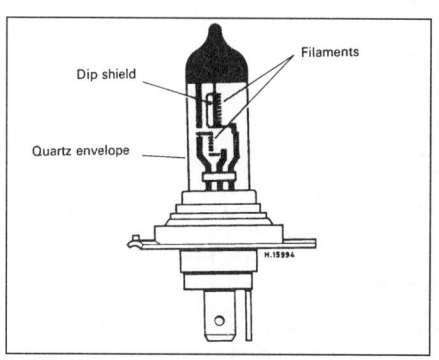

Quartz halogen headlight bulb construction

R

Rack-and-pinion A pinion gear on the end of a shaft that mates with a rack (think of a geared wheel opened up and laid flat). Sometimes used in clutch operating systems.
Radial play Up and down movement about a shaft.
Radial ply tyres Tyre plies run across the tyre (from bead to bead) and around the circumference of the tyre. Less resistant to tread distortion than other tyre types.
Radiator A liquid-to-air heat transfer device designed to reduce the temperature of the coolant in a liquid cooled engine.
Rake A feature of steering geometry - the angle of the steering head in relation to the vertical **(see illustration)**.

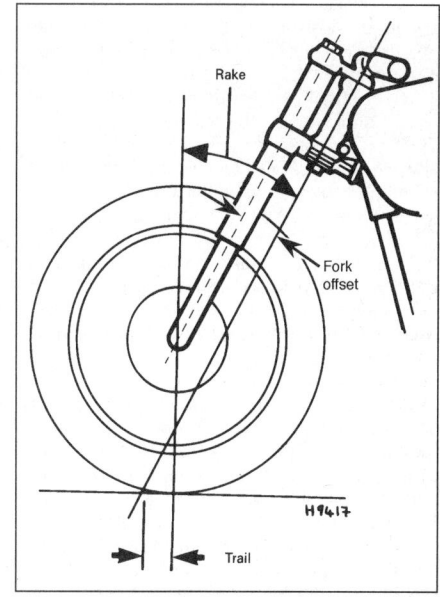

Steering geometry

Technical Terms Explained

Rebore Providing a new working surface to the cylinder bore by boring out the old surface. Necessitates the use of oversize piston and rings.
Rebound damping A means of controlling the oscillation of a suspension unit spring after it has been compressed. Resists the spring's natural tendency to bounce back after being compressed.
Rectifier Device for converting the ac output of an alternator into dc for battery charging.
Reed valve An induction system commonly used on two-stroke engines.
Regulator Device for maintaining the charging voltage from the generator or alternator within a specified range.
Relay A electrical device used to switch heavy current on and off by using a low current auxiliary circuit.
Resistance Measured in ohms. An electrical component's ability to pass electrical current.
RON (Research Octane Number) A measure of a fuel's resistance to knock.
rpm revolutions per minute.
Runout The amount of wobble (in-and-out movement) of a wheel or shaft as it's rotated. The amount a shaft rotates 'out-of-true'. The out-of-round condition of a rotating part.

S

SAE (Society of Automotive Engineers) A standard for the viscosity of a fluid.
Sealant A liquid or paste used to prevent leakage at a joint. Sometimes used in conjunction with a gasket.
Service limit Term for the point where a component is no longer useable and must be renewed.
Shaft drive A method of transmitting drive from the transmission to the rear wheel.
Shell bearings Plain bearings consisting of two shell halves. Most often used as big-end and main bearings in a four-stroke engine. Often called bearing inserts.
Shim Thin spacer, commonly used to adjust the clearance or relative positions between two parts. For example, shims inserted into or under tappets or followers to control valve clearances. Clearance is adjusted by changing the thickness of the shim.
Short-circuit An electrical condition where current shorts to earth (ground) bypassing the circuit components.
Skimming Process to correct warpage or repair a damaged surface, eg on brake discs or drums.
Slide-hammer A special puller that screws into or hooks onto a component such as a shaft or bearing; a heavy sliding handle on the shaft bottoms against the end of the shaft to knock the component free.
Small-end bearing The bearing in the upper end of the connecting rod at its joint with the gudgeon pin.
Spalling Damage to camshaft lobes or bearing journals shown as pitting of the working surface.
Specific gravity (SG) The state of charge of the electrolyte in a lead-acid battery. A measure of the electrolyte's density compared with water.
Straight-cut gears Common type gear used on gearbox shafts and for oil pump and water pump drives.
Stanchion The inner sliding part of the front forks, held by the yokes. Often called a fork tube.

Stoichiometric ratio The optimum chemical air/fuel ratio for a petrol engine, said to be 14.7 parts of air to 1 part of fuel.
Sulphuric acid The liquid (electrolyte) used in a lead-acid battery. Poisonous and extremely corrosive.
Surface grinding (lapping) Process to correct a warped gasket face, commonly used on cylinder heads.

T

Tapered-roller bearing Tapered inner race of caged needle rollers and separate tapered outer race. Examples of taper roller bearings can be found on steering heads.
Tappet A cylindrical component which transmits motion from the cam to the valve stem, either directly or via a pushrod and rocker arm. Also called a cam follower.
TCS Traction Control System. An electronically-controlled system which senses wheel spin and reduces engine speed accordingly.
TDC Top Dead Centre denotes that the piston is at its highest point in the cylinder.
Thread-locking compound Solution applied to fastener threads to prevent slackening. Select type to suit application.
Thrust washer A washer positioned between two moving components on a shaft. For example, between gear pinions on gearshaft.
Timing chain See **Cam Chain**.
Timing light Stroboscopic lamp for carrying out ignition timing checks with the engine running.
Top-end A description of an engine's cylinder block, head and valve gear components.
Torque Turning or twisting force about a shaft.
Torque setting A prescribed tightness specified by the motorcycle manufacturer to ensure that the bolt or nut is secured correctly. Undertightening can result in the bolt or nut coming loose or a surface not being sealed. Overtightening can result in stripped threads, distortion or damage to the component being retained.
Torx key A six-point wrench.
Tracer A stripe of a second colour applied to a wire insulator to distinguish that wire from another one with the same colour insulator. For example, Br/W is often used to denote a brown insulator with a white tracer.
Trail A feature of steering geometry. Distance from the steering head axis to the tyre's central contact point.
Triple clamps The cast components which extend from the steering head and support the fork stanchions or tubes. Often called fork yokes.
Turbocharger A centrifugal device, driven by exhaust gases, that pressurises the intake air. Normally used to increase the power output from a given engine displacement.
TWI Abbreviation for Tyre Wear Indicator. Indicates the location of the tread depth indicator bars on tyres.

U

Universal joint or U-joint (UJ) A double-pivoted connection for transmitting power from a driving to a driven shaft through an angle. Typically found in shaft drive assemblies.
Unsprung weight Anything not supported by the bike's suspension (ie the wheel, tyres, brakes, final drive and bottom (moving) part of the suspension).

V

Vacuum gauges Clock-type gauges for measuring intake tract vacuum. Used for carburettor synchronisation on multi-cylinder engines.
Valve A device through which the flow of liquid, gas or vacuum may be stopped, started or regulated by a moveable part that opens, shuts or partially obstructs one or more ports or passageways. The intake and exhaust valves in the cylinder head are of the poppet type.
Valve clearance The clearance between the valve tip (the end of the valve stem) and the rocker arm or tappet/follower. The valve clearance is measured when the valve is closed. The correct clearance is important - if too small the valve won't close fully and will burn out, whereas if too large noisy operation will result.
Valve lift The amount a valve is lifted off its seat by the camshaft lobe.
Valve timing The exact setting for the opening and closing of the valves in relation to piston position.
Vernier caliper A precision measuring instrument that measures inside and outside dimensions. Not quite as accurate as a micrometer, but more convenient.
VIN Vehicle Identification Number. Term for the bike's engine and frame numbers.
Viscosity The thickness of a liquid or its resistance to flow.
Volt A unit for expressing electrical "pressure" in a circuit. Volts = current x ohms.

W

Water pump A mechanically-driven device for moving coolant around the engine.
Watt A unit for expressing electrical power. Watts = volts x current.
Wear limit see **Service limit**
Wet liner A liquid-cooled engine design where the pistons run in liners which are directly surrounded by coolant **(see illustration)**.

Wet liner arrangement

Wheelbase Distance from the centre of the front wheel to the centre of the rear wheel.
Wiring harness or loom Describes the electrical wires running the length of the motorcycle and enclosed in tape or plastic sheathing. Wiring coming off the main harness is usually referred to as a sub harness.
Woodruff key A key of semi-circular or square section used to locate a gear to a shaft. Often used to locate the alternator rotor on the crankshaft.
Wrist pin Another name for gudgeon or piston pin.

Index REF•51

Note: *References throughout this index are in the form - "Chapter number" • "Page number"*

A

Air filter – 1•9
Air filter housing – 4•5
Air induction system (AIS) – 1•12, 4•21
Alternator rotor and stator – 8•19
Atmospheric pressure sensor – 4•12

B

Battery
  charging – 8•4
  check – 1•23
  removal and installation – 8•3
Bearings
  main and big-end – 2•39
  steering head – 1•20, 5•18
  swingarm – 1•20, 5•25
  wheel – 1•19, 6•20
Bodywork – 7•1 *et seq*
Brake
  bleeding – 6•16
  calipers – 6•4, 6•11
  discs – 6•6, 6•13
  fault finding – REF•42
  fluid change – 1•19, 6•16
  fluid level check – 0•14
  hoses and unions – 1•19, 6•15
  light switches – 8•9
  master cylinders – 6•6, 6•13
  pads – 1•18, 6•2, 6•9
  pedal – 5•2
  seals – 1•19
  specifications – 6•1
  system check – 1•17
  torque settings – 6•2
Brake/tail light LEDs and licence plate bulb – 8•8
Bulbs – 8•2

C

Cable lubrication – 1•13
Cables
  clutch – 1•13, 2•23
  throttle – 1•12, 4•19
Calipers – 6•4, 6•11
Cam chain tensioner – 2•11
Cam chain, tensioner blade and guides – 2•18
Camshafts and followers – 2•13
Camshaft position (CMP) sensor – 4•10
Catalytic converter – 4•22
Charging system testing – 8•19
Chain (cam) – 2•11
Chain (drive) – 1•6, 6•23, REF•18
Clutch – 1•13, 2•24
Clutch switch – 8•14
Component access – 2•5
Connecting rods and bearings – 2•40

Conversion factors – REF•26
Cooling system
  check – 1•14
  coolant level check – 0•14
  fan(s) – 3•4
  general information – 3•2
  hoses – 3•8
  radiator – 3•2
  reservoir – 3•3
  specifications – 3•1
  temperature display, warning light and sensor – 3•5
  thermostat – 3•6
  torque settings – 3•1
  water pump – 3•6
Crankcase separation and reassembly – 2•38
Crankcases – 2•38, 2•55
Crankshaft and main bearings – 2•46
Crankshaft position (CKP) sensor – 4•10
Cylinder bores – 2•55
Cylinder head – 2•19

D

Dimensions (model) – 0•11
Discs – 6•6, 6•13
Drive chain – 1•6, 6•23, REF•18

E

ECU (Engine Control Unit) – 4•24
Electrical system – 8•1 *et seq*
  alternator – 8•19
  battery – 1•23, 8•3
  brake light switches – 8•9
  brake, tail and licence plate bulbs – 8•8
  clutch switch – 8•14
  fault finding – 8•3, REF•42
  fuses – 8•2, 8•4
  general information – 8•3
  handlebar switch – 8•12, 8•13
  headlight aim – 8•7
  headlight and sidelight bulbs – 8•6
  headlight unit – 8•7
  horn – 8•14
  ignition (main) switch – 8•12
  instruments – 8•10, 8•11
  lighting system – 8•5
  neutral switch – 8•13
  regulator/rectifier – 8•21
  relay assembly – 8•14
  sidestand switch – 8•13
  specifications – 8•1
  starter motor – 8•15 to 8•17
  tail light assembly and licence plate light – 8•8
  torque settings – 8•2
  turn signal – 8•8, 8•9
  wiring diagrams – 8•22 to 8•30

Engine – 2•1 *et seq*
  camchain tensioner – 2•11
  camchain, tensioner blades and guides – 2•18
  camshafts and followers – 2•13
  connecting rods and main bearings – 2•40
  crankcases – 2•38, 2•55
  crankshaft and main bearings – 2•46
  cylinder bores – 2•55
  cylinder head – 2•19
  general information – 2•5
  oil and filter change – 1•16
  oil cooler – 2•33
  oil level check – 0•13
  oil pump – 2•36
  oil sump, strainer and pressure relief valve – 2•34
  overhaul – 2•10
  pistons – 2•43
  piston rings – 2•45
  removal and installation – 2•6
  running-in procedure – 2•56
  specifications – 1•2, 2•1
  starter clutch and gears – 2•29
  torque settings – 2•4
  valves – 1•23, 2•10
  wear assessment – 2•5
Engine management system – 4•1 *et seq*
Engine number – 0•9
EVAP system (California models) – 1•12
Exhaust system – 4•19

F

Fairing and bodywork – 7•2
Fan(s) and fan relay – 3•4
Fast idle system – 4•17
Fault finding – REF•35 to REF•46
Filter
  air – 1•9
  engine oil – 1•16
  fuel – 4•4
Footrests – 5•2
Forks
  adjustment – 5•21
  oil change – 1•20, 5•7
  overhaul – 5•11
  removal and installation – 5•7
  specifications – 5•1
Frame inspection and repair – 5•2
Frame number – 0•9
Front brake caliper – 6•4
Front wheel – 6•18, 6•20
Fuel injection system
  components – 4•10
  fast idle system – 4•17
  fault diagnosis – 4•7
  general information – 4•6
  pressure regulator – 4•18
  rail and injectors – 4•16
  throttle bodies – 1•10, 4•13

Index

Fuel level warning light and sensor – 4•5
Fuel pressure regulator – 4•18
Fuel pump – 4•4
Fuel pump relay – 4•13, 8•14
Fuel rail and injectors – 4•16
Fuel system check – 1•11
Fuel tank – 4•3
Fuses – 8•2, 8•4

G

Gearbox shafts – 2•48, 2•49
Gearchange lever – 5•2
Gearchange mechanism – 2•31

H

Handlebars and levers – 5•5
Handlebar switch – 8•12
Headlight and headlight aim – 8•7
Headlight bulbs – 8•6
Headlight relay – 8•5
Horn – 8•14
Hoses
  brake hoses and unions – 1•19, 6•15
  coolant – 3•8
  fuel – 1•11
HT coils – 4•23

I

Idle speed – 1•10
Ignition
  ECU – 4•24
  coils – 4•23
  crankshaft position sensor – 4•10
  (main) switch – 8•12
  system check – 4•22
  timing – 4•24
Immobiliser system – 4•25
Instruments – 8•10, 8•11
Intake air pressure sensor – 4•11
Intake air temperature sensor – 4•12

L

Levers (handlebar) – 5•5
Licence plate bulb – 8•8
Lighting system – 8•5
Lubricants and
  fluids – 1•2, REF•23 to REF•25

M

Main and big-end bearings – 2•39
Maintenance schedule – 1•3
Master cylinders – 6•6, 6•13
Mirrors – 7•5
MOT Test Checks – REF•27 to REF•30
Mudguards – 7•6

N

Neutral switch – 8•13
Nuts and bolts – 1•22

O

Oil cooler – 2•33
Oil and filter change – 1•16
Oil level check (engine) – 0•13
Oil level sensor – 8•15
Oil sump, strainer and pressure relief valve – 2•34

P

Pistons – 2•43
Piston rings – 2•45
Pressure checks
  cylinder – 2•5, REF•43
  oil – 2•6
  tyre – 0•16
Pressure relief valve (oil) – 2•34
Pump
  fuel – 4•4
  oil – 2•36
  water – 3•6

R

Radiator – 3•2
Rear brake caliper – 6•11
Rear shock absorber – 5•18
Rear sprocket coupling/rubber dampers – 6•22, 6•24
Rear suspension linkage – 5•20
Rear wheel – 6•19, 6•20
Regulator/rectifier – 8•21
Relay assembly – 8•14
Running-in procedure – 2•56

S

Safety first – 0•12
Seats – 7•2
Security – REF•20 to REF•22
Selector drum and forks – 2•53
Sensors
  atmospheric pressure sensor – 4•12
  camshaft position (CMP) sensor – 4•10
  crankshaft position (CKP) sensor – 4•10
  coolant temperature sensor – 3•5
  fuel level warning light and sensor – 4•5
  intake air pressure sensor – 4•11
  intake air temperature sensor – 4•12
  oil level sensor – 8•15
  speed sensor – 4•13
  tip-over sensor – 4•12
  throttle position sensor – 4•11
Sidelight bulbs – 8•6
Sidestand
  general information – 1•22, 5•4
  lubrication – 1•13
  switch – 8•13
Spark plugs – 1•2, 1•8
Specifications – 0•11, 1•2, 2•1, 3•1, 4•1, 5•1, 6•1, 8•1
Sprockets – 1•5, 6•23
Stand – 1•13

Starter circuit cut-off relay – 8•14
Starter clutch and gears – 2•29
Starter motor – 8•15 to 8•17
Starter relay – 8•15
Starter safety circuit – 1•22
Steering head bearings – 1•20, 5•18
Steering stem – 5•16
Storage – REF•32 to REF•34
Suspension
  adjustment – 1•21, 5•21
  checks – 1•19
  front forks – 1•19, 5•7, 5•11
  rear shock absorber – 5•18
Swingarm
  bearings – 1•20, 5•25
  removal and installation – 5•22
Switches
  brake light – 8•9
  clutch – 8•14
  handlebar – 8•12, 8•13
  ignition (main) – 8•12
  neutral – 8•13
  sidestand – 8•13

T

Tail light unit – 8•8
Technical terms
  explained – REF•47 to REF•50
Thermostat – 3•6
Throttle bodies – 4•13
Throttle body synchronisation – 1•10
Throttle cables – 1•12, 4•19
Throttle position sensor – 4•11
Tip-over sensor – 4•12
Tools and workshop tips – REF•2 to REF•19
Torque settings – 1•2, 2•4, 3•1, 4•2, 5•2, 6•2, 8•2
Transmission shafts – 2•48, 2•49
Tyres – 0•16, 6•23
Turn signals – 8•8, 8•9

V

Valves clearances – 1•2, 1•23
Valve cover – 2•10
Valve overhaul – 2•19

W

Water pump – 3•6
Weights – 0•11
Wheels
  alignment check – 6•17
  bearings – 6•20
  check – 1•19
  front wheel – 6•18
  inspection and repair – 6•17
  rear wheel – 6•19
  specifications – 6•1
Windshield – 7•5
Wiring diagrams – 8•22 to 8•30

Haynes Motorcycle Manuals – The Complete List

Title	Book No
APRILIA RS50 (99 - 06) & RS125 (93 - 06)	4298
Aprilia RSV1000 Mille (98 - 03)	♦ 4255
BMW 2-valve Twins (70 - 96)	♦ 0249
BMW K100 & 75 2-valve Models (83 - 96)	♦ 1373
BMW R850, 1100 & 1150 4-valve Twins (93 - 04)	♦ 3466
BMW R1200 (04 - 06)	♦ 4598
BSA Bantam (48 - 71)	0117
BSA Unit Singles (58 - 72)	0127
BSA Pre-unit Singles (54 - 61)	0326
BSA A7 & A10 Twins (47 - 62)	0121
BSA A50 & A65 Twins (62 - 73)	0155
DUCATI 600, 620, 750 and 900 2-valve V-Twins (91 - 05)	♦ 3290
Ducati MK III & Desmo Singles (69 - 76)	◊ 0445
Ducati 748, 916 & 996 4-valve V-Twins (94 - 01)	♦ 3756
GILERA RUNNER, DNA, Ice & SKP/Stalker (97 - 04)	4163
HARLEY-DAVIDSON Sportsters (70 - 03)	♦ 2534
Harley-Davidson Shovelhead and Evolution Big Twins (70 - 99)	2536
Harley-Davidson Twin Cam 88 (99 - 03)	♦ 2478
HONDA NB, ND, NP & NS50 Melody (81 - 85)	◊ 0622
Honda NE/NB50 Vision & SA50 Vision Met-in (85 - 95)	◊ 1278
Honda MB, MBX, MT & MTX50 (80 - 93)	0731
Honda C50, C70 & C90 (67 - 03)	0324
Honda XR80/100R & CRF80/100F (85 - 04)	2218
Honda XL/XR 80, 100, 125, 185 & 200 2-valve Models (78 - 87)	0566
Honda H100 & H100S Singles (80 - 92)	◊ 0734
Honda CB/CD125T & CM125C Twins (77 - 88)	◊ 0571
Honda CBR125R (04 - 06)	4620
Honda CG125 (76 - 05)	◊ 0433
Honda NS125 (86 - 93)	◊ 3056
Honda MBX/MTX125 & MTX200 (83 - 93)	◊ 1132
Honda CD/CM185 200T & CM250C 2-valve Twins (77 - 85)	◊ 0572
Honda XL/XR 250 & 500 (78 - 84)	0567
Honda XR250L, XR250R & XR400R (86 - 03)	2219
Honda CB250 & CB400N Super Dreams (78 - 84)	0540
Honda CR Motocross Bikes (86 - 01)	2222
Honda CRF250 & CRF450 (02 - 06)	2630
Honda CBR400RR Fours (88 - 99)	◊ ♦ 3552
Honda VFR400 (NC30) & RVF400 (NC35) V-Fours (89 - 98)	◊ ♦ 3496
Honda CB500 (93 - 01)	◊ ♦ 3753
Honda CB400 & CB550 Fours (73 - 77)	0262
Honda CX/GL500 & 650 V-Twins (78 - 86)	0442
Honda CBX550 Four (82 - 86)	◊ 0940
Honda XL600R & XR600R (83 - 00)	2183
Honda XL600/650V Transalp & XRV750 Africa Twin (87 - 02)	♦ 3919
Honda CBR600F1 & 1000F Fours (87 - 96)	♦ 1730
Honda CBR600F2 & F3 Fours (91 - 98)	♦ 2070
Honda CBR600F4 (99 - 02)	♦ 3911
Honda CB600F Hornet (98 - 02)	◊ ♦ 3915
Honda CBR600RR (03 - 06)	♦ 4590
Honda CB650 sohc Fours (78 - 84)	0665
Honda NTV600 Revere, NTV650 and NT650V Deauville (88 - 05)	◊ ♦ 3243
Honda Shadow VT600 & 750 (USA) (88 - 03)	2312
Honda CB750 sohc Four (69 - 79)	0131
Honda V45/65 Sabre & Magna (82 - 88)	0820
Honda VFR750 & 700 V-Fours (86 - 97)	♦ 2101
Honda VFR800 V-Fours (97 - 01)	♦ 3703
Honda VFR800 V-Tec V-Fours (02 - 05)	♦ 4196
Honda CB750 & CB900 dohc Fours (78 - 84)	0535
Honda VTR1000 (FireStorm, Super Hawk) & XL1000V (Varadero) (97 - 00)	♦ 3744
Honda CBR900RR FireBlade (92 - 99)	♦ 2161
Honda CBR900RR FireBlade (00 - 03)	♦ 4060
Honda CBR1000RR Fireblade (04 - 06)	♦ 4604
Honda CBR1100XX Super Blackbird (97 - 02)	♦ 3901
Honda ST1100 Pan European V-Fours (90 - 02)	♦ 3384
Honda Shadow VT1100 (USA) (85 - 98)	2313

Title	Book No
Honda GL1000 Gold Wing (75 - 79)	0309
Honda GL1100 Gold Wing (79 - 81)	0669
Honda Gold Wing 1200 (USA) (84 - 87)	2199
Honda Gold Wing 1500 (USA) (88 - 00)	2225
KAWASAKI AE/AR 50 & 80 (81 - 95)	1007
Kawasaki KC, KE & KH100 (75 - 99)	1371
Kawasaki KMX125 & 200 (86 - 02)	◊ 3046
Kawasaki 250, 350 & 400 Triples (72 - 79)	0134
Kawasaki 400 & 440 Twins (74 - 81)	0281
Kawasaki 400, 500 & 550 Fours (79 - 91)	0910
Kawasaki EN450 & 500 Twins (Ltd/Vulcan) (85 - 04)	2053
Kawasaki EX500 (GPZ500S) & ER500 (ER-5) (87 - 05)	♦ 2052
Kawasaki ZX600 (Ninja ZX-6, ZZ-R600) Fours (90 - 00)	♦ 2146
Kawasaki ZX-6R Ninja Fours (95 - 02)	♦ 3541
Kawasaki ZX600 (GPZ600R, GPX600R, Ninja 600R & RX) & ZX750 (GPX750R, Ninja 750R) Fours (85 - 97)	♦ 1780
Kawasaki 650 Four (76 - 78)	0373
Kawasaki Vulcan 700/750 & 800 (85 - 04)	♦ 2457
Kawasaki 750 Air-cooled Fours (80 - 91)	0574
Kawasaki ZR550 & 750 Zephyr Fours (90 - 97)	♦ 3382
Kawasaki ZX750 (Ninja ZX-7 & ZXR750) Fours (89 - 96)	♦ 2054
Kawasaki Ninja ZX-7R & ZX-9R (94 - 04)	♦ 3721
Kawasaki 900 & 1000 Fours (73 - 77)	0222
Kawasaki ZX900, 1000 & 1100 Liquid-cooled Fours (83 - 97)	♦ 1681
MOTO GUZZI 750, 850 & 1000 V-Twins (74 - 78)	0339
MZ ETZ Models (81 - 95)	◊ 1680
NORTON 500, 600, 650 & 750 Twins (57 - 70)	0187
Norton Commando (68 - 77)	0125
PEUGEOT Speedfight, Trekker & Vivacity Scooters (96 - 05)	◊ 3920
PIAGGIO (Vespa) Scooters (91 - 06)	◊ 3492
SUZUKI GT, ZR & TS50 (77 - 90)	0799
Suzuki TS50X (84 - 00)	◊ 1599
Suzuki 100, 125, 185 & 250 Air-cooled Trail bikes (79 - 89)	0797
Suzuki GP100 & 125 Singles (78 - 93)	◊ 0576
Suzuki GS, GN, GZ & DR125 Singles (82 - 05)	◊ 0888
Suzuki 250 & 350 Twins (68 - 78)	0120
Suzuki GT250X7, GT200X5 & SB200 Twins (78 - 83)	◊ 0469
Suzuki GS/GSX250, 400 & 450 Twins (79 - 85)	0736
Suzuki GS500 Twin (89 - 02)	♦ 3238
Suzuki GS550 (77 - 82) & GS750 Fours (76 - 79)	0363
Suzuki GS/GSX550 4-valve Fours (83 - 88)	1133
Suzuki SV650 & SV650S (99 - 05)	♦ 3912
Suzuki GSX-R600 & 750 (96 - 00)	♦ 3553
Suzuki GSX-R600 (01 - 02), GSX-R750 (00 - 02) & GSX-R1000 (01 - 02)	♦ 3986
Suzuki GSX-R600/750 (04-05) & GSX-R1000 (03-06)	♦ 4382
Suzuki GSF600 & 1200 Bandit Fours (95 - 04)	♦ 3367
Suzuki 700, 750, 800 Intruder, Marauder, Volusia & Boulevard (85 - 06)	2618
Suzuki GS850 Fours (78 - 88)	0536
Suzuki GS1000 Four (77 - 79)	0484
Suzuki GSX-R750, GSX-R1100 (85 - 92), GSX600F, GSX750F, GSX1100F (Katana) Fours (87 - 96)	2055
Suzuki GSX600/750F & GSX750 (98 - 02)	♦ 3987
Suzuki GS/GSX1000, 1100 & 1150 4-valve Fours (79 - 88)	0737
Suzuki TL1000S/R & DL1000 V-Strom (97 - 04)	♦ 4083
Suzuki GSX1300R Hayabusa (99 - 04)	♦ 4184
TRIUMPH Tiger Cub & Terrier (52 - 68)	0414
Triumph 350 & 500 Unit Twins (58 - 73)	0137
Triumph Pre-Unit Twins (47 - 62)	0251
Triumph 650 & 750 2-valve Unit Twins (63 - 83)	0122
Triumph Trident & BSA Rocket 3 (69 - 75)	0136
Triumph Bonneville (01 - 05)	♦ 4364
Triumph Daytona, Speed Triple, Sprint & Tiger (97 - 05)	♦ 3755
Triumph Triples & Fours (carburettor engines) (91 - 99)	♦ 2162
VESPA P/PX125, 150 & 200 Scooters (78 - 03)	0707
Vespa Scooters (59 - 78)	0126

Title	Book No
YAMAHA DT50 & 80 Trail Bikes (78 - 95)	◊ 0800
Yamaha T50 & 80 Townmate (83 - 95)	◊ 1247
Yamaha YB100 Singles (73 - 91)	◊ 0474
Yamaha RS/RXS100 & 125 Singles (74 - 95)	0331
Yamaha RD & DT125LC (82 - 87)	◊ 0887
Yamaha TZR125 (87 - 93) & DT125R (88 - 02)	◊ 1655
Yamaha TY50, 80, 125 & 175 (74 - 84)	◊ 0464
Yamaha XT & SR125 (82 - 02)	◊ 1021
Yamaha Trail Bikes (81 - 00)	2350
Yamaha 250 & 350 Twins (70 - 79)	0040
Yamaha XS250, 360 & 400 sohc Twins (75 - 84)	0378
Yamaha RD250 & 350LC Twins (80 - 82)	0803
Yamaha RD350 YPVS Twins (83 - 95)	1158
Yamaha RD400 Twin (75 - 79)	0333
Yamaha XT, TT & SR500 Singles (75 - 83)	0342
Yamaha XZ550 Vision V-Twins (82 - 85)	0821
Yamaha FJ, FZ, XJ & YX600 Radian (84 - 92)	2100
Yamaha XJ600S (Diversion, Seca II) & XJ600N Fours (92 - 03)	♦ 2145
Yamaha YZF600R Thundercat & FZS600 Fazer (96 - 03)	♦ 3702
Yamaha YZF-R6 (99 - 02)	♦ 3900
Yamaha YZF-R6 (03 - 05)	♦ 4601
Yamaha 650 Twins (70 - 83)	0341
Yamaha XJ650 & 750 Fours (80 - 84)	0738
Yamaha XS750 & 850 Triples (76 - 85)	0340
Yamaha TDM850, TRX850 & XTZ750 (89 - 99)	◊ ♦ 3540
Yamaha YZF750R & YZF1000R Thunderace (93 - 00)	♦ 3720
Yamaha FZR600, 750 & 1000 Fours (87 - 96)	♦ 2056
Yamaha XV (Virago) V-Twins (81 - 03)	♦ 0802
Yamaha XVS650 & 1100 Drag Star/V-Star (97 - 05)	♦ 4195
Yamaha XJ900F Fours (83 - 94)	♦ 3239
Yamaha XJ900S Diversion (94 - 01)	♦ 3739
Yamaha YZF-R1 (98 - 03)	♦ 3754
Yamaha YZF-R1 (04 - 06)	♦ 4605
Yamaha FZS1000 Fazer (01 - 05)	♦ 4287
Yamaha FJ1100 & 1200 Fours (84 - 96)	♦ 2057
Yamaha XJR1200 & 1300 (95 - 03)	♦ 3981
Yamaha V-Max (85 - 03)	♦ 4072
ATVs	
HONDA ATC70, 90, 110, 185 & 200 (71 - 85)	0565
Honda Rancher, Recon & TRX250EX ATVs	2553
Honda TRX300 Shaft Drive ATVs (88 - 00)	2125
Honda TRX300EX, TRX400EX & TRX450ER/ER ATVs (93 - 06)	2318
Honda Foreman 400 and 450 ATVs (95 - 02)	2465
KAWASAKI Bayou 220/250/300 & Prairie 300 ATVs (86 - 03)	2351
POLARIS ATVs (85 - 97)	2302
Polaris ATVs (98 - 06)	2508
YAMAHA YFS200 Blaster ATV (88 - 02)	2317
Yamaha YFB250 Timberwolf ATVs (92 - 00)	2217
Yamaha YFM350 & YFM400 (ER and Big Bear) ATVs (87 - 03)	2126
Yamaha Banshee and Warrior ATVs (87 - 03)	2314
Yamaha Kodiak and Grizzly ATVs (93 - 05)	2567
TECHBOOK SERIES	
ATV Basics	10450
Twist and Go (automatic transmission) Scooters Service and Repair Manual	4082
Motorcycle Basics TechBook (2nd Edition)	3515
Motorcycle Electrical TechBook (3rd Edition)	3471
Motorcycle Fuel Systems TechBook	3514
Motorcycle Maintenance TechBook	4071
Motorcycle Modifying	4272
Motorcycle Workshop Practice TechBook (2nd Edition)	3470

◊ = not available in the USA   ♦ = Superbike

The manuals on this page are available through good motorcycle dealers and accessory shops.
In case of difficulty, contact: **Haynes Publishing**
(UK) +44 1963 442030   (USA) +1 805 498 6703
(FR) +33 1 47 17 66 29   (SV) +46 18 124016
(Australia/New Zealand) +61 3 9763 8100

MCL21.9/06

Preserving Our Motoring Heritage

The Model J Duesenberg Derham Tourster. Only eight of these magnificent cars were ever built – this is the only example to be found outside the United States of America

Almost every car you've ever loved, loathed or desired is gathered under one roof at the Haynes Motor Museum. Over 300 immaculately presented cars and motorbikes represent every aspect of our motoring heritage, from elegant reminders of bygone days, such as the superb Model J Duesenberg to curiosities like the bug-eyed BMW Isetta. There are also many old friends and flames. Perhaps you remember the 1959 Ford Popular that you did your courting in? The magnificent 'Red Collection' is a spectacle of classic sports cars including AC, Alfa Romeo, Austin Healey, Ferrari, Lamborghini, Maserati, MG, Riley, Porsche and Triumph.

A Perfect Day Out

Each and every vehicle at the Haynes Motor Museum has played its part in the history and culture of Motoring. Today, they make a wonderful spectacle and a great day out for all the family. Bring the kids, bring Mum and Dad, but above all bring your camera to capture those golden memories for ever. You will also find an impressive array of motoring memorabilia, a comfortable 70 seat video cinema and one of the most extensive transport book shops in Britain. The Pit Stop Cafe serves everything from a cup of tea to wholesome, home-made meals or, if you prefer, you can enjoy the large picnic area nestled in the beautiful rural surroundings of Somerset.

John Haynes O.B.E., Founder and Chairman of the museum at the wheel of a Haynes Light 12.

The 1936 490cc sohc-engined International Norton – well known for its racing success

The Museum is situated on the A359 Yeovil to Frome road at Sparkford, just off the A303 in Somerset. It is about 40 miles south of Bristol, and 25 minutes drive from the M5 intersection at Taunton.
Open 9.30am - 5.30pm (10.00am - 4.00pm Winter) 7 days a week, *except Christmas Day, Boxing Day and New Years Day*
Special rates available for schools, coach parties and outings Charitable Trust No. 292048